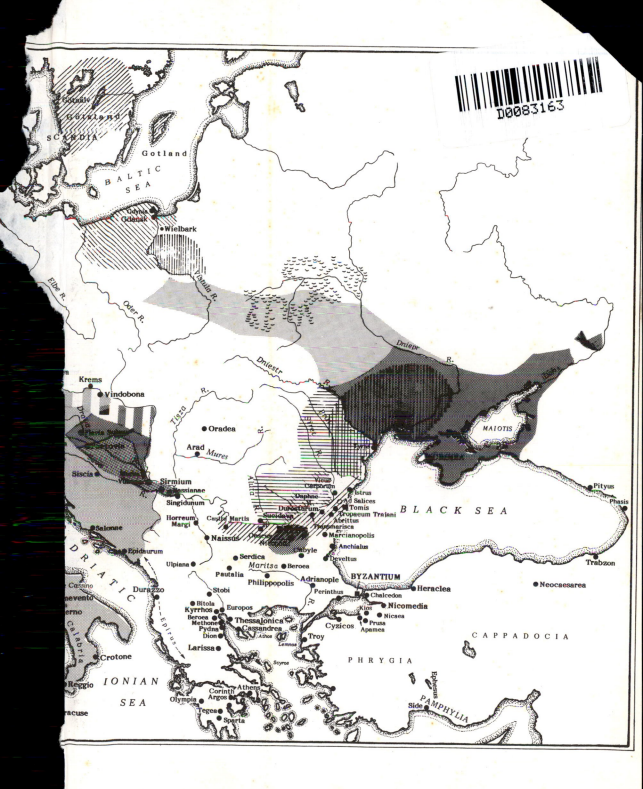

SCANDIA

Cotaals

Gotland

Gotland

BALTIC
SEA

Gdynia
Gdansk

Wielbark

Elbe R.

Oder R.

Visula R.

Dniepr R.

Dniestr

Krems

Vindobona

Tisza R.

Oradea

Arad   Mures

MAIOTIS

Siscia

Sirmium
Bassianae
Singidunum

Castra Martis

Horreum
Margi

Naissus

Serdica

Ulpiana

Pautalia

Stobi

Durazzo

Bitola
Kyrrhos
Beroea
Methone
Pydna
Dion

Krems

Salonae

Epidaurum

Cassino
Benevento
Salerno

Calabria

Crotone

Reggio

Syracuse

ADRIATIC

IONIAN
SEA

Vicus
Carporum
Daphne
Durostorum
Sucidava
Transmarisca

Istrus
Ad Salices
Tomis
Tropaeum Traiani
Abrittus
Marcianopolis
Anchialus
Develtus

Cabyle

Maritsa   Beroea

Philippopolis

Adrianople
Perinthus

BLACK SEA

Pityus
Phasis

Trabzon

BYZANTIUM
Chalcedon
Heraclea

Neocaesarea

Nicomedia
Kios   Nicaea
Cyzicos   Prusa
Apamea

CAPPADOCIA

Europos
Thessalonica
Cassandrea

Athos

Larissa

Lemnos

Troy

PHRYGIA

Scyros

Athens
Corinth
Argos

Olympia

Tegea
Sparta

Ephesus

Side   PAMPHYLIA

18—

History of the Goths

History
of the Goths

Herwig Wolfram

Translated by Thomas J. Dunlap

New and completely revised
from the second German edition

UNIVERSITY OF CALIFORNIA PRESS
BERKELEY LOS ANGELES LONDON

University of California Press
Berkeley and Los Angeles, California

University of California Press, Ltd.
London, England

First published in Germany © 1979 by C. H. Beck'sche
Verlagsbuchhandlung, Oscar Beck, München.

Library of Congress Cataloging in Publication Data

Wolfram, Herwig.
  History of the Goths.

  Translation of: Geschichte der Goten.
  Bibliography: p.
  Includes index.
  1. Goths. I. Title.
D137.W6213   1987   940.1   85–29044

Printed in the United States of America

To my American friends and students

Contents

Preface

 The overwhelming positive reception of the original German edition of this work among readers and reviewers alike exceeded the fondest hopes of the publisher and the author. The book was widely praised for combining scholarliness and readability. In response, leading foreign scholars, especially the late Professor Raoul Manselli of Rome, Professor Gerhart Ladner of Los Angeles, and Professor Michel Rouche of Paris, suggested that the book be translated. While the Italian edition, published in 1985, gave me a first opportunity to take into consideration the most recent scholarship and to review and, if necessary, revise my ideas, this English edition is a thoroughly revised and partially rewritten version of the original German text. Among the many changes and improvements the reader will find above all a radically new explanation of the circumstances and arrangements under which the Goths were settled in Gaul, Spain, and Italy. This problem, hitherto discussed only among specialists, is of crucial importance in understanding the political, legal, and socioeconomic structures of the emerging medieval world. The nonspecialist should therefore not be scared away by the difficulties that are involved in any discussion of these issues. The general reader might also encounter a flood of unfamiliar names. Any attempt on my part to identify every individual involved in a given event would have necessitated a second book. Fortunately there is no need for that, since

the reader can consult the excellent two- and soon three-volume prosopography of A. H. M. Jones and John R. Martindale.

I will be delighted if this book stimulates further research in the field of
early medieval ethnogenesis, thus adding to and strengthening the debate
about a historical period that a recent University of California Press publication so aptly called "The Transformation of the Roman World."

I wish to express my gratitude to the translator, Thomas Dunlap, whose
historical and linguistic talents made our joint venture a memorable experience. Many thanks also to Shirley Warren and Stan Holwitz and my editor
Amanda Frost for their endless patience and efforts. I am deeply indebted
to my assistants in Vienna, especially Brigitte Merta, Harald Krahwinkler,
Brigitte Resl, Anton Scharer, and Andreas Schwarcz. Without their help this
book would never have appeared. Last, but not least, I must thank my
friends and colleagues all over the world, to whom I am bound not only
by shared scholarly interests but also by deep personal friendship. Evangelos
Chrysos of Ioannina, Greece, shall here stand for all of them. Everyone
mentioned contributed to making this English translation a new book.

Introduction

Gothic History as Historical Ethnography

Anyone in the field of Gothic history must expect to be misunderstood, rejected, even stigmatized. This is hardly surprising, for the subject is burdened with the ideological weight of a readiness throughout the centuries either to reject the Goths as an embodiment of everything wicked and evil or to identify with them and their glorious history.[1] Sympathy and antipathy have taken grotesque forms right down to the present: "Goths go home" (*fuera godos*) adorns the walls of many houses on the Canary Islands today, demanding the expulsion of the mainland Spaniards. Jan Sobieski, king of Poland and in 1683 commander of the relieving army that saved Vienna from the Turks, was glorified as a Gothic Mars. That was hardly surprising, since there had been a long-standing tradition of equating Slavic peoples with East Germanic tribes. It is often necessary, however, to remind Central Europeans of the plain fact that a history of the Goths is not part of the history of the German people and certainly not part of the "history of the Germans in foreign countries." No such ideological controversy surrounds the Celts, for example, and everyone will gladly claim them as ancestors, because from the Irish, Scots, and Bretons there has been "no threat of annexation or war."[2] Clearly the Goths are no threat either. Today no one can seriously boast of being their descendant, and no such descendant

would frighten people. Because nowhere in Europe did the Goths achieve
the status of a nation,[3] they dissolved at their downfall into a myth accessible
to everyone. The result has been a long history of attempts to lay claim to
the Gothic tradition.

At the Council of Basel (1431–1449), for example, a quarrel erupted
between the Austrians and the Swedes when each side claimed to be the
true descendants of the Goths and thus to outrank the other in questions
of protocol.[4] Barely one hundred years later, Wolfgang Lazius, court historian of Ferdinand I, sought to prove that the Gothic migration all across
Europe had unified the region from the Black Sea to Cadiz so that "these
countries are now with full right once more united under the dominion of
the Habsburgs."[5] The pro-Gothic attitude reached its height of absurdity
in Sweden under Olaus Rudbeck (1630–1702), professor at Uppsala. He
actually claimed to have rediscovered Gothic Sweden in Plato's Atlantis. He
identified Old Uppsala as the acropolis of the Atlanteans and the pagan
temple of the Svears as the temple of Apollo.[6] Still today the second crown
in the Swedish royal coat of arms stands for the *regnum Gothorum*. Rudbeck was also responsible for popularizing a doctrine of Greek ethnography
in which the north enjoyed a virtually inexhaustible wealth of people, its
inhabitants enjoying sound health and begetting children to a ripe old age,
men of sixty retaining their procreative power, and women of fifty still bearing children.[7] Rudbeck and his students, among them men like Montesqieu
and Chateaubriand,[8] could fall back on Jordanes' description of Scandza as
an *officina gentium aut certe velut vagina nationum* (factory of tribes and
surely a mother of nations), which had brought forth the Goths and many
other peoples.[9] But of special importance right up to the time of Montesqieu
was the tradition that the strong kingship of the Goths had remained rooted
in the consent of the people, which meant that the Gothic king was popu-
larly elected: "Les Goths conquérant l'empire romain fondèrent partout la
monarchie et la liberté" (in conquering the Roman Empire the Goths laid
the foundations for monarchy and freedom everywhere).[10] Whereas most
postrevolutionary Frenchmen today prefer their national hero, the comic-
strip character Astérix, and care little about Goths living or dead, Chateaubriand called them *nos ancêtres* and even concluded: "Theodoric reste
grand bienqu'il fait mourir Boèce. Ces Goths étaient d'une race supérieure"
(Theodoric remains "great" even though he had Boethius executed. These
Goths were of a superior race).[11]

Even Anglo-American voices were not missing from the chorus of Gothi-
cists. In 1843, for example, George Perkins Marsh announced the Gothic
origin of England, the Pilgrims, and the heroes of the American Revolution,

all this in a book with the revealing title *The Goths in New England*. When the terms *Gothicism, Germanism,* and *Teutonism* had already begun to disappear from historians' workshops, the Dane Johannes Jensen in 1907 expected *den Gotiske Renaissance* from the North Americans.[12] Heinz Gollwitzer has shown that these isms with all their variations had passed out of use, or very nearly so, when National Socialism made possible a nightmarish and ghastly resurgence.[13] Thus the Polish port Gdynia-Gdingen became the city Gotenhafen in the Reichsgau Danzig-Westpreussen. Even during the war Nazi bureaucrats deliberated on how the formerly Gothic territory of the Crimea could be settled with Germans and whether Simferopol should be renamed Gotenburg and Sevastopol Theoderichshafen.[14] This criminal madness involved the transmutation of the pro-Gothic tradition into a historical argument. In motivating concrete action, the pro-Gothic sentiment had exposed itself as an attempt to turn back time and history, indeed to destroy them. And yet this anachronistic perversion was already behind the jubilant outburst of the usually level-headed Beatus Rhenanus: "Ours are the triumphs of the Goths and Vandals!"[15]

Of course the German and Scandinavian humanists were only reacting to the doctrine of Gothic barbarism propagated by the Latin humanists, especially the Italians. For Latin humanists everything "Gothic" had become a term of abuse, a general concept for lack of culture and education, for deficiency in way of life and in classical notions of architecture, for monkish hypocrisy and backwardness. The humanists north of the Alps therefore mistrusted their "Romanist" predecessors and colleagues and sought to return to the original sources.[16] In so doing they followed a method which the prescientific study of the past had already developed and which Hans Messmer has aptly called "the [moral] ethnographic approach."[17] The foundation for all their efforts was a detailed study of the *origines gentium,* among them especially the *Origo Gothica,* the work of Cassiodorus in the version of Jordanes.

The highly educated Cassiodorus, a Roman in the service of the Gothic kings of Italy, composed an *origo gentis,* an account of the origins of a people.[18] His work formed part of a classical genre in which two separate approaches had coexisted from the time of Caesar. Greek ethnography preferred to derive the origins of the barbarians from primordial deeds of Greek gods and heroes. In contrast, ever since Caesar, the Romans not only accepted native traditions but on occasion even preferred them to the familiar speculations of Greek mythographers. Indeed, a historian like Tacitus would say nothing about the origin of the Britons because he knew of no relevant native tradition.[19] Although Latin ethnographers were therefore

more open-minded about barbarian traditions than their Greek predecessors, they did subject these traditions to an *interpretatio Romana*.[20] This
interpretatio did not go so far as to present the stories of tribal origins as
a sort of second-rate Roman mythology. But because barbarian concepts
and institutions were equated with or actually integrated into their Roman
counterparts, Roman history became the goal of every *origo gentis*. As a
result, anyone who seeks to write a history of the Goths takes on an impossible task: the sources present a history of the later Roman Empire into
which the history of the Goths has been thoroughly absorbed. To recapture
Gothic history the historian must write it as historical ethnography. But a
historical ethnography of the Goths turns Cassiodorus's historical structure
upside down and seeks to allow the *Origo Gothica,* the particular origin
of the Goths, to reemerge from the *historia Romana.*

Through assimilation, barbarian traditions became Roman history: "Ori-
ginem Gothicam fecit esse historiam Romanam" (he made the story of
Gothic origins to be Roman history); this is what Cassiodorus has Athalaric
say about his *Origo Gothica,* which is known to us in Jordanes's version
under the title *Getica.*[21] But because Roman history was also Christian, the
Gothic pagan origins were absorbed into the Christian notion of history as
God's plan of redemption for mankind—what is often called providential
history. For the genre of the *origines gentium,* the Gothic history of Cassiodorus was therefore no less revolutionary an innovation than Caesar's
ethnographic excursus in the *Bellum Gallicum* had been. In the formal
structure of his work, Cassiodorus, as compiler of ancient and barbarian
traditions, is unoriginal.[22] But the content is unique, for Cassiodorus has
provided the first *origo* of a people that had originally not been part of the
ancient world yet, paradoxically, was now ruling a portion of the empire
with imperial recognition.[23]

Cassiodorus's incorporation of Gothic history into the ecumenical *historia Romana* created the model for the medieval *origines gentium,* the last
of which was that written by Saxo Grammaticus around 1200. Such works,
most written in classicistic Latin, elevated the prehistory of a Germanic-
Celtic-Slavic *gens* to the providential history of the *populus,* the *historia
Romana.* An *origo* of this kind was seen as a legitimation of power. Consequently the *origo* and the *lex scripta*—the tribal origins and the tribal
law—were put into writing at the same time.[24]

In turning to the individual tribal histories, above all the rediscovered
Germania of Tacitus as well as the *Origo Gothica,* the German humanists
abandoned the approach of the medieval world chronicle. The latter had
combined secular with sacred history and eschatology and had presented

between its covers the history of all mankind as the Christianized *historia Romana*.[25] Consequently, whoever isolated a particular *origo gentis* from such a historical scheme secularized world history. In this effort the German humanists rediscovered the term *gens,* as for example in Wolfgang Lazius's *De gentium aliquot migrationibus*.[26] The notion of tribal migration entails a belief in continuity, survival, and the transfer (*translatio*) of historical claims and rights, and it opposed the Italian humanists' concept of catastrophic barbarian invasions. Needless to say, both camps equated *Germanus* with *deutsch,* as is still evident in the English "German" and the Greek Γερμανός.[27] Since the German humanists mistrusted ancient historiography, they used archaeology and philology to develop the notion of healthy, strong, and young migratory peoples.

The concept of young peoples renewing the decadent Roman world is a secularized by-product of the classical-Christian idea of renewal. While French romanticism and German historicism could still agree in the nineteenth century that the invading Germanic peoples "freshened the blood" of the West,[28] today none other than archaeologists and anthropologists have put forth exactly the opposite argument: namely, that we are not dealing with young, vigorous peoples or a "healthy past."[29] Furthermore, putting the word *gens* into the context of the migrations was by no means tantamount to understanding its real historical significance. In his *History of the Germans* (1778) Michael Schmidt equated for the first time the phrase *migratio gentium* with 'tribal migration' (*Völkerwanderung*), a loan translation which Johann Christoph Gottsched already rejected with good reason on linguistic grounds.[30] Schmidt's equation is indeed semantically suspect, if not altogether false. Even during the Early Middle Ages the meaning of the term *gens* changed to such an extent that it came to embrace a wide spectrum of meanings, sometimes even contradictory ones. A Carolingian *gens Francorum* is closer to a modern nation than the *gens Francorum* of Clovis's time. And to complicate matters, we have no way of devising a terminology that is not derived from the concept of nationhood created during the French Revolution.[31]

Words such as *gens, genus*/γένος, *genealogia,* and *natio,* refer to a community of biological descent.[32] The tribal sagas, however, equate *people* with *army* and thus remain true to historical reality.[33] In addition, the sources attest the polyethnic character of the *gentes.* These *gentes* never comprise all potential members of a *gens* but are instead always mixed. Therefore their formation is not a matter of common descent but one of political decision. Initially this implies not much more than the ability to unite and keep together the multitribal groups that make up any barbarian army. The leaders and chiefs of "well-known" clans, that is to say, of those families who derive their origins from gods and who can prove their divine favor through appropriate achievements, form the "nuclei of tradition" around which new tribes take shape. Whoever acknowledges the tribal tradition, either by being born into it or by being "admitted" to it, is part of the *gens* and as such a member of a community of "descent through tradition."[34]

The history of a *gens* is the subject of ethnography, and ethnography, as the name implies, deals "descriptively with peoples." By definition these ἔθνη or *gentes* do not belong to the observer's superior culture. They remain outside the civilized world. They are barbarians;[35] their language does not sound human, more like stammering and mere noise.[36] The barbarians also speak diverse languages all at once or side by side, for in their eyes language is no criterion of tribal membership.[37] Under the assault of their horrible songs the classical meter of the ancient poet goes to pieces.[38] Their religion is superstition, and though not actually pagan, it is hardly more than corrupted Christianity, heresy and worse.[39] For barbarians can neither think nor act rationally; theological controversies are Greek to them. If a storm approaches, they fear the heavens are collapsing, give up any advantage they may have on the battlefield, and flee. At the same time, they are dominated by a horrible death wish: they actually look forward to dying. Even their women take part in battle. Barbarians are driven by evil spirits; "they are possessed by demons" who force them to commit the most terrible acts.[40] Barbarians simply resemble animals more than they do human beings, concluded contemporaries, wondering whether barbarians shared in human nature at all. How tenaciously such ideas persist is revealed by the association of the department of prehistory with the Viennese Museum of Natural History. As "two-legged animals" the barbarians were viewed as incapable of living according to written laws and only reluctantly tolerating kings. Barbarian customs are described as strange, unpredictable, and dangerous in an evil person, "splendid vices" even in the virtuous. Their lust for gold is immense, their love of drink boundless. Barbarians are without restraint. They embrace one another for the kiss of brotherhood but are faithless to the alien. For just as civilized observers deny that barbarians are human, to the barbarians only the community of their unwritten customary law is considered the "world of humans."[41] But whether they are Germanic peoples or not, barbarians are generally considered good-looking. They are blond and tall, if dirty and given to strange customs of personal hygiene.[42] They grease their hair with butter and do not mind its rancid smell.[43] Only the Huns are ugly, the sons of evil spirits and Gothic witches.[44] The reproductive energy of the barbarians is inexhaustible. The northern climate of their native land, with its long winter nights, favors their fantastic urge to procreate. If a barbarian people is driven back or even destroyed, the next one already emerges from the marshes and forests of Germany or the greater Scythian steppe. Indeed, there are really no new barbarian peoples—descendants of the same tribes keep appearing.[45]

In actuality, a tribe comprised surprisingly few people. Fifteen to twenty thousand warriors—which means a total of perhaps a hundred thousand people—are the greatest numbers a large people can muster.[46] In defiance of the facts, the literary topos of overpopulation persists to this day. The various migrations are explained by the assumption that a given territory could no longer feed the people, whereupon the entire population, or a part of it, was forced to leave the land. Of course the notion of a *ver sacrum,* a "holy spring," when a tribe sent out its young men in search of land, is not mere fiction. It is also beyond doubt that a barbarian economy provided poorly for its people. After a good harvest, the people could hope to get through the winter without going hungry.[47] Actual surplus, however, was either nonexistent or useless because reserves could not be stored. Everyone ate the same monotonous diet; the Huns were not the only ones who devoured their meat raw. If anyone was richer than his neighbor, if he had a bigger share of the "surplus" of the barbarian economy, he could use his wealth to purchase gold and hang it around his neck or that of his horse or wife.[48] Hunger and want constantly threatened barbarian existence. Such privation did not arise because the population was multiplying wildly—in fact the numbers remained remarkably stable[49]—but because barbarian society was in a constant state of war and because the enemy was not only the people living beyond a broad border zone but was as close as the neighboring village, the next clan, or another kin group of the same tribe. After the capitulation of Cumae, for example, Teja's brother sought to become a Roman to escape the dangerous life of a barbarian. We may wonder why tribal traditions saw such chaotic conditions as harmonious. This could be so only because the barbarians lived the pathos of heroism to the fullest.[50]

Barbarian history is the tale of the "deeds of brave men";[51] only the warrior, the hero, matters. Tribe and army are one, the *gens* is the "people in arms."[52] When the tribe migrated an extraordinary social mobility prevailed in its ranks. Any capable person who had success in the army could profit from this mobility, regardless of his ethnic and social background. In the kingdom of Ermanaric there were—apart from Greutungian Ostrogoths— Finns, Slavs, Antes, Heruli, Rosomoni, Alans, Huns, Sarmatians, and probably Aesti as well.[53] In the western "Gutthiuda" we find, besides the domi-

nant Tervingi (the Visigoths, as we call them), Taifali, Sarmatians from
the Caucaland, and minorities from Asia Minor; in addition we must assume a considerable contingent of former Roman provincials, more or
less strongly Romanized Daco-Carpian groups, other Sarmatians, and Ira-
nians.[54] The polyethnic structure of the Gothic peoples remained intact even
within the Roman Empire. The Gothic army that settled in southern Gaul
in 418 had the following composition: Tervingian-Vesian and Greutungian-
Ostrogothic tribal elements; non-Gothic groups that had been Gothicized
to varying degrees, among them Alans, Bessi from Thrace, Galindi from the
Baltic Sea, Varni, probably also Heruli, and maybe even Saxons from the
Loire and Garonne rivers. Among the elements of non-Gothic origin we
must also list the barbarians from the settlements of the *dediticii* and the
laeti, the Sarmatian, Taifalian, and Suevian colonies of the late Roman
Notitia dignitatum.[55] The kingdom of Theodoric the Great was no less
polyethnic. As a Roman high magistrate and king of his Goths, he was
actually in the best position to turn his army into a Gothic people, but the
ethnogenesis itself involved non-Gothic elements. In his army marched Rugians, Vandals, Alans, Heruli, Sarmatians and Taifali, Gepids, and Alamanni. Apart from the Romans who served in Theodoric's army and who
were "Goths at heart," there were also former Roman subjects, like the
wild Breoni in the Tirol, who became federates of the Gothic federates.[56]

From the first appearance of the Gothic hordes on Roman soil, they
attracted people from the native lower classes. At the time of migration this
attraction was a great advantage because it alleviated a constant shortage of manpower. But in southern Gaul, Spain, and Italy the *coloni* were
needed in the fields, not on the battlefields. Because Theodoric had staked
his future on consolidation and stabilization, he prohibited the Roman
peasant from joining the Gothic army. But the old attraction had not yet
disappeared when the Ostrogoths were fighting for their survival. Totila
not only accepted slaves and *coloni* into the Gothic army—and apparently
in large numbers—but even turned them against their senatorial masters by
promising them freedom and ownership of land. In so doing he permitted
and provided an excuse for something that Roman lower classes had been
willing to do since the third century: "to become Goths" out of despair
over their economic situation.[57] The principle of the time is clear: whoever
proves himself as warrior is lord; whoever works, whether as a peasant,
skilled craftsman, or merchant, is and will remain a slave.[58] The fate of two
Roman prisoners illustrates the social mechanism. The first, formerly a rich
merchant, is taken prisoner by the Huns, changes his life-style and, though
initially completely untrained, becomes a capable warrior. He wins riches

and freedom, contracts a "Hunnic" marriage, and climbs the social ladder of the army. The other Roman captive is an outstanding builder who uses Pannonian spoils to erect a beautiful bath for the same master his fellow prisoner originally served. But when the building is completed the architect does not gain his expected freedom. Instead, the Hun turns him into the lowest-ranking slave, a bath-attendant for the Hun and his family.[59]

This social order and the value judgments and attitudes on which it was based were out of tune with Roman social thought and practice. They had to be abandoned if the tribe wanted to establish a kingdom on Roman soil. The surrendering of the primitive tribal structures initiates the process of assimilation, and former barbarians become part of the Roman world.

The institution that accomplished this transition in the face of all dangers was the Gothic military kingship. Rebounding from all setbacks and near catastrophes the Gothic kings, Amali as well as Balthi, repeatedly managed to prove and reaffirm themselves as a "race of gods and heroes." Their success derives from their ability to adapt to circumstances better than their aristocratic competitors and, ultimately, to gain imperial recognition.[60] Moreover, Balthic and Amal Goths each had to endure a forty-year wait: forty years lie between the autumn of 376, when the ancestors of the Visigoths crossed the Danube, and the signing of the Roman-Gothic *foedus* in 416, and forty years separate the battle of Adrianople in 378 from the imperial decision in 418 to settle the federate Goths in Aquitaine. Thus the Visigoths resembled the Chosen People, who remained in the desert for forty years after receiving the law before they were allowed to enter the Promised Land. Ostrogothic tradition draws this comparison only by way of allusion: forty years the Ostrogoths are said to have mourned the death of their king before they chose Valamir, Theodoric the Great's uncle, as successor.[61] Such an interregnum, however, did not entail any loss of legitimacy. On the contrary, a forty-year wait shows that God has tested and elected the people concerned; it marks and legitimizes God's people.[62] Kingship, *gens,* and election by God form the *populus,*[63] which in the case of the Arian Goths only a mean-spirited *homousian,* a "Catholic" as we say, would have denied.

In the end, however, the Gothic military kingship was successful only when it "annulled" itself, in other words, when the kings succeeded in subordinating their peoples to Roman statehood and integrating them into larger territorialized units (*patriae*). Only the creation of a Latin-barbarian *regnum*—of a lasting successor state to the Western Roman Empire—restricted the possibilities of new tribal formations. With the creation of these *patriae* the free play of barbarian forces lost its dangerous effects.[64] Around

590 the Visigoths gave their *gens vel patria Gothorum* the name *Spania, Gallia et Gallaecia*.[65] Of the same order was the *Italia* of the Ostrogothic kingdom which Theodoric the Great created.[66] The relatively swift fall of this state reestablished the Ostrogothic *gentilitas* as the army of the Goths with a military king struggling in vain for imperial recognition. Thus the last Ostrogothic kingdoms seem like the first; they are as easily shifted geographically as they are able to take on the most diverse territorial dimensions. At one time these *regna* consisted of a few *civitates* in Pannonia, Macedonia, Thrace, or Moesia. Then the Goths were masters over substantially more than twenty provinces in Illyricum, Italy, and Gaul. After that a force composed of "only Belisarius and his retainers destroyed the power of Theodoric."[67] Defeated and robbed of their Amal legitimacy, the Ostrogoths of the year 540 would have been only too happy to have their kingdom limited to the transpadane provinces of Liguria and Venetia-Istria. For one year they repeated their offer to the emperor, while their dominion was shrinking further and finally comprised no more than the old royal city of Pavia. Then, almost out of nowhere, came the mighty rise of the "tyrant" Totila and the recapturing of "Gothic rule over the Italians." In 550, finally, two years before the destruction of the Ostrogoths, Totila would have been content with a kingdom made up of the Italian peninsula without her adjoining lands and islands.[68] Compared to this "accordion state" of the Ostrogothic army, the Visigothic kingdom seems remarkably stable, which is all the more surprising since the loss of Balthic legitimacy[69] was accompanied by heavy losses to the Byzantines and the Franks. Precisely the way in which the army of the former "Alaric Goths"[70] overcame these catastrophes and setbacks shows how deeply it was rooted in the prefecture of Greater Gaul. For two generations—counting from 507—the Visigoths lost land and battles to the Franks and Byzantines. Yet their kingdom retained a remarkable territorial extent. Here Goths from the lost provinces could find a new homeland;[71] from here reconquest and future expansion could begin. Although the king was killed and the royal city lost, the defeated kingdom of Toulouse did not dissolve into a mobile Gothic army; it simply shifted its center, first to the Mediterranean coast and finally to Toledo. The kingdom named after this city consolidated into a higher political entity, an early medieval *regnum* in which the notion of *gens* was given the new meaning of a legally constituted "national people."[72] There is no indication that the Spanish Visigoths still saw themselves as a community of descent through tradition.

Modern language fails to grasp conceptually the origins of such a community and the changes it underwent. This leaves an alternative that should not be carelessly adopted: that of retaining the Latin term *gens*, taken from the sources. A *gens* is a large group as much as a clan, a fraction of a tribe as much as a confederation of several ethnic units. The *gens* of the migrations had no *patria*. Therefore it had no distinct national identity; it was still an open process. A *gens* in the *origo* stage is always wandering—*in peregrinatione*—in order to grow through the kingship and the faith, whatever that may be, into a *populus*. *Stammesbildung und Verfassung* (tribal formation and political constitution), the duality which Reinhard Wenskus described in 1961, is the subject of an historical ethnography. As for Gothic history, we are here dealing with the confrontation between a tribal society and a state. There are familiar analogies for us to understand what the term *state* means historically. Without reviving the fruitless debate over the use of the term *state* prior to modern European history,[73] we can say that the *imperium Romanum* of late antiquity as well as the Carolingian empire had the characteristics of a state. In these states the territorial element, the *patria*, remained the vital component; the *gens* had to establish its legitimacy by becoming the *patria*.[74] This is what the Visigoths in Spain expressed in the classic phrase *patria vel gens Gothorum*.[75] These Goths had transcended the "Scythian character" of the migratory *gentilitas*.[76]

The original, that is, the "Scythian," *gentes* had no fixed structures. That explains how Synesius of Cyrene could tell his emperor Arcadius that there were really no new barbarians. They did in fact constantly invent new names and disguise their appearance to deceive the Romans—the civilized world—but strictly speaking the Scythians had remained the same since the days of Herodotus.[77] Less than a hundred years after Synesius it had become possible to replace the traditional Scythian name with that of the Goths: polyethnic bands of mounted warriors who came from northeastern Europe were now considered Goths, just as they continued to present themselves as Scythians to traditional ethnography. According to this view, all of Ludwig Schmidt's East Germanic peoples, including the non-Germanic Alans, belong to the Gothic peoples and profess the same heretical religion.[78] It is true that by 600 the tribal structure of the Goths had changed significantly: their "statehood" was limited to the realm of the Spanish Visigoths, and they were a "national people" of Catholic faith. Nevertheless, the Goths of Toledo continued to be called a *gens*, as if they were merely a community of descent to which even a soldier of the Byzantine army could belong.[79] The difficulty of putting into practice Otto Brunner's request that historians take their terms from the language of the sources is clear.[80]

Whoever uses the word *gens* must be aware of the many variations it embraces.[81] If we recount the "Gothic saga" with all this in mind, it would sound something like this:

Once upon a time there was a small people—because of the story's uncertain origins, one is tempted to begin the account like a fairy tale—calling itself Goths, which means "men."[82] It stepped onto the stage of history at the time when the Romans were penetrating into free Germania. In those days the Gothic settlements were strung along the southern coast of the Baltic Sea from Pomerania to the East Prussian Passarge river. Archaeologists equate the earliest history of the Goths with the artifacts of a culture named after the East Prussian town Willenberg-Wielbark. In this distinct, apparently indigenous culture there appears a "guiding fossil" that accompanied the Goths everywhere on their extensive wanderings: the body of a dead Goth was placed into the grave without weapons. This presupposes a belief in an afterlife vastly different from that of other peoples and cultures. As far as we can tell, these early Goths had nowhere reached the river Oder in the west. In fact, it is disputed whether this river ever bore the name Guthalus, despite the claims of some scholars that the Oder was a "Gothic river" and the counterpart to the Scandinavian Götaälv.[83] The tales of this early period, however, are all but lost, in spite of, or in fact because of, the Amal saga of the Scandinavian origin of the Goths.[84] In any case, the Goths—or Gutones, as the Roman sources called them[85]—were initially under foreign domination or formed at best a semiautonomous group within a tribal confederation,[86] a *nomen antiquum*.[87] The Gutonic peoples differed from their closest neighbors neither in their weaponry nor in their institutions; even the kingship they all had in common. According to the Hippocratic school of Greek ethnography this latter fact should indicate an advanced level of "statehood" among the Gutones. Moreover, these kings were special: for Germanic standards they had an unusual amount of authority. From the time we hear of these kings they rule more like the kings of the migratory army than the tribal kings of the last centuries before Christ.[88] To join the Gutonic kings one did not have to be a Guton or a free man, one had only to be a good warrior and follow the king faithfully.[89] In this way a body of royal retainers developed, an *exercitus Gothorum,* which soon surpassed the military capabilities of the surrounding peoples. This explains the apparent contradictions accompanying the early history of the Goths: they were originally a dependent and for a long time a small people who nevertheless occupied a large area extending from the Passarge river in Prussia through eastern Pomerania nearly to the Oder. Then the Gutones fought against the great powers of their time. In the end—no later than five generations after we first hear of them—they settled on the eastern, Sarmatian bank of the central Vistula.[90] There they formed the core of that "barbarian avalanche" that rolled over the Roman border along the Danube in the last third of the second century and brought about enormous changes as far as the Black Sea. Taking the Roman point of view, we still speak of the Marcomannic wars, a term that does not do justice to the full dimensions of the events. The Gutones who penetrated into the region between the lower Danube and the Don at the end of the second century were in any case no longer a small people. They asserted themselves successfully against barbarian rivals and soon stood at the head of polyethnic federations, of course still under royal leadership. From 238 the Gothic assaults devastated the eastern provinces of the Roman Empire for more than forty years. Compared to this the Marcomannic wars had been merely a weak prelude. The Goths of the third century were considered a new people to whom the old Scythian name applied. No ancient ethnographer made a connection between the Goths and the Gutones. The Gutonic immigrants became Goths the very moment the Mediterranean world considered them Scythians.[91]

This first large kingdom of the Goths outside the empire fell apart in the late third century when it was defeated and almost annihilated by the emperors Claudius II Gothicus and Aurelian,[92] whereupon the *gens* split up permanently. East of the Dniester it was probably the Amali who succeeded in preserving the royal Goths—the Greutungian Ostrogoths—while along the lower Danube/Ister there grew up the powerful oligarchy of the Balthic-Tervingian Vesi. This oligarchy developed a political system with multiple centers, which made possible the first territorialization of the *gens* at the doorstep of the Roman Empire. The invasion of the Huns destroyed both the eastern kingdom as well as the western oligarchy of the Goths. Those among both peoples who did not want to become Hunnic Goths and who were able to escape subjection crossed over into Roman territory. There they became *foederati* of the empire, that is to say, they became members of the Roman military forces. As such they could maintain ethnic and political identity only when commanded by their own chieftains. In keeping with Roman constitutional practice, however, these chieftains had to be "kings" as well as military "officers" recognized by the emperor. Thus a new barbarian kingship was established and at the same time such kings took their place within the highest levels of the Roman military bureaucracy. The oldest tribal creation of this kind of kingship was that of the Visigoths. This book emphasizes this process of integration, that is, the history of the Gothic ethnogeneses on Roman soil. In this kind of Gothic history the following elements are only of peripheral importance: (1) mere lists of the names of Gothic tribes, as, for example, Cassiodorus's linguistically significant catalog of Scandinavian peoples;[93] (2) the history of the Crimean Goths between the invasion of the Huns and the time of Justinian;[94] and (3) the fate of individuals who had gone over to the Romans.[95]

Both the Visigothic and the Ostrogothic *regna* did have their roots in barbarian tradition, but they were Roman institutions linked to the highest Roman magistracies with vice-imperial powers.[96] Consequently, the Gothic *gentes* are not only *exercitus Gothorum* but at the same time Roman federate armies. As successors to the Roman imperial forces they possessed a modified right of transferring power: the Goths do not raise up an emperor but a king.[97] From the point of view of the Roman constitution, the barbarian monarchy therefore represented that anomaly that reconciled the practice and theory of late antique statehood. Thus the *gens* is institutionalized or, if one prefers, imperialized. It had to give up its original "Scythian" ways if it was to form a permanent state. Thus Theodoric the Great took the *imperium Romanum* as the model for his *regnum*,[98] and Leovigild did the same in Visigothic Spain.[99] But if the barbarians were Romanized, the ancient world was barbarized. In politics and law the Roman name lost its ecumenical meaning and came to designate only one *gens* among many; a *gens* to which a Flavius Amalus Theodoricus belonged by law,[100] to which a "common" Goth had social ties,[101] and whose founding father was the same as that of the Burgundians and Franks.[102]

The Goths as outsiders, as barbarians, form the subject of historical ethnography. Law and cult, *lex* and *religio*, were considered synonymous. The last account that attests pre-Christian, if already thoroughly ecclesiasticized beliefs among the Visigoths dates from the fifth century.[103] In Italy under Theodoric the Great, remnants of the old *religio* were abolished without further ado, unless they served to enhance the "splendor" of the Amal clan.[104] Thus the king ordered his retainers, the *saiones,* to put an end to the Gothic custom of burying precious metals as grave furnishings. It is true that the *saiones* were told to proceed carefully, to try to recover the treasures entrusted to the earth without destroying the graves. Yet it was no longer the Gothic tradition but the Roman model that was to be the norm for burial customs and hence also for the ancestor cult.[105] The old religious beliefs must have been in an advanced state of decay if a royal decree could abolish them. While the Christian king Theodoric was taking steps against the last remnants of heathen practices, he was, however, using his own line of ancestors as the basis for the legitimacy of the Amal clan believed to be *Ansis*-Aesir. The source and foundation of the ancestral line is the "saga" that spans seventeen generations of Gothic history and thus covers nearly half a millennium. From the Ansic tradition, from the descent from Gaut/Gapt, Amal, and Ostrogotha—heroes and half-gods who "were no mere mortals"—emerges the justification for including the Amali among the nobility of late antiquity.[106] What Alaric I had once achieved in purely economic terms, namely, a top senatorial salary,[107] the Amali surpassed many times over and were, like the "younger" Balthi, admitted into the circle of the leading families of the ancient world.[108] The collective memory of the Goths did know pre-Amal and pre-Balthic "deeds of brave men," but this memory came to an end along with the history of the royal Amali and Balthi in the fourth decade of the sixth century.[109] It shared the fate of these clans, and after their end it was transformed into a general heroic legend that belonged to no specific people. One generation before their fall the Amali had succeeded in monopolizing the entire Gothic tradition. From this tradition they derived their justification for their claim to the first place, "the highest nobility," within the Latin-barbarian world of "kings and peoples."[110] At that time Cassiodorus Senator composed the *Origo Gothica*, which Jordanes, a Goth from the Balkans, shaped into its present form in Constantinople during the winter of 551.[111] This history tells of the "origin and fall" of kings and kingdoms.[112] It structures its account "from ancient times to the present day following the generations and successions of kings" and for this draws on the "songs of the ancestors," the tribal memory.[113] The Italian *regnum*, which Cassiodorus already considered a part of the ancient world, was destroyed by Justinian's reconquest. Nevertheless, Jordanes remained faithful to the attitude of Cassiodorus: the younger Jordanes, "as someone who derives his descent from the Gothic *gens*," lets the history of the Goths end with a "fortunate defeat." In his eyes, with the fall of the Amal kingdom, Gothic history ended in the victory of Belisarius over King Vitigis and his wife Matasuntha, Theodoric's granddaughter. Freed from her defeated husband by his death shortly thereafter, the last of the Amali could give her hand in marriage to the emperor's nephew Germanus and thus unite the glorious tradition of her clan with that of the Anicii. In this legitimate way took place the transformation of the Amal-Balthic *origo Gothica* into the *historia Romana*.[114] Whoever wanted to become king of the Goths after 540 lacked the symbols of power, both the concrete symbols as well as the "splendor of the clan."[115]

Remarkably enough the Visigoths, from 531 on, were able to come to terms with the problems that destroyed the Gothic kingdom of Italy during the dramatic fifteen years after 540. Neither the kings of the transition period nor the rulers of Toledo could fall back on an ethnic *memoria* that would have reached back to a time before the invasion of the Huns. In fact, the Visigothic kings had to fight this *memoria* as the political tradition of the nobles.[116] The only remnant permitted was the *lex Gothica* as a law code written in Latin, changed and greatly expanded through Roman additions, and enriched with biblical *exempla*.[117] Some of this law, though by no means all of it, made its way into the royal laws of the *leges Visigothorum*.[118] Gothic law, however, survived not only the fall of the Visigothic kingdom but that of the Italian *regnum* of the Ostrogoths as well. Far into the Middle Ages Goths from Italy, Catalonia, and southern France professed their own law.[119] But the Gothic "songs of the ancestors" that are mentioned from the mid-sixth century[120] are fundamentally different in content and political significance from the oral traditions to which the *Origo Gothica* referred. The disappearance of the royal bearers of tradition marked a deep break in the history of the Goths. From the diverse *memoriae* of the *gens* were preserved only the concepts of a Gothic community of law and, only until the sixth century, that of a Gothic religious community; both concepts together, as well as each by itself, formed the community of all those who recognized the *lex Gothica*.[121]

While early medieval "tribalism" acknowledged the diversity of peoples within a community of law, it had already absorbed enough Catholicism to exclude the diversity of religious beliefs. "Gothic law" could therefore survive the sixth century only if it separated itself from the Gothic cult and remained simply the basis of a community of law. Pagan Roman ethnographers had noted as barbaric such archaic institutions as human sacrifice or cult secrets.[122] Still around 400 many a pagan even saw the barbarian as a companion in arms from whom he expected support in the struggle to preserve the "religion of the forefathers."[123] To the Christian observer of that time, in contrast, paganism was fundamentally barbarian; for him it was the superstition of the "internal and external proletariat."[124] When the barbarians accepted Christianity there disappeared one of the most important obstacles to their integration into the Christian world. But since the Gothic peoples—unlike the Franks—initially became Arians, the *lex Gothica* seemed to serve as a sort of tribal religion. But Gothic Arianism could never truly fulfill the function of a tribal religion. Reports of Goths supporting the Roman Arians and vice versa are rare after 430.[125] The pagan tribal religion embodied the belief in the divine descent of the *gens* and its royal clan; it preserved the notion of a legal and religious community that embraced the living and the dead and that was constantly renewed through the cult. Only when this religious and political identity was threatened did the Gothic leaders react with severe persecutions, as was the case with the fourth-century Tervingian aristocracy and in the period immediately preceding the Visigothic conversion to Catholicism.[126] It is true that Gothic Arianism preserved a sense of separateness between Romans and Goths much longer than was necessary. But we know of no instance when a Goth who had become a Catholic lost his tribal membership on account of it. Conversion—*mutata religio*—also rarely led to discrimination, let alone persecution. Already two popes of the sixth century are considered Goths and Roman citizens: Sigisvult's son Boniface II (530–532) and Hunigild's son Pelagius II (579–590).[127] The third council of Toledo in 589 spelled the end of Visigothic Arianism.[128] Traces of the Ostrogothic religious traditions can be found among the Lombards as late as the seventh century,[129] but those who adhered to these traditions were as little a people as the Gotho-Arian soldiers in the Byzantine army.[130]

From the moment the Goths gave up their native language and dress, there vanished another important reason for contemporaries to see them as barbarians. Around 430 Romans and barbarians differed in their religion (*ritus*), their language (*lingua*), their dress and personal hygiene. To be sure, even in those days many Romans—subject to heavy taxation and weary of the state—would probably rather have endured the "stench of barbarian bodies and clothes" than the "mad injustice" of their own countrymen. A generation later Sidonius Apollinaris jokes that the barbarian Burgundians were afraid of committing barbarisms in their own barbarian language in front of a Roman noble, so proficient had he become in their tongue. At the same time the barbarians learned from him the Roman law, improved speech, and a Latin spirit.[131] But the Latin West was in fact more intolerant toward the dialects of the ethnic minorities than the Graeco-Slavic East. There the Gothic language, though in a foreign environment and without royal protection, survived the centuries, whereas in Spain, Gaul, and Italy Gothic as a living language probably did not see the opening years of the seventh century. The same goes for barbarian dress. The "Scythian furs" of the fifth-century Goths appeared barbaric. A century later, long before the last evidence for a spoken Gothic language, we have no more reports about this unusual Scythian costume, unusual because unsuited for the Mediterranean region.[132]

The Goths did not disappear, even after they had lost their kingdoms. But they had long ceased to be barbarians, let alone barbarian federates.[133] The Gothic people, which presented itself as a Gothic army, became an early medieval *gens* that stopped wandering through Europe. In the West and the East they had become Roman Goths, who attracted the attention of the still largely pagan *gentes* beyond the Roman frontiers in a peculiar way. Among these peoples Theodoric of Ravenna was remembered either as the exemplary Dietrich von Bern or looked upon as the demonic personification of the god of war.[134] Indeed, in the realm of myth and saga the Gothic name disappeared completely; one spoke of the descendants of the Amali, the *Amalungi*, if one meant the Goths.[135] But the Goths themselves, from the middle of the sixth century, are no longer the subject of historical ethnography; from that time we must write about them in a different way.[136]

1

The Names

The Gothic Name

Classical ethnography applied the name Suevi to many Germanic tribes.[1] In a similar fashion the appellation "Gothic" constantly gained in importance until the sixth century. As soon as late antique ethnographers noticed common elements of language, way of life, or geographical origin,[2] they spoke of "Gothic peoples."[3] It was known that these peoples had originally lived on the lower Danube and at the Black Sea, exactly where traditional, Greek-oriented ethnography had located the Scythians. Whoever wanted to be more precise also distinguished in this area Getae and Daci, Sarmatians and Sauromates, "Blackmantles" and Amazons, and whatever else could find room in the barbarian north. The fourth book of Herodotus's *Historiae* supplied the basic information and terms for this classification. But the literary game with the conventional terminology became deadly serious when the ancient world was no longer able to seal off the border along the lower Danube. The "Scythians" then threatening the Roman Empire were called Goths and Huns; soon only Goths remained after the Huns had disappeared.[4]

The name Goths, which replaced that of Scythians, embraced the most diverse Germanic and even non-Germanic peoples: the Goths in Italy, the Vandals, the Goths in Spain, the Gepids, Rugians, Sciri, and Burgundians, indeed, even the Alans.[5] The common faith and law, the *lex Gothica*,[6] and the common language were the most important reasons for lumping these peoples together. On linguistic grounds, for the purposes of classification, modern scholarship invented the artificial term *East Germanic peoples,* which is today commonly used.[7]

The Amal *Origo Gothica,* however, limited the number of Gothic peoples. It based its classification on a Scandinavian origin and counted among the Goths the Ostrogoths, Visigoths, and Gepids.[8] Before the end of the third century the Gepids broke away from this community "in disregard of their former bonds of blood kinship"[9] and became a separate people. The two tribes commonly called Visigoths and Ostrogoths, however, remained Goths[10] and therefore form the subject of the present book.[11]

The Gothic name appears for the first time between A.D. 16 and 18. We do not, however, find the strong form Guti but only the derivative form Gutones. Both Latin and Greek authors spoke of the Gutones until the middle of the second century A.D. The Greek geographer Ptolemy, who mentions this people for the last time around 150, was also aware of a people called Guti on the island of Scandia. Between him and the sixties of the third century no contemporary source mentions a tribal name that could be "Gothic."[12] In 262 Shapur I "the Great" had the famous trilingual inscription carved, and in it there appear Germanic and Gothic peoples among the Roman troops he had defeated in 245.[13] From the year 269 comes the oldest Latin-Roman evidence for the Gothic name: at that time Claudius II assumed the triumphal name Gothicus.[14] The same period also witnessed the appearance of the first Greek text mentioning the Goths.[15] In other words, around 270 a people bearing the name Goths was noticed by the Persians, the Romans, and the Greeks. The early epigraphic sources in particular used the strong form Gut(th)-, which had replaced the weak form Gutones for good. Both forms, however, have in common the stem *Gut-,* which is also attested by the vernacular tradition in the words *Gutthiuda* (land of the Gothic people) and *Gutans (Goth). From around 300 we find in the ancient languages almost exclusively the spelling Got(th)-.[16]

The chronology of the names causes difficulties because the strong name forms of the Scandinavian Guti as well as those of the Pontic Guti-Goths are attested later than their weak derivation, the name Gutones.[17] This last name contains the suffix -*one*, which can express contradictory meanings. Accordingly, it is linguistically possible to see in the Gutones either the "young" Goths or the "great" Goths.[18] Historically there is evidence both for the second, boastful name (in that the Gutones had a strong kingship)[19] and against it (in that the Goths were at their first appearance a dependent people and when last mentioned still a small people).[20]

Classical geography of the first century after Christ knew a continental river that flowed into the Baltic Sea and was called Guthalus. If a Gothic river is meant, the name presupposes the strong *Gut-* form, attesting it on the continent; but the name is also found as the Swedish Götaälv, as the river of the Scandinavian Guti-Gauts is called.[21] Procopius, who is the first to speak of the Gauts in Thule, knows about their veneration of Ares. He writes about it as if he is speaking of the Scythians, Thracians, Getae, or even of the Goths themselves.[22] A similarity between the Goths and the Gauts is probably also expressed by the tribal name Gauthigoths, which appears in Cassiodorus's Scandinavian list of peoples.[23]

What the names Goth and Gaut actually mean, how they are related, and how they differ are popular topics of etymological discussion. The aim of the scholarly efforts is "to make understandable the uses of *gautaz,* which would otherwise be difficult to explain." Does the root *Gut/Gaut*—which means "the one who pours out"—derive from the Scandinavian river that drains the huge Lake Vener into the Kattegat, or are the Goths and Gauts the "men" or even the "stallions" in the sense of "seed spreaders"? Or are the Gauts and Goths perhaps the sons of Gaut, the god of war, who is the leader of war bands both in Scandinavia and in Germania? Since the Gothic tradition provides evidence for all of these interpretations, to select one and exclude the others is arbitrary. But of greater historical importance than etymology is the linguistic insight that "the tribal name Goths means the same as Gauts."[24] So why not end the fruitless quarrels and "believe" Theodoric the Great, who derives his origins and those of his Goths from Scandinavia?[25]

The native Lithuanians of tsarist Russia mocked the Russian Lithuanians and the White Russians with the derisive name Gudas (i.e., Guddes). Linguists assume that this is "the vernacular name of the Goths." Though the Guddes are attested only from the sixteenth century on, they are said to be "very old." Gdec, which can be first attested for the eleventh century, Gdynia-Gdingen, and even Gdańsk-Danzig are supposedly Guddic names. This linguistic material is further supplemented by the place-name Graudenz-Grudziądz which is said to conceal a special Gothic name.[26] The historian reads such timeless reports from the past only with detached interest but must consider them impossible to interpret scholarly.

During the third century Roman and Persian contemporaries became acquainted with the name and the people of the Goths. A populous *gens* had formed along the northwestern shore of the Black Sea between the mouth of the Danube and the Don, and no one thought of deriving this people from the Gutones or the Ptolemaic Guti. The first Gutthia-Γοτθία of ancient ethnography is therefore located on the shores of the Black Sea; either in the Crimea or on the Kerch peninsula or, more probably, in present-day Romania. Among the participants of the ecumenical council of Nicaea in 325 was a bishop of the Goths, whose name appears in the protocol right next to that of his colleague from the Crimea.[27]

Around 480 there existed along the Caucasian coast of the Black Sea the Gothic-speaking people of the Eudusi. But they were certainly not Goths; more likely they were Eutes from the Cimbrian peninsula who had come to the Black Sea with the Heruli.[28] Only Procopius speaks again specifically about the Crimean Gothia where in the sixth century lived the Tetraxites and Trapezites. They had originally settled on the Kerch, but under severe pressure from the Hunnic Utuguri had exchanged this place for the Taman peninsula, which, Procopius says, they inhabited "still today."[29]

Of all Gothic territorial names the Dacian Gothia developed the strongest literary afterlife. As a geographic term it was spread especially by orthodox hagiographers and church historians. The earliest records come from the period just after 372 and between 383 and 392. They are, however, preceded by the imperial coinage of the years 332–334, even though the Gothia that Constantine subdued comprised at best parts of the old Trajan's Dacia. Not until about 400, when it seemed to Romans and Goths alike that the left bank of the Danube was lost, was Dacia equated with Gothia.[30] Since this was primarily a literary remembrance, it was widely adopted by historiographers. Although on occasion some authors allowed Gothia to be replaced by Gepidia,[31] Isidore of Seville best exemplifies the medieval view when he identifies the Goths as the original inhabitants of the province of Dacia and called the Daci only their descendants.[32]

To Gothia belonged also the settlement region of the *Gothi minores,* the "minor (i.e., Roman) Goths." This was the name Jordanes gave to the followers of Ulfilas. Ever since the middle of the fourth century they had occupied the northern slopes of the Haemus-Balkan mountain range. But as late as the ninth century Walahfrid Strabo believed that "there are Goths in the Greek provinces" who live side by side with "Scythian peoples" and speak the "Germanic" language.[33]

That the Thracian Goths called their lost homeland Gutthiuda—"land of the Gothic people"—is attested at the beginning of the fifth century after an older source.[34] Its counterpart was probably *Oium*—"in the fruitful meadows"—as the eastern Goths called their land.[35] But Gothic tradition also preserved two other place-names in the vernacular, namely, *Gothi-scandza* (Gothic-Scandia or Gothic coast[36]) and *Gepedoios* (fruitful meadows of the Gepids), as the island of Spesis in the mouth of the Vistula was called in Gothic. Cassiodorus claims that both names were in current use in his time. Supposedly the mixed people of the Vidivarii—composed of Gothic-Gepidic-Baltic elements—arose from the "meadows of the Gepids."[37] All these reports would cause no problems if the *Origo Gothica* did not claim at the same time that the Goths had gone ashore in Gothiscandza in precisely the year 1490 B.C.[38]

The invasion of the Huns destroyed the Gothic lands at the Black Sea. Gothia now became the Gothic army, the people in arms.[39] A new *patria Gothorum* arose only with the creation of the kingdom of Toulouse.[40] This patria outlasted the Aquitanian *regnum* as well as the Visigothic kingdom of Spain. Its subkingdom of Gaul, or Septimania, became in the eighth century the *Gotia* of the Carolingian Empire.[41] At about the same time Gothogreeks—Γοτθογραικοί—are still mentioned on the western coast of Asia Minor across from Lesbos, but by the tenth century at the latest they had been hellenized.[42]

To this day there are European regions bearing the Gothic name. Spanish Catalonia is certainly not a Gothia-Alania but merely means "land of castles."[43] Swedish Västergötland and Östergötland, however, as well as the island of Gotland, are not merely Gothicized but actual Gothic-Gautic names. The similarity of the name of the Gothic people and that of the island of Gotland seems to support the migration legend of the *Origo Gothica*. This area was also the home of the medieval Gutasaga, which relates that overpopulation led the people to draw lots and the inhabitants thus chosen emigrated. Their wanderings are said to have taken them across southern Russia into Greece.[44] Swedish "Gothicism" was always very vigorous. But in the Later Middle Ages it was believed that Austria too had once been called Gothia.[45]

The special forms of the Gothic name mark periods in the history of that people; they designate various Gothic ethnogeneses, among which the Scandinavian Gautic one lacks almost all evidence. It is therefore possible to attach a geographical and chronological meaning to the ethnic terms. Hereafter, whenever the Gutones and Guti are mentioned, these terms refer to the Goths on the Continent before their migration to the Black Sea. The people of the third century before the division will simply be called Goths. Thereafter, in the fourth century, appear the double names of the western and eastern divisions—the Tervingi-Vesi and the Greutungi-Ostrogoths[46]— and these are finally replaced by the conventional names for the Gothic peoples on Roman soil: Visigoths and Ostrogoths. The Gothic-Gautic peoples of the Baltic-Scandinavian north will be mentioned for the sake of completeness, but a historical discussion of these peoples can hardly go beyond the listing of their names.[47]

The Dual Names of the Two Gothic Peoples

The division of the Gothic people, first attested in the spring of 291,[48] produced two groups, the western one called Tervingi-Vesi and the eastern one called Greutungi-Ostrogothi. This nomenclature remained in use until shortly after 400; thereafter the pair Tervingi/Greutungi lived on only in the heroic saga. The name Vesi continued unchanged—as did the name Ostrogoths—until Cassiodorus "improved" the name to match that of the Ostrogoths and created the term Visigoths.[49] Nevertheless, many problems remain in understanding these names.

The oldest mention of the Tervingi comes from the spring of 291.[50] The three other Gothic names are not attested until the last decade of the fourth century, more or less simultaneously, but still one hundred years after the Tervingi. The *Notitia dignitatum* referring to the time between 388 and 391 contains not only the earliest mention of the Vesi but also attests the ethnic identity of the Tervingi and Vesi. The same certainty does not exist for the pair Greutungi-Ostrogoths, but it is highly probable that these peoples too are identical.[51] But how do we bridge the gap between these first references? Ammianus Marcellinus, who "discovered" the Greutungi, did not write before 392, if not actually after 395. Although he based his ethnographic discovery on a Tervingian chieftain who had been a commander as early as 376, barely two decades are gained in this way. And the oldest datable mentioning of the Ostrogoths appears in September 392 in Milan.[52] All attempts to complete the chronology must have recourse to conjecture, and it is precisely the name of the Ostrogoths that allows the first inference. According to the *Origo Gothica,* Ostrogotha ruled over the Ostrogoths or over both peoples—Cassiodorus was not quite sure[53]—when the Tervingi first became known in other sources. But while the saga speaks of an Ostrogothic king as "father of the Ostrogoths," historical reality works the other way round: Ostrogotha presupposes the existence of an Ostrogothic people.[54]

The sources never "mix" the names of the peoples. They either speak of the pair Tervingi/Greutungi or the Vesi/Ostrogoths. This scheme is not even upset when all four names are used. For instance, the order of the pairs is preserved even in the following sequences: *Ostrogothi mixtique Gruthungis,*[55] or *Gruthungi, Austrogothi, Tervingi, Visi.*[56] Finally, the pair Greutungi-Tervingi is geographically determined and consists of names that were initially used by one tribe to describe the other; they disappear half a generation after the Goths had been driven out by the Huns.[57] The pair Ostrogoths-Vesi, however, were boastful names chosen by each people and therefore the names survived the Hunnic invasion. In sum, the names Greutungi-Tervingi as well as Ostrogoths-Vesi must have been formed at the same time; each pair presupposes the other.

As to the etymology of the names, let us confine ourselves to a simple statement of fact: the Vesi are "the Good, the Noble," and the Ostrogoths are the "Goths of the rising sun"—hence "East Goths"—or the "Goths glorified by the rising sun." The Tervingi are the "forest people" and the Greutungi the "dwellers of the steppes and pebbly coasts."[58] This will suffice; otherwise the discussion will be endless.

As soon as the great migration begins all the special names fade out. After 400 the geographically determined names are mentioned only by authors who, like Zosimus, relied on sources predating the beginning of the fifth century.[59] The best example is Ammianus Marcellinus, who distinguished the Goths outside the empire according to their special names, but soon after their admission into the empire he knew only as Goths.[60] On January 1, 456, Sidonius Apollinaris is the last to attest that the king and the Goths of Toulouse saw themselves as Vesi. The same author is also aware of the Ostrogoths, the descendants of that *gens* that Ammianus Marcellinus calls the Greutungi.[61] Hence we are following contemporary terminology if we use the pairs Tervingi-Vesi and Greutungi-Ostrogoths for the history of the Goths from their division to the end of the fourth century.

Visigoths and Ostrogoths as Western Goths and Eastern Goths

Everyone knows that the Goths split "into the two peoples of the same tribe."[62] But the idea that the Visigoths are the western Goths and the Ostrogoths the eastern Goths is no older than Cassiodorus's entrance into the service of Theodoric the Great. What had once been the boastful name of the eastern Goths was used by Cassiodorus to make a geographic distinction. He clearly understood the Ostrogoths as eastern Goths, and to match their name he created the artificial term Visigoths in the sense of western Goths.[63] From the simplifying perspective of the sixth century the history of the Goths had always been that of a western and an eastern tribal division.[64] But this classification served only literary purposes. When it came to political concerns Cassiodorus monopolized the term Goths for Theodoric's people, whereas the Goths of Gaul were labeled the Visigoths. Theodoric thus usurped the entire Gothic tradition. Hence any geographical qualification, such as "western Goths," classified the Gallo-Spanish Goths as a mere subgroup of inferior standing.

Procopius and the other Byzantines make the same use of terms. A single testimony from the seventh century proves that Cassiodorus's terminology had been taken over by the Spanish Goths for their diplomatic communications with Italy.[65] A later "Germanic" addition to a source that is most likely Byzantine/Italian mentions the Romanized Goths of Spain or Italy as Valagothi (i.e., Roman Goths).[66]

In the second half of the fifth century the peoples we call Visigoths and Ostrogoths were also personalized. In 484 the Ostrogoths appeared as the Valameriaci (the "men of Valamir") because they were under the leadership of Theodoric, who was considered the son of Valamir. Only a little before, on the occasion of the events of 469, a Byzantine remembered the Alaric Goths, who were now under the sway of King Euric in Gaul.[67]

The Epic and the Derisive Names of the Goths

The Gepids traveled to the mouth of the Vistula in the last of Berig's three boats; for this reason the other Goths mocked them as "the lazy and sluggish ones"—*gepanta*.[68] It is possible that the Gepids took revenge by spreading a distasteful story: they said that the Goths had been in bondage in "Britannia or on some other island" and that they had been set free for the price of a horse.[69] Like the words "Arab" and "Walachian," "Goth" too can mean horse. The real point of the story is the claim "that for the horse people of the Goths only the price of a single horse—namely, that of a single Goth—had to be paid to free them all from bondage." If the reproach that they had once been slaves is serious, the insult is magnified if their freedom was purchased at a ridiculously low price. According to this story, one Goth would be worth as much as the entire people and vice versa.[70]

Hostile brothers may mock each other in this way, but the threatened neighbor uses stronger terms. To the Vandals the Goths seemed like τροῦλοι, trolls, as the Scandinavians still call the demons and monsters of the other world.[71] But there are indeed mentioned in Scandinavia Gauthigoths and

Greutungi, who lived "like animals in carved out, castlelike rocks."[72] This is an odd agreement between two sources as different as Cassiodorus and Olympiodorus, who are separated by more than a century.

To be sure, the name of the Greutungi, which originated in southern Russia, came to Scandinavia only as part of saga; for this the *Origo Gothica*, if a suggested emendation is correct,[73] would contain the first evidence. The original meaning of the name-pair Tervingi-Greutungi lived on in the *Hervarasaga* and its concluding section, the "Battle of the Goths and the Huns." The Gothic land is here called Týrfingr ("the Tervingian"), the same name that is given to the mythical hereditary sword of the Goths. This presupposes that the Thraco-Scythian Ares-Mars, who was seen as the incarnation of the people and the land and who also manifested himself in the shape of a sword, had been accepted as a Gothic god. And in fact this sort of acculturation can be demonstrated only for the Tervingi. Now the "Battle of the Goths and the Huns" also knows the Greutungi name, but here it does not refer to an object or a land but instead to the "Greutungian Warrior," a demonic-divine person, namely, Odin himself. Thus the Nordic epic poetry preserved the geographically determined names of the Goths with remarkable accuracy. The Greutungi survived as the surname of the Ansic Gaut, who is at the head of the Amal genealogy, while the Tervingian designated the land and the sword, the objects in which is embodied the Scythian-Thracian and from the fourth century the Gothic Ares-Mars.[74]

This difference in the way western and eastern Goths were remembered was taken a step further by epic poetry. For epic poetry to have a theme, there had to be the heroic pathos of a sacral tribal kingship being threatened. And since the historical Ermanaric sacrificed himself, his reward was a place in the heroic saga. The fall of the Greutungian kingdom seemed to repeat itself in the ruin of Theodoric the Great, and the memory of Dietrich von Bern (Theodoric of Verona) is as ambivalent as that of his legendary antagonist Ermanaric.[75] The combining of the power of fate with the deeds of kings leads to the creation of the heroic saga.[76] At first sight Vidigoia-Witige seems to be an exception. The *Origo Gothica* does count him among the Visigoths, and his name reflects that.[77] But the hero finds his way into epic tradition only as one of the retainers of the "Ostrogothic" king Ermanaric. At his court Vidigoia-Witige is received as a foreign refugee, which could indicate that he came from the kingless West. But the tragic conflict he faced arose from his alliance with both Ermanaric and Theodoric, whom the saga makes contemporaries and mortal enemies. All other names of the Goths refer directly to the Ostrogothic *memoria*.[78]

In medieval poetry and historiography the Goths are the Amalungi, the descendants of the Amal Theodoric.[79] In addition, the popular etymology of various languages created numerous other names as well.[80]

Biblical and Classical Names for the Goths

From the terms invented by "popular etymology"[81] we must distinguish the classical names given to the Goths to describe their settlement in an ancient land or their connection with a classical people. Examples are the Bosporanian Trapezites-Tetraxites and the Gothogreeks of Asia Minor;[82] both will not be discussed here.

Greek ethnography in particular continued to apply to the northern peoples the names it took from the Scythian book of Herodotus. This had already happened to the Sarmati and was now happening to the Goths.[83] The Athenian Dexippus wrote his work a little after 270 and dealt with the Gothic assaults that began in 238.[84] If we did not know from later excerpters of Dexippus's work that the Goths arrived at this time,[85] there would be no direct report about them, for Dexippus speaks only of Scythians. Still Orosius listed the three wildest Scythian peoples of his day: the Alans, Huns, and Goths.[86] It is no surprise that soon the Amazons—who had always been linked to the Scythians—were rediscovered in the Gothic women and that to them was attributed a mythical matriarchy in the prehistory of the Gothic people.

Then the Goths are identified as the "Scythian" Sauromates and the Melanchlainoi—the "Blackmantles." Finally the most effective connection again made use of the similar sound of the names: the designation of the Goths as Getae.[87] Before this "etymology" appeared, however, the Bible had been used for the first time to classify the Gothic peoples from the north. Around A.D. 93 Josephus Flavius equated the biblical Magog with the Scythians of Greek ethnography. Bishop Ambrose followed suit when he consoled the Emperor Gratian in the winter of 377/378, promising him that God would grant the Romans the victory over *Gog iste Gothus*. Less than half a year later Ambrose was strikingly refuted by the defeat at Adrianople. Although it was "only" the Arian emperor Valens who had lost the battle and his life, for the time this interpretation was discredited. A little after 392, St. Jerome already called it precisely the kind of poor eschatology it in fact was, and St. Augustine agreed with him. Jerome then introduced as an "antidote" the assertion that "all earlier scholars had called the Goths Getae rather than Gog and Magog."[88] With this he probably invented the identification of the Goths as Getae, which made its way via Orosius and many authors of the fifth century to Cassiodorus and Isidore of Seville.[89] During the Gothic Wars of the sixth century, mythographers in Rome still drew from the Sibyline Books the prophecy that the Getae, that is, the Goths, would be defeated.[90]

Up to and including Cassiodorus the names Getae and Scythians had still pushed back Gog and Magog but had not quite replaced them. Just as the Christian conception of Rome had to come a long way from regarding Rome as the whore of Babylon to seeing it as the earthly Jerusalem, so the mere mention of the "Gothic peoples Gog and Magog" offered the possibility of turning their original negative meaning into a positive one. In the seventh century Isidore of Seville made use of this in an elaborate and unambiguous way. It seems that Cassiodorus was not only aware of this idea but thought well of it. Cassiodorus's only regret was that Josephus Flavius had nothing more to say about the Goths than that their name and origin identified them as Scythians. Isidore supports the presumed descent of the Scythians and Goths from Magog, the son of Japhet, with a peculiar etymological operation: the homophony of the names of the Scythians and Goths. He even manages to discover the homophony of Getae and Tecti, which is linguistically interesting but without basis in fact. Furthermore, he uses the eschatological speculation Gog-Magog-*tectum* to turn *tectum*-house to *Tecti*-housed, protected (Goths). And to make things even worse, Isidore had found in Jerome a word-list in which Gaza (*fortitudo*) and Gog appeared in sequence. These words have nothing whatsoever to do with each other. Nevertheless, Isidore used this accidental, alphabetical closeness to the Goths' advantage: they were said to be Gog, that is, "covered" or "protected" and to have courage (Gaza-*fortitudo*). It is interesting that Libanius already called the Franks Φρακτοί and derived their name from φράσσω: "to protect, to arm, to fortify." The same approach, however, is used by scientific etymology, for which the word *free* carries the meaning "protected," "spared." As a final example we may mention that Isidore saw the name of the Daci (Da-Gi) as derived from "from the Goths," and he consequently declared them their descendants. In this case, as well, he was aided by an obviously not yet detected Romanism.[91]

Gothic Royal Houses and Their Names

"For many centuries the Goths were united in one realm under the leadership of kings. But because the kings are not recorded in the chronicles, nothing is known about them. They entered into the historical sources only from that time when the Romans began to feel their martial valor." With these words Isidore of Seville justifies his version of Gothic history, which he could only write with the help of Roman historiography.[92] It may well be that Cassiodorus, as he himself claims, "gained from reading historical sources a knowledge, *notitia,* that even the white-haired elders [of the Goths] barely remembered,"[93] yet in writing his Amal Gothic history he nevertheless relied also on "songs and stories," *carmina, cantus maiorum, fabulae.* The migration story, the heroic epic, and above all the Amal genealogy can be explained neither through the classical nor any other non-Gothic tradition; rather, they are part of an indigenous tribal tradition. Foreign sagas and stories that belittled the Goths Cassiodorus understandably rejected. In such cases the oral nature of the tradition was considered an argument against its credibility.[94] Whereas Isidore begins Gothic history with the Scythians outside the empire, Cassiodorus preserves the Amal memory not only of pre-Roman but also of pre-Scythian history. Thus he could link the history of the Goths in the Balkans, on the Sarmatian steppes, along the Vistula, and in Scandinavia. The bearers of this tradition were the "nuclei of tradition," the royal clans of the Goths.[95] Sisenand, the king of the Spanish Visigoths to whom Isidore dedicated his *Historia vel Origo Gothorum,*[96] found in the "old songs" no legitimization of his rule and nothing to motivate his Gothic identity. Although Isidore recommends the heroic songs as a tool for educating the nobility, he gives no indication that he knows the content of any genuine oral tradition.[97] It is not surprising that we learn all the names of the Gothic royal clans from Cassiodorus's *Origo Gothica.* Theodoric the Great had monopolized virtually every Gothic tradition and thus made it impossible for these traditions to be used by anyone else or any differently after the downfall of the Amali in 540.[98]

What stands out clearly is the tendency of the *Origo Gothica* to present the Amali as the legitimate royal house of the Ostrogoths and the Balthi as that of the Visigoths: this situation was said to have existed ever since the Goths migrated to the Black Sea, where they divided into these two tribes.[99] The Balthi were of "wonderful descent," their name *baltha* meant "bold," but their nobility ranked among the Goths only in second place, since membership in the Amal clan was considered "the highest honor among the [barbarian] peoples."[100] These statements correspond to the belief that "every family had a special rank peculiar to itself, one family was more noble than another."[101] The Amali and Balthi are families of "kings and heroes";[102] each of the two clans personifies its people. Thus the Amali are the *genealogia Ostrogotharum,* the "family of the Ostrogoths."[103] When this branch of the Goths recognized the divine charisma of its Amal leaders, *proceres,* it acclaimed and revered the Amali as *Ansis,* as Aesir. This is probably why Cassiodorus does not bother to explain the name of the Amali.[104]

The Ansis stand for the divine descent of the Amal clan. Their genealogy begins with Gaut, the Scandinavian god of war and ancestor of many peoples. His son is Humli-Hulmul, the divine founding father of the Danes. Amal is mentioned only in the fourth generation. The next eponymous hero is Ostrogotha, two generations younger than Amal and already at home in the Pontic area. Between these two stands Hisarna, who perhaps represents the Celtic-dominated layer of the Gothic ethnogenesis. As the "noblest of the Amali," Ermanaric belongs to the tenth generation; he is the first of his family who is mentioned by a source other than the *Origo Gothica* and the first to be noticed by Roman contemporaries. With him the *catalogus Amalorum* begins to become historical. The names that previously reflected theogony, ethnogeneses, and charismatic power are now replaced by names that once belonged to human beings of flesh and blood. Whereas the theogonic part contained only a relative, though highly important, chronology of the Gothic ethnogenesis, the generations after Ermanaric can be synchronized with historical events. But the first to step fully into the light of history are the Amal brothers Valamir, Thiudimir, and Vidimir, who around 450 were the leaders of the Hunnic Ostrogoths. Thiudimir's son is Theodoric the Great. Theodoric's grandson Athalaric, son of the Visigothic Amal Eutharic and Theodoric's daughter and heir Amalasuintha, concludes the genealogy, which was certainly drawn up before Theodoric's death in 526. In early 533 Cassiodorus chose from the genealogy ten of Amalasuintha's ancestors in order to legitimize her as queen of the Gothic army through the royal ancestral line: *tot reges quot parentes.* The shortened family tree of this highly educated woman lets the Gautic/Scandinavian origins recede into the background and it drops altogether the pagan barbarian Ermanaric. Though Ermanaric does appear in Athalaric's family tree, he does not belong to the direct ancestral line of the Ostrogothic king. Athalaric was legitimized through his descent, which taught him that he—like another Romulus, the founder of Rome—"possessed the royal dignity in the seventeenth generation."[105]

Cassiodorus presents Theodoric's family tradition. The great king decided who belonged to the Amal clan. His marriage policy is seen as the emanation of Amal splendor. Cassiodorus's rhetoric certainly did much for the high esteem the Amali enjoyed in East and West alike. But an Amal tradition already prevailed in Theodoric's clan at a time when Cassiodorus—whose birth is dated around 490—either had not yet gained office and honor or had not even been born. The two daughters of the king—Ostrogotho who was married in 494 and Amalasuintha who was born shortly after 493—were given Amal names, and Theodoric's eldest sister was called Amalafrida. Perhaps the special emphasis on Amal identity goes back to the time of the conflict between the two Theodorics. The *Origo Gothica* denies the hostile Theodoric Strabo membership in the Amal clan. But Strabo, the son of Triarius and rival of Theodoric the Great, was the brother-in-law of the Alan Aspar who named one of his sons after Ermanaric, "the noblest of the Amali."[106] This clearly shows that the family of Aspar's wife—and of her brother Theodoric Strabo—was more noble than Aspar's own family. Thus there is a high probability that Aspar had married an Amal woman and thus that Theodoric Strabo was also an Amal. It is in keeping with this evidence that Theodoric, son of Thiudimir, had killed in Rekitach, son of Theodoric Strabo, a "blood relative" (ἀνεψιός). Finally, even the *Origo Gothica* admits that some Amali did not move to Italy with Theodoric but stayed behind in the Balkans. We are told something about the Andela-Andagis family, which was related to the Alans; it was counted among the Amali, and during the lifetime of Attila it was subject to King Valamir.[107] Apart from them there was certainly at least one other family that had gone off on its own and had broken away from the Amal "nucleus of tradition." And the Visigothic Amali as such are a separate problem altogether. In the third and eighth decades of the fifth century Goths under Amal leadership came to Aquitaine. Among their descendants Theodoric the Great "discovered" his son-in-law Eutharic.[108]

Unlike the frequent name appearances for the Amali, there is only one positive testimony about the Balthic clan. Writing about Alaric's elevation to kingship, Cassiodorus claims that he is a Balth.[109] It is possible, however, to trace the descendants and ancestors of the first Visigothic king. First, a mere observation: the island that Pliny the Elder called Basilia ("land of the king") is also given by him the name Baltia, after a different source. It was said to be an enormously large island situated a three-day journey by ship from the "shore of the Scythians." It is not entirely impossible that the Balthic clan derives its origins from the "royal Baltia" and that the Balthi were initially Baltis. The Visigothic personal name Galindo is evidence that Baltic traditions not only survived the migratory period but were still alive in the ninth century. Another connection is established by considerations drawn from the historical development of names and institutions: the three Tervingian judges Ariaric, Aoric, and Athanaric probably represent three Balthic generations of the fourth century. But it is impossible to say in what way Alaric was related to this group. We do notice, however, that the Balth

had an older namesake in the Herulian king who was subdued by Ermanaric. One suspects a cognatic relationship of the two Alarics. Then one
should mention that the chieftain who led the Tervingi across the Danube
in 376 was called Alaviv. Little is known about him other than his name,
which represents the type of variation on Alaric's name which could make
Alaviv Alaric's father. In either case Alaric's name could be explained by a
Balthic tradition marked by alliteration, variation, and rhythm. There is no
reason to think that the name Alaric came to the Balthi from a foreign royal
clan.[110]

   As for Alaric I's descendants, the sons of the Visigothic king Theoderid
were his grandchildren. Theoderid, who succeeded King Valia in 418 and
whose family ruled until 531, is now considered the progenitor of the
"younger Balthi." Alaric I had a wife and children. Perhaps a daughter of
the conqueror of Rome became the wife of Theoderid; had the latter been
Alaric's son, contemporaries would no doubt have recorded it.[111] In any
case, Theoderid's grandson was given the name Alaric. For Cassiodorus the
Visigothic kingdom is so obviously a Balthic *regnum* that in order to describe its founding through Alaricus Magnus—Alaric the Elder—and its end
under Alaric II, he uses the analogy of Augustus and Augustulus and the
beginning and end of the Roman Empire.[112] The last of the younger Balthi
to assume the reins of power was the great-grandson of Theoderid and the
grandson of Theodoric the Great. He was called Amalaric, and his name
proves that the Amali were ranked higher than the Balthi, whose history
ends with his murder in 531.[113] Apart from the royal clan of Toulouse, the
successors to the Burgundian Nibelungs, who had been exterminated in
434, perhaps also belonged to the Balthi. The Burgundian king Gundiok is
called a descendant of Athanaric.[114] For a long time it was believed that he
had been put into power with Visigothic help and that he came from the
family of Theoderid. This view has recently been challenged.[115] But another
possibility is that Gundiok was related to the Visigothic king Valia. Gundiok's son Gundobad is considered the *nepos*—the grandson, nephew, or
in general the "relative"—of Ricimer, whose mother was the daughter of
Valia.[116] If one does not want to make Valia himself into a Balth, he too
might have married a Balthic woman, thus establishing his fitness for the
royal dignity in 415, which is similar to what happened to Athaulf when
he became Alaric's brother-in-law five years earlier[117] and what happened
to Theoderid possibly three years later.[118] But there were Gothic traditions
that reached back to a time before the invasion of the Huns and for which
the Visigothic Balthi were not necessarily directly responsible. Modares-
Modaharius, a Tervingian Balth who became a Roman officer,[119] has a

Gallic namesake in an Arian-Gothic priest of Euric's time.[120] Whether a Frankish rebel by the name of Munderic revolted against the Merovingians because he was actually a Goth and a descendant of a Tervingian chieftain of 376 of the same name must remain an open question.[121] But the *patricius* and descendant of the Burgundian royal house who rose against the Merovingian was called Aletheus.[122] Unless this was a Latin-Greek name,[123] this rebel was a namesake of the Greutungian chieftain Alatheus, the commander of the Gothic horsemen who decided the battle of Adrianople.[124]

The Scandinavian heroic saga sings of the deed of Hamdir and Sörli, who took revenge on a tyrannical king Jörmunrek-Ermanaric for the cruel death of their sister Swanhild-Sunilda.[125] This motif was already available to Cassiodorus, and it may have been the reason why he struck Ermanaric from Amalasuintha's ancestral line. In the *Origo Gothica* the author of course takes the side of the Amali. The "unfaithful race of the Rosomoni" takes advantage of the danger to the Ostrogothic kingdom and becomes guilty of criminal acts against its king Ermanaric. The unnamed husband of Swanhild-Sunilda commits treason, whereupon Ermanaric has the woman drawn and quartered. Her brothers Ammius and Sarus then inflict the mortal wound on the king, and he dies in the face of the Hunnic invasion like a biblical patriarch.[126]

A certain Sarus, frequently attested around 400, is as bitter an enemy and rival of the reigning royal clan as his Rosomon namesake: the legendary Sarus fights the Amali, the historical one the Balthi. This latter Sarus, and after his death his brother Sigeric, are the most vehement opponents of Alaric and his clan.[127] Nevertheless, we must not see the two Saruses as identical, the Rosomon of legend and the Goth of history. This does not imply, however, that the Rosomoni cannot be linked historically to the Heruli.[128] In the Rosomoni one could see Herulian opponents of both the Amali and the Balthi. They could have been a royal clan and would thus embody, as do the Balthi, Visigothic-Herulian connections. But reflections of this sort raise more questions than they answer.

The *Origo Gothica* speaks also about two other royal families of the Goths without giving their names. One we might name the Berig clan, after its progenitor. Berig is the king who supposedly led the Goths from Scandinavia onto the continent. After him there is a gap of two generations; then come Gadaric "the Great"—a surname that presupposes somewhere in Gothic history a younger Gadaric—and finally, as "approximately fifth king," Filimer. The latter is said to have begun the Gothic migration from the Vistula to the Black Sea.[129]

The second nameless royal clan can be called after Geberic. Although

Geberic is not the first but the last known member of the family, he is at the same time the only one about whom the *Origo Gothica* has anything to say. In its scheme he is one of those heroes celebrated in song before the time of the Amali. The tribal tradition remembered Geberic as a great victor over the Vandals. His father was Hilderith, his grandfather Ovida, and his great-grandfather Nidada.[130] Behind the last two names one has suspected, and not without reason, the Gothic king Cniva, who—again according to the *Origo Gothica*—defeated the emperor Decius in 251. Based on biological considerations—Geberic defeated the Vandals about eighty years after Cniva's victory over the Romans—and in view of linguistic and palaeographic arguments, the equation Nidada (Cnivida) = Cniva is more likely than the other alternative.[131] A problem, however, is raised by the identification of Cniva with Cannabas-Cannabaudes of the *Scriptores historiae Augustae;* given the dates of the available sources, this would presuppose a not impossible, though highly unusual versatility and longevity on part of the old warrior.[132] Although in a formal sense we may be dealing with an equation with two unknowns, a hypothetical solution would be as follows: Cniva, a successful Gothic commander and king of the army in the western tribal territory, is killed in battle as Cannabas against Aurelian. With him perish his people, supposedly five thousand men; the kingship is extinguished, the "western" Goths form themselves into the Tervingi in "Dacia" and do not recognize the "eastern" Amali when they take over the kingship. The abandonment of the kingship weakened but did not destroy completely the group of royal families—the many-layered *stirps regia,* the βασιλεῖον γένος—of the Tervingi. Among these the Geberic clan formed only one division, for it is certainly not identical with the group around Ariaric, Aoric, and Athanaric and it cannot be claimed for the Balthi. Royal families are attested also in the aristocratic societies that followed the fall of the kingships that these families had supported. This is true both for the Gallic and West Germanic tribes around the time of the birth of Christ and for the Tervingi of the fourth century.[133]

2

The Formation of the Gothic Tribes before the Invasion of the Huns

Gutones and Guti

From this island of Scandza, as from a factory of tribes or a womb of peoples [*officina gentium aut certe velut vagina nationum*], the Goths are said to have migrated long ago under their king Berig. As soon as they had disembarked from their ships and had set foot on land, they gave the place a name; for even today it is said to be called Gothiscandza. From there they soon advanced against the settlements of the Ulmerugi, who at that time lived on the shores of the sea, made war upon them, engaged in a battle, and drove them from the land. At that time they subjugated their neighbors, the Vandals, and by their victories forced them to join the Gothic tribe. . . .

This is the beginning of the *memoria*, the Amal tribal history of the Goths, which Cassiodorus recorded and which Jordanes preserved for posterity.[1] As late as the sixth century[2] Theodoric the Great insisted that his family had originated in Scandinavia and had made the long trek from there by way of eastern Pomerania and the Vistula to the Black Sea, thence to Pannonia and Moesia, and finally to Italy. In view of the enormous energy that scholarship has invested in defending or refuting the Scandinavian origin of the Goths, one could ask why we do not believe Theodoric and accept his claim—of course not as hard fact but as motif of a saga, the more so since the picture of a Gothic migration from one end of Europe to another certainly does not do justice to historical reality.[3] But after profound changes in the composition of the tribes and catastrophic collapses of Gothic kingdoms and realms—in short, throughout a history that stretches over more than half a millennium—formations of Gothic tribes were possible only because they were based on this saga, which was kept alive by "nuclei of tradition"[4] like the Amal clan. It was these nuclei who preserved the Gothic name. We should therefore take seriously, if not as hard fact, at least as a motif, the saga (*memoria*) of the Amali, which forms the background to their achievements. Although as a motif the Scandinavian origin had a strong afterlife—and made history—it is a saga, a story that even a modern historian can tell only in the words of the *Origo Gothica*. Moreover, the question is not whether Scandinavia was the "original homeland of the Goths"; at best it is whether certain Gothic clans came from the north across the Baltic Sea to the Continent.

The Amal genealogy gives an answer; it contains three eponymous tribal founders, who were related to one another in the male line: older than Ostrogotha, king of the Black Sea Goths,[5] is Amal, "with whom the history of the Amali begins."[6] But older still than Amal and the Amali are Gaut (sometimes pronounced and even written "Gapt") and the Scandinavian Gauts. This scheme is supported by the mention of Humli, the son of Gaut, and Hisarna, the son of Amal. Humli, the father of the Danes, stands for Gautic-Scandinavian relations. Hisarna, "the iron one," is a reminder of the earliest Gothic acculturation to the Celts, a process that occurred before the Amali became Goths or even Ostrogoths and reached the Black Sea. It is in keeping with the "logic" of the Amal family tree to place Hisarna in line as the father of Ostrogotha, the king of the Ostrogoths.

A second answer to the question raised could be given by comparing the *Origo Gothica* with its source, the work of Ptolemy. The Greek geographer mentions the Gutae, Γοῦται, as one of the seven peoples inhabiting the island of Scandia-Scandinavia. Unless we are dealing in this case with a double name for the Gutones, whom Ptolemy located along the Vistula, there must have been two Gothic peoples, namely, on both shores of the Baltic Sea. According to their genealogy the Amali became a group of continental Goths—and the leading group at that—only under Ostrogotha. But Ostrogotha belongs to the Ukrainian period, around 290. The Ptolemaic Gutae, however, already existed before 150.[7] Thus the creation of the *gens Amalorum* precedes the Ostrogothic tribal formation by several centuries;

the Amali could be derived from Ptolemy's Gutae. This would be in keeping with the evidence that Amal is a descendant of Gaut and the Amali descendants of the Scandinavian Gauti, whom Procopius perhaps also knew. Thus, with caution, we can say that at the beginning of the Amal tradition stood a Scandinavian ethnogenesis that the family tree of the Amali presented as a theogony.[8]

This theory, however, contains a major difficulty that is also raised by the *Origo Gothica*. The Gothic landing on the Continent is attributed to the Berig clan, which clearly did not belong to the Amali. Even in the structure of the *Origo Gothica* one notices a clear break between Filimer, the last of the Berig clan, and the first mention of Amali and Balthi.[9] And the first kings and heroes of the Gothic invasions of the third century did not come from either of the two royal families. Rather, it is explicitly reported that before the Amali there had been heroes whose deeds were also celebrated in song. In line with this statement in the *Origo Gothica* are the two "primordial" deeds that are said to have led to the creation and recreation of the Gothic tribe: first, the landing on the Continent; second, the Amali's assumption of the Gothic kingship about 440 years or seventeen generations before Athalaric's accession to power in 526. But Jordanes himself removes this distinction again by presenting the capitulation in 540 as the end of an Amal history that was said to have lasted 2,030 years. This contradiction reconciles the "Scandinavian origin" of the Amali—as contained in their genealogy—with the pre-Amal Berig saga. In the end Jordanes equates the history of the Goths with that of the Amali and thereby supports the memory of the Scandinavian origin of the tribe.[10]

No matter how one assesses all these attempts to reconcile different traditions, the Gutones certainly had nothing to do with the Amali. They were first mentioned by Strabo and last by Ptolemy, that is, roughly between the birth of Christ and the middle of the second century. This time span corresponds to the "approximately five generations" during which—according to the *Origo Gothica*—the Goths had settled in Gothiscandza.[11] Regardless of whether we take this name to mean "Gothic coast," or more likely "Gothic Scandia," this land might well have been identical with the area of the archaeological Wielbark culture in the East Pomeranian-Masovian region.[12] There are no doubt methodological reservations about equating too readily the accounts from the classical period with Cassiodorus's geography. For him both Gothiscandza and the island Spesis-Gepedoios in the Vistula were terms current in the sixth century. The coastal area at the mouth of the Vistula is the place where the Vidivarii, the inhabitants of the Witland/Woodland, appeared. Baltic peoples as well as Gothic-Gepidic groups contributed to the Vidivarian ethnogenesis. But Cassidorus thought that his geographic knowledge was valid "still today."[13] It is not surprising, though, that the people of medieval Scandinavia remembered the area of the Vistula as a Gothic land.[14]

Ancient ethnographers had scant knowledge of the Gutones, but we should be grateful for the little they did know because that includes some revealing information.[15] A century and a half after the geographer Strabo, Ptolemy was the last author who spoke of the Gutones. He was also the only one who clearly located them. According to Ptolemy, the Gutones lived northwest of present-day Warsaw on the eastern, Sarmatian bank of the Vistula. Since there is no reason to dismiss this information, regional shifts and changes must have accompanied the ethnogenesis of the Gutones.[16] Thus the Gutones were located in the very region from which they advanced to the Black Sea.[17] Ptolemy mentioned not only the Gutones on the mainland but also the Gutae, whom he lists as one of the seven Scandinavian island tribes. The question now arises whether the two "Gothic peoples" are not one of the author's numerous ethnographic doublets.[18] Of course the problem cannot be definitely resolved, but it appears that this is not the case. The Ptolemaic Gutones had been part of the ethnographic tradition; Ptolemy's Gutae, in contrast, seem to be an ethnographic novelty. Whether they were the predecessors of the Gauti who appear in Procopius some four hundred years later is a mere guess. Though the Gutae were not actually identical with the contemporary Gutones, it seems unlikely that there was no connection at all between these two peoples.[19] Regardless of where and how peoples crossed from Scandinavia to the mainland and vice versa, the Baltic Sea was not an obstacle. That certain cultural connections and clues to migrations across the Baltic Sea are not ethnically identifiable is a result of the methodology and the material of archaeology. Archaeologists consider the Wielbark culture autochthonous. But since no one wants to claim that the Gutones as such migrated from Scandinavia, it is entirely possible that there was a Gutic immigration. This would be reflected in the name Berig, just as Ostrogotha is mentioned for the appearance of the Amali in the Ukraine.[20]

Does this mean, after all, that the Goths originated in Scandinavia? Reinhard Wenskus has already given an answer, which ought to be slightly modified: not entire peoples but small successful clans, the bearers of prestigious traditions, emigrated and became the founders of new *gentes*.[21] In this sense it is possible that a group of Gutae, which the Gothic *memoria* identified with King Berig and his followers, left Scandinavia long before the Amali and contributed to the ethnogenesis of the Gutones in East Pomerania-Masovia.[22]

POLITICS AND INSTITUTIONS OF THE GUTONES

The Gutones, whom Tacitus clearly counted among the eastern tribes of the Germanic peoples,[23] had relations with three larger barbarian groups. Of greatest consequence was the close contact between Gutones and Vandals. The Gothic saga reflects the centuries-long conflict between the two peoples. True to its bias it celebrates the very first clash as a Gothic victory.[24] In reality this was probably not an isolated incident but part of a struggle that finally freed the Gutones from dependence on the Vandals. Pliny the Elder still mentions the Gutones as a subgroup of the Vandals-Vandili.[25] Moreover, Strabo connects the Gutones with the Lugians,[26] and even Tacitus names the Lugians and Vandals in one breath.[27] The most likely explanation—though one that has been challenged—is that the Lugians and Vandals were basically the same people who lived in the interior south of the Gutones and east of the Oder. Until the birth of Christ they were considered Celts and went by the name Lugians, but a century later they were considered Germanic. The Lugian name was preserved for a while, and so Tacitus could, all at once, recognize the importance of the Vandals, locate the Gutones—from the perspective of the Danubian line—"beyond the Lugians," and include many Lugian subtribes among the Vandals.[28] A Gutonic ethnogenesis within the Lugian cultural community (the Hisarna layer of the Amal genealogy) would have also offered the first opportunity for close contact between the Goths and the Celts.[29] In such cultural exchange the Gutones, a people periodically subject to other tribes[30] and as late as A.D. 150 still very small, were clearly on the receiving end. But they had already at that time developed a cultural characteristic setting them apart from all their neighbors: dead Gutonic warriors were buried unarmed, apparently because they had no battles to fight in the hereafter.[31] If these reflections are correct, we can suggest the following approximate chronology for the political history of the Gutones: during the first half of the first century A.D. the Gutones were part of the Celtic-dominated Lugians; then in the second half of the century the Germanic Vandals became predominant. At the turn of the first century the Gutones broke away from the Lugian-Vandal community and expanded their territory east of the Vistula.

Since the Lugians stood under the overlordship of the Marcomanni at the beginning of the first century, the Gutones were at that time also subject to King Marbod of the Marcomanni.[32] The Gutonic settlements, however, remained at the fringe of the sphere of Marcomannic influence, because it was there that opposition to Marbod's greater kingdom formed. The Roman general Drusus established contact with a Marcomannic refugee, the young noble Catualda, when the latter lived in exile among the Gutones. From there Catualda returned to his homeland "in great strength"—which probably means with Gutonic support—and overthrew Marbod. This took place in A.D. 18 or shortly thereafter.[33] About a year and a half before Catualda's uprising, the Cheruscan chieftain Arminius had forced his way into Bohemia, moving southward along the Elbe at the head of a Germanic coalition that tried to oust Marbod. Like Marbod, Catualda was unable to maintain his position, and both met the same fate: they were received in the Roman Empire as refugees. Their retainers, however, first remained outside the empire and were given a king and settlement land north of the Danube between the Morava and the Vah. Among those who settled in what is today Slovakia there might have been some Gutones.[34] During this continuous tribal warfare Catualda was clearly supported by the Gutones, who were trying to end their dependence on the Marcomanni.

The third ethnic group with which the Gutones had contact was the Rugians and Lemovians, who probably lived west of them at the mouth of the Oder, in modern-day West Pomerania. The tribal saga, which remembered only the name of the Ulmerugi ("island Rugians"), speaks inevitably of armed conflict. The heroic *memoria* depicts relations between tribes as warfare.[35] But in the eyes of the contemporary Tacitus, the Gutones, Lemovians, and Rugians, characterized by the same armaments and institutions, formed one East Germanic group. It is said that they used mostly round shields and short swords;[36] taken literally, this would represent an incomplete set of arms and a strange mixture of cavalry and infantry weapons. Archaeology tells us that round shields and short swords were by no means limited to the Gutones and the other eastern tribes. Tacitus, moreover, noticed that the Gutones, like their neighbors, were ruled by kings who had considerable power by Germanic standards.[37]

The strength of the Goths lay in a kingship whose authority noticeably surpassed that usually found among Germanic peoples. As the central authority of the wandering tribe,[38] the king could employ the resources of his smaller tribe more effectively than the leading stratum of larger, kingless tribal groups could use theirs. The Goths developed a great attraction for non-Goths—as, for example, for the Galindi from the Baltic area—because the Gothic kings decided questions of tribal membership quickly and on occasion against tradition.[39] Finally, the Gothic kingship had the ability not only to form the *exercitus Gothorum* as a polyethnic group but also to structure it on the basis of retainership. Ptolemy may not have always brought his information up to date before he entered it into his *Geography*,[40] but the small tribe of the Sarmatian Gutones from the Vistula must have had an especially efficient organizational structure if it could start the Marcomannic wars and cause the enormous unrest that affected generations of Europeans on both sides of the *limes*. This people obeyed kings who combined the sacred prestige of the *thiudans* with the power of the *reiks*.[41]

The Trek to the Black Sea

Old songs tell the story of the trek of the Goths from Gothiscandza to Scythia: the tribe supposedly suffered from overpopulation, so "the army of the Goths together with women and children" left its homeland on the decision of King Filimer. It was said that soon afterward the Goths passed through a vast swamp. While crossing a river, the bridge they were using collapsed and split the people forever. Some stayed behind, while others, who had already crossed the river, moved on and invaded the territory of the Spali. Eventually the Goths settled in Oium ("in the rich meadows") on the shore of the Sea of Azov.[42]

The emigration of an entire tribe is just as much a topos as the notion of overpopulation, despite what seem to be impressive examples from ancient ethnography.[43] What the separation resulting from the collapse of the bridge means can only be conjectured. Perhaps Cassiodorus wanted to anticipate the Gothic division into western and eastern Goths, a division for which he never tired of suggesting new explanations.[44] But it is also possible that this story preserves common barbarian experiences during the migrations. Modern archaeology assumes a slow shift of the East Pomeranian-Masovian Wielbark culture into the archaeological region that has been named, since the turn of the century, after the village of Cherniakhov near Kiev. The advance of the Polish culture into the Ukrainian area thus presents itself as a process that lasted from the end of the second until far into the third century. According to our ethnogenetic criteria the immigrants were still Gutones. The often described "trek to the Black Sea" can therefore have occurred only in stages, whereby Masovia, Podlachia, and the area around Brest were the earliest areas of expansion. To this stage belongs also the early phase of the Cherniakhov culture in Wolhynia. The river that separated the Goths was probably the Dnieper. But the story of the collapse of the bridge surely does not refer to the Goths' living on both banks of the river.[45] For the Dnieper in no way impeded communication and is nowhere described as an uncrossable border of the two tribal territories; had this been otherwise, we would have read as much in the *Origo Gothica*. Perhaps the story of the bridge contains nothing more than the memory of an event that took place during the Gothic, as well as other, tribal migrations and in this way silently corrected the notion of a "migration of the entire people." Moreover, according to the *Origo Gothica*, the various ethnogeneses of the Gutones never take place in deserted areas, and in this it is entirely trustworthy. Just as the Berig Goths at one time had to fight for their independence against East Germanic-Celtic predecessors and rivals, so in Scythia the Gutones met the Iranian-Sarmatian peoples.[46] As an example of a hostile confrontation the *Origo Gothica* mentions the fight against the Spali.[47] In Slavic their name means something like "the giants."[48] Such an unfriendly name is typically used to label foreigners,[49] and thus the Spali were probably not Slavs.

The Goths at the Black Sea

THE GOTHIC INVASIONS OF THE THIRD CENTURY

The history of the Goths in the "global crisis of the third century A.D."[50] makes for monotonous reading. Usurpations, wars in Persia, and attacks by the Germanic tribes in the West force the imperial government to pull back the capable Danubian army. The Goths seize the opportunity and cross into the empire. They plunder and devastate the land and make off, laden with booty. The Romans frequently intercept the attackers and inflict heavy losses, but at the next opportunity the barbarians are back again. The land is destroyed; the people the enemy has not killed or driven from the land succumb to famine and "plague."

About two generations after the last mention of the Gutones, there were increasingly signs that something was going on among "the barbarians sitting above Dacia."[51] The Romans had never succeeded in closing down the "funnel of peoples" between the Danube and the Tisza in the west or in safeguarding in the east the "wet border" along the Prut river. Quite the contrary: the greater part of Muntenia-Greater Walachia was already outside the frontiers of the empire, not to speak of Moldavia.[52] There had always been problems in this area with peoples of all kinds, who appeared for the most part as free Daci or Carpi.[53] We also hear of Kostobokoi and Roxolani. Finally, for centuries the Bastarnic element had been part of the ethnic mosaic of that area. The Germanic-Celtic Bastarni were also called Peukini after the Danubian island of Peuke.[54]

A new stage is reached in 238 when the rumblings along the border erupt into a massive Gothic onslaught. The attackers plundered and pillaged Histros-Histria south of the mouth of the Danube and then withdrew again. A year of historic significance marks the beginning of this "Scythian war."[55] Whereas until this time the Romans could only suspect the formation of a new greater-Scythian *gens* behind the attacking groups, that *gens* now emerged into the open, assuming leadership in the hostilities against the empire. The Goths had not always held this position of preeminence. Even as late as 238 the Carpian allies proclaimed themselves superior to the Goths. In return for the withdrawal of the army and the release of prisoners, the imperial government was ready to grant, if not renew, annual payments to the Goths. In this arrangement the Carpi were to receive nothing. On hearing this they threatened: "We are stronger than the Goths."[56] These words reflect the former strength of the Carpi. Even the *Origo Gothica* acknowledges the Carpi as an "especially warlike people."[57] It must have therefore taken some time before the Goths became dominant in the Dacian-Sarmatian community of peoples. Accordingly, the acculturation of the Goths to the Pontic area and their ethnogenesis "at the shores of the Black Sea" are simultaneous and mutually dependent processes. In other words, we should speak of the Goths only after the Gutonic immigrants had become "Scythians" at the Black Sea. Greek ethnography had already given this traditional name to the Sarmatians, whose way of life did not differ from that of their predecessors. Now the same thing happened to the Goths. The repeat of this ethnic identification was the basis for the distinction the ancient world made between Goths and Germanic peoples.[58] In the Roman army that the emperor Gordian III led against the Persians in 242, there were Germanic and Gothic peoples. The annual payments that had been negotiated in 238 were obviously not paid to the Goths without a return service. It appears that in the same year treatylike agreements, if not an actual *foedus,* had been concluded. In their first engagements in the service of the Romans, however, the Goths were involved in a defeat. In 262 Shapur I the Great celebrated his victory over the Roman army and its barbarian troops from east and west.[59]

In the decade from 238 to 248 no Gothic but instead several Carpic invasions are reported. Both in 246 and on New Year's Day in 248 the emperor Philip the Arab (244–249) celebrated triumphs over the Carpi. A Dacian era was dated from the first victory and coins were once again minted in the province. Because of these successes Philip thought that he too could revise his policy toward the Goths. He stopped the annual payments and renounced the agreements with them. But the emperor would have acted irresponsibly and rashly had he provoked the Goths without being militarily prepared. In 248 he sent the capable soldier Decius to Moesia to supervise the Danubian forces and above all to quash a temporary usurpation. It is difficult to say what Decius actually did or accomplished.[60] Nonetheless, he did win the support of the army and then dared to try to seize power for himself. In the summer of 249 the Danubian troops marched with him to Italy, leaving the frontier undefended and the empire exposed to the invading Gothic forces.

In the spring of 250 three columns of barbarians from north of the lower Danube thrust into Roman territory. The attack was aimed at the provinces of Dacia and Moesia, which were devastated in a campaign that lasted several years. The operation was led by the Gothic king Cniva, who was able to muster a number of other tribes in addition to his own people.[61] The Carpi are of course mentioned first among them, next Bastarnian, Taifalian, and Hasdingian Vandal contingents. Even Roman deserters must have joined.[62] The course and the outcome of the expedition show the Goths at an early peak in their power and reveal the attraction they exerted on other tribes. Now they were clearly predominant among the attacking peoples of Germanic-Sarmatian origin. As for Cniva, he proved himself a leader who possessed more than just a primitive knowledge of tactics and strategy. And his kingship was so strong that he could accept losses and defeats without having his people desert him immediately. We are reminded once again of Tacitus and his description of Gutonic kingship.[63]

After breaking through the transultanian *limes* Cniva's main army forced the crossing of the Alutus. As late as 248 the town of Romula-Rechka located west of the river had been fortified.[64] After the crossing the Carpi separated from the Goths and marched upstream along the Alutus into Dacia. Cniva crossed the Danube from modern Celeiu to Oescus-Gigen, veered east, and moved downstream into lower Moesia. A third detachment, led perhaps by the chieftains Argaith and Gunteric,[65] had already crossed the lower Danube and invaded the Dobrudja; this group then marched on to the gates of the Thracian city Philippopolis-Plovdiv. To keep in touch with his southern army, which was now beginning the siege of the city, Cniva executed a pincer movement. The Moesian legate Gallus drove the Goths back from Novae-Svištov, at the mouth of the Jantra. Cniva, however, did not turn back but moved south, upstream along the Jantra, in order to join the group encamped before Philippopolis. The emperor Decius had in the meantime cleared the Carpi out of Dacia. Now he tried to catch and defeat the Goths. He made a surprise appearance at Nikopolis-Stari Nikub, but Cniva, after plundering the city, had already disappeared into the mountains of the Balkan range. Decius pursued the Goths across the mountains and was hoping to relieve Philippopolis within a few days. Cniva suddenly turned around and attacked the imperial army, which was resting at Beroea-Stara Zagora after having crossed the Shipka pass. Decius had to beat a hasty retreat to a prepared rear position that Gallus had fortified at Novae. Here and in nearby Oescus he reorganized his defeated troops. But this took several months, and the Roman Danubian army was not ready for action again until spring 251. Philippopolis, however, was lost in the summer of 250. The Thracian troops in the city declared Priscus emperor so that he could come to terms with the united Goths. He offered to hand over the impregnable city to the Goths and fraternize with them. But the Goths did not keep their end of the bargain: once inside the city they went on a bloody rampage. Those Romans who were not killed were led away as captives, among them many of senatorial rank. Nothing more is heard of the usurper.

The fall of the city allowed the Goths to take a thorough look around Thracia and probably neighboring Illyricum as well. They were apparently in no hurry to return home, despite the proximity of both Decii—father and son—and Gallus encamped at the Danube. Cniva began his march back no earlier than the spring of 251. Laden with booty, the Goths moved northeast, in reverse direction along the route their southern group had taken the previous year. Meanwhile, the emperor's son Herennius Etruscus had been named augustus by his father. After some initial successes the Romans met the Gothic main force in the middle of summer 251 at Abrittus-Hisarlak near Razgrad in modern Bulgaria. Cniva lured the enemy into a marshy and treacherous area he himself seems to have been familiar with. He divided the Gothic army into several tactical units with which he tried to encircle the imperial troops. This maneuver was successful, and Decius and his son were killed. With great difficulty Trebonianus Gallus saved what was left of the Roman army, which subsequently proclaimed him emperor. He had to allow the Goths to move on with their rich human and material spoils and even had to promise them annual payments. This is why he is charged to this day with treason and incompetence. But in fact his actions were forced upon him by circumstances. After the defeats at Beroea and Philippopolis, and especially after the catastrophe at Abrittus, the new emperor had no other choice. He had to get rid of the Goths as quickly as possible. At the same time a plaguelike epidemic broke out, ravaging the land for many years. The empire's strength was nearly exhausted.[66]

The number and chronology of the Gothic invasions after the death of Decius are difficult to determine. The traditional notion of annual large-scale attacks by the Goths disregards the biological and military capabilities of barbarian peoples. At the next confrontation following Cniva's victory the Gothic land forces ran into trouble. The Roman military command had adopted the concept of the late Decius, namely, to maintain the Danubian border or, in case it was breached, to seal it off and fight the invaders with inverted fronts. Even an offensive into the barbarian land now seemed possible.[67] The Goths had to cross through a zone of "scorched earth" created by their previous invasions. The devastation of Roman territory now worked against the attackers, who of course could never count on supplies and who had to live off land they or their predecessors had despoiled. Consequently, the Goths suffered severe supply problems soon after the start of the campaign. The booty they had won spurred them on to new expeditions, but at the same time the previously plundered areas were avoided if at all possible. The entire Gothic strategy must have rested on this simple consideration. Barbarian recklessness, indeed their longing for death, assumed outrageous dimensions, especially from the moment when Gothic attacks from the sea introduced an entirely new element into their warfare.[68]

Along with the growing mobility and the extended radius of Gothic actions came an increased vulnerability of their armies, which now moved from the bases ever more daringly. The goals of the barbarians in search of booty were primarily the cities and large sanctuaries of the Romans. The Goths could always count on help from the rural population, which was hostile to the cities. They were also supported by social and religious minorities, as, for example, some Christians, who were conspiring against the Roman state and its social order and who seem to have been trying their hand at being Goths themselves. But it remains doubtful whether the support of the native fifth column was in fact part of the strategic concept of the attackers. The evidence speaks an entirely different language, if we consider the heavy losses of the Goths, who had to fight their way back home on foot from wherever they had been dropped off by their boats. But even when the cooperation with the "internal proletariat" was successful, it appears to have been accidental and temporary. The Goths were supported primarily before they attacked but not when they were returning home loaded with booty; before an attack, collaborators could hope to share in victory; afterward, the Goths themselves became the target of plunder lust. Members of the Roman upper stratum organized regional militias, which in general operated successfully because of their familiarity with the local area. But the Roman optimates often used the threat from the enemy to build veritable dominions of their own at the expense of their countrymen.

The next confrontation between Romans and Goths probably took place in 253. Hostilities commenced in the area where Cniva had campaigned. The governor of Moesia, Aemilianus, suddenly refused to pay the yearly sum that Gallus had promised, whereupon the Goths invaded Moesia and Thrace. To meet them Aemilianus himself took the offensive and, on the northern side of the lower Danube, gained a victory against the enemy. Although this did not force all the plunderers to leave imperial territory immediately, in the eyes of his soldiers Aemilianus had legitimized himself as a soldiers' emperor. They proclaimed him *imperator*.[69]

The new emperor moved immediately to Italy and, following the familiar pattern, the Danubian army went with him. Paradoxically, the success of Roman arms made the situation in the Balkan provinces worse. It is true that everywhere, even in Macedonia and Greece, at the pass of Thermopylae and at the isthmus of Corinth, new fortifications were constructed and old ones repaired; even the walls of Athens were restored. But after only a few months Aemilianus lost his claim to power and his life, and the Goths returned. While in 253 Dexippus could still boast that the damage caused by the Goths was "not worth mentioning,"[70] in 254 the attackers penetrated all the way to Thessalonica. Though they had to turn back, their failure must not deceive us as to the damage they inflicted. The open country suffered considerably. It was primarily western Goths who participated in the invasions of the years 253/254. Thereafter the eastern Goths made their appearance on the scene.

The years 255, 256, and 257 saw the first "Scythian" attacks by sea. Once again Sarmatian peoples preceded the Goths in this new theater of war.[71] The Roman client kingdom on the Crimea was weakened by internal tensions brought about by the waning of Roman support, the decline of once flourishing trade, and the increasing threat from the Ukrainian heartland. As a result the Gothic-Sarmatian neighbors gained control of the Bosporanian kingdom. Whereas until this time the Bosporanian navy, in cooperation with the Romans, had been able to safeguard navigation on the Black Sea and as a consequence had also been able to protect the Greek cities situated at the mouths of the large rivers, the fleet now became the first victim of the attackers. First we hear of Borani who took the fleet and its crews away from the Bosporani in order to sail against Pityus-Pitzunda on the western slopes of the Caucasus mountains. The first expedition failed; indeed, it was nearly a catastrophe for the pirates. The Borani had simply ordered the Bosporanian sailors to set them ashore; then the Borani sent the sailors and ships home. They would have all perished had the survivors not found, more or less by chance, Roman ships that they used to sail home. Having learned from this mistake, the second Black Sea expedition in 256 kept the confiscated fleet close at hand. This time a Gothic contingent also sailed along. The goal was to plunder the sanctuary of Rhea Cybele at Phasis. The raid failed, and the pirates headed once again for Pityus. The city—now without the successful defenders of the previous year, whom the Emperor Valerian had withdrawn—could no longer defend itself. Then, to everyone's surprise, the rich city of Trebizond on the northern coast of Asia Minor fell; caught by surprise, the garrison simply ran away.[72]

The attack in 256—and probably that of 257 as well—was reflected in the "canonical letter" of Bishop Gregorius Thaumaturgus (d. c. 270) of Neocaesarea-Niksar in Pontus Polemoniacus.[73] The letter denounced the general degeneration of morals, the isolationism, and the lack of solidarity among Roman citizens. The bishop addressed his letter—which reacted directly to a current event and must therefore have been written shortly after it—to his Pontic Christians. He urged that measures be taken to restore the religious and social peace that had been disturbed by the invasion. Above all he discussed the type and severity of ecclesiastical punishment for offences the Christians had committed during the Gothic invasion. This canonical letter stands at the beginning of practical legislation by ecclesiastical authorities who tried to control the devastation caused by the barbarian invasions. To that end they employed traditional measures that had been used to keep up ecclesiastical discipline during the persecutions by the Roman state. Now the threat came from a different enemy, who also attacked the empire at whose hands the church itself suffered. This twofold strain is reflected in the style of the letter. Gregori calls on his parishioners' sense of solidarity, not as Romans and citizens of the empire but as Christians and Pontici.

As expected, the barbarians had taken captives to relieve their chronic manpower shortage. Bishop Gregorius was concerned about the conduct of these individuals during their captivity. Should they regain their freedom, the bishop stipulated the conditions under which they could rejoin the community of Christians. This concern itself is puzzling, and one wonders even more about the apparent incongruity between the offence and its extensive treatment in the bishop's letter. The central theme of the first chapter of Gregoris's letter is his fear that the captives may have been forced by the barbarians to eat sacrificial meat. But the bishop knew that the enemies had not sacrificed at all in the pagan sanctuaries. And in any case a Christian would have been free of guilt if he had been forced to eat sacrificial meat and had done so without the proper religious attitude. The Goths and Borani had indeed visited the places of sacrifice but only for the sake of the riches piled up there, as the unsuccessful assault on Phasis shows. Why then the elaborate discussion of an offence the bishop knew did not occur? This contradiction and the discussion of the question of spiritual attitude lead us to assume that among the freed captives—who certainly existed—there was actually concealed an even larger group of Christians who had apostatized during a Roman persecution and who now wanted to return to the Christian community. The Gothic invasion gave them a chance to gain a general pardon for their conduct during the terrible persecution of Decius under which Gregorius and his Pontic community had suffered. The persecution that Valerian initiated in 257 is not yet meant here.[74]

Second, the bishop asks what is to be done with Christian women who had been raped. His answer is clear and in keeping with the best tradition. Whoever had not led a virtuous life before that moment had no reason to complain about degradation at the hands of the Goths. For all others, the saying of the Old Testament applied: Whoever suffers violence through no fault of his own has not thereby excluded himself from the community of believers. Once again, attitudes and convictions are the criteria for measuring innocence and guilt.[75]

Next, offences against property and collaboration with the enemy take up a large part of the pastoral instruction. There is no question that members of the lower classes collaborated with the enemy, acted as guides, and shared, or tried to share, in their booty. On occasion some even became active themselves and plundered on their own. All such people are said to be Christians and Pontici no longer; rather, they have behaved toward their countrymen like "Goths and Borani." The excuse that such individuals only wanted to recoup their losses is of course rejected. But the invasion of 256/257 was a signal not only for the poor and oppressed to upset the existing social order to their own advantage. Members of the upper stratum as well sought to enrich themselves and to use their social and economic power at the expense of their fellow citizens. We hear of captives who passed from the hands of the Goths into those of their Roman "liberators" without regaining their freedom. The bishop condemned in the strongest terms such "totally unacceptable" behavior, which the community of Christians could not tolerate under any circumstances. Here we see condemned on moral grounds a development that accompanied the dissolution of the Roman Empire: powerful landowners gathered private armies with which they increasingly took over state functions, such as the preservation of peace, policing authority, and enforcement of the law. Indeed, considering the ignominious role Roman soldiers had played in the capture of Trebizond and Chalcedon, the powerful had to take over these functions. The result was a growing state of dependency, especially for the rural population; we can observe the tendency, perhaps the necessity, to seize people and money wherever possible. But still in the fifth century, Roman legislation tried in vain to impress upon the leaders of successful militias that they had to return to their rightful owners all booty recovered from the barbarians.[76]

In 257 the Gothic pirates ravaged the southwestern coast of the Black Sea for the first time. In addition, they penetrated into the Propontis. While the land forces were moving southward along the coast, the Gothic fleet set sail from one of the Ukrainian river mouths. The fleet sailed past Tomis and Anchialus, and within sight of Lake Terkos it received such a large reinforcement of fishing boats that the available vessels were sufficient to ferry the Gothic warriors across the bay of Phileatine to the northern tip of the headland of Asia Minor. Afterward the Gothic fleet sailed through the Bosporus and met the land forces at Chalcedon. The Roman garrison of the city left without offering a fight. The combined advance of fleet and land forces opened to the Goths the rich province of Bithynia. In addition to Chalcedon, the barbarians succeeded in taking Nicomedia, Nicaea, Cius, Apamea, and Prusa. When their thrust toward Cyzicus was stopped by the flooded Rhyndakos-Orhaneli River, they returned to Nicomedia and Nicaea and destroyed these two cities. A Greek by the name of Chrysogonos supposedly betrayed Nicomedia into their hands.

The Gothic invasion of 257 started from a base that was clearly located west of the Crimea. In 256, in contrast, the Gothic-Boranian ships had set sail from the harbors of the Cimmerian Bosporus. This time the pirates intended to sail to a country not yet plundered; moreover, a repetition of the Armenian-Pontic invasion seemed too dangerous to them. But the shift of the Gothic starting positions to the western coast of the Black Sea presupposes that the Greek cities on the southern Russian river mouths—Olbia-Nikolajev and Tyras-Akkerman (Romanian: Cetatea Alba)—were in Gothic hands. Their inhabitants were probably the Roman traders and captives who are said to have supported the Gothic campaign of 257.[77] The barbarians could equip their ships in their home ports. In 268, at the latest, Tyras is attested as such a port.[78]

Until 257 the Goths had always acted and appeared together with Carpi and Borani, with Bastarnian Peukini, and with Vandal-Sarmatian groups. The Urugundi had also joined them. Modern scholars identify this last tribe as mounted nomads or "Gothic Burgundians." Be that as it may, their settlements were located in the Crimea or along the Don. Of course, the chronology and context of the traditional accounts contain many contradictions.[79] But even if we allow for a controversial emendation and with it the existence of Gothic Burgundians, these *gentes* had always had close connections with the Goths at the Black Sea.[80] This changed in the year 267, when an entirely new element became active in the Pontic area, namely, the Heruli at the Sea of Azov. If this group initially competed against the Goths—and there is good evidence that they did—there must have occurred a disruption of the barbarian balance of power similar to that which the Gothic-Sarmatian confrontation had caused at the beginning of the century.[81] At the same time a kind of "preformation" of the later tribal division seems to have emerged, for there are events that can be linked to what was to become one of the two Gothic tribes. Thus it was probably "western" Goths who carried off the ancestors of Ulfilas.

The capture of the Cappadocian Christians from whom the Gothic bishop is descended is generally associated with the events of 264 or 267, in any case, with one of the Gothic invasions that took place shortly before the death of Odaenathus, king of Palmyra in 267. During this campaign Pontic Heraclea was supposedly destroyed. Since serious historiography included the fall of this city we can assume the historicity of these battles.[82] But the city was destroyed by barbarians who came "from across the Black Sea," attacked the northern coast of Asia Minor, and then pushed into Galatia via Cappadocia.[83] The *Origo Gothica* also reports this, even though it scrambles the events of several successive years. For example, it names as leaders of the expedition in 267 the Gothic chieftains Respa, Veduco, and Tharuaro, who supposedly penetrated into the Aegean.[84] There are good arguments against this report. First, the Goths did not succeed in crossing the straits before 268. Second, in this particular year, "eastern" Goths were on the move; however, the ancestors of Ulfilas were not taken to the Crimea or southern Russia but to the Danube area. The tradition that raises so many difficulties must therefore be rearranged.[85]

THE GOTHIC ADVANCE INTO THE AEGEAN

A barbarian invasion of unprecedented size began in the spring of 268.[86] A large fleet that set sail from several bases—the Sea of Azov is mentioned for the Heruli and the mouth of the Dniester for the Goths—attacked the Roman Empire. Contemporaries knew only these two tribal names, but they counted the Heruli among the Goths. Additional ethnic differentiations are anachronisms and, moreover, ignore the large-scale nature of this attack by sea; only later did part of the invasion turn into a land expedition, then merely out of necessity. In any case, the Danubian border was successfully held, and Dacia too was better protected against the barbarians than the persistent pessimism of the ancient historiographers and their modern followers would have us believe. The combined band of the Goths could very quickly test the situation in Moesia when it went ashore at Tomis with the intention of attacking Marcianopolis and was forced to retreat immediately. The Roman hinterland, however, was much less protected.

After the failure on land the Goths sailed through the Bosporus against Byzantium, when their fleet suffered its first losses, either through unskillful maneuvers or a successful Roman defense.[87] Thereafter the Gothic-Herulian armada withdrew to Hieron. Soon after, the reorganized units forced the passage through the straits. In the Propontis Cyzicus was once again the target of an unsuccessful attack. Although the combined fleets withdrew from the city, they had managed for the first time to break through the Dardanelles and into the Aegean. On their way to Mount Athos the invaders devastated the island of Lemnos. After a rest stop on the eastern coast of the Athos peninsula, at the latest, the barbarian fleet split up into three squadrons, which thereafter operated independently.

Bands composed mostly of Heruli were dropped off at Thessalonica and Cassandrea on the Chalcidice. Meanwhile the "Hellas group" attacked Attica and probably also the Peloponnesus. In these groups the Goths must have been dominant. But if we consider that Dexippus both dealt with the Hellas group in person and may also have been the first ancient author who mentioned the name of the Heruli,[88] then it is likely that this group also contained Heruli. On their way to Greece the Goths ravaged the island of Scyrus/Skyros; on the mainland Athens and probably also Corinth, Argos, Sparta, and Olympia fell victim to the invaders. The third division, which was either made up from the start of Goths and Heruli or was reinforced by the Heruli only in 269, turned toward Asia Minor: Rhodes, Cyprus, Crete, and Side on the Pamphilian mainland were the targets of their attacks. The mixed fleet probably also pillaged Troy and the temple of Artemis at Ephesus, even if the well-fortified city of Ephesus itself could not be harmed. The leaders of this plundering expedition had already been mentioned in connection with the events of 267, but they most likely belong to the Aegean adventure.[89]

The first penetration of the "Scythians" into the Aegean presented them with difficult problems; the solutions they found were remarkably technical and logistical accomplishments. To be sure, the barbarian naval resources were vulnerable. The fleet is said to have consisted of some two thousand boats, but this was by no means enough to take all warriors and their booty home again. The seaworthiness of the boats and rafts as well as the nautical abilities of the crews had already been severely tested in the straits and especially in the Aegean. The experience gained by navigating in the Black Sea was no longer sufficient. Thus the Hellas group was exposed to the northeast trade winds—the Meltemi winds—as soon as it had stopped hugging the coast of Athos and it was apparently blown straight to Skyros. The Goths had to learn the hard way, suffering serious losses without any interference by the superior Roman fleet. But they learned quickly; at Philippopolis, Thessalonica, and Side they even employed siege engines,[90] and most of those who never left the boats lived to see their country again.[91]

It is remarkable how quickly and efficiently the Roman defenses responded, considering the large number of invaders and the various directions of their advance. The Roman army of the third and fourth centuries could in general repulse large-scale barbarian attacks more easily than small plundering expeditions. Gallienus's heavily-armed cavalry was a terrible weapon if put into action—and it was.[92] The emperor himself with his Dalmatian horsemen encountered the Herulian "Thessalonica group." The latter contingent had probably split up shortly before, since its units were operating both in the area around Doberos northwest of Thessalonica and along the Thracian river Nestus-Mesta. It was here that the greater part of the invaders were caught and destroyed. Herulian dead were said to have numbered three thousand, a figure equivalent to an entire tribal army. Their leader, Naulobates, entered Roman service and was honored with the consular insignia.[93]

Fate would not allow Gallienus to take advantage of this great victory. The commander of his field army in Italy deserted him, and the leader of the troops that were to block the road for the Hellas group conspired against the emperor. Apparently a few minor successes had gone to the general's head. While the Goths who had landed in Greece were turned aside by Dexippus and his Attic militia and veered off toward Epirus, Gallienus lost his power and his life, then the rebellious commander met his death, and finally Claudius II established himself as emperor. He gained a great victory over the Goths at Naissus-Nish, which eliminated the Hellas group but which also doomed the western unit of the Thessalonica group to destruction. The similarity in sound between Naissus and Nessus-Nestus as well as identical reports of barbarian losses for both battles have raised doubts about the historicity of Claudius's victory. But with all due caution we can keep both Gallienus's victory on the Nestus in 268 and the annihilating battle of Naissus in 269.[94]

This victory of Claudius II initiated the mopping-up operation on the Balkan peninsula. The remaining Goths next moved again in the direction of Macedonia, that is, into the interior of the empire, probably because this was the only place where they could hope to survive the winter. Hunger, disease, and inclement weather claimed many victims among the empire's defeated enemies, who dissolved into subunits. They were constantly threatened by Roman cavalry, which eventually forced the Goths to change their route of march. Those of the barbarians who were still alive and had not yet been captured were eventually encircled at the Thracian Mons Gessax, a mountain that should be located either in the country of the Bessi or in the Rhodope range. The besieged were at first able to repulse an assault by the Roman infantry with heavy losses to the attackers. Two thousand legionaries paid with their lives because their commander spurned the new military branch, the offensive cavalry, and attacked the Goths without its support. But in the end only the Roman horsemen could prevent an even worse rout of the infantry.[95]

The surrounded Goths finally surrendered and were either taken into the Roman army or settled as *coloni* south of the Danube. Only a minority of the Gothic warriors operating on land made it home again. The bloodletting affected especially the western Goths who would become Tervingi by the end of the century.[96] It thus appears like an act of desperation when in the spring of 270—after the death of Claudius and still before the elevation of Aurelian—the Goths undertook a sort of revenge expedition against Moesia. Warships supposedly also set sail to join the expedition.[97] The Goths were first attracted to Anchialus and its warm springs. Next they left the coast and captured Nikopolis-Stari Nikub. But local militias put an end to this scare.[98]

The Gothic-Herulian fleet in the Aegean operated with somewhat better fortune than the two divisions that had gone ashore. Although its crews also suffered heavy losses through Roman counterattacks and through hunger and cold, many returned to their homeland. As soon as the Egyptian prefect Probus had begun clearing the Aegean, several successful naval battles were fought by the Romans. These expeditions belong to the year 269, but they resulted in the loss of Egypt to the ruler of Palmyra.[99] In that same year additional Heruli reinforced the barbarian fleet. The bases of the naval units were the Crimea and the Sea of Azov.

Claudius II was the first Roman emperor who assumed the triumphal title *Gothicus,* or more precisely, on whom the title was bestowed by the senate. This triumphal name can be taken as a guide for Roman-Gothic confrontations during the next decades. With the tetrarchy, however, the granting of this name began to be a routine matter. The next to be celebrated as victors over the Goths were Aurelian, Tacitus, and Probus.[100]

AURELIAN AND THE DIVISION OF THE GOTHS

Claudius II died in the winter of 269/270 from the "plague," and Aurelian—he, like his predecessor, was commander-in-chief of the court cavalry—was made emperor after the brief reign of Claudius's brother Quintillus.[101] In 270 Aurelian defeated the Vandals on the Hungarian plain as well as the Germanic Iuthungi who had forced their way into Italy. In the spring of 271 the emperor marched with his victorious army east to subjugate Syrian Palmyra. On the way the Romans cleared Illyricum and Thrace of hostile warrior bands, who were probably mostly Carpi. But wherever the latter appeared, the Goths were usually not far off. In fact an encounter between Goths and Romans did take place, but it remains unclear whether the enemies were caught before penetrating into the empire or on their return from a plundering expedition. In any case, the emperor pursued the Goths and won several engagements on their territory north of the Danube.[102] Eventually the Goths suffered a devastating defeat. Five thousand warriors and their king Cannabas-Cannabaudes were killed.[103] The Gothic danger seemed averted forever. Aurelian certainly deserved his triumphal title *Gothicus maximus,* for he had not only gained a victory over the enemy but had also won peace.[104] "Defeated by Aurelian—that brave man, the avenger of their misdeeds—they [the Goths] kept peace for many centuries";[105] this statement by Ammianus is not exaggerated if we take "peace" to mean the sealing off of the Danube border and if we reduce "centuries" to the singular. But even one hundred years of peace is a long time. From a position of strength the emperor decided to give up Trajan's Dacia, which until that moment he still had in firm control.[106]

How correct Aurelian's decision was became clear during the following decades. The "western" Goths were fully occupied taking possession of the northern Danubian region on both sides of the Carpathians, dividing it with the Taifali, and keeping control of it. In the process their former allies, the Dacian Carpi, the Bastarnian Peukini, and the Vandal groups, became their rivals.[107] The Bastarni had to give way: in 280 Probus admitted what was probably the greater part of that tribe into the Roman Empire and settled them in Thrace; in 295 the rest followed. Thus ended the nearly five-hundred-year history of the Bastarni.[108] A little later a similar fate overtook the Carpi. In 295 they pushed southward in large numbers. Galerius, who was conducting the war against them on orders from Diocletian, was hailed *Carpicus maximus* by his troops no less than six times. Very soon Carpic groups were settled south of the Danube; in 303 they were joined by fellow tribesmen who had been driven out by the Goths.[109] Finally, the Gepids arrived; their appearance around 290/291 also sealed the permanent division of the Gothic tribe. For a century the Vesian Tervingi would live west of the upper Dniester and lower Prut; to the east lived the Ostrogothic Greutungi.[110]

Aurelian had placed the defeated Vandals under contract.[111] Whether the emperor concluded a similar *foedus* with the Goths, and if so with what group, remains controversial. The Goths who attacked Pontus, Galatia, and Cilicia in 276 and 277 came from the Sea of Azov. They claimed that they wanted to support the emperor—who was long dead—against the Persians. If they were referring to a *foedus,* it must have applied to the entire *gens* between the Danube and the Don. But this story is probably just a duplication of reports about the events of 297, when federate Goths did take part in Galerius's Persian campaign, whereas the Goths of 276/277 were simply plunderers from the eastern groups. Aurelian and his successors would hardly have concluded a *foedus* with a *gens* that was divided and fighting for its survival.[112] In the 290s, however, a *foedus* was possible since both divisions were stable, even if still threatened.[113]

The Tervingian-Vesian Confederation at the Danube

In the spring of 291, almost two decades after the Goths' catastrophic defeat by Aurelian and the end of their first greater kingship, the Tervingi are attested for the first time. They were considered "another part of the Goths," which indicates that they had split off from the main tribe. In the following century it was the Tervingi who were meant when the Romans spoke of Goths; the eastern group was entirely forgotten.[114] The Tervingi, who probably preferred to call themselves Vesi,[115] were as Goths the eponymous group of the polyethnic community north of the Danube.[116] The statement that "now Taifali, Victu(f)ali, and Tervingi possess the former Roman province of Dacia" reflects the situation of 350 at the very latest.[117] To be sure, the Goths must have been dominant in Transylvania—probably already before the middle of the fourth century—if Trajan's Dacia could become the Gothia of literary tradition.[118]

THE EVENTS OF 291 TO 364

In the spring of 291 the Romans considered it current news that the Tervingi had joined with the Taifali to fight the Vandals and Gepids.[119] The Vandals were the Hasdingi, and for a few generations they had shared the Tisza plain with the Sarmatians. At least one of the Hasdingian subdivisions, if not the entire tribe, also bore the name Victu(f)ali, who pushed all the way to the west of Transylvania after the Roman government had abandoned Trajan's Dacia.[120] They probably reached the upper course of the Three Körös, as well as the Maros-Mureş, up to the line between Oradea and Arad. The Vandal expansion, which ran counter to that of the Goths, began in the last decades of the third century and was finally stopped by the Tervingi in the fourth decade of the fourth century.[121]

Not only the Tervingi and Taifali but also the Gepids were mentioned for the first time in 291. They were fighting with the western "section of the Goths." But where did they come from? The *Origo Gothica* describes in detail the confrontation between the Gepids under King Fastida and the still unified Ostrogoths and Visigoths of King Ostrogotha. The "lazy ones" who had once again arrived too late demanded land from their Gothic brothers because their own settlements in a wooded mountain region could no longer feed them. The Gepids had recently inflicted a devastating defeat on the Burgundians and were accordingly arrogant. Ostrogotha rejected the demand of Fastida, whereupon a battle took place near the *oppidum* Galtis at a river called *Auha*. Because the two groups had similar weapons and fighting style, a tough struggle ensued, which the Goths won because they had the "better cause and greater cleverness." Both groups, the defeated Gepids and the victorious Goths, then returned to their homelands. This puzzling account of the *Origo Gothica* allows many different interpretations.[122]

There are two major problems: first, the chronology and the location of the battle, and second, the question of which Goths engaged in it. In the *Origo Gothica* Ostrogotha is at one time the last king who ruled over both Gothic peoples and at another time he is the first Ostrogothic king.[123] If he ruled only over the eastern Goths, the clash with the Fastida Gepids must have occurred east of the Carpathians. One archaeologist has suggested that the Galtis battle at the Auha should be located on the middle or upper course of the Prut.[124] But this takes too little account of the report in the *Origo Gothica* according to which the Gepids were "closed in by the roughness of the mountains and cramped by the thick forests" when they demanded new settlement areas from the Goths. Moreover, a panegyric that was delivered on April 1, 291, reported that Tervingian and Taifalian warriors had offered resistance to a Vandal-Gepid coalition. Indeed, both reports lead one to think of northern Transylvania. There now remains the problem of finding a modern name for the Auha river, which refers to a river of considerable size. One could think, if not of the Tisza, at least of the Maros-Mureş, especially since it was there that a generation later additional confrontations between Vandals and Goths occurred.[125] Hungarian archaeologists think that "the Gepids fought with the Tervingi and Taifali over possession of Transylvania, probably somewhere in the valley of the Szamos," and they consider the northwestern Transylvanian culture of the fourth century already Gepidic. This sounds reasonable. But a historian's task is to reconstruct history; to do that he needs written evidence, which for now is exhausted.[126]

When the tetrarch Galerius attacked the Persians in 297 he was accompanied by Gothic auxiliary troops. From this time tradition dated the special relationship of the Goths to the empire, in whose army they were included as federates "to this day," as Jordanes says.[127] Only the word "federates," however, had remained the same: there was a significant difference between the imperial federates of the fifth and sixth centuries and their predecessors. Nevertheless, from this tradition we may infer that the Bastarnic and Carpic war of 295 had ended with a regular Gothic *foedus*.[128] For one generation, until 323 exactly, the Goths honored the treaty. To be sure, there were violations by barbarian raiders, which gave new fuel to the fear of the Goths.[129] But in general peace and quiet prevailed along the lower Danube, until the system of the tetrarchy broke down in the civil war between Constantine and Licinius. Constantine had already adopted the title *Gothicus* in 315 and 319, which could be explained in a number of ways. Constantine's desire to honor his "adopted" ancestor Claudius II Gothicus certainly played a role in this. Another reason could have been some victorious battles with the Goths, who had fought on the side of Licinius in the first armed hostilities between the two emperors. There is some evidence for this inference: While the inscription on the restored Tropaeum Traiani-Adamklissi, which mentions both Constantine and Licinius, celebrates a general victory over barbarian peoples, it does not mention the title Gothicus or the Goths. Scholars now date the completion of the restoration to 318/319, when the damage done in the late third century, possibly in 295, was finally repaired. In any case, this joint appearance of the two emperors postdates their first armed confrontations. In not mentioning the Goths as defeated allies of Licinius, Constantine may have intended to signal a reconciliation.

On March 1, 317, the rival emperors Constantine and Licinius made peace. The diocese of Moesia with its provinces from Achaea to Dacia ripensis fell to Constantine, while the diocese of Thracia and its provinces remained in Licinius's sphere of power. The unity of the Danubian border was now destroyed. An effective defense against the Gothic attackers was now possible only if the two rivals got along with each other. If they did not, either nothing at all was done or any activity on the part of one emperor gave the other a casus belli, for an effective defense could not be conducted without violating the colleague's sovereign territory. The division of the empire also cast an adverse shadow on the future; imperial politics often referred back to this unfortunate arrangement.

Constantine spent the following years almost exclusively in the Balkans. His vigorous measures secured the peace in this area, but first they led to civil war with Licinius. In 322 Constantine punished a Jazygian incursion into Pannonia with a punitive expedition across the Danube; subsequently he armed against his rival. Licinius withdrew the border troops from the "Gothic bank," and in the spring of 323 a Tervingian contingent under Rausimod launched an attack. Although the Goths at first ravaged Licinian territory, Constantine conducted all the countermeasures.[130] He passed a law on April 28, 323 threatening all Roman collaborators with death by burning, and he pursued the enemies across the Danube into barbarian territory, where Rausimod met his death.[131] With this victory the Western army had violated the territory of Licinius, and the defeated Goths had again become allies of the Eastern emperor. Led by a certain prince Alica, the Goths stood by Licinius in the battles of the summer 324 and kept in contact with him even after he had suffered a devastating defeat. Licinius was deposed by Constantine, but he tried to regain his power with Gothic help. His plans were discovered and he was sentenced to death. The former emperor then arranged his escape to the Goths. Our source speaks of an escape into the "Serric Mountains," that is, into the southern Carpathians. The attempt failed and Licinius was apprehended in Thessalonica and executed.[132] The *Origo Gothica* distorts the events into the tendentious claim that the Goths killed Licinius on orders from the "victorious Constantine."[133]

With the death of his opponent, Constantine became sole ruler in 324. He was left with more than a decade of undivided responsibility for the Gothic front. During this time the emperor organized not only the defense against Sarmatians and Goths from Pannonia to the mouth of the Danube but he also resumed the offensive, as he had done in 322 and 323. Constantine shunned no unusual measures, as long as they promised success. Contrary to the old maxim of Roman foreign policy never to meddle in tribal feuds by force of arms, the imperial army offered support on request. Later observers described this as a principle of Constantine's barbarian policy.[134] When the emperor lay dying in 337, it seemed to him, at least, that things had worked out as planned. The command over the *ripa Gothica* could be handed over to the lowest ranking caesar among his successors, his nephew Dalmatius.[135] His plan of division was overthrown by the army, which tolerated only sons of the great emperor and killed everyone else. But his arrangement reveals that the diocese of Thrace was considered secure and no longer endangered.[136]

And now for the events in detail: On July 5, 328, Constantine opened the stone bridge across the Danube between Oescus-Gigen and Sucidava-Celeiu. At the same time the fortress Daphne-Spanţov near Olteniţa was erected downstream and linked by means of a large ferry with Transmarisca-Tutrakan, opposite the mouth of the Marisca river. Good roads leading from the hinterland to the fortified positions were repaired or newly built. The construction of the bridge was considered a first-rate military event: Constantine was celebrated as the renewer of Trajan's Dacia. While the bridge at Oescus linked the empire with Oltenia-Little Walachia, which was intended as a buffer zone and was for the most part successfully held, Daphne protruded like a thorn into the territory of the Tervingi and Taifali.[137]

Driven away from the Danube, the Goths changed their direction of advance. Around 330 probably began the increasing Gothic infiltration of Transylvania, a process that archaeologists interpret as the expansion of the Sîntana-de-Mureş culture. This advance led to a confrontation with the Tisza Sarmatians in 332.[138] The attackers were possibly led by Vidigoia, "the bravest among the Goths," who lost his life near the Tisza "through the cunning of the Sarmatians" and was buried there. In its arrangement of the events the *Origo Gothica* indicates a quick Gothic success, which was in fact only of short duration.[139] The emperor sent his son Constantine across the Danube with a strong army, which attacked the Tervingi in the rear and inflicted a disastrous defeat.[140] Five hundred Taifalian horsemen did offer the attacking Romans a successful running fight but were not able to escape the Tervingian catastrophe. Indeed, it appears that the Taifali in particular lost a part of their people to the empire at this time.[141] While Taifalian captives were deported and settled in Phrygia, the Tervingian group that had penetrated into the Sarmatian land perished along with women and children, if the reported number of "nearly one hundred thousand people starved and frozen to death" bears any relationship to reality. The Gothic offensive very quickly turned into a fight for survival under the leadership of Ariaric. He is the first Gothic chieftain whose name both the *Origo Gothica* and another ancient source have handed down reliably and independently.[142] He is also most likely the first Tervingian judge (*kindins*) known to us. With him Constantine concluded the *foedus* of 332, which required the Goths to provide a certain number of auxiliary troops in return for an annual payment and which permitted them to resume vital trade with their Roman neighbors across the Danube. As coin finds indicate, the border traffic was concentrated largely at the two fortified river crossings that Constantine had built.[143] The Goths had probably become *foederati* before 332. Treaties are conceivable in 238, 251, 271, and the years between 295 and 297.[144] It is possible that Licinius also demanded the support of the Goths on the basis of their status as *foederati* and in so doing anticipated the Procopius episode of the late sixties.[145] But the Constantinian *foedus* of 332 is the first treaty between Rome and a Gothic people which is clearly recorded by a contemporary source.[146]

A victory statue was erected for the emperor. Its inscription, "To fortune that has once again returned, on occasion of the victory over the Goths," still today announces the great deed.[147] Perhaps it was also at this time that the "Gothic Games," which were usually celebrated in Constantinople between February 4 and 9, were introduced.[148] The great military success, however, did not change Constantine's willingness to conclude a negotiated peace with the Tervingi. Gothic princes were rewarded and honored. Ariaric's son came to Constantinople as a hostage. It is highly probable that his name was Aoric, a Gothic chieftain who was identical with Athanaric's father, to whom a statue was erected in the antechamber of the curia in Constantinople.[149] The memory of Constantine was always revered among the Tervingi. After thirty years it was still so strong that it guided the Goths in making political decisions, and the responsibility for carrying out these decisions was given to Athanaric, who was probably the grandson of Constantine's *foederatus* Ariaric.[150] The Tervingi, trusting in the peace with the Roman Empire, conducted a punitive expedition against their northwestern neighbors, the Sarmatians, through whose fault they had recently suffered such a serious defeat. A part of the "free Sarmatians" had probably fled in 334 to the Hasdingian Vandals under King Visimar. Thereupon Geberic led Gothic warriors into the valley of the Maros-Mureş, where, according to the *Origo Gothica,* "the Gepids live today." The Tervingi, "after defeating and plundering the Vandals, returned home again." The *Origo Gothica* locates the Vandal settlements between the rivers Maros-Mureş and the Three Körös. Hungarian archaeologists can discover no traces of these settlements; the finds seem thoroughly Sarmatian. Be that as it may, from written records two facts should be noted. First, Geberic undertook his expedition in order "to expand his realm at the expense of the Vandal *gens.*" Second, at that time the Maros-Mureş did not yet form the boundary of a heartland of Gothic settlement. Rather, this central Transylvanian river was within reach of the Tervingian army, which was operating from a base much farther east. Supposedly it was Constantine who allowed the defeated Vandals to move their settlements to Pannonia. This is in fact not correct, but it does allow a chronological arrangement of the events.[151]

The flight of the *Sarmati Agaragantes,* the "master" (*domini*) Sarmatians, to the Vandals-Victu(f)ali[152] was the result of tribal conflicts that were to influence Gothic history nearly a quarter of a century later. The Tisza Sarmatians could not long enjoy the victory they had gained over the Goths with Roman help. Threatened by the enemy, the ruling Sarmatae Agaragantes had armed the subject Limigantes. Afterward the "master" Sarmatians were overwhelmed by their numerically superior slaves and were defeated in a bloody civil war in the year 334. Most of them were admitted into the empire by Constantine, while a minority sought refuge with the Vandals. What appears to have been a social conflict probably goes back to ethnic differences that had already surfaced after the Marcomannic wars. At that time the Roxolani probably subjugated the Jazygi and thus set the stage for the constantly recurring unrest in the Hungarian "funnel of peoples." In 358 Constantius II led the Agaragantes who were living with the Vandals back into the Banat, where they settled as Roman federates under royal leadership. The Limigantes, however, were decisively defeated in 358 and 359 by a Roman army with help from barbarian allies.[153] Among the horsemen needed for this campaign were also Taifali, who launched their attacks directly from their own settlements. But it is unlikely that they had to be given Oltenia-Little Walachia in return for their services, which allowed them to reach the Sarmatians more easily.[154]

Thus the Taifali fulfilled their duties as federates, and the relationship of the emperor Constantius II to the Tervingi was also friendly. Yet in the forties a conflict of sorts arose between the empire and its Danubian federates. Tervingian raiders had crossed the frozen Danube during the winter and invaded Moesia. The emperor, who was occupied with the Persians, attempted to settle the differences more by giving in than by taking drastic measures.[155] These disturbances may have been related to the persecution of Christians which Athanaric's father Aoric seems to have carried out in 348.[156] War against the Romans and persecution of Gothic Christians, who were considered Roman sympathizers, was renewed during the period of Athanaric's judgeship.[157] In any case, Constantius II extended an "honorable" reception to those who had been driven out (among them Ulfilas) and settled them at Nikopolis-Stari Nikub in modern-day Bulgaria. Here they formed the "numerous and unwarlike people of the Gothi minores."[158]

It was these Roman Goths who accepted Constantius II as their monarch (*thiudans*), thus equating the ethnic "monarchic king" with the emperor. The use of *thiudans* is all the more significant since the Tervingi did not have a king of this type.[159]

Julian, the successor of Constantius II, was ambivalent in his judgment of the Goths: at one time he considered them enemies unworthy of an emperor's attention because they dared only undertake plundering raids; on another occasion, before setting out on his march east—a march in which Tervingian federates dutifully participated—Julian did not expect the tribe to keep quiet much longer. To be sure, the second remark sounds like hindsight, a *prophetia ex eventu*.[160]

THE ERA OF ATHANARIC, 365-376/381

Tervingian history during the decade before the invasion of the Huns is dominated by the figure of Athanaric, who has fascinated posterity as much as he did his contemporaries. The Visigoths of the seventh century still remembered Athanaric as their "founder king." Even in the scheme of the Amal *Origo Gothica* the non-Amal Athanaric holds a special place. He is the first Gothic prince whose words Cassiodorus cites in direct speech. Athanaric's resistance against Rome and his reconciliation with the emperor at the end of his life seemed exemplary for the history of Gothic identity in West and East. Because the Gothic prince persecuted the Christians, the church historians of the fifth century condemned him. He was also involved in Gothic tribal feuds during his entire life. Nevertheless, his memory was blackened only in sources thoroughly hostile to the Goths. Today Athanaric is considered the first representative of Gothic political life "about whom we are told more than his name": the ancient authors do not merely mention him or his activities but also ascribe to him varied motives. There were also Roman contemporaries who knew the Goth personally or through reliable sources. And finally there appeared legends of saints who had suffered martyrdom under this Gothic prince.[161]

Athanaric was the head of the "royal clan of the Scythians,"[162] that is, he was head of the family that is probably rightly called the "older Balthi."[163] Alliteration, variation, and rhythm in the line of names Athanaric, Aoric, Ariaric resemble the "ideal type" of Hadubrand, Hildebrand, Heribrand. Since a functional comparison also shows great similarities among the three Tervingi, it has been assumed that these Gothic princes were the representatives of three Balthic generations of the fourth century and at the same time judges of the Tervingi. Constantine the Great had a statue of honor erected for Athanaric's father—who had come as hostage to Constantinople, probably in 332— in order to win him over to his side. The plan must have failed, at least in the long run, for the Goth later bound his son on oath never to set foot on Roman soil. Although we can explain this prohibition as an obligation linked to the office of judge rather than as a personal enmity toward Rome, it did—like the oath imposed on Hannibal by his father— cast its shadow over Athanaric's life.[164]

At Nish in the early summer of 364 Valentinian I and Valens divided the army and the empire "in fraternal concord." The older emperor took over the West with its capital at Milan, the younger brother took the East with Constantinople. In the spring of 364 the emperors, "after a calm winter," had marched through Thrace toward Illyrian Nish.[165] At that time no Goth could have been plundering on a large scale south of the Danube: it would have been suicidal to cross the river while the combined court armies were marching near the Danube.[166] Small incursions must have occurred, however, for on June 19, 365, Valentinian gave the commander of the province of Dacia ripensis the order to restore watchtowers or have new ones built.[167] Valens took similar measures for his section of the "Gothic bank." The setting up of a chain of stations was to prevent the intrusion of transdanubian raiders.[168] The relevant decree sounds like an answer to Gothic provocation. Yet the itineraries of the two emperors exclude the possibility that the Goths became restless before the spring of 365. Valens was on his way to Syria and had already reached Bithynia when in mid-summer 365 he received this ominous report from his border commanders: "The Gothic people, for a long time unmolested and therefore extremely wild, are combining into a confederation and preparing to attack the neighboring Thracian provinces."[169]

Valens reacted immediately, sending horsemen and foot soldiers to the threatened areas. While marching through Constantinople, however, the elite units were won over by Procopius, who made himself emperor with their help. While Valens was awaiting the abating of summer heat in Asia Minor, the usurper accomplished a double feat. Taking advantage of the alleged or real Gothic danger, he managed to annex all of Thrace and order the Tervingi to fulfill their obligations as federates.[170] At this time Athanaric was already the negotiating partner of the Romans; that is to say, he was the man with whom Procopius established written contact. The Roman observers described Athanaric more as a spokesman or the executive agent of a number of "Gothic kings" rather than as a royal or princely monarch. In the presence of the widow of Constantius II and with that emperor's small daughter on his arm, Procopius had presented himself to the army as a member of the Flavian house. Likewise, he demanded military support from the Goths by insisting on his relationship to Constantine the Great and Constantius.[171] In response, three thousand Tervingian elite warriors came to the usurper's aid.[172] On their way to Constantinople they probably behaved no worse than any other army on the march.[173] But when they arrived they found Procopius no longer alive; he had been executed on May 27, 366. His relative Marcellus then tried to make himself emperor with the help of the Gothic corps but had just as little luck. The Tervingi then tried to return home, though they still considered themselves allies, not enemies of Rome. Nonetheless, on their march back to the Danube they were overpowered by Roman troops without bloodshed and at first interned in various Thracian cities. Eunapius tells us that "the king of the Scythians demanded back these noble warriors. The case was embarrassing and difficult to settle justly." Athanaric was in fact able to present to the envoys of the emperor Valens, who demanded information about the Gothic support for the usurper, Procopius's written and apparently impressively reasoned plea for help.[174] Valens, who was taking bloody revenge on the followers of his enemy,[175] had not the slightest intention of sparing barbarians and did not hand over the captives. Nothing more is heard of them.[176]

The excuse of the Tervingi was to no avail. Valens did not accept it and in agreement with his brother he prepared for war.[177] This step shows that the emperor was consistent in continuing the measures he had already taken along the Danubian front before the episode with Procopius. His inflexible attitude and his determination for war raises doubts about alleged Gothic plans for attack. Who was really the aggressor, Athanaric or Valens? It is true that Valens did not want a war with the Goths while he was marching to Syria in 365, and the Tervingian marauders had opened hostilities on their own. But could the Romans legitimately assume in 365 that the Gothic peoples had formed a confederation in order to attack the empire? At the request of the border commanders Valens sent only two elite units as reinforcements and continued his march eastward. Either the emperor despised the Goths in the same way Julian was said to have done[178] or the problem was merely one of punishing a band of retainers operating on a small scale, not of repelling an attack of the entire barbarian confederacy.[179] A number of additional reasons also argue against the assumption of a Gothic offensive in 365. When Julian had marched against the Persians, the Tervingi had met their obligations as federates and had sent contingents to Syria as late as 362/363. The Roman army, however, wanted to move against the "Dacian" Goths, not against the Persians. But Julian insisted on his large-scale campaign against the Persians, who were guilty of nothing more than minor border violations; indeed, the war was undertaken against an enemy willing to make peace. The tribal warriors who returned from the Persian campaigns with the news of Julian's death must have known the mood of the Roman army. A Roman offensive could now be expected along the Danubian border, which had been extremely well fortified by the deceased emperor. The Goths felt threatened. They formed a confederation of all tribal divisions and placed themselves under the authority of a barbarian chief whom the Roman sources call a judge and who was probably called *kindins* in Gothic. But this "judge" was not allowed to leave the tribal territory, which made him the most unsuitable leader for an offensive war. Rather, he was responsible for the defense of the *Gutthiuda* (land of the Gothic people) against domestic and foreign enemies.[180]

In the spring of 367 everything was ready; after careful preparation Valens opened hostilities, which lasted into late summer 369. At Transmarisca-Tutrakan, where Constantine the Great had built the large ferry with the fortified bridgehead at Daphne, a pontoon bridge was thrown across the river. The Romans crossed the Danube and advanced into the Walachian heartland of the Tervingian-Taifalian settlement.[181] Athanaric, however, skillfully managed to evade the Roman army again and again, and he withdrew with the greater part of the barbarian confederacy. Taifali are not specifically mentioned, but it is likely that they were among Athanaric's warriors, considering how mobile they were. The Romans ravaged the land, went head-hunting after dispersed groups, but had to suffer themselves from partisan activity. "Thereafter," claimed Ammianus Marcellinus, "the emperor returned unopposed with his troops, without having inflicted any serious damage on the enemy or having suffered any himself."[182]

The floods in the summer of 368 interrupted hostilities, for Valens could not cross the Danube. This time he had planned to catch the Tervingi farther east. The Romans' choice for a base of operations fell on Vicus Carporum-Hirşova in the Dobrudja, in other words, exactly where the Danube comes closest to the Carpathians. The Bărăgan steppe, probably Taifalian, was to be bypassed in the east. Because of flooding, however, the emperor had no choice but to give up his base on the Danube at the end of the season and take up winter quarters at Marcianopolis. Valens would not have wasted the entire summer of 368 if Constantine's stone bridge in Dacia ripensis had still been intact.[183]

The campaign of 367 had already caused devastation, and flooding in 368 made the situation of the Tervingi even worse. The loss of the harvest in the previous summers could not be made up; moreover, there was no more trade with the Romans, which was always needed to keep up supplies.[184] Despite the danger of being starved out, Athanaric continued his strategy—to which the swollen "holy *Dōnaws" himself had now given his support[185]—into the third year of the war. This time Valens crossed the river at Noviodunum-Isaccea. The emperor had another pontoon bridge thrown across the river and invaded what is modern-day Bessarabia-Moldavian S.S.R. The Roman army first encountered the Greutungi, who had possibly come across the Budjak steppe to aid the Tervingi, just as the Tervingi would try to help the Greutungi against the Huns in 376. The Greutungian horsemen withdrew quickly, and the imperial forces marched on. The deeper they penetrated into the area between the Prut and the Dniester, the stronger Tervingian resistance became, until Athanaric finally faced the Roman army. Remarkably enough the Tervingian judge accepted battle with only a part of his tribal warriors.[186] The notion that he needed a reserve against his rival Fritigern, who was allied with the Romans, is incorrect, for armed conflict between the two Gothic princes did not break out until the 370s.[187] More likely, Athanaric had no intention of offering the Romans a decisive battle, which his tribal confederacy could hardly win.[188] The Goths did lose the engagement, but under the leadership of Athanaric they escaped annihilation. After a clever evasive maneuver the Gothic judge opened negotiations with the Romans. The unsuccessful attempt to encircle and decisively defeat the highly mobile tribal group prompted Valens, who had already returned to Marcianopolis, to accept Athanaric's offer of peace. The end of hostilities was also very much in the Goths' own interest, since their precarious economic situation would not have allowed a continuation of the war.[189]

In September 369 Valens had to make peace with Athanaric as an equal; he had to recognize Athanaric's refusal (on religious grounds) to set foot on Roman soil and he had to negotiate for an entire day on a boat anchored at a "suitable place" in the middle of the Danube. The manner in which the peace was concluded prompted lasting annoyance among the Romans. Athanaric had to conclude a new treaty on less favorable terms but still establishing *amicitia*. On the Roman side the previously open trade between the Danubian provinces and the Tervingi was restricted to two border points and the payments to the federates were halted. The Goths handed over hostages, and the emperor returned to Constantinople and assumed the triumphal Gothicus-title.[190] Athanaric was given a free hand to persecute Christians—in other words, to make war against the internal enemy—which he did until 372. One can hardly speak of a Roman victory in this peace or of a Gothic defeat in the military sense. It was therefore difficult for the imperial spokesmen, above all for the rhetorician Themistius, to justify the "philanthropic" nature of Valens's Gothic policy. Themistius, who had taken part in the peace negotiations as an envoy from the senate in Constantinople and who had come to know Athanaric personally, did not conceal his high regard for the Gothic judge.[191]

The second Gothic persecution of the Christians lasted from 369 to 372 and was conducted far more systematically than the first one in 348.[192] The Gothic persecutors were not content with isolated actions or the exiling of Christian tribesmen but instead aimed for complete extermination.[193] The persecution was directed by Athanaric, who conducted it in the same way in which he had been leading the Danubian-Gothic confederacy since 365: on the resolution of the Tervingian optimates. For the Christians of the following generation the Gothic judge was simply *the* persecutor; but what specifically he did is rarely mentioned, nor was anyone concerned about his motives; he was simply a "limb of the devil."[194] Only authors of the fifth century recognized certain connections between the persecution and the hostility toward Rome that a majority of the Goths felt. Church historiography of the fifth century did differentiate the political conflicts more strongly but at the same time presented it from an apologetical point of view. Thus Ulfilas was made into the opponent of Athanaric, who feared the destruction of the "faith of the fathers" through the Christian teachings.[195] Not unlike the way in which the pagan emperors reacted to this problem, the Gothic judge forced the Christians among his people to worship a common tribal idol. He ordered his people to carry "something like an image of god" through the countryside on top of a wagon and to offer sacrifices to it. Whoever refused to do so was burned along with his dwelling;[196] in other words, he suffered the punishment of someone who had violated the "divine law" of the tribe. There was probably no common idol; instead, each Tervingian subtribe had its own cult object. Perhaps the stake idol in Athanaric's *kuni* (subtribe) had counterparts in other *kunja*. The stake idol or idols—which were associated with the Ansis-Aesir— would then have represented nothing other than the divine ancestors or founding heroes. Whoever did not honor them denied the Gothic *origo,* the belief in the divine origins of the ancestors and the tribal community and thus forfeited his Gothic identity.[197] But Athanaric's conservative policies were directed not so much against things Graeco-Roman as against Christianity mediated by the Romans.[198] He feared that Christianity would dissolve the traditional social order of his people.[199] Yet the brutal persecution could not heal the differences within the tribe. Although the majority of the Danubian Goths were still pagan, the Christian faith could no longer be exterminated. The split among the Tervingi was deepened, and this contributed considerably to the catastrophe of 376.[200]

While those Goths who adhered to Catholicism would win the praise of posterity, the 360s and 370s saw the rule of Emperor Valens, who promoted the Arian faith. The Gothic prince Fritigern, Athanaric's rival and later the victor at Adrianople, must have realized the possibility of profiting politically from the Christian persecution by switching sides.[201] The judgeship of Athanaric, which represented a monarchical institution limited in time, had to be renewed repeatedly because the Tervingian confederation from 365 was constantly exposed to internal and external threats.[202] But unless the power of the judge was curtailed, the establishment of a strong kingship was to be feared. Athanaric could have set up a *regnum* that would have threatened both the Tervingian aristocracy and the Roman imperial government.[203] Fritigern therefore contacted Valens, gained imperial support in return for the promise that he would become an Arian Christian, and attacked Athanaric. The hostilities must have begun sometime between 372 and 375/376; the confused tradition does not reveal the exact date.[204] After varied success on both sides, Athanaric once again gained the upper hand, for we find him organizing as judge of all Tervingi the defense against the Huns.[205]

In the summer of 376 Athanaric led a strong army from Moldavia through Bessarabia to the western bank of the Dniester. Here, at the old border between the two Gothic peoples, the Gothic judge built a Roman-type fortified camp.[206] The position of the Tervingi was located quite a distance from a region called "the valley of the Greutungi." Two noble chieftains, Munderic and Lagariman, led a vanguard "about twenty miles" east across the river; they were to observe in "foreign countries" the advance of the Huns. There was, however, no contact between the Tervingi and the Greutungi, even though a part of the Ostrogoths who had been defeated by the Huns detached themselves carefully from the victors and moved west. The Huns let these Greutungi go, just as they despised the bait the Tervingi had laid out. Then, on a moonlit night, they crossed the Dniester—showing great familiarity with the region—and fell unexpectedly on Athanaric. The Gothic judge managed once more to retreat without suffering any losses worth recording. In the war against Valens he had already proved himself a master at such maneuvers.[207] The Tervingian line of retreat was also covered by the Bessarabian forest zone into which the Huns could not carry their pursuit. Moreover, the Hunnic force was probably not very numerous; it seems that only an advance detachment had been given the task of forcing Athanaric from his defensive position. A larger Hunnic army probably would not have let either Munderic's vanguard[208] or the Greutungian fugitives get away. Finally, the Tervingian judge would have had no time to think about building a redoubt on the central plateau of Moldavia if the Huns had been able to apply massive pressure. The early Hunnic stronghold at Conceşti on the upper Prut must have therefore grown up only after the retreat of the Tervingi. And so Athanaric gathered together between the Siret and the Prut a large part of the Tervingian confederation and began to fortify the exposed southern flank of the central plateau of Moldavia with a long rampart. A great many attempts have been made to identify its archaeological remains. Some suggested remains presuppose a labor effort of pharaonic scale. While these identifications thus seem rather unlikely, Athanaric must have nevertheless made great efforts to organize the defense. He did, however, exclude the Taifali from the protective measures. Every increase in the danger from the Huns deepened the divisions within the polyethnic community of the Tervingi: everyone became his own best friend. While Athanaric was pushing ahead with his "well-planned work," the Huns made another completely unexpected attack. This time the Tervingi would have met their fate had the enemies not been encumbered by the booty they were dragging along.[209]

The clash took place at the northern edge of the wedge between the Siret, Prut, and Danube, right where the forest zone turns into open country and the territory of the Taifalian horsemen began.[210] If the Huns appeared there loaded with booty, they must have been on their way home from a raid that had led them as far as Muntenia. It follows that the Huns, notwithstanding other Tervingian-Taifalian pockets of resistance mentioned only in passing,[211] had destroyed the basis of the food supply for Athanaric's Goths. Since all further political and military decisions were made in the entourage of the Gothic judge, it is likely that the greater part of the tribal group gathered at the redoubt in Moldavia. In contrast to the Roman war of 367–369, when the Goths escaped supply problems until the third year of hostilities,[212] this time the supply lines collapsed immediately.[213] One can point out several reasons why this happened. But the decisive factor, which the Roman campaign of 369 had also shown, was probably that Athanaric's power was centered in Moldavia and Bessarabia.[214] A Gothic judge who gave up this land obviously lost his backing. Apart from religious and political considerations, there was also the concrete problem of threatening famine. The Goths had barely recovered from the battles against the Romans when tribal conflict between Athanaric and Fritigern broke out;[215] in its wake came the Hunnish invasion causing a tremendous devastation of the land, the psychological effects of which made a bad situation even worse.

The Tervingi had no hope of surviving in a ravaged land that a new type of enemy could destroy at will, practically without advance warning. No one knew how to defend against the Huns, not even Athanaric who in his days had outmaneuvered the Romans. At this critical time the leaders of the opposition—the friends of Rome and the Christians, that is, the former enemies of the Tervingian judge—offered a credible alternative. They took the initiative, probably boasting of connections at the highest levels,[216] and promised flight into the Roman Empire as the only means of salvation. The majority of Tervingi thereupon deserted Athanaric, thus bringing the Tervingian judgeship to an end. Though single groups may have remained in the country, they were too weak to renew the institution that was tied to the Gutthiuda, to the Gothic people in its land.[217] The main body of Tervingi, led by Alaviv and Fritigern, was admitted into the empire. Fritigern had good reason to expect much from the emperor's goodwill, since Fritigern represented the party of Gothic Christians and was perhaps even bound to the emperor by a treaty, factors that must have increased his reputation and standing. Nevertheless, it appears that the otherwise un- known Alaviv was the higher ranking prince; not until after his death did Fritigern become the leader of all the Tervingi on Roman soil.[218] Fritigern became a barbarian *dux,* in the true sense of that word a leader of the army "who ruled in place of a king."[219] He never held the "office" of Gothic judge, but his mandate already represents a preliminary stage to the kingship of the army.[220] Thus Fritigern had the authority to negotiate and conclude treaties with the emperor as well as with other barbarian groups.[221]

The events leading up to the admission of Fritigern's Goths into the empire stretched over an extended period of time during which the Huns kept quiet. Most refugees had to cover no great distance to reach the borders of the empire. The second assault on Athanaric must therefore have taken place within sixty miles of the north bank of the Danube. But before the Goths could be admitted, permission had to be obtained from Valens, who was at that time in Antioch.[222] And so it was autumn before the emperor's answer arrived at the "Gothic bank." In the meantime the Romans allowed no one to cross the Danube. Those who tried were forcibly turned back. Eventually the bands of Alaviv and Fritigern were allowed to cross over. Athanaric, who had originally wanted to follow them, learned of the difficul- ties that all other Gothic refugees had faced and gave up his plan. The former Gothic judge remembered his strained relations with Valens and therefore decided to leave only his immediate homeland. The abandonment of the Moldavian redoubt had become necessary because the Tervingi who had remained loyal to Athanaric were in need of food and shelter for the winter. In the long run, however, he would have to provide an economically healthy and militarily secure settlement area.

The Caucaland, the *Caucalandensis locus,* "which was rendered inaccessible by high mountains and deep forests," was just such an area. It was inhabited by Sarmatians, whom the Tervingi simply had to drive out in order to occupy their houses and use their stores to get through the winter.[223] It is not certain where this "promised land" of Athanaric's Tervingi was located, but we should probably look for it in the upper Alutus valley in Walachia or in Transylvania.[224] As he had previously done with the Taifali, Athanaric broke with the Sarmatian minority in the territory under his rule. Ambrose comments with unsurpassable brevity on the chaos caused by the Hunnic onslaught: the Huns fell upon the Alans, the Alans upon the Goths, and the Goths upon the Taifali and Sarmatians.[225] Zosimus, as well, shows that the "Scythian" community of the "Goths, Taifali, and other peoples who had previously lived with them" was destroyed by the Huns.[226] When this community grew up again on the Roman side of the Danube, it did so only while giving up its old structures.[227]

Athanaric's conquest of the Caucaland was a success, if by success we mean the safety of his tribe at the expense of another. During the terrible disorders of the next four years, Athanaric's Goths remained lost behind the Carpathians; they were in a sense passed over by history. Actually there must have been Tervingi who had lived in Transylvania prior to 376 and who therefore had at first nothing to fear from the Huns. But we hear so little about the Dacian Goths that one would doubt their existence were it not for the well-documented archaeological sites at Sîntana-de-Mureş. One report—though difficult to interpret—speaks of the Arimir Goths, who must have existed north of the Danube sometime between 383 and 392. This group was certainly not identical with Athanaric's Goths. Through Gaatha, the mother of chief Arimir, the group had established contact with Christians in the Roman Empire without paying any attention to Fritigern's Goths.[228] At that time Athanaric was, of course, no longer alive. His own people, possibly his relatives (*proximi*), had driven the former Gothic judge out of Caucaland in late 380. An intrigue engineered by Fritigern, which, for whatever reason, fell on fertile ground among the Goths who had until then stood aloof from the power struggle, probably led to Athanaric's fall. But Fritigern could not prevent his rival from making his way, after all, into the Roman Empire.

Valens had now been dead for two years, and Theodosius received the head of the "Scythian royal clan" with great honor. The former Gothic judge came to the emperor in Constantinople as a refugee, ἱκέτης. He who had seemed invincible now surrendered to the Romans of his own free will. On January 11, 381, Athanaric enjoyed a splendid reception in Constantinople. The emperor came out in person to meet him at his entrance into the city of the great Constantine.[229] Perhaps even in the presence of the honored guest, Themistius, who had come to know Athanaric at the peace negotiations in 369, discussed the emperor's Gothic policy.[230] But two weeks later, on January 25, the Gothic prince died.[231] Even more than Athanaric's royal reception, his official funeral, which Theodosius arranged according to Roman rites, offered an opportunity for an impressive display of imperial power and splendor. The honors paid to the deceased were meant as an illustration of Theodosius's Gothic policy—which was reminiscent of the efforts of the early seventies—and they had their intended effect.[232] Political gestures of this sort lined the path toward the pacification of the Goths and the conclusion of the historically most important *foedus* in October 382. Later tradition, as, for example, the *Origo Gothica*, which was in this instance dependent on Orosius, saw in these events a direct relation of cause and effect: Athanaric was believed to be the Gothic king who entered Constantinople as Fritigern's successor and regretted his stubborn opposition to Rome and the emperor. After the death of their chief, the Goths submitted to the authority of Theodosius, who renewed the Constantinian *foedus*.[233] Orthodox bias and Christian apologetics were responsible for this distortion of the tradition. Men such as Ambrose and Orosius were interested in giving a meaningful structure to the events; they wanted to prove that Christianity as such, and Catholic Christianity in particular, offered the best protection for the empire. Chronology and historical details had to fall victim to such bias. Something similar happened with the history of Ulfilas. Most contemporary sources report more briefly about Athanaric and Ulfilas than did later generations. Nevertheless, they provide us with the necessary dates to correct many traditional notions. Ulfilas died only a short time after Athanaric, also in Constantinople. Like Athanaric he was given a splendid funeral. At his death the bishop had been a septuagenarian.[234] Athanaric's death, in contrast, had come as something of a surprise; there were even rumors of a violent end,[235] which means that the former Gothic judge was probably not an old man like Ulfilas. If we assume that Ulfilas was born in 311,[236] then all we can say about Athanaric is that he was probably born later than that and was in the prime of his life in the 360s and 370s.

The end of the era of Athanaric meant also the end of the ethnic identity of the Tervingi. The two Roman auxiliary units Vesi and Tervingi were perhaps levied already from among Athanaric's retainers in 381, but no later than after the peace treaty of 382. While the Tervingian name is attested historically for the last time as the name of this Roman military unit, Visi-Vesi was linked in folk etymology with the Gothic name and survived the migrations in the form Visigoths.[237]

Ulfilas and the Beginning of the Conversion of the Goths

Ulfilas's aim in life was certainly not "to lay the foundation for 'Grimm's Law' of the transmutation of consonants."[238] Nor did he intend to supply medieval constitutional historians with the badly needed Gothic equivalents of political terminology. Ulfilas was simply the good shepherd of his flock and a confessor of the Christian faith as he understood it.[239] Moreover, the translation of the Bible undertaken by Ulfilas and his helpers created the basis for their missionary work. Out of a Gothic language—which was, however, well prepared—they created a subtle instrument that immediately won its place among the classic languages of the Bible.[240] Ulfilas's independent theological achievement, however, ranks much lower. In accordance with the "fundamentalism" with which all translators before Jerome approached the original, Ulfilas and his assistants paid scrupulous attention to bringing the Gothic Bible as close as possible to the Greek source.[241] A translation was made of both the Old and the New Testament, but only the greater part of the latter has survived.[242] According to Philostorgius, Ulfilas deliberately left out the Book of Kings, "which contains the history of the wars, in order to dampen the battle lust of a people who delighted in warfare, instead of stirring them up for it."[243] What strikes us as intentional could be the result of incomplete survival. Yet biblical Gothic does lack certain military terms, the reason for which one could assume to be deliberate omission.[244] It is also possible that Philostorgius's story was meant to emphasize the pacifying effect of Ulfilas's mission on his Gothic followers. Consonant with this interpretation is the refusal of the *Origo Gothica* to blame the Gothic bishop for the pernicious "Arianism" of the new converts.[245]

Philostorgius, to whom we are indebted for much important information about Ulfilas, was a Cappadocian. He knew that the ancestors of Ulfilas had also come from Cappadocia, a region with which the Gothic community had always maintained close ties. Ulfilas's πρόγονοι were captured by plundering Goths in the village of Sadagolthina in the city district of Parnassus and were carried off to Transdanubia.[246] This supposedly took place in 264.[247] But, first, there was probably no Gothic incursion in that year.[248]

Second, the information is dated in such a way that it cannot be placed after 260: the abduction is said to have occurred "during the reign of Valerian and Gallienus," but Valerian became a prisoner of the Persians in 260, whereupon his son Gallienus dissociated himself from his father.[249] The dating of a joint reign, especially one in which clear precedence is given to the father, is therefore likely only between 253 and 260. Third, the raiders must have been "western" Goths. It follows from this that the ancestors of Ulfilas were captured in 257 by a band of Danubian Goths.[250]

For the Gothic identity of Ulfilas, however, plus or minus seven years makes no difference. His birth is placed around 311.[251] Whenever it was that his Cappadocian ancestors came to the Goths, Ulfilas himself was already of the third generation. His name is Gothic and means "little wolf,"[252] a diminutive that reveals nothing about his social standing. It is generally believed that the bishop was Cappadocian in his mother's line and Gothic through his father; this is probably not more than an inference from analogy, for Ulfilas's successor Selenas was in fact the son of a Gothic father and a Phrygian mother.[253] Whatever Ulfilas's Cappadocian ancestors meant to him, he was by birth a Goth, about whose grandparents we have reliable information, in contrast to the ancestry of many of his fellow tribesmen.

The Romans saw in Ulfilas the Gothic bishop and tribal leader, *pontifex ipseque primas*.[254] Constantius II is said to have called him the Moses of his time. Ulfilas was also compared to Elijah, which reflects similar notions.[255] The young Goth made his first trip to the imperial city between 332 and 337. This date can be derived from the statement that "the barbarian peoples were at that time subject to the emperor," which was the case only after the *foedus* between Constantine and Ariaric. It is possible that the two men who were probably enemies in 348, namely, Aoric (given as a hostage in 332) and Ulfilas, even lived in Constantinople at the same time for a while.[256] The purpose of Ulfilas's visit was to accompany a delegation of the Gothic tribal federation, of "the peoples," to the imperial city. The young man was in his late twenties. As a bishop he composed theological tracts and exegetical writings in both Latin and Greek; thus he not only learned the classical languages but must have also enjoyed some kind of rhetorical training.[257] Moreover, we may assume that Ulfilas was not a nameless upstart. He could never have become a member of the Gothic delegation without a certain social standing; otherwise the emperor would have been insulted.[258] Ulfilas did not win renown among Goths and Romans only as a result of his priestly office and the way he administered it; rather, he became bishop because he already possessed some standing. He was, for example, able to rise from lector to bishop without ever having been a deacon or presbyter. To be sure, because of the shortage of ecclesiastical personnel, the opportunity for rapid rise for competent people had existed ever since 332, when "the Goths, under the impact of their defeat by Constantine, first believed in the Christian religion."[259] Since Ulfilas's episcopal commission was apparently valid not only for the Gothic *gens* but for all of the "Getic land," he must have been recognized also by the non-Gothic peoples of the Gutthiuda, above all by the Romans.[260]

How then are we to determine Ulfilas's social position using the biblical Gothic he created?[261] Saint Saba was apparently someone we would call a "free" Goth. But he was poor and could "neither harm nor help anybody." Ulfilas, in contrast, made quite a different impression on his contemporaries.[262] His career was only possible because he already had certain financial resources. In the archaizing terminology of the sixth century he certainly was no *reiks,* but he must have belonged to the economically strongest stratum of the "curly-haired."[263] In the eyes of Auxentius-Mercurinus, the bishop of Durostorum-Silistria, Ulfilas was a saint, and so he wrote his biography after classic models:[264] Ulfilas was consecrated bishop at the age of thirty. He stayed north of the Danube for seven years, was then driven away to Moesia where he settled and led the Gothic community for another thirty-three years. Ulfilas died after having been a bishop for a total of forty years. This biography follows the model of David, who stepped into public light at age thirty, ruled over Hebron for seven years and over all of Israel for thirty-three years.[265] Christ too began to preach the gospel at age thirty.

When Auxentius was writing his pro-Arian tract, the Arians were already a beleaguered minority and had to make credible points to back their cause. Auxentius must therefore have avoided excessive invention. Still, we may expect that he did somewhat manipulate his figures. But on the whole this biography of Ulfilas, which could have been easily checked by any contemporary reader, must have been reasonably accurate.

When the lector Ulfilas came to Constantinople with the Gothic delegation, he was consecrated bishop "by Eusebius and the bishops who were with him."[266] This report raises some puzzling chronological problems. The Goths came to see Constantine in his imperial city, which they could have done in 337 at the latest. But it was not until 338, one year after the death of his father, that Constantius II made Eusebius, then bishop of Nicomedia, the imperial bishop of Constantinople. If we calculate the date of Ulfilas's consecration as bishop from the forty-year period he served in that capacity, we once again come up with a date when the great Constantine was already long dead.[267] It is generally believed that Ulfilas was made bishop in 341 at the council of Antioch. In the presence of Constantius II and presided over by Eusebius, the fathers at the council were trying to reach a compromise between the Nicene Creed and heretical doctrines. Ulfilas's dogmatic doctrine, to which he adhered throughout his life, agrees conspicuously with the theological position of the council. Thus Ulfilas must have come into the Roman Empire once as a member of the Gothic delegation before 337 and then in 341 to Antioch where the imperial bishop Eusebius ordained him "bishop of the Christians in the Getic land." Ulfilas's ordination reveals that an imperial mission to the Goths was planned. This decision of the emperor had such a lasting effect that even the second ecumenical council under the Catholic Theodosius still had to confirm it.[268] Expelled to Moesia during the first Gothic persecution of Christians, Ulfilas did not change his conception of his mission, namely, as the Christian leader of his *gens* to resolve *in Christo* the ethnic difference between Goths and Romans. Thus the parents of the Roman provincial Mercurinus—who later in Milan called himself Auxentius—brought their son to Ulfilas, who raised him and was in return loved and revered by Mercurinus beyond his death.[269]

Ulfilas's consecration as bishop in itself attests the existence of a Christian community in the Gothic land, and the translation of the Bible also reflects earlier efforts of both Latin and Greek missionaries among the Goths.[270] Thus the Cappadocian Eutyches, whom the anti-Arian apologetic made into "the apostle of the Goths," was probably an older contemporary of Ulfilas's.[271] Of course the beginnings of the Christian teachings reach back as far as the third century. Supposedly in 251 Cniva's Goths dragged off Roman Christians who then turned "their masters into brothers."[272] Where precisely the captured Christians were taken at first is difficult to say. The majority of Gothic plundering expeditions of the late 250s started in the Crimea,[273] so many captured Romans were transplanted into the area of the Tauric peninsula and its hinterland. In addition, the Bosporanian kingdom had recognized Christianity as the official religion around 300. Among the fathers gathered in Nicaea in 325 a Theophilus from Gothia is mentioned right after the bishop of the Crimea. Although it was Catholic apologetics, who made him Ulfilas's predecessor and teacher, this report might be true.[274]

Certainly, there was a Gothic community in the Crimea which developed a remarkable vitality at the edge of the world. It was spared serious conflicts—either because of its "backwardness" or for reasons of geographic isolation—and remained loyal to the Nicene Creed and to Constantinople. In 404 the Crimean Goths turned to the patriarch of the imperial city, John Chrysostom, and asked him for a successor to Bishop Unila, whom he had once appointed. John even preached to the strong Gothic community in Constantinople to confirm them in Catholicism. His open-mindedness toward barbarian souls recommended him to the Crimean Goths. Archaeological finds attest the continuity of Christianity, but the written sources are silent for a long time about life on the Bosporanian Chersonesus.[275] Theodoric the Great wished the Crimean Goths to join his army on the march to Italy, but they declined with thanks. Then two more generations passed before the Crimea reported again to headquarters. In 548 the Goths of the peninsula requested a successor to the deceased bishop. At the same time they also asked for political and military aid against their Hunnic neighbors, referring to similar measures Justinian had taken for other peoples.[276] Thereafter reports once again became sparse. But each subsequent century has at least one mention of Crimean Gothia.[277]

Gothic Crimea probably preserved Catholicism, even if a somewhat "reduced" version. The Balkan Goths, in contrast, were labeled Arians. Ulfilas had no choice but to follow the decision of the council of 360 which settled on a compromise formula. Thus he no longer discussed the nature (*substantia, οὐσία*) of the divine persons. This decision brought the young Gothic church into opposition with the Catholic majority. The latter labeled all mediators as adherents of Arianism, which subordinated the Son to the Father and taught their substantive difference. Although Ulfilas rejected the Catholic position and regretted the Arian doctrine,[278] neither his contemporaries nor the next generation were ready to accept his middle-of-the-road theology. At most contemporaries would concede either that Ulfilas was originally Catholic and well meaning in his error, or that he was intellectually incapable of understanding Christology;[279] not very flattering and reminiscent of Procopius's judgment of the Crimean Goths.[280]

Constantius II sent the aged Mesopotamian Audaios into exile in the province of Scythia minor (the Dobrudja). The Audaians, a sect named after him, advocated obsolete ideas about the corporeality of God (anthropomorphism), rejected the new regulation of Easter made by the Council of Nicaea, and distinguished themselves through their ascetic way of life. From the Dobrudja Audaios began his mission across the Danube among the pagan Goths. His austere bearing exerted a great attraction on the Tervingi. Audaios's place was taken by a certain Silvanus; a Uranius is also mentioned. The Audaian sect suffered greatly under the persecution of Athanaric. Their way of life seemed to pose a particular threat to Gothic tribal tradition. After their expulsion the Audaians went to Mesopotamia, the homeland of the founder of their sect, or to Syria, because their community was considered part of the Syrian church.[281]

The first persecution of Gothic Christians took place in 348, most likely after a war with the Romans.[282] Ulfilas was among those expelled, and for the remainder of his life he bore the honorary title "confessor."[283] It was said that this persecution also claimed some lives, but we know no details or names.[284] In the story of the martyrdom of the Gothic saints Inna, Rhima, and Pina, we read about a bishop—no doubt Catholic—with the name Goddas, which is probably Gothic. Seven years after the martyrdom of these saints he saw to it that their bones found a safe and worthy resting place. The three Goths, who were also considered Catholics, had resisted all persuasion and threats from the "prince of the barbarians" and had remained loyal to their faith. As punishment they were drowned in a river. Recently this story of martyrdom has been linked to the first persecution of Christian Goths, but placing it in the time of Athanaric seems more plausible.[285] These events were the prologue to the Gaatha story, the last episode of which took place between 383 and 392 in a Gothic land north of the Danube.[286]

In the mountainous country of Moesia around Nikopolis Ulfilas probably exercised the same office he had already held in transdanubian Gothia, that of *chorepiscopus,* an ecclesiastical functionary responsible for a rural area, χώρα.[287] Attempts to make Ulfilas the bishop of Nikopolis so that he could have used the city's "research library" to translate the Bible are based on a false chronology and overestimate the extent of Roman urbanization along the lower Danube.[288] Ulfilas's followers were shepherds.[289] His chorepiscopacy does not necessarily go back to Cappadocian models, but the great importance of this ecclesiastical institution in the homeland of his ancestors reveals how Christianity organized itself in thinly urbanized regions.[290]

Little is known about Ulfilas's Moesian period; he preached in the three languages he knew and wrote much.[291] The majority of his theological works as well as the translation of the Bible were probably written during this period. The task of inventing and spreading the Gothic alphabet, which added to its base of Greek characters elements from Latin and runic writing, must have taken some time[292] before he could start the translation. Ulfilas translated from the Greek; his source for the New Testament "should be sought in the so-called koine version of the fourth century."[293] Our knowledge of biblical Gothic rests primarily on the famous Codex Argenteus, which was written in Ostrogothic Italy and which shows the influence of the *vetus Latina.* Surviving fragments of parallel passages confirm the impression of a subsequent Latinization, which probably reached its height at the time of Theodoric.[294] Essentially, however, "the Gothic Bible offers only in part an idiomatic and for the most part a Graecizing Gothic."[295]

Auxentius claims that Bishop Ulfilas participated in many synods,[296] but his presence is attested only at the "Arian" Council of Constantinople in

360, where he gave his assent to the creed that had been formulated in the previous year.[297] Ulfilas was the ecclesiastical and worldly leader of the Moesian Goths; his words "were like law to them."[298] Ulfilas's worldly responsibilities do not seem to have grown into an institution,[299] but he did succeed in safeguarding the Gothic identity of his followers so that it survived for centuries. Not only Jordanes in the sixth century but even Walahfrid Strabo in the ninth century mentions these Goths.[300] Ulfilas's successor was the Gotho-Phrygian Selenas.[301] But first came Fritigern, whose bands tried in vain to force the *Gothi minores* to join them.[302] The "peace-loving and unwarlike" Balkan shepherds refused to leave their homeland, indeed, they offered refuge to newcomers tired of wandering around. Rural people from the villages north of the Danube[303] must have been only too glad to join them, for the natural increase in population alone would not explain why the Gothi minores seemed an "incredibly large people" to Jordanes, who was a Balkan Goth himself and therefore knew what he was talking about. The same goes for the name Gothi minores which he gave to the Ulfilas-Goths. In Roman political and geographical terminology the adjective *small* was added to those peoples and lands that were part of the imperium, while *large* was tantamount to "foreign, not subjected, free." Thus the "minor" Germanic provinces of the empire were contrasted with *Germania magna* or *libera* east of the Rhine, *Scythia minor* of the Roman diocese of Thrace with the enormous *Scythia magna* north of the Black Sea, and Roman *Asia minor* with the non-Roman continent of Asia.[304]

The Catholic authors of the early fifth century turned Ulfilas into a supporter of Fritigern and an enemy of Athanaric. The latter was probably true, although there is as little proof for such enmity as there is for the direct cooperation between Fritigern and Ulfilas before or after 376.[305] Besides, Fritigern acted an Arian role solely to please Valens and gain his support against Athanaric. Although Fritigern's Arianism was not entirely in line with Ulfilas's theology, the bishop's Moesian Goths were vital to Fritigern if he wanted to live up to his promise that the Tervingians would accept the imperial creed. Only Ulfilas and his people had the personnel and the means to carry out missionary work. Fritigern's decision in favor of Arianism represented the first internal Gothic encouragement for the work of conversion that Ulfilas had begun long ago.[306]

In 369 Athanaric took up the policy of his reputed father and on behalf of the Gothic oligarchy conducted the second persecution of Christians. The fury raged for three years and was directed indiscriminately against Arians, Catholics, and Audaians. But the written sources are biased in selecting the events. Since Fritigern opposed Athanaric and adopted the faith of the Arian emperor, he gave the missionaries from the Gothi minores a chance to regain lost ground. Thus the sequence of events was reversed. Although Athanaric's persecution took place earlier, it was understood as a reaction to the mission of Ulfilas supported by Fritigern.[307] While Augustine claimed to know only Catholic martyrs,[308] according to other sources only Arians suffered the fate of martyrdom.[309] But in fact confessors of all three faiths were victims of the persecution.[310] Of the Catholic faith were certainly Saba, who suffered martyrdom on April 12, 372; the two presbyters Sansalas and Gutthikas; possibly also Inna, Rhima, Pina; and Bishop Goddas, who recovered their remains and brought them into the empire.[311] Niketas probably adhered to the Catholic faith, but his *passio* has little historical value.[312] The Catholic Goths, who according to Isidore refused to follow Fritigern, owe their existence to Isidore's wish to explain something he did not understand, namely, a struggle among Arian Goths who held different attitudes toward the Roman Empire.[313]

But who was the princess Gaatha, reported to have been "an orthodox Christian?" Is this to be understood to mean Catholic, in the sense of 381, or to mean Arian, from the standpoint of a conservative Roman? If we start from the second possibility, the difficult Gaatha story seems far less puzzling. Between 383 and 392 the Gothic lady traveled in the company of her daughter Dulcilla and the Goth Wella from Gothia into the Roman Empire, having first transferred "dominion" to her son Arimir. The aim and purpose of the trip was the transfer of the remains of twenty-six martyrs to Cyzicus, where Roman Arians were still to be found. The Gothic martyrs who had been burned to death by the chieftain Winguric—the "colleague" of Gaatha's deceased husband—had been Arians and had met their deaths between 367 and 378. No less than three different sources, among them the liturgical calendar of the Goths, report this "murder by burning." After accomplishing her mission, Gaatha returned home; she left her daughter behind in Cyzicus, informed her son that he should pick her up at the border, and went together with Wella into old Gothia. There her companion was stoned to death. The murderers must have still been pagans of Athanaric's type. It is safe to see in this story a bypassing of Fritigern's Arian Goths and of Ulfilas's people. Obviously Arian Goths who lived north of the Danube directly approached like-minded believers in the Roman Empire. The Gothia of the princess Gaatha was not situated in Moesia or in Dacia ripensis; it was also full of pagans, even though the Huns had not yet arrived. Finally the act of the Gothic lady was part of the religious tradition of both the Visigoths and the Gothi minores. Her martyrs became the saints of all Roman Goths.[314] As it was, the Visigoths were badly in need of divine protection. Having penetrated farther into the empire, they were caught up in the fierce controversy that Ambrose and his supporters were waging with all means at their disposal. Only now did Ulfilas's legacy assume its historical significance.[315]

The Catholic mission, however, had already achieved some successes in transdanubian Gothia. Vetranio, the anti-Arian bishop of Tomis, supported by the commander of the Dobrudja, the *dux* Soranus, was Ulfilas's competitor for the Gothic souls. Needless to say both Roman dignitaries came from Cappadocia; Soranus, moreover, had previously recovered the relics of St. Saba from the Gothic land and had had this saint's legend written down for the Cappadocian church. The bond between the Gothic church and the church of Asia Minor was very close.[316] The foundation for this relationship had been laid during the Gothic invasions of the third century. Perhaps the Christians of Asia Minor regarded Gothia—which had become a missionary country with the abduction of their ancestors—as their special responsibility. But in general there were still no Christian missions across the imperial borders. Nevertheless, Christendom in Asia Minor seems to have offered a constant supply of messengers of the faith. Among them were laymen, monks, and also priests. The Phrygian mother of Selenas was certainly not carried off to the Goths.[317] The twenty-six martyrs under Winguric have partly Gothic, partly Phrygian, Cappadocian, and Syrian names.[318] The harsh punishment inflicted on them shows that they must have been considered Goths. The same goes for Inna, Rhima, and Pina, who suffered the same fate as Saba. In contrast, Saba's companion, the presbyter Sansalas, was obviously no Goth, as is revealed by the remarkably mild treatment he received from the same warriors who killed the saint. There were therefore among the transdanubian Christians people who belonged to a village community and thus to a Gothic tribal group and others who were considered outsiders and who were punished during the persecutions with various degrees of severity.[319] Athanaric's persecution did not succeed in exterminating the Gothic Christians. Christian dignitaries were among the Goths who crossed the Danube in 376.[320] The priest whom Fritigern sent to Valens was a Goth like Ulfilas, though the two are not identical.[321] If our interpretation of the report about Goddas is correct, there must have been a Catholic chorepiscopus among the Goths at that time, even if he did not stay with the main tribe at all times.[322]

According to Saba's *passio* the Christians formed only a minority. But Saba's martyrdom occurred in the Gothic hinterland, whereas the situation on the Danube could have been very different. The persecution that Athanaric and other Gothic chieftains carried out shows that the majority of Tervingians were still pagans who felt threatened by an ever growing Christian minority. The pagan Goths were more inclined to leave individual Christians alone, especially if they had completely isolated themselves through their behavior and their inferior economic status. The story of Saba reflects this as well. Only those who could be "dangerous or helpful" were persecuted,[323] in other words, only those whose actions presented a threat to the *gens* and its gods.[324] But a single person could be such a threat if he violated the *religio* with impunity. It is therefore probable that it was only Fritigern's decision that brought about the "breakthrough of Christianity."[325] Eunapius reports about the Tervingian tribe's sacred objects in the keeping of pagan priests and priestesses. In his opinion the Tervingian refugees had only feigned their Christianity in order to be admitted by the Romans.[326] He might not have been far from the truth as far as the majority of the Tervingi was concerned.

One would think that the religious conversion and actual migration of Fritigern's Goths into the empire crowned Ulfilas's life work. The number of Roman Goths now seemed vastly increased. Among Ulfilas's Gothi minores were those people who out of "brotherly affection" started the internal Gothic mission. No doubt it soon spread to the Roman Goths. It is much more difficult, however, to reconstruct where and when the Gothic peoples outside the Roman Empire, as, for example, the Ostrogoths and Gepids, were Christianized.[327] But the Goth Ulfilas himself was too much integrated into the imperial church[328] to have approved the tumultuous events that accompanied the Gothic crossing of the Danube. And when open warfare erupted, Ulfilas surely placed Christian solidarity with the Romans above any other allegiance, and this is in fact what the reports say about the behavior of the Gothi minores.[329]

The Ambrosian offensive received imperial support in its battle against conservative Arianism. But Theodosius had to act cautiously lest he drive the Gothic barbarians and the Roman opposition into each other's arms. Nevertheless, the emperor took the first anti-Arian measures and in the spring of 381 convened a synod at Constantinople which is known as the second ecumenical council. Among the Arian bishops who interceded with Theodosius was Ulfilas. The emperor had called for him expressly, which would at least indicate some sort of connection of the Gothic bishop to the warlike bands of Fritigern. The Arians were also promised a new council in 382. Ulfilas probably died in Constantinople in 383 during the third synod convened on this religious controversy.[330] On his deathbed he declared his creed: "There is one eternal, unbegotten, and invisible God, who before time existed alone. Within time he created the Son, the only-begotten God.

He is the creator of all things, the Lord of the Holy Spirit whom the Father created through the Son before all things. The Holy Spirit is obedient and subject to the Son like the Son to the Father."[331]

With large-scale participation by the people of Constantinople and perhaps also by the authorities, Ulfilas was carried to his grave.[332] His cause was doomed, for the synod followed the second ecumenical council in condemning Arianism. But the second canon of the general synod of 381 had already decreed that the "churches of God among the barbarian peoples . . . are to be governed in the manner that already existed among their forefathers"[333]—and that is where the matter rested. In this way a space was created within which Arianism, now driven underground, could and in fact did spread. The standardizing force of Ulfilas's translation of the Bible; the religious zeal of the new converts; the support of the Roman crypto-Arians in the settlement areas of the Gothic federates;[334] a "Gothic" faith as a means of preserving ethnic identity—all these circumstances might be responsible for the conversion to Arian Christianity of the overwhelming majority of the Goths who had penetrated the empire, even though, or precisely because, their Roman environment became more and more radically Catholic.

In the following decades, until about 395, the Moesian Goths and the Goths in the capital, though the latter to a lesser extent, were able to lay the foundation from which the highly successful Germanic mission started. Initially it reached only the other "Gothic peoples"—the Ostrogoths, Gepids, Vandals—but later it extended to the greater part of Germania so that even the Frankish king Clovis very nearly became an Arian.[335]

The Ostrogothic Greutungi until the Invasion of the Huns

From the early summer of 291 the ancient world had been aware of the existence of two Gothic tribes. At that time the main tribal element was still made up of "eastern" Goths. They fought along the Don with the Alans and another tribe that either belonged to a group of nomadic horsemen of uncertain origin or was composed of East Burgundians.[336] Thereafter the Goths of southern Russia disappeared from view of the ancient world. North of the lower Danube, there existed a Christian Gothia—sometimes identified with abandoned Dacia, which now belonged to the Tervingi.[337] Only at the end of the fourth century was there talk once more of the existence of Gothic steppe dwellers, the Greutungi. Their name was considered an ethnographic novelty. This people constituted a branch of the

Goths. The emperor Valens encountered them during the last year of his Tervingian war. It remains unclear, however, whether the Greutungi came to the aid of the Tervingi in 369 or whether they simply wanted to protect their own territory against the Romans. Both interpretations would be possible: the report of Ammianus Marcellinus is ambiguous. He passes from the Greutungi to the Tervingi without a break. One could therefore think of a joint action by both Gothic tribes.[338] In addition, Munderic, Ammianus Marcellinus's Gothic source,[339] mentioned a Greutungian place-name west of the Dniester. On the Tervingians' march against the Huns in 376 the greater part of the tribe halted before this place, thus respecting the territory of their neighbors. Athanaric pitched his camp on the bank of the river, "a good distance from the valley of the Greutungi."[340] Therefore the lower course of the Dniester, from its exit out of the forest zone down to its mouth, probably was the "Greutungian valley." Accordingly, the upper course of the river must have formed the border between the Tervingians and the Greutungi, while the Bessarabian Budjak steppe served as the largely deserted border zone of the Greutungi. It was only after days of "uninterrupted marches" that Valens was able to find the Greutungi, that is, provoke open resistance.[341]

ERMANARIC'S GREUTUNGIAN KINGDOM AND ITS DISSOLUTION

The first Amal king of the Goths in southern Russia was Ostrogotha.[342] Beset by foreign peoples and by the ethnically related Gepids,[343] the "royal Scyths" probably reemerged as the Greutungi or Ostrogoths.[344] Both designations are names for the same tribe: The Greutungi are "the steppe-dwellers"; the Ostrogoths are the "shining" or the "splendid" Goths. To be sure, Ermanaric is the first who is attested as king of the Greutungi and king of the Ostrogoths. This "warlike king" ruled a "warlike people" in the "wide and fertile lands of Scythia," Ammianus Marcellinus reports, and was "feared by the neighboring peoples on account of his many and varied deeds of valor." And Cassiodorus adds: Ermanaric is the "noblest of the Amali," and "some forefathers have justly compared him to Alexander the Great." Ermanaric came close to the great model of all ancient conquerors because his armored lancers penetrated far into the Russian and Baltic areas and created a great barbarian kingdom that held a good many polyethnic communities in a more or less loose state of dependence. Among the peoples mentioned are the most diverse "northern peoples," the Maeotic Heruli at the mouth of the Don, the Antes, and Sclaveni, and finally perhaps even the Aesti along the Baltic Sea. A summary of the "numerous and very fierce northern peoples" whom Ermanaric forced to live "according to his laws"[345] can be found in a "memory list" that probably follows the itinerary of traders and merchants. The catalog in the version of the *Origo Gothica* reads as follows: *Golthescytha Thiudos Inaunxis Vasinabroncas Merens Mordens Imniscaris Rogas Tadzans Athaul Navego Bubegenas Coldas.*

Golthethiudos would be the "gold peoples" of the Urals, while *scytha* should be understood as the interlinear gloss of a copyist. The *Inaunxis* cannot be identified, but they can be located in the vicinity of the "gold peoples" since the catalog lists the peoples according to geographical proximity. The *Wasinabrōkans* are the inhabitants of a "flat country with rich pastures, plentiful irrigation, and some swamplands." *Merens* and *Mordens* have always been identified as the Volga Finnish peoples, the Meriens and Mordwines. To that same ethnic group belong the *Imniscaris,* the "bee-keepers," who are called Mescera in Old Russian. The *Rogas* and *Tadzans* should be seen as the *Roastadjans,* meaning those people who live on the bank of the Volga. In the case of *Athaul, Navego, Bubegenas,* and *Coldas,* even the best interpretative effort has to capitulate.[346]

The dwelling places of these northern peoples lead us into areas that are separated from the Greutungian heartland in southern Russia by twelve hundred miles and more: "This implies for Ermanaric's realm geographical dimensions that seem entirely implausible."[347] Nevertheless, there are good reasons why the Greutungi should have ventured to undertake such a vast expansion. Because of "valuable metals, honey, wax, and superior furs," the area that stretches from the upper Volga to the gold-rich mountains of the Ural had always been the goal of traders.[348] The control and exploitation of this trade could well have been the purpose of Greutungian expeditions and they could in fact have achieved their aim. At any rate, the peoples of the Cherniakhov culture certainly had the military and logistical capability to enforce their authority in the vast expanses of Russia.[349] In any case it is impossible to judge Ermanaric's "greater state" by modern criteria; we should speak rather of Gothic protectorates. Behind the enumeration of the peoples subjected by Ermanaric one has quite rightly suspected a relative chronology of events.[350] After the northern peoples had been reduced to a state of dependence, there followed the conquest of the Herulian kingdom of the lower Don. This time the *Origo Gothica* describes in detail the bitter battles Ermanaric had to wage against the Herulian king Alaric. The movements of the Goths, who first swung far into the northeast and then turned back to defeat the Heruli close to the Gothic homeland, may have been prompted by the need to destroy the economic base of the Heruli (by depriving them of the long-distance trade with the Volga peoples) before they could be brought to their knees. Thus the Greutungi would have succeeded in gaining control of the entire trade route from the Volga bend downstream as far as the Don and the Black Sea.

After Ermanaric had attached many peoples of Finnish-Caucasian stock to his Gothic kingdom, the Baltic Aesti apparently also fell under his sway. The *Origo Gothica* reports that the king ruled over "all peoples of Scythia and Germania as if they were his own."[351] But since these two ancient regions were separated by the Vistula, Ostrogothic influence must have extended westward across this river. It is possible that the Ostrogoths came upon kindred groups to the northwest of Scythia. Thus Cassiodorus, who in general took a scientific interest in the Aesti, places the Gothic-Gepidic-Baltic ethnogenesis of the Vidivarii in the immediate vicinity of these groups. The Vidivarii are said to have formed through the "converging of peoples" at the mouth of the Vistula after the retreat of Fastida's Gepids. Even in the sixth century their settlement area was known as the island of the Gepids (*Gepedoios*).[352] Of course the expansion of Ermanaric's realm as it appears in the sources cannot be supported by archaeological finds. The northern line of the Cherniakhov culture moved at this time neither in the direction of the Baltic nor toward the Urals. But just as the *Origo Gothica* differentiates between "his own peoples"—the Ostrogoths of Ermanaric—and the peoples of Scythia and Germania subjected by him, there was a difference between the actual Ostrogothic-Greutungian settlement areas—the culture of Cherniakhov—and the area controlled by Ermanaric.[353]

But the *Origo Gothica* described in Ermanaric certain personal traits and behavior that in the heroic saga developed into the theme of the king as a demonic tyrant and destroyer of his own race. Cassiodorus was still able to let the controversial Gothic prince die with biblical quotations on his lips, thus concealing obvious contradictions. Yet it was not possible to suppress the embarrassing story of Sunilda, who had been drawn and quartered, and the king's suicide, which was probably the reason why Ermanaric was not included in Amalasuintha's genealogy. Sunilda, her unnamed husband, and her brothers Ammius and Sarus belonged to the "faithless" *gens* of the Rosomoni. They all had Germanic names, and their reception into the heroic legend shows that they were considered to be of Germanic stock, which is undoubtedly true.[354] The historical interpretation of the name Rosomoni causes some difficulty. Among recent explanations two seem most plausible, all the more so because they are not mutually exclusive. The meaning of *gens* is flexible: it can refer to peoples, war bands, and great clans. It therefore seems rather unimportant whether we describe the Rosomoni as a people or a clan that "Ermanaric had, among others, in his following." Accordingly, the Rosomoni—whose name, like that of the Heruli, could mean "the fast," "the impetuous"—would be identical with the Heruli or their *stirps regia* subjected by Ermanaric. The Don river marked the extent of Rosomoni territory in the east. It is therefore entirely conceivable that they sought to escape from the power of Ermanaric at the very moment when the Huns attacked and crossed the Don. The other plausible etymology sees in the Rosomoni "the reds." This designation could be derived from the custom of dyeing the hair red, which is known to us especially from war bands who pledged themselves to a divine ancestor as their warlord.[355] In this case, too, such a group could be linked to the Heruli, who perhaps wanted to offer, at the time of the Hunnish threat, an alternative to the Amali, an action similar to that of the Rugian Eraric when he seized the Gothic kingship after the murder of Hildebad in 541.[356]

The affair involving the Rosomoni cost Ermanaric his life. The king had Sunilda drawn and quartered because her husband had deserted him and had escaped his reach. Thereupon Ammius and Sarus revenged their sister, wounding the king. From this injury and out of grief over his defeat by the Huns Ermanaric was said to have died at the biblical age of 110.[357] Yet Ammianus Marcellinus, a contemporary of Ermanaric's, discovered and recorded the following details. After subjecting the Alans at the Don, the Huns together with the Alans invaded the "wide and rich territories" of the Greutungian king. For some time Ermanaric resisted, but the sudden and no doubt overestimated threat from the Huns drove him to such despair that he committed suicide to "escape his fear of making crucial decisions."[358] There is much to support the notion that the Greutungian king sacrificed himself at the moment of defeat.[359] After the death of Ermanaric in 375 the tribe and the royal clan split. The majority submitted to the Huns, the rest resisted. It took about a year before the free Ostrogoths had either been subjugated or had moved away.[360]

Political Organization and Culture of the Goths at the Danube and the Black Sea

During the fourth century the eastern Goths, the Greutungi, disappeared from the Romans' view. At the same time the interest in the western Goths, the Danubian Tervingi, increased to an unexpected degree, and the sources multiply accordingly.[361] The ancient observers examined the political and cultural institutions of the Tervingi, their social as well as economic levels of development and patterns of behavior, together with the military-strategic possibilities and expansionary tendencies that they entailed. The relatively great abundance of sources is further increased by Ulfilas's translation of the Bible, which offers a wealth of information, even though the events of the Bible took place in Roman Palestine around the time of the birth of Christ. Jewish traditions were at that time in conflict with the culture of the great Hellenistic Roman state. There was a multiplicity of political jurisdictions, such as, for example, the Roman emperor and his governors, the Hellenistic kings, the ethnarchs, the tetrarchs, and the oligarchic organs of Jewish self-government. In addition there was the personal power of the rich and noble, and various tribal institutions existed. Finally, Jewish law held sway, a law that separated the peoples, the heathens, from the *populus,* the people chosen by God. This heterogeneous New Testament "politics" unfolded before the backdrop of a Mediterranean culture based on public literacy, a culture that knew an advanced money economy with a banking and taxation system but that also experienced the tensions between the city and its surrounding countryside.

The way in which the Gothic language translated the biblical text and thus interpreted this foreign world, the question of whether Gothic terms were available or whether foreign or borrowed words and loan translations were necessary and from which of the classical and nonclassical languages they came—all this conveys information about the Goths' social and material level of development, in other words, about the tribal culture of the Danubian Goths. The historian runs into serious problems, however, if he wants to derive hard facts from this data. With all due respect for etymology and its achievements, we have to recognize its methodological limitations in arranging chronologically and topographically historical events that stretch over a period of, say, only a hundred years. A significant difference can exist between the meaning of a Gothic word at any given time and its original root, and to ignore this difference would mean ignoring the limitations of etymology. Etymology does, however, throw light on the Goths' earlier—though chronologically not absolutely determinable—relations to and dependence on other peoples and cultures. Traces of these relationships can be found in Ulfilas's translation. The biblical vocabulary can be compared with the information about the Tervingi which contemporary or near contemporary observers supply. Since this corrective is for the most part not available for the Greutungi, and since Ulfilas was not born east but west of the Dniester, the Black Sea Goths must get rather shorter treatment in this chapter.

THE *GUTTHIUDA*: THE LAND OF THE TERVINGI AND TAIFALI

Though *Gutthiuda* means etymologically nothing other than "Gothic people," in the fourth century it designated not a community of descent but the territory ruled by the Tervingian-Taifalian tribal confederation. Only part of the area delimited the Gothic settlement in the narrower sense of the word; nevertheless, the entire territory was considered *genitales terrae,* the "country of origin" of the Tervingi. Its southern boundary was determined by the course of the Danubian *limes.* How far west of the Alutus it extended and to what extent it occupied Oltenia (Little Walachia) is difficult to say. In the first half of the fourth century the Tervingi occupied large parts of Transylvania, in the process pushing back barbarian rivals, such as the Vandals, but receiving into their tribal confederation smaller groups like the Sarmatians of the Caucaland. The political centers of the Tervingi were clearly located in Muntenia (Walachia) and Moldavia, not merely because these regions facing the *imperium* attracted the greatest attention from Roman observers. The Gothic judge Athanaric had his seat in Moldavia, while his rival Fritigern was probably at home in the Moldavian-Muntenian border region. The word Gutthiuda comes from the tradition of the Christian Goths, who applied it to the heathen land of the Goths. If we leave aside this religious dimension, Gutthiuda means the same as the *Got(h)ia* of the Greek and Latin sources. That a barbarian territory is called "the people" or "the family" is not unusual. Visigothic Spain was considered the "land or people of the Goths"—*patria vel gens Gothorum.* Nonetheless, mutatis mutandis, Gutthiuda also included all non-Gothic peoples who lived in Tervingian tribal territory.[362]

This is true above all for the Taifali. From the first appearance of the Tervingi the Taifali were associated with them and stayed with them until the invasion of the Huns in 376 destroyed their alliance.[363] At that time the Taifalian territory extended from the west as far east as the Siret, so that its eastern boundary coincided with the eastern border of modern-day Walachia.[364] Less than two decades earlier, in the year 358, to be exact, the Taifali in Roman employ attacked the territory of the Tisza Sarmatians located "right next to their own settlements."[365] This would mean that the western boundary of the Taifalian territory extended far westward, perhaps even beyond the Alutus all the way into Oltenia. But the archaeological evidence for the fourth century is interpreted in such a way that Oltenia, if not actually part of the *imperium* itself, was at least within its immediate sphere of influence. In any case, the finds so far recovered argue against permanent *sedes Taifalorum* west of the Alutus.[366]

In all likelihood, however, the question of where the Taifali were permanently settled during the fourth century should not even be raised. The Taifali were nomadic horsemen and accordingly had few permanent abodes. Within the Gothic "commonwealth" on the Danube they constituted the cavalry. Taifalian horsemen fought in 332 against the troops of Constantine the Great;[367] in 376, after having been displaced from their homeland, they joined the mounted Greutungi led by Farnobius, were involved in his defeat,[368] and at the end of the fourth century they supplied first-rate cavalry contingents for the Roman court army—very much unlike the Tervingian-Vesian foot warriors.[369] Within the possible boundaries one would thus most likely look for the Taifali in the expanses of the Bărăgan steppe in Muntenia.[370]

The Taifali are said to have borne a Celtic "cult name" and to have been identical with the Lacringi, a Vandal people. Evidence for this identification is—by way of analogy to the Victufali—the name-ending in –fali and the mention in pairs of Lacringi and Hasdingi, on the one hand, and Taifali and Hasdingi, on the other.[371] The later history of the Taifali within the Roman Empire shows their close association with Sarmatian units. Those Taifali who escaped annihilation in 377 were partly settled in Italy—namely, in the region around Modena, Reggio, and Parma in Emilia,[372] where still in the time of the Lombards there was a town called Taivola[373]—and partly sent to Gaul. It was there that the *Notitia dignitatum* of the West mentions at least one Sarmato-Taifalian barbarian unit. When the Visigoths settled in Aquitania many Taifali became subjects of the king of Toulouse. Despite this association the Taifali never became Goths nor did the two peoples establish closer contact that would have been even remotely reminiscent of the fourth century.[374]

Even after the expulsion of the Carpi[375] we have to count on the existence of Sarmato-Dacian, in any case non-Tervingian, peoples in the Gutthiuda.[376] If we associate the Taifali with these peoples, the ethnogenesis of the former should be described as follows. Acculturation did not flow in one direction only. Ethnic groups tried to imitate whatever group was dominant within their polyethnic community. Thus groups of the Iranian Alans were associated with the Goths and with the Vandals and in the sixth century they had been Gothicized to such a degree that they were included among the Gothic peoples.[377] In like manner it is possible that a Sarmatian core group first associated itself as Taifali with the Vandals but then entered into a close alliance with the Tervingi. Yet political misfortune, economic, social, and religious differences—in short, history itself—destroyed this unity, which had lasted from the late third century until the invasion of the Huns.

In the chaos caused by this invasion there began in 376 a war of all against all which revealed the weaker, if not subordinate position of the non-Tervingians.

The expulsion of the Sarmatians of the Caucaland by the Goths of Athanaric clearly reveals this process of disintegration. Ptolemy knew of a tribe called Caucoenses in Transylvanian Dacia, and a mountain range of the Transylvanian Carpathians is epigraphically attested as Caucasus. To these names belongs also the Caucaland; as the Germanic *–land* reveals, the Goths used this name to designate the abodes of a foreign minority. Here lived Sarmatians who were not considered Tervingi but whose land was in Gothia, in the *genitales terrae* of Athanaric. The pre-Gothic inhabitants of the Caucaland are presented as Sarmatians, but they bear a Dacian name. It is therefore probable that the Daco-Carpian elements who penetrated along with the Tervingi into the old province contributed to a revival of old barbarian traditions. The Caucaland was certainly not located in the Banat but rather in the Carpathian mountains along the Alutus river.[378]

Although other non-Tervingian peoples are not all named, the Gutthiuda contained numerous peoples apart from the Taifali and the Sarmatians of the Caucaland. There is evidence for minorities from Asia Minor among the Christian Goths. But in addition there were people of similar background who were legally and politically considered strangers (*gasteis*). A considerable number of former Roman provincials, more or less strongly Romanized Daco-Carpian groups, Sarmatians, and other peoples of the most diverse names, must have existed there. Of course we must be wary of distributing and assigning tribal names too liberally. The polyethnic character of the Gutthiuda is attested by both written and archaeological sources. Where archaeological and historiographical interpretation coincides we may mention names;[379] where this is not the case we must refrain. Strong Tervingian groups can be assumed above all in upper Bessarabia, in Moldavia, and in Walachia.[380] There must have also been Tervingi in Dacian Transylvania, considering both the warfare with the Vandals and Sarmatians in the plain of the Tisza[381] and the Germanic name of the Caucaland, which presupposes a Tervingian majority in its vicinity.[382] The middle and upper course of the Dniester must have formed the boundary between Tervingi and Greutungi,[383] whereas the lower course of the river was called "valley of the Greutungi," the western bank of which was occupied by the Greutungi. In the west the Alutus and the Munţii Apuşeni were not crossed to any significant extent.[384] We cannot say anything about the northern frontier of Tervingian Gothia; only in the south was it clearly marked off "in Roman fashion" by the Danube.[385]

Politically the Gutthiuda was composed of several "peoples."[386] In times
of danger the Gothic subdivisions formed a confederation, they acted as
conspirantes in unum.[387] The Tervingi had no monarchic kingship; there
was no *thiudans* among them.[388] The individual subdivisions (*kunja*) were
ruled by chiefs (*reiks*).[389] At those times when the common policy of the Gutthiuda was at issue they made up the tribal council. If we may draw an analogy to the Jewish Sanhedrin, this tribal council was called *gafaurds*. Since
the unfree as well as the free underclass was excluded, the council was
composed of the chiefs (*reiks*) and representatives (*sinistans, maistans*) of
each *kuni*.[390]

To meet both external and internal threats, the oligarchic council could
reactivate a kind of monarchy, the Tervingian judgeship. Although the
judge's authority covered the entire barbarian confederation, it was intended
to be temporary and territorially limited. The Tervingian judge was not
allowed to leave the tribal territory. When Athanaric was negotiating a
peace settlement with Valens in 369 the emperor addressed him as king.
To this the Gothic prince replied that he preferred the title judge, since
the judge embodied wisdom (σοφία), the king only power (δύναμις).[391]
With this differentiation the unity of the phrase in the Gothic Bible "God's
power and God's wisdom" (*gudis mahts jah gudis handugei*) is broken.[392]
Athanaric would not have objected to being a *thiudans*, but this monarchic kingship did not exist among the Tervingi. When the Latin-speaking
Valens addressed him as *rex*, Athanaric had to understand it in the sense
of *reiks*. The title *reiks* would have limited Athanaric's authority.[393] He
was more than that, he was a *iudex gentis*, a judge of the whole tribal
confederation, indeed a *iudex regum*, "judge of kings" (*reiks*).[394] It is possible that the Gothic Bible had the Tervingian judge in mind when it described
the functions of Pontius Pilate. He is usually the *kindins*, but he also
carried the more general name of *ragineis*, "counselor." In deviation from
the etymology, *kindins* means no longer the lord of a *kind*, "kin," community of descent, but the person with authority over an entire barbarian
confederation. He receives his commission from the Roman emperor in his
role as "judge among the children of the Jews"—as he is still called in the
Saxon *Heliand*. We can therefore see reflected here the constitutional reality
of the Danubian Goths of the fourth century.[395] Like the Jews, they have
no *thiudans* of their own; instead, for them, Christians or pagans, the
emperor is the "king of the Roman people," the *rex Romanorum* or
thiudans.[396]

The title *kindins*—like that of *thiudans*, like that of the Burgundian
hendinos (king), like that of the Latin *tribunus*, and like that of a possible
Gothic *drauhtins*—is an age-old name for a tribal leader. Since there was

no Tervingian *thiudans* and since the imperial *thiudans* did not exercise direct authority in the Gutthiuda, the Tervingian tribal council bestowed upon each Gothic judge the mandate for the Gothic land. In this capacity Athanaric dispatched *reiks* with tribal forces across the frontiers, conducted in person war against the Romans in the Gothic territory (like his reputed grandfather had done), made peace with Valens, persecuted the Christians (like his reputed father had done), and tried in vain to resist the advance of the Huns inside the Gutthiuda.[397]

Among the Tervingi there was a preeminent "royal family" that we may perhaps identify as the Balthi. The Romans, however, noticed other people among the Goths who wore the "royal insignia" and who assumed a special position because of their "dignity and descent." Gothic leaders certainly did not form an exclusive stratum, let alone a class. Rather, ancient authors noted that the tribes had two divisions in their leading stratum which they called "kings and chieftains." Perhaps the Goths expressed this duality with *reiks,* on the one hand, and *maistans* (the magnates) and *sinistans* (the elders), on the other. But whereas the *maistans* together with the "leaders of one thousand warriors" were among the retainers of a biblical *thiudans,* the Jewish elders were both an authority of political self-government as well as the bearers of the national tradition. The high priest, pharisees, and elders of the people (*sinistans manageins*) form the high council (the *gafaurds*) that persecuted Christ, condemned him, and finally handed him over to the *kindins* Pilate.[398] Into this pattern fit the two actual persecutions of Gothic Christians: in the first Ulfilas and his followers were driven from the land by a "godless and law-breaking judge of the Goths";[399] the second began when a "prince of injustice" enforced the decisions of the aristocratic *megistanes* (the tribal council) against the religious minority.[400]

The Gothic judge functionally resembles the Gallic ἡγεμών and the *vergobretos* of the Haedui. As in Gaul at the time of Caesar, the Danubian Tervingi assigned certain duties to a quasi-monarch, a judge. But the Gothic judgeship is a dead end from the point of view of institutional history; it does not have a future. Instead the *reiks,* whose army followed him anywhere, was on his way to becoming a king of the army. Vidigoia against the Sarmatians and Geberic against the Vandals could have been the first such *reiks* who led the tribe in offensive wars.[401] But what is significant is that this military mandate of a nonroyal leader is attested only south of the Danube, at a time when the Tervingian judgeship had already ceased to exist. Alaviv and Fritigern called upon the "entire people" to leave the tribal territory, and they led the people into the foreign Roman land.[402] Both men were *reiks* and thus occupied a position derived from their initial role as chiefs of Tervingian subdivisions (*kunja*). Fritigern's rule over a Tervingian *kuni* can be inferred from his confrontation with Athanaric. Although Alaviv is not directly attested as a *reiks,* it is almost certain that he was one, since Alaviv was initially at least of equal rank with Fritigern, if not actually higher.[403] The Gothic *reiks* might also have been called **drauhtins* if military authority was emphasized.[404]

THE *KUNI*: COMMUNITY OF DESCENT AND SUBDIVISION OF THE GUTTHIUDA

Undoubtedly the *kuni* formed the most important political unit, but it was at the same time also a community of descent, unlike the Gutthiuda to which it was subordinated. The etymological relationship between *kuni* and *gens* was thus semantically preserved. A Goth belonged to the *kuni* as an *inkunja,* συμφυλέτης. The head of a *kuni* was the *reiks.* No *reiks* could claim monarchical power.[405] A *reiks* owned a "house"; as lord of the house—*frauja*—he exercised authority over his dependents, among whom were armed retainers. The latter were called *andbahtos* and *siponjos.* Latin and Greek sources give them the usual names for dependents.[406] Within the confederated *kunja* a royal family was dominant; but here, as well, we can detect no monarchical selection. Instead, "numerous gradations" existed. The memory of this early political organization survived in the sixth-century belief that the Balthi had held only the second rank after the Amali.[407]

The number of Tervingian *kunja* is unknown. Only some of them can be located. The group led by Atharid had its home along the river Musaeus-Buzău in Muntenia,[408] whereas Athanaric's own *kuni* was probably settled—before it moved into the Transylvanian Caucaland[409]—in Moldavia on both banks of the Prut. In the neighboring region to the west, with its rear secured by the Danube, probably lay the territory of the subtribe that Fritigern represented.[410] The region where the twenty-six martyrs were burned to death was ruled by Winguric, and very close to him must have been the land of the unnamed *reiks* whose wife Gaatha brought the remains of the martyrs into the Roman Empire. Since Gaatha's son Arimir still inherited his father's position, Arimir's Goths apparently belonged to those Tervingi who continued to live north of the Danube even after 376.[411]

Each *kuni* had its own shrines and priests and no doubt its own cult. With the fall of the old Gothic monarchic kingship the Tervingi seem to have lost much of the common tribal religion. This would explain why the concept of a community of descent shifted from the level of the Gutthiuda down to that of the *kuni*. Although the Tervingian tribal confederation was thereby opened to non-Gothic elements, it was at the same time politically

and culturally fractured. It was the task of the judge to prevent the dissolution of the *gens* in times of crisis; accordingly, we know from Athanaric's
period both politico-military and religious measures aimed at stopping the
disintegration of the tribe or even reversing it.[412] Like the Gothic special
names, like the Tervingian Gutthiuda and its judgeship, the *kuni* and its
independent leadership also fell victim to the great migrations.[413] The *gens*
became the *exercitus Gothorum,* the polyethnic Tervingian community
became the army of the Goths, still polyethnic but led by a "real" king.[414]

THE *HARJIS,* THE TRIBAL ARMY

As long as the Tervingians enjoyed a "barbarian" state of peace their tribal
armies were small[415] and composed of specialized elite warriors.[416] Already
a single Roman legion of Ulfilas's time (about three thousand men) was
considered an army, a *harjis*.[417] It was not by mere chance that only a biblical *thiudans* had twenty thousand warriors at his command, and it was
also a greater king of this kind whose generals led contingents of a thousand
soldiers.[418] When tribal armies of the Goths—and not only of the Goths—are
mentioned without exaggeration, the number three thousand appears almost as a rule. Only Cannabas was destroyed along with five thousand
warriors. But that event was a catastrophe of such magnitude that the Goths
lost their first greater kingship and forever their tribal unity.[419]

When the Tervingians fulfilled their duty as federates and sent their 3,000
men, the Romans soon got the impression that all the Gothic warriors were
noblemen. According to Eunapius, they wore a coat of mail that made them
look like wasps with "an abstriction in the middle, just as Aristotle says of
insects." These huge fellows, said Eunapius, are comical and useless; if one
gets to know them better one is no longer afraid of them.[420] When the
Roman army attacked, the Gothic forces withdrew into the interior or, if
they offered resistance, were defeated even on their own territory.[421] Such
experiences created an overwhelming sense of superiority in the Roman
army, expressed, for example, in the statement that "Galatian slave-traders
were sufficient to keep them [the Goths] in check."[422] But when the Hunnic
storm caused a *levée en masse* and even the last peasant able to carry a
stick became a warrior fighting for his life, it still took until the battle of
Adrianople before the Romans realized what the total militarization of a
gens meant.[423]

Armies were raised by the individual *kuni* as well as the Tervingian
Gutthiuda. We know of the conflict between Athanaric and Fritigern which
is described explicitly as a war between two subtribes.[424] Also, the slave

hunts organized by the Romans are only conceivable if those who undertook them were participating in Gothic tribal feuds, which were again fought with small armies.[425] Furthermore, Gothic raiders from the Danube attacked their Roman neighbors at a time when not all Tervingi had confederated.[426] In such cases we are dealing with expeditions of individual chiefs (*reiks*). But if the Gutthiuda was in a state of war, the Gothic judge had the supreme command over the army, insofar as the defense of the tribal territory was concerned. Operations outside this territory, such as the support given to Procopius or the thrust across the Dniester eastward to counter the Huns, were led by Athanaric's officers. The financial subsidies the Romans paid to the Tervingi as part of the treaty probably also went through the hands of the *kindins* and the *reiks,* thus contributing to economic and social inequality among the members of the tribe.[427] In 376 the chieftains Munderic and Lagariman were put into action.[428] "Much earlier" there must have been a Gothic force that stood under the command of Colias and Sueridus when it was admitted by the Romans and integrated into the imperial army. This group had sister units stationed in Asia Minor in 376.[429] The war against Valens and the defense against the Huns inside the Tervingian territory, however, were conducted by Athanaric himself. Thus the ancient sources record the judgeship primarily as a military institution, which the *Origo Gothica* later linked to the legendary Ostrogotha.[430]

A subdivision of the *harjis* (army) is the *hansa* (horde), a term that remains completely undefined as to size. It can refer to military units as diverse as the Roman maniple and cohort.[431] The Vandal army was organized into groups of one thousand, and the bands that joined Alaric I on his march were probably also regrouped into such formations. The Visigothic army of Spain was still structured according to the decimal system. The Scandinavian *Hervarasaga* has probably preserved the Gothic-Hunnic military organization in historically reliable form: the hostile armies appear here drawn up in units of peoples, "one thousand" and "one hundred," but this division did not correspond to a hundred warriors or exact multiples of one hundred. The numerical formations of the Gothic army could therefore go back to non-Roman influences.[432] This is supported by the following observation drawn from Priscus: when a Hunno-Gothic unit was cornered by the Romans in the gorges of the Balkan mountains its organization differed significantly from that of the Roman army. The latter must therefore be ruled out as a model for the formation of the Gothic army.[433]

The Tervingian tribal armies were composed of unmounted warriors.[434] In the Danubian homeland the Taifali had provided the cavalry for the Tervingi.[435] After 376 that cavalry was no longer available, which is why

Fritigern allied himself with the Greutungi.[436] Whatever else we are told about the tactics of Tervingian commanders is sparse enough. Athanaric was a master of retreat maneuvers; he organized guerrilla attacks and let the Romans waste their energy in unopposed thrusts. When he was cornered by Valens, he did not join battle with all forces at his disposal. The ancient source recording the events creates the impression that the Gothic judge had freedom of action in choosing this course. In this case Athanaric could have formed a tactical reserve whose task it was to construct the second line of defense, to which he in fact fell back after losing the battle. Interpreted differently, the decision could have been forced upon the Gothic judge by his inability—for whatever reason—to mobilize all Gothic warriors. In any case, Athanaric's tactical measure led to the retreat of the Romans and the peace of 369. When seven years later the Gothic prince tried to use a similar strategy against the Huns—in this case even supporting it with fortifications—he failed, but more from lack of provisions and panic among his people than from the inadequacy of his measures.[437]

Athanaric's attempt to defend against the Huns in fortified camps and behind ramparts seems evidence that the Danubian Goths were not horsemen. But perhaps it was exactly this type of defense that caused the conflict between the Tervingi and the Taifali; south of the Danube the latter immediately joined up with those eastern Goths who would let them ride out again until the Romans put an end to their doings.[438] The Crimean Goths, who were also unmounted, had quickly become familiar with the Huns' style of fighting. They formed a wall of shields and held out behind it until the attackers had spent all their missiles.[439] During migration Fritigern's Tervingi employed the fortified circle of wagons to protect themselves against surprise attacks and long-range missiles. The use of the circle of wagons was at that time considered such a typical element of Gothic warfare that the Gothic word for it—*carrago*—has been preserved. It is possibly a combination of Celtic *carrus* (cart) and Germanic *hago* (fence).[440]

In general, as Reinhard Wenskus explains, "The archaeological evidence forms the most important source for our knowledge of the armament of the Germanic peoples."[441] The Tervingi, however, like their Greutungian neighbors, buried their dead without weapons. Thus the written sources offer not only "valuable supplementary information" but are the very basis for the study of Gothic weapons and armament.[442] From Ulfilas's Bible we know the word for armament—the neuter plural *sarwa*—as the general term that included *brunjo* (coat of mail, armor), *skildus* (shield), *hilms* (helmet), and *meki* (sword). *Sarwa* probably refers to "the artistic panoply" and has related words in the Old Prussian and Avestic languages. *Brunjo* could be a Celtic import, although other etymological derivations are also under consideration. *Skildus* means a split wooden board and reveals a significant fact about the construction of the shield. *Hilms,* which actually means "wrapping," is "archaeologically well attested among the Germanic peoples since the Bronze Age."[443] Still, the ancient writers were always amazed at how little use the northern peoples made of armor and helmets. But, as Helmut Birkhan reminds us, "even what is seldom worn must have some kind of name."[444] *Meki* could be a drift word, originating perhaps in the Caucasus; in any case, it was adopted by a large number of peoples, but it is not the only Gothic word we know for sword. *Hairus* appears much more frequently. Two such completely different names could have designated two different objects. If we trust the somewhat unreliable etymology we could assume that *hairus* described at least an early form of the *sax* (one-edged sword). The use of two swords was for a long time considered customary of the Huns. Finally, *meki* may be the *spatha,* the longsword.[445] But the nomadic horsemen's combination of weapons, longsword and *sax,* were not adopted by the East Germanic peoples before the first half of the fifth century.

Biblical Gothic lacks the word for the long lance, the *contus.* This weapon was later the characteristic feature of a Gothic warrior, whether he was on horseback or not.[446] In an engagement that preceded the battle of Adrianople the Goths pelted their Roman enemies with enormous, fire-hardened wooden clubs. Much later Charlemagne felt compelled to prohibit this type of weapon, which reveals the persistence of such a primitive weapon and the economic conditions that produced it.[447] The bow also served the Goths of the fourth century as a long-range weapon, but it was more likely to be used by the lower classes, and the Goths never employed it the way the Huns did.[448] Fire arrows are mentioned only once by Ulfilas.[449] The figures on the famous sacrificial bowl of Pietroasa are as remarkable as they are difficult to interpret. One of them represents a foot soldier in plated armor.[450] His armament, like the sacrificial bowl itself, resembles eastern models. Yet it is probably true that the Persian type of armor, the "caftan cuirass," was in fact adopted by those Tervingian tribal warriors who belonged to the elite.[451]

GARDS, BAÚRGS, SIBJA: LORDSHIP, RETAINERS, COMMUNITY OF LAW

It may appear odd to combine *baúrgs* with *gards* and not with *haims* (village). But the biblical pair of opposites—city and rural settlement—had

no real counterparts among the Tervingi. Neither the people of the Gutthiuda nor the Gothic bishop and his followers were city dwellers in the legal sense; because the translation adhered faithfully to its source it spoke of
cities, which did not exist north of the Danube. Petrus Patricius claims that
the Goths compared the Roman city-dwellers to birds "that had abandoned
the nourishing earth and relied more on walls than their own strength."
Thus Ulfilas's "city" corresponds no doubt to the fortified residence of the
Gothic *reiks*. More often than not such a *baúrgs* was surrounded not by a
stone "wall" but only by a "stockade." A Gothic *baúrgs* was the center of
the dominion of a tribal king. He would have set himself apart economically
and socially from a regular noble, who might have lived in an unfortified
Roman manor house (*gards*). In any case, in a legal sense the *baúrgs* differed from its surrounding lands (*gawi*) so little that Ulfilas could not
translate the Greek word for "cityvillage," or perhaps he did not even
understand it and rendered it as both village *and* city. If *baúrgs* itself did
not describe the keep that housed the living quarters, it contained such a
structure in the *kelikn,* a term borrowed from the Gallic *cilicnon.* A person
belonged to the castle as a *baúrgja,* as a burgher in the true sense of the
word.[452]

The *gards,* the house, is both the *frauja's* (the lord's) dwelling and family:
it includes his wife, children, relatives, and all his dependents. His authority
over the house was organized on the principle of retainership. The house
comprised the person born into it, that is, the actual family member *(in-
nakunds),* as well as the "housemate" and retainer *(ingardja).* Occasionally,
though, these two terms were used synonymously, which indicates that
there was little political difference between these two groups. In any case,
to the house belonged also the servants, the *gasinth(j)os* as "road companions," and the armed retainers *(andbahtos, siponjos)* as well as the dependent freemen living in their own huts. The ancient sources speak of
the *servi et familiae* of the Goths. These include the freedmen and the
swarms of slaves for whom biblical Gothic has a rich terminology. There
are (1) the *skalks* (slave); (2) those slaves whose names belong to the word
family **thius;* (3) the day laborer *(asneis)* who was used at harvest time;
and (4) probably also the *magus.* A Celtic origin has been suggested for
magus, while such an origin is clear for "retainer-lord" (*reiks*) and "retainer" (*andbahts*). The word for disciple might have also had a Celtic origin, although *siponeis* originally meant "accomplice."

Gards is also the basic word in such different concepts as garden and
vineyard, in the terms for kingdom and royal castle, and finally in the word
for world, where, however, the influence of the οἰκουμένη is clearly visible.

But even if the influence of the Greek model may have been quite significant, *gards* loses nothing of its central importance. *Midjun-gards,* "the house in the middle," is how the Goths conceived of the world; they are the first of the Germanic peoples for whom this concept can be attested. In like manner it accords with the political experience of a barbarian society to think of a kingdom as the "house of the king," *thiudans-gardi.*[453]

The difference between *reiks* and *frauja,* in the sense of "lord of the people" and "lord of the retainers," lies in their different functions. According to the Gothic Bible a ruler over the "peoples of this world" is a *reiks.* Yet Christ—δεσπότης-*frauja*—is the lord of his "retainers" (disciples)-*siponjos.* Likewise there was a Tervingian of royal blood called Atharid whose retainers call him their lord δεσπότης and demand that St. Saba do the same. But St. Saba acknowledges as δεσπότης only the heavenly lord. In response an angry retainer nearly runs him through with a lance. Athanaric, the former judge, *kindins,* entered the Roman Empire in 380 as the head of his house, after he had been the *reiks* of the *kuni* of the Caucaland for more than four years.[454] Of course every *reiks* was a *frauja,* but not vice versa. Retainers are bound to their lord by an oath, which established a mutually binding loyalty, a pact. The word for inheritance, *arbi*; for oath, *aiths*; another expression for a pact in the special form of a marriage, *liuga*; finally the word for obligation and duty, *dulgs*: all these terms are, if not Celtic imports, at least Celtico-Germanic or even Celtico-Gothic isoglosses. Succession is also indicated by the name given to the landholdings that provided the basis for the individual's physical and political life: the land bequeathed within the family, the house, was called *haimothli.* In this we can recognize, apart from the elements of retainership described above, the first signs of the formation of landed lordship, an institution that became possible especially after the occupation of Roman provinces. The inequality in the distribution of property and thus in the distribution of power is attested by the story of St. Saba's martyrdom. Landed lordship, authority over a family, and its corollary, authority over a band of retainers, are the three pillars on which rested the power of the aristocracy of the *reges Gothorum,* the Gothic *reiks.* They all stood for the Gutthiuda, while a single *reiks,* who was "rich," *faihu habands,* represented a Tervingian subtribe.[455]

The *Origo Gothica* of the sixth century still remembered the Gothic leaders of the early period, the *generosi,* as a stratum that it falsely equated with the Getic-Thracian nobility of the *pilleati.* These *reges* of Getic prehistory were in fact subordinated to an authority clearly resembling the Tervingian judgeship. Ulfilas's *reiks* and Cassiodorus's Gothic kings personify the upper stratum from which the *Origo Gothica* distinguished "the middlings" (*mediocres*). In the sixth century these are called "the long-haired or curly-haired" (*capillati*); their equivalents are the free men of biblical Gothic, the *frijai,* who were described in the fourth century as "hair-shaking" tribal warriors. The hair (*skuft*) of the Goths was bound into a knot. Even the princely warrior on the Pietroasa bowl sports the same hairstyle; his rich hair is tied in three knots. Comparable to the Gothic "curly-haired" are the Vandal Hasdingi, before the name was monopolized by the royal family of the Vandals, after the fashion of the Merovingian "long-haired" kings. The contrast between Goths and Romans emerges from the Gothic verb *kapillon,* which in the Tervingian "military slang" meant something like "getting a Roman-type military haircut," so that the Goth wore his hair (*capilli*) in the Roman manner.[456]

The rise of a realm with multiple political centers is linked to the *baúrgs,* the fortified residences of the lords, and the result was the growing dependency of free peasants living in villages. A polarization of this kind also derived from the displacement of the clan (*sibja*) by vertically structured groups, like the *kuni* and the *gards.* Nevertheless, the *sibja* as a legal community remained important. The act of adoption, so important for barbarian society, the reconciliation with one's brother, as well as states of lawlessness and outlawry are described in terms and phrases that either use the word *sibja* or compounds that include it. Although the Bible of course does not mention the blood feud, a clan member was no doubt bound to pursue it. Significantly, the cases of blood feud known from the sources primarily involve ties of retainership, with the lord taking up the cause of his retainers and vice versa. And the two slayings for which Theodoric the Great exacted blood vengeance were more political acts than revenge for a violation of the clan's honor. Nonetheless, when "the judge was far away," regardless of whether he was a Goth or a Roman, a strong clan took the law into its own hands. A Goth who had married the Syrian girl Euphemia did not dare admit this to his first Gothic wife because he feared her powerful relatives.[457]

HAIMS (VILLAGE): THE SOCIAL WORLD OF
THE GOTHIC FREEMAN

The army and territory of the Goths, the subtribe, the castle, and the house were ruled by the Gothic upper stratum. The magnates ruled by virtue of their lordship over retainers in which the differences between free and unfree disappeared because every retainer *in expeditione*[458] had to obey his lord.[459] In competition with these forms of lordship was the communally organized village, the *haims* or *weihs*.[460] Here the people lived by cultivation of the land. The stereotype of the peaceful Gothic peasants was obviously more than mere rhetoric. The language of the Gothic Bible has a rich agricultural terminology. The non-Tervingian population in particular was rooted in peasant agriculture. In the village the free Goth, the *freis* or *mediocris,* must have felt *anahaims* (literally, "at home"). Outside of the village he was away from home, *afhaims* (exiled). Even the free villagers, the "relatives and neighbors," took no part in the decisions of the tribal council. In the Tervingian political structure there is no sign of a Tacitean assembly of all the people. Since Ulfilas had only the oligarchic Sanhedrin to translate, we would know nothing about this differentiation of political authority were it not for the martyrdom of the thirty-eight-year-old Goth, Saba, on April 12, 372, in the river Musaeus-Buzău, and the writing down of his *passio.*[461]

Although Saba was poor and, in the eyes of a member of the Gothic upper stratum, politically insignificant, he was nevertheless a freeman who took part in the decisions of his fellow villagers and could resist them successfully even as an individual. The place of assembly, where the people "ran together" (*garuns*) to discuss affairs, was probably the village square. The village assembly (*gagumths, gamainths*) is clearly dominated by a group that makes suggestions, guides the decision-making process, and, above all, acts as the executive organ. Moreover, the same people are in charge of the consecration of the sacrificial meat, which implies that they are also responsible for cult and rituals. The term for these men, however, is so vague that we cannot distinguish them as delegated members of a village council from the rest of the village assembly. Instead, they must have been individuals who stood out by virtue of their prestige and economic power but who would not decide without the other villagers, even if those, like Saba, owned nothing more than the shirt on their backs. We could imagine these notables as spokesmen (*faúramathljos*). They were all heathens, which is shown both by their names and by their role in preparing and conducting sacrifices. It appears, therefore, that Christians became unfit to exercise any function on the village level. Yet the villagers demanded from their dignitaries that they protect those Christians whom they considered their relatives, προσήκοντες. Saba too would have been among these and could have enjoyed the peace of the village had he not been so stubborn.[462]

Led by the village spokesmen, Saba's village decided to serve the Christians unconsecrated meat during the sacrificial meal prescribed by the *reiks-megistanes.* Because Saba resisted this "pious trick" vehemently, he was banished from the village. Exile is the form of punishment that a clan society inflicts for incest and sorcery. Incest we may disregard in this case—and not only because we are dealing with the *vita* of a saint—but the other violation of the tribal norm appears much more likely, for sorcery represents nothing other than foreign and therefore forbidden religious practices.

After some time, however, Saba returned to his village; no doubt his exile was not meant to be permanent. The village elders then acted vigorously to protect Saba against the powerful *reiks,* who came from outside the village. There had been a change of sentiment in favor of this steadfast Christian. We can see how sensitive the notables were to public opinion in the village. Now they were even ready to commit perjury: they denied the presence of any Christians in their area. But Saba sabotaged this attempt as well, whereupon the village elders swore that there was only one Christian in the village. In this way they protected their relatives but at the same time abandoned the saint. Saba's second banishment was pronounced by the same *reiks* who had mocked him for his poverty. But Saba survived this exile also, returned once again to the village, and fell victim finally to the third persecution under Atharid.

No one in Saba's village thus participated in the process of formulating the political objectives of the *kuni.* If the village assembly of free Goths did not agree with the decisions of the tribal council, it had only the timeless methods of peasant resistance: jointly to deceive the authorities and to sabotage their decrees. But if a delegate of the tribal council came into the village with his armed retainers, he had the power to overrule the communal self-government while he was actually present. There would then be no room for villager self-government or the institutions through which it was expressed.

The sociocritical attitude of the author who left behind in his saint's life a "hagiographical gem" is readily apparent. He sides not only with the persecuted Christians but also with the pagans of the lower classes. Despite the weakness of the villagers, he feels sympathetic toward them and grants human feelings to Atharid's *andbahtos,* who kill Saba most reluctantly and only when he reminds them of their orders. He draws a picture of the woman who set Saba free when his pursuers had fallen asleep and who in return enlisted him to help cook breakfast and wash the dishes until Atharid's retainers caught up with him. One can hardly escape the conclusion that the author, or at least his source, was at home (*anahaims*) in a Gothic village.[463]

CULT AND RELIGION AMONG THE GOTHS

The cult of the Tervingi was centered in the individual villages and was determined and regulated by the *kuni* and its *reiks*. The village was the special sphere of peace established and preserved by the ritual sacrificial meal of the villagers. Whoever excluded himself from that meal broke his religious ties to the community, which responded with the banishment of the sacrilegious person on the grounds that he or she had denied the divine origin of the *gens*. But such an apostate could be more readily accepted by and integrated into a communally organized village, where everyone was in fact related, than by vertically structured *kuni*. The denial of the tribal tradition necessarily threatened the upper stratum of *reiks*, who saw themselves as the bearers of the ethnic traditions, which they tried to monopolize. The political importance of the leading stratum rested on its social prestige. From its midst had come the heroes whose deeds the people celebrated in songs and sagas, thus accepting and legitimizing the rule of the aristocracy. The Gothic Bible reflected social reality when it said that a man of good family (*godakunds*) was capable of conquering a kingdom. A nobleman had "family": we know of the Amals' deification of their ancestors as *Ansis*-Aesir but the Tervingi too opened battle with songs of praise for their forefathers. The "Getic gods" and the "spirits of [Alaric II's] forefathers" were one and the same element of the cult.

During the persecution of the Christians Athanaric ordered a wooden idol to be led through his land so that it could be worshipped. This idol perhaps represented *the*—or, better, *an*—original ancestor of the Tervingi. Every Gothic subtribe had its own special sacred objects, which were looked after by priests and priestesses. Tervingian paganism was an exclusive tribal religion. One did not talk about it with outsiders, and outsiders had no part in it. The priest Sansalas, who was persecuted along with Saba, escaped with his life because he was not a Goth. As a non-Goth he could not violate the tribal law just as he could not become the object of missionary activity.[464]

Although linguistically a neuter noun, the word *guth,* which means the Christian god, is masculine. Only its perverted form, the "idol," had retained the old identity of grammatical and natural gender. Gothic thus made the same connection between the Christian god and the pagan false god as did Old Norse. From *guth* is derived *gudja,* the name for the priest. The hierarchical differentiations that biblical Gothic makes for the Jewish priesthood do not reflect the situation among the Goths. But the words for sacrificing and for he who sacrifices—*blotan* and *blostreis*—reflect reality. Of course, with Ulfilas these terms lost their pre-Christian meaning and came to mean "to worship" and "priest." Among the Gothic refugees in 376 there were said to be bishops and monks. But these individuals looked like clowns to the pagan Romans, and they utterly scandalized the Roman Christians. The Tervingian presbyters probably followed the custom of pagan priests and wore bracelets and necklaces as signs of dignity. St. Ambrose tried to discredit a Roman Arian colleague by accusing him of dressing in this fashion and of thereby relapsing into paganism. In any case, no pagan priests participated in the persecution of the Christians in the fourth century. Measures concerning religious policies and their execution were the responsibility of the leaders, the Gothic judge for the Gutthiuda and the *reiks* for the different *kunja,* as had been the custom since "time immemorial."[465]

The Gothic witches, the *haliurun(n)ae,* the "women who engaged in magic with the world of the dead," had to be expelled from the tribe by the migration king Filimer, whereupon they entered into union with the evil spirits of the steppe and gave birth to the Huns. The historical significance of the witches is comparable to that of the persecution of the Christians. Banishment was the punishment a pagan society meted out for violation of the norms through sorcery, by which we must understand rituals and practices not recognized by the tribe. It is possible that necromantic practices, which were seen as very sinister and dangerous, gave such offense that the majority of the Goths turned against them. A comparison with the Scandinavians, for whom the Finnish sorcerer and his shamanic skills were always suspicious and detestable, is probably permissible. The Gutones must have felt similarly when they reached the Black Sea around the year 200 and came across shamanic cults there.

We must not, however, see the entire "Gothic special vocabulary"— namely, all words that have no direct corresponding words in Germanic or Indo-European languages—as the "genuine remains of the shamanic vocabulary." By no means must everything that remains unexplained be a reminder of a shamanic experience. Such a generalization would certainly be greatly exaggerated. But the intoxicating "cannabis sauna," which Herodotus noted among the Scythians, was not unknown to the Thracians and probably also sent the Gothic shamans on the desired "trip."[466]

The acculturation of the Gothic peoples to Greater Scythia is also attested by the religious beliefs of the Taifali. Like the Heruli, they are said to have practiced pederasty, a term by which the *interpretatio Graeca* usually described the association of warriors with boys. The slaying of a bear or a wild boar, however, freed the Taifalian boy from this "uncleanness." This account perhaps reflects the memory of a "magic ritual" that took place during the rite of passage into manhood. Something similar is found among Siberian peoples, who accepted a boy into manhood as soon as he had proven himself a "slayer of a four-legged animal." Not so much from Gothic as from the Gothicistic tradition of late medieval Scandinavia comes the legend according to which the Goths were the descendants of a bear and a young woman.[467]

A possessed person was described either as someone who "has an evil spirit" (*unhulthons habands*), who is "raging mad" (*woths*), or simply "demonic" (*daimonareis*). The opposite of an evil possession is the power to work a miracle, *taikneis* or *faúratani*.[468] "White magic," the power of doing good, pervades Tervingian-Vesian society as a force of life. The charisma of the Burgundian *hendinos*-king and the *quasi fortuna* of the Ansic Amali worked in a similar way. But Alaric I, too, must have possessed a special grace that destined him to become the conqueror of the Eternal City. Sacrificial meals and processions of the gods to weed out Tervingian Christians were, of course, intended to preserve the favor of the gods. Pagan "luck" was no doubt also meant if one wished another person *hailag*, a formula attested by the runic inscription on the necklace from Pietroasa. Ulfilas, in any case, avoided that word and used almost exclusively *weihs* to translate "holiness" in the Christian sense. In the eyes of the Christian Romans Alaric I was therefore also demonic, "possessed by a demon who forced him to destroy Rome."[469]

This sacral polarity, the change from a blessing into a curse, was part of the nature of the oath. The Gothic oath (*aiths*) contained an appeal to fate and a curse on the oath-taker in case he violated the oath; this meaning is also attested by the story of Athanaric's oath. We are told that his father put him under obligation never to enter Roman territory. His "religion" as well as a "terrible and dreadful oath" were to prevent him throughout his life from crossing the *limes*. Before the battle "At the Willows" the Tervingi also bound themselves on oath "according to their custom" to come to one another's aid. Several contemporary sources know of thoroughly false oaths. Eunapius even claimed that the Tervingi who crossed the Danube in 376 came with the express intent of breaking the oaths they had sworn to the emperor as a surety. Only the Roman side is said to have always kept its promises. Such an observation is justified to some extent, since a barbarian society was not obliged to be faithful to the alien, the *gasts*. When the Tervingi did not know what to do in their despair and were being continually put off by the Romans, they are said to have united in oath never to rest until they had destroyed the empire. But by no means did all Goths keep this oath, and it is questionable whether one may infer from this fact the existence of two Gothic "parties." When the Huns' power was waning, the Ostrogoths swore sacred oaths never to cooperate with their former oppressors. In 469 they had to be reminded of this oath by, of all people, a Hun in Roman services. Their reaction was in keeping with "barbarian logic": when asked about their old oath the Goths responded by attacking their Hunnic allies. But those ties that grew from obligations of kinship proved stronger than all formal oaths. The Goths in Saba's village were only too willing to commit perjury to protect their Christian relatives.[470] They swore by their gods, which is nothing unusual. The Danubian Goths probably preferred to swear by the Δούναβις-*Dōnaws; however, we do not know whether the river was among the chief gods of the Tervingi, although it evidently received human sacrifices.[471]

Whoever inquires about the names of Gothic gods will fare like an animal "on a meager pasture." The demons lead you around in a circle, you sense the fertile pastures but cannot find them. That Ares-Mars, in the form of the sword, was the divine father of the Scythians, Getaes, Goths, and Gauts was known to ancient ethnography, which never tired of mentioning it. Among these peoples the god of war had been born and now had died there as well, as a Christian-Gothic apologist smugly remarked. The notion of Ares-Mars as divine ancestor was appealing, and from it was derived a kinship between Goths and Romans. The Christian apologist's sardonic remark, however, was forgotten: it was most unwelcome if one celebrated Mars as the common father of Goths and Romans.

But what did the Goths name this god? The answer is surprising. The false identification of Goths and Getae now became a serious matter. The Gutonic god of war, probably a manifestation of the Germanic *Tiwaz*, took on the additional name of a Gothic Mars or Ares. The latter is attested still today in the Bavarian *Irchtag* (Tuesday) while a Gothic *Teiws* (read: *tēoos*) can be derived from the runic alphabet. West of the Dniester this high god may have been called "the Terwing," for the Scandinavian *Hervarasaga* transmits the name Týrfingr as the designation for both the Gothic land and the Gothic hereditary sword. The sword incarnation, however, is neither a Germanic nor an especially Scandinavian phenomenon; instead, it is the characteristic epiphany of the Black Sea Ares-Mars among all ethnic groups. The *Hervarasaga* appears as credible evidence for such an intensive cultic acculturation because it faithfully preserved Gothic traditions.

The second Gothic high god might have been called *Faírguneis* as well as Jupiter. This assumption would be substantiated if we are correct in reading this meaning into the famous runic inscription of Pietroasa-Bucharest. If the sawed-up golden bracelet is in fact inscribed with the words GUTAN(E) IOWI HAILAG, the dedication would read: "Holy to the Jupiter of the Goths." It is true that this reading by Richard Loewe is rejected by most German Germanists. But if we follow him, the bracelet would carry a unique Latin-runic inscription and the only evidence that the Goths also called their high god by the name Jupiter. Let us recall here that the Goths, like the Celts and the Bastarni, feared the collapse of the heavens, the realm of the Jupiter ("the thunderer"). So it might have been more than mere *interpretatio Romana* when Augustine reports that the Ostrogothic chieftain Radagaisus made human sacrifices to Jupiter when he invaded Italy in 405. In agreement with this view is the modern assignment of the treasure of Pietroasa to the Ostrogoths rather than the Tervingi.

When new Gothic peoples reached the lower Danube after 400, they went through the same acculturation as their Tervingian predecessors. The famous imitative medallions of Szilágy Somlyó-Şimleul Silvaniei (Transylvania), in fact both the shape of the medallions as well as the creative use of the Latin language in the legends, are evidence for this process. Here the Roman emperor is called *rex Romanorum*. The praise that the Neoplatonist Eunapius bestowed on Fravitta presupposes a Gothico-classical syncretism. Fravitta was in religious convictions "a Greek," still a young man but already the leader of pagan Goths who were "pleasing to God." He revered the gods "in the traditional custom of his fathers" and remained faithful to them even after he had made a splendid career in Roman service. Eunapius must have discovered kindred features in the belief of the barbarian he praised, features with which an intellectual of late antique paganism could identify.[472]

While Ares and Jupiter no doubt became familiar to both Gothic peoples, there were some Gothic gods who remained Goths: for instance, the Ansic Gaut, the first ancestor of the Amali. Although the Balthi were a race of "heroes and kings," the tale of their divine origins was lost. "The family of the Ostrogoths," in contrast was not only of greater nobility than the Balthi but had not forgotten its divine ancestor Gaut.[473] In Scandinavia he was considered a manifestation of Odin. At first glance this seems to accord with the presentation of Gizurr, the "Greutungian Warrior" in the *Hervarasaga*, as Odin.[474] The historian, however, must question the legitimacy of such an interpretation. Ulfilas knew the adjective *wods-woths*, the root of the name Woden-Odin. It has been remarked, and rightly so, that it would be asking too much if "one wanted to find the [Woden] name in the Gothic Bible or the Skeireins."[475] In the Scandinavian sources Odin comes from the Russian region.[476] Although these sources may be late, they give us something to think about. Nevertheless, we must ask how "wodenistic" was Gaut? He is the original Ansic ancestor, and the Gothic runic name *ansuz provides early evidence that the ancestral cult of the Amali was not a mere literary construct. Through this cult they legitimized their kingship.[477] But was Woden already "alive" at that time?

Woden and Odin had explicit ideas about the duties of the warriors who became their retainers. For example: when the Norwegian king Haakon the Good, a Christian among pagans, was mortally wounded he first asked to be moved into a Christian land. Should he die among pagans, however, he requested burial in the customary way. Haakon did die in a pagan land; his friends threw up "a great mound in which they laid the king in full armour and in his best clothes, but with no other goods. They spoke over his grave, as heathen people are accustomed to, and wished him to Valhalla." There he experienced what only a pagan king could hope for. Christendom had thus "reduced" the custom of burial goods as far as it concerned Haakon's "property," that is, the objects of daily life as well as his royal possessions. But the change in faith could not prevent the interring of the king with his most magnificent robes and with his weapons. Where he was going he needed weapons, even as a Christian.[478] But Gothic graves, whether of the Christian or the pagan period, are recognizable precisely by the absence of weapons. Apparently they were of no use to the deceased Goth in the hereafter.[479]

That Theodoric the Great took on Odinlike features in the northern memory reflects the *interpretatio Scandinavica* and says nothing about the Amal Gaut. If King Valamir, who was considered Theodoric's father, could emit sparks of fire, this skill may indicate the Amal charisma, which no one denies in any case; but no path leads inevitably from the flames to Woden-Odin.[480] In sum, it is safe to conclude that the Gothic Gaut and Odin-Woden were different gods. Only after the "heroic" end of the Goths in Italy did the two gods become identified in Scandinavia.

A Gothic runic name *enguz indicates an *Ing* god, for whom there is, however, no other evidence. During the tragic crisis of his sacral kingship Ermanaric committed suicide. He probably sacrificed himself to a god with whom he was closely associated. Nevertheless, we cannot say what this god was actually called in Gothic. And in any case, what was said concerning the evidence for the *Ing* god would apply also to an *Irmin* god inferred from Ermanaric's name. Not only the Vandals but also the Goths had a Dioscurian pair of divine helpers.[481]

With due caution we can thus trace the following high gods of the pagan Goths: the Ansic Gaut for the Greutungian Ostrogoths and especially for the Amal royal clan; a *Teiws, who was very soon also called Ares-Mars and perhaps Terving among the Vesi; a *Faírguneis in the role of the "thunderer"-*thunaraz, whom the Goths apparently also called Jupiter; finally, an *Ing* god and an *Irmin* god, who, insofar as they actually existed, resembled each other but were not identical.[482] The assumption of a Gothic Woden does not seem likely, and the same goes for a differentiation into a Vanian pantheon of the Tervingi and an Ansic pantheon of the Greutungi.[483] Both Gothic peoples probably did know an Ansic ancestral cult, symbolized by idols in the form of carved posts. What place the Tervingian *Donaws held among the Gothic gods remains uncertain.[484]

A passage from the Epistle to the Colossians has received much attention and has long been used to show the existence of a Tervingian moon cult. In the epistle the apostle Paul opposes, among other Judaizing tendencies, the observation of the new moons. The usually accurate Ulfilas turns this, however, into a prohibition of the worship of the full moon, an undoubtedly intentional deviation from the original. But Ulfilas probably did not so much demonize the moon divinity as condemn a pagan calendar of feast days for calculating certain days (*certi dies*) according to the full moon. These special days were probably the time when feasts took place, during which an animal (*hunsl*) was sacrificed and the sacred meat (*tibr*) consumed by all. Such a feast was the *dulths*; an expression that the Austro-Bavarian *Dult* has to this day guaranteed a boisterous afterlife. Finally, from the vernacular calendar of saints we know the designation for the eleventh month, which had the Latin-Gothic double name *Naubaimbar*-November and *fruma Jiuleis* (the first month of Jul). The Jul feast, which celebrated the winter solstice, was therefore observed in December.[485]

LANGUAGE AND DAILY LIFE

Biblical Gothic reflects various layers of language which correspond to different influences and cultural contacts. The word for "fig," *smakka*, which comes perhaps from the Caucasus, attests by the object it describes and the word used a period before the Goths came into contact with Mediterranean culture. At an even earlier stage the Goths were affected by a strong Celtic influence, which left its mark above all in their political life. There are Celticisms in the important military and political vocabulary which appear among the Germanic languages only in Gothic. In principle such an acculturation was already possible in the Wielbark culture, where the Gutones belonged to the Lugian cult league, which was originally dominated by the Celts. Of course this assumption presupposes the continuing existence of the Gutonic language stratum in fourth-century Gothic. Moreover, the Lugian period by no means explains why only the Goths and the Celts have these elements in common, for the Gutones formed only a small tribe within the Celto-Germanic confederation. If, however, the Goths met Celts or Celtic elements mainly on the lower Danube, this would explain the exclusiveness of some Celtic-Gothic connections. The mediators could have been the Balkan Celts and possibly also the Bastarni, although it is controversial how "Celtic" the Bastarni were. In any case, Celts, Bastarni, and Goths had similar notions about the collapsing heavens. That the Goths drove the Bastarni from their homeland at the end of the third century does not argue against contacts two or three generations earlier. Bastarni were fighting in the army of the legendary Ostrogotha, even if the Gothic tradition made them only auxiliary troops.[486]

Biblical Gothic drew specialized Christian liturgical terminology from Greek, either directly or through the mediation of Latin. The terms for the cultural achievements of Mediterranean civilization, however, rest almost exclusively on a Latin basis. In this linguistic heritage is reflected the life of a barbarian society, whose peasants, traders, and warriors came into contact with the greater Roman state and its civilization. Especially noticeable are the words from the Roman *sermo castrensis* (the "army slang") which the Gothic mercenaries, who had served in the Roman army as federates, brought home with them.[487] In this way the Latin technical term for military pay, *annonae,* came into the Gothic Bible as the military loan word *anno.* The loanword *anno,* however, has a Gothic equivalent in *mizdo.*[488] The same goes for "raging mad"—*woths* and *daimonareis;*[489] for *militon* and *drauhtinon*—"to serve in the army"; for *laigaion* and *harjis*—"legion or army"; for *Naubaimbar* and *fruma Jiuleis*—"November"; for *rex* and *reiks,* in the sense of a nonroyal king; for *rex-imperator* and *thiudans*; for Jupiter and *Faírguneis,* Mars-Ares and *Teiws*; in other words, this phenomenon applies to words that attest a bilingual political and religious terminology among the Goths. This terminology formed the basis for Ulfilas's work as a translator and thus gives us a better understanding of his great accomplishment against the background of its historical preconditions. A syncretism of this sort presupposes that it was supported by the upper stratum and that it could count on widespread approval. Anti-Roman attitudes and policies of several Gothic judges do not refute this argument. Even the bloody persecutions of the Christians were in the Roman tradition; they would have been unthinkable in a barbarian society far from the Roman frontiers. Ambivalent behavior toward Rome also characterizes the Burgundians. They saw themselves as relatives and descendants of the Romans, and yet "when they had been deceived by them they killed their Roman prisoners."[490]

The Gothic federates learned to "buy" things (*kaupon*); they went to the innkeeper (*caupo*) from which we can infer trade connections that originally existed with socially less respectable Romans. The Latin "dealer" had in the Gothic language the role that in other Germanic dialects was assigned to the slave traders (*mangones*).⁴⁹¹ Hair was cut in the Roman fashion (*kapillon*),⁴⁹² and luxury goods were nearly all physically and linguistically imported.⁴⁹³ The biblical parables paint a remarkable picture of the lives of people who lived from agriculture, cattle breeding, and fishing. Ulfilas needed no loanwords to translate these scenes into Gothic.⁴⁹⁴ Nearly all the terms in biblical Gothic for fruit, grain, weeds, for manure and plow, for all other tools and peasant activities, are based on purely Gothic words. From the Gothic roots came the rich terminology of cattle-breeding herdsmen, that is to say, of those people who moved with Ulfilas into the Roman Empire and as Gothi minores still adhered to their seminomadic way of life two centuries later. That wealth literally meant "livestock" (*faihu*) is something Gothic has in common with other ancient languages.⁴⁹⁵ But horticulture and viticulture, as well, seem strongly Gothicized, with the exception, however, of vinegar (*aket*).⁴⁹⁶ Among the names for Mediterranean fruit-bearing trees, that of the olive was borrowed early, perhaps from the Illyrian-Venetian languages.⁴⁹⁷ The "palm tree" was the "pointed tree," the "fig tree" possibly came from the southeastern Caucasus, and only the "mulberry," the "berry tree," was a Gothic creation.⁴⁹⁸ According to its shape the carob was simply called "horn."⁴⁹⁹ Purely Gothic once again are the terms for cattle, fowl, and the dog as well as the names for all types of game. Donkey and camel, the latter mistaken for an elephant, were, in contrast, derived from the ancient languages.⁵⁰⁰ The physician, *lekeis,* "the one who casts spells on the disease," used herbs and spices, the former derived from the Gothic tradition, the latter supplied by Rome. The cloth the physician used was a Gothic word, the sacks and bandages he cut from it betray the ancient loanword.⁵⁰¹ It is actually remarkable how few foreign elements Ulfilas needed to translate into Gothic the great number of biblical artisans and craftsmen. Although he does not always get by without borrowed concepts, even taxes and tax collectors, money changers and scribes, are wrapped in Gothic garb. The only Slavic loanword in Gothic possibly has to do with dancing; perhaps it came from an originally foreign and therefore conspicuous ritual.⁵⁰²

THE OSTROGOTHIC-GREUTUNGIAN KINGSHIP

Long ago, seventeen generations or about 440 years before Athalaric, the Goths won a great victory through the "good fortune [*fortuna*] of their nobility." The Goths then realized that these men were no ordinary human beings but semidivine heroes and Ansis-Aesir. The songs of the Italian Goths of Theodoric still recounted this saga. This is what Cassiodorus tells us about the origins of the Amali and their royal authority over the Ostrogoths. If this period of time—in a merely chronological sense—takes us back not only to the Black Sea era but even to the Gautic-Scandinavian period, Cassiodorus does correct himself by mentioning Ostrogotha, with whom at the end of the third century the Ostrogothic kingship of the Amali probably began.[503] It has rightly been said that "as soon as it [the kingship] becomes more clearly visible it bears all the traits of a kingship of the army."[504] Under its leadership the Scythization of the eastern Goths is completed: the armored lancer, who covered incredible distances and fought on horseback; the practice of hunting with falcons; shamanism; the adoption by the Amali of the Sassanian royal vestments; in short, the life-style of the Iranian-Turkish peoples of the steppe became part of the Gothic world.[505] This world is ruled by Ermanaric, the great king of the Ostrogothic-Greutungian army. His conquests and the extent of his dominion suggest a comparison with Alexander.[506] Ermanaric committed suicide because his struggle against the Huns ended in defeat. It is not impossible, indeed it is very likely, that Ermanaric's death had a ritual character and can be considered the king's final act. After his death the Greutungi chose a new king who was certainly related to Ermanaric but was definitely not his son. This king too died in battle against the Huns, whereupon most of the Ostrogoths submitted to the victors. But the entire tribe did not take this step. The dead king had left behind a small son; despite his young age he was already king and embodied the Amal charisma. The nonroyal *dux* Alatheus took in the royal child, combined his Greutungian retainers with Alanic and Hunnic deserters and led this confederation from the homeland into the Roman Empire. Nevertheless, Alatheus and his Alanic ally Safrax did not become kings, neither by virtue of this act of rescue, nor on account of their decisive intervention at Adrianople, nor by their conquest and settlement in Pannonia. Rather, they seem like Amal legitimists who derived their authority from their recognition of the Amal kingship.[507] There existed, therefore, besides the Greutungian greater kingship also the tribal mandate of the nonroyal *reiks* or *drauhtins*.[508] This still leaves open the question of whether Ostrogotha, Ermanaric, Vithimiris, or the little Videric were monarchic ethnic kings with the title or rather character of a *thiudans*.[509] Their descendant Theodoric, however, was a *reiks,* even if a monarch. The migration and the formation of a kingdom on Roman territory had apparently brought about the creation of a new Latin-Gothic military kingship to which the biblical *thiudans* no longer corresponded.[510] Yet Gothic polyethnicity, which can already be attested in Ermanaric's kingdom, remained unchanged: Finns, Slavs, Antes, Heruli, Alans, Huns, Sarmatians, and no doubt also Aesti are mentioned.[511]

3

The Forty-year Migration and the Formation of the Visigoths, 376/378 to 416/418

 Forty years lie between the autumn of 376, when the Goths crossed the Danube in large numbers, and the conclusion of the *foedus* in 416. And forty years separate the battle of Adrianople in 378 from the imperial decision in 418 to settle the Goths in Aquitania. Within this period a people emerged whom Cassiodorus first called the Visigoths.[1]

The Invasion and Settlement of the Goths in Thrace

FROM THE CROSSING OF THE DANUBE (376) TO THE
BATTLE OF ADRIANOPLE (378)

From Antioch came the imperial order to admit the Tervingi led by Alaviv and Fritigern. After a lively debate in the imperial consistory the opinion prevailed that the groups of friendly Gothic princes—who were considered Christians—could justifiably be settled in Thrace since the advantages clearly outweighed the disadvantages. The Goths of Alaviv and Fritigern were seen as *dediticii,* that is, they placed themselves as "supplicants" at the emperor's mercy. With his permission "they were given the opportunity to cross the Danube and settle in parts of Thrace." After temporary provisioning by the Roman authorities they were to live from the cultivation of the soil and would receive no further subsidies.[2] The imperial consistory expected in return to call upon large numbers of Goths to serve as Roman soldiers, which would increasingly allow the government to forgo forced levies among the Roman *coloni* and demand a money payment instead. In Ammianus Marcellinus, usually the most detailed and competent Roman observer, we encounter two problems in trying to understand the events: first, the author nowhere addresses the question of whether the Goths were disarmed or not; second, he is silent about the exact legal status the Goths were to receive within the empire. But the impression that Ammianus Marcellinus did not report accurately is deceptive. He did not see the admission of the Goths as unusual from the point of view of Roman law; instead, he condemned the emperor's decision because of its catastrophic consequences, which culminated in the battle of Adrianople. What caused this disaster was the enormous number of Goths and the incompetence of the Roman officials in charge. The author found a precedent for the decision of 376 in a request made in 359 by Sarmati Limigantes, to which emperor Constantius II had responded in the same way as Valens did in 376. The advantage of being able to avoid drafting Roman recruits and receive payment instead was even brought up at the meeting of the imperial council in 359. Inevitably the imperial authorities talked of *coloni* status for the immigrants, which included "settling them in far-off regions" at the discretion of the imperial government. But what exactly the act of "submission" (*deditio*) meant and in what way it was carried out is described by Ammianus Marcellinus in the following story: The "master" Sarmatians "came humbly to ask for peace." They drew up in battle formation. At first their leader took off his arms, threw himself to the ground, and asked to be forgiven. When the emperor indicated to him that he should rise, his people also "threw away their shields and weapons and stretched out their hands in supplication." All these proceedings show that *deditio* meant disarmament, reception with *coloni* status, settlement in areas determined by the emperor, and unlimited recruitment. It goes without saying that no treaty, *foedus*, was to be concluded between the emperor and those *Sarmati dediticii*. The difference between 376 and 359 is not that the affirmations of peace by the Sarmatians were mere pretense, for the Goths too were not especially serious about their promises, but that in 376 the Goths had already set their sights on Thrace before negotiating with the emperor, and they got their way. Furthermore, the general situation probably made it impossible even to begin settling the Goths according to *coloni* law. In fact, Valens asked for soldiers among the Goths for his war against the Persians, which he need not have done had the Goths been mere *coloni,* whom he could have levied at will.[3] Fritigern was perhaps personally bound by a treaty with Valens which he had entered into when he was seeking help from the emperor against his rival Athanaric.[4] The generation after 376 often asked itself why the Goths had not been disarmed, following Roman political and legal traditions. The emperor's order from Antioch probably did include disarming as a precondition for admission, but the Roman officials failed to enforce it.[5]

The admission of "an entire tribe" created considerable problems. The management of these problems and the opportunities to grow rich at the expense of the Gothic refugees and their amazing treasures[6] overtaxed the moral and administrative abilities of the Romans in charge of the operation. Moreover, despite continuous use, the available transportation was not sufficient to ferry this mass of people across the Danube. Roman ideas about the order of embarkation destroyed or threatened the family and clan structure of the Goths. An inadequate supply of foodstuffs—a shortage that was not necessarily intentional—also did not help to calm the hungry tribe. Roman observers described the misery of the Tervingi and complained about their exploitation by dishonest officials and generals. Despair led to self-enslavement, to the separation of families, and the handing over even of noble children.[7] In this chaos tensions mounted. Lupicinus, the Roman commander in Thrace, was forced to delegate a part of his troops as an escort for the Goths. This was done at the expense of the unbroken line of watch along the Danube, where the Roman fleet discontinued its patrols. Subsequently, at least three tribes, to whom entrance had previously been denied, forced their way into the empire: the mostly Greutungian confederation of Alatheus and Safrax;[8] the probably also Greutungian groups of Farnobius; and the Taifali from Walachia.[9] Once they had arrived south of the Danube, the last two groups joined together,[10] while Alatheus and Safrax somewhat later established contact with Fritigern.[11]

It would be interesting to know where all these Gothic peoples crossed the Danube. In view of the danger from the Huns and the prevailing famine, they must have moved from their settlements to the Danube by the fastest possible route. If that was the case, the following scenario emerges: the Tervingi under Alaviv and Fritigern crossed the Danube at Durostorum-Silistr(i)a. Evidence for this is (1) the refugees' starting point between the Siret and Prut rivers; (2) the limited possibilities of crossing the lower Danube, which at this time was once again at flood level; and (3) the Moesian road network, which determined the course of the first operations of the Tervingi on Roman territory. And the Taifali, the Greutungi, and the Farnobius group as well had no alternative but to penetrate into the Roman

Empire from Muntenia. The Greutungi used rafts and "pitched camp" on the right bank of the Danube "at a considerable distance from Fritigern,"[12] which implies that the Greutungi did not cross the river in upper Moesia, let alone Pannonia.[13] Since Athanaric, who was still holding out in his Moldavian redoubt, knew about the problems the Romans had caused for the Greutungi, they must have effected their crossing close to his position.[14]

Initially Fritigern followed imperial orders.[15] With the Greutungi at their rear, the main body of the Tervingi marched slowly up to the gates of Marcianopolis-Devna, the headquarters of the Thracian troops. Lupicinus invited the two leaders Alaviv and Fritigern to a sort of reconciliation feast. They accepted the invitation. But distrust and a poor handling of the situation soon led to uncontrolled reactions on both sides. A quarrel broke out between the Gothic escort and the Roman guards which greatly disturbed the mass of Tervingi encamped outside the city. They demanded the opening of the gates and permission to supply themselves with food. In response Lupicinus had the escort of the Gothic princes cut down. Fritigern managed to escape in the general chaos, but Alaviv's name is mentioned for the last time on this occasion. What is surprising is that the same applies to the name of the Tervingi: from this time Ammianus Marcellinus speaks only of the Goths.[16] Be that as it may, Fritigern escaped from the city, placed himself at the head of his people, and an open revolt broke out. The pent-up hatred and fears about survival burst forth with great violence. The Goths swept across the land, burning and plundering everything in their path. It was early 377, and Lupicinus raised all available troops to put down the revolt. But only nine miles from his headquarters he suffered a serious defeat. Lupicinus was killed, and with one stroke the Thracian regional forces had been eliminated. The raging Gothic warriors had simply trampled them.

The first Gothic victory on Roman soil gave a signal to others. Fritigern was now joined by Thracian miners, overtaxed Roman underclasses, and Gothic-barbarian slaves. At the same time a Roman unit composed entirely of Tervingi changed sides. It was under the command of Colias and Sueridus, who initially had had no intention of joining their newly arrived tribesmen. The Gothic unit was in its winter quarters near Adrianople when it was ordered to move immediately to Asia Minor, where its sister units were stationed. Colias and Sueridus demanded the travel expenses (*viaticum*) they were entitled to, supplies and a two-day delay in their departure. But since they had engaged in some plundering in the suburbs, along the way ravaging the estates of the head of the city administration, the *duumvir* in charge refused to meet their legitimate demands and incited the local proletariat, among them workers from the weapons factories, against the Goths. The Gothic troops, drawn up in ranks, struck back, revolted, and joined Fritigern for a joint—if unsuccessful—siege of Adrianople. But not all Moesian Goths switched sides.[17] Ulfilas's people placed religion above ethnic solidarity and "remained loyal to the Romans." As a result they were attacked by the Tervingi and were only able to hold out in the highlands.[18] Nevertheless, the number of deserters from all quarters was large, and through them Fritigern's people received valuable information about the countryside and acquired new and different skills.[19] The Goths took a special interest in Roman war material, which they won as booty and seized from the weapons factories.[20] Of course the captured stores could hardly meet the great demand for weapons. At the battle "At the Willows" the Goths used as ersatz missiles huge wooden clubs they had hardened in fire.[21] Although the Tervingian refugees had kept their weapons in 376, their logistical inferiority became apparent just a few months after the outbreak of the Thracian war.[22]

The emperor Valens and his court still misjudged the extent of the danger. During the emperor's first Gothic war between 367 and 369, the enemy had constantly retreated, even though the Romans were fighting north of the Danube and were threatening the barbarian homeland.[23] Less than ten years had passed since then. Why should the Tervingi now pose a serious threat? Just recently the emperor had recruited Gothic soldiers for his planned campaign against Persia;[24] was he now to abandon all his plans and preparations? This misjudgment of a situation so completely different from that in 367-369 would be costly. The Roman military leadership merely reacted piecemeal to the gradual increase of danger, thus frittering away forces and surrendering the initiative to the Goths. Minor Roman successes merely obscured the magnitude of the threat and prevented the necessary abandoning of the adopted strategy.

The first to appear on the Thracian battlefield were the infantry commander Traianus and the cavalry commander Profuturus at the head of some of the troops called up in Armenia. Valens asked his nephew and coemperor Gratian for support from the Western empire. In response came Frigeridus, the proven commander of Pannonia Valeria, who was not especially pleased with his new mission. At first the measures taken seemed entirely adequate. Even before the arrival of Frigeridus the few elite units of the Eastern army had done valuable preliminary work by forcing the Goths into the Dobrudja. There it was expected that hunger would soon compel them to surrender.[25] Moreover, the two Roman divisions at hand were reinforced by some Gallic units led by the *comes domesticorum* Richomeres. But the Roman troops remained numerically inferior to the Goths, and their leaders could not agree on how to fight the enemy.

The Tervingi, encamped "At the Willows" (*Ad Salices*), remained safely sheltered behind their fortified circle of wagons. In the face of this dilemma, Frigeridus suffered an attack of gout and left the supreme command to Richomeres.[26] His battle plan was simple enough: at some point lack of food would force the Goths to move their circle of wagons, and at that moment, while they were on the march and most vulnerable, he would attack. But Fritigern either realized what the Roman plan was or found out about it from deserters. He remained in his impregnable circle of wagons and recalled all the predatory detachments within reach. Finally, the Romans decided to wait no longer, and the Goths too launched an attack, after having "sworn mutual oaths of loyalty according to their custom."[27]

The Roman army opened battle with the *barritus*. This battle song of barbarian warriors began quietly and gradually swelled to a thundering roar, revealing just how Roman the troops really were. The Goths struck up a song in praise of their ancestors. Already in this respect the two armies were equal. The battle, which took place in the late summer of 377, was not decisive. Both sides suffered serious losses: the Goths did not emerge from their circle of wagons for an entire week, while the Romans withdrew to Marcianopolis. But the Romans did manage to block the Balkan passes. They also concentrated their food reserves in cities that remained inaccessible to the Goths.[28] The Romans concluded that they had gained time and could afford to hold on to the current strategy. Richomeres went to Gaul to obtain reinforcements, while Valens still hesitated to go to Thrace in person.

Frigeridus too had left the theater of war and was in familiar Illyricum awaiting new orders from his emperor Gratian. Valens sent Saturninus, the vice cavalry commander of the Eastern army, to support Traianus and Profuturus. The efforts to cut off and isolate the enemy were effective, the attempt to starve out the Goths in the triangle between the Danube, the Balkan mountains, and the Black Sea seemed to be succeeding because the Tervingi were not prepared for a war of position. In this critical situation Fritigern pulled off a coup de main: he persuaded Alatheus and Safrax to join him.[29] The Greutungian, Alanic, and Hunnic horsemen quickly loosened up the hardened fronts. The first contact between these groups and Fritigern's Tervingi had taken place as early as the fall of 376.[30] Subsequently, Alatheus and Safrax had probably moved from the area of lower Moesia and Scythia minor upstream along the Danube. They did not participate in the battle "At the Willows." In order to aid the Tervingi, who were encamped in the northeast of modern Bulgaria, the horsemen must have then moved back into the region of the lower Danube. And in fact Saturninus was soon compelled to abandon the blocking of the passes. The consequences of this Roman retreat were disastrous. Since Saturninus was not criticized for his action, his position must have become untenable. All of Thrace from the Rhodope mountains to the Black Sea was now at the mercy of the barbarians, who began a war of revenge against everything Roman.[31] It was alleged that "in their homeland" they had sworn in their misery an oath to harm the empire any way they could without relenting.[32] Now they seemed to be redeeming this promise: "Like animals who had broken their cages, the barbarians raged unrestrained across the wide expanses."[33] Such words were not mere rhetoric; the devastating Gothic invasions of the third century had found their sequel.[34]

The addition of mounted warriors provided the former Danubian Goths with a new and effective element of warfare. Their foot warriors and the Greutungian cavalry complemented each other. At Dibaltum-Develtus, near modern-day Burgas on the Black Sea, a Gothic raiding force surprised a Roman elite unit that was throwing up trenches. Its commander was killed and the unit was wiped out, but only after a larger Gothic cavalry detachment appeared on the scene of battle.[35]

By order of Gratian Frigeridus, who was at this time probably promoted to commander-in-chief (*magister militum*) of the Illyrian army, once again moved into action in Thrace.[36] At Beroea-Stara Zagora he tried to set up a fortified defensive line. In other words, he wanted to continue the Saturninian concept of defensive warfare, especially along the important road leading from the Shipka pass into the valley of Maritsa. The strategic importance of this area had been revealed by the victory here of the Gothic king Cniva over the imperial army that had followed him from the north, thereby forcing his break-through to Philippopolis-Plovdiv.[37] Thus the Goths had to dislodge Frigeridus from central Thrace before the beginning of winter 377 if they wanted to survive that season safely. And so they moved against his position from all sides. To avoid encirclement the Illyrian commander-in-chief cleared the area around Beroea and withdrew once again to the West. On his way across the mountains, Frigeridus came upon Farnobius's Greutungian-Taifalian band. Farnobius had split off from the other Greutungi and had entered into an alliance with the Taifali. The engagement ended with Farnobius's death and the total defeat of his detachment. The survivors, evidently mostly Taifali, surrendered to Frigeridus and were settled in upper Italy and Aquitania. There is no point in trying to guess their numerical strength, but they must have been more than a small splinter group since these Taifali both continued the tradition of the transdanubian tribe and also gave their name—which still existed centuries later—to some of the barbarian settlements.[38]

When in the winter of 377/378 Gratian wanted to hasten to his uncle's aid, the Alamanni invaded Raetia. While on home leave an Alamannus who was serving in the imperial guard had revealed the imminent departure of the Romans into Illyricum. Thereupon his tribe attacked; Gratian, however, not only stopped them but answered with a counteroffensive.[39] Meanwhile Frigeridus had fortified the Succi pass between Serdica-Sofia and Philip-popolis-Plovdiv. The so-called "gate of Trajan" (*Trojanova vrata*) consti-tuted at that time the boundary between the two parts of the empire.[40] If the Romans could occupy and hold this strategically important position, they would be able to stop the Goths from spreading westward. At this decisive moment the experienced general Frigeridus was replaced by a man who proved a failure in the battle for the Succi pass.[41] A change also took place in the high command of the Eastern army; the undoubtedly incompe-tent Traianus was relieved as infantry commander, but he remained with the Thracian army. His successor was Sebastianus, who came from the Western empire.[42] Valens made this arrangement in Constantinople, where he had arrived with the main body of his forces at the end of May 378.[43] "From everywhere the armies were massed to achieve something great and extraordinary," wrote Eunapius.[44] Older estimates probably set the strength of Valens' troops too low; today one calculates thirty to forty thousand men who gathered in southern Thrace for the strike against the Goths.[45]

In early June Sebastianus had begun his operations in the area around Nike, a small town about fourteen miles north of Adrianople. In Constan-tinople a Catholic revolt had forced the hated Arian emperor Valens to leave his capital, a bad omen for an army that was marching out against the enemy and only one of the many disquieting and even terrifying portents that frightened Valens on his march against the Goths. By June 11 the em-peror had covered the distance from Constantinople to the imperial domain of Melanthias, located about seventeen miles from the city. There he estab-lished his headquarters.[46] Meanwhile Sebastianus had pulled off a successful coup de main. With only two thousand chosen troops he destroyed near Adrianople a Gothic column composed primarily of men who had plun-dered the southern Thracian province of Rhodope.[47] In addition, the Gothic details that had moved into the positions abandoned by Frigeridus on the road to the Shipka pass were afraid of being cut off and left. The Gothic retreat was further accelerated by an order of recall from Fritigern, who was trying to concentrate his forces at the city of Cabyle.[48] This important crossroads at the bend of the Tundja river, near modern Yambol, dominated the approaches from Beroea to the Black Sea and from Novae on the Danube to Adrianople.[49] In mid-July 378 Valens reached the city.[50] Good news, in fact all-too-good news, awaited him there: the success of Sebastianus; the approach of Gratian, who, even though suffering from malaria, had already arrived in Castra Martis in northwestern Bulgaria; and, moreover, the message from reconnaissance units that the Goths were marching toward the town of Nike with only ten thousand men. Now Valens urged haste. A minor successful engagement with the Goths not only strengthened the confidence of the victorious Sebastianus but inspired the entire Eastern army.[51] To this we must add Gratian's impressive victory over the Alamanni, which the older and higher ranking augustus wished to equal. It is not surprising that the majority of the officers of the Eastern army supported the idea of a separate offensive, even before the memorable war council made the decision on the eve of the catastrophe.[52]

Around August 7 it suddenly seemed as if the preconceived plans of the leaders would change. Richomeres, who was returning from Gaul, conveyed Gratian's urgent request to attack Fritigern only after the two imperial armies had united.[53] There was good reason for this warning. A predominantly Alanic detachment of the Greutungian cavalry, which Fritigern was eagerly awaiting, had attacked Gratian's lightly armed troops at Castra Martis and had inflicted some losses. At worst the fight was a minor disgrace for the Romans, but the suddenness with which the new enemy had attacked and disappeared must have created a vivid impression of the dangers of the coming battle.[54]

But the war council, presided over by Valens, decided to seek battle. The infantry commander Sebastianus, who could point to his recent victory, prevailed against the cautious councillors and their speaker, the cavalry commander Victor, even though the latter, as a Sarmate and a former envoy to Athanaric, knew only too well what he was talking about.[55] Valens decided to attack, and his decision was further strengthened by apparent signs of Fritigern's weakness: on August 8 Fritigern had sent a (presumably) Arian priest to the emperor, who gave him a friendly reception but did not take seriously what he had to say. Fritigern demanded all of Thrace—including crops and livestock—as federate territory for the Goths. In a secret letter delivered at the same time, however, he offered himself as a friend and ally of the Roman Empire. Fritigern advised the emperor to draw up his troops and with this demonstration of strength bring the rebellious Gothic army to its senses.[56]

It is unclear how serious this offer was, but it takes its place in a series of similar ones extending from Alaric and Theodoric (II) all the way to Theodoric the Great and Theodahad.[57] Ammianus denies that the offer was meant seriously, and to this day many have followed his view, despite obvious contradictions in Ammianus's assessment of the Gothic priest's embassy. First, Valens initially gave the legates a friendly reception, even though the presbyter and his companions came from the Tervingian lower stratum, a fact the emperor considered an insult on the next occasion.[58] Second, the priest is described as a "confidant of secret plans and a loyal follower of Fritigern" and at the same time his dismissal and failure is explained away by his "not [being] authorized." These statements simply do not fit together. Fritigern's proposal, however, seems entirely plausible and logical: all of Thrace, together with its livestock and its harvest, was to be surrendered to the Goths as federate territory, (habitanda Thracia sola). This would have meant that Fritigern was seeking to make a considerable improvement in the immigration stipulations of 376 the basis of peace talks. Instead of coloni status in dispersed settlements, the Goths would have achieved the status of imperial federates and would have formed compact settlements under their own tribal organization. In this way a Gothia could have arisen very close to the imperial city, and this would have invariably opened to the Gothic nobles the highest careers in the imperial service and through them power and influence in the empire.[59]

Before the battle on August 9 Fritigern tried twice more to establish contact with Valens.[60] On these two occasions the Gothic chief was probably only seeking to gain time, to wear down the resilience of the Romans, and to wait for the arrival of the Greutungian cavalry. It must have been these delaying tactics that led Ammianus Marcellinus, as he was looking back on these events, to color his account of the negotiations on August 8. When he first sought contact before the outbreak of hostilities, Fritigern surely wanted to make peace with "his" emperor, which must have seemed to him more advantageous than any victory. A Gothic noble would, in any case, have better prospects for a career in a functioning Roman state than in a heap of rubble. The events of the following decades would prove Fritigern right. For the time, however, his short-term calculations were also successful.[61]

On the morning of August 9 the imperial army left the city of Adrianople, leaving behind under guard the baggage train and the imperial treasure and insignia. As usual the Goths awaited the Romans in and around their circle of wagons. But this meant that the Roman troops had to cover a distance of almost eleven miles in scorching heat before contact with the enemy could be made. Men and animals suffered from hunger and thirst, the road was in poor condition, and the Goths had set fire to the withered grass and brush to add to the heat of the early afternoon hours. Worse, the Roman advance detachment discovered that the Goths were far more numerous than had been assumed. Envoys from Fritigern appeared, but they were only insignificant individuals and therefore not authorized negotiation partners for the emperor. Valens wanted to negotiate with the Gothic leaders. Had the emperor changed his mind at the last minute? Some time passed and then a Gothic herald appeared and accepted the imperial request but demanded in return a high-ranking Roman as hostage. After some hesitation Richomeres agreed to remain with the Goths for the duration of the talks. The choice had initially fallen on a relative of the emperor, but since that relative had recently been a hostage with the Goths he declined the dubious honor. When Richomeres was finally ready to go he could no longer be received by the Goths. Two Roman units had begun hostilities without orders, and they dragged along the rest of the army in a more or less disorganized fashion.

The battle had hardly begun when the day was carried by the "blitz," a lightning-quick attack of the Gothic cavalry. Alatheus and Safrax had no sooner returned from foraging than they launched a surprise attack. As from an ambush the Greutungian and Alanic horsemen fell upon the right flank of the Romans and rolled it up from the side or perhaps even from the rear. Then one detachment of the Gothic cavalry withdrew, went round the Romans and attacked the left flank, where it repeated its tactics. In the meantime Fritigern's foot warriors had left the circle of wagons and were attacking from the front. The Roman cavalry fled immediately—who can blame them—and the tactical infantry reserves did the same. There was no possibility of reestablishing the battle lines. Surrounded on all sides the Roman army was cut down, and with it the emperor, most of his generals, and no less than thirty-five high-ranking officers. Only a third of the Roman soldiers managed to escape, among them the cavalry. Whoever was saved owed his life in large part to the late start of the battle, which had only begun in the late afternoon, and to a moonless night, which made pursuit difficult.

The battle of Adrianople has been considered the turning point in the history of western warfare. At this time the thousand-year reign of the knight is said to have begun. Such chiliastic notions, however, have little historical meaning. Above all, it is not true that Gothic horsemen were from this time invincible, and it is equally inaccurate to infer from the disaster of Adrianople a fundamental superiority of cavalry over infantry.

Just as the battle of Adrianople by no means changed military history as decisively as has sometimes been suggested, its impact on the history of the late empire can also be easily exaggerated. The Romans of the fifth century, who had experienced many horrors in their generation, saw Adrianople as the beginning of the end. But contemporaries of Adrianople thought differently.[62] The emperor Valens died among his soldiers, probably struck by an arrow.[63] Ammianus Marcellinus, however, recounts a more memorable story of the emperor's death. Some people believed that the mortally wounded emperor had been carried to a log cabin where he and his companions were burned to death.[64] The fact that the body of the Arian emperor was never found was linked with the story of his death by burning, symbolic of the eternal flames of hell. It was obvious to every Catholic Christian that the devil had taken Valens.[65] But the pagan Ammianus Marcellinus did not think in the terms of Catholic apologists.[66] He did not record the story to have it exploited as an example of providential history. Ammianus discussed secular events as a contemporary, and his historical comparisons are therefore of great interest. The battle of Adrianople reminded him of the death of the emperor Decius and his son in the battle of Abrittus in the year 251 when the Gothic king Cniva annihilated the Roman army.[67] And Ammianus further compares Adrianople with Cannae.[68] The meaning of these comparisons is clear: Cannae was followed by the battle of Zama where Hannibal lost the war. After Abrittus came the victories of Claudius II Gothicus and Aurelian, who between the years 269 and 271 destroyed the first Gothic kingdom, put an end to the unity of the Goths, and nearly wiped them out completely.[69] Against Rufinus's famous dictum that "this battle [of Adrianople] meant for the Roman empire the beginning of the calamities at that time and since,"[70] Ammianus's hope for recovery was entirely justified. The Goths by no means exploited their victory; indeed, despite help from "traitors and deserters" they were unable to capture even Adrianople, where the imperial treasure was kept. Fritigern, who would have preferred to try to take the city peacefully with the help of a Christian fifth column, was outvoted by the other Gothic chiefs, whereupon the barbarians attacked the city from August 10 to 12. They were repulsed with bloody losses and once again confirmed the experience of the first assault on Adrianople in early 377, after which Fritigern had declared that he would from now on "keep peace with stone walls."[71] Philippopolis-Plovdiv and Perinthus as well held out against the Goths, and a drive toward Constantinople was condemned to failure from the start. The Goths won their only victory at Nikopolis-Stari Nikub, whose garrison did not want to fight. Everywhere else local militias defended the fortified cities.[72]

The Roman defenders were supported by heavy artillery that hurled huge rocks against the attackers. The impact of these technical "marvels" was supplemented by a number of events whose supernatural interpretation aroused great anxiety among the Goths. For example, when they attacked Adrianople a subtropical downpour drenched them, and the Goths thought the heavens were collapsing.[73] The Gothic drive against Constantinople shows no clear grasp of reality. The enormity of their undertaking seems to have dawned upon the attackers only when they actually stood before the walls of the capital. Moreover, strange things happened there. All of a sudden one of the city gates was thrown open and a group of Saracen horsemen galloped toward the Goths. One of them, a Nazir, rushed at a hugh Gothic warrior, cut his throat with a dagger, and drank his blood. The Goths understandably withdrew, horror-struck.[74] And meanwhile, behind their backs, the imperial treasure was taken from Adrianople to safety in Macedonia and imperial Dacia.[75] This indicates that the Gothic army was not a large one. The barbarians were never able to actually control an area through which they had moved. The Goths could pillage and burn the land, slaughter and enslave the population, they could already feel "at home" in Thrace and imperial Dacia, they could even thrust forward as far as the Julian Alps, and still the Romans would not give up.[76] What is more, the Goths had neither the necessary equipment nor the experience to capture fortified towns.[77] As they had done in the third century,[78] they now tried to learn in a hurry, but successes did not follow. We read about the building of siege engines, which had to be destroyed because the Goths did not know how to use them properly.[79] And in the cities was stored not only the wealth of the Romans but also the food the Goths so urgently needed. Once again the tribe began to go hungry.[80]

Paradoxically, victory fragmented Fritigern's army and weakened his position. For the Gothic leader was neither able to keep together his warriors nor to follow a specific plan. The short-lived coalition of barbarians which had been formed under the threat from the combined Roman court armies fell apart. Just as before the battles of Adrianople and "At the Willows," raiding parties once again roamed through the land.[81] In this way the lust for booty could be more easily gratified and the problem of obtaining provisions more easily resolved. Nevertheless, the imperial government— despite a catastrophic shortage of troops—gained enough time to take measures that would at least prevent the spread of the Gothic "brushfire." Thus Iulius, the commander of the Eastern army, ordered the Gothic garrisons within his sphere of command in Asia Minor to be overpowered and cut down. In this way he nipped in the bud any possible repeat of the events of winter 377 when a Gothic unit of the Roman army had rebelled before the battle of Adrianople and gone over to Fritigern. It is probable, however, that this bloody action—which already belongs to the time of Theodosius and for which the eager general had obtained authorization only from the senate in Constantinople—cost Iulius his office.[82]

The events that led up to the battle on August 9, 378 had developed like an ancient tragedy: ἄτη and ὕβρις, fate, blindness, and arrogance, decided the course of events. There is even a messenger—Richomeres to Valens—who tries to overcome the blindness of the doomed but is not able to avert their downfall.[83] Yet tragedy and history differ in that no curtain descends on historical life, there is no end of the play and no final resolution. This is true above all for Adrianople, which was certainly not a decisive battle. Nevertheless, it introduced a change in Roman policy. First, it laid the foundation for the battle at the Frigidus in 394 and thereby for the final Christianization of the Roman Empire, however paradoxical this may sound.[84] Second, in its wake a new Gothic ethnogenesis began: out of the Danubian Tervingi emerged the Visigoths as horsemen whose model was the victorious Greutungi and their allies. All at once there is a change in the archaeological finds in the *castra* and *castella* from the estuary of the Danube to that of the Inn. It is often impossible to say whether an artifact comes from the Crimea or from obscure Untersiebenbrunn east of Vienna. These archaeological remains have led to the conjecture that an enormous Visigothic kingdom existed in the fifth century. This is a fanciful conjecture, which as such is wrong because it can be understood only in political-institutional terms. But as far as way of life and *Weltanschauung* are concerned, a "Scythian" koine—carried by the Goths—did in fact spread over the Roman provinces of the middle and lower Danube. Tervingian accultu-ration to "Scythian" eastern customs continued even after Alatheus and Safrax separated from Fritigern's Goths. Third, the battle of Adrianople brought a change in Roman policy toward the imperial barbarians. The accommodation that Constantine the Great had initiated between the clas-sical and the nonclassical worlds experienced another fundamental shift. Certainly, in times to come the Romans would succeed often enough in subduing the barbarians beyond the frontiers; but with the assimilated groups within the empire they had to find a modus vivendi, even if they had conquered them. New paths had to be taken to solve the barbarian problem. It would seem that Theodosius and his advisers had learned the lesson of the battle of Adrianople and tried to pass it on to posterity. No supernatural power—whether a god or an anonymous law of history—determined the fall of Rome. There was still freedom to act. The man who conceived the necessary alternatives to answer the challenges of the time was Theodosius, "the friend of peace and of the Gothic people."[85]

THEODOSIUS AND THE SETTLEMENT OF THE
GOTHS IN THRACE

In 378 Gratian recalled the Spaniard Theodosius, who had withdrawn to his native country after the violent death of his father. Reconciled and promoted to commander of the Illyrian cavalry, this capable general went to the *limes* in upper Moesia and Dacia, which he knew from earlier commands. By the end of the year he had managed to defeat the Tisza Sarmatians, who had penetrated into the empire; the morale of the troops rose. On January 19, 379, in Sirmium-Sremska Mitrovica Gratian appointed Theodosius coemperor and handed over to him the East, including the prefecture of Illyricum with the dioceses of Dacia and Macedonia.[86] As early as the spring the new augustus could enter Thessalonica unopposed, for the plague had driven the Goths out of Macedonia. The most pressing task of the emperor was the raising of a new army. Peasants, miners, Asian and African federates, even Goths, were recruited and enlisted. The Goths were offered such attractive terms that the large number who responded threatened the maintenance of Roman military discipline. The Goths seemed to come and go as they pleased. Theodosius tried to control the chaos by exchanging Gothic contingents for Egyptian troops. Nonetheless, the Goth Modares-Modaharius was a real gain for the Romans when he entered their army.[87] If we take Zosimus literally, Modares-Modaharius belonged to the same clan as Athanaric.[88] Illustrious descent always provided a good start to a career in the Roman army, and in fact Modares rose very quickly. Perhaps his kinship with Athanaric explains the hatred with which this infantry commander fought against the Goths of Fritigern. In 379 Modares succeeded in destroying a large column of Gothic plunderers. And it was not long before the Goths were once again confined to the area between the Balkan mountains and the Danube, where they could maintain themselves in the long run only if there was peace and the Romans supplied them with food. Thus it seemed for the moment as though there had never been a catastrophe at Adrianople. On November 17, 379, the victories over the Goths, Alans, and Huns were proclaimed in Constantinople; we can probably assume that even the groups led by Alatheus and Safrax had suffered defeat.[89]

The reverses of these years led the Gothic tribes to modify their strategy.

The authority of Fritigern, as well as that of the two cavalry commanders Alatheus and Safrax, increased once more, whereupon two large-scale campaigns were prepared. The mounted three-tribe group had already thrust into Illyricum after rather than before the battle of Adrianople in summer 378; subsequently it had to withdraw to the Thracian area from where it undertook individual plundering expeditions.[90] Now, in 380, the horsemen arrived in closed formation.[91] Gratian realized that a military solution was impossible and that the operations of one of his generals were threatening to undo the narrow defensive victories of the previous year. Thus the Western emperor—after consultation with Theodosius—settled the Greutungi and their allies as federates in Pannonia II and probably also in Savia and Valeria.[92]

While the Greutungi were moving upstream along the Danube, Fritigern gathered his band and set out toward Macedonia, where in the spring of 380 the Goths almost captured Theodosius. It was pure luck that the emperor escaped Fritigern's troops, who were always well informed through their fellow tribesmen serving in the Roman army. Subsequently Fritigern plundered the land as far as Thessaly. Gratian answered Theodosius's call for help and sent a powerful force under Bauto and Arbogast into the threatened area. The two generals added the remainder of the Theodosian army to their own troops and drove the attackers back to lower Moesia, from where they had set out. The game of the previous years was repeating itself, the first signs of the coming stalemate in the following months.[93]

Athanaric must have fallen victim to a plot by Fritigern quite some time before Theodosius—who had recovered from a serious illness—entered Constantinople in triumph on November 24, 380.[94] The former Gothic judge was driven from the Caucaland "by the conspiracy of his relatives and closest friends." In order to free his rear Fritigern had probably overthrown his former rival in his place of refuge. Athanaric may have contacted Theodosius and offered his services against Fritigern. Whether Modares was involved in all this or not, his decision to join the Romans showed just what the Thracian Goths had good reason to fear. When Athanaric arrived in the imperial city, the arrangements unfolded so splendidly that one has to assume previous contact between him and Theodosius. Athanaric clearly had been driven out by his own people. But he did manage to upset Fritigern's plans with his flight to Constantinople. Theodosius used the arrival of his former enemy and his death in the capital soon after for an impressive demonstration of Rome's strength and willingness for peace.[95] This did not put an immediate end to hostilities; merely to survive, the Goths had to keep plundering. It would also take another eighteen months before the negotiations would come to a successful conclusion. But on October 3, 382, a treaty was ratified, probably the most momentous *foedus* in Roman history:[96] "the—or better: an—entire tribe of the Goths together with its king surrendered to Romania," wrote an unknown chronicler.[97] With this a new page was turned in the history of Roman institutions.

To be sure, when Gratian settled the three-tribe confederation in Pannonia in 380, he did create a precedent for the *foedus* of 382.[98] Nevertheless, the conclusion of the treaty of 382 loses nothing of its epochal significance. The two *foedera* really belong together, since Theodosius not only approved the solution to the Greutungian problem but perhaps even suggested it. Moreover, Fritigern's Goths formed an entire people, whereas the Pannonian Goths never developed into one. The best accounts of the peace settlement of 382 mention a bipartite Gothic leadership as negotiation partners of the Romans. Fritigern's name does not appear.[99] This raises the question of whether he was still alive at that time and whether it was he whom the Roman considered king of the federate Goths.[100] Fritigern had the mandate for the military leadership of a wandering, homeless tribe. He was a barbarian *dux,* a king of the army without royal standing, a Gothic Vercingetorix, just as Athanaric had been a Gothic *vergobretos.*[101]

Although the exact details of the *foedus* of 382 are not known, the following points can be discerned: (1) the Goths became subjects of the empire but remained barbarians and as foreigners had no *connubium* (right of marriage) with the Romans; (2) in the northern part of the dioceses of Dacia and Thrace, that is, between the Danube and the Balkan mountains, they were allotted tax-exempt land (γῆ), though not property in the Roman legal sense; (3) the assigned land remained Roman sovereign territory but the Goths were considered autonomous; (4) the Goths were obligated to render military assistance to the Romans, but their own tribal leaders were to receive only subordinate commands; thus the Balth Alaric in 394 stood under the supreme command of a Roman general; (5) as partners in the agreement the Goths lived with the provincials "under one roof"; historians have no doubt rightly inferred from this provision the use of the Roman institution of *hospitalitas* (billeting of soldiers); the Goths' livelihood was no doubt to be secured by the land that was assigned to them and that they had to work themselves. This solution did not have much of a future and was in any case radically different from the later modalities of settlement in Gaul and Italy; (6) the Gothic federates were entitled to annual payments in an unknown amount.

One can compare the treaty of 382 with the arrangements of 376. Nevertheless, there are significant differences: (1) in 376 the Goths were to be settled not along the Danube but in central Thrace; (2) they would not be settled as a compact group; and (3) they would not constitute an autonomous Gothia, a state within the state. All these points were conceded to the federates in 382; in addition, they were exempted from taxation and received a yearly payment. On the positive side there was the emperor's hope that the Gothic treaty partners would behave as well as Ulfilas's people and the other "previously settled [Roman] Goths"; moreover, he was hoping that they would be a substantial boost to the military forces along the Danubian frontier.[102]

As imperial federates the Moesian Goths behaved not much differently than they had in their homeland across the Danube. In serving the emperor they were as reliable as was (or seemed to be) compatible with their own interests. Among themselves in their settlement area and with the Roman provincial population they kept peace to the extent that this was at all possible for a barbarian society. If the Goths felt that their rights had been violated by the Romans, in whose midst they lived, they took the law into their own hands and settled the issue according to their own customs, since the regular Roman "judge was far away" from autonomous Gothia.[103] Theodosius was remarkably tolerant of the Gothic mentality, which must have seemed utterly lawless to imperial authorities. When Gerontius, the commander in Scythia minor, took action against the Gothic federates, whether justified or not, he was taken to task for it by the emperor and could barely save his own skin.[104] Yet no judgment was rendered on the quarrel between Fravitta and Eriulf which broke out at the imperial table and ended with the slaying of Eriulf, the Christian enemy of Rome, by the speaker of the pro-Roman "Gothic party," Fravitta, who was a determined pagan. After the murder the imperial guards merely separated the fighting Goths: the lives of the federate warriors had simply become too valuable.[105]

As for the defense of the frontier along the lower Danube, it served in equal measure the interests of the empire and the Visigothic federates, who in this way protected their own settlement areas. The Huns had not yet consolidated their power north of the river. Time and again "Scythians" tried to break loose from the Hunnic grip and cross the Roman borders. During the winter months of 384/385—or perhaps in the year after—unnamed "barbarians"—perhaps Goths—crossed the frozen Danube and arrived in the area at the mouth of the river. But apart from the occupation of the small site of Halmyris, at Lake Halmyris, nothing is known about this event.[106] The defense of the frontier was strained more severely in 386. In the vast expanses of the "northland" a polyethnic confederation had arisen around a Greutungian core commanded by the chieftain Odotheus. He led his bands across the Danube and into Thrace, where the general Promotus was in command. With the help of warriors proficient in the barbarian language—probably Visigothic federates—the Roman general lured the newcomers into a trap. Some barbarians were killed, others were taken captive on strict imperial orders. But Theodosius, who was nearby, separated the survivors from the Goths in Moesia and settled them in Phrygia.[107] The emperor did not necessarily take this step in order to prevent a possible strengthening of the Visigoths; it is entirely possible that he was eager to maintain peace between the two Gothic groups. The Greutungi of Alatheus, for example, had separated again from Fritigern's Goths of their own volition, without any Roman involvement.[108] Tribal differences continued to be responsible for the separation of various groups from the main tribe. Even after 376 there were Tervingian groups north of the Danube. But neither the new Visigoths south of the river nor the new Hunnic rulers of the *barbaricum* had an interest in allowing the independent existence of these bands.

The fall of Athanaric in the second half of 380 and the death of Gainas in late 400 reveal to what extent independent groups were seen as troublemakers and were fought by both the imperial Goths and the Huns outside the empire. These two events also mark the end of the period of a relatively pluralistic tribal development.[109] Thereafter only two ethnogeneses were possible: that of the Roman Goths within the empire and that of the Hunnic Goths at its doorstep.

During this same period, between 383 and 392, the Princess Gaatha traveled from a transdanubian Gothia into the Roman Empire and back again. This bypassing of the Gothic federates in Moesia, probably for political reasons, throws a revealing light on a group of Tervingi linked to the name of Arimir, Gaatha's son. The Gothic lady, accompanied by her daughter with the Latin name Dulcilla, brought relics of martyrs to Cyzicus and then returned home with her companion Wella, while her daughter remained behind. Upon their return Wella was stoned to death by pagan Goths. Little had thus changed since the time of Athanaric. The majority of the Tervingi north of the Danube still linked hostility toward Rome with hostility toward Christians, despite the Romanization and Christianization of some of the highest members of their own upper class. Meanwhile the Gothic colony in and around Constantinople grew in size, and the newly raised Eastern army consisted increasingly of Goths.[110]

As had once happened during the early phase of Athanaric's career, the Gothic federates in Moesia were soon involved in internal Roman affairs.

Two acts of usurpation took on a fateful significance: first, the final phase and epilogue of the career of Maximus and, second, a few years later the pagan reaction of Eugenius. In 388 Theodosius could no longer delay the confrontation with Maximus and his well-armed Western forces. The imperial army was composed of contingents of the most diverse ethnic backgrounds and must have been a rather colorful troop, claims to the contrary notwithstanding. Moesian Goths undoubtedly marched among the unnamed tribes. By the Pannonian federates are probably meant the Goths, Alans, and Huns who served as horsemen in the Eastern army. They decided the outcome of the first engagement at Siscia-Sisak on the Sava with a surprise cavalry charge reminiscent of Adrianople. Shortly thereafter Theodosius won a victory in the battle of Poetovio-Ptuj. Maximus's resistance collapsed like a house of cards; the usurper himself was executed on August 28, 388.[111] Nevertheless, the consequences of his usurpation were not immediately undone. The propaganda of Maximus had infected the Eastern army even before it had set out westward. Unnamed barbarians, among them no doubt also Moesian Goths, deserted when it became known that they had been bribed by the usurper. They entrenched themselves in the barely accessible area around the estuary of the Axius-Vardar west of Thessalonica. Even when the emperor returned to the East in the middle of 391 the deserters in the Macedonian marshes were still a dangerous troublespot.[112]

In the late summer or fall of 391 polyethnic confederations crossed the Balkan range and advanced southward; it is likely that they had contact with the barbarians at the Axius.[113] The leader of this expedition was the Moesian Goth Alaric, whose name appears here for the first time. And for the first time since 382 the treaty between Theodosius and the Gothic federates was broken. Fravitta and Eriulf had quarreled about the wisdom of such a move. But now the decision had been made. The emperor himself at the head of his army marched out to meet the invaders, but just as in Macedonia in 379 he once again neglected to protect his army on the march. The Roman troops were caught by surprise at the Hebrus/Maritsa river and suffered such a serious defeat that the capable Promotus barely managed to extract his emperor from the fighting. As a reward for his valor Promotus, who had defeated the Greutungi in 386, was given the command to continue the campaign against Alaric, which cost him his life before the year was out.[114] Promotus's successor was Stilicho, who defeated and encircled Alaric in 392 but on orders from the emperor let him go. And so these two adversaries began that cat-and-mouse game that is as weary to the reader as it was shocking to contemporaries and that would repeat itself four times between the years 392 and 402. One is tempted to believe in a literary convention when one reads Claudian's description of the events at the Maritsa (392),[115] at Thessalian Larissa (395),[116] on the plateau of Pholoë in Elis (397),[117] after Pollentia, and finally at Verona (402).[118] But there is no doubt that all these near-catastrophes for Alaric and his Goths did in fact take place. It is not only today that some have tried to explain these seemingly absurd events with the help of a sort of "stab in the back" legend, making either Rufinus or Stilicho responsible for the betrayal.[119] Very fitting in this regard is the characterization of these events by Orosius: "I will keep silent about King Alaric, who was so often defeated and surrounded together with his Goths and yet was set free again every time."[120] To be sure, there were already ancient observers who attributed Stilicho's failure to lack of discipline among his forces and to Gothic gold and Gothic promises that had a big impact on the barbarian soldiers in the Roman army.[121]

All these considerations, however, start from the false assumption that Roman policy at the end of the fourth century still had the option—indeed, that it was in its interest—to destroy an army of imperial federates. Gratian, for example, was killed fighting the army of Maximus; nevertheless, his coemperor Theodosius granted the rebellious troops an amnesty after the death of their leader because he needed them as soldiers.[122] Stilicho could just as little afford to do without Alaric's Goths, the most Romanized barbarians of his time.[123] Even when Theodosius and the men who after him determined imperial policy had long been dead, the official attitude toward the Gothic federates had changed very little.[124] It is instead likely that some feeling of solidarity developed between the Romans and their barbarian federates against the barbarians beyond the frontiers. In any case, they worked together in defeating the "wild Getae," the "dirty Huns," and the "savage Alans,"[125] a cooperation attested by the fall of Odotheus and Radagaisus and even at the battle on the Catalaunian Fields in 451.[126] The imperial government could neither destroy nor drive back the barbarians and federates it had admitted, as Synesius of Cyrene demanded in the style of the old pagan Libanius or as Ammianus Marcellinus might occasionally have dreamt about. There was no meaningful alternative to the policy of appeasement toward the imperial, assimilated foreigners. Despite their panegyrical intentions, Themistius and Pacatus showed greater insight when they advocated the Theodosian approach.[127]

Listed among the peoples who supposedly fought on Alaric's side in 391 we "find" many who no longer existed. We are dealing here with one of those "catalogs of peoples" common to late antique ethnography, a catalog in which an author's literary knowledge can be distinguished from accurate observations only with great difficulty. For example, Promotus is said to have been killed fighting the Bastarni, and this confuses us. The Bastarni had disappeared for an entire century, and now they are mentioned as allies of Alaric? They are thus either deserters from *laeti* settlements in northern Thrace or merely a name the author gleaned from his readings, like the Daci, Getae, Gelones, Massagetes who are also mentioned. Huns and Sarmatians appear as comrades-in-arms of the Vesi. Be that as it may, we may safely infer from this statement that the Moesian federates had been joined by migrants from the transdanubian north.[128]

In 391 it was still possible to drive Alaric back, and the old order seemed reestablished. When Theodosius tried to put down the usurpation of Eugenius by force of arms in 394, the Gothic federates followed his command. Their contingents must have represented the greater part of the arms-bearing men of the Goths if it is true that they provided twenty thousand soldiers. Alaric led them, but he received neither an independent command nor a Roman military office. Instead he was placed under the command of Gainas, who was a fellow-tribesman of Alaric's but had "no lineage." Though still in his early twenties, the Balth felt slighted. The events of late summer 391 fully justified Theodosius's suspicions concerning Alaric, but the latter's disgruntlement was a factor not to be underestimated in the future policies of the Gothic federates in Moesia.[129]

The dissatisfaction of one of the noblest chieftains and the crisis that took hold of the entire tribe when shortly thereafter the Huns crossed the Danube for the first time raised fears of more serious problems. During the last months of Theodosius's life the special relationship between the emperor and his Goths was exposed to a test it did not survive. On September 5 and 6, 394, Theodosius defeated the usurper Eugenius; the battle took place at the Frigidus-Vipava, a left tributary of the Isonzo. On its descent from the Hrušica ("Birnbaumer Wald") the Eastern army had to struggle through the narrow pass of the Hubl. Arbogast, the supreme commander of the Western army, awaited in the plain below the undeployed columns of the imperial forces. The first day of battle ended with dreadful losses to Theodosius's vanguard, which was composed of Goths. Half of them are said to have been killed. It began to appear that the commanders of the imperial army had planned this decimation of the Gothic troops. One can imagine the rising discontent among the Gothic federates. Nevertheless, they remained with the combined Roman army, at least after January 17, 395, that is, after the death of Theodosius; it was Stilicho who eventually discharged them. Then, before the end of January, they began their march home, undoubtedly already under Alaric's leadership. The circumstances of their march further increased the existing tensions. The supplies for the Eastern army had been used up; apparently they had been meant to serve only as one-way provisions. The returning Goths therefore had to requisition supplies, no doubt taking more than the absolute minimum of what they needed. Thus their march through Illyricum, including Dalmatia, quickly turned into open plundering. Fortunately for the provincials, the Goths had little time to do a thorough job.[130]

The Balkan Campaigns of 395–401

The death of Theodosius annulled the *foedus* of 382, since the emperor as the primary party to the treaty had dropped out. But in 395 no one seemed honestly interested in the alliance any longer. The Visigoth Gainas led the regular Eastern army under the supreme command of Stilicho; for that very reason Alaric and his former federates could not be kept in service. But the Balth managed to lead his Visigothic contingents back home to lower Moesia in less than ten weeks, plundering southern Pannonia, parts of Dalmatia, and all of upper Moesia along the way, and finally to persuade the Goths at home to join him in Thrace. Stilicho reacted to this Gothic rebellion by the middle of spring 395, mobilizing the combined army of the Eastern and Western courts. Such a rapid succession of events would be unthinkable unless both sides had been preparing for them.[131] It would be easier to understand what happened if the Moesian federates at home had also been urging an attack, even before Alaric had returned. And in fact it does appear that both the units with which Alaric had marched down the Danube and the Goths who had remained behind in northern Thrace revolted at the same time. The returning troops had to hurry to reach Moesian Gothia, or what was left of it.

In the middle of winter 394/395 all of Thrace was ravaged by Hunnic hordes. This was the first time the Huns had crossed the Danube in large numbers. That winter the river was so thickly frozen that the invaders could attack and return across the ice. To be sure, the Hunnic winter campaign into Europe was only a short prelude to the events of the following summer, when Asia Minor was assaulted by hordes coming from the Caucasus. Nevertheless, the Goths must have felt seriously threatened.[132] There was probably no danger that the river would lose its protective function every winter, although the Goths could hardly rely on the hope that the "frozen Danube" was only a literary convention. Already a decade earlier unnamed barbarians had taken advantage of the lakes and swamps at the mouth of Danube, which froze more easily than flowing water. But those who crossed at that time were only part of a small-scale expedition of individual groups.[133] And even in 391 contingents of Hunnic cavalry were probably most welcome to the Goths, who then launched a joint attack on the Romans.[134] But now there was ominous evidence for the growth of Hunnic power north of the Danube and the Black Sea. The Huns consolidated their dominion and in a sweep of solid expansion reached the lower Danube.[135] While Gothic warriors were fighting in foreign countries their own land lay unprotected. In order to conquer the West the emperor exposed the frontier of the Eastern Empire and practically invited the Huns in.[136] The Goths were thus doubly affected by the "traitorous" policy of the imperial government. Decimated in battle and threatened at home, the Gothic federates could well ask themselves whether the alliance with the empire, which was supposed to guarantee the existence of the tribe on Roman territory, was still valid. In 395 the mood among the Goths was probably much like it had been in 376: the Goths were exasperated and ready for just about any action.

Fear of the dreaded Huns would also explain the seemingly aimless and unplanned wanderings of the following years. The movements of the Goths were actually based on a clear strategic concept: they were fighting for a homeland that would be both militarily safe from the Huns and economically healthy. Thus all the dwelling places the Goths sought in the lands of the Balkan peninsula had one thing in common: they were protected by the mountains and were close to the sea; in other words, they were places where the Huns could not follow them but where provisioning with food could be guaranteed even if the actual settlements could not feed the newly arrived people. This strategy, however, was conditional upon the availability of transport ships and the absence of a Roman blockade.[137] In 416 the *patricius* Constantius was able, largely through a naval blockade, to force the Visigoths to surrender.

Led by Alaric, the former federates left the Danubian provinces. The only ones who stayed behind in Thrace were Gothi minores and individuals who had previously split off from the main tribe.[138] The goal was Constantinople, where Alaric wanted to conclude a new and substantially better treaty. To back up his demands he led his plundering army right up to the gates of the imperial city. Stilicho's keenest rival, the praetorian prefect and top imperial advisor Rufinus, declared himself willing to negotiate and went unaccompanied into Alaric's camp. Rufinus probably had long-standing ties with the federates, who supposedly left his land holdings untouched. In any case, he understood their mentality; he went to meet Alaric in Gothic costume and military dress and he concluded a *foedus* with the Gothic leader. It is possible that in the treaty Alaric was granted a high military post, perhaps that of *magister militum per Illyricum,* which would have overturned the most humiliating clause in the treaty of 382. In this way the prefect brought about the withdrawal of the Goths from the diocese of Thrace, with the result that the direct threat to Constantinople diminished.[139] Of course this masterly diplomatic move came at the expense of eastern Illyricum: at first Greece—the diocese of Macedonia—suffered from this arrangement, while its neighboring diocese of Dacia was spared for the time being.[140] Alaric and his army then marched to his assigned region. He probably moved westward on the coastal route, which is still today much traveled; then he swung toward the south and only stopped again when his attempt to break through the valley of Tempe was repulsed with heavy losses. But the Goths were able to get around the defense of the Thessalian militias and penetrate the plain of Larissa by moving along the foothills of Mount Olympus. Once they had reached the plain, they immediately entrenched themselves behind their circle of wagons to await the arrival of the expected Roman armies under Stilicho's command.[141]

The Romans and the Goths must have stood facing each other for several months, during which time Stilicho did not seek battle nor did Alaric regain his mobility. Eventually Stilicho was forced to give up his position in Thessaly on orders from Arcadius, and he withdrew to Italy with only the Western troops of the army. In recognizing the authority of the eastern emperor, the commander-in-chief of the West also bound himself to return the Eastern army and moreover to give up the two eastern Illyrian dioceses. Though this did not put an end to the troublesome quarrel over these dioceses, Rufinus was already giving orders for the next steps to protect Greece. But he met with no success: Thermopylae was taken, there were rumors of treachery, and the Goths overran Boeotia. Thebes held out, but Piraeus was captured. Athens was able to buy off the enemy with huge payments that impressed Alaric's people no doubt far more than the appearance of Pallas Athene and Achilles on the walls of the city. The Goths then moved into the Peloponnesus. Along the way they plundered the temple of Demeter at Eleusis, but inexplicably they met with no resistance at the isthmus. The largely unfortified cities of the peninsula now lay open before them: Corinth, Argos, and Sparta were sacked, only the small town of Tegea in Arcadia was able to defend itself successfully thanks to the initiative of a local noble. The Goths also reached Mycenae and Olympia. For more than a year Alaric and his hordes remained in the Peloponnesus, creating the impression that they intended to settle there.[142]

In the spring of 397 Stilicho again marched east with strong forces. He was to assist the emperor Arcadius against the Huns and Alaric. Stilicho landed on the Peloponnesus on the southern coast of the Gulf of Corinth and began to outmaneuver the Goths.[143] On the plateau of Pholoë in Elis he was able to encircle the Goths, who began to suffer from lack of water, hunger, and epidemics. Everyone expected the decisive blow, but once again—for the third time—it did not come. Stilicho entered into certain unknown agreements with Alaric and withdrew. Several reasons were given for this decision: the unreliability of the Roman army, the revolt of the African governor Gildo—which, however, broke out only after Stilicho's retreat—or in general the quarrel between the two parts of the empire. In 397 Stilicho was declared a public enemy of the Eastern empire. All this must have caused considerable uncertainty, which could have led Stilicho to fail to drive home the victory that was so close at hand. The assertion, however, that Stilicho was at that time pursuing his own policy toward Alaric is not plausible.[144]

THE *FOEDUS* OF 397 AND THE SETTLEMENT OF THE GOTHS IN MACEDONIA

Alaric waited until Stilicho had left, then broke the agreements and crossed into Epirus. There he wrought such havoc that he forced the imperial government to come to terms with him. Nonetheless, in 397 Arcadius and Alaric entered into a *foedus,* which allowed the Goths to settle in *Emathia tellus,* the central Macedonian heartland between the Haliacmon and Axius rivers, in other words, exactly where in 474 the Ostrogoths of Thiudimir and Theodoric were to be settled. At the same time Alaric was probably appointed *magister militum per Illyricum* rather than merely *dux.* In any case, the purpose of the arrangement was twofold: first, the intention was not so much to place Illyrian troops under Alaric's command as to integrate him into the Roman hierarchy; second, the imperial authorities wanted to designate the Roman territory that was to support the Goths. In this way an institutional model was created which would be used again in the future. Within a larger Roman administrative unit, which was placed by imperial orders under the authority of a barbarian leader, a few relatively small centers of compact barbarian settlements were formed. Since the federates came under military administration, it was natural that their leader would be given a high military post. But even as commander-in-chief of Illyricum Alaric would not have been able by himself to safeguard the survival of his tribe. For this the tribe also needed the support of the civil bureaucracy, which was responsible for arming and provisioning the military. Thus, in order to preserve the infrastructure of Illyricum after the Gothic settlement the emperor had to institutionalize Alaric's authority. A *magister militum per Illyricum,* however, stood in rank beneath the Illyrian praetorian prefect, the head of the region's civil administration. Details about the stay of the migrating tribe are known only from Claudian, but even this poet could not avoid Roman political terminology. We read that Alaric conducted the civil administration in the region. The Illyrians are also said to have made him their *dux* and to have placed him in a position to control "with legal authority" (*legitimo iussu*) the weapons factories and storage depots as well as to collect raw materials as taxes from the cities. Arcadius was certainly concerned "to legalize and thus control the de facto rule of a Germanic prince on Roman soil." But the Eastern Roman government did not do this at the price of violating the constitution. Just recently, on July 9, 397, the emperor had defined the authority of the praetorian prefect for precisely those administrative functions that were handed over to Alaric a few weeks later. No commander of the army, let alone a *dux,* could legitimately exercise these functions unless Constantinople, in bestowing on him the military office, recognized a barbarian mandate that the tribe had granted him for both war *and* peace. Constantinople could thus avoid the question of what should be done in this case with the late Roman practice of separating the spheres of military and civil authority. But for us the question arises: in what capacity did Alaric lead the Goths and what title did he hold? [145]

ALARIC'S ELEVATION TO THE KINGSHIP

The decision as to whether Alaric I was a king follows a sort of fashion. Reinhard Wenskus in 1961 not only affirmed the royal elevation of the Balth but even depicted it as typical and exemplary for the future Latin-barbarian military kingship. At present, the older scholarly opinion denying Alaric's royal status is returning to undeserved favor. [146] Scholars who insist that the Tervingian ancestors of the Visigoths did not know the greater kingship and at the same time reject Alaric's election as king are forced to assume that the introduction of the new institution "happened" to Alaric's Goths [147] somewhere and sometime on the march, because no one doubts any longer that Athaulf, Alaric's brother-in-law and successor, was in fact a king. Such an argument seems illogical in itself, and its justification certainly is. One can in fact quarrel about the value of the reports in the two Gothic histories—[*Alaricus*] *ordinatus super se rex; rex creatus; regem sibi constituerunt* [*Alaricum Gothi*].[148] It is, however, far less easy to downplay the explanation of the *Origo Gothica* that Alaric was made king principally because of his Balthic background: for this statement establishes a connection to Athanaric and the "royal race of the Scythians," who had occupied the first rank among the Vesi, had held the Tervingian judgeship for at least three generations, and had possibly already proved its royal ability among the Pontic Heruli. Alaric I was a namesake of the Herulian king whom Ermanaric defeated, so it is possible that he was named after him.[149] Moreover, a Roman poet tells us that Alaric came from the Danubian island of Peuke, and though this need not be taken literally, it does make it more likely that the Balth had a Pontic rather than a Muntenian-Moldavian origin.[150] In any case, he was not born inside the borders of the empire; perhaps Alaviv was Alaric's father.[151] Finally, we must investigate what name Roman contemporaries gave the Gothic prince or, in other words, whether Alaric appeared to them as a monarchical king.[152]

Before making decisions of greater importance, Alaric had to consult the representatives of his people; compared to the time of Fritigern, nothing had changed in this regard.[153] Even after 395 the successors of the Tervingian *reiks* did not voluntarily give up their duty and right to participate in the decision-making process. But under Alaric I the gradual centralization of power and the curbing of independent authority had begun.[154] Especially valuable is the testimony of Olympiodorus, whose knowledge of barbarian institutions was based on close examination and personal experience. During an embassy to the Huns before Attila's time, he discovered among them a large number of chiefs, subrulers, and leaders of subgroups. He gave them the same name he had given the Pannonian Gothic prince who had fallen victim to Athaulf: ῥήξ [read: *rēx*]. This leads one to think that Olympiodorus still knew the Gothic word *reiks* [read also: *rēx*] in its original meaning.[155] But his extant work contains not a single passage that uses the term ῥήξ [read: rēx] for the leader of a large barbarian group. Whoever rules a whole tribe, φυλή, is a tribal ruler, φύλαρχος, if he is not altogether called *hegemon,* which refers to a tribal mandate of wide authority. From Alaric I to Valia, all Visigothic "monarchs" were either a φύλαρχος or a ἡγεμών.[156] But the same names were also given to Gundahar, who had asserted himself as sole ruler of the Burgundians against a number of petty kings.[157] Olympiodorus's terminology permits only one conclusion: either all tribal rulers mentioned were representatives of the new greater kingship or none of them. A difference in rank among them cannot be detected.

The differentiation between a multiplicity of ῥῆγες and a single φύλαρχος reveals the fundamental change in political terminology since the days when

Ulfilas translated the Bible and Eunapius described the Tervingian refugees of 376. At that time the φυλή corresponded to a tribal subgroup, namely, the *kuni* of biblical Gothic, which was ruled over by a *reiks*.[158] But the migration dissolved the Tervingian community of descent, with the exception of the clan of the Balthi.[159] The confederation on the northern bank of the Danube which had been divided into *kunja* turned into one people on the move under Balthic leadership.[160] The Goths appeared like a single φυλή under a single *reiks,* Alaric, and even like a body of royal followers—structured after the decimal system—whom observers called the Alaric Goths.[161] The process of "leveling" was no doubt lengthy and painful. Not a few Goths from the leading stratum must have still believed they were as much princes as Alaric and had the same right to independent authority. But except for the case of Sarus, an *eparchos* of the Goths, we hear of no open resistance to Alaric's rule.[162]

Ulfilas's Bible kept teaching the Goths through the example of the Chosen People that "anyone who makes himself *thiudans* opposes the authority of the emperor." Three verses later, in that part of the Gothic gospel of St. John which has been lost, it must have said: "We have no *thiudans* except the emperor!"[163] Consistent with this attitude is the Moesian Goths' revering of the emperor as their *thiudans*. Because the tribal structure of the Danubian Goths did not know a monarchical king, it was not difficult for the Tervingian federates to submit to the authority of the "Roman king."[164] Especially Theodosius, that mighty emperor of the army whom the Fritigern Goths had followed "because of his ability and kindness,"[165] must have been for them the quintessential *thiudans*-emperor. But Theodosius was dead, his successor a child. Who would now satisfy the need of the Gothic federates for food and security? A rebellion was inevitable if the empire failed in its obligation toward "its" Goths.

In this situation Alaric appears a *tyrannus Geticus,* an apt description of his position. The designation of Alaric as "Gothic usurper" was an institutional novelty,[166] a designation that in the age of usurpations against the rule of "child-emperors" says everything. The Romans conceded to Alaric his claim to exercise civil and military authority inside the empire and to take the place of an augustus—a claim that should not be taken less seriously because of its presumption.[167] This claim was raised on the basis of a tribal mandate and in order to safeguard the tribe's ethnic identity, but it needed imperial recognition: ever since the days of Constantine the Great such recognition was seldom granted, but whoever received it was a *rex gentium,* a king.[168] Alaric, however, was not made *thiudans* in place of the emperor. Just as the φυλή now represented the entire tribal group, its ruler had become a monarchical *reiks*. The enormous increase in the importance of this biblical Gothic term can be explained largely by the Latinization of the Goths' political language. Very soon no difference was seen between *rex* and *reiks*. Moreover, Ulfilas had already understood the dominion over the peoples as *reikinon thiudom*. Thus the new Gothic monarch did not become a *thiudans*.[169] He was a greater *reiks,* whereas a *thiudans* ruled in heaven.

When the Goths penetrated more deeply into the Roman Empire, they needed a centralized authority; in other words, the Goths had to develop precisely the kind of "office" whose occupant the Romans called a *tyrannus Geticus*. The previous twenty years had shown that monarchical leadership was needed even after a direct threat had been overcome or a current campaign concluded. Not only a defeat but also too great a victory could cause the dissolution of the tribe, everyone going where he liked best.[170] It was only as the holder of a tribal mandate that was absolute and unlimited in duration—precisely as a Gothic king—that Alaric had the right to declare the "escape to the Romans"[171] a criminal act of desertion and to inflict punishment when the occasion arose. Until this time even Gothic chiefs changed sides at will and for their own advantage and conducted feuds in the accustomed fashion.[172] Such options and alternatives, however, were not open to a Gothic king. After 395 Alaric could no longer join the Romans because they would have regarded him as a usurper.[173] He did have contact with the Roman leadership, which was aware of his personal wishes and gave them positive credit.[174] But Alaric himself no longer had Fritigern's option of entering into secret negotiations with an emperor, negotiations that, regardless of how we look at them, included in their calculations a weakening of the Goths.[175] All that a Gothic king could do for the empire was to offer the emperor help against all his enemies, combined with the demand for a fusion of Romans and Goths into one people.[176] But to put this plan into practice, Alaric first had to find an emperor who would go along. Initially none of the "collaborating" usurpers could fill that role. But from the moment the Visigoths established a monarchy, the possibility of splitting the *gens* into separate groups diminished, so that at the end of the migration all that was left was one political identity, and this was embodied by the younger Balths.[177]

FRAVITTA AND ERIULF

Fravitta and Eriulf were the leaders of two Visigothic groups whose hostility to each other grew out of opposing attitudes toward the Roman Empire.

Eriulf, the chieftain of the Christian majority, hated the Romans and represented the "Gothic party" hostile to assimilation. This group relied on a common oath never to seek reconciliation with the empire. Nevertheless, Eriulf appeared at the rich table of the emperor Theodosius and indulged liberally in the wine. Until shortly before his death, Athanaric had been more steadfast in his opposition to Rome. The pagan Fravitta, in contrast, supported assimilation and worked for adherence to the treaty the Goths had concluded with Theodosius and had affirmed on oath. Over this issue a quarrel arose in the course of which Fravitta killed his opponent with his own hands. Eriulf's followers struck back and a general brawl ensued. The fight had begun at the emperor's table, but Theodosius was "not very angry about it."[178] Fravitta and Eriulf as leaders of their respective groups remind us of Athanaric and Fritigern. Yet they do not seem to have possessed a tribal mandate. Rather, the bloody feud between Fravitta and Eriulf reveals signs of the disintegration that afflicted the *foedus* of 382 from the early 390s. Zosimus probably dated the conflict correctly to the eve of the war with Eugenius. Alaric's first rebellion in 391 is apparently also connected to these events.[179]

Fravitta was young—we are not told Eriulf's age—when Theodosius courted him and other chieftains. He had at that time already married a Roman woman with imperial permission which indicates that he did not yet have Roman citizenship. The young Goth Fravitta was of noble birth, a fact his Roman father-in-law, who took pride in his own ancestry, especially appreciated. Immediately after the murder of Eriulf—a deed by which Fravitta cut himself off from the tribe—he probably went over entirely into Roman service. His subsequent fate, however, is not reported by the sources until after the death of Theodosius. Simultaneous with Alaric's election began Fravitta's rapid rise in the services of Arcadius. The Goth gained the highest Roman military offices, finally even the consulate, which was bestowed on him in gratitude for his suppression of dangerous Gothic unrest and which made him a Roman citizen. Thus his career resembles that of a Modares or a Munderic, although he was more successful than either of them. Fravitta, the pagan friend of Rome, was regarded as a hero especially by the Neoplatonist Eunapius and his successor Zosimus. After the victory against his rebellious tribesman Gainas, Fravitta asked for no other privilege than to be allowed to continue living as a real "Greek," that is, as a pagan. His rival Eriulf, however, a Christian who hated Rome, embodied the fusion of barbarian culture and the new faith.[180] Zosimus was to follow his model Eunapius in his judgment of these men, and even Edward Gibbon still accepted it.[181]

GAINAS AND TRIBIGILD

A tribal history of the Goths depicts primarily the process of ethnogenesis and neglects the fate of those people who cut themselves off from it. The Theodosian policy of reconciliation had induced many Goths, among them especially Visigoths, to associate themselves directly with Rome. Nevertheless, quite a few Gothic magnates who seemed entirely integrated as Roman imperial officials kept open the alternative of a barbarian career. Thus they could improve their position in the Roman hierarchy by using the pressure of a position of tribal authority or vice versa. Yet there never was the possibility of making a complete exchange of Rome for Gothia; whenever this step was taken, it inevitably led to destruction. The prime example for such a quid pro quo is the activities of the Vesian Gainas and his relative, the Greutungian Tribigild.[182] The scene of action was Constantinople, the surrounding Thracian lands, and Asia Minor. Here, in the heartland of the Eastern empire, there were many Goths even among the free and unfree lower classes. Whenever barbarian officers rebelled they could therefore count on support not only from the Gothic troops in the Roman army but also from settled Gothic *coloni* and slaves. At the same time the successes of Alaric's Goths aroused great hopes among all the other Gothic peoples of the eastern half of the empire. They all wanted to raise their socioeconomic and legal status to a level equal to that of the favored "royal" federates of Illyricum.[183]

In 399 the Greutungi settled in Phrygia thought their time had come to act. This group was composed mainly of the survivors of the Odotheus group that had been defeated in 386. From among their ranks a "Roman legion" was recruited; from this we might infer the existence of Greutungian-Ostrogothic cavalry units, similar to the well-recorded Tervingian-Vesian units.[184] In any case, the leader of the Greutungian horsemen was the *comes* Tribigild, who had done a great service fighting the Huns in 398.[185] When his demand for an appropriate reward was insultingly rejected by the imperial government, he rebelled and began to lay waste the provinces of Asia Minor. His victorious advance came to a temporary halt in Pisidia. The Greutungi were lured into an ambush by a local militia and disastrously defeated. Tribigild himself with three hundred men managed to escape only because an officer of the Roman regulars that were supposed to support the irregulars allowed himself to be bribed and cooperated with the Goths.[186] This event shows how problematic it was to fight rebellious barbarians with barbarian troops. There were many dissatisfied Goths in Asia Minor, the Roman army was full of them, making it possible for Tribigild to use their presence to his advantage whenever the Romans marched against him. After another Roman army had been defeated, or, rather, had changed sides, Gainas was charged with conducting the war against Tribigild. The maneuvers of Gainas are difficult to understand: the Roman observers, at any rate, saw in them the game of two traitors who avoided hurting each other.[187] Tribigild no doubt wanted to gain a position similar to that of Alaric, which would have entailed the creation of a Gothic people in Asia Minor.[188] Gainas, however, rebelled to stay alive; his kinsman Tribigild, along with other barbarian princes, was for him probably only a means to that end.[189]

In the winter of 399/400 Gainas dropped his disguise, joined the rebels in Asia Minor and crossed the Bosporus into Europe. Whereas Tribigild was killed shortly thereafter while fighting in Thrace, Gainas marched to Constantinople and occupied the city. There he soon showed great insecurity: his policies seemed half-hearted, brutal, and short-sighted. Constantinople was simply too complicated for a military man who, despite his high imperial offices, had deep down always remained a subordinate troop commander. It is possible that his low birth handicapped him. At any rate, he did not understand life in the big city. The demand of the zealous Arian Gainas that the Goths be given a Catholic church met with vigorous opposition from John Chrysostom and aroused the displeasure of the populace. Either Gainas did in fact order banks to be plundered or someone deliberately spread the rumor that he was planning to confiscate the cash boxes of the money changers. Then all of a sudden the imperial palace went up in flames. The general unrest led to street fighting that turned into a panic. Only one half of Gainas's troops, which were numerically far inferior to the urban populace, were stationed in the city. In an attempt to unite his troops, Gainas committed serious blunders. The crowd disrupted the retreat of the troops and launched a manhunt after the Goths. On July 12, 400 seven hundred Goths fled into a church, not, as one would assume, an Arian but an Orthodox church of the Goths near the palace. There they were surrounded and on the personal order of the emperor Arcadius either cut down or burned to death. Gainas, however, managed to escape; his attempt to gain a foothold in Thrace was thwarted by the locals. Thereafter he wanted to cross back into Asia Minor with his troops, because he could still count on a strong Gothic element among the population there. But the barbarians had no ships; their crossing turned into a disaster when Fravitta, Gainas's successor and fellow tribesman,[190] appeared with a Roman fleet and destroyed the Goths' primitive rafts. In judging the events that then followed the ancient observers reveal considerable confusion. If we believe Zosimus, who offers the most detailed description, the Gainas story developed in this way: Gainas next turned north, marched through Thrace, and sought to return to the transdanubian homeland. Even Roman soldiers followed him all the way to the Danube, but he had them killed after entering the *barbaricum*.[191] The accounts generally state that Gainas was intercepted and killed by the Huns under Uldin. The treatment of the Roman soldiers and outbreak of hostilities north of the Danube suggest a different explanation. The Goths probably tried to create at home an independent dominion that the Huns considered a threat to themselves.[192] The returning Vesi could have all too easily become a rallying point for the subjected Gothic peoples. When Gainas was killed in action on December 23, 400,[193] the Hunnic-Gothic war immediately came to an end.

There is a clear and direct connection between the number of existing sources for an event and its significance for contemporaries. Measured by this criterion the Gainas-Tribigild revolt was a scandal of the first order. Although Tribigild was no Alaric, and Gainas too operated amateurishly, if bravely, the shock they caused was enough to bring about in the East a change of policy. Constantinople broke with its hitherto friendly policy toward the Goths. Certainly Gainas as an Arian barbarian did not want to make himself emperor. But his downfall ushered in the new course whose next victim was Fravitta, the conqueror of Gainas.[194] A direct result of this sudden reversal was the cooperation of Rome with Uldin's Huns, and this not only in the East but also in the West. The first known ruler of the European Huns sent the head of Gainas to Constantinople. The package arrived there on January 3, 401, and Uldin was rewarded with presents and a treaty.[195]

The Goths in the Western Empire, 401–418

ALARIC'S ITALIAN WARS

In the fall of 401 the Goths left their Macedonian *patria* in the Illyrian prefecture.[196] Again Alaric broke a *foedus*, but his partner to the treaty, the Eastern imperial government, felt, if anything, relieved, indeed, confirmed in the new policy it had adopted. The fate of Gainas showed the willingness of the new men in power to bring the Hunnic card into play against the Gothic hegemony. Nothing, however, could have made a greater impression on Alaric and his people. Once again the Goths were ready to depart, though they did await the harvest and the end of the hot weather. But Alaric was already invited to attack the West because an invasion by the Vandals and Alans had forced Stilicho to concentrate his troops in Raetia and

Noricum.[197] And so the Macedonian federates marched north past Sirmium and upstream along the Pannonian Sava into Italy. Although this is not mentioned in the sources, along the way Alaric's Goths must have met their Greutungian cousins. The last time they had fought under joint command had been in the battle of the Frigidus. Now they had another opportunity for a joint campaign, and this time they were fighting for themselves. There is some indication that the opportunity was taken, but it is not attested.[198]

By November 18, 401, Alaric was already in Italy, without having encountered any real resistance.[199] If this interpretation is correct, fighting took place only in the area around Duino. There was, however, no defense at the pass through the Julian Alps, the Hrušica; surprisingly enough the military fortifications there were no longer intact or were at least not defended. Still, the defense put up at the Isonzo and Timavo rivers was bound to fail.[200] Thus the Goths advanced almost unopposed as far as Aquileia, which, however, was able to hold out successfully.[201] In the course of the winter the Goths captured several unnamed cities and the plain of Venetia.[202] Next they threatened the capital city of Milan. Apparitions in the sky and millenarian expectations caused great anxiety among the Italian population.[203] In Rome the Aurelian city walls were hastily repaired.[204] Honorius got ready to escape to Gaul, but Stilicho prevailed upon him to stay. The Roman army, strengthened through the addition of Alanic cavalry from Pannonia and newly received Vandal federates, arrived in time to relieve Milan.[205] At the beginning of March 402 Stilicho forced the crossing of the Adda, which compelled Alaric to give up the siege of the capital.[206] The shock caused by the appearance of the Goths before the walls of Milan led to the transfer of the imperial residence to Ravenna, an impregnable city that could easily be supplied by sea.[207]

In February or March 402 the army of the Goths moved westward upstream along the northern bank of the Po. It seemed that they wanted to march into Gaul. But suddenly Alaric crossed the river at its upper course and veered south. His goal was now the Ligurian Apennines, but perhaps also rich Tuscany and Rome itself, as contemporaries claimed.[208] Most likely, though, Alaric was at this time neither in the mood nor able to open a large-scale offensive. On the contrary, he had to try to avoid getting caught between two fronts. From Gaul the Rhenish and Britannic troops were approaching, while Stilicho stood in the rear.[209] The Goths' attempt to take the city of Hasta-Asti on the Tanaro failed, whereupon Alaric's subsequent moves turned into a retreat. The Goths pitched camp upstream, about two kilometers below the estuary of the Stura di Demonte. The town was called Pollentia-Pollenzo, and at some distance from it flows the Urbs-

Orba, a river that bears the name "city" and symbolizes Rome. Here Alaric had a date with destiny.[210]

On Easter Sunday, April 6, 402, Stilicho handed over the supreme command to the pagan Alan leader Saul. He then made a surprise attack on the Goths, who did not expect a battle on such a day.[211] Alaric lost his camp and all the booty; he suffered losses among his foot soldiers but was able to preserve the cavalry intact. In the counterattack the Alans were driven back and Saul was killed. The battle ended in a draw. Stilicho intervened in the action and held the Roman position, allowing the Roman panegyrist to declare him the victor; the Goths, however, moved south into a fortified position in the mountains.[212] Then, as so often before, negotiations were begun. Claudian claims that at that time a regular *foedus* was concluded, which Alaric soon broke again. In fact Claudian was probably trying to use this argument to counter the criticism of those who saw Stilicho's apparent leniency toward Alaric as a sign of treason and incompetence.[213] Thus Claudian contradicts himself in a later passage where he explains that the lenient treatment of the Gothic king was a result of the "constraints of the circumstances."[214] At any rate, Stilicho was able to use diplomatic means to win the victory that armed force denied him. Alaric and his Goths left Italy south of the Po, and not even the Gothic prisoners were returned to him. But near Verona the Gothic king stopped. We do not know exactly why. Did he intend to put pressure on the imperial government in order to regain lost territory or was he at that time already thinking of moving through Raetia into Gaul?[215] It is possible that Stilicho provoked Alaric so as to have an opportunity to silence criticism at home. This time he wanted the Gothic king dead or alive.[216] And so in July or August the second great battle of the year was fought.[217] Again the Alans rushed forward, again they upset Stilicho's tactical concept, and once again the Goths withdrew into a fortified camp in the mountains. But this time Alaric lost his mobility, for Stilicho was able to block the road leading north. The Roman general's trap had closed. As in the days on the plateau of Pholoë, the Gothic army, encircled on a hill near Verona, was plagued by hunger, disease, and desertion. Horsemen and foot soldiers left Alaric in droves;[218] the events after Pollentia repeated themselves on a larger scale.[219] Perhaps Pannonian Ostrogoths were among the deserters, but Visigothic units also left. At this time, at the very latest, Ulfilas, later to become *magister militum,* and the Gothic chief Sarus joined the Romans. Alaric's defeat was probably only the pretext Sarus needed in order to break with the Balthic king.[220]

Without doubt Verona was Alaric's most serious defeat; although he may have been able once again to preserve the core of his tribe, he did suffer great losses.[221] One often reads that Stilicho took Alaric into Roman service at that time, but this is probably not true. The Visigoths abandoned Italy and settled down "in the barbarian land next to Dalmatia and Pannonia."[222] From there they ravaged eastern Illyricum, an area to which the West, however, did not lay claim in the years before 403/404. At this time Honorius was sincerely sorry about what the Visigoths were doing in the Illyricum territory of his imperial brother.[223] Only when Stilicho wanted to break with Constantinople did he persuade Honorius to conclude a *foedus* with the Gothic king and declare him *magister militum per Illyricum*. That decision was a serious violation of the sovereignty of the Eastern empire. Even the prefect of Illyricum was appointed by Ravenna in violation of the Illyrian agreement of the two imperial brothers.[224]

But Stilicho's plans were not carried out. First of all, in 405 the invasion of Radagaisus prevented them from being implemented; but apparently it also upset Alaric's schemes, since he kept quiet.[225] Not until 407 could Stilicho once again think of attacking the Eastern empire. Alaric, who had invaded Epirus after being appointed once again *magister militum* of Illyricum,[226] was to be supported by a fleet. At that very moment the defense of the empire along the Rhine collapsed completely. It seemed impossible to stop the hordes of Alans, Vandals, and Suevi who poured into Gaul,[227] whose desperate population sought salvation from the Britannic usurper Constantine.[228] To make matters worse, rumors of Alaric's death spread in Ravenna.[229] Stilicho now abandoned his hostility toward the East, and as early as 408 the Eastern imperial consul was also recognized in the West. Though the policy of reconciliation between East and West made only slow progress,[230] Alaric and his Goths had now become unnecessary. That lead to a break of the *foedus,* whereupon Aëtius and the other hostages who had since 405 guaranteed the treaty between the empire and the Goths[231] probably returned home. In the spring of 408 the Goths once again marched against the West. They turned first toward Emona-Laibach, which, as a city in the Julian Alps, already belonged to Italy. The Goths did not advance farther, however, but occupied both the Norican part of modern-day Slovenia, Carinthia, and southern Styria and the adjoining upper Pannonian area of western Hungary.[232] At the same time Alaric demanded an indemnity of four thousand pounds of gold, threatening to invade Italy if he failed to receive it.

In considering this enormous sum of 288,000 solidi, two observations are in place. First, more than ninety thousand people could have lived from it comfortably for a year. This figure confirms the presumed size of the tribe, which is generally estimated at about a hundred thousand people. Second, four thousand pounds of gold amounts to the yearly income of a senator of the wealthy, though not the wealthiest, class. Was Alaric trying to "purchase" the rank of a Roman noble? Whatever the answer, the Roman senators in particular resisted Alaric's demands.[233] Though posterity regarded Stilicho's good relations with the senate as exemplary, he managed to push through Alaric's demands only with the greatest difficulty and against the vehement opposition of that venerable body. Stilicho succeeded and once more took the Balth into Roman service. But it was a Pyrrhic victory. As military commander of Gaul Alaric was now to lead regular Roman troops and his Goths against the usurper Constantine.[234] In the previous year Sarus had achieved some success against Constantine's generals, but in 407 he had been forced to return across the Alps and along the way had to abandon all his booty to the Bagaudae of Savoy.[235]

Alaric never became *magister militum* of Gaul,[236] and he undoubtedly never saw an ounce of the gold he had demanded.[237] On August 14, 408, Stilicho was toppled on August 22; thousands of barbarians who were living in Italy and trying to assimilate[238] fell victim to the subsequent manhunt. At this moment a king of the army at the head of his warriors stood ready—as it were, within striking distance—to present himself as the savior of all persecuted barbarians: it is said that thirty thousand non-Romans joined Alaric, among them probably the twelve thousand elite troops Stilicho had taken over from the "assets" of the "bankrupt" Radagaisus and who were now looking for a new master.[239] Only Sarus remained with the Romans; apparently all bridges between him and the Balth had broken down. Although Sarus was Stilicho's confidant to the very end, he changed his position in a flash after the overthrow of Stilicho at Pavia and he had the Hunnic bodyguard of his former master murdered at night. It is possible that Sarus was hoping to become Stilicho's successor. Perhaps this act of perfidy against the Pannonian Hunnic warriors was one of the reasons for the deep hatred between Sarus and Athaulf, who had himself commanded Huns in Pannonia.[240]

Alaric, however, thought his time had come: he was still negotiating with Honorius, who was temporarily residing in Milan again. The Gothic king lowered his demands, called for a renewed exchange of hostages—among them once again Aëtius—and was willing in return to vacate Noricum and to withdraw to Pannonia. When his offer was rejected he acted quickly. Without awaiting the arrival of his brother-in-law Athaulf, who was commanding the Goths and Huns of upper Pannonia, Alaric moved back into Italy. Zosimus describes Alaric's march like a present-day summertime road trip. On the Via Postumia past Aquileia and farther along the main road, which touches Verona, the Goths moved through transpadane Italy as far as Cremona. Perhaps they wanted to bar the emperor's route to Ravenna. But for that it was already too late. Near Cremona the Goths crossed the Po "like some festive procession" and then took the Via Aemilia through Bologna to Rimini on the Adriatic. They bypassed Ravenna and marched along the Flaminian coastal road via Ancona as far as the land of the Piceni. There the army turned westward—probably at the mouth of the Tronto—and moved along the Via Salaria by way of Ascoli and Reate/Rieti to the gates of Rome. It is said the Alaric's march through Italy took only the month of October 408.[241]

The Eternal City was completely cut off from all supplies. Famine and epidemics afflicted the city. At the same time rumors and prophecies spread promising salvation at the last minute: relief would soon arrive from Ravenna; pagan rites had saved a city in Tuscany from the Goths with thunder and lightning: all one had to do, therefore, was to reinstate the old religion, possibly following the Tuscan example, and the enemy would take flight. Even Pope Innocent I is said to have acted as a Roman patriot and to have listened to such ideas.[242] After all, everyone knew that the Gothic king was possessed by a demon driving him to his furious assault against Rome.[243] Meanwhile attempts were made to negotiate with Alaric. Among the envoys was an acquaintance of the Balth who had once cooperated with him in Illyricum. But the Roman spokesmen were torn between assuming a threatening or a submissive stance; legend and rumor had spread such confusion and misinformation that they were not even certain whether they were in fact negotiating with Alaric or someone else. But the Gothic king was very much alive and made the Romans pay very dearly. This time we read of five thousand pounds of gold, thirty thousand pounds of silver, four thousand silk robes, and three thousand purple-dyed furs as well as three thousand pounds of pepper. The tribute was raised from public and private sources; some came from the ornaments of the statues of the gods. To determine the true value of these sums, to whose payment the emperor agreed, one must, however, compare them not only to the economic resources of the state but also to those of the senatorial class. The impoverished treasure alone is not an accurate indication of the empire's entire wealth since the senatorial class had amassed enormous riches.[244]

As an additional condition Alaric demanded that a Roman embassy pledge itself to obtain from Honorius a lasting peace between the empire and the Goths. This was promised, and in the following months sincere though fruitless attempts were made to bring about this peace. During the siege thousands of barbarian slaves had gone over to Alaric. Their lack of discipline and thirst for vengeance caused problems. Until the handing over of the tribute the Gothic king allowed a three-day market to supply the city with food. At the end of the year 408 Alaric marched to Tuscany and there established a permanent camp.[245]

The Balth was never again able to attain, let alone surpass, the great success he had achieved during the fall of 408; even the conquest of Rome two years later added to his problems instead of solving them. Honorius, moreover, was not willing to make peace with the Goths. With the inconstancy that was his peculiar trait, he sometimes drew support from the anti-Germanic court party and sometimes from its opponents. The rival political powers ruling the Western empire kept each other in check in such a way that the legitimate emperor could avoid making any decision. As long as he played off the Germanists and the anti-Germanists against each other, they all remained in the camp of the legitimate ruler and on the side of the house of Theodosius.

Alaric, however, despite, or precisely because of, his military success, had by no means the same mobility as his imperial opponent. With the Roman booty he satisfied his people's sense of prestige, their desire for luxuries, and their thirst for gold. But he could not guarantee their daily bread. The Goths ravaged precisely those regions from whose fruits they were supposed to live. The value of their booty was eaten up by inflation, which they caused themselves by destroying the markets where their gold had value and could be exchanged for a better—a Roman—life-style. If the *exercitus Gothorum* kept up this sort of behavior, the Goths would have to hang the gold around their necks to get any use from it: there was thus the danger of a relapse into their primitive economy.[246] As long as the Goths had no solid ground under their feet and ruined the economy of every region assigned to them, their existence was at stake in everything they did. Every move could be their last: Alaric could cut off Rome in 408 and 409, take the city in 410, capture the emperor's sister, threaten Africa, Italy's granary, even devastate Italy, yet in the end he and his Goths would be destroyed by all their victories unless they succeeded in establishing a permanent Gothia on Roman soil.[247]

Several embassies from the city of Rome sought out Honorius in Ravenna in early 409 but were unsuccessful. Even though Pope Innocent I interceded in person, the emperor refused to make peace with Alaric. Honorius's firmness had been considerably strengthened by the arrival of six thousand Dalmatian elite troops. They immediately marched out to relieve Rome, but the Goths intercepted them on the way and almost completely destroyed this sizeable force. At the same time Athaulf tried to fight his way through to Alaric with his Gothic-Hunnic horsemen. The appointment of Generidus as commander of a newly created military district stretching from Raetia all the way to Pannonia and eventually also embracing Dalmatia must have hastened Athaulf's move from the middle reaches of the Danube. Although he ran into resistance near Pisa and suffered some losses, he was able to meet up with Alaric's Goths, a union that had been planned in the fall of 408.[248] The defeat of the Dalmatian troops and the arrival of his brother-in-law strengthened Alaric's position. In Rimini he presented his new demands: he wanted Noricum and Venetia inclusive of Dalmatia as well as annual payments and a guaranteed supply of grain to meet the needs of the Goths. Alaric himself wanted to be *magister militum* again. What he probably had in mind was the elimination of the recently created regional command of Generidus.[249] Intrigues by court cliques and clumsiness on the part of the Roman negotiators led to a breakdown of the talks; once more both sides armed for war. Honorius engaged a large contingent of Hunnic cavalry, who are said to have numbered ten thousand. Since the supply problems of the Goths did not improve, Alaric sent a number of bishops to submit new proposals to Ravenna. This time he demanded only the two Norican provinces and grain supplies, expressly renouncing military office and payments.[250]

The imperial government interpreted Alaric's mediation attempt as weakness and broke off the negotiations. For the second time Alaric then marched against Rome. At the port of Ostia the Goths found the enormous stores of grain that had been feeding Rome. The Gothic king then renewed negotiations. In November or December 409 Alaric wanted to reach an agreement with the senate, and in this regard he showed himself Stilicho's able student. In the end the Balth got the senate to declare the urban prefect Attalus emperor. Apparently Attalus had been working since 408 for a reconciliation between the empire and the Goths. His first measures, however, must have been deeply disappointing to Alaric. The Balth was once again made commander-in-chief but had to share this dignity with an open enemy of the Goths; the same thing happened to Athaulf as commander of the cavalry. And to make things even worse, Attalus appointed the speaker of the anti-Gothic senatorial party to the highest civilian office of Italy. To personnel decisions of this sort he added a persistent refusal to conquer Africa with Gothic help. Relying on prophecies that were as inspiring as they were groundless, Attalus decided to forgo Alaric's assistance in his attempt to win the African province which every Italian government desperately needed. African grain fed Rome and the heartland of the Western empire. But it appears that Attalus preferred failure to yielding on this issue, which in fact presented an insoluble problem. For if the Goths gained a foothold on the other side of the Mediterranean, they would no longer need Attalus or the senate. But if the expedition was attempted without the Goths it would lack the necessary military power to force the African governor into union with Rome. A weak consolation remained to Alaric in that the emperor was kind enough to give up paganism and convert to the Gothic faith. Attalus was baptized by the Arian bishop Sigesar.[251]

As expected, the African venture collapsed; Attalus's rule could not last much longer, for the Gothic people were again starving.[252] To gain recognition for his emperor Alaric advanced as far as Ravenna but fought with only moderate success in the Po Valley.[253] In this way the first half of the year 410 went by. Then the Gothic king's patience ran out and he once again drew closer to the legitimate augustus. In the camp at Rimini Alaric had Attalus publicly stripped of his office and sent the diadem and the purple robe to Ravenna. The usurper himself, however, remained with the Goths, who guaranteed his personal safety.[254]

This made it possible for Alaric once more to negotiate with Honorius. In a small town called Alpes, about eight miles from Ravenna, the Roman emperor and the Gothic king met face-to-face for the first time. An agreement on the hoped-for peace seemed within reach, a recognition of a Gothic state on Italian soil possible.[255] At this moment Sarus, with a band of only three hundred desperados, attacked the unprepared Gothic army, which suffered a setback in the ensuing action. A few things seem strange about the report: Sarus, the Gothic enemy of Alaric, was fleeing from Athaulf, who had chased him out of Picenum. If the brother-in-law of the Gothic king was conducting a private war near Ancona which surprised the main army involved in peace talks, communications between Alaric's Goths and the Pannonian horsemen of Athaulf must have been unclear. In any case, Honorius immediately changed his policy: the reckless Sarus was received honorably, and Alaric for the third time marched against Rome, this time ready to take the siege to the bitter end.[256]

On August 24, 410, the Goths forced their way into the Eternal City. The swift capture was—as usual—explained by treason. A certain lady of high rank was even suspected of having opened the gates for humanitarian reasons.[257] During the three-day plundering of the city the Goths seized vast riches, among them probably part of the Jewish temple treasures that Titus had brought from Jerusalem to Rome.[258] Athaulf himself captured Galla Placidia, the emperor's sister, unless the report we have was made up later because she eventually became his wife. It is likely, however, that the Roman princess came to the Goths before 410.[259]

The capture of the city was a profound shock to Latin contemporaries. "What will remain standing if Rome falls?" St. Jerome had already asked anxiously in 409. Was this the punishment of the Christian God or were the pagan gods avenging themselves for the abandonment of the old religion, the foundation of *Roma aeterna*? In the great unrest of the time many answers emerged, but only one person managed to offer Christian hope. Augustine created in his *City of God* an eschatology in which the fall of Rome became an event of providential history.[260] While this interpretation was truly Christian, on a more profane level some contemporaries downplayed the Gothic "plague" and its terror. Christian apologists and opinion-makers began to point out to themselves and the pagans how humanely Alaric and his warriors had plundered Rome and that in any case they had left the city after only three days. But for many Romans, and especially Roman women, these three days were an eternity; and it was impossible to calm the pagans.[261]

It is true that the Goths did not stay in Rome for very long. The capture of the city had been forced upon Alaric by an evil spirit, so it was said. Possibly he was driven to do it for the sake of his own destruction. Since Alaric died in 410, there emerged from these two facts—the capture of Rome and the fall of its captor—a motif that determined the course of future actions.[262] It is conceivable that Alaric himself vacated the city out of some "mythical" fear, although more concrete reasons may have been important in the quick withdrawal. There was still the unsolved problem of supplies, the threat of famine and epidemics, and the constraint to get somewhere before the onset of winter, possibly to conquer the grainlands of Africa via Sicily. The march to the south was successful, cities like Capua and Nola were taken, but time was running short. And then the Straits of Messina presented an insurmountable obstacle. Ridiculous attempts to get at least to Sicily failed. The Goths lacked the necessary ships, and the autumn storms were setting in. Gainas's debacle at the Bosporus repeated itself, even though this time the Roman fleet was not involved. The Gothic army then began its retreat; the march went north toward Campania. Perhaps Alaric wanted to seize a larger port like Naples—which he had already besieged in vain on his march south—in order to equip a suitable fleet. What is certain is that the Goths spent the winter there and at first did not give up their African plan even when Alaric died in Bruttium before the end of the year.[263]

Klaus Düwel tells us that "Alaric is considered one of the most important and attractive Germanic figures of the age of migrations."[264] Or as Ludwig Schmidt puts it: "He was one of the most powerful, sympathetic hero figures of Germanic antiquity."[265] To the present little has changed in the special fondness of German historiography for Alaric I. The sources of his period do not allow us to describe in detail the character and personality of the Gothic king. According to the *Origo Gothica* "his people mourned out of their love for him."[266] Such sentiments were usual for the Goths, and not only for them. When Attila died his people mourned, and the death of an Amal ruler supposedly caused such intense grief that the Goths did not elect another king for forty years.[267] Part of the topos is also "the grave in the Busento river." Thus the *Origo Gothica* reports that Alaric was buried in the Busento near Consentia-Cosenza, after the riverbed had been drained. The laborers who accomplished the work were killed. The "nocturnal" burial of the "young Gothic hero" became part of the cultural tradition of romanticism through Platen's well-known poem. The type of burial chosen for the migratory king—who was of course already forty years of age at his death—indicates that the Goths wanted to leave Italy. But we must be careful in interpreting the story of the death of the Balth historically. There are numerous parallels for the "grave in the river." The entire story of Alaric's mysterious grave in the Busento, which has occupied the imagination of treasure hunters to this very day, is the stuff of legend and not historical fact. The origin of the saga goes back to the region of the lower Danube and the Black Sea, thus reflecting the acculturation of the Goths to their Scythian homeland.[268]

The importance of Alaric for his tribe emerges from his ability to keep his people together in the wake of serious defeats. Alaric was no longer a savage. But he was ambitious, proud of his ancestry, and prevailed with his Balthic identity against Romans and Goths. If he or his people were offended he turned into a barbarian who precipitately ordered the march on Rome. In those moments he was guided by an inner voice, a demon.[269] But Alaric was a good organizer and recognized the value of Roman administration. He was aware of the importance of regular supplies, and he solved the kind of logistical problems that had been the undoing of even a Radagaisus within a short time. Even in the Roman sense, Alaric proved himself a good, though not a superior, general. He was never completely defeated, but then he was also never able to defeat a Roman army that was halfway intact.

Alaric's group was at the stage of a "community of migration" before it developed once again into a people. From Tervingian, Greutungian, and non-Gothic elements there emerged under Alaric's royal leadership a new Visigothic people. But just as he was not able to establish a royal clan (*stirps regia*)—something that was achieved only by the "younger" Balths after serious setbacks—Alaric I also did not solve the question of how the imperial power and a barbarian kingship could be reconciled on Roman soil. Alaric's unsuccessful attempts to integrate Gothic statehood into the empire were also the reason why his policies alternated so abruptly, as it seemed, between enmity toward Rome and readiness for compromise. Now and then one gets the impression that the Gothic king was at one time dominated by a "Gothic nationalist party" and at another time by the "friends of Rome" among his people. In fact these groups hardly existed in the sense of parties that fought each other; they were political alternatives that Alaric would try to use according to need and possibility.[270] Like his successor he can therefore be seen as a pragmatist in the "game of kings" in which every move drew a countermove, in which one could threaten the "king" yet never be able to turn check into checkmate but only into a draw.

ATHAULF AND THE GOTHIC TREK WESTWARD

Alaric died without leaving an appropriate heir, so his brother-in-law Athaulf was made king of the Goths. There was probably some sort of election but history does not tell us how it took place, who participated, and whether there were other candidates.[271] The Goths remained in Italy beyond the year 411 and ravaged the country.[272] No details about the devastation are known, for the sources suddenly lose the power of a comprehensive view and continuous narrative. Even when the sources are completely preserved they seem fragmentary, as if composed only of headlines. Even in the East, where the art of telling a story was still alive, there was no real interest in the events in the western half of the empire, and the sympathy aroused by the fall of Rome remained within limits.[273]

In 411 Iovinus, a member of the highest Gallic nobility, usurped the imperial authority. A barbarian coalition under Burgundian-Alanic leadership formed the background to this usurpation. As a result the Burgundians were permitted to establish a kingdom on the left bank of the Rhine. The new emperor thus seemed to understand the signs of the time; he permitted in Gaul what the Goths had in vain tried to obtain by force in Italy. But in Iovinus's eyes Athaulf too had something to offer. With his help the usurpation could perhaps be carried into Italy. Eventually Attalus got involved and established the link between the Goths and Iovinus; it might be possible for Attalus to play the role of the *tertius gaudens*.[274]

The Gallic-Gothic coalition did not last long. Iovinus quarreled with Attalus because he brought the Goths with him. But apart from that, Iovinus's hopes were based on a fundamentally false assumption. Like the last Gallic "provincial emperor," Avitus,[275] Iovinus in 412 also underesti-

mated the inner resilience of Italy and the difficulty of ruling it from beyond
the Alps. Athaulf, however, knew the situation from three years of experience and only too gladly followed Attalus's advice to leave the Apennine
peninsula. Moreover, in so doing the Gothic king carried out a plan that
his predecessor had devised as early as 402.[276] In 412, probably some time
before the imperial law of May 8, 413, which was to provide tax relief for
Campania, Tuscany, Picenum, Samnium, Apulia, and Calabria as well as
Lucania and Bruttium, the Goths vacated central and southern Italy and
moved across the Alps to the west.[277] Iovinus had expected something else.
His irritation increased when Athaulf intercepted and destroyed Sarus's
shrunken band. The latter had broken with Honorius because of a blood
feud, and with the last of his loyal followers he had gone over to the Gallic
usurper. On the way he fell into Athaulf's ambush and was killed. Contemporaries emphasized the brave resistance the Gothic "dissident" put up.[278]

Thereafter Iovinus made his brother coemperor without consulting
Athaulf. It is significant to note that the Gothic king saw in this an encroach-
ment on his rights. This would mean that he had negotiated for actual
participation in Iovinus's rule. In anger he dropped the Gaul and returned
once more to the camp of the legitimists, who promised in Honorius's name
to settle the Goths in Gaul and to secure their grain supply. These people
must have been authorized to negotiate with Athaulf, so we get the impression that the Goths were established as Aquitanian federates as early as
413. And in fact Bordeaux opened its gates and received the Goths peacefully. In the same year the Gallic usurpation collapsed, not without causing
a split in the senatorial class and afflicting especially the Auvergne, where
Iovinus had his headquarters. Iovinus himself was captured by the Goths
near Valence and handed over to his enemies.[279] But Honorius once more
broke his promise to the Goths. The pretext was the demand that Galla
Placidia be released before the treaty could be implemented. In response
southern Gaul suffered Italy's fate. The land was ravaged, cities burned and
conquered. Narbonne and Toulouse were captured, but a Gothic attack on
Marseille failed. During the unsuccessful assault the Gothic king was
wounded so seriously that he called off the attack.[280]

At the beginning of the year 414 both sides were ready for compromise,
even if they agreed to it without consulting the emperor. The general famine
in Gaul left no choice.[281] In January 414 Galla Placidia, "the queen of the
south, married the king of the north," Athaulf, as some contemporaries
sought to interpret the event according to the prophecy of Daniel.[282] The
wedding took place in Narbonne in the house of a Roman nobleman. A
legitimist officer and intimate confidant of Placidia had advised her to

consent to the marriage, and he himself had organized the ceremony. Among the guests was also the former emperor Attalus, who was allowed to recite the wedding poem. Athaulf wore Roman robes and deferred to his bride, the daughter and sister of Roman emperors, allowing her the honor of heading the procession. It was appropriate that the rich gifts with which he honored her came from Roman booty. Where else could Athaulf have got them, if he wanted to do everything entirely the Roman way? The provincials and Goths who were present seemed deeply impressed; much less so the man in Ravenna who had become Athaulf's brother-in-law much against his wishes.[283]

Supposedly at this wedding were spoken those famous words in which the king declared that at first he had wanted to replace Romania with Gothia in his desire to become for a Gothic *imperium* what Augustus had been for the Roman Empire, namely, the eponymous founder of a universal empire. But he had realized that the Goths would never be able to abolish the Roman state—that is, the *res publica* based on law—because of their "unbridled barbarism." He was therefore ready to make peace, to become the renewer of Rome instead of its destroyer. Of course it was said that Athaulf's change of mind was brought about largely through the influence of Galla Placidia. Orosius claims that a respectable citizen of Narbonne, a former military officer under Theodosius, had reported Athaulf's words to St. Jerome in Bethlehem. The quarrel about the authenticity of this story seems pointless, because the Gothic king changed his policy in a way that was very much in line with the spirit of his statement.[284]

When Galla Placidia gave birth to a son—probably at the beginning of 415—the child received at baptism the imperial name Theodosius. It reminded Athaulf's people of the man who had been a "friend of peace and of the Goths,"[285] and for the Romans it meant legitimacy. The child died within a short time and thus fulfilled for the experts another part of Daniel's prophecy, namely, that the couple from north and south would have no offspring. But Athaulf's policy remained unchanged and clear, and it was further confirmed by the "legacy" he soon entrusted to his brother: "He asked him to return Galla Placidia to Honorius and to establish, if he could, friendship with the Romans."[286] What Athaulf had desired beyond peace, namely, admission into the house of Theodosius, his successful rival Constantius was to achieve. The victory over the Goths in the following year (416) brought the future emperor Constantius, the third of that name, the patriciate and made him the heir of Stilicho and Athaulf because he was a Catholic Roman.

In the year 416 Galla Placidia was "freed"; on January 1, 417, Constantius married Athaulf's widow, who would have happily done without another marriage. Through her Constantius became the father of the emperor Valentinian III, and in order to better secure the succession he even made himself coemperor of his brother-in-law Honorius.[287] But the forty-year migration of the Goths was nearing its end.

Orosius—rhetoric notwithstanding—aptly described the Gothic position at the beginning of the fifth century. The former Danubian *gens* had become one party among the many fighting for leadership in the empire. The more clearly a history of the new Visigoths emerges, the more the historical ethnography of their ancestors fades away. The Visigoths were now part of the *imperium*.[288]

Constantius cut the Goths off from supplies by land and by sea, whereupon they vacated famine-ridden Gaul.[289] Terrible scenes took place during the retreat; even Bordeaux, which was friendly to the Goths and where Attalus could once more act as puppet emperor, went up in flames. Like a piece of booty Attalus was dragged along across the Pyrenees and lost on the way, whereupon he was captured by imperial troops. A man like Paulinus of Pella was swept up and crushed by the events, although there were also people who "with Gothic favor" made their fortunes. Memories of a not too distant past come alive with these words. The quick collaborator is a permanent part of the *conditio humana*. Although Paulinus lost much in Bordeaux, he was lucky to make his escape to Vasates-Bazas together with his family and a large part of his fortune. But there also the situation became critical. Goths, Alans (whom Athaulf had taken over from the fallen Iovinus), and Bagaudian bands from the neighborhood combined to form an explosive mixture that gave Bazas reason to fear the worst should it explode. But Paulinus was personally well acquainted with the Alanic king, whom we identify as the unsuccessful emperor-maker Goar, and knew especially how to stir up Alanic-Gothic differences. He split the besiegers and led the Alans into the city as protection against foreign and domestic barbarians. Thereupon the Goths withdrew.[290] In the beginning of 415 the Goths were still in Narbonne. Vacating the Mediterranean coast of Gaul was probably the last thing Athaulf did. Young Theodosius had already died in Barcelona, where his father was assassinated in late August/early September of the same year. When news of his death reached Constantinople on September 24, 415, it was celebrated with games and fireworks.[291]

ATHAULF'S CONTRIBUTION TO THE VISIGOTHIC ETHNOGENESIS

We know only the last seven years of Athaulf's life. Within that period he developed from a tribal chief into a late antique statesman. The influence of Roman leadership, already attested for Alaric's Macedonian kingdom, increased steadily from 409 and reached it first climax in Athaulf's marriage to the emperor's daughter Galla Placidia.[292] Nevertheless, the Gothic king could never deny his origins, and the cause of his death is related to this fact. In the fall of 408 Alaric wanted his brother-in-law who was in upper Pannonia to join him in the invasion of Italy. It is on this occasion that Athaulf's name first appears in the sources. What he had done before this time can be reconstructed only vaguely. In any case, we hear that he was in Pannonia commanding a sizable force of Goths and Huns. This was almost certainly a Gothic-led mixed cavalry contingent,[293] which reminds us of the polyethnic three-tribe confederation of 380.[294] In 401, at the latest, Alans had split off from that confederation, so the mention of a Hunnic-Gothic group in Pannonia in 408 seems to present no problem of identification. Was Athaulf thus the successor of Alatheus and Safrax or even of Videric, whom he supposedly had killed? Unfortunately the story of the federates who lived in Pannonia for about half a century is one of the most obscure, perhaps even deliberately obscured, chapters in the Amal Gothic history.[295]

We can say that Athaulf, as the brother-in-law and blood relative of Alaric, undoubtedly belonged to the extended Balthic family and was therefore of Moesian Gothic origin.[296] The argument that it was impossible for Athaulf either as a Visigoth to command Ostrogoths or as an Ostrogoth to become king of the Visigoths is certainly wrong.[297] Rather, it is entirely possible that after the Radagaisus episode Alaric entrusted his brother-in-law with gaining control of Pannonia; for if the neighboring federates and other Gothic groups remained loyal to the Romans, Alaric's position would become difficult. The best evidence for this is the attitude of the Alans, who were so enthusiastic in their cavalry attacks at Pollentia and Verona that they caused Alaric serious problems.[298]

Athaulf was murdered while he and his retainers were inspecting the horses. The deed was committed by one of the men in his entourage; his name was Dubius or/and Eberwolf. He is said to have been short and therefore the target of ridicule. Insofar as this motive is historical it only triggered the crime; the actual cause was revenge for the murder of a former lord, the "rhix (ῥήξ) of a Gothic subtribe," whom Athaulf had killed "a long time ago."[299] We can identify this unnamed chieftain as Sarus, but only if we attach greater importance to the events after Athaulf's death than to the source itself, according to which an "ancient crime" was revenged on the Gothic king. Sarus's brother Sigeric was in fact able to act the part of Gothic king, if only for a week, after the death of his mortal enemy. From this we must conclude that under Athaulf Sigeric belonged to the main

Gothic tribe, and this fact gives rise to two considerations: first, Sigeric was in a position to plan a conspiracy against Athaulf; second, if the brother of the slain chief Sarus could move freely within the immediate entourage of Athaulf, it must have been just as easy for a former retainer to do so. It is possible, however, that the murdered chief had been a Tervingian *rhix* who had resisted the attempt of the Balthic leadership to force him into line.[300] Finally, the Greutungian Videric has also been suggested as the unnamed *rhix*. But Videric, the son of Vithimiris, is mentioned for the last time in the fall of 376 before the admission of his group into the empire. The story of Videric's fate on Roman soil can therefore only be written if one invents it.[301]

The one-week kingship was long enough for Sigeric to have Athaulf's children of his first marriage murdered in the arms of Bishop Sigesar and to humiliate the royal widow, Placidia.[302] But the election of a brother of Sarus as king over the brother of Athaulf, who had apparently designated him as the successor, indicates the existence of a certain degree of support for the Sarus clan[303] in the army of the Balthic Goths. We first heard of Sarus when, together with the Walachian Hunnic chief Uldin, he was supporting the Romans against Radagaisus. In 405 Sarus must have had a respectable retinue under his command, if, as *dux* of the Goths, he was of equal rank with the *dux* of the Huns.[304] Sarus made a career for himself when in Roman service, and at his own expense he fought against Alaric and also caused the fall of Stilicho. On the latter occasion many Huns lost their lives. Sarus was the opponent of the two Balths, but there was deadly enmity between him and Athaulf. Why? One possible answer could be that the fall of Radagaisus or the slaughter of Stilicho's Hunnic bodyguard made Sarus and Athaulf enemies in a case of blood feud. How seriously Sarus himself took the obligation of blood feud—placing it even higher than his own safety—is revealed by his break with Honorius and by his death.[305]

Athaulf, more so than Alaric I, appears to have been caught up in the bloody fight for the Visigothic kingship. In Pannonia Athaulf had been a *reiks* with all the increasing importance attached to this office since Alaric's election as king. In the army of his brother-in-law he could therefore assert a remarkable degree of independence. First, Athaulf was conspicuously slow in complying with the request to join Alaric.[306] The reason is unknown; perhaps Athaulf's decision had something to do with the extension of Generidus's sphere of command. Still in 409 the Goths' emperor Attalus had to appoint Athaulf commander of the mounted bodyguards. He thus became one of the first *comites domesticorum equitum* we know. Although he did receive his military office at the same time that Alaric was made commander-in-chief, a *comes* of this type ranked only slightly lower than the *magister militum* and was always qualified to hold an independent command.[307] It seems that a Roman institution was being used in an effort to settle internal Gothic questions of rank. In any case, Athaulf derived from his new position the continuation of his old privileges. Through his pursuit of Sarus in the middle of 410, as unsuccessful as it was unauthorized, he caused a serious disruption of Alaric's plans; nevertheless, we read nowhere that this action got him into trouble.[308] Rather, it was exactly this independence as well as his position as brother-in-law and blood relative of Alaric which recommended him as the latter's successor. But Athaulf had already proved himself a future king quite independently of such considerations. The authority he had held in Pannonia had been so extensive that after his departure he obtained that Roman military office that served as a direct stepping-stone to the supreme command. A man of such authority clearly ranked as a king.[309]

THE VISIGOTHS BECOME HORSEMEN

Athaulf himself symbolizes the end of a development that had changed the nature of the Tervingian tribe: in increasing numbers the Alaric Goths fought on horseback. This entailed not merely new equipment and techniques but also a far-reaching transformation of the traditional mentality. The Visigothic ethnogenesis had begun. The change in fighting technique was brought about by personal experience and foreign example.[310] Fritigern had awaited the arrival of the Ostrogothic cavalry before he had opened battle at Adrianople. Less than two decades later Alaric's horsemen were operating in the mountains of the Peloponnesus, and the Romans were suffering from Gothic cavalry: the Goths trampled everything in their path with such force that even "iron-reinforced walls were threatening to collapse."[311] And at Pollentia Alaric not only stopped the frontal cavalry attack of the Roman Alans but even drove them back successfully. (Because the Goths at first turned in flight, we conclude that it was probably Alaric's foot warriors who were unable to resist the attack.) In contrast the Roman infantry was still an elite troop. With its help Stilicho succeeded in turning around the cavalry engagement he was losing and to stand his ground. But that was all he could do, for Alaric, "surrounded by cavalry, withdrew unharmed into the mountains along with the remainder of his troops."[312] After the battle of Verona Alaric's ranks were greatly reduced; to heavy losses was added the desertion of various groups, among them entire squadrons. Perhaps Alaric sent Athaulf to Pannonia to recruit new horsemen to make up for the bloodletting of the year 402.[313] These horsemen could have been Ostrogoths. We do know that Ostrogoths were received by Theoderid and Euric.[314] At decisive points in his life Athaulf was involved with horses, and he even met his death among them.[315]

By 400 the cavalry of the Alaric Goths was qualitatively superior to that of the Romans. And it was at least equal to the heavy Alanic horsemen of Stilicho, both in battle tactics and armament, which consisted of a coat of mail, a helmet, and a lance (*contus*) wielded with both hands. The same tactics that had won Adrianople and Sisak—overwhelming the enemy with a lightning attack—were now characteristic of Alaric's crack division. Where did this fundamental change come from? There can be no doubt that the Greutungian-Ostrogothic element provided a model, even though Alatheus and Safrax later parted again with Fritigern. But the successes of the eastern Goths forced the Roman federates of Tervingian origin to adapt—or better: readapt—themselves to the fighting techniques of the peoples of the steppe. It sounds like an irony of history that it was on Roman soil that the descendants of the Danubian Goths returned to the Sarmatian-Scythian fighting style of their eastern neighbors.[316]

The evidence for the far-reaching transformation of the Gothic army is clear-cut: from this time the cavalry set the tone and indeed made up a larger and larger portion of the actual fighting force. In the battle of the Catalaunian Fields, the Visigoths faced the mounted Ostrogoths, from which we can once again infer a parity in armaments and tactics.[317] Near Vouillé a Gothic cavalry force was defeated by Frankish foot warriors.[318] In the *Historia vel Origo Gothorum* of Isidore of Seville the mounted Gothic warrior is the rule,[319] and even from the ninth century comes the statement that Gothic duels were fought, according to ancient custom, on horseback.[320] Compared to their Daco-Thracian ancestors the mounted Visigoths had become a new people, in large measure because the dominant Danubian traditions had been changed and altered by the experiences of the Black Sea. Athaulf contributed so much to this process that his name—next to that of the even more important Alaric—must be remembered.

RADAGAISUS AND HIS CONTRIBUTION TO THE VISIGOTHIC ETHNOGENESIS

To speak in this context of Radagaisus, this barbarian pagan and "true Scythian,"[321] may seem a little farfetched. All the same, he contributed—even if unwillingly—to the Visigothic ethnogenesis. To this day it is unclear where he and his swarm of "locusts" originated.[322] What is certain is that he and his people were considered Goths.[323] His aggressive heathenism was one reason why he was called a Greutungian, the successor, so to speak, of Odotheus; but it was also said that Arian Christians joined him. If the latter is true, it would mean that the Gothic Christian mission had at that time already extended beyond the Danubian region.[324] Like Odotheus, Radagaisus was also a leader of Gothic tribes seeking to escape Hunnic domination. No details, however, are known about the composition of these tribes.[325] But all Roman observers noted the suddenness and magnitude of the avalanche of Gothic peoples. Yet its devastating force was not felt in northern and central Italy until the end of 405.[326] At first the blow fell on Illyricum, and crowds of Roman refugees poured into Italy. Radagaisus must have crossed the Danube, which indicates that Pannonia and Noricum were the first areas to suffer.[327] But what exactly happened there, which cities were ruined, and how the Pannonian federates reacted to their "wild" relatives—all this is only speculation. The great south Styrian city of Flavia Solva is said to have been largely burned down and abandoned during that period, and about the same time Aguntum was supposedly devastated by a catastrophic fire.[328] If a historian employs archaeological dating he runs the risk of succumbing to a *petitio principii,* because the dates of the archaeologists are in most cases merely borrowed from the historians.

It is astonishing how little surprised contemporaries were that the Radagaisus Goths were defeated with the help of Alans, Danubian Uldin Huns, and the Sarus Goths who had split off from Alaric, while the Balth himself—committed in Illyricum by a treaty—remained inactive.[329] Merely because Orosius apologetically placed the heathen Radagaisus and the Christian Alaric face-to-face, Isidore's *Historia vel Origo Gothorum* could turn this fact into a Visigothic double monarchy.[330] In actuality the years 405 and 406 saw a repeat of the political constellation of the Gainas-Tribigild rebellion. As before, Alaric remained neutral, a Roman Goth defeated the Gothic enemy of Rome in the decisive battle, and Uldin destroyed him. The Huns were interested in the elimination of any transdanubian Gothic kingdom and in the destruction of the Radagaisus group. Uldin was always ready and willing to destroy other Gothic groups, but he never sought a direct confrontation with Alaric.[331] The fury of Radagaisus was stopped at the Florentine city of Faesulae-Fiesole, where no less than a third of the Gothic warriors were killed, and it ended with the death of their leader by the hand of the executioner on August 23, 406.[332]

Radagaisus is said to have been a king. He did in fact hold a charismatic position reminiscent of the Burgundian *hendinos,* and he was a truly inspiring leader.[333] He still strikes us as an archaic king of the army but one who lacked all Roman or Hunnic recognition. Instead, Radagaisus upset the barbarian equilibrium both in the Roman Empire and in the Hunnic realm. Thus both powers united to fight him and took measures to prevent any future attempts at breaking away. To that end the Gothic peoples under Hunnic overlordship were probably given a kingship whose consolidating function resembles that of the Balthic kingship in the Roman Empire. The beneficiaries of this development were the ancestors of Theodoric the Great.[334]

Alaric's Goths benefited, of course, more directly than the Amali from the fall of Radagaisus. His hordes supposedly had a strength of several hundred thousand men. This figure is certainly exaggerated, since Stilicho easily defeated his enemy with only thirty units (*numeri*), that is, thirty thousand men at the very most. Nevertheless, Radagaisus's forces must have been numerous; when the captured Radagaisus Goths were sold into slavery the slave market collapsed.[335] And twelve thousand crack troops were taken by Stilicho into the imperial army, from where they went over to Alaric after Stilicho's downfall.[336] Even as such remnants the hordes of Radagaisus strike us as gigantic. The question of their absolute strength is wisely not raised. Whoever is so inclined can examine the figures, which are given in only one source.[337] In any case, we can understand both the great relief, indeed, the exaggerated joy, of the Romans when the nightmare was over and the anger of the future patriot Zosimus that Alaric was the real beneficiary of the poorly exploited victory of Stilicho.[338]

VALIA AND THE GOTHS "IN ROMAN SERVICE"

Around the middle of September 415 Valia was chosen Gothic king over several other candidates.[339] He was originally supposed to continue the war against the Romans, but to do that he would have first had to overcome the problem of hunger. Mocked by the Vandals and their allies, but otherwise left alone, the Goths marched through the Iberian peninsula.[340] Their goal was Africa. This time Alaric's plan, which promised a solution to all problems, was to be finally realized. But during the past ten years the Goths had not become seafarers, and as a result even the merely "twelve thousand foot wide" Straits of Gibraltar became an insurmountable obstacle. A Gothic advance party perished in a storm. Valia called off the expedition. Probably at this time the first of those Gothic groups that later followed the Vandals to Africa split off from the main tribe. For the moment, however, there was no alternative but to surrender to the Romans. In the spring of 416 the Gothic king gave himself up to Constantius, the commander-in-chief of the West; in return he received a supply of grain that would feed about fifteen thousand warriors along with their families and followers and he was given the task of clearing Spain of domestic and foreign enemies.[341] For their part the Goths had to hand over Athaulf's widow and provide hostages from among the nobility.[342] The federates went to work with remarkable enthusiasm and success. That the Goths had to go primarily against the hated Vandals and the Alans—who were considered deserters[343]—made the entire mission even more appealing. Of the Siling Vandals who had occupied Baetica in southern Spain, only a kingless remnant survived, which went to join their Hasdingian cousins. Valia next marched against the Alans who, after the death of their king in battle, also joined the Hasdingi. The still intact Vandal tribe of the Hasdingi was living in northwestern Spain with the Suevi. It seems that both these people were not molested by the Goths; why this was so we are not told. Valia's daughter was the wife of a Suevic noble, and this might have been one reason for the diminished Gothic aggressiveness.[344] But the Hasdingi, as well, were spared, and they especially were the hereditary enemies of the Goths. Thus it seems more likely that Valia simply did not get around to settling the old score, as a result of which the Vandal king became the beneficiary of the Gothic victories. The Goths had unintentionally caused the creation of a Vandal-Alanic tribal confederation.[345] And the Suevi too escaped unharmed, no doubt because Valia had to break off the campaign on orders from Constantius. For two years the Gothic king had conducted the Spanish war "on behalf of the Romans"—*Romani nomini causa*.[346] Now he returned with his people to Gaul. The *foedus* of 416 was to be followed by a settlement that was contractually guaranteed and carried out according to Roman law. But Valia did not see it implemented—he died in 418.[347] In Spain the Goths had proved their fighting ability; now they were needed somewhere else.

4

The Kingdom of Toulouse,
418 to 507

The *regnum Tolosanum* is mentioned for the first time in the sources at its fall in 507. In reality, however, we can place the beginning of the Toulousan kingdom of the Visigoths at the time of their settlement in 418, when they made Toulouse the center of their dominion.[1] What is more, their leader was a king, even though his *regnum* consisted until that time not of a Gothic land, a *patria Gothorum*, but of an *exercitus Gothorum* that roamed through Europe.[2] At times it seems that the absence of ties to a distinct homeland encouraged the locating of Gothia in a political dreamland, as Athaulf's unrealistic alternative between the renewal and destruction of Romania reveals.[3] If the Goths therefore wanted to preserve their ethnic identity, they had to accept the economically adequate offer of 418 and settle permanently in Aquitaine. But it was also in the interest of the Roman imperial government to find a permanent solution to the Gothic question. The new *foedus* had to be economically better secured to fulfill its purpose. This was the only possible way of raising the army necessary for reestablishing a Roman Gaul. The first attempt to resolve the problem of the Goths led directly to the creation of the Toulousan kingdom, but indirectly it initiated the process that has recently been called the "transformation of the Roman world."[4]

The Aquitanian Federates, 418–466

Valia was permitted to conclude his Spanish summer campaign of 418, but then Constantius "recalled" the Goths to Gaul. This move was not extorted from the Romans but was decreed by the all-powerful *patricius* in the name of his imperial brother-in-law. The Gothic federates were assigned to the valley of the Garonne "from Toulouse to Bordeaux" and were allotted in addition the Atlantic coastal strip extending from Les Landes and the foothills of the Pyrenees in the south just barely to the Loire in the north.[5] From the Roman point of view the Gothic settlement area included the entire province of Aquitania II as well as some *civitates*—including Toulouse, above all—of the neighboring provinces of Novempopulana and Narbonensis I. But the Goths were excluded from the Mediterranean coast.[6] Aquitaine and Novempopulana were considered the richest areas, the "marrow" of Gaul.[7] Although the Romans were free to decide where to settle the federates, they still chose these areas. Indeed, it appears that the imperial government had long planned on this location and had arranged it with the inhabitants of the provinces in question. For on April 17, 418, the general assembly of the seven southern Gallic provinces was reestablished by imperial decree. The praetorian prefect of Gaul, whose seat had recently been moved to Arles, had asked for the reestablishment of the assembly and had gained the support of Constantius. From August 13 to September 13 of every year the assembly was to be in session at Arles and bring together the functionaries of the Roman imperial government and the representatives of the provincials.[8] The first meeting of the *concilium* took place in the year it was reestablished. Constantius probably attended. If he did, the assembly convened shortly before the recall of the Gothic federates from Spain. It is hard to imagine that the Gothic question was not on the agenda, for deliberations focused on the reestablishment of Gaul. Constantius would hardly have reorganized the provincial assembly of southern Gaul only to go over its head shortly thereafter to make a unilateral decision that might have run counter to the interests of those affected.[9] But then the recall of the Valia Goths before the last barbarian enemies in Spain had been destroyed in itself is inexplicable. The usual "legend of the stab in the back," according to which Constantinus did not want to let the Goths become too powerful on the other side of the Pyrenees and so decided to preserve a sort of barbarian equilibrium,[10] is just that, a legend. Ravenna gained nothing in Spain by withdrawing the Gothic federates; indeed, it alienated the Spaniards it had thus abandoned.[11] This leaves us with the conclusion that the imperial government, in agreement with the senatorial leadership in southern Gaul, decided that the Goths were more urgently needed north of the Pyrenees than in distant Spain.

Federates were usually settled along threatened borders.[12] But neither in Aquitania II nor in Novempopulana was there at that time a border that had to be defended against an external enemy. The Suevi of northwestern Spain could not threaten Aquitaine; rather, that area served as a marshaling zone against them and against the surviving Vandals, insofar as the Basques did not already serve as a *cordon sanitaire*.[13] Aquitaine's Atlantic coast was being ravaged by Saxon pirates. But no matter how troublesome these raids were, the remarkably unseaworthy Goths would have been the last people to entrust with a naval campaign against the pirates. Even the mighty Gothic king Euric had handed over the protection of the coast as well as the command of his fleet to local senators.[14] It thus seems that the Gothic federates were supposed to fight a domestic Roman enemy; in other words, they were employed for the preservation of the existing social order. But this was something in which the senatorial nobility also had a lively interest. The many "popular movements" springing up from among the "internal proletariat" had to be separated from the barbarian threat, the "external proletariat," as Paulinus of Pella clearly realized at the siege of Bazas.[15] The rebarbarized Bretons and the various Bagaudian bands had to be kept away from southern Gaul. Whoever wanted to regain this Roman heartland for the *imperium* could not allow its constituent parts to break away from the empire, refuse to pay taxes, and expropriate, expel, and kill the ruling class, which believed it owned the state the same way it did its latifundia.[16] But if the interests of the Gothic king and his magnates were combined with those of the Aquitanian senators, the danger could be defeated.[17] Both groups had the common desire to preserve the existing order, for they had become for each other *consortes vel hospites*.[18] It is not clear how permanent Constantius and his advisors intended the Gothic settlement to be. It is also not certain whether the imperial government in 418 or 419 entered into another *foedus* with the Goths when it ordered them settled in Aquitania II. Our sources either combined the treaty of 416 with the Gothic settlement in 418 or they accurately reported that the death of Valia, the royal partner to the treaty, necessitated a new *foedus*. That the local nobility had to give hostages to the federates supports the second possibility, for such a stipulation must have been set down in a contract in some way or another.[19] After Valia's death there was apparently no tribal crisis, and Theoderid, son or rather son-in-law of Alaric I, "became the next man to assume power."[20]

Nothing is known about the earlier life of the new Gothic king. The

Roman observers were interested exclusively in the fate of the treaty and the Goths' loyalty to it. In 422, Gothic federates marched in the Roman army against the Vandals in Spain. In the moment of victory the Goths deserted their allies and the Romans suffered a serious defeat.[21] Theoderid himself may have ordered this step. In any case, this act of treason had no consequences whatsoever. In 423 the emperor Honorius died; the question of the succession was problematic,[22] and two years later the Goths appeared before the walls of Arles. With this the Goths began their tiresomely regular marches to the Gallo-Roman capital,[23] but the city itself was never taken nor the *foedus* ever broken. At times other cities as well, for example, Narbonne,[24] became the goal of Gothic summer excursions. Bloody conflicts—and the Gothic-Roman clashes were bloody—must not be downplayed, but they were not meant to destroy the existing order; they aimed rather at raising the "market value" of the Gothic federates. This is revealed by the general outcry when a Roman commander did not adhere to the rules of the game and wanted to take Toulouse and destroy the Goths.[25]

When the Goths appeared before Arles in 425 they were intercepted by Aëtius.[26] With his Hunnic mercenaries Aëtius established a barbarian equilibrium in Gaul during the next decades which worked remarkably well.[27] His antagonist Bonifatius, whose defense of Marseille had nearly cost Athaulf his life,[28] was in Africa in 427 commanding a Gothic federate army.[29] In 430 the Goths once again marched on Arles. But Aëtius was on the spot and the Goths withdrew; their leader was captured by the Romans. At the same time Aëtius defeated the Iuthungi and the rebels in Noricum, who would occupy his attention once more in 431.[30] In that same year Theoderid entered into "treacherous" negotiations with the Spanish Suevi. The negotiations led to nothing, but the Romans may have had a different idea of what loyalty to a treaty meant.[31] In 433, however, the Goths were ready for action when their former queen Galla Placidia called for their aid against Aëtius. She commanded the primarily Gothic *buccellarii* of her two former husbands, and this was the reason why she was exiled to Constantinople after the death of her brother: she had simply become too powerful. It is not known whether Toulousan federates also came to Italy to help her at that time. Aëtius, in any case, lost neither his position nor his authority— he had the Huns on his side.[32]

The Goths, the "poison of the state," welcomed every problem of the Romans as an opportunity to improve their own position. When in 435 a great revolt of the Bagaudae shook the region of central Gaul between the Loire and the Seine, the Aquitanian federates got involved, just as they later took advantage of the unrest that was caused by the downfall of the

Burgundians.[33] On the latter occasion, in the year 436, Theoderid wanted to reach the Rhone. He led his army in person against Narbonne, where he remained until 437 in order to lay siege to the city. Just when it was about to fall, the general Litorius, second in command after Aëtius, appeared on the scene, smashed through the Gothic siege lines with his Hunnic horsemen, put the enemy to flight, and for the time supplied the starving population with grain.[34] The year 438 brought no victories for the Goths, and in 439 Litorius stood before the walls of Toulouse.[35] Theoderid now resorted to negotiations and even called in Catholic bishops to help. The last time we heard of such a diplomatic move by the Goths was when the victorious Alaric was trying to force the government of Ravenna to yield to his demands.[36] Now it was a question of survival. Litorius, however, declined to negotiate and continued fighting. Despite some significant initial successes he was unexpectedly captured by the hard-pressed Goths, thus losing the battle and soon after his life.[37] It is surprising to read in the biography of Bishop Orientius of Auch—who had so loudly lamented the devastation of Gaul at the beginning of the century—that its hero had led the delegation to Litorius and had even prayed for the victory of the Goths. Moreover, this source celebrates the defeat and death of Litorius as the liberation from foreign oppression and as the downfall of an evildoer who had trusted in pagan practices. Litorius was indeed a pagan and for that reason had already incurred the contempt of his contemporary, Salvian of Marseille, who could fit Litorius very nicely into his image of the "world turned upside down": the piety of the Gothic king versus the godlessness of the Roman leader.[38] The value of the late *Vita Orientii* as a source was long disputed and has been positively established only in recent times.[39] The land under Gothic rule was also the homeland of the Romans, and they preferred the Gothic "Getae" to the Hunnic "Scythians."[40]

An exception to the common trend is a report from the year 439 which says that a certain *Vetericus*-Videric remained loyal to the Romans and distinguished himself through his military abilities. This Goth was probably an Amal who was pursuing a policy toward Rome which was independent of the Balthic king Theoderid at the very time when the existence of the Visigothic kingdom stood on the razor's edge. Was he perhaps planning to overthrow Theoderid with Roman help and become king himself, as Jordanes seems to indicate?[41]

Avitus, who had become praetorian prefect of Gaul in 439 and who had already proved himself in a diplomatic mission to Theoderid, once again negotiated a peace.[42] Then in 442 the Vandal nobles rose up against their king, an event that nearly caused the collapse of the African kingdom. It is possible that Gaiseric's son Huneric had married a daughter of Theoderid's as early as 429. The Visigothic princess no doubt became involved in the revolt of the nobility—Huneric was living at that time as a hostage in Ravenna—and was sent back to her father with her nose and ears mutilated. In view of the carefully cultivated enmity between Vandals and Goths, a *renversement des alliances* never lasted very long. They showed much greater enthusiasm for fighting each other, even though Goths had gone to Africa in the army of Gaiseric. But these groups had probably split off from the main Gothic tribe, indeed, had become its opponents, when Valia eliminated a series of rival claimants to the throne.[43] In general, however, Gothic-Vandal alliances were always short-term affairs.

In 444 a high-ranking fugitive arrived in Toulouse: this was *magister militum* Sebastianus, who had fallen from favor. It is no wonder that he became a nuisance to the Gothic king, who held the same rank and who got rid of him by sending him to Spain. For some time Sebastianus led a wild, adventurous life, eventually ending up in Africa, where he was eliminated by Gaiseric.[44] In 446 there was another Roman campaign against the Spanish Suevi in which the Gothic federates participated. Booty was a great temptation, and the expedition also gave the restless young warriors something to do.[45] But this did not keep Theoderid from seeking an accommodation with the same Suevi two or three years later. His wealth of daughters allowed him to supply the Suevic king Rechiar with one in 449, and he had the couple married in Toulouse. On the way home from the meeting with his father-in-law and possibly supported by a Gothic contingent, Rechiar ravaged the area around Zaragoza and captured Ilerda.[46]

The Gallic community of Romans and barbarians appeared to outsiders as a "union of discordant peoples."[47] But the year 451 showed that this community survived its severest test. Gaiseric was stirring up trouble, and Attila was using diplomacy in an effort to split apart the Gallic peoples.[48] And then Attila attacked. His adversary was Aëtius, *patricius* and *magister utriusque militiae*, with whom the Huns had kept up a strong friendship for decades. Now the commander-in-chief of the Roman troops opposed the former allies with all his might. His forces comprised all the peoples who had found a home in fifth-century Gaul, both those who had immigrated and those who had developed into a people there. In addition to the Visigoths, the *Origo Gothica* lists Rhenish Franks, Bretons, Sarmatian and Germanic *laeti*, Burgundians, and Gallic Saxons as well as members of former Roman military districts. To these were added the Alans from Orléans under the leadership of their federate king Sangiban, an unreliable fellow when it came to fighting Attila. To keep the Alans from deserting or running away, Aëtius had to wedge them in between his own people and the Goths.[49]

At first the Goths had hesitated to join their old enemy Aëtius. But on his third great diplomatic mission to Theoderid, Avitus succeeded in persuading them to do their duty as federates.[50] In the summer the king and his two eldest sons, Thorismund and Theodoric, marched with the Gothic army into Champagne.[51] The great battle took place on the Catalaunian (or more precisely, the Mauriacan) Fields between Troyes and Châlons-sur-Marne.[52] Although the battle ended in a draw, or was perhaps even intentionally left undecided by Aëtius,[53] the epochal confrontation destroyed Attila's aura of invincibility. Theoderid was killed in action, and Thorismund, who was nearly captured by the Huns, was in a hurry to get back to Toulouse.[54] Most details of the battle are insignificant for a history of the Goths, but it is important to note that here Goths fought against Goths. For the Huns had been joined both by the Gepids[55] and by those Goths who lived outside the empire and whom we call Ostrogoths. Led by the three royal brothers, Valamir, Thiudimir, and Vidimir, the Amali directly confronted the Balthi. Indeed, an Amal called Andagis supposedly hurled the spear that killed the Visigothic king Theoderid.[56] More than twenty years later the son of the youngest Amal prince went to visit the fourth son of the Visigothic king whom his father had fought so vigorously.[57] But Euric—and the *Origo Gothica* states this quite explicitly—had been too young to participate in the battle on the Catalaunian Fields.[58]

Thorismund had too many ambitious brothers: he and his kingship did not get very old. In the years of his rule, from 451 to 453, he made war on the Alans of Orléans and marched again on Arles. Aëtius was militarily unable to prevent him from doing this. The praetorian prefect Ferreolus did not admit the Goths into the city but invited the king for a meal. The king was lavishly entertained and perhaps also received a heavy, gem-studded bowl, with which he returned home, supposedly satisfied. Other reasons for Thorismund's return would have been news of a conspiracy of his brother or the desire to prepare a general offensive against Roman Gaul.[59] But that plan was never realized in any way. The victory over the Alans at Orléans was also not complete, since Childeric's Franks were left with plenty to do there.[60]

Theodoric (II), the third Toulousan king, did not actually reestablish the *foedus,* since it in fact had never lapsed, but he undoubtedly made the treaty with Rome effective.[61] Already in 454 his brother and vice-king Frideric "on Roman orders" destroyed Spanish Bagaudae,[62] and in the following year Theodoric even tried his hand at "making" emperors. Avitus, a frequent guest at Toulouse since 418/419, arrived in the city once again in the spring of 455 on an important diplomatic mission. Avitus had held high Roman office and had just recently been made commander-in-chief.[63] After the violent end of the Theodosian dynasty—in March 455 Galla Placidia's son Valentinian III was murdered—the new emperor also had to gain the recognition of the federates. A special problem in this regard was the "legitimistic" Visigoths. The personal talks were effective: Avitus was convincing, and with Theodoric on his right and Frideric on his left he entered Toulouse in a festive procession. The treaty was now confirmed.[64]

But when it became known shortly thereafter that Avitus had achieved success for a dead man, Theodoric urged his former teacher to assume the purple himself. The royal brothers led him to Arles, where Avitus was proclaimed emperor by Roman soldiers, in keeping with the proper procedure, but not without having first obtained the support of the Gallic aristocracy in lengthy negotiations. Finally the Goths made a peaceful entrance into the Gallic capital, which they had so often assaulted without success, and the Roman-barbarian community seemed to prove its viability once more.[65] At the end of summer Avitus marched to Italy with a Gothic corps among his troops. The subsequent fate of the last "Gallic" emperor was bitter, for there was not enough Gothic support. If Theodoric (II) was planning to pursue an Italian policy, it would have overtaxed his kingdom's forces, even if he had not divided them. In fact the king became involved in Spain under circumstances that remind us of the time of Valia and that prevented him from giving urgently needed help to his emperor in 456.[66] The only goal that seemed important to the Goths was their "imperial mission" to take action south of the Pyrenees. In this they were supported by the other federates of southern Gaul, the Burgundians under their leader Gundiok, who is "suspected of being a Goth." But the evil brother-in-law Rechiar, the Catholic king of the Suevi, paid with his life for his resistance to the emperor; apparently the Goths had soon conquered his kingdom, so that Theodoric could install a non-Suevic, the Varnian Ag(r)iwulf, as governor.[67] The losses of the Suevi were so severe that their *regnum* was considered "destroyed and finished."

The news of the death of Avitus reached the Gothic king in Mérida-Emerita, where he was encamped with his army at the beginning of 457. As he was undoubtedly concerned about the security of his position in Gaul, Theodoric immediately returned to Toulouse and handed over the Spanish war to his subordinate officers, who conducted it with great cruelty against the Suevi and the provincials.[68] The hostilities would continue for many years. Agriwulf deserted the Gothic camp and made himself king, but he was captured and executed in June 457.[69] In 461 the Suevic claimant to the throne, Rechimund, would try unsuccessfully to gain the support of Theodoric. From 458 to 462 Gothic troops fought in Spain alone and with Roman troops. Indeed, in the end the Gothic king Theodoric even appointed a Roman commander-in-chief, which shows how well Toulouse had weathered the anarchy that had meanwhile broken out.[70] Avitus had been succeeded by the able emperor Majorian, who came to Gaul in the winter of 458/459 and took vigorous measures.[71] His actions had to be all the more surprising since the Goths, Burgundians, and Gauls from the south had agreed to sulk and not accept a "foreign" emperor. But Aegidius joined his friend Majorian. Appointed commander-in-chief and *patricius,* Aegidius for a while played the role in which Aëtius had been cast until his murder. But while Aëtius had sought to preserve the equilibrium within the Gallic community with the help of the Hunnic warriors from outside, Aegidius drew his support largely from the Salian Franks under Clovis's father Childeric.[72] Killing and burning, Aegidius marched down the Rhone, got control of Lyons in 458, and in the next year allowed himself to be shut up in Arles by the Goths.[73] The Goths thought that they were supposed to perform the usual federate ritual outside the walls of the Gallic capital, but they were rudely awakened from their daydreaming by an attack of Majorian and the "Frankish" Aegidius. After suffering heavy losses they withdrew and remained loyal federates;[74] at that time St. Martin is reported to have performed his first anti-Gothic miracle.[75]

The emperor next planned to attack the Vandals by way of Spain. The Goths gladly participated in the expedition, that is, they followed him for half the way only to split off and march once again against the Suevi with imperial authorization and Roman troops. Gaiseric, who had already tried to mediate between the Suevi and the Goths in 457 in an effort to forge a triple alliance against the empire, defended himself successfully. Off Cartagena Majorian lost his fleet and his "luck." He was dead by 461.[76] The master of Italy was now the half-Goth Ricimer; the upshot of his coup was that the empire nearly lost Gaul. Aegidius rebelled, whereas the Goths supported the new emperor Ricimer had installed, hoping to receive in return some sort of reward. There was total chaos: Romans fought against Romans and made deals with the barbarians. A general who was besieged in Narbonne by Aegidius called on Toulouse for assistance, and the Goths entered the coastal city in 462. Frideric was given the task of occupying and organizing the conquered territories, but already in the following year, 463, he had to protect the northern border of the Gothic realm. In 463 Aegidius attacked with his Franks via Orléans and defeated the Goths; Frideric was killed in action. Thereafter Aegidius was seriously planning a move against Toulouse, while he encouraged Gaiseric to attack the Italy of Ricimer, who had caused all these calamities. It was a stroke of great good fortune for the Visigoths that Aegidius died in 465; as a result they were able to launch a counteroffensive and conquer Roman territory along the Loire.[77]

About the same time that the Visigothic kingdom was in great distress, the Spanish Suevi recovered. Their new king Remismund first overcame the tribal conflicts among his people and was then able to establish himself as an equal negotiating partner of the Goths. Around 465 Remismund married a Visigothic woman and probably became the "son in arms" of Theodoric (II). In return, in 466 the latter sent him an Arian missionary with the Homeric name Ajax, and in matters of church policy the Catholicizing Suevi and the Goths were joined together.[78]

Theodoric was murdered by his brother Euric in the year 466.[79] This deed annulled the Roman-Gothic *foedus* that had just reached the half-century mark, and it suspended for nearly a decade the union of the Toulousan *regnum* with the empire. But this also meant that the marches on the Gallic capital of Arles, which had been the ritual procedure for amending the *foedus* of 418, came to an end. Without glossing over those marches against the city—for this game was deadly, especially for third parties—we can say that these "parades" resembled the posturing that goes on today during collective bargaining. In the fighting against the Bretons, Bagaudae, Alans, and Suevi, the Gothic kings made sure that the army acquired booty and at the same time released the excessive energy of its warriors. Moreover, the operations against the popular uprising of the Bagaudae both north and south of the Pyrenees served the purpose of maintaining the existing social order. For the representatives of the Roman imperial government the *exercitus Gothorum* was often the only "executive body" that could—insofar as it was in the Goths' own interest to do so—preserve peace at home and abroad.[80] This was also the reason why Roman generals spared the often defeated Goths of Aquitaine; the commander who did not adhere to this rule could count on being defamed, even by the Romans.

The Visigothic "Superpower," 466–507

EURIC (466–484) AND THE BREACH OF THE *FOEDUS* OF 416/418

In the year 466 Theodoric lost the throne and his life. At that time the Visigoths controlled extensive territories that lay outside the area assigned to them in 418 and therefore did not legally belong to their federate kingdom.

This was especially true in Spain, whereas the Gallic acquisitions since 418 were not very significant. Both north and south of the Pyrenees the Toulousan kings ruled over a land composed of administrative units of the Roman Empire and considered part of the imperial dominion. Once in power, Euric did not change the course his predecessor had charted so much as pursue it on a larger scale: the result was the creation of the most important successor state to the Roman Empire, a Gallo-Spanish *regnum* in which perhaps close to ten million people lived within an area of almost three hundred thousand square miles. The new kingdom was nearly six times the size of the old federate realm.[81] The life span of Euric's creation was about equal to the forty-year wandering that had led the Goths to Toulouse.[82] But comparisons of this sort combine coincidence with symbolic numbers; the historian is therefore really not entitled to make them.

Euric's older brother had fought for decades in Spain as loyal federate of Rome. His actions against the Suevi and Bagaudae were undertaken on imperial command and in the Goths' own interest. In Gaul this policy became possible after 461, when several emperors were struggling for recognition and Theodoric could choose in whose name he would profit.[83] South of the Pyrenees all that was at stake for a long time was booty or on occasion a fortified base. In Gaul, however, the Gothic kings tried to extend their territory, fighting for every inch of land that would increase the *regnum*. The wars had created a powerful Gothic army that even before 460 had become so attractive that high-ranking Roman military officers offered their services:[84] ". . . for the victors grow steadily in power and strength," says Procopius, describing with this timeless comment the attraction of successful kings of the army.[85]

Theodoric had made the fullest possible use of his *foedus* with Rome and had thereby secured both his military operations and his conquest. But as imperial authority declined "on account of the frequent changes of Roman princes,"[86] Gothic policy had to adjust to new circumstances. Euric surely did not kill Theodoric because of his Roman sympathies. Nor did the murder take place because Theodoric was persisting in the old course—this is shown by the conquest along the Loire after 464.[87] Rather it was motivated by a thirst for power. For shortly after Euric began his reign, the moment came to put an end to Roman rule in southern Gaul.

Initially we hear only of a diplomatic offensive of the new king. In 466 and 467 envoys were sent to the Suevi, the Vandals, and the emperor, thus indicating the three powers Euric had to reckon with.[88] No one knows the content of these negotiations.[89] In any case, when the Romans threatened Carthage in 467, the Gothic as well as the Suevic envoys who had accompanied the Romans, withdrew in a hurry.[90] They probably did not have an altogether clear conscience, which should reveal a good deal about the purpose of their missions. We do not know if Euric formally abrogated the *foedus,* but it is certain that he took action regarded as a breach of the treaty.[91] Anthemius's accession to power in 468 occurred at a time when no treaty existed and the Visigothic union with the empire was suspended. But even in 475, after the conclusion of a new treaty, the Visigothic kingdom remained beyond the pale of imperial law. Anthemius's *novellae* were the first laws that were not incorporated into the *lex Romana Visigothorum.*[92] Mere coincidence can be ruled out, particularly since Anthemius had special support among the Gallo-Roman notables.[93]

The new emperor was from the East, and as a "puny little Greek" and a "hot-tempered Galatian" he was at first not taken seriously.[94] But in fact Anthemius was a capable general. He had once fought the Pannonian Ostrogoths and he immediately recognized how dangerous Euric was. In Gaul the Bretons, the Burgundians, and Aegidius's successors Paulus and Syagrius joined with the Salian and perhaps also the Rhenish Franks to form an anti-Gothic coalition, which the emperor intended to reinforce with a regular army from Italy.[95] South of the Pyrenees the Suevi and the Roman provincials were probably also to conclude a similar alliance.[96] From the imperial perspective the plan had been properly conceived, but it was put into effect only hesitantly and without coordination. The pitiful failure of the large-scale Roman offensive against the Vandals[97] took so much pressure off Euric that in 468 he began war in Spain. Remismund tried to negotiate, but Euric acted so quickly that the advancing Gothic army almost caught up with the Suevic envoys on their way home.[98] To the year 468 belongs the treason of Arvandus, who rejected the "Greek emperor" Anthemius and made an agreement with the Gothic king. As prefect of Gaul he advised Euric to attack the Bretons, not to make peace with the imperial government, and to divide Gaul between Goths and Burgundians.[99] No mention was made of the Romans and the Franks of northern Gaul, either because they were underestimated, disliked, or both. Even Sidonius Apollinaris felt threatened by the Frankish Mars on the Rhine while he praised the Gothic Mars on the Garonne.[100]

Since Romans and barbarians could come to no agreement among themselves or with each other, events took the course they had to: those whom Arvandus designated the enemy of the Goths were the first to suffer defeat. The Bretons of King Riothamus,[101] Sidonius's friend, tried to protect the still Roman Aquitania I from the Loire, but near Deols, today a suburb of Châteauroux on the Indre, they suffered such a crushing defeat that the survivors had to seek refuge with the Burgundians.[102] The second line was defended and held by Paulus with his Franks under Childeric.[103] Thus Tours and Bourges either remained in Roman hands for the moment or soon became Roman again temporarily.[104] Despite the setback in the north the Gothic invasion continued. Paulus was killed in action against the Saxons near Angers,[105] and the emperor Anthemius needed all his forces to maintain his position in Italy against his *patricius* Ricimer. But how seriously the emperor took the war in Gaul can be seen from his haste in sending an army across the Alps at the slightest easing of tensions between him and Ricimer. This was to be the last such force.[106] Euric crossed the Rhone and destroyed the imperial army, whose commanders, among them the emperor's own son, were killed.[107] This battle probably took place in the early part of summer 471.[108] Now the south of Gaul stood open to the Goths; their warriors appeared in the *civitates* of Arles, Riez, Avignon, Orange, Apt, Valence, and St. Paul-Trois-Châteaux. At this very moment the Burgundians finally remembered their duty as federates and drove the attackers back. In their retreat the Goths left behind a broad strip of scorched earth. The result was a severe famine among the Roman population.[109]

THE CONQUEST OF THE AUVERGNE AND TARRACONENSIS

Only a few areas of the declining Western empire offered the barbarian conquest such obstinate resistance as did the Auvergne in Aquitania I and the Tarraconensis in the Spanish Ebro valley. After the withdrawal of the Roman imperial authority the local nobility led the fight in each case. The leading strata of these two regions show a strong resemblance.[110] These people saw themselves as Romans, even though their Latinity often did not amount to much. In the Auvergne even the "better circles" still, or once again, spoke Celtic[111] but were at the same time convinced that they, like the Romans, were descended from the Trojans.[112] The strong ties of retainership that bound the Auvergnian lower strata to the landowning nobility also appear a Celtic trait.[113] Although the common people—"encircled on all sides" and without imperial support—could obviously think of something more reasonable than fighting the Goths, they nevertheless remained loyal to their masters.[114] They were persuaded because the notables had at their command well-armed private soldiers and had gained in Ecdicius, the son of the former emperor Avitus, a capable commander. Ecdicius was always good for a surprise move; with eighteen horsemen he hacked his way through "thousands of Goths" and successfully combated their tactics of attrition.[115] Support from the Burgundian federates was also enlisted, even though at Clermont their allies were not always entirely pleased with them.[116] The ideology of resistance was developed by Ecdicius's brother-in-law Sidonius Apollinaris. Bishop of Clermont since around 470, he defended Latinity and Latin Christendom as a unified concept against barbarians and heretics.

Sidonius Apollinaris was above all a rhetorically trained member of the higher nobility—"and a poet to boot." The reader will not take everything he says too literally, especially since he can be full of contradictions. Sidonius strikes us as a true intellectual: biased and not always consistent. But he conducted the fight against the Visigoths vigorously and—despite favorable kinship connections[117]—uncompromisingly, even at the risk that a Gothic victory could mean the end for him and his class.[118] His rousing words to a group of imperial negotiators whom he contacted before they went to Euric to discuss the fate of the Auvergne were spoken with such conviction that they had the intended effect.[119] At that time Sidonius could not have known that his fate after Rome's final abandonment of the Auvergne would take a more positive course than he had feared. Euric, however, had to control Clermont, which was driven like a wedge between his conquered territories and provided an open corridor of invasion for the Burgundians. The king, as Sidonius reports, would rather renounce the Mediterranean coast of Septimania than the Auvergne.[120]

The abrogation of the *foedus* had put an end to the fiction that the Goths were serving the *imperium,* not their own interests. The war that followed brought about a "late Roman awakening," but in the end Euric was victorious. First the Goths attacked Spain in 468, and although they pushed on in a hurry, they did not arrive in time to "protect" Lisbon against the Suevi: the besiegers and the besieged had already come to terms. The Roman commander handed the city over to the Suevi and soon after traveled at the head of a delegation of his former enemies to the emperor Anthemius to request assistance. It is possible that the Suevic-Roman action hastened Euric's decision and his preventive war in Gaul in 469.[121] For the next two years the main forces of the Goths were tied up north of the Pyrenees. In 472 Euric reduced the conflict in that area to minor battles in the Auvergne[122] and instead sent two Gothic armies to Spain in 472 and 473: one captured Pamplona and Zaragoza in the west, the other occupied the coastal cities, including Tarragona. One of the two commanders of the eastern army was the Visigothic *dux Hispaniarum* Vincentius. Barely a decade earlier he had still commanded as a Roman *dux.* Now he was fighting against the nobility of the Ebro valley, against his own countrymen. In a pitched battle the last Ibero-Roman resistance came to an end.[123] With the exception of the Suevic northeast and a few Basque pockets in the north Spain was under Gothic control. The attention now shifted back to the Auvergne.

Euric's war aims in Gaul were from the start known to friend and foe alike: all the land between the Atlantic, the Loire, and the Rhone was to become Gothic.[124] The chronology of events between 471 and 475, when the king actually achieved his aims, is unclear.[125] In 473 Arles and Marseille fell into Gothic hands, but we do not know the details.[126] Moreover, the rich sources for the Auvergnian war distort events and make it difficult for us to assess them properly. The *civitas* of Clermont was only one section of the Gallic theater of war, indeed, only one of eight *civitates* of the province of Aquitania I.[127] Supposedly all other seven *civitates* were in Euric's hands before 475. For the king appointed (probably as early as 471) as governor of Aquitania I the *dux* Victorius, who was, like the Spaniard Vincentius, a Roman and a Catholic.[128] This means that in the newly conquered territory along the Ebro as well as in Gaul local Romans held command as Visigothic *duces,* even though the war there was not yet over. There was at least one other Auvergnian senator who fought—supposedly involuntarily—in Euric's army against his countrymen.[129]

This makes us wonder just what criteria Sidonius Apollinaris and his friends used to judge their fellow Romans. People like Arvandus and Seronatus were considered traitors in 469/470, at the beginning of the war, when, in a situation that was "constitutionally" unclear, they gave administrative support to the Gothic expansion. Yet Vincentius and Victorius drew no condemnation when only a few years later they fought, weapon in hand, for the Gothic cause. The former Roman *duces* seemed to have gone over to Euric with their entire staffs. Arvandus lost his office and his status, Seronatus even his life, but the two generals were largely spared defamation.[130] And this was the case even though Victorius ruled as Euric's governor in a region where the Goths conducted campaigns year after year, in summer as in winter. Moreover, Victorius—who was not loved by all his countrymen[131]—captured Clermont, where he must also have decreed the banishment of Sidonius Apollinaris.[132]

In the spring of 475, after two previous unsuccessful negotiation attempts, Bishop Epiphanius of Pavia arrived in Toulouse. He had clear imperial orders to make peace at all costs. By concluding a new treaty Nepos accepted Euric's conquests without relinquishing his legal claim to the prefecture of Gaul. The emperor came to terms with Euric's conquests, but this did not establish legally the sovereignty of the Gothic kingdom. A formula was devised which in Ennodius's account would seem to indicate that the emperor was content "to be called friend, *amicus* [by the Visigothic king], even though he was entitled to be addressed as lord, *dominus*." In interpreting this passage we must bear in mind that Ennodius lived in Ostrogothic Italy of King Theodoric, whose policy called for an emperor with precisely such an attitude. In any case, Nepos was willing to recall Ecdicius from Gaul.[133] The *civitas Arvernorum* was handed over to the Goths, and Victorius established his headquarters there;[134] the city of Bourges itself was no doubt too exposed to serve as the center of Gothic administration.[135] Sidonius went into exile. For about two years he remained in confinement in the stronghold of Livia near Carcassonne.[136] Euric's measures were neither harsh nor mild—they were political: eliminating the leaders of the resistance without creating irreconcilable antagonism. In his place of exile Sidonius was busy throughout the day, but he does not tell us exactly what activities occupied his time.[137] The nights, however, were terrible: two perpetually drunk Gothic women disturbed his sleep by quarreling and bawling below his window every night.[138] Such living conditions are unpleasant (as any insomniac will readily understand). But after Sidonius had returned home, he cooperated well with the *dux et comes* Victorius[139] until the latter's downfall over internal conflicts. What then explains Sidonius's lenient attitude toward the Roman commander in Visigothic service? Victorius was a member of the noble clan of the Apollinares. Hence much of what strikes us as high-level politics and Roman-Gothic animosity was in reality a function of intergroup rivalries within Gaul's leading stratum. The fate of the Spaniard Vincentius will have been no different. Treason in this context seems not only a question of timing but also of party allegiance. But when in 479 Victorius had an Auvergnian nobleman killed, he was forced to flee to Italy where he met a tragic end. He was accompanied by none other than Sidonius's son Apollinaris, the same man who under Alaric II probably also became *comes* of the Auvergne, who fought at Vouillé against the Franks, and who followed in his father's footsteps when he became bishop in 515. But when the younger Apollinaris left his homeland in 479 with Victorius, his father had to face great difficulties.[140] Contradictory statements come from the poet's pen about his relations with the nobleman Victorius had slain. On one occasion Sidonius praises the Auvergnian for his courage in the fight against the Goths. On a different occasion he thwarts the man's candidacy for the bishopric of Bourges, the see of the metropolitan of Aquitania I, Sidonius's own superior. In this case, too, we note internal Auvergnian conflicts that probably date back to the days of the Gallic emperor Iovinus at the beginning of the fifth century.[141] In any case, Euric made use of such conflicts to strengthen his authority. Where the Gothic conquest met with resistance by local notables, the king gave one of them the task of first breaking the opposition militarily and then bringing about an administrative accommodation with the Gothic state. Men like Victorius built Catholic churches. And even as Visigothic *duces* they remained Romans.[142] Salla built bridges,[143] and Vincentius was even considered a *quasi-magister militum* of the Gothic king.[144]

THE LAST BATTLES WITH THE EMPIRE

The Visigothic armies had just won great victories in Spain and were still fighting in the Auvergne when Emperor Glycerius unintentionally sent much-needed reinforcements to Gaul. Italy had in 473 suffered an Ostrogothic invasion. The attackers came from Pannonia and were led by the Amal king Vidimir. He died shortly after his arrival in Italy, whereupon his son Vidimir the Younger inherited the army but not his father's kingship.[145] This group, which had split off from the main Ostrogothic tribe and which fought unsuccessfully in Italy after the death of its king, raised no opposition when the emperor got rid of them by sending them off to join the Visigoths.[146] Their leader—like his predecessor Videric in 427—was no serious threat to the king of Toulouse.[147] But just to be safe, Euric kept some of his Pannonian cousins within sight among his retainers[148] while others received border patrol duties along the Loire.[149] After 485 we probably hear of Vidimir on two other occasions. Bishop Ruricius of Limoges exchanged letters with a member of the high nobility by the name of Vittamar and sent him and his wife each one hundred pears. The shipment of such a perishable gift would point to the Limousin as the place where Vidimir settled, provided we are right in identifying him with Vittamar.[150]

The peace concluded in 475 with the *imperium occidentale* had lasted barely a year when the Western empire came to an end. Orestes, whose task was to contain the Visigoths after the departure of Ecdicius, was directly responsible for letting the southern province on the left bank of the Rhone, the remainder of imperial Gaul south of the Durance, fall into Gothic hands. Then in 475 the *patricius* Orestes chased out the legitimate emperor Nepos and made his own son Romulus *imperator*. But the *imperium* of this Augustulus, petty Augustus, was no more than an intermezzo, shorter and less significant than that of his immediate predecessor. After this, Odovacar stepped onto the Italian stage, where the drama "West Roman Empire" was being performed. In 476 the regional federate army made him king. Odovacar came from the Scirian royal clan, which had been at odds with the Orestes-Romulus clan since the days of Attila.[151] Now the day of reckoning had arrived. But Euric had made no treaty with the Italian king Odovacar, and the Gothic war began anew. The Burgundians, as loyal imperial federates, did try to stop Euric's expansion as best they could. But their efforts ended in defeat, and the Visigoths took Arles, the capital of Roman Gaul, in addition to Marseille. Thus the prefecture of Gaul disappeared until the Ostrogoths reestablished it.[152] It was probably also during this time that Vincentius met his end. Euric had sent him to Italy "like some sort of *magister militum*." There he was killed while fighting at the head of a Visigothic army against two commanders with the East Germanic names of Alla and Sindila. If these two men were Odovacar's generals, one would have to date this event to 476. In any case, "around 477" Odovacar accepted the reality of Euric's Gallic conquests.[153] The Visigothic king thus acquired nearly all of the bankrupt empire's "assets" in the "seven provinces."[154] Even the *civitas* of Vivier, located between the Massif Central and the Rhone, was now part of the Toulousan kingdom.[155] At this time the land south of the Pyrenees did not serve as a settlement area for the Goths.[156] But controlling it meant wealth and security, support, and a base to fall back on in case the geopolitical situation changed. In the enormous expansion of Euric we can also see an overextension of the Gothic *gens*.[157] But judgments of this sort are based on the catastrophe of 507 and are unhistorical. Whoever makes them wants to be more perceptive than the people of the past. What Euric certainly did not intend was the establishment of a universal monarchy, the realization, so to speak, of Athaulf's dream.[158] Although Sidonius Apollinaris sees the entire world assembled at the Visigothic court and even speaks of Persian envoys, the kingdom of Euric nevertheless rested on the Latin-barbarian particularism to which the future belonged.[159] The aim of the royal policy was the establishment of a compact *patria Gothorum,* with the Loire, the Rhone, and the Durance as the "wet border" against the rest of Gaul, the Mediterranean Alps as the border with Italy, and the open Iberian peninsula as the Gothic hinterland. This extensive core area, comprising nearly the entire Gallic prefecture, was to be shaped, consolidated, and ruled by Toulouse.

THE ORGANIZATION AND DEVELOPMENT OF DOMINION

After making peace with Odovacar, Euric turned to consolidation of his rule.[160] We even hear of roadblocks and police actions to impede free communication,[161] measures that strike us as unpleasantly modern. But it is possible that the Gothic government confined such measures to the border area between Provence and Burgundy, where tensions persisted. When

Sidonius was at the royal court at Bordeaux, probably in 476, he met a "Burgundian who forced his seven-foot-tall body down on its knees and sued for peace." In addition he came across an "old Sygambrian" who was letting his hair grow again after having it cut as a sign of defeat. It is believed that at that time a Gothic-Burgundian peace was concluded. The Sygambrian was probably a Frankish prince who had been taken captive by the Goths when Euric was supporting the peoples along the Waal against their mighty Frankish neighbors. For before 475 the Salian Franks had attacked the kingdoms of the Heruli, Varni, and Thuringians on the lower Rhine but were beaten back by a Gothic fleet. Thereafter Euric supposedly extorted a *foedus,* but it is more likely that he made this treaty with the western Heruli, the Varni, and the Thuringians rather than the Franks.[162] Clues to Gothic-Varnian relations can already be found during the reigns of Euric's predecessor.[163] Now the king strengthened the small peoples in the Frankish rear. The ties to the Belgian/southern Dutch coastal region must have had a lasting impact, since on the eve of the battle of Vouillé it was still possible to remind people of them.[164] Euric, in any case, recognized the danger that the Franks posed and found a way to contain their expansionist drive. But the attack by sea also reveals the considerable military potential the new Gothic power had at its disposal. Its Atlantic fleet, led by Roman commanders, thus did not merely set sail to catch Saxon pirates off the coast of Aquitaine.[165] Euric's intervention in the north of Gaul was the first Gothic victory over the Franks, and on top of that it was won far from the Goths' own base in the Franks' "back yard." Moreover, Euric's course of action is reminiscent of Roman practices. The king could therefore appear to Sidonius as a universal monarch, not unlike the way in which Cassiodorus looked upon the Amal king Theodoric. The consolidation of the greater Gothic state, however, would have required a corresponding ecclesiastical and legal policy, but such a policy was implemented only under Euric's successor and son, Alaric II.

Before the end of 484 Euric died at Arles, of a natural death, as later reports took pains to emphasize, since no other ruler of Toulouse was so fortunate.[166] That this city was the king's last stop has led to speculation that he was planning to invade Italy from there and pursue, after all, a policy of universal dominion.[167] But there is no good evidence for this.

ALARIC II (484–507)

On December 28, 484, in Toulouse, Alaric took his father's place. The new king was young, probably the same age as his Frankish antagonist Clovis.[168]

Alaric's reign gets no full treatment in the sources, and the little they do contain is overshadowed by his death in the battle at Vouillé and the downfall of the Toulousan kingdom. Alaric was therefore considered a weakling, an unworthy successor to his father whose "iron rule"[169] would have been needed to maintain the Goths' position as a great power.[170] A judgment of this sort has little value; moreover, it is also false.

In 486 or 487 Clovis attacked the realm of the Roman king Syagrius, conquered it, and forced the defeated ruler to flee. Syagrius was received in Toulouse, but when Clovis threatened war he was handed over to the Franks, who killed him. This chain of events seems to prove Alaric's "timidness, which in no way reflected the actual balance of power."[171] But it is nowhere written that Syagrius was in fact handed over in 486 or 487. At that time Clovis got no farther than the Seine; only after several more years did the Franks succeed in occupying the rest of the Gallo-Roman buffer state north of the Loire.[172] Clovis's threat of war would have been ineffectual unless the Franks and Goths were actually neighbors. No later than 490 the Visigoths fought on the side of the Amali against Odovacar. After the latter had been defeated in 493, Theodoric married the sister of Clovis, evidently making an attempt to be on good terms with the Frankish king.[173] It is conceivable that the other Gothic state demonstrated its willingness for peace by handing over Syagrius. Both steps could be seen as a response to the advance of Clovis, who according to this interpretation would have reached the Loire border shortly before or around 493.

In Spain in 494 and then again in 497 we can observe the first real signs of a Visigothic immigration.[174] Previously this large country had been a sort of mix between a crown colony and a military training ground. Now the Goths themselves began to arrive, and it seems easy to guess why. By 496 the Franks had already crossed the Loire; in that year they were expelled from Saintes deep inside Gothic territory. In 498, shortly after the second wave of Gothic settlers is recorded in Spain, the Franks even occupied Bordeaux and in the process captured the Gothic *dux*.[175] The expedition for the recapture of Saintes took place at the same time as the outbreak of serious unrest in the Spanish Ebro valley which was put down in 497 with great brutality. Discontent flared up again a decade later in the area around Tortosa, apparently in the Bagaudian tradition.[176] It is possible that this unrest reflected attempts by regional groups of the middle and lower classes to defend themselves against Gothic newcomers. For the new settlers were all notables—the poorer Goths remained behind in Gaul—and they increased the pressure that was already felt by the native population from the owners of latifundia. Thus the hostilities around 500 provide late evidence for why Constantius had recalled the Goths to Aquitaine in 418.[177] But Alaric's military activity in Spain at a time when he was also winning victories against the Franks is evidence for the fighting power of his army. His father and uncle had also conducted wars on two fronts.[178] Only a commitment in three areas, as happened in the early 490s when the Amal Goths needed help, overextended the military resources of the Toulousan kingdom and therefore had to be avoided. In this way we can explain Alaric's attempt to appease Clovis in the disgraceful Syagrius affair.

Eventually the Franks retreated and the Goths switched to the offensive. When the Franks in 500 attacked the Burgundians—quarrels within the royal clan offered an opportunity to meddle in Burgundian affairs—Alaric supported the legitimate royal party. The Franks were defeated, Frankish prisoners were sent to Toulouse, and the victorious Burgundian king Gundobad ceded Avignon to the Goths in 501. The Toulousan kingdom clearly did not lack the energy for expansion, another reason not to explain the collapse in 507 as the logical consequence of persistent weakness. It does appear, however, that Alaric II eventually did strain the economic resources of his realm, for he had to raise new revenues by issuing debased coinage. Moreover, on the eve of the great Visigothic-Frankish war, Theodoric the Great showed concern about the effectiveness of his son-in-law's army. We would really like to know on what basis he made this assessment of the Visigothic army. The statement that the Toulousan army had suffered a decline in fighting strength from the days when it defeated Attila on the Catalaunian Fields sounds too literary and conventional to be taken all too seriously.[179]

Alaric II and Clovis met in 502 for direct talks on an island in the Loire near Amboise. Here they ended the warfare between their two kingdoms which had flared time and again since the second half of the 490s.[180] Peace talks in the middle of a border river and an agreement on an *amicitia* are reminiscent of 369 when the emperor Valens and the judge Athanaric negotiated with each other on the Danube. Did the Gothic tradition still remember this in 502? This time the Goths were "the southerners." But the events that followed the talks in 378 and 507 become comparable only in retrospect. When the two parties met in 502 the purpose was merely to furnish proof that the two kings were equal in rank and power.[181]

The peace lasted for a few years. Then in 507 Theodoric the Great not only had to intervene for some of the defeated Alamanni but also had to admonish Clovis to keep peace and warn Alaric against provoking the Franks. The western Heruli, the Varni, and the Thuringians were also reminded of the debt they owed Euric, and were asked to exert pressure on the Salian Franks along the lower Rhine. Finally, Theodoric advised the Burgundians to abandon their suicidal alliance with Clovis.[182] All these efforts were to no avail: Clovis kept his Burgundian allies and penetrated into Visigothic territory. Alaric's restraint, which met with Ravenna's approval, was not rewarded.[183] Theodoric's threat to intervene on behalf of his son-in-law did not scare Clovis.[184] Since Byzantine warships were cruising along the Italian coast and dropping off land forces, the Ostrogoths were not able to intervene in Gaul in time.[185] Alaric was aware of his difficult position, but the magnates forced him to offer resistance in a pitched battle.[186] At Vouillé near Poitiers the two armies led by their kings met in the late summer of 507. The Goths, who were perhaps numerically inferior, were not able to charge over the enemy: the Frankish infantry was too numerous and too stubborn to be confused by a lightning-quick "nomadic style" cavalry attack with feigned retreats and other maneuvers. Alaric II was killed, supposedly by Clovis himself. The death of the king and the destruction of the army ended the Toulousan kingdom, but Gothic history continued.[187]

The Legal and Ecclesiastical Policies of Euric and Alaric II

Any discussion of the legal and ecclesiastical policies of the last two Toulousan kings must deal with four questions: first, the problems revolving around the enactment and scope of the *Codex Euricianus*, whether it is to be seen as a codification from the period around 475 or as a step parallel to the *Breviarium Alaricianum;* second, the *Breviarium Alaricianum* itself, which was probably promulgated on February 2, 506; third, the anti-Catholic measures of Euric and Alaric II; fourth, Alaric's attempt to bring about a reconciliation between the Arian Gothic minority and the Catholic Roman majority, for which purpose he summoned a council at Agde, the protocols of which were signed on September 10, 506.[188] The cancellation of the *foedus* of 418 had made Euric lord of his Roman subjects. Then the empire accepted the reality of the situation by the new *foedus* of 475. While the Visigothic king, as the highest-ranking military official of a Roman region, had up to that time already been in charge of supervising the Catholic church,[189] his quasi-magisterial responsibility now changed into an emperorlike rule over the church. The same development took place in the field of law. All legislation, especially the further development and adaptation of Roman law, was in the hands of the Visigothic king. Within his sphere of authority the Catholic Romans were just as much subject to him as were the "confessors" of the *lex Gothica*.[190] The *lex Gothica* not only regulated cult and religion among the barbarian Arians but also embraced the Gothic community of law. The creation of a uniform stratum of subjects, however, presupposed the solution to a number of problems,[191] including the organization as well as the territorial structure of the Roman church in the Gothic state and the "territoriality" or "personality" of royal legislation.

THE LEGISLATION OF EURIC AND ALARIC II

Once the Gothic federates were settled in Gaul they lived according to their customary law. They may have called the law *belagines*, but we do not know whether the term described a legal reality for both Gothic peoples or only for the Ostrogoths. It is said that the *belagines* were written statutes, but there is no basis whatsoever for this assumption in Visigothic tradition.[192] Moreover, it is also disputed whether the Goths' barbarian law was in fact so extraordinarily resilient that it lived on even in the Spanish-Septimanian "customals." To be sure, the *lex Gothica* of the post-Toulousan era was more extensive than the royal law of the *Leges Visigothorum*. But only the latter was the *lex scripta*; still in the High Middle Ages in Catalonia and Septimania it was cited not only frequently but usually with meticulous accuracy, and it had a greater validity than the Gothic customary law, which would have much too readily allowed recourse to judicial duels.[193]

Not long after 418 the traditional Gothic customs were no longer sufficient to regulate all the problems posed by Goths and Romans living side by side. And so Theoderid had to promulgate written statutes concerning inheritance and private property, statutes that were certainly expanded by Euric's predecessor and brother Theodoric.[194] The structure and scope of pre-Eurician legislation is a popular subject of dispute among legal historians; especially whether or not it was the Visigothic king Theodoric (II) or the Ostrogoth Theodoric the Great who had issued the *Edictum Theoderici*. Moreover, it has been questioned whether the *Codex Euricianus* in its present form was in fact codified by Euric. What is beyond dispute is that around 475 the Visigothic king enacted laws, and no doubt a considerable portion was absorbed into the oldest Visigothic *lex scripta*, which is today generally considered the *Codex Euricianus*. But there is a good possibility that the act of codification itself belongs to the time of Alaric II.[195] Be that as it may, the legislation of all Gothic kings could not get by without

Roman lawyers. It goes without saying that the language of the lex was the Latin of "the laws as they were practiced in the provinces." This vulgar Roman law differed from classical or classicistic jurisprudence in its strong tendency toward simplification, popularization, and adaptation to the realities and needs of a "smaller space." It runs counter to that universalism that characterizes the legal work of Justinian. The Visigothic codification brought about the victory of Roman vulgar law and the final "turning away from the legal developments in the Eastern empire, which were influenced and determined by the emperors."[196] Thus the *Leges Visigothorum* were never the written fixation of a whole Gothic tribal law but always selective and statutory royal law. At the beginning stands the *Codex Euricianus,* which shall retain its accustomed name despite the problematic attribution.

A palimpsest from the sixth century transmits only fragments of the *Codex Euricianus,* probably about one-sixth of the original length. There have thus been numerous attempts to reconstruct the missing portions. These efforts are based on the later laws of the Visigoths and even on the southern Germanic "tribal laws," among them especially the Bavarian *lex.* Although the results remain controversial, they do attest the epochal and exemplary achievement of this legislation, which, together with the *Breviarium Alaricianum,* was as important for the future as Ulfilas's translation of the Bible.[197]

The fragments deal with disputes arising from the cohabitation of Romans and Goths. They regulate questions of custody, loans, purchases, and gifts and convey to the Goths such important devices as the last will, loans at interest, and the use of charters, the *frabaúhtaboka,* as they are called in Italy in the mid-sixth century. Moreover, Euric, and not Alaric II, was probably the first legislator in the Roman world who recognized the institution of "private" retainers.[198] Many have puzzled over the identity of the Gallo-Romans who assisted in drawing up the Eurician legislation, and many have tried to find the *consiliarius* Leo among them. Certainty on this question is impossible.[199]

The greatest problem raised is whether the *Codex Euricianus* promulgated personal or territorial law, in other words, whether the codex was valid only for the Goths or for all Gallic and Spanish subjects of the Visigothic kingdom. In discussions on legal history the general historian can participate only as an interested listener. Nevertheless, he may be allowed to make a few comments. If the *Codex Euricianus* was in fact enacted around 475 and provided adequate territorial law, Alaric II could have spared himself the trouble of promulgating the "Roman law of the Visigoths." In fact Alaric's act was a necessity, and the *Breviarium Alaricianum* was made law the year before his death. But if Euric codified only Gothic personal law, two questions arise: (1) why did the Gothic kings let more than a generation pass after 475 before making themselves legal lords of their "Roman subjects," and (2) why were the Romans satisfied to live by a legislation that had not been amended in over forty years? Such a gulf between legislation and legal reality is hard to imagine. The problem could be instantly solved, however, if it were assumed that the *Codex Euricianus,* analogous to the Burgundian dual legislation for both the tribe and the Romans, was chronologically close to the *Breviarium Alaricianum* and was therefore also drawn up under Alaric II. Otherwise, one must resort to complicated explanations, as, for example, the assumption that the *Codex Euricianus,* which in any case incorporated Roman law, was initially territorial but was unable in the long run to fulfill this function and therefore became secondary personal law for the Goths as soon as the personality of Roman law was recognized in the *Breviarium Alaricianum.*[200] But that Eurician legislation did have territorial application is attested by Sidonius Apollinaris, the only contemporary who wrote about it: "Just as the august king within the borders of his expanded realm forced the people to submit to his arms, he now submits his arms to the yoke of the law."[201]

We know far more about the *Breviarium Alaricianum* than the *Codex Euricianus* because the letter of authentication sent to each *comes civitatis* along with a copy of the code has survived. We learn from it that a commission of legal experts (*prudentes*) under the direction of one of the highest ranking *comites,* the *vir illuster Goiaricus,* drew up the legislation, which met with the approval of the bishops and selected Romans (*electi provinciales*). The promulgation was then undertaken by the king himself— probably on February 2, 506—before an assembly of bishops and magnates. As the case of Goiaricus shows, there must have been, at least among the *nobiles viri,* Gothic notables and dignitaries in addition to senatorial nobles. The original copy of the *Breviarium Alaricianum* was authenticated by a certain Anianus *vir spectabilis* and was deposited in the royal treasury for handy reference. Every *comes civitatis* was ordered on penalty of death to permit the use of no other Roman law. As the sender of the royal decree— *auctoritas Alarici regis*—there appears once again Anianus. The *Breviarium Alaricianum* explicitly names as its source the *Codex Theodosianus* of 438 as well as "various law books," that is, post-Theodosian novellae and several decrees from the *Codex Gregorianus* and the *Codex Hermogenianus.* To nearly all the borrowed laws were added interpretations, which were not drawn up especially for this occasion by Alaric's commission but were taken from independent commentaries on the *Codex Theodosianus.*

These interpretations vulgarized the wording of the law but in so doing frequently clarified it. "No body of Roman law takes on greater significance for understanding the culture of Roman law which prevailed in the early medieval world than that which forms the Visigothic-Roman law code, the *Breviarium Alaricianum.*" Thus, for example, as late as the eighth century it provided the model for the Carolingian *Lex Romana Curiensis* from St. Gallen in Switzerland.[202]

THE ECCLESIASTICAL POLICIES OF EURIC AND ALARIC II

When the Goths settled in Aquitaine the majority of them professed the Arian faith. One characteristic of Gothic Arianism was a certain religious tolerance of or indifference to Catholics or even pagans. As late as the sixth century, it was considered "Gothic" to show reverence toward Christian churches as well as pagan temples.[203] Of course such an attitude did not exclude conflict with the Catholic Roman population. For example, the Goths repeatedly tried to appropriate Catholic churches in order to conduct their own services in them. This happened in Milan in the year 385 during the time of St. Ambrose, in the hot summer of 400 in Constantinople, and probably also during the Visigothic settlement in Rions (in the district of Bordeaux). Those who took over Catholic churches "could invoke Valentinian II's edict of 386 that expressly granted the Arian barbarians the freedom to practice their cult." In addition, there were overzealous believers who baptized the children of Catholic parents. It would be no surprise if the Goths also put a stop to Catholic pilgrimages to their capital of Toulouse. On a different occasion an Arian priest was said to have caused the destruction of a Catholic church. But all these reports and more of this kind are difficult to date and can by no means be clearly traced to the orders of any particular Visigothic king.[204]

Those Goths who separated themselves from the main tribe were easily Catholicized, as, for example, Sunnia and Fretela, who discussed the translation of the Bible with St. Jerome.[205] We know of a Catholic woman, a *comitissa* with the latinized name Glismoda, who in 455 donated money for the construction of a church in Narbonne, that is, for a Catholic church in an area that was at that time still outside the Gothic kingdom. She could have been the wife of a Roman rather than a Gothic comes.[206] When Braga was captured during the Spanish campaign of 455, churches were plundered and the clergy harassed. But at that time there was a state of war, and in Spain the Visigoths never imposed any special restraints on themselves.[207] Moreover, we know the attitude of Frideric in the quarrel over filling the vacant bishopric of Narbonne after the city had become Gothic. The Gothic vice-king, who as a quasi-regular *magister militum* had to concern himself also with ecclesiastical matters, was scrupulously exact in regarding the appointment as a Roman prerogative, and he even consulted the pope on the issue.[208] A pronounced respect for everything Roman characterizes the era of Theodoric. But this attitude could easily change into the opposite, as is revealed by a comparison of Euric's policy of conquest with that of his predecessors. Before 466 the Goths had expanded both in Spain and in Gaul and on imperial orders had "liberated" the native Romans from their imperial government. After 466 this legitimization vanished and open hostility erupted. A similar development took place in the Goths' relationship to the Catholic hierarchy, which, after the defeat of the Roman armies, remained the only Roman institution still functioning on a large territorial scale. Sidonius Apollinaris expresses the task of the church in a dramatic way: the Roman negotiators must get Euric to guarantee the free appointment of bishops "in order that we may be able to maintain, at least with the help of the faith, if not on the basis of the *foedus,* the *Romanitas* of the peoples of Gaul who live in Gothic territory." But with these words the champion of Gallic *Romanitas* had himself stated the reason why conflict arose between Euric and the Catholic hierarchy.[209]

During the first decades of the Toulousan kingdom the Catholic episcopacy was by no means considered an enemy of the Goths. In 439 a Catholic bishop tried to intervene on behalf of the federates, who were under severe pressure from the Romans.[210] There was no need to fear one another: the Goths ensured some kind of order and the members of the Catholic hierarchy did not belong to the upper classes.[211] Around 440 a priest still lost the "dignity of noble status";[212] a generation later, not only did the bishop rank above the senator but the lowest cleric counted for more than the highest secular dignitary.[213] The frequent entrance of members of the Gallic upper stratum into the clerical order, their readiness "to lose their hair" and to become bishops,[214] also healed the social conflict between them and the majority of the population. These notables, the "descendants of the hated tax collectors and owners of latifundia" of the early fifth century, had now become the leaders of their *civitates.*[215] This is how Sidonius Apollinaris characterizes his candidate for the vacant see of Bourges: the *comes* and *vir spectabilis* Simplicius is descended from the city's nobility;[216] he has "family." His ancestors were bishops and prefects. He possesses excellent moral and intellectual qualities and the ability to represent the city "before barbarian kings clad in furs as well as before emperors dressed in purple." Already once before "the heavily bolted door of a barbarian dungeon was opened for him by an act of God."[217] Simplicius had probably got into trouble when the Goths temporarily occupied Bourges in 469. All the more understandable would be his banishment when the city became permanently Gothic around 474/475.[218] Here, on the border threatened from two sides, Euric did not need an anti-Gothic martyr and miracle worker while he was still at war. Moreover, Simplicius was the candidate of Sidonius, who himself had to go into exile after the capture of Clermont and who won his release after two years only on the intercession of Leo, Euric's "Cassiodorus." Perhaps the king also pardoned him because he was hoping for a Gothic history from the highly praised rhetorician. Sidonius Apollinaris maneuvered himself elegantly out of this affair and declined with thanks.[219] Unfortunately for us, the king did not keep him locked up until he would complete the task. The reader of this book could be spared much conjecture if we possessed the work Euric requested, for Sidonius knew a lot. The few lines of his panegyric on Euric as well as his description of Theodoric reveal accurate knowledge.[220]

Did Euric then systematically persecute the Catholic church? From a barbarian who did not even know Latin properly,[221] who combined pagan magical beliefs with what he presumed to be orthodoxy,[222] such hostility would no doubt be expected. But since the days of Alaric I and Theoderid it had been part of a bishop's activities to negotiate peace between the Goths and the empire. In 474/475 a number of bishops were sent on similar missions.[223] The second episcopal delegation included Basilius, who was probably bishop of Aix-en-Provence, Leontius of Arles, Faustus of Riez, and Graecus of Marseille. All four were respectable colleagues and correspondents of Sidonius Apollinaris.[224] Sidonius's letter to Basilius paints a gloomy picture of Euric, to whom the Auvergne was now being handed over: the king is taking steps against everything Catholic such that one cannot tell whether he is the leader of a people or a sect. All his recent victories, which he had only gained through "luck" (*felicitas terrena*), he ascribes in his blindness to the alleged orthodoxy of his faith. He prevents the appointment of new bishops to the vacant sees of Bordeaux, Perigueux, Rodez, Limoges, Mende, Eauze, Auch, Bazas, St. Bertrand-de-Comminges, and other cities. Churches and parishes are being deserted. A certain Bishop Crocus, from an unknown diocese, as well as Simplicius, no doubt the metropolitan of Bourges in whose appointment Sidonius had played a significant role, are said to have been banished. This would mean that about one-fourth of all Gothic-Gallic dioceses were vacant. If we add to this the banishment soon afterward of Sidonius himself and of one of the negotiators, Faustus of Riez, the comparison of Euric with pharaoh and Ashur

seems appropriate. The impression we get is further intensified by the opening passage of the letter to Basilius. Sidonius reminds him of his victory in
the disputation against the Gothic Arian Modaharius, which seems to indicate that Euric had begun and accompanied his military offensive with a
campaign of Arianization.[225] All the more so, since even Theodoric, who
was friendly toward Rome, had converted the Suevi to the Gothic faith with
the help of the Arian Ajax[226] and since in 470/471 there were also Roman
Arian candidates for the appointment to the bishopric of Bourges.[227] Finally,
"it seems fairly certain that Euric also made it impossible for the Catholic
bishops of his realm to communicate with Rome."[228]

Yet Euric cannot be described as a systematic persecutor of Catholics,
even though in saying this we contradict prevailing notions.[229] Euric tried
to achieve a gradual "shutdown of the ecclesiastical institutions," but he
did so without proselytizing. Thus it cannot be shown that Modaharius was
connected to Euric, let alone that he acted on royal instructions or that
there was official support for the Roman Arians at Bourges. Euric's anti-
Catholic policy remained purely negative and therefore stopped halfway. It
tried to "eliminate the Catholic church politically as long as its positive
integration into the Gothic state was not possible."[230] Euric therefore ceased
his openly anti-Catholic policy soon after the Romans recognized his conquests. Whatever the king's motives may have been, he certainly did not
wish to engage in a religious war.[231] But his measures invariably sowed
dissension between the Catholic episcopacy as the leading stratum of Gaul
and the Gothic monarchy. Although one must not overrate the resulting
tensions—for the senatorial nobility itself and hence the ecclesiastical hierarchy were divided into factions and parties[232]—a certain strain on Gothic
policy did result and cannot be denied. Many members of the Roman upper
stratum were active at the court on royal business.[233] But the best organized
group remained estranged from the new state and persisted in a position of
at least silent opposition. It is true that Euric's policy was dictated by the
pressure of circumstances in the Gothic expansion of the late 470s. But it
was not completely revised even when the necessity for it had disappeared.
Above all, Euric was not able to fit the territorial structure of the Gallo-
Roman church into the boundaries of his realm.[234]

Alaric next tried to solve the problems he inherited from his predecessors.
His *Breviarium* is directly related to the summoning of a Gothic-Gallic
regional council at Agde. Like the codification of the law, this council was
also the first of its kind in the barbarian successor states of the Western
empire. Today both events are viewed in a rather positive light,[235] even
though—in retrospect—they may be seen as signs of a *fusion manquée*.[236]

Nonetheless, the king, as the representative of the Gothic state, had declared the *utilitates populi nostri*,[237] the law and religion of his Catholic Roman subjects, to be his concern and had furthered their active development. The Catholic hierarchy was at long last to be integrated into the Visigothic kingdom as a "national church"; it had rested far too long on the Gallo-Roman territorial structure that historical developments had rendered obsolete. It can therefore be no coincidence that only a little less than seven months after the promulgation of the *Breviarium Alaricianum* the assembled church fathers signed the protocol of the Council of Agde (September 10, 506). Roughly three-quarters of the bishops of Gaul either participated in the synod in person or sent their representatives to Septimania. Another meeting was planned for the following year in Toulouse; this time the Spanish *confratres* were also to attend. In Toulouse the regional council of Gaul would have thus expanded to become a council of the entire kingdom. The Frankish invasion wrecked the plan; nevertheless, Agde pointed the way to the future.[238] Alaric II's abilities as a statesman are clearly attested by the codification of the law and by the council, which was opened "with the permission of our lord, the glorious, all-powerful, and pious king," and in which prayers were said "for the kingdom, for a long life for the king, and for the people." The church of Narbonne received from Alaric II a charter in confirmation of its property. This is hardly the only instance where this was done.[239]

Agde also put an end to a series of measures that suggest a revival of Euric's antichurch policy. Probably in 495 or 496 the bishop of Tours, Volusianus, on suspicion of being in league with the Franks, was banished to Toulouse, where he died. (By no stretch of the imagination can Clovis be regarded at that time as the champion of the Catholic faith.) Verus, the successor to Volusianus, suffered the same fate and was exiled in mid-September 506. Similar difficulties developed along the Gothic-Burgundian border, where in 505 even the famous Caesarius of Arles had to leave his bishopric temporarily and move to Bordeaux. A notary of his chancery—a Roman, of course—had denounced him, charging that he wanted to hand over the city to the Burgundians. But the Burgundians were Arians, like the Goths, so Caesarius's opposition to the Goths must have been a question of church politics, not one of religion. On September 29, 500, Arles had received papal confirmation of its rights as a metropolitan see. But Caesarius could enforce these rights only to a limited extent as long as much of his district belonged to the kingdom of the Burgundians. Yet Caesarius could not renounce the Burgundian portion of his bishopric, and later, when Alaric II was long dead, he was again under suspicion of treason. The cases of the two bishops of Tours were similar. Tours was also a metropolitan see, composed of mostly "foreign" bishoprics. As soon as the Franks had reached the Loire border, Tours had either to cooperate with them or renounce its metropolitan rank. This then exhausts the list of all the attested measures of Alaric II against the Catholic episcopacy in his kingdom. (While Caesarius was still in exile, the Gothic king instructed him to prepare and summon the council at Agde.) Whatever else is reported or conjectured about them does not belong here. Thus the problems of the Gothic king appear like obstacles on his "way to a clear conception of domestic and ecclesiastical policy."[240]

The King and the Royal Clan

THE ROYAL FAMILY

With Theoderid, sometimes also called Theodoric I, the "younger Balthi" gained the Visigothic kingship. Theoderid had six sons: Thorismund-Thorismud, Theodoric (II), who is attested as grandson of Alaric I, Frideric, Euric, Retemeris-Ricimer, and Himnerith.[241] The first four came to power either successively or—as Theodoric and Frideric—jointly; of the last two we know only the names. Retemeris-Ricimer had the same name as the all-powerful Italian *patricius* who on his mother's side was the grandson of Valia. In addition to the sons we also know of two daughters of Theoderid:[242] one was married to the Vandal Huneric in 429,[243] the other became the wife of the Suevic king Rechiar in 449.[244] The dates of the marriages no doubt indicate something about the relative ages of the two princesses. The elder returned to her father mutilated and probably remained without offspring. We know of no children of the younger daughter, either, but the Suevic royal family probably did not die out with her husband Rechiar.[245] The offspring of Theoderid's sons is nearly as meager: Thorismund left no children.[246] Around 465 Theodoric, the second-oldest son, did give a Visigothic woman in marriage to the Suevic king Remismund when he made him his "son in arms," but she is today no longer considered to have been his daughter.[247]

Only in the case of Euric himself do we know of a male offspring, namely, his son and successor, Alaric II. Euric married Ragnahild, the daughter of an unknown king. We might conjecture to what tribe she belonged. We can suppose that Euric would have married an Arian woman. Moreover, she had a Latin education, for a petitioner by the name of Evodius not only gave her a heavy silver bowl but asked Sidonius to compose some verses to accompany his gift.[248] When Sidonius complied with Evodius's request (around 466 or 467),[249] Alaric had already been born. In his verses Sidonius expressed the wish that the queen's son should one day reign with his father and as his successor. These lines do in fact apply to a small child. When Euric assumed power he was about twenty-six years of age.[250] Only at that time could he have married the daughter of a foreign king. If we consider the joint Gothic-Suevic actions around and after 466, a Suevic princess seems the most likely candidate, even though Euric's relation to Remismund was tense because of the latter's leanings toward Theodoric. Now if Euric had already married before the murder of his brother, the guessing game goes on. But could it have been in Theodoric's interest to boost the standing of his restless brother by allowing him to contract a fully valid marriage and thus establish ties with a foreign royal clan?[251]

Theoderid reigned from 418 to 451. During this unusually long rule grew up a royal clan, a Visigothic *stirps regia,* which from that time monopolized the kingship.[252] Though there was no fixed rule for the transmission of power comparable to that which existed among the Vandals, there did in fact develop a sort of succession based on seniority.[253] Without trouble from Goths or Romans the four eldest sons of Theoderid succeeded each other on the throne; only the first of the line was not guilty of fratricide. First Thorismund became king after the death of his father in battle, reigning from 451 to 453. He was murdered by Theodoric and Frideric. Frideric was during the remainder of his life vice-king to Theodoric, who in 466 lost the kingship and his life to the fourth brother, Euric. Then the line broke off: the two youngest sons of Theoderid are not mentioned. Euric was succeeded in 484 by his son Alaric II, who died in the battle at Vouillé in 507. Then Alaric's sons Gesalec (507–511) and Amalaric (526–531) tried to be kings for a time. When, unusually enough, Euric himself died a natural death, Alaric II received from the Goths the same "confirming recognition" that had been given to the regicides who reigned before him, to his uncle Theodoric and probably also to his own father Euric. Only from 507 do we hear of elections for the king, so unquestioned was the rule of Theoderid and his descendants down to the catastrophe of Vouillé.[254]

The exceptional status of the royal family was revealed in its successes. The Goths believed in them, since even the Romans knew that the Balthi "were descended from kings and heroes."[255] The Balthi themselves believed in the charisma that God had given them as a reward for their orthodoxy.[256] But under Alaric II, at least, they recognized the higher nobility of the Amali. Around 494 the Visigothic king married Thiudigot(h)o, the daughter of Theodoric the Great.[257] Their son received the name Amalaric in recognition of the family of his mother.

THE KING

Shortly after Euric had assumed power he annulled the *foedus* with the empire. In nine years of hostilities he forced the Romans into a new treaty; in it the imperial government accepted the factual independence of the much-enlarged Visigothic kingdom without, however, recognizing Euric's creation as a sovereign state. De jure Toulouse did not separate itself from the empire.[258] But the treaty with Nepos had important consequences: before 475 there is no source that opposes the Gothic *regnum* to the Roman *imperium,* but then the terminology changes overnight. Now the empire and the kingdom of Toulouse are two polities equal in rank and prestige.[259] Even Euric himself distinguishes the *regnum* of his predecessors from the Gothic kingdom of his own time.[260] As Sidonius Apollinaris noted a few weeks before the conclusion of the new *foedus,* "the peoples of Gaul, who live in the Gothic land," had remained Roman because of the old *foedus.* Looking back in 476 Sidonius is altogether of the opinion that in the early 460s Gaul was still "largely unscathed."[261] Nor did this change in practice by the fact that the Gothic kingdom very quickly became a state within the state. In part of the "seven provinces" of Gaul the Gothic king was the holder of the sole functioning executive authority. The entire income from the provincials' taxes remained "at home"; it served to maintain both the Gothic army and the regional Roman administration. The regular administration of the Gallic praetorian prefect at Arles as well as of the vicar of the "seven provinces" was therefore *via facti* considerably reduced, if not actually eliminated.[262] It is, however, difficult to grasp chronologically the stages in the territorialization of the Gothic royal power. Perhaps in the mid-420s, when the death of Honorius put in question the *foedus* that had been concluded with him, the next step was taken in the formation of the kingdom. If the Gothic settlement had ever been intended as a temporary arrangement, there was now no longer any doubt that the *sortes Gothicae* had become a permanent solution.[263] This actual tie to a defined territory led to the appearance of a new *patria Gothorum.* It is not surprising that the phrases "borders of the Gothic land assignment," "land of the Goths," and "territorial kingdom" eventually came to be synonymous.[264] The Romans now also belonged to all these political entities and formed within them a separate group specifically described as such.[265] No later than Thorismund the Romans called the Gothic king their lord (*dominus noster*) and dated according to regnal years, as they had been accustomed to do for the emperor and vice-imperial magistrates.[266] The Latin titles bestowed upon the Gothic king show that his rank was considered equal to that of the vice-imperial magistracies. Signs for this development are visible from the early years of Theoderid's rule.[267]

After Valia had died, Theoderid succeeded him "as next in power." How the succession took place we are not told, but a Greek observer who until this time had commented on every change of rulers considered the Gothic kingship at this time an ἀρχή,[268] that is to say, a magistracy of equal rank with, though not identical to, the highest Roman magistracies.[269] The Gothic king appears like a Roman general who did not need imperial appointment. In contrast to what we find among the Burgundians, the Toulousan kings did not take over Roman military offices.[270] Valia too had conducted the Spanish war as a federate king of Rome.[271] The Visigothic *reges* were used as "patrimonial officials" of the imperial government. In this way it was possible to establish a barbarian *regnum* that did not threaten the territorial integrity of the Roman Empire.[272]

Toulouse was from the very beginning the capital of the Visigothic *regnum*, a fact that greatly helped in the consolidation of the kingdom.[273] In addition there were royal residences in Bordeaux, where Euric is known to have spent some time, and Narbonne, where Alaric II had a palace. In a similar building in Arles, possibly the residence of the former prefect, Euric spent his last days before his death in 484.[274] The importance of Toulouse was not diminished by the other cities. Credible estimates indicate that the city covered about two hundred acres and offered living space for about ten to fifteen thousand people.[275] Where the Toulousan palace was located is still debated. Today we are inclined to agree with the view of the local historians of the eighteenth and nineteenth centuries, who located the Gothic *palatium* not in the "Porterie" or the "Daurade"[276] but in the "Château Narbonnais."[277]

By 418 and 439 the city and the Gothic kingdom seemed to be identical,[278] and this is confirmed at the first succession. After Theoderid was killed in battle the army proclaimed his oldest son Thorismund king. But this act, which was basically constitutive, was not considered enough. Instead, Aëtius was able to persuade Thorismund to withdraw quickly by advising him to hurry back to Toulouse to "take possession of the kingship that his father's death had left vacant in order that his brothers would not seize the paternal treasure and the kingship of the Visigoths."[279] Incidentally, this is the only known case of Roman "interference" in the Visigothic succession. Whether the question was only one of gaining possession of the city and the treasure or whether there was also the need for an "additional ceremony in Toulouse" is not specified.[280] Possession of the royal city and the treasure that was kept there was synonymous with possession of the entire kingdom.

Not without good reason was a public inspection of the treasure part of the king's daily routine.[281] Although Euric died in Arles, Alaric II was proclaimed king in Toulouse.[282] Until the end of the Toulousan kingdom the center of Gothic settlement was therefore in an area that did not extend beyond a radius of one hundred kilometers around the city.[283]

From the period before 507 no official document carrying a royal title has survived; the closest thing is the inscription *Alaricus rex Gothorum* on the Viennese seal ring that probably belonged to Alaric II. All other known titles either imitate those of the emperor or were of the same rank as the vice-imperial *patricius* of the West. In their role as legislators Euric and Alaric speak of their imperial predecessors as *principes,* as they themselves were occasionally called. But this title could easily be barbarized and would then mean the "prince," the first among his people. Moreover, as long as the Visigoths still spoke Gothic,[284] they would not have noticed the difference between the Latin *rex* (read then: *rēx*) and their customary *reiks* (read also: *rēx*), because the two terms had become identical in sound and meaning.[285]

How a Gothic king would appear to a Roman senator is shown by Sidonius Apollinaris's classic portrait of Theodoric. It is addressed to the son of Avitus, under whom the king in his younger days had studied Virgil and Roman law and whom he had eventually made emperor.[286] Since Avitus was also the author's father-in-law, there was no Gothic king to whom Sidonius was more favorably inclined than Theodoric. It must have been in 455[287] that Sidonius lived in Toulouse and composed these lines, whose afterlife seems as impressive as their vividness and descriptive power.[288] We read the following:[289]

Sidonius to his dear Agricola, greetings

1. Seeing that report commends to the world the graciousness of Theodoric, king of the Goths, you have often asked me to describe to you in writing his appearance and the character of his life.[290] I am delighted to do so, subject to the limitations of a letter, and I appreciate the honest spirit that prompts so nice a curiosity. Well, he is a man who deserves to be studied even by those who are not in close relations with him. In his build the will of God and nature's plan have joined together to endow him with a supreme perfection,[291] and his character is such that even the jealousy that hedges a sovereign has no power to rob it of its glories.

2. Take first his appearance. His figure is well-proportioned; he is shorter than the very tall, taller and more commanding than the average man. The top of his head is round, and on it his curled hair retreats

gently from his even forehead. His neck is not soft but erect and sinewy. Over each eye arches a bushy eyebrow; when his eyelids droop, the tips of the lashes reach almost halfway down the cheeks. The tips of his ears are hidden by strands of hair that are brushed back over them, as is the fashion with them. His nose is most gracefully curved; his lips are delicately molded and are not enlarged by any extension of the corners of the mouth. Every day he shaves the bristles that grow beneath his nostrils. His facial hair is heavy in the hollow of his temples, but on the lowest part of the face the barber constantly shaves it from the cheeks, which retain their youthful appearance.

3. His chin, throat, and neck suggest not fat but fullness; the skin is milk-white, but on close inspection it takes on a youthful blush, for this color is frequently produced in his case by modesty, not by ill temper. His shoulders are well-shaped, his upper arms sturdy, his forearms hard, his hands broad. The chest is prominent, the stomach recedes; the surface of his back is divided by a spine that lies low between the bulging ribs; his sides swell with bulging muscles. Strength reigns in his well-girt loins. His thigh is hard as horn; the upper legs are full of manly vigor; his knees are completely free from wrinkles and full of grace; the legs are supported by sturdy calves, but the feet that bear such mighty limbs are small.

4. And now you may want to know all about his everyday life, which is open to the public gaze. Before dawn he goes with a very small retinue to the service conducted by his priests, and he worships with great earnestness, though—in confidence—one can see that this devotion is a matter of routine rather than conviction. Administrative duties of the kingdom take up the rest of the morning. Nobles in armor have places near his throne; a crowd of fur-clad guards is allowed in so as to be close at hand but is excluded from the presence so as not to disturb; and so they keep up a hum of conversation by the door, outside the curtains but within the barriers. Meanwhile deputations from various peoples are introduced, and he listens to a great deal of talk but replies briefly, postponing business he intends to consider, speeding that which is to be promptly settled. The second hour comes: he rises from his throne to inspect his treasures or his stables.

5. When a hunt has been proclaimed and he rides forth, he considers it beneath his royal dignity to have his bow slung at his side; but if in the chase or on the road a bird or a beast appears within his range, he reaches back and an attendant places the bow in his hand, with the string or thong hanging loose; for he thinks it childish to carry a bow in a case and womanish to take it over ready-strung. When he takes it he either holds it straight in front of him and bends the two ends and so strings it or he rests upon his raised foot the end that has the knot

and runs his finger along the loose string until he comes to the dangling loop; then he takes up the arrows, sets them in place, and lets them fly. Or he may urge you first to choose what you wish to have struck down: you choose what he is to strike and he strikes what you have chosen. If he ever misses your vision will mostly be at fault, and not the archer's skill.[292]

6. If one joins him at the dinner table—which on all but festival days is just like that of a private household—there is no unpolished conglomeration of discolored old silver set by breathless attendants on sagging tables; the weightiest thing is the conversation, for there is either serious talk or none at all. The couches with their spreading draperies show an array sometimes of scarlet cloth, sometimes of fine linen. The food attracts by its skillful preparation, not by its costliness, the platters by their brightness, not by their weight. The goblets or wine bowls are refilled at such long intervals that there is more reason for the thirsty to complain than for the drunk to decline.[293] To sum up: you can find there Greek elegance, Gallic plenty, Italian briskness; the dignity of state, the attentiveness of a private home, the ordered discipline of royalty. But as to the luxury of the festival days I had better hold my tongue, for even the lowest person cannot fail to note it.

7. To resume the story: after satisfying his appetite he never takes more than a short midday sleep and often goes without it. In the hours when the gaming board attracts him he is quick to pick up the dice; he examines them anxiously, spins them with skill, throws them eagerly; he addresses them jestingly and calmly awaits the result. If the throw is lucky, he says nothing; if unlucky, he smiles; in neither case does he lose his temper, in either case he is a real philosopher. As for a second throw, he is too proud either to fear it or to make it; when a chance of one is presented he disdains it, when it is used against him he ignores it. He sees his opponent's piece escape without stirring and gets his own free without exaggerated rejoicing. You would actually think he was handling weapons when he handles the pieces on the board; his sole thought is of victory.[294]

8. When it is time for play he lays aside for a while the stern mood of royalty and encourages fun and freedom and goodfellowship. My own opinion is that he dreads being feared. Furthermore, he is delighted at seeing his defeated rival disgruntled, and it is only his opponent's ill temper that really satisfies him that the game has not been given him. Now comes something to surprise you: the joy that overcomes him on these trivial occasions often speeds the claims of important transactions. At such times the haven of a prompt decision is thrown open to petitions that for a long time have been in distress through the foundering of their advocates. I myself at such times, if I have a favor to ask,

find it fortunate to be beaten by him, for I lose my pieces to win my cause.[295]

9. About the ninth hour the burden of royal business is taken up again. Back come the importunate petitioners, back come the marshals to drive them off; everywhere the rivalry of the disputants makes an uproar. This continues until evening; then the royal supper interrupts and the bustle fades away, distributing itself among the various courtiers whose patronage this or that party enjoys; and thus they keep watch until the night watches. It is true that occasionally (not often) the banter of low comedians is admitted during supper, though they are not allowed to assail any guest with the gall of a biting tongue.[296] In any case no hydraulic organs are heard there, nor does any concert party under its trainer boom forth a set performance in chorus; there is no music of a lutenist, flautist, dance conductor, tambourine girl or female guitarist; for the king finds charm only in string music that comforts the soul with virtue just as much as it soothes the ear with melody.

10. When he rises from the table, the night watch is first posted at the royal treasury and armed sentries, who will keep guard through the hours of the first sleep, are set at the entrances to the palace.

But I have already exceeded my part, for I promised to tell you a little about the king, not a long story about his rule; it is also fitting that my pen come to a stop because you desired to hear only of the tastes and personality of the great man and because I took it upon myself to write a letter, not a history. Farewell.

COURT LIFE: RELIGION, LANGUAGE, AND CULTURE

Just as the king did not differ from other Goths in his habits, at sport or play, he did not set himself apart by dress[297] or appearance. The Goths preserved from their former Danubian "habitat" certain attitudes and customs rather than concrete objects. At this time, however, we are unable to identify either the settlements or the burial grounds of the Toulousan Goths; as a result we lack the most important source for writing their cultural history.[298] Contemporary poets and writers noted the wide use made of Gothic furs.[299] Linguistic evidence seems to indicate that Goths early gave up their peculiar dress, but this is refuted by finds in the Spanish Gothia where the Gothic costume is still clearly identifiable in the first half of the sixth century.[300] The Goths' delight in hunting on horseback with the falcon or the bow remained unchanged. Not only the king, for whom this was one of his social duties, but also his magnates and the Gothic warriors went hunting with such fervor that on one occasion it even took the prayers of a saint to chase away the game and the uninvited hunting party; otherwise the Gothic lords would have totally ruined the area around Arles that was rich in wild boars.[301]

On several occasions we read of an Arian court clergy. Of course the exclusively Catholic Roman observers speak disparagingly of them,[302] and it seems that at times even the king did not take them all that seriously.[303] Still, we must believe that these men were capable of assiduous Bible studies and the preservation of Ulfilas's heritage through the spoken and written word.[304] We do not know whether Modaharius, who debated with Roman bishops, was part of the court or was even sent to the disputation by Euric.[305] Modaharius's name, however, is in the best Balthic tradition,[306] and so it cannot have been mere coincidence that he spoke up for the *lex Gothica,* the Arian faith and law.[307] Toulouse, to be sure, served not only the Suevi[308] but also the Burgundians in matters of the faith.[309] Modaharius and his friends, among whom a few must have written Ulfilian texts, had mastered not only the Latin of their time but undoubtedly also the Gothic language.

At what time the Visigoths gave up their own language is a matter of debate.[310] The deep sigh of a Latin poet, who had picked up at least a few Gothic words, points to the Toulousan kingdom.[311] His excuse for not composing any decent poetry reminds us of the affected despair of Sidonius Apollinaris, whose six-foot-verses (hexameters) were destroyed by wildly dancing seven-foot-tall Burgundians. While Sidonius suffered from the smell of his "guests'" pomade of rancid butter,[312] the unknown poet declared: "In the midst of Goths who are constantly exclaiming 'Hail! Let's eat and drink!' no one can write decent poetry."[313] The royal court certainly continued to be bilingual for some time.

Few reports about the court's artistic activities have come down to us. The usual troop of jugglers and guitar players is a far cry from a court theater.[314] And the Gothic epic songs, last attested at Theoderid's death in battle, are not art but a cultic veneration of ancestors and a tool for educating young nobles.[315] Even Isidore of Seville, who wrote so much later and who undoubtedly no longer met Gothic-speaking persons, saw the *carmina maiorum* as educational tools.[316] Theodoric enjoyed a Latin upbringing for which Avitus was responsible. Avitus's son-in-law Sidonius Apollinaris also spent a lengthy period of time in Toulouse in the early 450s.[317] From Euric's court we know of the Roman-Latin court poet Lampridius, who received back from the king his confiscated property but who eventually met a bad end: he was murdered by his own slaves.[318] Euric would probably have been delighted to attract to his court Sidonius Apollinaris, the brightest light in Gaul's intellectual circles. But the bishop of Clermont declined with thanks.[319] This same king, who together with his wife Ragnahild took pleasure in the overrefined poetic art of the Gallo-Roman poet,[320] used a translator to communicate with the Italian imperial envoy Epiphanius. From this we should not infer (as is occasionally done) that the king had an inadequate knowledge of Latin but rather, the other way round, that he *still* spoke Gothic. Why he would have done so in front of an imperial negotiator is easy to guess: like the Persian king, the Visigothic prince could thus emphasize that he and his kingdom were equal to both the emperor and the empire.[321]

That the Ostrogoths spoke Gothic until the end of their Italian *regnum* is attested. On the Balkan peninsula as well the language had not become extinct;[322] indeed, it perhaps survived into the Early Middle Ages.[323] Under Theodoric the Great the Ostrogoths had come to the West, in fact both to Spain and what remained of Visigothic Gaul.[324] This linguistic "infusion" could have temporarily interrupted or at least slowed down the Romanization of the Visigoths. From this we could infer that after the middle of the sixth century the Visigothic language disappeared.[325] But it had probably already lost the ability to create new words and terms. If that was the case, specialized Gothic terminology was created at the latest during this period, regardless of the date of the source in which it has survived.[326]

The Kingship: Its Functions and Functionaries

Like all barbarian *regna* on Roman soil, the Visigothic kingdom grew out of the kingship of a migratory army.[327] But the world into which the Goths sought to integrate themselves was much too complicated for them to survive without roots in the structure of the Roman state. Alaric I was not only a successful leader of the "people in arms,"[328] he also knew Roman administrative practices. It is not surprising that he was eager to integrate his barbarian kingdom into the *imperium*. If he could succeed in gaining the recognition of the imperial government, the ethnogenesis of the "Roman" Goths would be secured.[329] Alaric I's policy remained unfinished, but the Toulousan kingdom consistently continued what the Balth and his immediate successors had begun. It was therefore not necessary that the greater Gothic state of Euric and Alaric II be born overnight. Long before Euric dissolved the treaty with Rome in 466 and renewed it in 475 under entirely new conditions, it had no other function than to legitimize the rule of the Gothic king in and over a portion of the Roman Empire.[330] When the provincial assembly of the "seven provinces" of southern Gaul was reestablished back in 418, it was decreed that those areas in which the Goths would settle a few months later could delegate their seats. Was this already a precautionary measure? In any case, we have no report that the vicariate of the seven provinces or the Gallic prefecture ever exercised any sovereign power in the area comprising the kingdom of Toulouse.[331]

The Gothic king and his staff became the "patrimonial officials,"[332] as it were, of the top-level Roman bureaucracy, while the administration of the individual *civitates* remained in the hands of the Roman *curiales*.[333] The rulers of Toulouse had the following responsibilities: (1) The Gothic king was the head of the Arian tribal church, a position derived from barbarian tradition.[334] But he also became head of the Catholic church of his Roman subjects.[335] (2) The king was commander-in-chief of his tribe's military forces. (3) The king functioned as the highest legislative authority and as judge. (4) He conducted foreign policy and supervised the domestic administration of his realm. In legal language the list of the king's tasks thus reads: "The essence of the royal power consisted in executive authority, the right to pass laws and statutory regulations, the power to tax and enforce the laws, and finally, jurisdiction over the church."[336] No wonder that in this Gothic kingdom there was no place for a presumed "assembly of the people." Furthermore, it would be rather odd to find this Germanistic "fiction" in Toulouse, of all places, considering that scholars have looked for it unsuccessfully in all previous Gothic history.[337] Although royal power during the fifth century increased steadily at the expense of the magnates, we hear of no resistance, no rebelliousness or rebellion by the nobility. External threats and expansion kept the nobles in line. Security and a share in the booty could be won by the Gothic nobleman only if he followed his king. The first time the Gothic leading stratum forced its will upon the king was when the Franks were devastating their lands and property. The Gothic army, that is, the royal *comites* and troop commanders, were eager to engage the Franks in battle. But Alaric II wanted to wait for his father-in-law before facing Clovis. This decision would have been the right one, but the reaction of the Gothic magnates shows them taking the initiative to exploit setbacks and weakness in the kingship. In other words, resistance to the Toulousan king arose only at the moment when the carefree policy of expansion came to an end.[338]

The Gothic magnates participated in political life when decisions directly affected them: the succession to the throne, the declaration of war,[339] the conclusion of a treaty,[340] or the promulgation of a new law code.[341] A single reference in Hydatius Lemicus has been interpreted to mean that a regularly convened assembly deliberated these issues.[342] That the assembly, according to Sidonius Apollinaris, met in the morning could have had purely practical reasons. Those assembled deliberated while standing, and the participants seem like a council of elders, a sort of senate. It is not impossible that the Gallo-Roman observer was generalizing and turned a few elderly chiefs into a *gerousia*. In any case, the assembly served to pass on information and to delegate joint responsibility to the magnates. By their acclamation they pledged themselves to implement the resolutions passed. A story recounts the following procedure: first the king spoke, then a Roman envoy with the rank of a king; finally those in attendance voiced their consent and the matter at hand was thus settled. The implementation of the decisions was merely a matter of time.[343] The *Origo Gothica* describes such a decision-making process with words that Tacitus or Ammianus Marcellinus might have used: "With loud acclamation the followers answer the king of the army, the people follow gladly" (*adclamant responso comites duci, laetus vulgus sequitur*).[344]

This story also reveals that the barbarian meanings for *comes* (follower) and *dux* (king of the army) were not lost even after the tribes had settled in the Roman Empire where similar, if much more sophisticated, political structures existed.[345] Ever since the reorganization of Constantine the Great, *comites,* as "followers of the emperor," had assumed a permanent place in the administration "with corresponding rank in the court hierarchy." They were civil and military representatives in the central imperial administration as well as in the provinces. As military officials the *comites* could also be called *duces.* But *duces* were also commanders of "dukedoms" (*ducatus*), military districts comprising one or more border provinces. From the moment that the creation of federate *regna* turned internal administrative boundaries into state borders or even created entirely new borders, the establishment of *ducatus* became necessary also within the empire.[346] That the Visigothic courtiers of the seventh century could still describe their military commissions with the double title *comes et dux* indicated that an adjustment between the various ancient traditions had already occurred.[347] In the same way the Ostrogothic *comites rei militaris* were the real generals who represented the king, the highest-ranking *dux* in theory, in the field and in this capacity were called *duces*; they have to be distinguished, however, from the *duces* who were not *comites* but only commanders of border militias.[348] In the Frankish kingdom of the Merovingians as well as among the Lombards in Italy the traditional terminology changes: the late antique *comes* disappears and in the end—the dates varying from region to region—

the *dux* takes his place. But the available title of *comes* could already in the sixth century designate a lower ranking agent of the Frankish king. By contrast, the Lombard *comes* remains an exception; his place is taken by the *gastaldus*.[349]

The kings of Toulouse left civil matters in the hands of the Roman administration, especially the curias and their personnel. Cooperation between the Roman central administration of Gaul and the Roman authorities of the Gothic kingdom was possible only through the court of Toulouse.[350] But the Gallic praetorian prefects and the vicars of the seven provinces of southern Gaul did manage to communicate with the Gothic kings, though not without difficulties.[351] The kings' "people," the *comites,* were to supervise the Roman administration within the Gothic kingdom. Primary concerns were protecting the royal revenues, regulating an orderly coexistence between Goths and Romans, and finally preserving the army's military strength. Analogous to the curias' sphere of activity the *civitates* offered themselves as the administrative units of the *comites.* The earliest permanent royal representative was therefore the Gothic *comes civitatis.* "After modest beginnings in the late Roman period," he became the most important government official of the kingdom of Toulouse.[352] A *comes civitatis* was in command of each of the nineteen city-districts the Gothic kingdom had grown to encompass after Euric assumed power.[353] If a war was being fought in which the king did not participate in person, he appointed a *comes* to take his place.[354] The entourage of the emperor had developed into permanent representatives and virtual magistrates through the practice of placing a *comes* at the head of a given administrative branch. In like manner the Visigothic *comes* showed a tendency to become "officialized" whenever the need arose.[355] But since the royal administration of Toulouse, even more so than its Roman model, developed from within—that is, it functioned as an extension of the royal court administration—the Roman career path was turned on its head: now the *cursus honorum* began in the retinue of the king and ended in the provinces.[356]

The earliest imperial *comites* in the provinces were special appointees with judicial functions. Moreover, it was in the nature of late Roman administration that nearly every individual who held a higher office was at the same time judge over those within his sphere of authority. Thus the military officers sat in judgment over their soldiers, and the heads of regional and local authorities presided over the Roman provincials. While the administration of law was thus among the duties of late Roman high-level bureaucrats, they were, to be sure, supported by "professional" lawyers. We must therefore in each case distinguish whether the word *iudex* is used for a bureaucrat or a lawyer.[357]

The Gothic federates could easily adopt the existing administrative structure because it corresponded somewhat to their tribal structure and because they themselves were Roman military personnel. It was nothing new that a Gothic commander passed sentence on his subordinates. The Roman *iudex* terminology could therefore live on in the Toulousan *regnum* and later in the Toledan kingdom. Since the *Breviarium Alaricianum* took over the greater part of those laws meant for the *rectores vel iudices provinciarum,* there must have been an actual need for them. *Iudices militares,* however, no longer appear in the *Breviarium,* for their function had been transferred to the Gothic *comites civitatum.* But Gothic officials are not the subject of the *Breviarium,* which is why their positions are not defined. Despite the formal preservation of the Roman order, the actual exercise of power was in the hands of the king and his agents. The *comes civitatis* possessed local executive power. In his city-district he was in charge of military affairs as well as jurisdiction and financial administration. The sources describe the Gothic *comes* as the man "whose command is obeyed by everyone who serves in the military and bears arms," and he is known as the person who "commands the soldiers." The *comes civitatis* was the head of all the *iudices* "to whom *civitates* and towns were entrusted." Among them was a lawyer in the rank of a *iudex mediocris,* the *defensor civitatis* who was elected by the curiales to look after the equitable collection of all tax revenues.[358] The judge from among the urban middle class had a sort of rural counterpart in the *numerarius.* This widely used and traditional title was also given to the top accountant of the royal domains. In the Kingdom of Toledo at the latest this *numerarius* was appointed by the *comes patrimonii,* the administrator of the royal estates, in agreement with the regional bishop. Whereas the *defensor civitatis* was thus originally the representative of an electoral body, the *numerarius* represented the government.[359]

The expansion of the Gothic kingdom, which began under Theodoric (II) and was basically brought to a conclusion by Euric, demanded organizational structures on a larger scale than those which existed in 418/419. At its height the *regnum Tolosanum* embraced not only a large number of city-districts but also many Roman provinces. Theodoric made use of the Roman *foedus* in such a way that he even deposed and appointed Roman imperial officials.[360] Euric made efforts to integrate the military territorial administration into the *exercitus Gothorum.* Now the *regnum Tolosanum* comprised not only many *civitates* but also entire Roman provinces. Yet, no separate Gothic provincial administration that combined several *civitates* was set up. Instead, many a *comes civitatis* was assigned an entire province as extended sphere of authority. In this capacity he could then be called either *comes* or *dux*.[361] When the *regnum Tolosanum* had, territorially and institutionally speaking, sunk its roots more deeply into the Roman Empire it comprised even former Roman *ducatus* that the imperial government had recently created against it. The function of the Roman *ducatus* was to protect endangered border provinces.[362] But ever since the beginning of the fifth century large parts of Gaul had become a border region.[363] Spain followed suit in the next decades. While initially there was still a Roman *comes Hispaniarum* in command in the peninsula,[364] his place was taken by a *dux Tarraconensis* no later than the early 460s when the last Spanish resistance to the Goths was forming. This *dux* eventually went over to the victorious Goths and continued his career as Euric's *dux Hispaniarum*. This man, Vincentius, on one occasion even described as a *quasi magister militum,* presents an excellent object for closer study:[365] he exemplifies both the transition of the Roman provincial *comitatus* to the early medieval "dukedom" as well as the modification within institutional continuity. A similar development can be observed in the Auvergnian part of Gaul. The imperial government seems to have rewarded the resistance of the *civitas Arvernorum* by establishing a military district where Ecdicius held command as *dux*.[366] At the same time, if not shortly before, a Visigothic *ducatus* was established in the conquered part of Aquitania I.[367] South of the Loire, however, both these institutions were the continuation of the *tractus (ducatus) Armoricanus et Nervicanus* that Constantius had reestablished in 417.[368] But while Ecdicius lost the war and his *ducatus* disappeared, his relative Victorius, the Visigothic *dux,* conquered all Aquitania I and turned embattled Clermont into his residence. Euric had thus taken over, both in Spain and in Gaul, Roman *ducatus,* that is, militarized provincial districts, together with their governors.[369] This is also why the first Toulousan *duces,* who were at the same time commanders and *rectores provinciae,*[370] were Romans in Visigothic service. After Vincentius and Victorius we hear also of Visigothic *duces* in Bordeaux, the capital of Aquitania II, and in Mérida, a *civitas* of Lusitania.[371] Euric probably took over the existing Roman institution as it was. After all, Aquitania II was also originally part of the old *ducatus* north and south of the Loire.[372] The need to combine several endangered border districts and place them under one military command remained unchanged throughout the centuries. In this way the *dux provinciae* took the place of a *comes* who commanded larger units. In other words, out of the function of the late antique and barbarian *dux* developed the rank and function of that *dux* who became the predecessor of the early medieval duke. But how tenaciously this office clung to its roots is revealed by the fact that *dux* and *comes* remained interchangeable and that right up to the beginning of the High Middle Ages every *dux* was in principle also a *comes*. In the fifth century the connection is visible in that one and the same person could exercise both functions, since a *dux provinciae* administrated his sphere of authority from a *civitas* whose *comes* he was.[373]

MILITARY ORGANIZATION

Contemporaries report little about the internal organization of the army of Toulouse.[374] Nevertheless, we may assume that the structures developed during the period of migration remained in use.[375] In the Visigothic army the cavalry had the greatest prestige and formed the core of the forces, as the conflicts with the Huns, Ostrogoths, Bretons, and Alans and certain Basque traditions attest.[376] From Ravenna's perspective the Visigothic army on the eve of the battle of Vouillé showed obvious shortcomings and had lost much of the power it had demonstrated in the battle against Attila. In any case, the Visigoths lost the great battle against an army of Frankish foot soldiers.[377]

Ideologically colored histories pretend that only the "real" Goth was allowed to carry arms and go to war, whereas the Romans were on principle excluded from military service and were considered "unworthy to bear arms." What is presented as an ethnic differentiation was in reality the outcome of constitutional developments. Imperial legislation had deprived the Roman provincials of the right to bear arms and had called them to the standard only when their country was directly threatened. The waging of war was the responsibility of the army, and in the kingdom of Toulouse this was the *exercitus Gothorum*. Those Romans who previously had been liable for military service or who had the right to bear arms—like the Roman upper class—also found themselves in the army after 418. The army was therefore composed of Goths, members of local settlements of *laeti* and barbarians, and senatorial nobles who had volunteered or had been pressed into service. The commander-in-chief was the Gothic king, who entrusted the positions of officers as *duces et comites* to his own people and to Romans of equal standing. If a special mission was involved, such as equipping and commanding a fleet, a task for which the Visigoths up to the time of Sisebut "lacked the necessary experience," then a Roman was appointed general or admiral, as the situation warranted. In fact, Euric's highest-ranking officer was a Roman by birth who had begun his career in the regular Roman army.[378]

Whenever the Visigothic king had himself replaced as commander of the army authorized *duces et comites* took his place. But wherever the Toulousan armies fought they moved within the Roman Empire and its organizational structure. Every royal commission was therefore combined with an administrative district that could be given a traditional Roman name. On rare occasions this administrative area could be composed of one or even several provinces, but usually it consisted of a city-district. Thus the top levels of the Visigothic military organization followed the lines of the Roman territorial division into *ducatus* and *civitates,* for which there were respectively *duces et comites* or *comites civitatum.*[379]

The structure of the *exercitus Gothorum* on the decimal system was not affected by these developments. King Sisebut (612–621) still described the common Gothic warrior as a "soldier serving in a group of one thousand" (*millenus miles*). What had perhaps appeared in the course of the migrations was formalized during the Toulousan period into a definite structure whose differentiated nature was without parallel. Though the terms for this structure can only be traced to the Spanish *regnum*, it is unlikely that they were not introduced earlier. Thus the Toledan legislation distinguished among the troop leaders the *decanus,* the *centenarius,* the *quingentenarius,* and the *millenarius-thiufadus.* While no group of five hundred men can be shown to have existed, units of ten (*decania*), one hundred (*centena*), and one thousand (*thiufa-thiufada*) are attested.[380]

The sources of the fifth century mention only the *millenarius.*[381] But a leader of this type was never entrusted with an independent command. Into such positions Toulouse placed men who are called *comites* or *duces* and on one occasion even a *quasi magister militum.*[382] Initially there is evidence only for the judicial authority and policing power of the *millenarius.* Thus the legislator of the *Codex Euricianus* assumed that those Goths who had suffered any damage to their property would turn for redress first to the *millenarius.* If, for example, a widow was squandering her deceased husband's property and thereby harming her sons, the *millenarius* was the first who dealt with the case. But the injured party could also plead the case before the *comes civitatis* or before a probably non-Gothic local lawyer.[383]

In the Visigothic realm of Spain paradoxically enough the Latin word *millenarius* was replaced by a Gothic one. The leader of a group of one thousand was now called *thiufadus-thiufaths.*[384] Judging from the name, this military rank must have already existed before the middle of the sixth century.[385] No later than 580 the *thiufadus* found his way into the Visigothic legal terminology.[386] By way of analogy the group of one thousand from that time had the name *thiufa-thiufada*.[387] But just as this word had nothing to do with the number one thousand, the *thiufadus* was also no leader of a group of one thousand (*thusundifaths*) but etymologically speaking a "lord of slaves." As a result far-reaching inferences have been drawn about the social composition of the Visigothic army in Spain.[388] That it was not merely made up of noble landholders and their slaves is revealed by the laws regulating the duties of the troop leaders. Among these leaders the *thiufadus* certainly has the highest rank, even though later he was counted among the *viliores personae*. He was thus definitely no "sergeant" of slaves but a commander of a unit of the Gothic army that ranked numerically above a group of one hundred, and he was the leader of warriors (*exercitales, milleni milites*), not of unfree men.[389] It is possible, however, to see the *thiufadus* as the "master of military servants," for quite often the younger, or in any case less heavily armed, warrior who supported the elite troops was looked upon as a servant or page, regardless of his social standing. If this view is correct, then we need not bother with the older etymology that interpreted the *thiufadus* as the "lord over the multitude."[390] The *thiufadus* was not only a judge but also a military leader and thus exercised a dual function that the Visigothic *millenarius* presumably also had, but that cannot be proved. The process whereby the Latin term was supplanted by the Gothic word could perhaps be explained in sociolinguistic terms. As long as Gothic was spoken the Latin technical terms possessed greater prestige and greater precision. With the abandonment of the Gothic language this relationship was reversed, and some Latinized Gothic words now appear for the first time as technical terms.[391]

THE COURTIERS

We do not know whether those very Roman-seeming *comites* who formed the entourage of the Visigothic king of Toledo had already existed at the court of Toulouse. The office of the *comes patrimonii* could not have come into being until ca. 500.[392] It is tempting but unacceptable to draw conclusions about conditions in the fifth century from these courtiers (*palatini*)[393] of the mid-seventh century. Although one may wonder how Roman continuity could have in a sense skipped over the kingdom of Toulouse and continued only at the court of Toledo, it is dangerous to draw a straight line of development across unknown periods; in other words, it is risky to say something about the profession of the father because we see the grandfather and grandson working in the same business. We are also advised to be cautious by the analogy of the Visigothic *ducatus* which also continued Roman institutions only from about 470, for until then there had been neither a need for it nor personnel to fill the positions.[394] Thus Leovigild probably consciously adopted much of Roman tradition when he fashioned his realm as an *imitatio imperii*.[395]

In contrast, only the following court positions can be attested or at best inferred at Toulouse:[396] the bearer of the arms, the treasurer, the marshal, and the cup-bearer. At the court of Theodoric there was a *comes armiger,* who did not leave the king's side and who stood out clearly against the other "fur-clad guards and troops." In Spain this armor-bearer was then called the *comes spatharius* after the Byzantine model. His title could also be bestowed as a mark of honor, so there soon existed a number of *comites spatharii,* but one of them actually exercised the function. This armor-bearer could have been a sort of "chief *comes*" whom the others obeyed as their superior.[397] The royal treasure was certainly older than the kingdom of Toulouse and its great significance is repeatedly emphasized.[398] We cannot say whether in Toulouse the treasure was already supervised by a *comes thesaurorum* or whether another functionary was responsible for it.[399] Yet it is likely that there was already a marshal, *comes stabuli,* at the court of Theoderid and his successors.[400] One would certainly have met there a *comes scanciarum* or several courtiers of equal rank who carried out the function of cup-bearers. This courtly position had a traditional Gothic name, which comes as no surprise: "They drink like Goths" had already become a proverbial expression. Men and women liked to get drunk, so why shouldn't the king himself create a separate office for that purpose?[401]

The administration of the kingdom of Toulouse could not function without Roman experts. Nevertheless, the senatorial noble Leo of Narbonne is the first who can be attested as a Visigothic official of the central administration. He had made a name for himself as poet, orator, and jurist. The entire flow of correspondence relating to administrative and foreign policy matters went through his hands. Leo negotiated with the foreign envoys and also assumed the position of mediator between the king and his Roman subjects. It is not clear whether the latter role had been officially assigned to him or whether it was a self-appointed one, but this does not really matter since in any case his sphere of duties would not have fit into the administrative structure of the Roman Empire. His contemporaries are like us in that they too had to *describe* his tasks and could not *define* them with the traditional terms of civil administration.[402] Leo was still active under Alaric II and then probably found a successor in Anianus,[403] but we do not know whether the latter followed him directly or whether there was someone else in between.[404] Both Leo and Anianus were *viri spectabiles,* that is, they belonged to the second late Roman class ranking. Since there was also at Alaric II's court a *comes* of the first rank who was placed above Anianus as a *vir magnificus et inluster,*[405] the classical ranking scheme was probably still in use. Thus Anianus seems in every way like a Merovingian *referendarius.*[406]

ROYAL ESTATES AND FINANCES

Later Visigothic legislation shows a remarkably strong continuity with imperial fiscal administration.[407] Nevertheless, there are doubts about how directly the system was taken over by Euric and Alaric II. In other words, we do not know which *comes*[408] with a staff of agents—such as *actores, procuratores, praepositi, vil(l)ici*—and the representatives of the cities kept watch over the revenues of the king.[409] The basis of the royal finances was the domain taken over from the imperial possessions. The credit rating and the splendor of the kingship were determined by the treasure at Toulouse. It contained valuable objects made from coined and uncoined gold and silver, precious objects such as the bowl dedicated to Ragnahild, and finally the riches of Rome and Jerusalem.[410] This treasure also included the archives.[411] Into the treasure flowed the king's share of the booty, the gifts and tributes, the taxes of the Romans—insofar as they were paid in bullion or coin and were not spent where they were levied—the tolls, fines, and the income from the minting of coins.[412]

The taxes levied under Euric and Alaric II were seen as exemplary in the period after 507/511. Thus the population of Spain and Septimania complained about Ostrogothic taxes and demanded from Theodoric the Great a return to the levels that had been fixed in writing by Euric and Alaric II.[413] No later than the 440s and probably two decades earlier the Visigothic kings had begun to keep the regular tax revenues of their Roman subjects. A simplification and easing of public expenditures—Toulouse could eliminate the military budget that was ruining the Western empire—and perhaps initial shortcomings in the administration at first made the kingdom of Toulouse a tax paradise for Romans and thus an attractive place to live. Things became different in the 470s when Euric conquered entire Roman provinces and taxed his new subjects. The Goths, however, were exempt from taxes as far as their *sortes* were concerned, and they did not lose this privilege even in 475 after a new treaty with the emperor had been concluded. Goths who owned property had to pay taxes.[414]

The monetary system of course remained Roman; nor was any separate coinage issued by the kings of Toulouse. The Constantinian gold solidus continued in circulation, seventy-two solidi making up a pound. Then there was the Theodosian tremissis, a third of a solidus, as well as silver coins. No full siliquae are known—twenty-four of which added up to a solidus—but only smaller monetary units.[415]

Since only a single royal clan ruled the kingdom of Toulouse, the possessions of royal families did not grow at the expense of a shrinking royal domain, as was the case later in Spain. The Toulousan royal demesne was composed of landed estates—the *domus regiae, dominicae (dominicales)*—which in the *Breviarium Alaricianum* are once again called *fiscus*.[416] The size of the royal landholdings clearly still surpassed that of the richest senatorial nobility.[417] One example as a comparison: the Arabs are said to have promised the heirs of the last Visigothic king the ownership of three thousand manors.[418] The royal estates were worked partly by slaves and partly by the *tributarii* who were close to the slaves in social standing; but land was also given to free owners, *possessores*, whereby use was made of the traditional form of *emphyteusis*.[419]

The Settlement of the Visigoths

In 1844 Theodor Gaupp advanced the thesis of an orderly policy of settlement in opposition to the theory of chaotic conquest. Since then the following model of the Visigothic settlement has developed into the predominant doctrine concerning the economic preconditions of the barbarian kingdoms on Roman soil.[420]

The disorder after the death of the emperor Honorius in 423 supposedly shifted the balance of power in favor of the Goths, and for the first time in Roman history barbarian co-owners proceeded to actually divide the land.[421] The Goths are said to have received two-thirds of the cultivated land. Add to this half of the fallow land, the virgin woods, and the pastures; however, if any of this land was developed or improved, the Gothic owners would have to pay an appropriate compensation. A third of the labor force is said to have fallen to the Gothic allotment, the *sors Gothica*.[422] Finally, it is possible that in the billeting the Romans were given the right of first choice.[423]

There are virtually no contemporary sources that support these assumptions, and many contradictory ideas have also raised doubts about the "*hospitalitas* system" as such.[424] This explanatory model therefore has to be abandoned, although it is only a new and better understanding of the late antique system of taxation and income that now decisively disproves it.[425] One impetus to a critical reexamination of the issue was the legitimate surprise that modern historiography so readily accepted the idea that the Romans would have given up one-third or even two-thirds of their property without any resistance. Moreover, the Visigoths and Burgundians did not come as conquerors; instead, they were settled deep inside the Roman borders on the command of the Roman general who had subjugated them. At least in the case of the Visigoths a prior agreement between the central military authorities and the Roman magnates affected by the intended settlement is almost certain. But on the whole the sources have so little to report about the modalities of settlement that we can only conclude that the method used was familiar and acceptable and by no means oppressive. In comparison, encroachments by the Loire Alans, who in fact expropriated, chased away, or even killed Roman landowners, led to the most serious complaints in the otherwise restrained and brief Gallic accounts of the fifth century.[426]

In addition, scholars have noted that the late antique laws on billeting refer in fact only to the accommodation of mobile units and not to the financing of their livelihood. The *leges de metatis* deal with the traditional, temporary *hospitalitas* that is considered the personal obligation (*munus personale*) of most homeowners.[427] What remained of this after the permanent settlement of the Gothic army was the language of the sources, which depict the relationship between Goths and Romans as that of "guests," *hospites*.[428] In reality no Roman was legally expropriated; instead, in the area of the kingdom of Toulouse two-thirds of the Roman tax revenues went as tax-exempt *sortes Gothicae* to the barbarians; the *tertia Romanorum*, the "third of the Romans," paid for the maintenance of the administration in the Roman *civitates*. The responsibility for the collection and distribution of the taxes fell on the urban curiales. Although the king could make gifts to his Goths from the *tertia Romanorum*, Toulouse was intent on protecting this share of the fiscal revenues from rapacious Gothic hands.[429] The Italian Ostrogoths were content with one third of the tax revenues. The Visigoths and the Burgundians took the same amount from the head-tax, *caput*, but claimed twice as much from the *annona*, the general tax. This is exactly how Jean Durliat explains the former assumption that the Visigoths and Burgundians received two thirds of the cultivated land and a third of the labor force. The reason probably lies in the fact that the usual distribution of the revenues—one third for the army, one third for the central government, one third for curial administration—was possible only in the Italy of Odovacar and Theodoric, for both had taken over

the entire Roman governmental apparatus. By contrast, the Gallic kingdoms were made up of *civitates*. Roman administration functioned here
only up to the level of the curiales, but the centralized institutions had
to be created—with Roman help, to be sure—and financed by the barbarian kings.[430]

The form of settlement devised in southern Gaul represented a viable
compromise between the demands of leaders such as Alaric I or Athaulf
and the imperial government's attempts, doomed to fail, to settle the barbarians at the borders or in uninhabited areas. The Gothic army was a
Roman federate army, the maintenance of which could in traditional fashion
be left to the curiae. The fundamental difference, however, was that the
Gothic army remained in the country for an extended period and formed
the basis of a kingdom.[431]

Who among the Goths was entitled to an allotment is nowhere stated.
Considering the social structure of the Gothic army, however, it is out of
the question that everybody had an equal claim. Both the free and the unfree
retainers, the *buccellarii* and the *saiones,* as well as the slaves remained
unhoused unless their lord provided for them during the time of their
service. He was the *dominus* of the unfree and the *patronus* of the free
men.[432] The idea that the Gothic army—or any Germanic army—was ever
composed of equals is a myth. The social differentiation was intensified
after the settlement, so that the upper stratum accumulated considerable
economic power. No doubt there were Goths who at times forcibly increased the taxes of "their Romans" and who tried to deprive their "co-owners" (*consortes*) of their property and their freedom.[433] But there were plenty
of legal ways to become a property owner (*possessor*). Just like the Romans
the Goths could buy property or receive it as a gift, but as a result they
probably became subject to taxation.[434]

The process of allotment and billeting witnessed injustice and violence.
Hospes, a "billeted Goth," became a dreaded word, as many a deep groan
of despair reveals.[435] The federates formed a state within the state, changing
the Roman environment: more often than not they caused old wealth to
disappear and new wealth to sprout.[436] But most senatorial nobles retained
their importance in the Gothic state and remained as powerful as before.
For this reason alone it seems unlikely that the senators of southern Gaul—
that is, the very group that must have agreed to the Gothic settlement and
allotment—were in 418 or the following years as radically dispossessed as
has often been assumed. The sources of the fifth century are silent about
any large-scale expropriation in Aquitaine, whereas there is an outcry
against the wild Alans from the Loire who seized senatorial latifundia and

expelled their owners. And it makes no difference that those events took place in the areas of Gaul where Roman social and economic structures were already weaker than in the south.[437] Even after 418 certain landed estates of Spanish and Aquitanian senators were so large that contemporary sources called them "kingdoms." This description was accurate: in the sixth century a Spanish lady of the senatorial class was wealthy enough for her husband Theudis to raise two thousand warriors and eventually gain the Visigothic kingship.[438] But already Ecdicius and his fellow senators had enough wealth to defy the Visigothic king Euric for four years.[439] Thus Gothic tax demands would have threatened the property and freedom of the curiales—the members of the urban middle class—far more than they did the senatorial class. But neither the emperor nor the Gothic king could have had any interest in seeing the curiales unable to pay the taxes or "running off into the woods."[440] Last, one should not forget that "even before the barbarians arrived" there were many deserted estates, which did not pay taxes.[441]

To strengthen the legal protection of property, Theoderid and his immediate successors issued decrees—*legum statuta*—dealing with possession and property. These decrees probably did not legitimize arbitrary proceedings in the past but set a date after which such proceedings were prohibited. Nonetheless, no one was allowed to raise claims based on conditions of ownership that had existed before 418, *ante adventum Gothorum*. The new era was to begin with a fixed date. Part of the new regulation was the incontestable validity of a division that had been carried out in the presence of "relatives and neighbors."[442] Such groups of people, guaranteeing the public nature of the act, were probably not merely ad hoc bodies assembled for each case but organs of local self-government, like the *conventus publicus vicinorum* attested at a later period.[443] We should beware of making an institutional connection between this body and the village council of the Tervingian Goths, but a functional comparison of the two institutions is possible.[444] The "assembly" only had powers of arbitration. If an offense had to be punished, if, for example, a Goth acquired a Roman *tertia* against the law—that is, without royal permission—the "judges of a given urban district" or the supervisors of the royal estates intervened.[445] Oaths and the testimony of witnesses were permissible as "evidence." The legal rights of the plaintiff, however, were protected not only through a trial by inquisition in the presence of the plaintiff and the judge[446] but also, in keeping with the Roman structure of the Gothic administration, by written records of the proceedings. The existence of such records is clearly assumed by Gothic legislation[447] and is revealed by the delightful story related by Paulinus of

Pella in his memoirs. The author, originally from Bordeaux, lived an impoverished and lonely life in Marseille, a city that was still Roman. Decades had passed since the Goths under Athaulf had entered his hometown for the first time. Out of the blue an unknown Goth sent him the purchase price for a small piece of property. The buyer must have discovered in the records that Paulinus was the legal owner of a field he had acquired. The recipient praised the unexpected money as a gift from his God.[448] Of course the story also shows that a "foreigner," a Roman provincial living beyond "the borders of the Gothic allotments,"[449] had no choice but to accept whatever was offered. There was no negotiating about the price or the Roman's intention to sell; a Goth simply sent the money and that was that. But Paulinus's title of possession could have been preserved only because it was entered in a land register—the *gesta municipalia*[450]—where the Goth discovered it and accepted it as legally valid.

The Gothic "guests" left barely any traces in the language and place-names and virtually none in the archaeological finds of Aquitaine.[451] But modern scholars even quarrel over the meager remains. The modern significance of the problem is slight. There never was in France a large-scale settlement of Goths comparable to that of Franks. By no stretch of the imagination can one therefore make them responsible for the creation of the French-German language boundary.[452] The Goths settled various areas of their federate kingdom in different stages and in varying degrees of density. Furthermore, the majority of the settlers were bilingual, which in itself accounts for the small number of place-names taken from their tribal language. Nevertheless, the conditions of Gothic settlement remains one of the thorniest problems in the "histoire régionale d'Aquitaine." "Germanic" researchers have found a lot of Goths in areas where their "Latin" counterparts deny their existence. Of course no one openly declares his biases but smuggles them in through the "most reasonable" of human inventions, statistics. The results are estimated tribal sizes of about one hundred to two hundred thousand Goths, at times a few more or less, who are said to have settled and multiplied in Aquitaine. The origin of all the problems is Gaiseric's count of his Vandals in 429 in his efforts to procure enough ships.[453] The Goths, in contrast, had always neglected to take such a precautionary measure when they wanted to cross the sea, which is why they never got across or left any figures about the size of their people.[454] Gaiseric had learned from their mistakes, which is why he counted his people, supposedly right up to eighty thousand. Historians then complete the calculation. If the Vandals had a certain size but still ran away from the Goths, the victors must then have been even more numerous: the results of such calculations are the statistics mentioned above.

Whoever estimates the size of a people and gives the number in absolute terms would also like to locate them in a specific area and at the same time secure their archaeological as well as toponymic traces.[455] Since a people such as the Goths were "foreigners," whatever they left behind is expected to stand out clearly against local remains. But if little or nothing has been preserved, it follows that the people were either "not very numerous" or that they "all fled to Spain after 507." The best example is the Visigoths.[456] Those who dislike even dead Goths simply reduce their toponymic legacy. Where a certain sympathy exists for Goths, the findings on place-names change: their number is allowed to rise. But the study of toponyms does not possess the methodological tools to determine population numbers, especially of Gothic migratory groups.[457]

Attempts to estimate the size of the federate army from the amount of grain that the Roman military administration supplied to the Goths yield more promising figures. Thus Valia could have fed fifteen thousand warriors for one year with the 600,000 bushels of grain he received through the peace of 416. This number does not diverge too much from the twenty thousand federate Visigoths of the time of Theodosius.[458] Archaeological tools permit us at best to deduce urban populations but not to distinguish between Goths and Romans. One assumes for each hectare of built-up urban space one hundred fifty to two hundred people. But since the majority of the inhabitants lived in the country, one cannot say anything about the total population of a region.[459] Anyone who then tries to fill in the gap with a "mixed calculation"[460]—that is, by lumping together the results of various disciplines—is necessarily disappointed by archaeology and toponymy.[461]

Both disciplines, however, remain indispensable for insight into general developments and phenomena. They yield qualitative rather than quantitative results. For example, they answer the question "Which barbarian groups inhabited a certain region?" but not the question "How many there were?" Comparative sizes and the multilingualism of a region can also be read from toponyms and archaeological finds.[462] On occasion they also convey insights into religion, as, for example, the nature of change in the cult and when it took place. The graves without weapons which we find among the Goths in the pagan *barbaricum* point to a special concept of the hereafter. Apparently a Gothic warrior had no need of weapons as he began his final journey.[463] Nonetheless, Theodoric the Great had to forbid the Ostrogoths to make burial offerings of precious metals because it made no sense to leave the dead with valuables that could be useful to the living. The custom itself indicates that the pagan Goths needed gold in order to "be someone" in the hereafter.[464] Eventually in the Gothic kingdoms of Italy and Spain there was a "reduced" custom of burial offerings: women in general and less frequently men were buried in the outfit they had worn during their lifetime.[465] Although we have no definite evidence for this custom in the kingdom of Toulouse, it probably existed.[466]

The starting point as well as stumbling block of all work on *Romania Germanica* is Ernst Gamillscheg's monumental work of that title.[467] Gamillscheg discussed the Germanic influence on the language of the Latin West, intending to provide a history of the language and settlements of the Germanic peoples in the territory of the former Roman Empire.[468] To this end an important, if not *the* most important, field of investigation for him was Germanic toponymy. As far as the Gothic place-names of the kingdom of Toulouse are concerned, Gamillscheg rightly started from the assumption that the federates were already largely bilingual when they entered that region in 418. But he argues that there already existed Gothic places inside and outside of the *sortes Gothicae*. This "earlier, peaceful" settlement was indicated by place-names that could be traced to *Gotos, Gotorum, Gotones, Gotiscum,* and similar forms.[469] Gamillscheg was a brilliant philologist and scholar of Romance languages but not a historian. Hence he did not ask himself where else these settlements, which of necessity would have been settlements of *laeti* and barbarians, were attested. The notorious *Scriptores historiae Augustae,* which claim that around 400 there was no Roman territory without its Gothic slaves, are insufficient evidence.[470]

Gamillscheg distinguished place-names of a first phase between 418 and 480 from those of the late period of the Toulousan kingdom, the formation of which continued in Spain. The first Toulousan phase he characterized by toponyms in which a Gothic personal name was combined with the word *villa* (estate, village) or with the suffix *-ingôs* (the people of). Both types of place-names are concentrated in the original settlement area around Toulouse. The *villa* names resemble the Frankish Avricourt type, that is, those hybrid forms that were formed, for example, like *Eberhardi curtis*. But the Gothic analogy is different in one important respect. The Frankish combination places the determinative word at the beginning, as a result of which the personal name is used in the manner of a Saxon genitive—that is, it is used in the Germanic fashion—but the name is declined in Latin through the formation of an oblique case. The Gothic *villa* names and their analogies, however, are combined with the personal names by means of the Gothic joining vowel *-a,* so that, for example, the form Amalavilla-Ambleville is created. From this Gamillscheg no doubt correctly inferred that the process of name-giving was not, as in the case of Avricourt, the work of Romance speakers but of Goths who knew not only Gothic and Latin but who also used the Latin term *villa* in place of the biblical Gothic *haims* or *weihs*. Anyone who believes in an extensive bilingualism of the Danubian Goths can easily concur with this assumption.[471]

The *-ingôs* names cause difficulties insofar as they have pre-Roman, that is, Ligurian-Iberian, precursors. Gamillscheg was aware of this and re-marked: "All interpretations that cannot base themselves on early medieval forms are therefore doubtful."[472] One who opposes the inferring of popula-tion size from place-names will in no way mourn the loss here and there of a few, indeed even of many, *-ingôs* names to the old pre-Roman *-incus* suffix.[473] The interpretation of the *-ingôs* names as "the estate/village of the people of so-and-so" also demands great caution, but it has this difficulty in common with all Germanic *-ingen* names.[474]

Certain "adjustments" also took place in the Gothic south as they did in the Frankish North.[475] Since the *-ingôs* ending remained in use for a long time in the Gothic heartland, it could even replace the suffixes in *-acum*, *-avum-*, *-arum* in old Roman place-names. At the same time there hardly existed here the possibility of the creation of hybrid forms: a Gothic personal name and a Latin ending are a real rarity in the area around Toulouse, but this combination does appear with greater frequency outside the actual Gothic land: "Where the traces of Gothic settlements are . . . weak or non-existent, these names can be attested."[476] While an Amalaville-Ambleville belonged to the name type of the Gothic heartland, Amaliavum-Amaillou and Amal(i)acum-Millac are situated in the north of Aquitania II.[477]

Gamillscheg detected a transition to the place-name formations of the late period after 480 in his Harjanisvilla type: here the Latin oblique case has replaced the Gothic joining vowel. In the next, third phase of Gamillscheg's analysis, the non-Gothic majority to which the increasingly Romanized Goths joined themselves changed the grammatical construction. The in-verted form *villa Harjanis* or simply *Harjanis* sounded right to them. Thus was created the Septimanian type, which was the only type used south of the Pyrenees.[478] The suppression of the word *villa* is reminiscent of place-name developments in the Waldviertel in parts of Austria. There we find place-names such as Gerungs, Otten, and Irnfrieds, from which words such as *-dorf* or *-schlag* have dropped off. Perhaps this comparison provides some suggestions for further research. The genetival place-names were used mainly as "colonization and expansion names" in lower Austria.[479] It seems not impossible that the Septimanian form reflects a similar process. After the conquest of the coast, Euric may have attempted a systematic penetration of the region,[480] a process that in the old settlement area would probably be indicated only by the *mark-gastald* (Margastaud) places, which undoubtedly reflect an early colonization of the Toulousan heartland. Although it would be conceivable that Gothic refugees after 507 occupied such places,[481] no intensified Gothic colonization in Septimania is attested at that time.

But the fifth century is only the first of many centuries of Gothic history or the history of the Goths in Gaul. It is true that in 507 Aquitania itself was lost and Toulouse as well was captured by the Franks. But the Goths held out along the urbanized Mediterranean coast between the Rhone and the Pyrenees, and they even gave the land around Narbonne their name of "Gothia."[482] Up to the middle of the twelfth century one could still "profess the Gothic law" here. The southern counterpart to the Gallic Gothia was Catalonia, the Spanish March of the Frankish kingdom and later of high medieval France. In this Gothia the authorities thought it was necessary as late as 1251 to formally abolish Gothic law.[483] It is no surprise that Gothic name-giving in this area has become an object of "scholarly" interest.[484] As late as 964 a mother and all of her eight children in the Gothic south had Gothic names.[485]

But it was not only Gothic personal names that remained attractive; it is likely that the Gothic place-names of the early Toulousan type also continued in use. It follows that an undetermined number of Gothic toponyms appeared only after the end of the kingdom of Toulouse.[486] There are names of the type "village of the Goths," or "mountain of the Goths"[487] which are reminiscent of the south German Walchen names. Those names were given by a German-speaking majority to a Romance-speaking minority. They do not appear in any of those areas where Romance place-names were preserved in compact clusters. A Strasswalchen east of Salzburg and a nearby village called Latein point to a time when the Romance speakers declined to a minority. Part of Strasswalchen is today also the village of Roithwalchen. Its name, however, does not mean that around the year 700 Walchen-Romans were here still clearing new land; rather, it points to the expansion of the land in the twelfth century,[488] when nobody there still spoke any Romance dialect. But without the old Romance base of Strasswalchen there would have been no Roithwalchen.

One would like to know whether the Toulousan toponyms reflect the integration of the Gothic notables into the late antique system of landownership. Is it permissible to make a distinction between a "real" -*ingôs* name, such as Wulfaringôs-Olfarencs,[489] and a *villa* place-name of the first generation? A distinction, perhaps, in the sense that the first form goes back to

Gothic dependents, such as retired *buccellarii* of a certain Ulfilas, whereas a village named Ambleville refers to an Amal landlord ruling over Romance-speaking peasants?[490] Does the existence side by side of Malarencs and Malaville permit such an assumption?[491] Questions of this sort must no doubt remain unanswered. It is possible that *villa* and *haims* are synonyms. The attempt to distinguish semantically between *-ingôs* places and *villa* places would then merely lead to the same dilemma that is already raised by the place-names in *-ingen* and *-heim*.[492] To speak of "slave villages" reveals less about ethnic identity and more about the social status of the settlers, and in this case we find side by side Skalkingôs-Esclaquens and the hybrid form Famulingôs-Famalencs.[493]

The Peoples of the Kingdom of Toulouse: Ethnic and Social Composition

The internal tensions unsettling the later Roman Empire were intensified by the "barbarization" of the *imperium*.[494] The admission of foreign peoples into the empire rendered the social problems insoluble.[495] The tribal kingship of barbarian or rebarbarized groups, however, seemed able to handle such problems better. For the moment it appeared as if a wandering army could ease the lot of many discontented and desperate provincials.[496] From the time when Gothic invasions into the empire began, many individuals and groups were ready to join the barbarians; they began by collaborating with the Goths and ended up as Goths themselves.[497] The constantly developing barbarian society proved receptive to other *gentes*. From the third to the sixth centuries the following maxim held true: a Goth was anyone who was allowed to fight with the tribe, irrespective of his ethnic or social background. But from the moment the Gothic army settled down, social mobility was restricted. Ethnic differentiations were then felt as social injustice and they increased the polarization of society.[498]

GOTHS AND ROMANS IN THE KINGDOM OF TOULOUSE

The legal sources for the period around 475—that is, about two generations after settlement—know only two ethnic groups: *Goti* and *Romani*.[499] The latter were the former provincials,[500] the locals, who set themselves apart from the Goths by calling themselves Romans. Barbarization took place everywhere on former imperial territory, in Gaul and Spain, as well as on the upper Rhine or the Inn and Salzach rivers. It is interesting that the

Romani concept could be further differentiated. Thus the Romani of Merovingian Aquitaine around 750 became the Aquitani of the Carolingian Empire. The ethnic distinction meant above all a legal separation of provincials from newcomers.[501] Both groups were kept apart by the prohibition of intermarriage which existed for Roman citizens and barbarians and which was taken over by the *Breviarium Alaricianum*. Even before the abrogation of this law in the sixth century it applied more to the middle and lower classes than to the upper stratum.[502] Social relations between Romans and Goths revealed for a long time a feeling of separateness, intensified by the religious differences: the Romans were Catholics, the Goths Arians.[503] In a well-known saying Sidonius Apollinaris stated that he avoided the barbarians even when they were decent people.[504] He also mocked those Romans of his own social class who had learned the foreign tongue so well that "the barbarians were afraid they might commit a barbarism in their own barbarian language."[505] But Sidonius's colleague Ennodius in Pavia also thought that the Gothic language of King Euric was mere "barbaric mumbling."[506] In appearance and behavior the barbarians were strange and unpleasant: the fur clothing they wore in southern lands and their strong body odor,[507] their drinking and eating bouts,[508] and their huge bodies.[509] But their fair skin and blond hair and their military parades also fascinated the Romans.[510] The barbarians were totally unpredictable characters. In a rage they could commit atrocities and then instantly turn around and protect a Roman.[511] Just as Paulinus of Pella had joined the Attalus group, his sons returned to their homeland, to Gothic Bordeaux,[512] "out of love of freedom." Other Romans also voted with their feet against the empire and fled to the Goths. And hardly because they valued the Goths' "rigorous morality" or wanted to share the life of a "noble savage" but rather because in the kingdom of Toulouse taxes were in fact lower.[513] A tax burden of any kind, however, could threaten the ownership of land and with it the freedom of the owner.[514] Moreover, the Visigoths were neither able nor willing to reverse the polarization of the late antique social structure. Their legislation speaks mostly of nobles and slaves, lords and servants, poor and rich, while the middle class recedes into the background.[515] It is possible that the urban population possessed a more effective communal self-government than the rural folk did. Thus as long as there were still cities in the legal sense, the social freedom of their inhabitants was better protected than that of the rural population. But these differences were eliminated in the seventh century, at the latest, to the disadvantage of the cities and urban communities.[516]

Romans were cooperating with both the migrating Goths as well as the

Toulousan kings.[517] Their motives were as diverse as all human behavior can be. Apart from collaborators and profiteers, we find lukewarm sympathizers who just went along and tried to support the "Gothic peace" in order to prevent worse from happening.[518] But anyone who saw the situation clearly had to realize that it was an illusion to hope that the empire could be saved with Gothic help. It is no surprise that since Euric's time there had been a tremendous increase in the number of prominent Romans entering Visigothic service. A great stir was caused by the intention of the Gallic prefect of 469 and the governor of the seven provinces to transfer the Roman administration of Gaul to the kings of the Visigoths and Burgundians and to divide the remainder of imperial Gaul between the two barbarian princes. This plan presupposes, however, the belief that the barbarian *regna* were part of the late antique state. If this plan, a reaction to the "Greek emperor" Anthemius, had been carried out, it would have anticipated administratively Euric's conquests without detaching them from the Roman Empire. But apparently Arvandus and Seronatus were not isolated phenomena. At least three Roman generals continued their careers as Gothic *comites* and *duces* during the course of Euric's expansion. There is good reason to ask whether Romans who served in the army were subject to full taxation. Perhaps it was out of this group of privileged people that there developed the Roman upper stratum of the *convivae regis,* the "king's table companions," who are attested both in Burgundian and Frankish law.[519] We also know the names of those Romans who stood at the head of the central administration developing in the growing state of Euric and Alaric II.[520] Roman court poets appeared in Toulouse, and even Sidonius Apollinaris, who at one time was frequently found in the entourage of Theodoric, once again gave voice to a timid panegyric after Euric had recalled him from exile.[521] A Roman was in command of the Goths' Atlantic fleet. It once again made sense for the Romans to fight, since "under the standard of an ever-victorious people" they were not fighting for a lost cause.[522] But Toulouse had already been a meeting place of Gallic notables during the early period. Not long after the Gothic settlement, Avitus entered into his relationship with Theoderid. The Auvergnian nobleman was allowed to call the king his friend and he was entrusted with the raising and educating of the king's son Theodoric.[523] Soon after 418 the sons of Paulinus of Pella must have also tried to embark on a "Gothic" career. They too considered themselves the king's friends. Unfortunately the sons died too soon to help their impoverished father, who had undoubtedly compromised himself.[524]

During the last days of the kingdom of Toulouse Apollinaris—Sidonius's son and Avitus's grandson and the companion and successor of the *dux et comes* Victorius—fought with his friends on the side of the Goths against the Franks. After the battle of Vouillé a son of the Merovingian king had to "visit" the Auvergne personally in order to annex it to the Frankish kingdom.[525] Apparently the new generation of the *civitas Arvernorum* was repeating the policy of its forefathers in refusing to submit without resistance to the changing situation; they wanted to remain Gothic even after the end of Gothic rule, just as their fathers had still held high Rome's flagpole after the flag itself had long been lowered. And the resistance of the Auvergne paid off at the beginning of the Frankish era, for the region retained its accustomed independence.[526]

JEWS, GREEKS, AND SYRIANS

At the council of Narbonne in 589 a distinction was made, from a religious and political point of view, between *Ghotus, Romanus, Sirus, Grecus vel Iudeus*. The Syrians, Greeks, and Jews lived of course according to the same laws as the Latin Roman majority; what set them apart from the Romans and from one another was their religion. The Syrians, who spoke Greek, were frequently mistaken for the real Greeks. All three eastern minorities were especially active in long-distance trading and in the money business. Thus places with a Roman-Visigothic mint usually had a Graeco-Syrian and a Jewish colony.[527]

The anti-Jewish legislation of Visigothic Spain codified frightful excesses of hate. But we cannot blame that on a "general Gothic mentality." Rather, Sisebut, Recceswinth, and Ervig continued the legal tradition of imperial legislation which could count on the approval even of the Church Fathers. In the correspondence of Sidonius Apollinaris we find echoes of a basic anti-Semitic sentiment, whereas Visigothic Toulouse did not persecute the Jews. Restrictions against overseas trade, which might go back to the time of Euric and Alaric II, affected all minorities who engaged in commerce and were not directed specifically against the Jews. But we do not find among the Toulousan Visigoths anything like the remarkable bond of loyalty between the Jews of Naples and the Ostrogoths who were under attack by the emperor.[528]

THE NATIVE BARBARIANS

Apart from Romans and Mediterranean minorities, the Visigoths also encountered other barbarian groups in Gaul, among them especially the Basques and Bretons. The second name is to be understood in the broadest sense of the word; it describes those inhabitants of Gaul who represented the native Celtic element. Since the third century the Bretons had returned increasingly to their ethnic identity and had become a linguistic, cultural, and especially a political force long before the Visigoths came to Gaul. Thus the Bagaudae based themselves on a rebarbarized particularism that sought to relieve by violence the socioeconomic pressures to which the lower classes were exposed. In the fifth century entire districts of Gaul detached themselves from Rome or entered into treaties as federates with the *imperium*. This movement was institutionalized by the Breton kingdom of Riothamus. With the consent of the imperial government he had established a federate kingdom on the northern border of the kingdom of Toulouse, and naturally it became the first target of Euric's expansion. The two enemies must have been similar. The Bretons were horsemen, like their Gothic-Taifalian neighbors. No doubt the Basques were also horsemen; after the retreat of the Visigoths they extended their territory all the way across the Garonne and thereby took possession of the wide plains, an excellent area for horsebreeding. The sources report nothing about Visigothic-Basque conflicts, but this in no way implies that the lords of Toulouse were also the lords of the Basques.[529]

THE IMMIGRANT BARBARIANS

What ethnic elements made up the Visigoths? Onomastics provides the following evidence: (1) in the kingdom of Toulouse we find pure Amal names;[530] (2) it is possible that a Thracian by the name of Bessa and more than a dozen Baltic Galindi appeared in the area of Toulouse;[531] (3) it is possible that not far from them a certain Sarus and a Gainas settled down;[532] (4) Alanic-Vandal groups have left traces;[533] (5) the Taifali, who along the Danube had had ties to the Tervingi, are found again in Gothic Poitou near the Garonne river and in the Burgundian-Frankish border region.[534]

The Gothic army that was settled in 418 was composed of Tervingian-Vesian, Greutungian-Ostrogothic, and originally non-Gothic elements now more or less Gothicized. The diverse composition of the Goths was noticed by contemporary authors, who spoke of the Toulousan federates as "peoples" (*populi*).[535] At times Gothic polyethnicism was also expressed through listing of all the tribes the Romans had ever dealt with.[536] Sidonius Apollinaris was a true Gaul, "highly decorated and without any sense for geography." Nevertheless, we owe to him the knowledge that the king of Toulouse and his magnates were Vesi. On January 1, 456, Sidonius delivered a eulogy on his imperial father-in-law Avitus in which he showed that the name "Vesus" was still alive at the court of Toulouse. The territorial name Tervingi had disappeared, but the Gothic magnates and their king were still "the Good" (Vesi).[537]

Greutungian-Ostrogothic groups repeatedly switched sides and joined the Visigoths. Perhaps not all Greutungian horsemen left Fritigern's Goths when in 380 they parted from their battle companions of Adrianople.[538] Most of the Pannonian Goths of Athaulf and the majority of the survivors of Radagaisus's group and of the former followers of Sarus probably also belonged to the eastern Goths, as did many of the nameless barbarians of Stilicho's persecuted bands who found refuge with Alaric in 408.[539] After 418 two waves of Amal reinforcements to the Ostrogothic group are attested among the Toulousan Goths. The first took place around 427, the second in 473 or 474. The older group was probably led to Gaul by the same Vetericus-Videric who is attested in the fateful year 439. The second wave came with Vidimir the Younger. The arrival of these Amal Goths was recorded by Gallic contemporaries. Thus Sidonius Apollinaris finds them in Euric's entourage, but he confuses the first wave of immigrants with the second. For he says that with Euric's massive support "the Ostrogoths at home defeated the Huns." But around 475 no Ostrogoths or Huns were living in Pannonia. Nevertheless, it appears plausible that the Ostrogothic refugees of 427 had to leave the Pannonian homeland in the face of the advancing Huns. The Ostrogothic groups went to join the free royal Goths in order to "form a people" with them.[540] Perhaps the two Ostrogothic waves of immigrants can even explain the Amal settlement names in the Toulousan kingdom. We know of an Amal place-name of the older type in the heartland of the kingdom of Toulouse, and two younger Amal settlements are located on the Loire border.[541] The Visigothic king no doubt employed the Amali in Spain.[542] In any case, Euric kept some of them in his immediate entourage, along with representatives of the other tribal groups.[543] Thus even Vandal-Suevic settlements were found in the area northeast of Toulouse.[544]

Euric had excellent relations with the western Heruli, the Varni, and the Thuringians.[545] Among the various peoples who came to his court of their own free will, Sidonius mentions first the Heruli "from the most distant shores of the ocean."[546] Is it possible that some of these "Vikings" were among the king's personal retainers? At least one such case is known from the Varnian neighbors. Euric's brother and predecessor Theodoric possessed in the Varnian Ag(r)iwulf a "personal dependent" (*cliens proprius*) whom he made governor of the seemingly subdued Suevic kingdom in 456. Agiwulf lacked "the nobility of the Gothic blood," but despite an allusion in the

Origo Gothica he was not necessarily an unfree man.[547] In any case, it was only in royal service that the Varni could play a role that his non-Gothic origin would otherwise not have allowed. Such an outsider remained basically dependent on his lord and formed some sort of counterweight to the Gothic establishment. In Agiwulf's case, however, the king had miscalculated. Agiwulf behaved like a true Gothic magnate: he rebelled and made himself king. In a certain sense Agiwulf reminds us of Theudis, whom Theodoric the Great entrusted with the government of the Visigothic kingdom of Spain. Theudis, however, was far more successful than Agiwulf; he took his time, married rich, and remained a "legitimist" until the extinction of the rightful dynasty, even though he may have hastened its end.[548]

Both Romans and Goths felt the greatest loathing for the Saxon pirates. They were dangerous, difficult to catch, and they were pagans who sacrificed every tenth captive to the sea and even thought they were performing a good deed. Under Euric an Atlantic fleet of sorts was built to stop the Saxons.[549] Nevertheless, Gothic-Saxon relations were not entirely hostile. For the Saxons did not sail from far across the sea, as one would at first assume, but had established themselves at the mouth of the Garonne as well as the Loire. The Gironde and the mouth of the Loire, however, were part of Aquitania II and thus belonged to the territory the Goths occupied at the very outset. Later on members of the Loire and Garonne groups are scattered through other parts of the former Gothic kingdom. This again raises the problem of the extent to which inferences from the Frankish period are permissible. As late as 673 a Saxon contingent supported the Visigothic rival king Paulus. But this tells us nothing about relations between the two peoples two hundred years earlier. Nonetheless, we are told that in the seventh century the Saxons formed a military unit employed by the rulers of Aquitaine. It is likely, however, that Euric had already succeeded in subduing the Saxons at his doorstep and in binding them to himself by means of a treaty,[550] as he did with "other peoples from beyond the sea."[551]

Among the barbarian elements of non-Gothic origin there were, finally, the barbarians from the settlements of *dediticii* and *laeti*. These people were already part of the Roman provincial organization when the Goths arrived, and they were taken over into the Gothic sphere of authority. Subjugated barbarians (*dediticii*) and their descendants (*laeti*) were, like the Goths, placed under Roman military administration, but a vast social gulf separated them from the privileged federates.[552] Within the territory that had now become Gothic, the *Notitia dignitatum* lists Sarmatian, Taifalian, and Suevic colonies.[553] Southern French place-names have preserved to this day the memory of Taifali and Alans.[554] Since the Alans were obviously not considered Sarmatians, we must ask where they came from and with what status they were settled. For we are dealing here with people who were not identical either with the Armorican Alans or with those of Orléans or Valence.[555] Their settlements were not only on the Roman Mediterranean coast but also along the road from Narbonne to Toulouse as well as in the area around the Gothic capital.[556]

Of all barbarian peoples the Alans were the most fragmented, which is why they appeared everywhere and nowhere. In 409 Royal Alans had moved to Spain with the Vandals and Suevi.[557] But five years later we find Alans led by a king outside of Bazas, south of Bordeaux. This group later settled in the area north of the Loire. But certainly not all members of this group left the south, and they remained even when the Goths returned after four years. Yet the Alans of 414 would have had good reason not to await the year 418 at the upper reaches of the Garonne. For they had broken away from the Athaulf Goths, and they had gone over to the Emperor Honorius under whom fellow tribesmen were already serving.[558] Some Alans, however, remained in the south. To illustrate primitive ancestor worship in Marseille around 425, one uses as an example the Alans, not the Goths.[559] They were still pagans, even when some had come under Gothic rule. And now Toulouse entered upon the inheritance of the Roman imperial government.

Much the same goes for the Sarmatians and Taifali. In the wake of one of the Roman barbarian settlements attested for the beginning of the fifth century,[560] there grew up the Frankish *pagus* Theifalia-Theofalgicus. Around 565 Gregory of Tours mentions the Taifali as a separate *gens*. He speaks of them in friendly terms, even though their behavior was not at all peaceful, and he even knows a miracle-working priest of Taifalian origin. Thus they cannot have been the sort of people Gregory considered Goths and heretics. They did kill their Catholic bishop, but not because as people of a different faith they had no use for him but because he had been forced upon them by the Frankish king.[561] This group seems to have been remarkably independent. Scholars have compared the Taifali of Poitou with the contemporary Saxons of Bayeux, who were serving as a separate contingent in the Frankish army.[562] The Taifali used to be under Gothic rule and at Gregory's time they were subjects of the Frankish king. But there is no indication that they had ever been Arians. Their conversion very likely took place around the middle of the fifth century, when the Romans launched a "religiopolitical" offensive that for a brief period even reached the Suevic kingdom in Spain.[563] Something similar is assumed to have happened to the Alans. As late as 400 imperial legislation happily noted that there were many people who "followed the fortune of Rome" and who let themselves be settled as *dediticii*. The Taifali who were mentioned in the Western empire served in cavalry units levied under Honorius. Alanic horsemen were already part of Gratian's entourage. But we cannot say at what time the first of these peoples found a permanent home in Aquitaine; at any rate, settlements of *Alani gentiles* (*dediticii*) are not attested.[564]

The Gothic kings took over subject peoples from Roman administration and thereby increased the number of their "personal dependents."[565] Taifalian place-names are attested not only in Poitou but also close to the Visigothic capital. Likewise there are Alanic names around Toulouse. Their origin might be of more recent date and could, for example, go back to settled captives from the Orléans group.[566] But in the same region is also a place where as late as the seventh century we still find Gothic *fiscalini* (people settled on royal estates) who had belonged to the villa of Trebosc near Rodez "since time immemorial."[567] After all, dependents did not leave their land simply because ownership of an estate changed hands. Since it was these dependents who worked the fields, they were precious to every new lord. They created, indeed, in a sense they were the land that the lord had won for himself.

CONDITIONS OF DEPENDENCY

Social and economic conditions among the Goths were as unequal as those of their Roman "hosts." A fundamental split existed between the free and the unfree; by no means did all free Goths become *consortes* of the Aquitanian nobility.[568]

Such a notion would be unrealistic for a number of reasons. Gothic society had already become strongly differentiated at the time when the Tervingi developed into a people in close contact with the Mediterranean world. Since not all of the peasant underclasses left the homeland in 376, initially a certain leveling off of Gothic society must have occurred.[569] But this situation cannot have persisted for long. That the *exercitus Gothorum* was in no way a socially homogeneous group is shown by its unfree members.[570] But even the so-called free warriors formed no uniform group, much less a class. Clearly separated from them was the nobility, which in the eyes of Goths and Romans alike was distinguished by wealth and illustrious descent.[571] Moreover, the Gothic federates formed part of the Roman army,[572] which, like military organizations at all times, had its own hierarchy. Incidentally, the influence of the Roman army extended so far that it even determined the nature of Gothic "retainership."

We read that "in the days of Honorius the title *buccellarius* was used not only for Roman but also for certain Gothic soldiers."[573] The *buccellarii* were elite troops who either did not have to subsist on the common rations and instead received the *buccellae* or who ate in the same "mess" as their lords. Thus far the etymological interpretation. They were retainers and were themselves again structured according to rank. Their highest-ranking members were called δορυφόροι. The *buccellarii* were in direct contact with their lord. Insofar as the latter was a commanding general or a commander-in-chief, such a unit of *buccellarii* remained part of the late Roman army; in fact it was the unit the commander could most rely on. *Buccellarii* could be inherited or bequeathed to someone else, they could be acquired through marriage, and they could be sold. One can well imagine the negative effect the existence of the *buccellarii* had on the morale of the army, which now had two kinds of soldiers. This "institution" presented an even greater danger in the hands of senatorial nobles or other wealthy people, even if they used it only to fill the vacuum in public authority left behind by the dying Roman state. The emperor therefore never grew tired of prohibiting the keeping of these retinues.[574] Almost simultaneously with the last imperial law against the institution of the *buccellarii*, Euric promulgated legal decrees[575] that institutionalized this form of warrior retainership as a Gothic practice.[576] But the decrees and the name reveal that nothing new was being created.

As a result of the social differentiation within the Gothic army the retainers remained with their lord when he settled down on a Roman estate. It was a sign of the Visigothic kingdom's undeveloped statehood that its lawgiver paid special attention to the practice of retainership instead of merely tolerating it. Thus there were two types of dependency for the "unhoused" free Visigoths.

The *buccellarii* were permitted for the duration of their service to use "weapons and other gifts they had received from their lords."[577] If they left service and looked for another employer, which no one could stop them from doing since they were free men, they had to return to their lord everything they had received together with half of what they had acquired. This obligation did not change even in the second or third generation, and it applied equally to male and female descendants of the *buccellarii*. Daughters could retain possession of the "loan" if they "remained in the power of the lord" and married a man who was acceptable to him.[578] The status of *buccellarius* was heritable, which "led to greater security for the retainer but also limited his social freedom."[579] In addition, the lawgiver could not conceive of a *buccellarius* without his lord. Even the economically weaker strata of the migrating Gothic tribe settled in Aquitaine not as peasants or craftsmen but as warriors; in this social system one either personally fought for the lord or brought arms in marriage to a man chosen by the lord.

Case law of Gothic legislation is based on the concept that obligations arising from the hereditary *buccellarius* status could extend to the second or third generation. This time span and the Latin name point "to the days of Honorius,"[580] when the Goths were still a wandering tribe. It is quite possible that in those days the Goths turned a late antique development into an institution of their own. This new retainership surpassed quite visibly the *saio* retainership, which had a Gothic name. Among the retainers the *buccellarius* was socially and economically the most prominent and remained so as late as the seventh century.[581]

Although the word *saio* does not appear in Ulfilas's Bible, it is nevertheless of Gothic origin and describes the retainer in the true sense of the word. As such the term is also used by the *Codex Euricianus,* and traces of this usage can still be found in later Visigothic legislation.[582] In a functional sense a *saio* appears like a Bible-Gothic *andbahts.*[583] The *saio* has full freedom of movement and receives his "tools," his weapons, in full personal possession. But whatever he acquires during the time of his service remains without exception his lord's property if the *saio* decides to look for another patron. Moreover, the *Codex Euricianus* lacks any regulation concerning the economic and social security of the *saio,* who, in contrast to the *buccellarius,* cannot acquire any property, (*possessio*). Even in case of a breach of loyalty the *buccellarius,* according to legislation of the sixth and seventh centuries, was still left with half of his *adquisitio.*[584]

The Visigothic *saio* of the fifth century could be a retainer of any lord, whereas the Ostrogothic *saio* was exclusively an agent of the king.[585] When Theodoric the Great was also king of the Visigoths, it is possible that Ostrogothic *saiones* went to Spain and influenced their Visigothic counterparts.[586] For in the sixth and seventh centuries the Visigothic *saiones* were acting as agents of the judges and the provincial governors. But there are problems with this scenario. First, there is no evidence that Theodoric sent one of his *saiones* to Spain. Second, even the later Visigothic *saiones* were not exclusively agents of judges and governors. Third, the judges and governors were lords who exercised patronage and took part in public affairs. When they assumed the duties of a "patrimonial official," their agents also exercised public authority. Thus the specialization that the Visigothic *saio* underwent during the sixth and seventh centuries can be derived from his basic function. Little wonder that Recceswinth still considered the regulations provided by the *Codex Euricianus* for the *saio* so current that he took them over into his own law code with few modifications.[587]

Like the slaves, the retainers of free status were also dependent on a lord. But the *buccellarii* and the *saiones* had a *patronus,* whereas the slave was considered a piece of property and had a *dominus.* This does not mean that the slave had no legal standing.[588] He could fulfill for his lord a variety of functions and tasks in the latter's absence.[589] At first, the Visigoths considered any possessions of the slave as the lord's property.[590] An improvement in the situation of the unfree probably went hand in hand with the great increase in their numbers. But the growth of unfree groups meant in return a heavy strain on the social structure of Visigothic Spain.[591] Thus the *saio* of the late period still had a patron but was whipped like a slave if found guilty of an offense. Nevertheless, social mobility had not been completely suppressed; there was movement between classes, and the king and the nobility did not rule over an amorphous mass of slaves and servants.[592]

In the last decades of the Visigothic kingdom of Spain we still find attested a royal retainer of high rank whose name *gardingus* could have come straight out of Ulfilas's Bible. The *gardingus* is the housemate of the king, although in the Visigothic kingdom both before and after 507 there were also others who owned "houses." The first appearance of the term around 680 is as puzzling as its absence on earlier occasions when the mention of the *gardingus* would have been proper. Yet, the word must have been created at a time when the Visigoths were still actively using their native language. Such was the case until the middle of the sixth century at the very latest. A possible explanation could therefore be that *gardingus*—like its biblical Gothic counterpart *ingardja*—referred in the kingdom of Toulouse to any retainer and housemate. As a nontechnical term this word—unlike *buccellarius* and *saio*—was not taken into consideration when the *Codex Euricianus* regulated the various forms of retainership. Eventually the term was Latinized, whereby, however, the *-ing* suffix emphasizing the association with retainership was preserved. The Latin of the Spanish Visigoths preserved the term as amber preserves an insect. At the same time fossilization increased the prestige of the word, which now referred only to the royal retainer. After the *duces* and *comes,* the *gardingus* also belonged to the people of the palace; all we know of this development is that it was concluded before 680. The Gothic *gardingi* correspond roughly to the Roman *domestici.*[593]

THE END THAT WAS NO END

It is widely believed that the defeat at Vouillé marked the end of the kingdom of Toulouse. Even contemporaries noted the fatal consequences of the battle.[594] Like a house of cards Euric's grand structure collapsed. Then in 507 his incompetent successor Alaric gambled away the kingdom and his life. Without further resistance the Visigoths supposedly retreated before the victorious Franks and abandoned their old settlement areas along with their capital of Toulouse. Thanks to Theodoric the Great at least the Mediterranean coast remained Gothic, the greater part of the Visigothic royal treasure was saved, and the formation of a new kingdom became possible.[595] How very differently the Italian Ostrogoths defended themselves and conducted their twenty-year "war for Rome," until they were defeated by a superior imperial opponent, not by a barbarian chieftain such as the Frankish king Clovis.

The heroic mood that usually infects the historian of the Goths when, secure behind his desk, he compares the fields of Vouillé with the "Milk Mountain of Naples" may seem macabre or even comical, but it is in fact unfounded; this belated heroism rests on false premises. The end is never absolute. Even after the battle at Mons Lactarius there were Ostrogoths who could decide whether they wanted to return to their "proper land," οἰκεία χώρα, as subjects of the emperor or fight on, even without a king.[596] To an even greater degree the kingdom of Toulouse possessed enough strength—despite some signs of weakness[597]—not to disappear entirely from the stage. Almost a quarter of a century passed before the Franks were able to consolidate their victory of 507. The Balthic dynasty could have continued to reign during this period had not the Amal Theodoric prevented it from doing so. Just as Dietrich von Bern in the heroic saga did not fight Romans or Huns but Germanic peoples, his historical predecessor fought his bitterest wars against barbarian rivals. These struggles culminated in the elimination of the Balth Gesalec and ended with the repression of the "real" son, the Amal-Balthic Amalaric, who was not allowed to rule independently during the lifetime of his Amal grandfather, even though the youth had long since come of age.[598] Besides Spain, the Visigoths were able to keep, admittedly with Ostrogothic help, that "narrow strip of land,"[599] as it has often been described, consisting of the economically strong and urbanized Mediterranean coast west of the Rhone. Here were located Narbonne,[600] Agde, Nîmes, and Carcassonne. Here a Gothia flourished and held its own[601] and even in the seventh century acted as an independent Gallic *regnum* that dared to declare war on the entire Iberian peninsula.[602] Whoever looks at an historical map with large modern states in mind will tend to overrate the importance of large territories in the past. Barbarossa had to use all the power of his empire to conquer Milan, and still he could not force it to its knees; the Medici of Florence could have bought the England of the fourteenth century had they felt like it.

More serious than the destruction of the Gothic army, than the loss of both Aquitanian provinces and the capital of Toulouse, was the death of the king. Alaric, who was about forty years old when he died, had made no provision for the succession.[603] Two women had each borne him a son: one was an adult but "illegitimate"[604] and the other was the offspring of a legal marriage but still a child.[605] The younger son was Amalaric; his name reflects Alaric's recognition that the highest rank among Gothic royal houses was held by the Amal clan,[606] which Amalaric's grandfather ruled at Ravenna and guided throughout the barbarian world.[607] Theodoric did not merely want to save the Visigothic kingdom, he wanted to gain control over it for himself.[608] But for the time he was content with the Visigothic selection of the older royal son, Gesalec, as ruler; after all, Theodoric's own descent had not been much better.[609] Gesalec was unable to hold Narbonne against the Burgundians.[610] He apparently also decided not to defend Carcassonne, where the greater part of the Visigothic royal treasure was stored and where his half-brother was probably living.[611] Such inaction on the part of the king gave Theodoric a pretext for intervening. Moreover, Gesalec had made enemies of some high-ranking Visigothic dignitaries. Thus Goiaricus, who in 506 had drawn up most of the *Breviarium Alaricianum,* was killed on order from the king.[612] When in the late summer of 508 the Ostrogoths had driven back the Frankish-Burgundian besiegers from Arles and had freed Carcassonne from the Frankish threat,[613] Theodoric tried to impose his own peace in the Gallic south. In 509/510 Provence became the Gallic prefecture of the Ostrogothic kingdom, the Franks withdrew from the Mediterranean coast, and the Burgundians were left to themselves and came away completely empty-handed. Of course the Burgundians had to consider themselves fortunate to hold on to their existing territory in the face of Gothic superiority. The stabilization of the situation and the retreat of the "barbarians"[614] allowed the Ostrogoths to contest Gesalec's claim to the Visigothic kingship. In 510 Ostrogoths and Visigoths fought each other for the first time since 451. This time the Visigoths lost; Gesalec was defeated, fled, and became a serious threat. First he enlisted the support of the Vandals and went with King Thrasamund's money to Aquitaine, where he raised a Gothic army. This nearly brought on a major Ostrogothic-Vandal war, if the later report that Theodoric's troops ravaged Sicily—that is to say, Amalafrida's dowry of Lilybaeum—is correctly dated to 513/514. That Clovis allowed or had to allow Gesalec's actions indicates that the Franks had not yet fully conquered Aquitaine, still strongly populated by Goths. Only the death of Amalaric in 531 gave the signal for a widespread exodus of the Gothic upper class and their retainers from Aquitaine. One more time, in 511/512 or 513/514, Gesalec tried his luck against the Ostrogoths. He lost the battle in what is today Catalonia and then played his last card, the Burgundians. But on his way to Gundobad he was captured "on the other side of the Durance" and executed as a rebel.[615]

In 511 Theodoric the Great became king of the Visigothic kingdom; it was his third elevation to kingship.[616] The Amal had the realm governed by his sword-bearer and governor, Theudis. The territory that had been lost to the Franks remained lost; any attempt to reconquer it was abandoned when Theodoric, in 512/513 or 514/515, that is, after the death of Clovis, concluded a peace with the heirs of the Frankish king. Amalaric married a Merovingian princess. The south of Novempopulana, Rodez, probably Albi, and even Toulouse remained in Gothic hands until 531. After Theodoric's assumption of power Ostrogothic troops were sent west and the Visigothic treasure was brought to Ravenna.[617] In church and tax policies Theodoric soon learned that he was expected to follow Alaric II and Euric.[618] After 526 Amalaric reigned five more years independently,[619] then his Ostrogothic helper Theudis inherited the rule.[620] The end of the Amal-Balthic dynasty intensified the latent Visigothic anarchy. The *morbus Gothicus* was raging: the Goths were eliminating their kings at will, as if in a fit of madness.[621] But none of these disturbances could destroy the viability of the Visigothic state. It is true that the period of reconstruction was only finished two generations later. But after Leovigild had come to power in 568 or 569, the Visigothic kingdom rose like a phoenix from the ashes. Leovigild's reign saw the conclusion of a development that turned the Visigothic *regnum* into a Spanish *imperium*. In Spain emerged the most complete successor state to the Roman Empire, a perfect replica in its strengths and weaknesses.[622] How this happened, how the Goths became Catholic in 589, after they had just subjugated the Suevi, how they expelled the Byzantines from the south of the peninsula and became true Spaniards, and how they finally lost their independence—all this forms the history of early medieval Spain. The remarkably complete victory of the Arabs and the swift conquest of the Gothic kingdom in the years after 711 must not blind us to the persistence of the Gothic tradition north of the Ebro and its strength sufficient to initiate the Christian *reconquista* of the peninsula.[623] When the reconquest began, the Goths who had joined the Carolingians asserted themselves also in the barbarian confederation of the Frankish kingdom. Gothic refugees and colonists again went north across the Pyrenees; Septimania became the Frankish *Gotia*. This land, that is to say, its nobility, saw itself as a Gothic community of law; the people considered themselves Goths. They formed within the Carolingian Empire a minority that was by no means in an inferior position or discriminated against.[624] The Merovingian Franks, together with the Romans, Bretons, and Alamanni, had traced their descent from an ancestor different from the progenitor of the Goths, Burgundians, Gepids, and Lombards.[625] By Carolingian times this feeling of separateness had vanished. The Goths formed a "Frankish tribe." Their law was recognized by the king;[626] their language, which had long disappeared in the Latin West, was still part of the *lingua Theodisca,* one of the two languages of the Carolingian king. The Gothic contingent joined up with the royal military levies and Gothic magnates had successful careers.[627]

5

The "New" Ostrogoths

 Friends of the Ostrogoths may wonder why only one chapter is devoted to them.[1] But the history of this people lasted only five generations: according to strict historical criteria precisely from 451 to 552. The Ostrogothic century is marked off by two defeats and the names of two kings. Valamir commanded the tribal contingent in Attila's army which was defeated on the Catalaunian Fields;[2] Teja was killed at the Mons Lactarius, the "Milk Mountain," and with him the kingdom and the ethnic identity of the Ostrogoths came to an end.[3] It is true that Valamir did not create the Ostrogothic people on the march to Gaul. Rather, at that time we can first name and date the outcome of a development that had begun at least a generation earlier. And after Teja's death the Italian Ostrogoths did not disappear into thin air. They remained a community of law and a military-political factor that the emperor and after 568 the Lombards as well had to take into consideration.[4] But too much is lacking from both the prelude and the finale for these periods to be real history and the history of a real people. Prior to 451 we have no certain date where and when Ostrogoths were active; after 552 there is neither a kingship nor a "constitutionalized" *gens* and thus no institutional criteria that Ostrogoths were in fact active.

The history of the origins of the Ostrogoths is poorly recorded. Theodoric the Great—a conventional name he deserves not only for the sake of identification—had emerged victorious in a tough process of selection as the Gothic king who combined in himself the entire tribal tradition. Thus he monopolized Gothic policy, selectively determined the tribal tradition, and ensured that his Amal group became *the* Goths:[5] his father's younger brother and his cousin had to make way, as did the "squinting" Theodoric, the Scirian "Gothic king" Odovacar,[6] and the Balthic pretender Gesalec. Eventually only those Goths under Theodoric's dominion mattered. The reality he had created was followed by the theory of "his" *Origo Gothica*. This work was to spin the guiding thread through the labyrinth of the Gothic past, but it often becomes, for the Theseus who follows it, Ariadne and the Minotaur in one.

The Division and Reunification of the Amal Goths, 375–451

PANNONIAN GREUTUNGI, HUNNIC GOTHS, AND OSTROGOTHS

The creation of the "new" Ostrogoths was the achievement of those Amali who can be attested for the first time in Attila's kingdom—in 451 at the very latest—as kings of all Hunnic Goths.[7] The prestige of the former Greutungian-Ostrogothic royal clan had suffered so little, despite subjugation, division, open civil war, even some interregna that lasted several decades,[8] that at least one branch of the Amali was able to regain power over the non-Roman Goths within the Hunnic commonwealth and strengthen their rule in the wake of the consolidation of the Hunnic dominion.[9] Their base of support was the majority of the Greutungian Ostrogoths who had been subjugated in 375/376 and who were "bound to the Huns by oath and loyally devoted to them."[10] That such support did not exist outside the Hunnic realm explains why the Amali failed in an early attempt to become kings of the Roman Goths of Toulouse.[11] Those Amal Goths who had joined the Balthi contributed to the Visigothic ethnogenesis.[12] Yet the Tervingi who had remained north of the Danube or had returned there were absorbed into the emerging Ostrogoths. Among them were the descendants of most of the Athanaric Goths from the Caucaland, the Arimir Goths as well as their fellow tribesmen from the Danube region, whom the Greutungi of Odotheus had met in 386 while passing through, and finally the emigrants who had been among the retainers of Gainas in 400 and had survived their return to the area north of the Danube.[13] The chaos that followed in the wake of Gothic defeats in the years 375/376 also prevented a Hunnic consolidation of power.[14] As a result the next generation witnessed the frequent breaking away of Gothic groups and their crossing into Roman territory. In fact, the story of Princess Gaatha, Arimir's mother, shows that as late as 392 regular border traffic between Romania and transdanubian Gothia was possible.[15] Nor do we hear in 386 of a Hunnic threat to the Greutungian Odotheus Goths.[16] Only the attempt of the Tervingian Gainas to return to the transdanubian land after an unsuccessful Roman career and to create a dominion for himself there brought the Huns to the scene. The forceful intervention of their leader Uldin thwarted Gainas's venture, and Uldin was also involved in stopping the last attempt by Hunnic Goths to get away, though not until the horde led by Radagaisus had already reached Roman territory.[17] In any case, after 404/405 Gothic barbarian "floods" of this sort no longer crossed the Danube, even though internal Amal conflicts may have continued to cause unrest among the non-Roman Goths. Thus in 427 "something" must have happened,[18] and the battle at the Nedao as well as the assignment of Pannonia to the Valamir Goths in 456/457 led to new divisions among the Amali and their Goths.[19]

A historical survey of this sort is certainly useful, and because it is so general in nature it is unlikely to contain too many errors. But it is vastly more difficult to write a real history of the Hunnic Goths. Between the defeats of the year 375/376 and Attila's expedition in 451 we lack virtually any data on the time and place of events. In addition, there are two traditions that agree only in general outline. Contemporary reports stand in contrast to the family history in the *Origo Gothica* and related statements by Cassiodorus in the sixth century. Cassiodorus reports the "deeds of brave men"[20] and their names; factual contradictions appear and dates and places are also confused. Contemporary reports, however, were dependent on the meager trickle of information that reached the Roman Empire from the *barbaricum*.[21] But since Cassiodorus in writing the *Origo Gothica* consulted the main source of the older tradition, the work of Ammianus Marcellinus,[22] it is possible to compare the two traditions.

Ammianus Marcellinus relates the following story. After the death of Ermanaric in 375, Vithimiris was made king of the Greutungi and for some time resisted the Hunnic Alans, to which end he engaged "other Huns" as mercenaries. He survived many defeats but was eventually killed in battle. Thereupon his young son Videric,[23] who was still under age, became king, apparently without election; however, the experienced *duces* Alatheus and Safrax assumed the rule in his name. Under their leadership grew up a three-tribe confederation of Greutungi, Alans, and Huns. This cavalry confederation was able to escape Hunnic encirclement, crossed the Danube in 376, and in 378 decided the battle of Adrianople.[24] With this event the report of Ammianus Marcellinus ends and other sources continue the history of the Roman Greutungi. In 380 they were settled in Pannonia as federates of the emperor Gratian. The Tervingian analogy of 382 would indicate settlement along the Danube, that is, in Valeria and Pannonia II and probably including Savia. As federates the people of Alatheus and Safrax fulfilled their obligations dutifully. In 383 Huns and Alans were sent to Raetia to defend it against the Alamannic Iuthungi. A Sarmatian incursion in 385 ran head-on into the Pannonian federates and was driven back. Gothic household troops are found in the entourage of Valentinian II at Milan and they tried unsuccessfully to "Arianize" an orthodox church. Like the highly valued Alans of the emperor Gratian, these warriors probably also came from Pannonia. Then in 388 and 394 the federates marched in the army of the legitimate emperor Theodosius against the usurpers. Not until his death are they likely to have participated in the general uprising of the barbarians against the imperial government.

The newcomers had initially forced their way into the empire by fire and sword: Mursa, Stridon, and numerous other cities were devastated, and in the following year as well the peacefulness of the Pannonian federates left much to be desired. For a while contemporaries had the impression that the imperial government was abandoning the Pannonian provinces. But by 383 the land along the Danube could once again export grain. Many big landowners continued to live in their villas. And in 397 St. Jerome found a buyer for his paternal property in Stridon. In addition, Amantius, the bishop of the Valerian city Iovia-Heténypuszta, was active during the last two decades of the fourth century among the "double people of the two duces." This is a puzzling statement. To whom does the term "double people" refer and who are the two duces? In the year 395 the devastation had reached considerable dimensions. Vindobona was burned to the ground, the circulation of money nearly dried up, and the economy virtually came to a standstill. At the same time Suevic Marcomanni found in northern Pannonia a new homeland. But before the Vandals moved through this area upstream along the Danube in the spring of 401 and before the autumn of that year when Alaric occupied the south of Pannonia as a springboard for his invasion of Italy, Stilicho had managed to reestablish some order in this region. With the Vandals, however, came the native lower classes (hostes Pannonii) and the Alans. At that time at the very latest the Alans must have abandoned their coalition with their former allies in the three-tribe confederation. In that case the "double people" of Bishop Amantius could now only refer to Gothic-Hunnic groups. In 408 at any rate Athaulf commanded such units in "upper Pannonia," by which is probably meant Pannonia I and Savia. But Amantius was active among the "double people" before the Alans broke away. In Pannonia the bishop converted two *duces* who are identified as Alatheus and Safrax. But a King Videric is nowhere mentioned, just as there is no evidence of any kind that this Amal ever entered the Roman Empire. Nonetheless, an inscription on a tombstone is considered evidence that the Gothic-Alanic coalition led by these two *duces* existed also in Pannonia as the core of the three-tribe confederation.[25]

The story according to the *Origo Gothica* is as follows. After the death of Ermanaric and the separation from the Visigoths, the Ostrogoths remained in their homeland, that is, "in their old Scythian settlements," under Hunnic rule. The Amal Vinitharius, however, retained "the insignia of his princely rank" and tried to escape Hunnic subjugation. To that end he invaded the land of the Antes and after an initial setback had their king, royal sons, and seventy nobles crucified "as a warning example." After about a year the Hunnic king Balamber put an end to what was left of Ostrogothic independence. Balamber called in the Amal Gesimund, the son of Hunimund the Elder. Gesimund stood "with a large part of the Goths under the dominion of the Huns" and marched with the Huns against Vinitharius, "after having renewed the [Hunnic-Ostrogothic] alliance." A long conflict ensued, in the course of which Vinitharius was twice victorious and inflicted heavy losses on the Huns. But in the third battle, which took place on the river Erac, Vinitharius was killed when he was struck in the head by an arrow. The deadly archer was said to have been Balamber himself. The Hunnic king then married Va(l)damerca, the dead king's niece, and thus gained dominion over all the Goths, "who lived peacefully in a state of submission, but in such a way that they always stood under their own leader even if he was selected by the Huns." The first to rule was Ermanaric's son Hunimund, after him his son Thorismund. Then a forty-year interregnum ensued because Thorismund's son Berimud had followed the Visigoths to the west "because he despised the Ostrogoths for their subjection to the Huns." He had taken with him his son Videric, who later became the father of Eutharic. In their kingless period the Ostrogoths never forgot their Amal king, so they eventually transferred the rule to Vandalarius's son Valamir, a relative of Thorismund. Thus Valamir gained the kingship "in succession to his forefathers" at a time when the Goths and other peoples were still subject to the Huns. Valamir's younger brothers Thiudimir and Vidimir participated in his dominion but did not share in his kingship.[26]

It would be easy to confine our criticism of this account, largely derived from Cassiodorus, to its many contradictions. Anyone who writes a history of the Goths ought to lay his cards on the table. So far there has been no successful attempt to sketch the broad outlines of Ostrogothic history between 376 and 451, much less to write such a history based on the available sources. A string of observations must therefore replace a running narrative.

First, the heroic saga depicts Ermanaric as the king who exterminated his own descendants.[27] In agreement with this view is the succession of Ammianus's Vithimiris, who was definitely not the son of his predecessor.[28] In addition, it was possible to drop Ermanaric, the "noblest of the Amali,"[29] from the list of Amalasuintha's royal ancestor's without impairing her legitimate claim to the kingship of the army.[30] The descendants of Ermanaric, as well as the entire "younger" Amal line traced from him, are probably the genealogical invention of Cassiodorus rather than actual historical figures.[31] The claim that the Visigoths split off from the Ostrogoths after the death of Ermanaric is another invention, unless the statement really refers to the Goths of Alatheus and Safrax who actually broke away and made it to the Roman Empire.[32]

Second, it is beyond doubt that the Ostrogoths split up after the death of Ermanaric, whereupon the majority of them probably fought with the Huns against an Amal king until his death in battle. The son of this king survived. Ammianus Marcellinus calls the two Amal kings Vithimiris and Videric, whereas in the *Origo Gothica,* which was familiar with Ammianus Marcellinus, they carry the boastful names Vinitharius, "conqueror of the Venedi," and Vandalarius, "conqueror of the Vandals."[33] The names alliterate not only with each other but also from one source to the other. As is usual with bynames, they were created by posterity. The Vendish victory of Vinitharius was originally a fourth-century victory over the Antes, for at that time the Slavs did not exist. Not until the *Origo Gothica* was composed were Venedi, Antes, and Sclaveni causing havoc "everywhere in punishment for our sins."[34] The Antes of the fourth century, however, had neither come that far west nor had they been Slavicized—the Vinitharius story is the only passage in the *Origo Gothica* where they are mentioned by themselves[35]— but belonged no doubt to the Alanic-Ossetic group of peoples between the Don and the Caucasus.[36] But the Vithimiris of Ammianus Marcellinus also fought against the Alans. The Greutungian king defeated them with the help of Hunnic mercenaries.[37] And when Vithimiris's son Videric was taken to the west by the *dux* Alatheus, the Greutungian-Hunnic allies were in fact joined by the Alan splinter groups of Safrax.[38] The attack of Vinitharius against the Antes is reminiscent of the expulsion of the Sarmatians of the Caucaland by the Tervingi of Athanaric,[39] and it is entirely possible that it occurred in the steppes north of the Caucasus. In view of these events it no longer seems impossible to equate the river Erac, where the Amal king lost his life, with the river Phasis in Colchis.⁴⁰ And in fact there were Goths who survived the Hunnic invasions on the Taman, Kerch, and Crimean peninsulas, on the route to and from the Caucasus.⁴¹ Based on all these observations, the current scholarly opinion is to equate Vithimiris with Vinitharius and Videric with Vandalarius. As long as the problem is treated only with onomatological methods and the results merely confined to genealogical charts, we can be quite happy with the findings. But if we try to fit this equation into an historical account, insoluble difficulties arise. While it is still possible to imagine Vithimiris as the great-grandfather of Theodoric the Great, his son Videric causes the entire structure to collapse. All we know of Videric is that in the fall of 376 he was taken by his guardians Alatheus and Safrax to the left bank of the lower Danube. There is no report whatsoever that he crossed the river. Furthermore, it is certain that in the Roman Empire the three-tribe confederation was led only by *duces*. Videric probably met his death while still a child. But the idea that someone who died at about age ten could ever become a grandfather is just a bit unlikely.⁴²

Third, it is true that the "younger" Amal line descended from Ermanaric is missing; but this does not imply that Gesimund, the son of Hunimund the Elder, must be excluded as a historical figure. We must also consider the meaning of the Hunnic king Balamber and his Amal wife Vadamerca. First, the linguistic usage of the *Origo Gothica,* which only a few lines earlier had distinguished Alaric I (the Elder) as *Alaricus magnus* from Euric's son Alaric II, forces us to apply the same diacritical criteria to the two cases where Hunimund is mentioned. The *Origo Gothica* did not see Gesimund's father and the alleged son of Ermanaric as one and the same person but distinguished the first-named as the "elder" Hunimund from the "younger" Hunimund.⁴³ This assigns Gesimund to the first generation after Ermanaric and gives his name to the first Hunnic vassal prince of the Ostrogoths.⁴⁴ As such he fights against the great-grandfather of Theodoric the Great, whereby the king of the free Ostrogoths is killed.⁴⁵ The events described took place in 376. In contrast, the Amal family tradition celebrates the exemplary deed of Gesimund, who "after being made a son only through arms linked himself to the Amali in great devotion." Even though Gesimund was pushed into the kingship, he did preserve it for the legitimate heirs who were still small children.⁴⁶ This group of heirs is believed to be the brothers Valamir, Thiudimir, and Vidimir. In that case Gesimund must have been active at least half a century after 376, around 430 or 440.⁴⁷ Two deductions can be made: either there were two Gesimunds, Hunimund's son who supported the Huns with the majority of the Ostrogoths in putting down the last Amal resistance, and the Amal "son in arms" who helped to bridge the Ostrogothic interregnum, or the Gesimunds are one and the same person, in which case only the "loyal Hildebrand"[48] of the generation of Theodoric the Great's father can be historical. The latter possibility would mean that Balamber and Va(l)damerca should be moved from 376 to the time of Valamir. In that case we would have to assume that the Hunnic Ostrogothic king Valamir and the legendary Hunnic king Balamber had "something to do with each other," even if that "something" may have been hardly more than an assimilation of their names in popular etymology. And in fact the names Balamber (read: Valamver), Va(l)damerca, and Valamir alliterate the way Amal names do. It is almost certain, however, that behind Balamber stands the Iranian name Balimber, which is already attested in the second century A.D. along the lower Danube.[49] Balamber and Valamir must therefore have been two different persons who belonged to two different centuries.

Fourth, we must identify the geographical setting of the history of the Amal Goths during the "forty-year interregnum," or more precisely, during the two generations after 376. According to the *Origo Gothica* the greater part of the Ostrogothic tribe remained in Scythia after the subjection by the Huns. This emphatic statement is no doubt historical fact.[50] As long as Greutungi, like the Odotheus group of 386, still appeared along the lower Danube, they came from southern Russia. But the breaking away of Radagaisus in 404/405 could indicate that the Ostrogoths had migrated westward; they were probably even forced to do so, for it appears that Radagaisus was trying to avoid the Huns rather than to break out of Scythia.[51] At any rate, three observations reveal that the Ostrogoths of Attila's time lived close to their master. All of Scythia was now the barbarian land under Hunnic rule. Thus the ancient "Scythia" had shifted westward and now referred to "Dacia and Pannonia, where the Huns were living with various other tribes they had subjugated."[52] Moreover, in Attila's multilingual camp Gothic held the rank of one lingua franca, "since the Scythians, a colorful mix of peoples, speak in addition to their native dialect either Hunnic, Gothic, or even Latin." This is confirmed by the fact that King Valamir as well as the Gepid king Ardaric were among Attila's magnates.[53] Their status of relative independence could be counterbalanced only by a certain proximity to the center of Hunnic power. By contrast, the Akatzires, who lived in southern Russia, were either ruled by Attila's oldest son or stood under the leadership of their own princes, who were careful, however, not to come too close to the Hunnic king. The marvelous treasures the soil of Romania has so far given up could have belonged to Hunnic Goths both west and south of the Carpathians. In Transylvania the Ostrogoths may have been the eastern neighbors of the Tisza Gepids, forming with them a line of defense for the nucleus of Hunnic dominion.[54]

Fifth, the identification of Videric with Vandalarius would mean that the grandfather of Theodoric the Great left the main tribe as early as 376 and, assuming he survived the crossing of the Danube, which is unlikely, was living from 380 among the Pannonian federates.[55] This of course would have been the place where until 401 an Ostrogoth could have won for himself the boastful name of "conqueror of the Vandals." But Pannonia is also the area where a victory over the Suevi by Hunimund, the alleged son of Ermanaric, would have taken place as well as the death of Thorismund in a battle against the Gepids. Both events are attributed to the Amali, who are explicitly listed in Amalasuintha's genealogy as the ancestors of Theodoric the Great and are there honored with epithets corresponding to equivalent bynames in the *Origo Gothica*. As much as we can sympathize with Ludwig Schmidt's indignation about the Amal genealogies, the Hunimund-Thorismund traditions cannot be pure fabrications. After all, with Thorismund's death began the forty-year interregnum that, regardless of whether we take it literally or not, had concrete historical significance.[56]

The actual history of events, in fact, leaves no room for the names and deeds of the Amal family tradition. Soon after the withdrawal of the Vandals in 401 the Balthic Goths arrived in Pannonia, where Athaulf in particular expanded his authority. He was even believed to have killed an unknown Gothic king there. Apart from the absence of even a single source attesting Pannonia as the scene of the crime, the victim could not have been Videric-Vandalarius. For there is no testimony of any kind that the royal child Videric came into the Roman Empire alive. The last report tells us of his arrival at the lower Danube where his Greutungi pleaded unsuccessfully for admission into the empire. Thereafter we hear only of Alatheus and Safrax. Moreover, Amantius, bishop of the Valerian city of Iovia from 380 to 400, was active only among the "double people of the two *duces*," a title that is also used on all other occasions to describe the two chieftains. Indeed, the *Origo Gothica* even goes so far as to mention Alatheus and Safrax—next to Fritigern—as explicit examples of tribal leaders ruling in place of kings; the first Gothic occupation of Pannonia took place under their leadership alone.[57]

Shortly after Athaulf had left Pannonia with his Goths and Huns, Ravenna established along the Danube a military district that comprised the Pannonian provinces, Noricum, Raetia, and a little later also Dalmatia. A general by the Germanic name of Generidus was placed in charge of this district in the winter of 408/409, but despite some initial successes his command was not blessed with a long life.[58] The Gothic domination in the plains of Pannonia was followed by the settlement of Huns, the allies of the generalissimo Aëtius.[59] Subsequently, in 427 to be exact, the Romans are said to have succeeded in regaining the Pannonian provinces after a nearly fifty-year occupation by the Huns.[60] In this way the first advance of the Ostrogothic-Alanic-Hunnic confederation, which probably in 378/380 reached modern Burgenland and the border of Styria,[61] is depicted as the Hunnic occupation of Pannonia. This occupation then came to an end in 427 when the Romans drove some groups of Greater Huns back across the Danube.[62] The details of this story are part of the history of the Roman Empire and could remain such were it not for the mention by later sources, among them the *Origo Gothica,* of Goths on the scene. For precisely in the year 427 the legitimate Amal heir is said to have left his homeland together with his son "out of contempt for the Goths' subjection to the Huns." The goal of the expedition was Visigothic Toulouse, where the Amal hoped, if in vain, to succeed Valia, who had died in 418.[63] At any rate, in 439 we find attested among the Visigoths a certain Vetericus-Videric,[64] that is to say, a namesake both of that Greutungian king who in 376 had appeared at the lower Danube[65] and of that son of Berimud who had gone to the Toulousan kingdom in 427. If there is good reason to identify the Videric of 427 with the Videric of the year 439 and thus to make the latter the father of Eutharic, we had better exclude the Greutungian royal child from all this. Otherwise this peculiar Videric would have stayed hidden in the dark for about half a century only to found a sizable family as a vigorous sexagenarian and would also have had two fathers, Vithimiris and Berimud. Still, Videric the son of Berimud did in fact come to Gaul in 427, where apparently not only his father presented himself as a rival to the Balthic kingship. The Toulousan Goths remembered for a long time that Ostrogoths had come to them seeking refuge from the Huns.[66] The same Videric assumed a pro-Roman attitude during the hostilities of 439, for which he undoubtedly got into trouble with Theoderid after the conclusion of the peace, but we hear nothing more of him.[67] Around this time Attila achieved the breakthrough that made the Huns into a great power, with all the corresponding attraction this had for the magnates and exiles of the Romano-barbarian world.[68] For that very reason the Ostrogothic participation in Attila's attack on Gaul seems like an Amal-Balthic quarrel, no matter how embarrassing the civil war may have been to the *Origo Gothica.*[69] Perhaps Valamir was the driving force behind the Hunnic war against the Visigoths. To be sure, the Amal efforts as early as 430/440 probably caused a constitutional crisis among the Hunnic Goths which generations later was still linked to the name of Gesimund.[70] The saga praised his deed as an unselfish yielding to the claims of the legitimate Amali. The adoption of Gesimund had analogies in the subsequent generations of the Amal kings.[71]

The narrative regains solid historical ground only with the generation of Theodoric the Great's father. Between the invasion of the Huns in 375 and the trek to Gaul in 451, two events certainly took place. First, a new people appeared who had in common with the Greutungian Ostrogoths nothing more than the name "Goth" based upon an old tradition.[72] Second, the Amal group with the highest prestige was able to prevail against numerous rivals. The Ostrogoths had developed a highly ambivalent relationship to their Hunnic masters during their long subjection.[73] Attila as well as his brother Bleda and many other magnates (λογάδες) of the Hunnic empire had Gothic names, and many Goths carried Hunnic names.[74] The Goths had become familiar with the practice of artificially deforming the skull; with Hunnic tools; with costume accessories; and also with the old custom as practiced in "Greater Scythia" of princes' hugging and kissing each other in front of the people.[75] They had adopted the Hunnic attitude that emigration and separation from the main tribe were serious crimes. Whoever ran away from the Huns showed his contempt for the Goths and lost his Amal identity, which was even more highly regarded than Attila's nobility. But at the same time the Gothic peoples ardently longed to regain their freedom. Negotiations between Romans and Huns dealt mostly with Attila's demands for payments and the handing over of deserters and escaped Romans and barbarians.[76] The Goths were bound to the Huns by oath and were loyally devoted to them, but at the same time they had sworn sacred oaths among themselves never again to have any dealings with them once they were free. The Goths acted accordingly, as happened on one occasion.[77] The story of the Haliurun(n)ae combines a sense of "kinship" to the Huns with a feeling of profound disgust. These sorceresses, the Haliurun(n)ae, were said to have been expelled from the tribe by the Gutonic migration king Filimer, whereupon they had intercourse with the evil spirits of the steppe and gave birth to the race of the Huns. The legend combines three different chronological layers: one from around 200, another from the end of the fourth century which tried to explain the demonic nature of the new enemy,[78] and the last one from the period of subjection to the Huns during which the legend portrayed the Goths as "somehow" related to the Huns.[79] It remains unclear whether Hunnic political institutions influenced the development of the joint rule of Valamir and his brothers. His kingship looks a little bit like that of the Burgundians, who were ruled by a high king with a number of petty kings below him. It is true that among the Huns Octar and Ruga, like Attila and Bleda, ruled jointly, if over different territories and tribes; but other brothers, as, for example, Attila's own father Mundzuc or his third uncle Oebarsius, had no share in the Hunnic kingship.[80]

The Ostrogothic Kingdom in Pannonia, 456/457–473

In 451 Attila marched to Gaul. Many tribal groups followed him, among them the Tisza Gepids who were commanded by King Ardaric and the Ostrogoths under the leadership of the royal brothers Valamir, Thiudimir, and Vidimir.[81] The Amal Andagis also made a name for himself: in his family, which had kinship ties to the Alans, the story was still told one hundred years later that he had hurled the spear that killed the Visigothic king Theoderid.[82] Nevertheless, the Amal Goths suffered a serious defeat at the hands of their Balthic cousins. Two years later Attila died. His unexpected death once again put the Amal Goths to the test, which they survived, but not without undergoing changes and suffering a decline in numbers. The Gepid Ardaric placed himself at the head of a tribal coalition fighting for its independence. The decision whether to stay loyal to the Huns split the tribal groups when it came to a battle at the river Nedao, which should probably be dated to 454 rather than 455. According to Jordanes the scene of the conflict lay in Pannonia. There is some evidence for a site on the Sava river in Savia. Yet one would rather expect the Huns to have attacked the rebels, whose center of strength lay along the Tisza. But since our reports speak explicitly of several battles, culminating in the engagement at Nedao, it would be possible to combine general considerations with traditional accounts: the battle fought at the Nedao, a tributary of the Sava, sealed the fate of Attila's sons and their retinues, who had already been forced on the defensive. Thus the Huns and their allies were defeated. The victors, especially the Gepids, took possession of the heartland of Attila's former realm.[83] In this way they not only extended their settlement areas southward but also gained in the east large parts of Trajan's Dacia. The Gepidia had replaced the Gothia.[84] Westward the other victorious tribes and subtribes established or enlarged their territories. Thus there arose (1) the Rugian kingdom in lower Austria north of the Danube; (2) a Herulian kingdom to its northeast in southern Moravia and on both sides of the March with extensions as far as the Danube and the Carpati minores; (3) until 470 a Pannonian *regnum* of those Suevi who had not left their homeland along with the Vandals and Alans. As for the Sciri, earlier efforts to locate them north of the bend of the Danube have recently been abandoned in favor of a location in the central sector of the plain of the Tisza (Alföld). The noble grave of Bákodpuszta is "probably linked to the Scirian princely family." As neighbors to the Sciri we find Sarmatians on either side of the Danube. Both they and the Sciri held their own in the forefield of the mighty Gepids. But just as the Rugians settled north of the Danube while they lived off the provincials south of the river, most of the other Danubian barbarians stayed outside the empire but encroached on Roman territory. Until about 470 only Suevi and Sarmatians were also settled on the right bank of the Danube, which was probably also where the centers of their power were located.[85]

There is hardly any doubt that at Nedao the Ostrogoths fought on the losing side. They did not like to remember it and did everything to make themselves and posterity forget this embarrassment, although the heroic saga *Lied von Frau Helchens Söhne* (Song of the Sons of Lady Helchen) faithfully preserved the Goths' role at Nedao.[86] At least until the battle of Nedao Valamir and his people had remained loyal to the Huns;[87] other Goths had still not had enough of their alliance with the Huns as much as fifteen years later.[88] The end of the realm of the Greater Huns had once more opened wide Pandora's box.[89] The vanquished sought refuge in the Roman Empire. The Huns, their unity now dissolved as each tribe placed itself under the leadership of one of Attila's sons, either returned to the Sarmatian steppes or placed their hopes in the *imperium*. A similar split occurred within the peoples that had once been subject to them. Thus a part of the Rugian tribe came to Thrace with the Roman Huns, and Valamir was not able to assert his kingship over all the Hunnic Goths. But his group remained strong enough to be of interest to the imperial government. The request for admission into the empire was granted with the understanding that the Valamir Goths were to form a *cordon sanitaire* along the Sava for the protection of Dalmatia and upper Moesia. It is also possible that the group of an otherwise unknown chief Tuldila was living in the central Danubian region. Regardless of whether this horde consisted mostly of Goths or Huns, it had already "lost its lord through war" when the emperor Majorian attacked and destroyed it in 458. The Andagis-Andela Amali, however, were settled in the Dobrudja and in northern Bulgaria with Alans, Sciri, and the Sarmatian Sadagares.[90] Not far from them was probably the stronghold of the Gothic king Bigelis, who was killed by Ardabur.[91] The latter was the son of the *patricius* and imperial general Aspar, who under Marcian and Leo I had for a time been all-powerful, who had boasted of

Alanic-Gothic descent, and who had drawn his might largely from Gothic troops. The Goths who had withdrawn their loyalty from Valamir at the very latest after the battle of Nedao and had become soldiers of Constantinople were initially led by an Amal with the Latin name Triarius. He was certainly related to the Valamir clan and married his sister to Aspar, which reflected his eminent position within the Eastern military hierarchy. Thus when he died, which was probably in the second half of the 450s, his son Theodoric Strabo could succeed him without danger.[92] But there was also another important relative of the Pannonian Amal who was in Roman services and who in 478/479 lived on his estates near Durazzo. His name was Sidimund and he could have arrived in 459 when Valamir was plundering Epirus. Sidimund, at any rate, did not belong to the Ostrogoths of Theodoric son of Thiudimir when, "mindful of the former kinship," he supported him in his conquest of the Adriatic province. A blood relative of Sidimund was the *comes domesticorum* Aidoingus, who must therefore also be considered an Amal. One man who remained an enemy of "Valamir's people" was the Goth Gento, who was married to a Roman and who in 479 fought in Epirus against fellow barbarian tribesmen, as Fravitta had once done in Thrace.[93]

Both the victors and the vanquished of Nedao became Roman federates. In the 430s Ravenna had withdrawn from Pannonia, in part in fulfillment of treaties, in part forced to do so. As a result, after the mid-fifth century the influence of Constantinople prevailed there among the many different types of federates. In the fall of 455 the Western "Gothic emperor" Avitus did try to take action in the disputed territories, but the emperor who had allowed Valamir to settle in Pannonia and who had concluded a *foedus* with him was the Eastern Roman Marcian, who had never recognized Avitus. It thus follows that the Ostrogothic settlement in Pannonia took place at the very latest prior to January 457, which is when Marcian died.[94] We must distinguish between a sphere of Gothic influence and the actual settlement area. The Goths were explicitly allocated the Pannonian provinces between Sirmium and Vindomina-Vindobona. But it appears that they felt responsible for patrolling the border stretching from the Moesian-Serbian valley of Margus-Morava up into Noricum ripense east of the river Enns.[95] Of course this settlement area along the border between the two halves of the empire offered not only opportunities but was also fraught with many dangers. Wedged between the barbarian enemies of Nedao and the *imperium,* Valamir and his brothers were caught in a precarious situation that they were not able to handle in the long run. Ricimer, the master of the Western Roman empire, tried to drive the Goths out of Noricum, while Constantinople made a pact with the federates outside the empire against Valamir's men.[96]

Corresponding to the division among the three Amal brothers, the Ostrogoths settled in three districts. Valamir was considered king and was the overlord of them all. The actual Gothic settlement area probably extended—in the shape of a crescent—from the southwestern tip of Lake Balaton to the river Drava, from there downstream to the mouth of the Karasica-Aqua Nigra west of Mursa-Osijek, and reaching finally Sirmium-Sremska Mitrovica west of the Scarniunga-Jarcina river. The westernmost of the three subkingdoms was ruled by Thiudimir; the weakest section was that of the youngest brother and was located in the center. Valamir as the strongest of the brothers took over the most endangered part in the east. In modern terms Thiudimir would have had the central and southern part of the county of Somogy as well as northeastern Croatia, while Vidimir would have had upper and Valamir lower Slavonia. In those days one would have spoken of parts of the provinces of Pannonia I, Savia, and Pannonia II (Sirmiensis).[97] Valamir and his brothers probably commanded nearly eighteen thousand warriors.[98]

The "united" Ostrogothic kingdom in Pannonia lasted only from 456/457 to 473.[99] Although there were still peasants among these Goths,[100] the Valamirian federates were not able to strike roots in their allotted settlement area. There was no curial system of taxation,[101] which could have provided the economic basis for a lasting *regnum*. The result was that the Ostrogoths engaged in destructive exploitation of the Pannonian economy and became increasingly dependent on Constantinople's willingness and ability to meet its payments.[102] Constant threats from outside accentuated the internal weaknesses of the state Valamir had created.

The Ostrogoths had barely concluded their treaty with the emperor when Hunnic horsemen once again appeared in the east. In 456 they attacked Valamir so unexpectedly that he had to fight without the help of his brothers. Nonetheless, he was able to defeat the Huns, "who were in pursuit of the Gothic deserters as if they were fugitive slaves."[103] The defeated attackers were said to have retreated all the way to the Dnieper. This could be true, for at that very time the Crimean Goths had to fight off a flood of returning Huns.[104] We are told that the message of Valamir's victory reached Thiudimir on the day Ereleuva-Erelieva gave birth to his son. Later she went with her son to Italy, where she was regarded as a queen. By then, at the very latest, she had been baptized a Catholic with the name Eusebia. As for her relationship to Thiudimir, our sources call her his *concubina*. It is difficult to say how we are to understand this statement. All that is certain is that the marriage between Theodoric's parents was not fully valid. Perhaps there was a religious difference between them—like most Ostrogoths of his time Thiudimir was an Arian—or perhaps they were of different ethnic background, which would have amounted to much the same. Although one source calls Theodoric's mother a Goth, it is possible that Ereleuva did not even have a Germanic name.[105] Theodoric, like the Vandal king Gaiseric, may even have had a mother of Roman origin.[106]

The date of Theodoric's birth is also problematic. If he was really born in 456, he could not have gone to Constantinople three years later as an eight-year-old hostage. Simple arithmetic and the use of a three-year-old as a hostage argue against it. But if we have Theodoric move to Constantinople after 459, his life falls into total disarray. Thus in 471 Theodoric would have had to succeed his deceased uncle Valamir and conquer Singidunum-Belgrade as a fifteen-year-old boy. The chronological problems can be avoided if Theodoric was five years older and was already born in 451.[107] In that case the news of the defeat of the Huns which arrived at his birth could have referred to the Catalaunian Fields. At that time the Ostrogoths were among the losers, so there was reason enough for the *Origo Gothica* to move the year of Theodoric's birth in order to preserve the point of the anecdote.

Leo I, who became emperor of the East in 457, tried to revise the *foedus* with the Pannonian Goths. The "usual yearly payments" (*consueta dona*) were stopped. After two years Valamir inquired of Constantinople what it thought loyal adherence to a treaty meant. Yet his embassy returned home with nothing but the report of how well Theodoric Strabo and his people were doing at the imperial court. Valamir thereupon opened hostilities; for the first time the Ostrogoths penetrated as far as Epirus, moving south and upstream through the valley of the Morava. Even the capital city Durazzo fell into Gothic hands. The Goths had thus achieved the purpose of the federate revolt, which reminds us a little of the early Visigothic "summer excursions" to Arles and Narbonne. The imperial government now specified the "usual payments" at three hundred pounds of gold a year, and the Goths returned to Pannonia.[108] At the same time little Theodoric went to Constantinople as a hostage. He would remain there from 459 to about 469, that is to say, he spent his childhood and his youth up to his eighteenth year in the imperial city. One needs only the most elementary knowledge of pedagogy to understand how important the years in Constantinople were in the development of the young Amal.

During this decade Theodoric caught up on all the Romanitas it had taken the Visigothic Balthi generations to acquire. Perhaps many of the instances of extreme and erratic behavior by Theodoric could be explained by the tensions to which he had been exposed as a barbarian child and a young man.[109] Theodoric is said to have enjoyed the emperor's favor. This piece of information from the *Origo Gothica* could be true, but it also agrees with the general bias of the source.[110] At any rate, the treaty of 459/460, which was guaranteed by the little prince, held for a remarkably long time. For a decade there was peace between Romans and Goths, or at least such a state of affairs as was considered peace. Gothic raids into the fringe areas between the *imperium* and the *barbaricum* were apparently not seen as a violation of the treaty.[111] Gothic predatory detachments perhaps appeared east of Noricum ripense as early as the middle of 456.[112] *Ostrogothus* next appears in the wondrous catalog of peoples describing the Western Roman army of 458. The description of the forces, which an unknown general supplied for his emperor Majorian, mirrors half a millennium of ancient ethnography, and we will therefore not take the report too literally. But the participation of Germanic contingents from Noricum and Pannonia—such as the Ostrogoths, Rugians, Suevi, and others—can be accepted.[113]

The Pannonian history of the Ostrogoths deals with princes and wars; more than any other history it recounts the memory of the "deeds of brave men."[114] Valamir and his people did not exactly become rich through the annual payments from Constantinople, but even the Huns had once started out on a modest scale.[115] On April 12, 467, Anthemius was proclaimed emperor of the West. That he was Greek rendered his situation even more difficult, for Greeks were not well regarded in the West.[116] As early as 459 Anthemius had already fought the Valamir Goths. He was an excellent general and personal experience had convinced him that the Goths were the number-one enemy of the empire and had to be eliminated in the West and the East. Shortly before his election, Anthemius, as Leo I's general, had successfully repulsed an attack near Serdica-Sofia by Attila's son Hormidac.[117] This diverted the Hunnic counteroffensive to a new direction of advance. Already at the outset of the new emperor's rule "his" *magister militum* Ricimer, a half-Goth and a royal Balth on his mother's side, succeeded in defending Noricum against the Amal Goths from Pannonia. This is the earliest date that Gothic raiders could have penetrated as far as the capital of Noricum mediterraneum, Teurnia-Tiburnia, and seriously threatened the city. Unable to capture the city, the Goths after long negotiations with the inhabitants, concluded a *foedus* and were sent off with a nonmonetary tribute of clothes. On January 1, 468, the Ostrogothic setbacks and the successful defense of Noricum were celebrated as recent events.

While Valamir was busy in 467/468 subjugating the Sadagares who had remained behind in the interior of Pannonia, a different son of Attila's, Dengizich by name, tried to capture the city of Bassianae between Belgrade and Sremska Mitrovica. Valamir turned back and defeated the Huns, who then "for ever after" left the Goths in peace.[118] While the latter were occupied in the east, Suevi from northern Pannonia moved through Gothic Savia into Dalmatia. They were able to march calmly through Thiudimir's territory, drive away the Gothic flocks, and set out for home loaded down with booty. But on the way they were caught by Thiudimir near Lake Balaton and all of them, including their leader Hunimund, were captured. In order to regain their freedom, the Suevic king agreed to become the "son in arms" of Thiudimir. But the Suevic king, now an "Amal-by-way-of-capture," was so little impressed by this unwelcome honor, which was to seal his dependence on the Goths, that he immediately began to conspire against them. His goal was above all to divide and weaken the Gothic forces.[119] Still in 468 or in early 469 the Tisza Sciri made a surprise attack on Valamir, who again had to fend for himself. The battle ended with the death of the Ostrogothic king but a victory for his people. Thiudimir succeeded his brother as king of all Pannonian Goths and also placed the districts of the dead king under his direct control until the return of Theodoric from Constantinople.[120]

In 469, Anthemius was planning that the Loire Alans, the Burgundians, and Paulus with his Franks should attack Euric's Visigoths—the former "Alaric Goths"—while Spanish Suevi and Romans would begin an offensive against them on the Iberian peninsula.[121] A comparable Roman-barbarian coalition directed against the Ostrogoths emerged in the Danubian region. The Suevic king Hunimund united his troops with the warriors of the second Herulian Alaric or rather with those of a Suevic prince called Alaric, with the Sciri under Odovacar's father Edica and his older brother Hunulf, and with their neighbors the Sarmatians of the kings Beuca and Babai; he then marched against Gothic Pannonia supported by Gepidic and Rugian divisions. At the same time the Eastern emperor Leo sent a regular Roman army to attack the rear of the Goths, who were being engaged by these tribes. Leo thus deliberately opposed his general Aspar, who had rejected any war of annihilation against the Goths as harmful to his own interests. A battle was fought at a river called Bolia. Once again it is difficult to locate the site. If we identify Bolia with the Slovakian-Hungarian border river Ipel-Ipoly, then we must correct the *Origo Gothica,* which assumed that the river was on the right side of the Danube in Pannonia. A possible solution would be to locate the battle site across from the confluence of the Ipel and the Danube, even though this would raise the question why the Danube itself was not mentioned.[122] When it comes to naming rivers, however, it is characteristic of the *Origo Gothica* when identifying Pannonian places to mention small rivers instead of larger ones.[123] The battle seems like a repeat of Nedao, but this time the Ostrogoths were victorious. On hearing of the outcome the approaching imperial army turned back. Leo I gave in and sent young Theodoric home with rich presents, without saying a word about a return service on the part of the Ostrogoths. Was the emperor already planning to elevate the Pannonian Goths as a counterweight to Aspar and Theodoric Strabo?[124]

The year 469 brought great successes for both Gothic tribes. Euric opened his Gallo-Spanish war in order to preempt the hostile coalition of Loire Alans, Burgundians, Franks, Suevi, and Roman provincials from Spain. The Amal Goths were equally successful in Pannonia. Unlike Euric, however, they did not win a great kingdom but instead created for themselves new tensions and new tribal unrest. They were running the risk of being too successful. It must have been exactly in 469 that a Hunnic-Gothic incursion into Thrace took place. Following a tested strategy, the Roman defenders shut up the invaders in the highland and cut them off from all supplies. Plagued by hunger the "Scythians" offered to surrender on the condition that they would be settled on Roman territory. But negotiations about such terms went beyond the authority of the Roman commander, so the emperor's decision was requested. In the meantime, however, the barbarians were to be supplied with food. To that end the Hunnic-Gothic division was to be subdivided into smaller, preferably homogeneous units, each unit to be overseen by a Roman detachment. The entire operation was supervised by Aspar's second-in-command, a high-ranking Hunnic officer in Roman service. He called in the chiefs of a predominantly Gothic unit and stirred them up against their allies. He gave weight to his polemic by mentioning his own Hunnic background and by reminding the Goths of how the Huns had always acted "like wolves," never cultivating fields but living off Gothic harvests. A joint settlement would therefore benefit only the Huns—for that very reason the Goths' ancestors had forsworn dealings with the Huns. If the Goths now insisted on their demands, they would be disregarding both their own interests and their fathers' oaths. The Gothic chieftains and their retainers were easily persuaded first to kill the Huns in their own units and then to fall upon the others. The survivors among Goths and Huns were then cut down by the imperial troops; only a few "Scythians" managed to escape.[125]

This story, which would have delighted Tacitus, should be in every "how to defeat the barbarians" handbook. We learn from it above all what the term "Hunnic Goths" meant, namely, a state of dependence that applies in a similar way to relations between Slavs and Avars.[126] But we also see that there were still Goths who cultivated the soil and were quite able to feed their Hunnic lords and themselves as farmers. Furthermore, they were bound on oath to avoid any association with the Huns. Such an oath was most likely sworn by the Pannonian Ostrogoths in the period between the battle of Nedao and the victory of Bassianae. But why, then, would Pannonian Goths have joined the Huns in the first place? The same chieftain Dengizich who in 467 or 468 had attacked Valamir was killed two years later on the lower Danube in a battle against the Romans. In the summer of 468 the imperial government issued new decrees against the use of "*buccellarii,* Isaurians, and armed slaves." This would mean that there had been a considerable rise in the number of barbarians—and among them especially Goths and Huns—who sought their fortune in the Roman Empire. The violent death of Dengizich and the story of the Scythian plunderers who were annihilated would thus fit together well.[127]

The signs of disintegration among the Gothic victors were insignificant compared to what happened in the camp of the defeated. First, the sons of the dead Scirian king Edica marched off; Hunulf, the older of the two, entered the services of the Eastern empire and the younger, Odovacar, became a soldier in Italy. So many Heruli and Rugians, but also Turcilingi, followed Odovacar that he was later considered their king.[128] In the winter of 469/470 Thiudimir went to war against his Suevic neighbors, who formed the core of the anti-Gothic coalition. Hunumund had had enough: he and his followers moved off upstream along the Danube to the west. The Suevic king Hunimund is probably identical with the chieftain Hunimund who attacked the city of Passau. If so, the by no means numerous Suevic refugees had joined the related Alamanni, and in so doing Hunumund had lost the kingship.[129] The majority of his people, however, remained behind in the two western Pannonias where they formed an ethnic substratum for foreign rulers up to the days of the Lombards Vacho and Alboin. Other Germanic groups from the Danube entered the army of Anthemius in 470 and suffered a crushing defeat at the hands of the Gallic Goths in 471.[130] Of those who had remained behind, the March Heruli best survived having the Goths as neighbors. If we may draw inferences from the time of Theodoric the Great, the Heruli could have entered into the Suevic heritage in northern Hungary at this time.[131] Those Suevi who had stayed in western and southern Pannonia fell under the dominion of the Goths, which caused the Rugians a good deal of anxiety. Their king Flaccitheus became frightened because the

Goths now controlled all lines of communication with Italy.[132] It must have been around 470 that Feletheus-Feva, the son of the Rugian king, married the Amal princess Giso. As the successor to his father he pursued an Ostrogothic course, but this led to a split within the Rugians and eventually brought them into a fatal confrontation with Odovacar, their former ally.[133]

On his return from Byzantium in 469/470 Theodoric son of Thiudimir took over the portion of the kingdom which his uncle Valamir had ruled, while his father succeeded Valamir in the kingship.[134] In Singidunum-Belgrade in upper Moesia, Babai, king of the Tisza Sarmatians, had extended his authority at the expense of Constantinople. The problems the Goths had faced during the previous years had certainly made it easier for him to do this. Now Theodoric crossed the Danube with the six thousand warriors from his third of the tribe, attacked the main Sarmatian force, and defeated and killed Babai, whereupon Singidunum surrendered. Through this successful campaign the young Amal legitimized himself as a lord in his own right, though without actually becoming king. Theodoric, to be sure, looked upon this as the beginning of his kingship. The war begun in 470/471 in the emperor's name ended with the last territorial expansion of the Goths. Theodoric kept Singidunum for himself.[135] Two years later the Pannonian Ostrogoths marched off. Had Theodoric intended to improve the starting point for his departure? Meanwhile Theodoric "the Squinter" had established himself so firmly in the Thracian threshold of Constantinople that in 473 he was "raised up to be king over all the Goths."[136] The incident in 469 when Ostrogoths had joined the Huns in order to get to Thrace had to be a cause for concern.[137] The departure from Pannonia was loudly demanded by the Goths, and the Amali kings seem like men forced to act the way they did.[138]

The abandoning of Pannonia can be aptly compared to Alaric's departure from Moesia. In both cases imperial federates left the Danubian border, the protection of which had been entrusted to them, and penetrated more deeply into Roman territory in order to integrate themselves more firmly and more profitably into the *imperium*. But whereas Alaric had done everything he could to concentrate the forces of his tribe,[139] the Pannonian Goths split up before their departure. This appears all the more puzzling because the split came at the initiative of that Amal clan whose unity the *Origo Gothica* always praised as its highest virtue. As if following the example of the Scirian royal sons Hunulf and Odovacar, the older brother Thiudimir turned to Constantinople and the younger Vidimir along with his son Vidimir went west. The Amal Goths split up because the success of the young Theodoric threatened no one more than his uncle and his cousin.[140]

The Vidimir group left Pannonia and invaded Italy,[141] where they suffered several defeats. When the elder Vidimir died, this splinter group of Amal Goths was too weak to renew the kingship. Instead they allowed the emperor Glycerius, who reigned from March 3, 473, to the spring of 474, to send them off to Gaul to the Toulousan Goths. The younger Vidimir probably settled down in the Limousin, where he still seems to have been living in the following decade.[142]

The Ostrogoths in the Balkans, 473–488

The chronology of the early history of the Ostrogoths is difficult, and it is not made any easier if one ignores the few absolute dates contained in the fairy-talelike Amal family tradition. According to this version the departure of Vidimir took place in the late summer or early fall of 473. This allowed the Goths to bring in the harvest and to await cooler weather, something the Thiudimir group undoubtedly also did. That the stronger group would have set out earlier is unlikely simply because Vidimir could not have held his position in Pannonia for a single day without his brother's support. Thiudimir's Goths, however, were needed in the Balkans only after 473 when Theodoric Strabo ("the Squinter") had engaged in an act of open rebellion, indeed, almost outright usurpation. Perhaps the Thiudimir Ostrogoths could march into upper Moesia with so little opposition because an order from the emperor prevented the Sarmatian federates and Roman border troops from offering resistance.[143]

The imperial commander-in-chief Aspar had been toppled in 471, but his party did not give up, and while having to accept heavy losses they tried to salvage what they could. But when the battle for the imperial court and the capital had been lost, it seemed that only Theodoric Strabo was in a position to take the place of the once almighty Aspar. This Theodoric was an Ostrogoth and an Amal, like the son of Thiudimir. As a relative of Aspar, "the Squinter" initially tried to pursue a "Roman" career. This plan failed, and Theodoric Strabo withdrew to Thrace, where he assembled an Ostrogothic army. His following grew rapidly, and soon the federate warriors felt strong enough to proclaim their leader king. His elevation as king in Thrace in 473 parallels the elevation of Odovacar in 476. Although less well known and far less significant, the kingship of Theodoric Strabo grew out of the same institutional basis as the rule of Odovacar would three years later. A Roman federate army sought to force through its demands by making its general king. Such a step did not necessarily strengthen the army's bargaining position with the imperial government, which regarded such a king as a usurper and tyrant, but it did increase the king's responsibility for the group that had elevated him to the royal dignity. And so Theodoric Strabo took the next logical step of demanding recognition as sole Gothic king to whom all deserters had to be returned—he had learned from the Huns—and he further demanded the settling of his people in Thrace as well as the surrender of the institutional and material inheritance of Aspar. It took more bloodshed and devastation before the emperor formally agreed to the demands and promised in addition to pay two thousand pounds of gold each year. If this sum had actually been paid, Theodoric could have assembled a gigantic army of some ten thousand warriors. He himself gained in the bargaining the office of commander-in-chief, declaring himself ready and willing to wage war with his people against everybody except the Vandals. "The Squinter" demanded this saving clause either because he was continuing Aspar's traditional friendship with the Vandals or because he was justifiably afraid of embarking on a "suicidal mission." For a campaign against the African Vandals led across the sea, which the Goths preferred to avoid.[144]

The ominous rise of Theodoric "the Squinter" had to force the Pannonian Goths to action and thus to an advance into the interior of the empire. For if Theodoric Strabo succeeded in monopolizing the Gothic kingship, then he could enter into the Amal inheritance and Thiudimir and his son Theodoric would be left with the role of poor relations. Numerically weaker and poorly armed and equipped, father and son had to avoid a direct confrontation in the meantime. Instead, Thiudimir marched unopposed as far as Naissus-Nish, where the Goths probably spent the winter of 473/474. His son Theodoric used this forced period of inaction for an armed reconnaissance mission, which led him across the Kosovo polje into the valley of the Vardar and from there all the way to the gates of Thessalian Larissa. Along the way the cities of Castrum Herculis-Kurvingrad Clisura, Ulpiana-Lipljan, Stobi near Gradsko, and Heraclea-Bitola, fell into his hands. Apparently satisfied with his son's success, Thiudimir planned a thrust toward Thessalonica for the beginning of the campaigning season. The king was not able to take this large city in 474, but he did extort a favorable treaty for his Goths. They were settled—as the Alaric Goths had been in 397—in the Macedonian *civitates* of Europos, Kyrrhos, Pella, Beroea, Methone, Pydna, and Dium. In one stroke they had thereby gained fertile settlement land and access to the Via Egnatia, the important road linking Durazzo and Thessalonica. Kyrrhos was the center of this short-lived federate kingdom. In this city resided Thiudimir; here he convened an assembly of Goths to designate his son as heir and successor, and here he died in 474. His Goths honored his last will and raised up Theodoric as their king.[145] Contrary to traditional practice Theodoric's younger brother Thiudimund was completely passed over; nor could he later offer any special evidence of his fitness for the kingship.[146] From 474 Theodoric was king of the Thiudimir Goths, or the Valameriaci, as they were called because of an understandable mistake.[147]

January 18, 474, saw the death of Leo I, the emperor who had made great sacrifices in his desire to get along with Theodoric Strabo. His successor Zeno was cast in a different mold and dropped "the Squinter." At the same time he perhaps urged the Macedonian Theodoric to attack his Thracian namesake. But it is possible that Theodoric Strabo's loss of the emperor's support was sufficient reason for Thiudimir's son to seek an open confrontation. These Gothic hostilities, however, probably did not break out until 476/477. And before that time other significant changes had taken place.

Between 474 and 476 Theodoric gave up the Macedonian federate kingdom and moved with his people back to the Danube, this time to lower Moesia. The center of this second attempt at creating a kingdom was the strategically well-placed city of Novae-Svištov. With interruptions Theodoric son of Thiudimir resided here until 488. Just what had induced him to shift his "road show" can only be conjectured: on the one hand, a small Gothic kingdom on the lower Danube would be the natural ally of Constantinople if it wanted to catch the rebellious Goths of Thrace in a pincer movement; on the other hand, Theodoric could expect support and emigration into his land from Gothicized lower Moesia, which had open borders with the *barbaricum,* if only he had appropriate successes to show. By contrast, on the Via Egnatia west of Thessalonica he would have remained a stranger.

But the Goths of lower Moesia did not become attractive to the imperial government as alliance partners before the middle of 476. Only then was Zeno once again in control and back in Constantinople. He began the offensive against "the Squinter" who had caused him great trouble and had done his best to help deprive Zeno of his emperorship and his life, an effort that very nearly succeeded. It must have been during the second half of 476 that a veritable flood of imperial gifts and honors poured out to Theodoric son of Thiudimir: following barbarian tradition Zeno adopted him as a "son in arms," called him his "friend," and appointed him *patricius* and commander-in-chief. At the same time the federate kingdom in lower Moesia was recognized and the government promised to subsidize it with

annual payments. Young Theodoric would have been well established had
all the provisions of the treaty been met. But as long as a federate kingdom
was dependent on the imperial treasury's willingness to pay, its economic
problems remained unsolved and its existence was subject to recall. The
Ostrogoths had learned this painful truth in Pannonia and in Macedonia,
and they now faced it once again in lower Moesia. The threat to their ethnic
identity was further heightened by the refusal of the "squinting" king of
the Thracian Goths to surrender. As late as 477 the capital received an
embassy from Theodoric Strabo offering his return to private status and
simultaneously denouncing the Moesian Theodoric as the scourge of the
Roman Empire. The first attempt at reconciliation failed: it was only too
well known that "the Squinter" continued to conspire with the anti-Zeno
party. Zeno therefore took a tough stance, and the senate and the army
declared Theodoric Strabo an enemy of the empire.

The grand gesture was not followed by appropriate action. Zeno punished
Strabo's supporters with nothing more than banishment, thus revealing his
insecurity, which then also affected his ally Theodoric son of Thiudimir. In
478 the Moesian Amal advanced only as far as Marcianopolis-Devna,
where he intended to await the imperial army. But neither intensive exchange of embassies nor grandiose promises could deceive the young Gothic
king as to his difficult situation. He insisted that the emperor and the
imperial government promise on oath never to become reconciled to "the
Squinter." His demand was fulfilled with transparent insincerity. When
Constantinople used Theodoric's delay at Marcianopolis as a pretext to
stop the vital payments, the Moesian Goths prepared to advance across the
Balkan mountains. They were then told that the money was waiting for
them south of the Balkans. Moreover, Theodoric was told that an enormous
force of Roman soldiers would meet him there. In addition, strong advance
detachments had been promised to the Goths for their march through the
Balkans. Of the promised eight thousand Roman cavalry and the infantry force of thirty thousand the Moesian Goths saw nothing. Instead, an
unpleasant surprise awaited them at Mount Sondis. As the "Valamirian"
Goths, led by Byzantine guides, were clambering up the mountain road that
connects Provadija and Ajtos, they encountered an obstacle: Entrenched
behind an impregnable position Theodoric Strabo had pitched his camp.
Minor skirmishes took place, but neither Gothic king sought a decisive
battle. Each dead Gothic warrior represented a loss to each Theodoric. If
each was trying to monopolize the Ostrogothic kingship, he had to try to
lure away from his rival as many living Goths as possible and thus increase
his own following.

In the propaganda war that followed Theodoric Strabo seized the initiative. At a safe distance from the enemy camp but still within hearing range, he rode back and forth and shouted accusations against the other Amal. He charged him with youthful inexperience and political clumsiness in dealing with the imperial government, called him a "traitor and enemy of their common race," expressed regret at the impending Gothic civil war that would benefit only the Romans, and lamented the wretched economic condition of the Moesian Goths. He reminded them that they had all left their homeland with two or three horses, whereas now they had to go on foot like slaves. And, he added, this was happening to the very Goths whose descent was equal to that of their leader Theodoric son of Thiudimir and whose goal had been heaps of gold measured out as booty. However literally we wish to take this impressive scene, the basic outline of Theodoric Strabo's speech is revealing. The passage shows that the Amal and Ostrogothic traditions were identical and of high prestige. Furthermore, it gives evidence of an exalted sense of prowess, a lust for gold, and the pride of owning herdes of horses in a people who as followers of Attila had had the world's treasures at their feet and who were now trying to defend their standard of living in Roman service. The precious furnishings of the grave of Apahida II reveal a princely warrior who during his lifetime could easily have spoken the words of Theodoric Strabo.

The performance of "the Squinter" made a great impression. Theodoric Thiudimirson's own people, the warriors as well as their women, forced him to seek reconciliation with his enemy. In accustomed fashion the two Gothic kings drew up their people facing each other across a river and entered into an agreement: from now on they intended to present their demands jointly to the imperial government. First, they needed food until the next harvest, a bargaining point that dates the events to the late spring or early summer of 478. In addition, they wanted the settlement area of the Moesian Goths extended southward all the way across the Balkan mountains. "As on the first occasion," the necessary steps could be supervised and carried through by Roman officials. With this demand Theodoric son of Thiudimir proved that he had not forgotten his years of apprenticeship in Constantinople and that he recognized the value of Roman administration. Decades later as king of Italy he would let the emperor know that he had learned in the Greek East how to rule Romans. Theodoric Strabo, in contrast, demanded only compliance with the treaty of 473, particularly the unfulfilled clauses, especially the retroactive payment of the promised yearly subsidy. The emperor's response, containing both reproaches and offers, followed the maxim *divide et impera*. Zeno ignored "the Squinter" completely and tried to bribe the other Theodoric with a large sum of money: one thousand pounds of gold, forty thousand pounds of silver, and a fixed annual sum of ten thousand solidi. From the yearly payments alone Theodoric could have paid for about two thousand federate warriors. Last, Zeno offered him an imperial princess or some other noble Roman woman in marriage, provided Theodoric would continue the war against Strabo. But Theodoric son of Thiudimir declined the offer and hostilities commenced.

The initial successes of the imperial army, which came at the expense of both Strabo and the younger Theodoric, seemed to justify the emperor's policy. But mistakes in judgment soon deprived Zeno of the fruits of these victories. Then Theodoric son of Thiudimir marched off westward through Thrace along the northern edge of the Rhodope mountains, plundering as he went along. But as he moved farther away from Constantinople he eliminated himself as a serious power factor, lost some of his following, and gave the imperial government an opportunity to strike a deal with Strabo. The latter received back his fortune, was given pay for thirteen thousand warriors, and accepted the command over two palace units and finally even the office of commander-in-chief, which was taken away from Theodoric son of Thiudimir. Furthermore, Strabo's relatives were to be rehabilitated. These were not empty promises, for the payments were actually made. The younger Theodoric now seemed doomed. He suffered further defeats in engagements against imperial officers, who clearly had orders to keep him alive. The Moesian Goths withdrew once again to the Vardar valley where they captured the city of Stobi, which had already been plundered once before, and massacred its garrison, probably as revenge for their humiliation. News of the atrocity spread far and wide; the population of Thessalonica revolted to express their sense of betrayal by the imperial government. The memory of the Gothic federate kingdom outside the gates of their city was still strong. In order to calm the tense situation and gain time the emperor dispatched envoys to persuade Theodoric to adopt a more sensible course. Among them was the man who had headed Theodoric's chancery when the Gothic king had been commander-in-chief. The imperial effort was successful: the Gothic king halted for a while at Heraclea-Bitola and sent off his own embassy to the imperial court. Because the bishop of Heraclea brought rich gifts and organized provisions for the Gothic army, the tension seemed to be easing. Zeno decided the time had come to advance serious proposals. He wanted to establish once again a federate kingdom with Theodoric Thiudimirson's Goths; the planned site for this third attempt was to be the fertile basin of Pautalia-Kjustendil. There in the interior of Dacia, between the military districts of Illyricum and Thrace, the emperor would have the Gothic federates at hand in case Strabo should cause new difficulties but could control them if Thiudimirson's Goths tried anything foolish themselves. The emperor placed two hundred pounds of gold at the disposal of the Roman officials who were to supervise the settlement.

But the emperor's well-laid plan failed, for in the meantime Theodoric had contacted his relative Sidimund. Sidimund had acquired rich land holdings near Durazzo while in imperial service; he was considered a friend of the Romans and was held in great esteem. But he had been involved in the anti-Zeno party at court, which is probably why he thought it wise to withdraw to distant Epirus. Sidimund probably had made his peace with Zeno, for the population and the two thousand-man garrison believed him when he claimed that Zeno's orders called for the evacuation of the territory to make room for the Goths. Everyone was advised to seek a safe place for himself and his possessions. The soldiers were even threatened with the emperor's displeasure if they offered resistance. After Sidimund's ruse had worked, he sent word to Bitola and invited Theodoric to establish his fourth federate kingdom. While Theodoric was using his sister's illness and subsequent death as an excuse to put off the imperial envoys, Sidimund's message arrived at the city. Thereupon the Goths marched off in a westerly rather than northeasterly direction. The inhabitants of Bitola probably got word of what was afoot, for they all withdrew into the citadel and rejected the Gothic king's demands for travel provisions. In return they had to watch the Goths set their city on fire in retaliation.

Circumstances forced the Goths to divide into three marching columns. The first was led by Theodoric, the second by the second in command, Soas, and the third by Theodoric's brother Thiudimund. An obstacle in the mountains, perhaps the Diavat pass, was successfully overcome, and then the Goths stood before Lynchnidus-Ohrid. This city, situated on Lake Ohrid, was well provisioned and ably defended, and Theodoric could accomplish nothing. Past abandoned Scampa the Gothic army then marched the last twenty miles to Durazzo without encountering any resistance. But Thiudimund's column was still missing.

Although the Romans were taken by surprise, their reaction was swift and effective. The operation against Theodoric son of Thiudimir was led by two men, the highly capable general Sabinianus and the *patricius* Adamantius. In modern terms Sabinianus would have been deemed a "hawk" and Adamantius a "dove." Whereas the latter wanted under any circumstances to sit down at the bargaining table, the general was looking for a confrontation. Adamantius suggested meeting places and demanded the handing over of hostages. Theodoric accepted the proposal; the princely general Soas would have even been willing to deliver himself up to the Romans. But when Sabinianus refused to provide any sureties the Goths broke off the talks. This is how things went back and forth between Durazzo, Scampa, and Ohrid, until Adamantius ran out of patience. He suddenly appeared with two hundred men before the fortress of Durazzo as if he had flown across the mountains. From a safe and secure place he began his negotiations with Theodoric, the bargainers once again separated by a river. In response to Theodoric's reproaches for the imperial government's betrayal in the preceding year which had forced him to make peace with "the Squinter," Adamantius enumerated all the benefits the emperor had showered upon Theodoric and his people. He reminded the Gothic chief of his high Roman offices and of his escape from Thrace even though he had been completely encircled. Finally, Adamantius threatened the Goths with the superior power of the empire, which would never accept Gothic settlement in Epirus. Above all the Romans feared that Theodoric might build up a naval force. The imperial envoy then described the territory of Pautalia, a deserted and fertile land where the Gothic army, if only it were willing, could easily feed itself.

Adamantius made a great impression. Theodoric accepted the offer in principle but argued for certain specifics. He and his exhausted army wanted to spend the winter of 479/480 in Epirus. Thereafter he would be willing to follow the imperial representative into the new federate land. He was also waiting for the emperor to specify in which Roman *civitates* his non-combatants and the baggage train should be left while he himself with six thousand warriors would clear Thrace of hostile Goths. This figure is interesting; obviously Theodoric son of Thiudimir had lost about half of his men, reducing his army to the numerical strength it had had at the beginning of his rule in 471. And there was a threat of new bloodletting. Even as the Gothic king was offering his mother and sister as hostages, they were already in great danger. Thiudimund had not yet arrived with the women, who were part of his column still marching through the mountains of Epirus. And now Sabinianus made his move, intercepted the Gothic rear guard, and took a large number of prisoners. Only by abandoning his people in a manner most unworthy of a king, and indeed only by tearing down at his rear a bridge to safety was Thiudimund able to escape with his mother. The Roman "hawks" had won; the negotiations with Theodoric were forgotten, his dream of a Roman career and a comfortable life "in the city" after victory over "the Squinter" dissolved into thin air, not to mention Theodoric's proposal to support Nepos in Dalmatia against Odovacar.

That offer Adamantius had already rejected, for he wanted to keep the Goths away from the Adriatic coast at all costs. Instead, Sabinianus was now allowed to conduct his war against Theodoric with the Goth Gento supporting him. Gento was married to a Roman lady from Epirus, perhaps came from that region himself, though surely not from Sidimund's clan, and had placed himself at the head of Roman troops. Sabinianus, who at first had had only a small contingent of *buccellarii* at his disposal, was given command over the regular troops of the neighboring districts and over the Illyrian army under Hunulf. The son of the Scirian king thus got another opportunity to fight against his old enemies. The chance was not seized in 479, however, and Theodoric survived the year 480 without further losses. The impending offensive of the Romans collapsed completely when Sabinianus fell victim to an intrigue in 481. Then the sudden death of Theodoric Strabo in the same year brought an end to the dual Ostrogothic kingship. The son of Thiudimir had survived the greatest crisis of his career.

But Theodoric owed his survival in Epirus from 479 to 481 to his "squinting" namesake. The army of Strabo had grown to a size of thirty thousand men and presented such a threat to the legitimate emperor that Zeno could think of nothing but mobilizing the Bulgarians against the Thracian Goths. Theodoric Strabo beat back this Turkish people, who in 480/481 made their first appearance in their future homeland. When Theodoric sought to drive home his victory and marched his army once again to the gates of Constantinople, he had to contend with problems in his own camp. His advance thus ended in failure, as did his attempt to cross over to Bithynia. Strabo's position in Thrace obviously became critical. On his way westward "to Greece" he stopped over at Stabulum Diomedis where he met his fate. While breaking in a horse, Theodoric Strabo was thrown off and impaled on a lance hanging from a tent. Thus ended in 481 the life of that Theodoric without whose timely death Theodoric son of Thiudimir would have never become "the Great." For more than a decade the Thracian Amal had kept his Pannonian-Moesian relatives from expanding and in the end he had even challenged their hold on the Ostrogothic kingship. Now the surviving Theodoric entered into the inheritance of the deceased, especially by learning from his mistakes. Theodoric's readiness to leave the Eastern empire may have been influenced by Strabo's long and hopeless fight against Constantinople. Although "the Squinter" left behind a wife, two brothers, and a son, Rekitach, none of these posed a threat to the other Theodoric. Rekitach had soon gambled away his father's position. He killed his uncles and lost the army, which went over mostly to Theodoric Thiudimirson. As a worn-out king's son he was slain in Constantinople in 484 by the consul of that year, *Flavius Theodericus,* with the emperor's knowledge. This spectacular crime, possibly a response to the murder of Strabo's brothers and carried out in broad daylight, would not remain the only blood feud in the life of Theodoric the Great.[148]

Freed from his most dangerous enemies and rivals, in 482 Theodoric began an offensive against Greece in the course of which he advanced once again as far as Larissa. The resulting devastation finally forced Zeno in 483 to conclude the treaty desired by Theodoric: the Amal was again made commander-in-chief, was designated consul for 484, and was given Dacia ripensis and parts of lower Moesia.[149] In 483 Theodoric returned to Novae, from where he had set out half a decade earlier. Did he now actually intend to lead a quiet life "at the Scythian border," something he had once dreamed of?[150] On January 1, 484, at any rate, he must have been back in Constantinople to begin his regular consulship. From that time, at the latest, he also possessed the citizenship, through which his Amal family also became Flavians. As consul the Gothic king received the usual honors, which the sources ignore because they were nothing exceptional. Whoever sticks to their literal testimony can report of Theodoric's consulship in Constantinople only the murder of Rekitach.[151] And yet it appears far more significant that the Amal received this high dignity *suo anno* ("in his year") when he was probably thirty-three years old, as if he had been from one of the leading Roman families.[152] The barbarian Theodoric and the Roman Theodoric are not two successive phases in the life of the same man but had been ever since his childhood two aspects of a single personality.

In the year of Theodoric's consulship Zeno thought the time was right to take energetic measures against the Isaurian rebels in Asia Minor. At the head of his tribal warriors and regular Roman troops Theodoric crossed to Bithynia. But he was recalled at Nicomedia or shortly after leaving that town when "it had occurred to the emperor that he could become disloyal."[153] To make things worse, Theodoric was replaced by none other than Ermanaric, the son of Aspar and cousin of "the Squinter." Ermanaric, bearer of the venerable Amal name,[154] stood at the head of a group of Rugians, not exactly the best friends of the Ostrogoths.[155] The sources for the years between 484 and 486 are full of contradictions; thus for the same period they report Theodoric's recall and replacement, the permission for his festive entrance into Constantinople, and the erection of an equestrian statue in his honor. Without any doubt in 486 hostilities opened between Zeno and Theodoric:[156] the Amal returned to his Danubian homeland from where he invaded Thrace on a plundering raid. Thereupon Zeno once more called in the Bulgarians to help, but they were defeated. In 487

Theodoric began his offensive against Constantinople. The Goths block-aded the city, occupied important suburbs, and cut off the water supply. There was no thought of actually taking the city. Rather, this was one of the usual acts of blackmail and a demonstration of power, a game at which the Gothic federates in East and West were masters. Zeno for his part knew the proper response: he called for Amalafrida from the entourage of the empress and sent her to her brother with rich presents. The way was now clear for a return to Novae.[157] The sources like to make a causal connection between Theodoric's last devastation of Thrace and the Ostrogoths' depar-ture for Italy. There may indeed have been such a connection, even though the motives appear more complex than the ones presented by the sources.[158]

Theodoric's Battle for Italy, 488–493

The precarious relations between Constantinople and the Italian kingdom deteriorated further when Odovacar prepared for an intervention in the East on the side of the anti-Zeno party. To defend against the threatening war on two fronts the emperor mobilized the "lower Austrian" Rugians, who now thought they were close to striking it rich and would move to Italy. But Odovacar reacted quickly. A bloody conflict within the Rugian royal clan was tantamount to a breach of the treaty, and the last Italian armies marched to the Danube in Noricum to punish and discipline the barbarian federates and at the same time to eliminate the Roman opposition that had found a home there after 476. In the late fall of 487 Odovacar attacked the Rugian kingdom and destroyed it. King Feletheus-Feva and his "evil wife," the Ostrogothic princess Giso, were captured by the victors and executed in Italy. Their son Frideric was able to save himself along with scattered Rugian survivors, but an attempt in 488 to reconquer their tra-ditional kingdom failed. This time Hunulf, who after 479 had left Byzantine service to join his brother Odovacar, appeared on the scene and chased the Rugian away. Those provincials whom St. Severin had gathered together and had placed under Rugian protection were forced by the victors to emigrate to Italy. In this way the enemies were deprived of an economic base and the formation of any other East Germanic state in this region was prevented. Seventeen years after the military abandonment of Gaul the same thing that had happened there was repeated on the middle reaches of the Danube: a former Roman province became a military deployment zone. It took a half millennium for the region between the Enns river and the Wienerwald to overcome this fate.

Expelled by Odovacar's military power and policy of scorched earth, Frideric and his followers—the pro-Ostrogothic party of the Rugians—sought help from Theodoric. They encountered no resistance as they marched downstream along the Danube.[159] Constantinople may have quietly arranged everything beforehand. But when Frideric arrived in Novae-Svištov in lower Moesia, the emperor and the Gothic king must have already been negotiating the attack on Italy. Without paying another visit to Constantinople, Theodoric concluded a formal treaty with Zeno which stated that "after the defeat of Odovacar Theodoric, in return for his efforts, was to rule [Italy] for the emperor until he arrived in person."[160]

THE OSTROGOTHIC MARCH TO ITALY

Once again—how many times had it now been?—Theodoric's Ostrogoths packed their belongings and set out. Estimates place their number at twenty thousand warriors, that is to say, about one hundred thousand people altogether, a figure that comes close to reality.[161] Not all Balkan Goths joined the trek. Theodoric, however, made every effort to obtain a consensus from as many Goths as possible. He was even in contact with the Crimean Goths, but they declined to participate in the Italian venture and stayed at home. The same course was taken by many, even high-ranking, Goths in Thrace. From that group would come some of the better soldiers that Justinian later sent against the Ostrogothic kingdom of Italy.[162] In the battle between the two Theodorics the Amal Goths had split up; wounds had been inflicted that had not healed even half a century later. Although many Goths refused to go along with their king, he was joined by numerous non-Gothic elements, such as the Frideric's Rugians and individual Romans, among them even relatives of the emperor.[163] Even if the sources did not explicitly state the reasons for Theodoric's departure from the Balkan peninsula, we could easily guess them. The Gothic king realized that in the long run he was no match for the imperial power.[164] Time, Zeno's ally, worked against him. If Theodoric proved incapable of solving the economic problems of his retainers, his people would desert him and he was certain to meet an inglorious end. It is true that by having himself sent against Odovacar he continued to be a tool of Zeno's seesaw policies, but at the same time he was given the chance to end his dependence on the imperial treasury. After at least four previous unsuccessful attempts, the establishment of a lasting kingdom now seemed within reach.

As usual the Goths waited for the harvest before they left the Danubian provinces and set out westward. They marched along the Roman road south of the Danube as far as Sirmium. Apparently Theodoric had promised not to live off the land while he remained on East Roman territory but to take along the necessary provisions. This clause in the treaty addressed the problem of their late departure and the dangers of the winter season. Theodoric's provisions did in fact still last when his people reached their former Slavonic homeland. This land, however, was no longer Gothic but since 474 had been part of Gepidia. Near modern Vukovar, near where the Vuka flows into the Danube, large bands of the hostile "cousins" had fortified the west bank of the river and barred the way. Whether the Gepids were in league with Odovacar or whether they were doing this on their own is unknown. It is true that Theodoric's march to the West was accompanied by diplomatic efforts. But we only know of Theodoric's demand that Odovacar help resolve the confrontation with the Rugians. Whether Odovacar on his part made efforts to gain allies and how he may have gone about it is also unknown. At any rate, the attack on Odovacar was meant to appear as a liberation of Romans from the yoke of a tyrant and as a barbarian campaign of revenge. Even Odovacar's murder, which Theodoric committed with his own hands, was justified by reference to the injustice the Rugian royal house had suffered. Whatever it was that prompted the Gepids to refuse passage to the Goths in 488, the first opposition that Theodoric encountered was dangerous and serious. The Amal king himself led the assault; the entrenchments were taken by storm, the enemy routed, and their supplies captured. Among the dead Gepids was possibly their king Thraustila-Thrapstila. After crossing the Vuka, which at that time probably formed the imperial border, the Goths could think of setting themselves up for the winter months without violating the treaty. In all probability they waited in the area of modern Slavonia for the new harvest of 489 before setting out again. It is possible that the Rugians joined the Ostrogoths at this time, for their leader Frideric had joined Theodoric at Novae in the preceding year, probably with only a small band. At some point between the battle at the Vuka and their arrival in Italy the Ostrogoths were attacked by Sarmatian nomads, an event that may have been connected to the march of the Rugians through Pannonia. Theodoric's bands then marched along the route that so many Gothic "travelers" to Italy had used. Coming from the plain of Emona-Laibach, the Gothic army crossed over the Hrušica into the valley of Wippach-Vipava, until they had reached the mouth of the river. There, at Pons Sontii (Isonzo Bridge) on the right bank of the river Odovacar's army had entrenched itself. The Goths had broken the resistance of the Gepids and had beaten back Sarmatian attacks, but now the thirty-eight-year-old Theodoric met his sixty-year-old enemy for the first time face to face. On August 28, 489, the Amal attacked and put Odovacar to flight. With the subsequent crossing of the Isonzo he entered the "empire of Italy" (*Italiae imperium*); a new era had begun. No more than a month later the Goths reached Verona on the Via Postumia where the Italian king offered the historical Dietrich von Bern a second battle. As on the Vuka, the Gothic king is said to have demonstrated his personal bravery. The panegyrist Ennodius describes the beautiful scene in which Theodoric, dressed in magnificent armor, takes leave of his mother and sister at the beginning of the battle. But Theodoric won the victory by skillfully outmaneuvering his enemy. The Gothic king's position as supreme commander was no empty title, for in the services of the Eastern empire he had also acquired the necessary military skills. The Adige river became a trap for Odovacar's troops, who were cut off from Verona, and on September 30, 489, the Italian king fled to Ravenna.[165]

THE BATTLES IN ITALY, 489–493

Theodoric's march to Italy seemed destined for a fast and decisive victory. In Milan, which Theodoric captured after Verona, secular and ecclesiastical dignitaries welcomed him as the emperor's representative. Even Odovacar's commander-in-chief Tufa and large numbers of the defeated army joined the victor. We could interpret Tufa's step as the submission of the highest ranking Italian general to the emperor's supreme commander Theodoric. Apparently Theodoric saw no reason to question Tufa's loyalty, and he dispatched the general to Ravenna with a band of elite troops. Theodoric was clearly counting on the impact the example of Odovacar's former commander-in-chief was bound to have on the remaining troops. Ravenna could be taken only by surprise or through psychological warfare. But Tufa changed sides, the Gothic elite force entrusted to his command was destroyed, and Theodoric suffered his first serious defeat on Italian soil. While the Amal fell back to Ticinum-Pavia where he shut himself up, Odovacar regained the open field and began to besiege the enemy. That each side kept the other tied down was an open invitation to the Burgundians to invade northwestern Italy. While Odovacar was occupying Cremona and punishing Milan, these Gallic barbarians plundered and devastated Liguria. A great many Roman captives regained their freedom about three years later when Theodoric finally bought them back from the Burgundians.

It was not until summer 490 that Theodoric was able to take the initiative. Then the tide began to turn in his favor. Alaric II gave one of the rare displays of Gothic solidarity and sent his warriors to Italy. At the approach of the Visigoths Odovacar raised the siege of Pavia and returned to the Adda river. Possibly near Acerrae-Pizzighettone, where the road from Lodi to Cremona crossed the river, he accepted battle on August 11, 490. He was once again defeated, and among his losses were such excellent men as the *comes domesticorum* Pierius. That Odovacar, in the euphoria in early 490, had marched to Rome to have his son proclaimed caesar, lost all its significance. Odovacar had to retreat once more to Ravenna. Not all the followers of the Scirian king, however, locked themselves up in the city. Thus the Goths were not able to eliminate Tufa. He held his ground in the strategically important valley of the Adige at Trent, where he even received unexpected reinforcements. Meanwhile Theodoric had to be content with minor actions: one area had to be secured and sealed off, in another area he had to take measures for internal pacification—a policy that was only too often upset by Theodoric's own followers. There was also the war in the Pineta south of Ravenna, and the neighboring tribes thought they could grab whatever they wanted during what seemed like a free-for-all in Italy. The Vandals followed the example of the Burgundians and invaded Sicily. But in 491 they suffered such a serious defeat that they not only withdrew but concluded a treaty renouncing the tribute Odovacar had been paying them.

No sooner had the Vandal problem been resolved than the alliance with the Rugians broke down. After Theodoric had regained his mobility in 490, Frideric and his people remained behind to protect Pavia. There they soon began to act like a true occupation army, harassing the population and bringing Theodoric's Roman policy into disrepute. But not until a year later, on August 18 or 22, 491, was Theodoric able to intervene in Pavia in person. The disciplinary action he took drove Frideric to "violate his loyalty" and to go over to Tufa together with his Rugians. The Gothic king had no choice but to isolate the two allies north of Verona and to await further developments. In 492, or perhaps 493, Tufa and Frideric quarreled and actually fought a battle somewhere between Verona and Trent. We know for certain that Tufa was killed, and Frideric probably met the same fate. At any rate, the Rugians rejoined the Gothic king. The name Tufa is East Germanic; perhaps he had been a Rugian who long ago had followed Odovacar into Italy. That Tufa and Frideric not only struck an alliance but also fought each other does not speak against their being relatives.[166]

Like the resolution of the Rugian problem, the capture of Ravenna also took a long time. All offensive warfare was frustrated by the impregnable defenses of the city, which, moreover, was freely provisioned by sea for two years. Not until August 29, 492, after procuring a sufficient number of ships in Rimini, were the Goths able to set up an effective blockade. Of course, at that point Odovacar must have long since given up hope of victory. On the night of July 9/10, 491, his last large-scale sortie failed. Though both sides had suffered serious losses, it was a much heavier blow to the numerically inferior defenders. Livila, Odovacar's commander-in-chief and Tufa's successor, was killed in action along with the best of his Herulian troops.[167] But that was by no means the end of the battle. Not until February 25, 493, did John, the bishop of Ravenna, mediate a treaty according to which Theodoric and Odovacar were to occupy Ravenna together and exercise joint rule over Italy. In agreeing to these arrangements Theodoric broke the *foedus* with the emperor, but in return he was able to enter Ravenna on March 5, 493. Ten days later Odovacar was dead,[168] slain by the hand of his coregent: during a common meal Theodoric killed the Scirian. Two motives were circulated as justification for the crime: first, that Odovacar had been killed in blood revenge for the Rugian royal couple (with this version it apparently did not matter that their son was at that very moment in open rebellion against Theodoric); second, that the Gothic king had merely preempted an ambush by his rival.[169] In fact the Amal broke the treaty deliberately and committed murder. Not even the "nice" words put into Theodoric's mouth can change the dark picture of his deed: Odovacar's question "Where is God?" drew the response: "This is what you have done to my people." While two of Theodoric's men who were acting as supplicants grabbed the victim's hands, the Gothic king ran his treaty partner through with his sword and is supposed to have said as he stood over Odovacar's body: "This wretch does not even seem to have bones in his body." The deliberate and methodical nature of Theodoric's act is clearly revealed by the subsequent events: Odovacar was not allowed to receive a Christian burial and his wife Sunigilda was starved to death. Odovacar's brother Hunulf sought refuge in a church and was used as a target by Gothic archers. The caesar Thela survived for a time; he went into exile to Visigothic Gaul but was eliminated when he made efforts to return to Italy.[170] On the day of Odovacar's murder his followers and their families were attacked. Wherever the Goths could lay hands on them they met their deaths. The noble Romans in Odovacar's party fared better. Theodoric did impose property restrictions, even confiscations, on them, but through episcopal mediation he was dissuaded from carrying out these measures. Moreover, the senate was spared a planned purge of Odovacar's supporters.

In the course of the year 493 Theodoric had become the unchallenged master of Italy.[171] The *exercitus Gothorum* responded to this situation by elevating him once more to the kingship; Constantinople, however, was slow to grant its recognition.[172]

Flavius Theodericus Rex: King of the Goths and Italians, 493–526

THEODORIC'S EFFORTS TO OBTAIN IMPERIAL RECOGNITION, 490/493–497

After the battle at the Adda there was hardly any doubt that Theodoric's mission would be crowned with success. That is why Festus, the spokesman of the Roman senate, was willing to go to Constantinople as Theodoric's envoy. But the negotiations for recognition, which were begun as early as the fall of 490, led nowhere. Theodoric made the next attempt after he had completely cut off Ravenna in August 492. Zeno had died in the spring of 491, and Anastasius had succeeded him. But the negotiations with Anastasius dragged on until Theodoric ran out of patience and allowed the Gothic army to proclaim him king in March 493 "without permission from the new emperor." The result was that the senatorial delegation in Constantinople achieved more for itself than for Theodoric. As a sign of imperial favor both consuls of 495 were selected from the nobility of Rome. But no progress was made on the question of Theodoric's recognition; among the reasons was the Gothic king's refusal to force Pope Gelasius to capitulate in his dispute with the emperor. This was followed by two years of ill-feeling; no one from the West was given the consulship. Then Gelasius died, and his successor showed himself willing to talk with the emperor. At that favorable juncture Festus once more led a senatorial embassy to Constantinople, where in 497 he gave the impression that the reconciliation was all but accomplished. In response a Western senator was again designated consul for 498, and at the same time Theodoric received recognition as the ruler of the West; Constantinople sent the *vestis regia*. Along with "all the insignia of the palace" (*omnia ornamenta palatii*), which Odovacar had dutifully sent to Byzantium in 476, there must have also arrived the message that Anastasius had "entrusted to the Amal the power and responsibility of the kingship."[173] It could not have been expressed more clearly: the king of Italy in 497 was very different from the king of Italy in 476; not even the faintest stain of tyranny seems to have tarnished Theodoric any longer.

SOME QUESTIONS

Theodoric's treaty with Zeno provided that (1) Odovacar, a formerly recognized king who had turned into a tyrant, had to be defeated; (2) Theodoric was then to rule in the emperor's name, that is, he was to exercise vice-imperial authority until Zeno could come to Italy in person. But now not only Odovacar but Zeno too was dead, and Anastasius had other things to worry about than traveling to Ravenna to play emperor. This meant that the clause of *praeregnare* took effect, that is to say, Theodoric had to exercise the *regnum* for a legitimate emperor. With what right and to what end did the victorious Gothic army then "confirm" its king as king after Odovacar had been killed in the late winter of 493?[174] Why did Constantinople regard this as an act of usurpation, as the unwanted exchange "of one tyrant for another,"[175] even though Theodoric assumed "neither the imperial dress nor the imperial title" but throughout his life had himself addressed as king after the barbarian custom?[176] Had not Theodoric himself cited the case of Aspar to show that "the elevation of an Arian and Germanic chief to the imperial dignity was impracticable"?[177] How could it then be said that although the Amal was in name a tyrant, in reality he had been like a "rightful emperor" and any other holder of the highest dignity?[178] Why did Anastasius in 497 nevertheless recognize the royal elevation of 493 and in 516 present Theodoric to the senate of Rome as the man to whom he had entrusted the dominion over the West? If Constantinople was engaged in short-term maneuvering and granted the recognition merely to gain an advantage in the field of church politics, why then did Justin, Anastasius' successor, call Theodoric a king, a *praecelsus rex*?[179] If the Amal kingdom in Italy was a tyranny, why did the Goths until 540 have the unchallenged right to proclaim someone "king of the Goths and Italians," a right that disappeared only with the capitulation of Vitigis?[180]

All these questions are based on the assumption that there existed two different political philosophies that Theodoric combined in his Italian kingdom.[181] Posterity gave Theodoric the title "the Great," even though the state he created was, leaving aside the Odovacar prologue, the most short-lived of all Latin kingdoms on Roman soil. Ostrogothic Italy remained part of the Roman Empire, yet its ruler overshadowed the seemingly "independent" tribal kings of his time. In the course of the fifth century the Western *imperium* had declined to the point of being the territorial and institutional junior partner of Constantinople. The vice-imperial military regime of the "Western" *patricius*, the roots of which reached back to the days of Stilicho, was not spared the barbarization that was taking place everywhere. All attempts to direct the development into the framework of Roman institutions failed sooner or later. It was precisely the most capable Western emperors who fell victim to "their" *patricii*. Thus among those who were involved in these events the notion could arise that the one emperor in Constantinople was also sufficient for the occidental empire, especially when the West comprised hardly more than the former Italian prefecture without Africa. The only question was whether the Western vice-emperor should be a supreme commander of patrician standing or a king. In other words, the issue was whether the barbarized army of Italy would permit an arrangement on the basis of a Roman magistracy or whether it would seek its own solution in a barbarian-type rule. When a kingdom was proclaimed in 476, the second option was adopted. Now there was no further need nor place for an emperor of the West. The adjustments made in the kingdom were imperfect and for centuries to come they sealed the division of Italy between foreign rule and autonomy. This division, however, affected only the highest levels; the inner structure of the state remained Roman. By continuing Odovacar's policies, Theodoric preserved the Italian prefecture as a Roman state and at the same time strengthened the claim of the *gentes* to determine the fate and government of the peninsula.[182]

THEODORIC'S KINGDOM: AN ATTEMPT AT A CONSTITUTIONAL ANALYSIS

Of all Gothic kings the Italian Theodoric is the most famous, yet he never called himself king of the Goths (*rex Gothorum*). His title *Flavius Theodericus rex* might be rooted in Odovacar's tradition, but it is attested in this particular form for the first time in 501.[183] The Flavian royal title was adopted by many other barbarian kings, at first in Theodoric's own family, then among the Visigoths and the Lombards. Even Charlemagne knew that the old imperial title Flavius was taken by kings "because of its great prestige." When Theodoric received the Roman citizenship, he became *Flavius Amalus Theodericus*. For a full royal title the term *rex* was still missing, a Roman term expressing the fact that Theodoric had been recognized by the emperor. It is in keeping with his political program that Theodoric dropped any reference to barbarian traditions, such as his family name and the name of the Gothic people. The final version is the title *Flavius Theodericus rex*. Just as Constantine had founded the second imperial Flavian dynasty, Theodoric founded the third Flavian dynasty of royal rank. And just as the imperial Flavians had possessed the emperorship, in like manner the Gothic royal Flavians sought to monopolize the kingship itself. This implied that Theodoric's kingship was "universal," ranking high above the kingship of the other *gentes*. But the *regnum,* though recognized by the emperor, was not bestowed on the king by a Roman but by a barbarian assembly. Thus the Italian kingdom, which remained part of the Roman Empire, was not founded on the principle that "the army makes the emperor"[184] but on the maxim that "the king is chosen by the federate army." Before Theodoric, Odovacar and Theodoric Strabo had tried to establish such *regna*. Under these circumstances it seemed only logical to replace the Roman army with a federate army. Theodoric Strabo's demand had been rejected not because of ethnic differences—barbarians and Romans served in the regular *exercitus* as well as with the federates—but because of the political consequences it would have entailed. In its wake a legitimate abolition of the Roman Empire would have been a distinct possibility.[185]

This very thing had been brought about by Odovacar's elevation to the kingship; in the Italian *regnum* there was no longer an emperor, and the army in Italy had been "content" with proclaiming a king. Twelve years later, with permission from the emperor, federates marched to Italy and conquered the western *regnum* without detaching it from the *imperium*.[186] In this way the *exercitus Gothorum*[187] acquired the right and the duty to decide over the *principatus Romanus*.[188] The army of Gothic federates could not elect an emperor—that would have been inexcusable usurpation—but only a monarchic, a *reiks*-ῥήξ, "as the barbarians usually call their rulers."[189] Under certain circumstances the emperor could get along with such a ruler, a king. But just as a Western emperor who was proclaimed by the Roman army had to receive the recognition of Constantinople, the king of the Italian federate army also needed imperial confirmation if he wished to avoid the stain of usurpation, the *praesumptio regni*.[190] The institution that functioned as mediator in this issue was the senate. Next to and jointly with the army it had always had the right of transferring the highest dignity. This is why Theodoric selected his envoys to the East carefully, sending the speaker of the senate and some of its highest ranking members. The rise in prestige of the venerable institution had begun under Stilicho and reached its high point under Odovacar; but Theodoric too supported the senate, which alone could accommodate the barbarian rulers' need for legitimacy.[191]

When the Amal Theodoric marched into Italy he had been designated by his father, he had established himself as king of a Gothic army, he had received Roman citizenship along with the consulship from the emperor, he held the office of supreme commander and the patriciate, and he was king of a federate army.[192] After victory over Odovacar the Gothic federates were the only army in the Western empire. This army then took the logical step, prematurely in the emperor's eyes but not illegally, of proclaiming Theodoric king of the Western empire. The elevation to kingship in 493 was as necessary as it had been after Thiudimir's death. In both cases the *exercitus Gothorum* had changed: in Kyrrhos in 474 Theodoric entered into his father's inheritance, at Ravenna in 493 the *exercitus* acted as the imperially recognized army of the West. In virtue of the contractually guaranteed right of *praeregnare*, the Gothic king had become "indeed a real emperor," a *princeps Romanus*[193] who called the Roman *imperatores* his predecessors.[194]

THEODORIC'S RULE IN THEORY AND PRACTICE

Theodoric tried to present his Italo-Gothic *regnum* as both independent of and subordinate to the unified empire: with God's help the king had learned in Constantinople how to rule justly over Romans. His kingdom was therefore an imitation of this model, the image of the empire. To the same degree that Theodoric stood in rank below the emperor he surpassed the other *gentes* and their kings.[195] The Romans called him another Trajan or Valentinian. The comparison reveals something about the impression Theodoric's rule made on contemporaries. Following the imperial custom his authority was publicly displayed, which is revealed above all by his appearance in Rome in 500. On the occasion of his tricennial, the Arian Theodoric paid his respects to Saint Peter "as if he [Theodoric] had been a Catholic"; he honored the senate, gave presents—probably like the famous three-solidi gold medallion of Senigallia—and pleased the populace with gifts of grain, circus games, and a festive entry into the city.[196] It is not surprising that statues and paintings were made for Theodoric, that the Romans acclaimed him their lord (*dominus*), and that at times they even called him augustus.[197] The Gothic king's rule over the Roman bureaucracy was also "imperial" in nature; he made appointments at the highest levels, but Constantinople's right to name senators, *patricii,* and the Western consuls—on the suggestion of Ravenna—was left untouched.[198] Theodoric possessed high justice and the right of pardon over all inhabitants of Italy; he also held in fact the supreme power in ecclesiastical affairs. All these responsibilities far exceeded Theodoric's former authority as *magister militum.*[199]

Because Theodoric secured peace within Italy, he could also keep house like an emperor. The still rich land filled Ravenna's treasury and prospered not least because Theodoric carried through sensible economic measures, such as a reform of the coinage, and took an active interest in economic policies.[200] The general welfare was also served by the promulgation of the famous Edictum Theoderici, which on the one hand modernized Roman imperial law and adapted it to the existing circumstances, but on the other hand in no way interfered with the prerogatives of imperial legislation. In Theodoric's Italy territorial law, from which no one was exempt, was in force.[201] How in conflicting cases this law was accommodated to the Gothic legal tradition, the *belagines*,[202] we are not told.

The surplus that very quickly accumulated was used for an intensive, if restaurative, building program. The government erected representational buildings and functional structures (such as aqueducts) as well as fortifications. The aqueduct of Trajan in Ravenna arose in new splendor. The royal city, however, saw more than renovation and restoration. Theodoric's magnificent architectural adornment of Ravenna is the foremost achievement of his era; more than any other action it deserves to be called "creative." Rome too still made an overwhelming impression on an African who visited the *caput mundi* during Theodoric's tricennial celebration in 500. In addition, we know of cities founded by the Gothic king, among which the mysterious The(o)doricopolis in Raetia even bears his name.[203]

On one thing the king and his Goths were agreed: the emperor's prerogatives, such as the assumption of the title *imperator,* the wearing of imperial robes, the appointment of consuls, *patricii,* and senators, and the right of legislating, remained in a formal sense untouched, even though Theodoric the Great must have looked almost like a real emperor. His royal monogram followed Eastern models, his glittering scale-armor was imperial, the figure of Victory on the orb in his left hand and his right hand raised in the imperial gesture of *adlocutio* have an air of universal dominion. But no matter to what lengths the *imitatio imperii* might go, significant characteristics of the royal image remained Gothic. Both the jewel of Bern and the gold medallion of Senigallia "show the king with the characteristic closely trimmed mustache of the Goths, and both artifacts depict him with a strong, totally un-Roman head of hair."[204] Theodoric also refrained from making any significant changes in the practice and structure of the internal administration. The possession of the royal city and the royal treasure had the same function among the Ostrogoths that it had in Toulouse. Ravenna was the most important royal residence on the peninsula, unless circumstances compelled the adoption of alternative arrangements. From 490 to 493 and after 540 the Ligurian fortress Ticinum-Pavia was the capital of the Gothic kingdom. Between 549 and 552 Totila tried to establish the city of Rome as a royal residence. And even after Teja's catastrophe, a remnant of Ostrogothic statehood held out in Cumae until the Franks arrived there in the winter of 553/554.[205]

Theodoric's state, the dominion over "Goths and Italians," combined the *principatus populi Romani* with a *regnum gentis*. The king wanted his Goths to recognize *civilitas,* the rule of law. In this regard the Goths were to imitate the Romans, not the reverse.[206] Thus the *exercitus Gothorum* had to give up some of its personal law. The tax exemption for the soldiers in the federate army was limited to the original allotments. The government compensated for the tax liability of newly acquired property by donatives.[207]

What remained of the barbarian tradition was pride in being an Amal Goth, which was celebrated in heroic songs extolling the divine origins of the royal clan. The "magnificent splendor of the Amali" could influence politics. Within the Roman Empire Amal blood became the ticket of admission into the nobility, and among the tribes Theodoric's race was the "most noble," as long as its charisma worked. It is true that the Gothic king owed this charisma basically to his Amal descent. But without his rise from chief of a wandering Balkan tribe to envoy of the emperor and lord of Italy, the widely branched family tree of the Ansis, which began with gods and demi-gods, would have remained dead capital. After all, Sidimund, the Andela-Andagis clan, Theodoric Strabo, and Vidimir the Younger all had the same ancestors as Theodoric the Great. Yet history knows them only in connection with the latter.[208]

Exercitus Gothorum

COMITES GOTHORUM, DUCES, SAIONES, MILLENARII, MEDIOCRES, CAPILLATI

Theodoric surpassed Odovacar not only in power but in time, for he had the opportunity to finish what his predecessor had begun. In other words, Theodoric's Italian kingdom was a more stable, richer, and stronger version of Odovacar's *regnum.*[209] This kingdom consisted of the Italian prefecture without Africa, a large area administered by Romans and certainly of imperial dimensions. Whereas the Goths of Toulouse grew only gradually into an *imitatio imperii,* Odovacar and Theodoric adopted this posture from the moment they became rulers of Italy, which is why they continued the late antique state without a break. That state possessed a highly specialized and differentiated bureaucracy.[210] It had always been the custom for the emperor to supervise official bureaucratic channels by means of special agents, *comites.* Theodoric appropriated this right, which the Goths of Toulouse also used, and consolidated it into the *comitiva Gothorum*.[211] Those who held these positions were all selected from the *exercitus Gothorum*. They placed themselves in deliberate competition with the Roman civil bureaucracy, the *militia Romana*.[212] A *comes Gothorum* had the right to use the staff of the Roman authorities. He was charged with military tasks and possessed the judicial power that accompanied them, but in disputes between Goths and Romans he could exercise such authority only in consultation with Roman lawyers.[213] In this way Theodoric had added an ethnic component to Diocletian's system of overlapping spheres of competence.

In times of peace a Gothic *comes* was usually responsible for a *civitas*, which was also the case in the kingdom of Toulouse. But in those *civitates* that had few or no Gothic-barbarian settlers *(millenarii, mediocres, capillati)* but instead had field units, the sphere of competence of the *comes Gothorum civitatis* could be extended to include the entire province. The idea that groups of several *comites civitatum* were subordinated to a higher ranking *comes Gothorum provinciae* is erroneous. Rather, the *formula comitivae provinciae* of Cassiodorus applied precisely to a *comes civitatis* who held an extended command: such was the *comes* of Salona who was in charge of the combined provinces of Dalmatia and Savia. Likewise, the *comes* of Syracuse had the command over all of Sicily, the *comes* of Naples over no less than the entire coast of Campania, and the *comes* of Marseille over at least the southern half of Ostrogothic Gaul, if not over all of it. Finally, following the example of the Dalmatian-Savian command, a *comes* was situated in Sirmium to oversee the province of Pannonia II (Sirmiensis). While Dalmatia and Savia also had civil governors, the *comes* of Pannonia Sirmiensis—established in 508—exercised both military and civil authority. *Comites* with an extended sphere of command were *viri illustres*, whereas the regular *comes civitatis* was only a *vir spectabilis*, unless he was sent as special envoy of Theodoric to Rome.[214]

The military and social structures of the Gothic army were almost identical. The rich and powerful were the *comites et duces*; the first title expressed affiliation with the royal entourage, the *comitatus*,[215] and the second the function of military leadership.[216] In war the title *dux* entailed an independent command in place of the king, who since the capture of Ravenna in 493—and probably following the imperial model—no longer went into the field in person. Only once, in 508, did Theodoric shift the court from Ravenna to Ligurian Pavia in order to be closer to the theater of the Gallic war.[217] *Duces* such as Pitz(i)a along the Sava, Ibba in southern Gaul and Spain, or Tuluin against the Burgundians, stood high above the commanders of frontier militias, such as the *dux Raetiarum*. While the latter probably came from a local Roman family and was a *vir spectabilis,* the Gothic generals of the mobile army were *viri illustres.*[218]

Although subjection to the Huns and the period of migration had not caused the old Gothic nobility to disappear, wealth and position determined an individual's rank, which was based largely on how close the individual was to the king. Thus the *armiger* or *spatharius* was a confidant of the king with the rank of *comes.* A sword-bearer could make a splendid career, even if he did not come from one of the best families. Until the middle of the sixth century nearly all non-Amal Gothic kings belonged to such "clans of sword-bearers."[219] The *comites et primates gentis,* the king's representatives and the "first" men of the tribe, formed the leadership stratum of the Gothic army. They determined the succession to the kingship and could even offer it to someone who did not belong to the tribe.[220] Theodoric's powerful rule exercised a strong, though not exclusive, influence on the composition of that elite. The personal style of the king's rule, however, aimed at addressing every free Goth and warrior of the Gothic army (*millenarius, mediocris, capillatus*) and at dealing with him directly. True, this goal was often nothing more than a good intention, but the possibility of getting to know capable men "among the common people" and of recruiting them into royal service existed and was utilized.[221] Theodoric did not pursue a hostile policy toward the nobility; most likely he sought to create a general and uniform class of Gothic and Roman subjects. A man's descent from a good family and his loyalty were frequently cited as reasons for his appointment to a certain office. Just as the royal house had ties of kinship to the leadership of both peoples, the king drew in equal measures upon the Gothic and Roman nobility.[222] If we leave aside the revolt of the nobility under Amalasuintha, the sources give only the names of two Gothic *comites* of high nobility whom Theodoric executed.[223]

Whoever wanted to make an illustrious career for himself had to go to court at a young age. There he was at first employed as a page. If he proved himself capable, he rose to the rank of an "eminent man of the royal house" (*maior domus*).[224] The men who gained the confidence of the king belonged to the nobility of the court, the *proceres palatii,* and were part of the king's permanent entourage, the *comitatus.* Although this group was not composed exclusively of Goths, they formed the majority.[225] The act of summoning a man to Ravenna to become a member of the *comitatus* even had a separate formula, which clearly reveals a Roman-imperial model. The most important task of the *comitatus* was its function as a palace court for both Romans and Goths. Although Pope Gelasius protested vigorously that clerics were allowed to appeal to a court that "even included barbarians," under Athalaric even the appointment of bishops was decided in the *comitatus*. The royal *comitatus* had decided in its own favor the rivalry with the traditional *consistorium,* in which the Romans formed the majority even though the highest ranking Gothic *comites* also belonged to it.[226]

Apart from the military-judicial positions, two other positions were open to Goths and presupposed a close relationship with the king: that of the *comes patrimonii,* the only exception in the civil administration, and that of the *praepositus cubiculi.* The patrimony had been created under Odovacar in order to separate royal property from the regular treasury. This innovation proved so successful that under the emperor Anastasius it became an institution of Roman government in the East. The Western patrimony, however, was in competition not only with the traditional financial administration but also with regular provincial government. Head of the provinces was the highest civil servant of the Italian prefecture, the *praefectus praetorio.* All the provinces that Odovacar had taken over when he assumed power remained subordinated to the prefect. But what the Italian king conquered within the Italian prefecture he regarded as his separate property. Thus in 476 Sicily and in 481 Dalmatia became part of the "royal house, which the Romans call *patrimonium.*" In 491 Theodoric redeemed the last claims of the Vandals to the island of Sicily and left the bipartite provincial administration as he found it. The Savia was probably organized only by Theodoric and then joined to Dalmatia. To the patrimony was added in 508 Pannonia Sirmiensis, which had been conquered a few years before and had "once formed the border of Italy." In the same year the territory as far as the Rhone became Ostrogothic and thus part of the "Italian Empire." In 510 at the latest Theodoric established a separate administration there by reviving the Gallic prefecture with its seat in Arles. From that time the Ostrogothic kingdom comprised two territorially unequal prefectures of the old *regnum Hesperium.*

From the prefecture and the *patrimonium,* both Roman administrative bodies, we must differentiate the *cubiculum* as a Gothic institution. The *praepositus cubiculi* was always a Goth. As the head of the "royal bed chamber" he supervised the chamberlains and eunuchs at the court and guarded the royal treasure. When Theodoric was king of the Visigothic kingdom between 511 and 526, the taxes of the *universa Hispania* went to the treasury and thus to the *cubiculum.*[227]

The head of the central administration at Ravenna was the *magister officiorum.* This high-level Roman bureaucrat exercised in traditional fashion a wealth of functions, of which some, however, had become empty formalities. Thus he "supervised" the palace guard, but its members had been sent into retirement by Theodoric and had been replaced by Gothic bodyguards. Naturally these men were placed under the command of the *comes spatharius,* who was a Goth. But the *magister officiorum* represented—at least in theory—a sort of controlling authority for the entire administration, a task for which he employed, in the king's name, the *comitiaci.* These emissaries were dispatched with direct royal orders and supervised their implementation in the civil sphere.[228] In keeping with the two-track nature of regal barbarian rule, there was also a Gothic counterpart to the *comitiacus.* Just as the holders of the *comitiva Gothorum* ensured that the interests of the king and the army were safeguarded even far from the court, there was also need for Gothic agents whom the king could send into the provinces. As Goths they were military personnel, but in the king's name they could exercise both military and civilian tasks. They were called *saiones* and thus had the same name as the lower-ranking Visigothic retainers whom any lord could keep in his entourage. In contrast, the Ostrogothic *saio* had taken on special significance: he was the messenger of the king and the bearer of direct royal orders. All officials were directed and controlled by the *saiones*; this also included the *praefectus praetorio.* *Saiones* came onto the scene especially when the king "had something to discuss" with his Goths: the movement of troops, the summoning of people before the palace court, even if they held rank, interference in Gothic practices and customs—all these things were properly among the tasks of the *saiones.* Only for a few was the position of *saio* the beginning of a career; careerists are rare among the *saiones.*[229] Above all a *saio* could be used to extend to a certain person the privilege of the king's protection, the *tuitio.* The state of late antiquity and the political system of the *gentilitas* outside the empire certainly had one element in common: they both posed a constant threat to the individual's liberty. Theodoric's *civilitas* was often enough preached to deaf ears.[230] The subordination of the Gothic army to Roman territorial law had to compete with the obsolete Gothic "customs," the *belagines;*[231] acts of violence and violation of the law by the powerful could be prevented only occasionally.[232] Even noble Gothic women beat each other until one of them succumbed.[233] The least sign of weakness could mean the loss of economic and legal status of the free man.[234] People such as Theodoric's nephew Theodahad did not shrink from cheating their Gothic brothers out of their property,[235] thereby exposing them to slavery. But if the man who faced such a threat could reach the king in time, he could possibly divert the danger for a while.[236] A final and important task of the *saio* was control over the means of transport and over the food supply.[237]

We have virtually no information about the commanders of the smaller divisions of the Gothic army. On one occasion they are given the rather colorless name *duces et praepositi,* "commanders and superiors." Nor are we in any position to say what the units under their command were called, provided they had a fixed name. Unlike the Toulousan *millenarius,* his Ostrogothic namesake was no "leader of a unit of one thousand men," no commander of a military *millena,* but the owner of a *sors* that comprised one or more *millenae.*[238] A contingent of Gepidic warriors on the march through Italy was made up of household units (*condomae*), but these were supply units assembled for this particular occasion.[239]

THE SETTLEMENT OF THE GOTHIC ARMY

In the introduction to his account of the Gothic war Procopius writes that Odovacar gained the victory over Orestes because he had fulfilled the demand of the federate warriors that they be assigned "the third part of the entire Italian land." After Odovacar's defeat Theodoric's troops then took over this property.[240] This is also what Cassiodorus seems to imply when he recalled the Gothic settlement about fifteen years after it had taken place: since 493, he says, "the landholdings of the Goths and the Romans, like their hearts, have been bound together through the assignment of the third-shares." The "community of landholding" (*praediorum communio*) had created such an atmosphere of harmony that "both peoples [*utraque natio*] lived together and desired the same." Goths and Romans had been joined together by the "division of the landed property" (*cespitis divisio*). "The friendship between the peoples grew in strength through this loss, and in return for a portion of the land [*pars agri*] a defender was gained, so that the complete protection of the property was assured." Other passages in Cassiodorus's *Variae* give us similar information, and bishop Ennodius's praise of Liberius says much the same.[241] It is therefore not at all surprising that historical interpretation, trained on literary texts, reached the "obvious" conclusion that the Romans had to turn over a third of the land to the Goths as the successors to Odovacar's troops.[242] But this view is wrong, and for the reconstruction of what really happened we are indebted primarily to the efforts of Jean Durliat and Walter Goffart.[243]

Theodoric had charged Liberius with carrying out the settlement of the Goths. As an Italian senator and a relative of those Romans of the high nobility who had early offered their services to Theodoric's regime, Liberius was the ideal man for the job, despite his youth. Although he had remained faithful to Odovacar until the latter's death, as early as 493 he became the

Italian praetorian prefect of the Gothic king, who immediately assigned to him the delicate task of organizing the settlement. The manner in which Liberius accomplished his task prompted great relief and lasting astonishment among the Romans. Apparently they had expected a much more oppressive arrangement.[244] As late as 535/536 King Theodahad still claimed that the settlement of the Ostrogoths could not be compared to that of the barbarian peoples, who also included the Visigoths.[245] And in fact the terms *hospitium* and *hospitalitas* were not used for describing the settlement of Theodoric's army. It is not impossible that the Cassiodoran *civilitas*, the social, legal, and economic coexistence of Romans and foreigners based on law, was deliberately opposed to the barbarian solution, to the *hospitalitas* in Gaul.[246]

All this leaves the conclusion that no landed property was confiscated in order to settle the Gothic army and provide its economic base. The needed resources were drawn instead from shares of the regular tax revenues. The difficulties that the terminology has caused our understanding of the issue can be explained by the fact that the language of Roman fiscal law can also use the various designations for landed property and its subunits to describe the expected tax intake from a given unit of land. In other words, according to fiscal law terms such as *praedium, c(a)espes, iugerum, iugum vel millena* do not indicate a landed estate or parts thereof (as in private law) but the tax owed on it. Hence, if an agricultural unit called *iugum vel millena* produced a yearly tax intake of two solidi, this sum of revenue could also be called *iugum vel millena*. Whenever it was possible and meaningful to do so, the tax money collected was spent by the local authorities on the spot to pay for public services and governmental salaries.[247] This arrangement followed old custom and was nothing new. Thus in the state's books the *annona* in the revenue column represented the regular tax and in the expense column the unit of payment for all servants of the state, civil as well as military *militiae*.[248]

The "third part of the entire land of Italy"[249] did not therefore consist of expropriated land but represented the third (*tertia[e]*) of the regular tax (*annona, canon*). This third formed the *sors* that was assigned as the basic tax-exempt provision to the allotted Goths (*Gothi deputati*). Insofar as this *sors* comprised one or more *millenae* (tax units), the Gothic recipients could also be called *millenarii*.[250] To this basic allotment were added extraordinary donatives which the king distributed in person in Ravenna at various times. On that occasion also, the courage of each one was examined, so that "no one would be deprived of what he had accomplished in battle."[251]

Although it could happen that a rich senator would support out of his own money (*patrimonium*) not only the army but also the "allotted Goths," thus easing the burden that weighed on the curias as well as on the royal treasury, the payment of the Gothic *sors* was, as in the Visigothic kingdom, in the hands of the city curiales. Ever since the reform of the fourth century, the curiales, "nerves of the state and entrails of the cities," as *possessores* were responsible not only for raising the tax revenue of their *civitates* but also for supervising the regional allocation of the revenues. The monies were divided between the local curial administration and the state in the ratio of 1:2. The taxes were paid in money, in kind, or in services. The sums at the disposal of the curiales were called *tertia* (*pars, portio*), while the central treasury (*sacrae largitiones*) administered the other two-thirds, the accounts of which had to be squared with the praetorian prefect, who represented the agency that set the tax and distributed the intake. The highest agency assigned half of the remaining two-thirds to the army and half to the court and its departments. The actual distribution of the money, however, took place in a decentralized fashion by the individual curias. The late antique state thus allocated one third of its tax yield to the army, one third to the court and its central departments, and one third for the local needs of the *civitates*. Hence, in Gothic Italy one could follow the example of Odovacar and assign the first third to Theodoric's army, as *sors* or *annona*, while the other two-thirds belonged to the *militia Romana*, the central top-level bureaucracy, and to the agencies of curial self-government. The royal court at Ravenna, in contrast, probably lived mostly, if not exclusively, from the royal *patrimonium*. This was facilitated by the fact that the *comitiva patrimonii* administered not only the former imperial domains but even entire provinces, namely, Sicily, Dalmatia, and southern Pannonia. Revealing are the efforts of those *civitates* that had seen no Gothic settlement to let the *tertia(e)* merge with the general tax instead of having to account for it as a separate offset item. Although such a move did not in any way change the tax liability, the local authorities were suspicious of the "name of the third." In all likelihood the point of the efforts was to prevent anyone from getting the idea to send Gothic warriors with their following to the *civitates* that were still free.[252]

Theodoric settled his Goths according to strategic considerations and, in view of the small number of his troops, in regional concentrations. Gothic Italy felt threatened above all from the east. The Gothic military settlements were therefore centered in modern-day Lombardy and Venetia. Tuscany and the Marches, where the outer fort of Auximum-Osimo was located, were safeguarded in a similar fashion. In addition, Goths were to be found in Dalmatia, both on the mainland as well as on the offshore islands. But the Goths did not settle everywhere as *vicini et consortes* of the Romans to live with or among them. In those areas that saw very little permanent settlement or none at all, mobile units were placed in garrisons: in Sicily and Italy south of the line that the Via Valeria drew from Rome to Pescara, in the outer fort of the Aosta valley, in the endangered border regions of Gaul, in Visigothic Spain, in inner Dalmatia, and in the "former home of the Goths," Pannonia Sirmiensis. Like their predecessors, the members of the Roman field army, these Gothic troops were called *milites* and received the *annona* as their usual pay. But we must distinguish them from the local militias who were also called *milites,* and who as successors to the *limitanei,* the soldiers of the Roman border troops, defended the Alpine region.[253]

In principle every Goth was liable for active military service. Exemptions were granted only in case of illness or old age. Theodoric had to struggle constantly against economic setbacks, but on the whole his economic policies seem to have been a success. Although on occasion it was necessary to prohibit the export of certain foodstuffs it is reported that during Theodoric's reign one solidus would buy as much as sixty bushels of grain or thirty amphoras of wine. If that is true, a Gothic soldier could have purchased with an extraordinary donative of, say, five solidi a one-year supply of grain for eight to ten people. The money had to be picked up in Ravenna in person, an arrangement that was entirely in keeping with the personal style of leadership of a king of the army. The march to Ravenna was considered active military service, and the soldiers received expense money (*exercituales expensae* [*annona*]), as compensation.[254] This was intended to reduce the plundering that a marching army might undertake. Apart from the review of the forces, movement of troops was of course also necessary for military reasons, and the provincials were compensated for such troop movements through their region. Nevertheless, the patience of the affected population was often sorely tested.[255]

Whatever the members of the Gothic army did not consume they could invest in landed property. This made them owners and subject to taxation, even if they resisted it. Together with his property the Gothic warrior received a charter (*pittacium*) drawn up by an authorized agent (*delegator*). King Theodoric set for this procedure the date of August 28, 489, the day he had crossed the Isonzo with his Gothic army. As early as the second decade after his entry into Italy Theodoric made all illegal or irregular acquisitions that had taken place prior to this fixed date subject to the thirty-year statute of limitation (*tricennium*). The king himself tried to contain encroachments by the Goths. He did not even shrink from twice summoning before the palace court his own relative Theodahad, the "king of Tuscany who was unwilling to tolerate any neighbors," in order to censure his greediness, which he had dressed up with Platonic philosophy and readings from the Church Fathers. The members of the royal family and possibly other Gothic magnates (*comites et primates gentis*) owned property in land and people, which was accordingly called *patrimonium*, like the senatorial family estates. It is hard to imagine that these *massae* were subject to taxation.[257] The king himself took over the royal *patrimonium* Odovacar had created. It comprised and administered the former imperial landholdings and, in competition with the *comitiva rerum privatarum,* the private property of the ruler, which might include entire provinces. The royal domains can be attested in the Po Valley, in Apulia, and in Sicily. In addition a very rich royal *patrimonium,* which Theodahad tried to appropriate illegally, lay in Tuscany. During the many negotiations Theodahad conducted with Constantinople when he was king, Justinian at one time even offered him the ownership of all Italian domains if he renounced the kingship. The royal estates were only in exceptional cases subject to taxation. For example, it was ordered that the domains share the burden of the construction of a fortification in the economically weak *civitas* of Tridentum.[256]

The settlement of the Gothic army could have varied consequences both for the individual Gothic warrior and his following as well as for the Roman "neighbors and partners" (*vicini et consortes*). Leaving aside the king, his family, and the most prominent members of the comitatus, the following arrangements were made to satisfy the "victorious Goths." (1) Entitled Goths were assigned to certain *civitates,* where they lived side by side with the Romans and received from the curiales lodging as well as an appropriate share (*sors*) of the third (*tertia*) of the regular land tax (*annona* or *canon*). Since the tax was calculated from the land unit *iugum vel millena,* the settled Goths were also called millenarii. Nothing is said about the size of the yearly payments, except that they "fed" the Goths. The sources are also silent on the criteria that entitled a Goth to such an allocation, but personal freedom as well as a certain level of wealth were no doubt prerequisites. (2) The customary salary, *annona,* was paid to the conscripted units, both to the troops (*milites*) quartered in barracks for an indefinite length of time as well as to any Goth millenarias, as soon as he served active time in the army. The milites stationed in the royal patrimonial provinces were paid from the *patrimonium,* which after all took in the taxes of the provincials who lived there. The Goths who made up the units quartered in barracks for extended periods, perhaps even permanently, may have been drawn from economically weaker groups, such as younger sons. (3) Extraordinary donatives were paid to the members of group one, who "were enriched" by them, and to special units such as the free sailors of the fleet built in 526. Between 511 and 526, Theodoric supposedly gave the entire income from Spain as a "yearly gift" (δῶρον ἐπέτειον) to the Spanish army made up of Ostrogoths and Visigoths. (4) Tax liability for all Goths and barbarians who had acquired property "no matter under what title." (5) Free and unfree retainers were to be maintained by their respective lords.[258]

POLYETHNICITY, SOCIAL STATUS, AND COMPULSORY MILITARY SERVICE

Theodoric led to Italy not the entire Ostrogothic people but a federate army composed mainly of Ostrogoths. As a Roman high magistrate and king of these Goths, Theodoric was in an ideal position to turn his army into a new Gothic people, but the actual ethnogenesis also involved non-Gothic elements.[259] Within the framework of this process the Rugi of Frideric preserved the greatest degree of independence. They had joined Theodoric's Goths but did not intermarry with them when they settled together in a northern Italian district. After the debacles of the years 540 and 541 they felt strong enough to proclaim one of their own king of the Goths.[260] Smaller groups and splinter groups of various tribes were of course integrated more quickly into Theodoric's people. The commander of Avignon in 508 was called Vandil, a *saio* of Theodoric's had the Alan name Candac, and a Milanese tribune the Celtic name Bacauda.[261] This fundamental polyethnic character of the Gothic army was intensified after the defeat of Odovacar's army. Considerable contingents of the Western army joined Theodoric, whereby additional Rugian, Herulian, Scirian, Turcilingian as well as Suevic, Sarmatian, and Taifalian elements became "Gothic." The same applies to the "old barbarians" (*antiqui barbari*) of Pannonia-Savia who owed taxes and military service. But they were not the only ones who had married Roman women: the wives of the Goths Brandila and Patza were called Procula and Regina and may have been Romans.[262] No doubt the victory over Odovacar also increased the number of Romans in the Gothic army. As provincials they were by late antique law excluded from obligatory military service, but there were Romans who were "Goths at heart" and who very much "belonged" to the Gothic army.[263] Furthermore, there existed a regional military organization. For the construction, maintenance, and garrisoning of the cities and fortresses not only the locally settled Gothic landowners were called upon but of course also the Romans. The

same was true for religious minorities such as the Jews. When Belisarius
was besieging Naples in 536, the Jews organized the supplies and acquitted
themselves well in open battle. Totila, however, accused the Sicilians of
having repaid with ingratitude the preferential treatment they had received
from Theodoric—Gothic troops had been stationed only in Syracuse and
Palermo—and of having failed to put up any resistance to Byzantine aggres-
sion.[264] No Goths were settled in and north of the Alps, but in this area
Ravenna could not allow a military vacuum to arise. In Raetia a native *dux*
commanded the native border troops (*limitanei*). Also under his command
were the wild Breoni of the Tirolian Alps. Needless to say, these unruly and
violent people were oblivious to the much praised Ostrogothic *civilitas*.
But as federates of the Goths they at least safeguarded important Alpine
passes. Noricum was organized in the same way as Raetia.[265]

In the first decade of the sixth century, three other Germanic *gentes* joined
Theodoric's army.[266] In the offensive of 508 the Gothic force captured the
Gepids, who had remained behind in Sirmium, the "former homeland of
the Goths." Thereafter Gepidic contingents served not only as frontier garrisons in the east but were also transferred to Gaul. Individual members of
that tribe even came to Italy.[267] The "old barbarians" of Savian-Suevic
Pannonia had already become Gothic by the time of Theodoric's assumption
of power in Italy, but they are not found outside their own region.[268] In
507 the "old barbarians" probably received an influx from the Alamanni.
Vitigis still called up the Pannonian Suevi in the war against Byzantium;
however, shortly thereafter they became Lombardic.[269] Almost simultaneously with the reception of Alamannic refugees, Ravenna was obliged to
accept one of the three Herulian units into which that tribe had split after
its defeat by the Lombards.[270]

To be a Goth, that is, to enjoy the "freedom of the Goths," and to march
in the Gothic army were the same thing. But no individual was immune
from losing that freedom. If a Goth was threatened with loss of his rights
and liberty, proof that he had served in the army was sufficient to protect
his personal freedom.[271] Whoever belonged to the Gothic army was automatically of age; in one instance a dishonest guardian was ordered to hand
over his nephew's property.[272] Those Goths who fulfilled their obligatory
active service far from home were entitled to special protection for their
families and their property.[273] We know the name of honor of Gothic
freemen from their songs: they were called the "curly-haired or long-haired
ones" (*capillati*). In Ravenna there was apparently a tendency to understand
by that term all able-bodied "barbarians." In this case the term would
herald the transformation of the Gothic army with its various peoples into

a general class of subjects bound to the king by an oath. Theodoric would have accordingly used the word *capillatus* in a way similar to the Carolingian kings' use of the word *liber*.[274]

The army on the march held out the promise of social mobility and attracted the native underclasses. At the time of migration this attraction was useful, for it helped to relieve the chronic shortage of manpower.[275] But in Italy the *coloni* were needed in the fields, not on the battlefields.[276] Since Theodoric had staked his future on the consolidation of his kingdom, he prohibited the Roman *coloni* from joining the Gothic army.[277] But the old attraction was still alive when the Ostrogothic kingdom was fighting for its survival. Totila not only accepted Roman slaves and *coloni* into the Gothic army but even mobilized them against their senatorial masters, promising them freedom and the ownership of land.[278] These measures are all too easily misread as a sociorevolutionary program of the Gothic king.[279] Totila merely made possible and provided a cover for something the Roman underclass had been prepared to do from the third century: to "become Goths" out of despair over their economic situation.[280]

OSTROGOTHIC WEAPONS AND FIGHTING TECHNIQUES

Like the Ostrogothic Greutungi in southern Russia and the Visigoths in France and Spain,[281] the Italian Ostrogoths were primarily horsemen. The mounted warrior enjoyed the highest esteem. Theodoric Strabo could heap no greater insult on the Goths of his cousin Theodoric than to ride up in front of their camp dressed in splendid armor, reminding them that they all had once owned two or three horses but now had to go on foot like slaves.[282] This mockery does not mean that a "real" Gothic army was composed exclusively of horsemen who only in an emergency switched to fighting as infantrymen. In Theodoric's army, as in that of his successors, there were foot warriors who had specific tactical tasks.[283] But even when the infantry fulfilled its tasks in a disciplined manner, it was the cavalry that dealt the decisive blow.[284] The Gothic horseman was much like the lance rider of other nomadic peoples.[285] He has a predecessor in the galloping Sarmatian seen on the tombstone of Tanais[286] and successors in the Lombards portrayed on the Florentine shield decoration and on the silver plate of Isola Rizza[287] or in the "victorious prince" on the famous gold jug of Nagyszentmiklós.[288] A warrior of this kind ideally wore a helmet with protection for his neck and cheeks[289] and was dressed in a flexible suit of armor, not necessarily of metal, which reached down at least to his knees.[290] He wielded with both hands the extra-long thrusting lance, the *contus,* to which a pennant was afixed,[291] and he carried a sword and buckler as secondary weapons for close combat on horseback or on foot.[292] The warriors sat on armored horses[293] and galloped toward the enemy "with long lances held in close formation."[294]

Gothic attitudes, such as their great esteem for the "white-spotted horse" or the "Thuringian" charger, their weapons, and the tactics of the Gothic armies remained relatively unchanged during their entire history. The Italian weapons factories, which maintained their complex production under Theodoric's special care, and the royal stables, which even in times of crisis remained remarkably productive, may well have provided war material in larger quantities and especially of better quality than what the Pannonian Ostrogoths and Scythian Greutungi had known;[295] yet a fundamental change in the type of armament or in attitudes and tactics did not occur. The fatal charge to which Totila ordered his lancers in the battle of Busta Gallorum in 552 sprang from the same mentality and tactics that in many earlier battles had led to victory. Procopius's books are full of such stories,[296] which do not differ fundamentally from the best known examples of success or failure of Gothic cavalry attacks, namely, the battles of Adrianople and Vouillé.[297] The many duels the author describes were fought in the same manner. They usually took place as single combat between a mounted Gothic barbarian and an identically armed Roman barbarian. Both charged and tried through skillful maneuvering to pierce the enemy with the lance. It is true that in Procopius the "Roman" always won, but only because he was more skillful and not because he used a different style of fighting. The same is true on a larger scale; the hostile armies used the same tactics.[298] Thus many times the charge of evenly matched enemies riding without stirrups[299] ended in "mutual suicide."

The characteristic elements of Gothic tactics are the lightning-quick attack launched from an ambush and accompanied by loud war cries; outflanking maneuvers to attack the enemy's infantry from the rear;[300] riding the horses hard and fast in the hope of dealing a decisive blow before the horses were exhausted;[301] quick retreat behind the lines of one's own foot warriors in case the attack failed; and gathering new forces for another attack, possibly reinforced by reserves.[302] Both the strength and weakness of the Gothic army lay in its one-sidedness. The relatively simple manner of fighting could be easily practiced and thoroughly trained, a fact of which Theodoric the Great used to satisfy himself in person.[303] If the enemy neglected the necessary reconnaissance[304] or lacked discipline, a Gothic cavalry attack could easily cause the intended panic. For if the enemy lines wavered or even broke, there was soon no way of stopping the attackers.

Just as the Heruli were used in all armies as light-armed troops,[305] the Gothic horsemen served not only in the Gothic army. The Eastern Roman armies of the generals Belisarius and Narses in particular were characterized by a high degree of specialization in their fighting techniques and tactics, the various tasks being carried out by different ethnic units. In the polyethnic confederation of such an army the Goths were often more successful than under Gothic leadership.[306] Even the great Theodoric was never able to defeat a Roman army that was well put together from different military branches—that is to say, different "peoples"—and led with determination. This is not to mention that in the long run Vitigis would have been no match for a Belisarius nor Totila for a Narses.

Belisarius is said to have attributed the decisive weakness of the Goths to the lack of heavily armed mounted archers.[307] This would also explain Totila's seemingly senseless order to his horsemen in the battle of Busta Gallorum to use only the lance. The attack collapsed in the shower of arrows launched by the "Hunnic" archers.[308] Procopius considered the mounted archer of his time—well protected by armor and equipped with a curved bow, sword, shield, and lance—the "miracle weapon" of the Romans.[309] In contrast, the Goths only had archers on foot; their mobility was limited and hence they were extremely vulnerable.[310] But we should not underestimate the Gothic foot warrior.[311] The Crimean Goths once resisted a Hunnic cavalry charge by forming a "fence" with their shields and thrusting their long lances against the attackers.[312] In mountainous Moesia Theodoric employed a large number of infantry against Bulgarian horsemen and was just as successful as his father Thiudimir, who had conducted a victorious winter campaign with an "army on foot."[313] But because the socially disadvantaged fought on foot, they were dependent for the most part on the supply of public weapons. When Theodoric's training stopped and his supply system collapsed—which did not happen, however, until after the capitulation of Vitigis—the training and equipment of the infantry became irregular and insufficient.[314] Perhaps this was one of the reasons why the Gothic infantry failed completely in the battle of Busta Gallorum even though under Vitigis before Rome it had fought effectively.[315]

A Lombard shield decoration of the seventh century might give us an idea of the appearance of the Gothic foot soldier: he would have had a *contus,* a sword along with a buckler, and a battle tunic that reached below the knees and served as protection against long-range weapons.[316]

Procopius's description of the Gothic style of warfare appears to contradict the description of Vegetius from the beginning of the fifth century. The latter considered it a "Gothic" tactic that mounted archers showered their enemy with arrows. But Vegetius is describing the three-tribe confederation of Goths, Huns, and Alans and shows that he uses the adjectives "Gothic" and "Hunnic" as synonyms. Thus at that time the Gothic cavalry already relied on the *contus* and the mounted nomads had become archers.[317] According to the *Origo Gothica* this was also the arrangement at the battle of Nedao.[318]

As seaworthy as the Goths may have seemed in the third century,[319] the sea remained foreign to them after their admission into the Roman Empire. This is true both for the Ostrogoths and the Visigoths.[320] Although it is likely that in Epirus Theodoric had thought of procuring ships,[321] as king of Italy he did without a fleet until shortly before his death. In naval matters the Amal relied on the Vandal kingdom until that doubtful ally deserted him for good. After the murder of his sister by the new ruler of Carthage, Theodoric ordered a campaign of revenge. Construction began on a gigantic fleet, but Theodoric died before it was completed.[322] Thereafter Ravenna had at its disposal only light sailing vessels for Amal queens eager to escape.[323] Moreover, the fishing fleet remained intact; Theodoric had exempted their crews from the naval buildup so as not to endanger this significant element in the Italian food supply.[324] Totila was late in recognizing the value of a fleet in the war against Constantinople, but this alone did not turn the Gothic landlubbers into real seamen. Even if the crews were made up of "able-bodied" warriors commanded by an officer corps of Byzantine deserters, they nevertheless remained Goths for whom water was an uncomfortable element. It is not surprising that they acted as "marine infantry" and tried to fight land battles at sea. The outcome was correspondingly disastrous.[325] In the end the last Gothic admiral deserted to the Romans and handed over the fleet that was protecting King Teja and the rest of his Goths in the bay of Naples. This betrayal sealed the fate of the last Gothic king.[326]

Only late do we read about an Ostrogothic artillery.[327] For the time of Totila and Teja we find evidence of strategic warfare: with the help of dikes and ditches the Via Postumia along the Po river and other routes as well were flooded, bridges were destroyed, and paths made impassable.[328] But the exploitation of environmental elements must have been easier for the Goths than the "city-hopping" that the Romans forced upon them and that required good siege engineers.[329] Starving out the enemy, hoping for treason within the city walls, and cutting off the water lines—this was almost the entire repertoire of Gothic siege techniques, even if Vitigis's destruction of the aqueducts profoundly influenced the future water supply of Rome and thus the future history of the Eternal City. But the greater the size of a city—after all, the Goths twice captured Rome and only Ravenna remained closed to them after 540—the greater the difficulty in holding it once taken.[330] When Vitigis lifted the siege of Rome in March 538, he dealt his kingship the fatal blow. And when in April 547 the imperial forces captured Rome for the second time, Totila's reputation among the *gentes* suffered irreparable damage.[331]

But Italy's wealth of cities was also an advantage for the Goths. Thus Verona, Theodoric's second residence, and the royal city Ticinum-Pavia, where as late as 552 Totila stored part of the royal treasure, remained Ostrogothic until the end of the war.[332] And Aligern, Teja's youngest brother, defended himself in fortified Cumae with the royal insignia and the remaining part of the royal treasure for more than a year, even after the death of the last king.[333] The fortifications on the peninsula, some of which were excellent, derive from Theodoric's efforts to preserve and, if possible, improve the existing system of defenses. The main fortress, Ravenna, was also the most important residence; but the Amal also spent considerable sums on maintaining Rome's city walls. Moreover, Theodoric probably took over and expanded the organization of the *tractus Italiae per Alpes,* the fortresses at the southern exits of the Alpine passes. At any rate, we know of several measures by the Gothic king to construct fortifications and supply camps at the Gallic Durance, in the Cottian Alps, in the Val d'Aosta, and near Como and Trent. The conglomerate hill Doss Trento, which Gothic coin finds also identify as a stronghold, was crowned by the fortress with the telling name "Wart." This Verruca and the Ligurian fortress of Dertona are the best known new constructions of Theodoric's time.[334]

Theodoric's Barbarian Policy and the Securing of Italy

It is easy to underestimate the important role Theodoric's "barbarian policy" played in safeguarding Italy. Its successes hardly survived Theodoric's death and, indeed, during his lifetime its possibilities remained limited. Thus one can hardly say that Theodoric reestablished the *regnum Hesperium* along its old boundaries. Nevertheless it would be wrong to use his failures in judgment against him. After the disorders of the fifth century, Italy and its neighboring provinces found peace for at least a generation. Theodoric accomplished not only the preservation of peace against domestic and foreign enemies but even succeeded in reconquering Roman provinces. Even though the territorial acquisitions were modest,[335] Theodoric's policy of restoration left a lasting impression. It has been compared to that of Diocletian. Moreover, Theodoric's accomplishment is not lessened by his debt to Odovacar in the sphere of barbarian policy.[336] His reference to imperial models did not remain a formal, literary imitation; rather, it proclaimed a political program. To the Romans Theodoric seemed another Trajan or Valentinian I, a comparison that was not meant merely to invoke the memory of the "good old days." Trajan was generally the model of a good ruler, and the mention of Valentinian calls to mind the imperial conquerors of the barbarians.[337] If Theodoric followed their example, he was "victor and triumphator," the "spreader of the Romans' name," and "ruler and conqueror of the barbarians,"[338] as he acclaims himself on the medallion he minted on the occasion either of his *tricennalia* or of an actual victory over barbarians. The legends correspond to the symbolic statement of the royal portrait, where Theodoric appears "with a gesture that is also found in imperial portraits, namely, with the right hand raised in the act of blessing, a gesture taken from the depiction of the unconquerable sun god." In the left hand the king holds victoria on an orb, reflecting the claim to royal authority. In this way Theodoric had deliberately drawn closer to the augustus, "who, after all, had made concessions to him by sending the *ornamenta palatii,* the insignia of power." "Unlike Odovacar, Theodoric wore the purple and, like other kings recognized by the emperor, a diadem, which of course must have differed clearly from that of the emperor."[339] But to the *gentes* Theodoric appeared just like an emperor;[340] in festive procession, as if in triumph, he entered Rome and Ravenna,[341] occasionally had himself called augustus by the Romans, and added that he was with every right an Alamannicus because he had saved that people from destruction, whereas another man, namely, the emperor in Constantinople, had assumed that title without right.[342] The notion of an imperial protector of peoples, which Themistius had once elaborated in Constantinople,[343] received new meaning in Theodoric *domitor ac victor gentium*: the Amal himself had become the executor of the Roman barbarian policy.

THE VANDALS

The Vandal kingdom of Africa had already passed the climax of its power when the Amal Goths occupied Italy. Nevertheless, Vandal naval power still dominated the western Mediterranean with the islands of Corsica and Sardinia. The aging Vandal king Gaiseric had come to an agreement with Odovacar about the possession of Sicily: in return for yearly tribute the island would belong to Italy. But with the Gothic victories over Odovacar in 490, the Vandals no longer thought themselves bound to the treaty and tried to recapture all of Sicily. Although Theodoric's main force was tied down before Ravenna, the Gothic contingent he dispatched in 491 was enough to destroy the Vandals' hopes. The defeat in Sicily must have been so decisive that Carthage renounced both its territorial and financial claims.[344] Thus Theodoric, like his grandfather, had become a Vandalarius, a conqueror of the Vandals.[345] Probably in the year 500, immediately after his Roman tricennial and only two years after a change of kings in Carthage, Theodoric married his widowed sister Amalafrida to the Vandal king Thrasamund. In return the Vandals had to be "content with an alliance of friendship instead of yearly tribute." With a retinue of one thousand elite troops and their five thousand servants the Amal lady went to Carthage as an element in Theodoric's policy of a barbarian balance of power. Her successes, however, were limited, even though she brought as a dowry the territory of Lilybaeum in western Sicily.[346] Thrasamund's fleet did not set sail in 507 to aid the Goths when the imperial navy was ravaging the coast of southern Italy and preventing Theodoric from marching to Gaul in time. In 510 and 511 the Vandal king sided with Gesalec, whom the Ostrogothic expeditionary force had driven out of Spain. The Visigothic claimant to the throne had fled to Carthage, where he was supplied with such ample resources that he was able to return to his homeland and renew his resistance against Theodoric. This led to considerable ill-feeling between Ravenna and Carthage; however, the tensions came to a head, if at all, only in a conflict that remained limited to the border region of Lilybaeum.[347] Thrasamund realized his weakness and apologized in word and deed. The gold he offered was turned down, but his written apology was accepted.[348] When in 519 Theodoric's son-in-law Eutharic held the consulship, Africa supplied the traditional wild animals for the hunting games at Rome.[349] This diplomatic kindness was also accepted by Ravenna. Thrasamund remained Theodoric's ally until his death. The successor king Hilderic broke with Ravenna and switched to the imperial camp. The royal widow Amalafrida protested this change of policy, but she and her retinue were outmaneuvered and eventually killed. Theodoric then prepared a campaign of revenge against Carthage. A hastily constructed fleet of no less than one thousand ships was to leave the Italian bases on June 13, 526, but the Ostrogothic warships remained in their ports because Theodoric died on August 30 of that year. His successor registered only a lame protest and left the punishment of the criminals to the divine powers.[350] Theodoric's reaction permits the inference that his sister Amalafrida and her people had been murdered at the latest in 525. The Vandal kingdom survived the break with Ravenna by only a little less than eight years. When Belisarius attacked the Vandals in the summer of 533 the Ostrogoths allowed him to make a crucial logistical stopover in Sicily. Thereafter the Goths occupied the district of Lilybaeum, Amalafrida's dowry, and held the territory despite imperial complaints until Belisarius conquered Sicily.[351]

THE VISIGOTHS

It was probably in 477 that Odovacar made peace with the Visigothic king Euric. Their agreement made the Alps the border between the two kingdoms.[352] Until 490 both sides respected this line of demarcation between their respective spheres of interest. But when Odovacar had surrounded the Ostrogothic army in Ticinum-Pavia, Alaric II intervened in Italy.[353] This was the second Visigothic expeditionary force that tried to determine who would rule Italy.[354] And this time the intervention of Toulouse was successful. With Visigothic help Theodoric regained his mobility, defeated Odovacar in battle at the Adda, and forced the enemy to shut himself up in Ravenna.

After Theodoric had become undisputed master of Italy in 493, he gave Thiudigotho in marriage to the Visigothic king Alaric II. This marriage united the two noblest Gothic royal clans, the Amali and the Balthi. By all human calculation this alliance should have secured a long peace between the Goths. Inevitably, history took a different course. Hindered by the aftereffects of his armed clash with the emperor,[355] Theodoric was not able to give his son-in-law timely support against the Franks, even though Alaric had based all his plans on such support.[356] In the catastrophe of Vouillé in 507 Alaric II lost the battle and his life, and his son Amalaric, Theodoric's grandson, was still too young to become king of the Visigoths. The result was an inter-Gothic war that lasted until 511 and ended with Theodoric's becoming king of the Visigoths. Already in 508 the Ostrogothic army had driven the Burgundians, allies of the Franks, out of formerly Visigothic Provence. The territory between the Alps and the Rhone was subsequently annexed to the Gothic kingdom of Italy. Theodoric took the acquisition of this region as the occasion to reestablish the Gallic prefecture with its seat in Arles. At the same time he announced that Provence had been freed from the barbarians and had become once again part of the Roman Empire. The term "barbarians," of course, referred not only to the Franks and Burgundians but also to the Visigoths. This attitude toward his sister-tribe was based on experience and would not be altered by future events.

Ravenna appointed the tried and tested Liberius as praetorian prefect of Gaul; he remained in office from 510 to 534, during the last two years even serving as supreme commander of the Gothic-Gallic troops with the rank of *patricius praesentalis*. Even before his appointment as general, this Roman was considered a "military man" (*exercitualis vir*) who had received "wounds." Sometime before 523, north of the Durance near Arles and thus close to where that river flows into the Rhone, Liberius fell into a Visigothic ambush, apparently in a time of peace. Visigothic warriors had probably invaded the Gallic prefecture via Burgundian territory, for until 523 the Durance formed the Ostrogothic border with the Burgundians. Only after 523 did Theodoric annex that region, at least up to the Drôme. Thus this strange incident in which Theodoric's praetorian prefect of Gaul was attacked by Visigothic warriors, of whom Theodoric was king, must have taken place between 512 and 523. This event throws a revealing light on the stability of the united Gothic kingdom and its internal concord.

At the head of the Visigothic kingdom, whose royal treasure was taken to Ravenna, Theodoric placed his shield-bearer and confidant, the Ostrogoth Theudis. The latter made a rich marriage: his Hispano-Roman wife brought so much money into the marriage that he could afford to keep two thousand private soldiers. With the help of this "domestic force" and a clever policy toward Ravenna Theudis soon managed to make himself ruler of Spain. Although, Amalaric, the son of Alaric II and Thiudigotho, ruled after his grandfather Theodoric's death for five years as independent king of the Visigoths, Theodoric's former governor nevertheless held the reins of power. After the violent death of Amalaric in 531, Theudis became king himself.[357]

Theodoric's Visigothic policy did not rest on reciprocity. We must wonder in all seriousness whether his intervention in Gaul did not harm the Gothic cause more than it helped it. The Ostrogoths always got more than they gave. Many of them joined Visigothic garrisons as "liberators," lording it over the locals and "needlessly" demanding from them services that threatened the locals' social and economic independence. The upheaval of 507/ 511 had apparently once again crushed a number of people: law and order was precarious, and there were acts of violence by the powerful who often enriched themselves with ecclesiastical property at the expense of the church. Moreover, abuses occurred during the collection of taxes, and the local bureaucracies acted as oppressors. Theodoric tried to take measures against such actions; in particular he ordered that laws and regulations that had been valid under Euric and Alaric II should be adopted as the standard for his own tax policy.[358]

During Theodoric's fifteen-year reign over both Gothic kingdoms he strove for the reestablishment of Gothic unity. Theodoric "discovered" the

Visigothic Amal Eutharic and made him the husband of his daughter and heir Amalasuintha.[359] Nonetheless, despite Ravenna's propaganda and royal policy, integration of the two Gothic peoples did not take place. When Theodoric died and his two grandsons took over the government as independent rulers, many Goths were compelled to choose one kingdom or the other. At the same time Athalaric returned the royal treasure to his cousin Amalaric; for the next eleven years the Rhone constituted the border between the two Gothic *regna*. After the murder of Amalaric in 531, the Visigoths were too preoccupied with their own affairs and with the Franks to come to the assistance of the Ostrogoths in their agonizing war against Byzantium.[360] Nevertheless, the hard-pressed Ostrogoths were hoping for support from Spain. The elevation of Hildebad to the Gothic throne took place in large measure because he was Theudis's relative. The same was the case for the more successful Totila, Hildebad's nephew.[361] But just as Theudis had refused to help the Vandals against Belisarius in 533, he hesitated for a long time before intervening in the widening conflict between the Goths and Byzantium. It was probably in 547, a year after Totila had reached the height of his power, that his great-uncle Theudis ordered his men to cross the Straits of Gibraltar and attack the city of Septem and the small imperial province of Tingitana. The expedition ended in a catastrophe and was one reason why Theudis lost the throne and his life in 548. This event also broke the last bond between the Visigoths and the Ostrogoths, who from that time fought on their own—and lost: the Ostrogoths lost Italy and their *regnum,* the Visigoths large parts of Spain. Even if it is true that Theudegisel, the murderer and successor of Theudis, is identical with Amalaric's Amal cousin of the same name, both the Amal *Origo Gothica* and Isidore's *Historia vel Origo Gothorum* were ignorant of this connection or else considered it unimportant.[362]

THE BURGUNDIANS

Because Theodoric did not lack for female family members, he could also honor the Burgundians with a marriage. One object of the deal, which was probably settled in 494, was the return of those Italians whom the Burgundians had carried off in 490/491. As the purchase price Theodoric offered his second daughter Ostrogotho—the Ostrogothic Areagne—through whose hand he tried to bind to himself Sigismund, the son of the Burgundian king.[363] The persistent tension between the three most important Gallic kingdoms tied down a considerable number of Ostrogothic forces on the northwestern border.[364] The Burgundians had suffered heavy losses in the

great Gothic war of 507–509; they had been the real victims of the Ostrogothic counteroffensive. Not only had they lost all their conquered territories and hope of acquiring Arles and Avignon but all their territory as far
as Orange had been devastated. These wounds were slow to heal, but
Theodoric seemed to have renounced any further offensive policy toward
the Burgundians. The Durance line received strong fortifications, as if he
planned to establish a permanent border there.[365]

Theodoric's Burgundian son-in-law Sigismund was coregent from about
501 and succeeded his father Gundobad in 516. Wedged between the aggressive Frankish kingdoms and the united Gothic "superpower," Sigismund looked to Byzantium for support. He emphasized that his Burgundian
kingdom was a federate *regnum* of the old style. Honored already before
his rise to the kingship with the dignity of a *patricius* because of his service
to the empire, Sigismund increasingly pursued a proimperial and hence
anti-Gothic course. For that reason Theodoric tried to stop the diplomatic
communications between Lyons and Constantinople, which effort did little to improve relations between the two neighbors. In actuality Sigismund
lacked the power for any anti-Gothic actions. The Burgundian king's positions as *patricius* and *magister militum* remained merely a latent threat.
That Gundobad, as successor to and nephew of Ricimer, had exercised
military authority in Italy many years before was no more than a pleasant
memory. Equally as unimportant was the Burgundian kings' vision of themselves as "soldiers of the emperor."[366]

It is clear that Theodoric and his Burgundian son-in-law were not on the
best terms. Nevertheless, peace prevailed along the mutual border for nearly
fifteen years. The situation changed very quickly, however, once Theodoric's
daughter died and Sigismund killed his son Segeric, born of his Ostrogothic
wife. The end of the Burgundian pro-Gothic party meant the end of Theodoric's defensive policy toward the Burgundians. Now he was forced to exact blood revenge for a slain Amal, a duty Theodoric always took seriously.
The impending Ostrogothic offensive also gave the Franks an opportunity,
so the Burgundians were caught between two fronts. While Sigismund was
trying in vain to beat back the Frankish invasion, the Ostrogothic army led
by the Gaul expert Tuluin occupied the region between the Durance and
the Drôme rivers, probably moving even as far as the Isère. Tuluin was also
married to an Amal woman, which was another reason for Theodoric to
entrust him with this expedition. As a result of the events of 522 and 523
the Ostrogothic possessions in Gaul reached their greatest territorial extension.[367] The last acquisitions were then lost around 530 when Amalasuintha
renounced the territory north of the Durance in the name of her son Atha-

laric. But the Burgundian-Ostrogothic treaty concluded on this occasion had no effect. When in 532 the Franks attacked their neighbors and in the process even occupied Ostrogothic Arles, the Gothic army did only enough to reestablish the violated borders. In 534 too, when the Burgundian kingdom met its fate, the Ostrogothic army remained in its garrisons.[368]

Ostrogothic-Burgundian relations had nearly always been tense. Only in the period between 501 and 507 do we discover friendly gestures. At Gundobad's request Theodoric sent to the Burgundian kingdom a water and sun clock, which had been made especially for the occasion, along with the necessary personnel to operate it.[369] The other instance was when Sigismund, who had converted to Catholicism, was given permission to undertake a pilgrimage to the apostles' graves in Rome and to visit Pope Symmachus. Theodoric's son-in-law's change of faith caused the Arian Amal some concern.[370] Caesarius of Arles had already twice had problems with Alaric II over his relations with the Burgundian kingdom, where the greater part of his diocese was located. He was again accused of high treason and deported to Italy in 513, but was acquitted through the intercession of Ennodius.[371] Something similar had already happened to the bishop of Aosta before the Gallic war of 507: he too was accused of conspiring with the Burgundians and was then relieved of his office.[372] After the Visigothic pretender Gesalec had lost Frankish support in 511, he had no choice but to take refuge with the Burgundians. But Ostrogothic guards captured him on the border river Durance and handed him over to the executioner.[373]

THE FRANKS

Before Theodoric married his daughters to the kings of the Visigoths and the Burgundians he himself—in 493 or 494—had taken as his wife Clovis's sister Audofleda. She gave birth to Amalasuintha and sealed the friendship between the two mightiest Latin kings of the time.[374] In fact they both avoided open confrontation. Only when Arles was relieved in the fall of 508 did Ostrogoths and Franks fight each other, and then only because the Burgundian besiegers had to be supported by a Frankish contingent. But when in 508 Theodoric's troops marched to Gaul, Clovis himself was no longer in the south. The Frankish king was already busy displaying in Tours and then in Paris his kingship, which equaled that of Theodoric.

Even if the two brothers-in-law caused each other some problems, neither one ever sought a real war. Moreover, their differences probably did not intensify until the year 506, which saw busy diplomatic activity. At that time the Alamanni, after a nine-year period of peace had risen up again against the Franks and had been defeated once more.[375] The Burgundians, who were allied to the Franks, subsequently extended their territory as far as Windisch-Vindonissa (Switzerland). But this buffer zone could not prevent the appearance of a military and political "gray zone," if not an actual power vacuum, between the Frankish and the Ostrogothic kingdoms. Theodoric, who as Odovacar's successor had organized the Raetian mountain region "as the bulwark and protective barrier of Italy,"[376] took the threatened Alamanni under his protection in 506. Ravenna demanded from the Frankish king that he abstain from any further persecution of the vanquished tribe, in return for which Theodoric guaranteed that the Alamanni would in the future respect Frankish territory. Theodoric advised Clovis not to push things too far, for, after all, "the king of the Alamanni had perished along with the haughtiness of his people." The panegyrist Ennodius saw the well-deserved downfall of the Alamannic kingdom in a similar light. He added, however, that the tribe should be happy in having received a new king in Theodoric.[377]

The Alamannic crisis did not prove serious enough for Theodoric to break off relations with the Frankish royal court. The embassy that was to negotiate with Clovis over the Alamannic problem[378] was accompanied by a guitarist, "an Orpheus who was to conquer with his sweet sounds the wild hearts of the foreign people." No less a man than Boethius had been instructed by the Gothic king to show his expertise by selecting the suitable person. The accompanying letter itself was one of the finest accomplishments of the new quaestor Cassiodorus.[379] At the same time Boethius began constructing for the Burgundian king "a device to measure the hours,"[380] and Cassiodorus wrote the explanatory remarks: the Italian kingdom had the duty and the ability to bring culture to the barbarian kings of Gaul. Of course this appealing picture can obscure the seriousness of the threat to the transalpine peace. Despite vigorous diplomatic activities, Theodoric was not able to break up the Frankish-Burgundian coalition and prevent an attack on the Visigothic kingdom. Nor was the appeasement policy he had recommended to Alaric II of any avail; without provocation Clovis launched his attack at the beginning of the campaigning season of 507.[381] After the Frankish king had conquered or brought under his control large portions of the Gallic part of the Visigothic kingdom, he pursued a more peaceful Gothic policy during the last years of his life. But Clovis, like the Vandal Thrasamund, tried to prevent Theodoric from becoming king of the Visigoths. To that end he allowed Gesalech to distribute his Vandal money among the Goths who had remained north of the Pyrenees and to raise an army. Only when the hapless Visigothic king had been defeated for the second time by the Ostrogoths under *dux* Ibba did Clovis discontinue any further support.[382]

Clovis died in 511 without having achieved total conquest of Aquitaine. In 512/513 or 514/515 his successors concluded a peace leaving the Goths with the south of Novempopulana and possibly also Rodez and Toulouse. The Visigothic king Amalaric married a Frankish princess. The Burgundian kingdom continued to function as a barrier between the Gallic and the Italian great powers. At the beginning of the third decade of the sixth century, however, when Theodoric had also died, the tide turned. Along a line that was at least a thousand miles long and that extended from central Germany to the Tyrrhenian Sea, the Frankish kings went on the offensive, simultaneously threatening the Visigoths on their southern flank. Already in 531 Amalaric had sustained such a crushing defeat by his Frankish brothers-in-law that his own people murdered him. Almost simultaneously the Franks conquered the Thuringian kingdom—which was allied to the Ostrogothic Amali—and occupied Burgundy, which in the years from 532 to 534 lost its independence permanently.[383] When the Byzantine-Ostrogothic war broke out thereafter, in 535/536 the Franks presented their "modest" demands: They were being courted by the emperor and an appeal had been made to their sense of Catholic solidarity, but they offered to remain neutral if Ravenna would pay in gold and land. In 537 Vitigis concluded the negotiations, which had begun under King Theodahad: he renounced Provence, transferred to the Franks by way of a treaty the Ostrogothic overlordship over the Alamanni, handed over to them the entire region north of the Alps and the Alpine region itself, and paid out two thousand pounds of gold.[384] To be sure, the last word in Ostrogothic-Frankish relations had not yet been spoken.[385] The barriers that Theodoric's barbarian policy had erected as a protection for Italy and that had been aimed principally against the Franks had been torn down by the Roman government of Constantinople itself. But the Gothic peace had outlived Theodoric by a decade and had lasted altogether more than forty years, something one can say of few security systems.

RAETIA AND WESTERN ILLYRICUM
UNDER OSTROGOTHIC DOMINION

The Alamannic question, which set the Ostrogoths and the Franks at odds, has remained to this day a controversial issue. Local historians seek to push the boundaries of the Ostrogothic kingdom as far north as possible, at least to the upper course of the Danube or even deep within the *barbaricum* at the modern boundary between the Swabian and Franconian dialects.[386] In contrast, general historians exercise far greater restraint, arguing that the exits of the Raetian-Norican Alps would have formed the farthest extension of the northern border of Theodoric's kingdom.[387] These opposing opinions are perhaps the result of different definitions of the term *border*. As part of the Roman Empire Theodoric's kingdom had fixed borders with the successor states as well as with Byzantium. Along these borders watch was kept by Ostrogothic troops;[388] a violation of these borders constituted a *casus belli* or at the very least led to diplomatic complications. Toward the *barbaricum*—part of which was also former Roman territory that Italy had given up—Theodoric's kingdom was protected not by a border but by a broad border zone composed of three sections.

The first line of defense consisted of the fortified southern exits of the Alps. Both Ostrogothic troops and local militias served in the fortresses located there.[389] Farther north, the Alpine zone, including modern Austria and eastern Switzerland, formed the second belt. In this section, over which Ravenna held sway,[390] were located Raetia I, the Alpine regions of Raetia II,[391] and those of Noricum ripense,[392] and former Noricum mediterraneum. Both Norican sections made up Ostrogothic Noricum, which preserved the old provincial name. This Italian province had been recently reorganized as *ducatus* and probably extended across the Alps northward to a geographically defensible outpost. Certain parts of the city-district of Iuvavum-Salzburg may have formed such an outpost. There is no other way to explain the Romania of the valley of Salzach, a Romania that reached to a line formed by the mountains in and around Salzburg. Here local militias, who were secure in their rear and who received only a little support from the south, could refuse passage to anyone coming from the north.[393] The population had the status of provincials[394] or, like the Breoni of Raetia II in the Inn valley, that of federates.[395] In Raetia the command was held by the *dux Raetiarum*, the *vir spectabilis* Servatus. He commanded over "soldiers" (*milites*) whom Theodoric considered part of his army. Nevertheless, these *milites* cannot have been Goths. The Raetian troops were no doubt recruited from the local population, and the same holds true for the Breoni, who rendered as federates the *militaria officia*. Although the wild "proto-Tirolians" thought little of the Italian-Gothic *civilitas*, they did not have to be forced to subordinate themselves to the Ostrogothic kingdom. Danger threatened from the north, not from Italy, at whose expense they lived and which provided the necessary protection.[396]

Both the Norican and the Raetian regions were no doubt organized the same way. Like his Raetian colleague Servatus, the *vir spectabilis* Ursus was also a Roman and a *dux*.[397] His residence was in Teurnia—the late antique capital of Noricum mediterraneum[398]—where shortly after 500 he and his wife donated the beautiful mosaic in the cemetery of the town church.[399] Ursus and Ursina, "bear" and "she-bear," have names common among the Alpine Romans.[400]

North of the second line of defense, which was held by the warlike mountain folk was a third security belt that had been established with the help of Germanic allies. The military effectiveness of these allies and their forms of political organization varied. In the "game" for Italy's security they were the pawns who were sacrificed without hesitation when they themselves needed help. Yet Ravenna exerted an extraordinary attraction for the northern peoples. Even the Baltic Aesti established contact with Theodoric. They brought their amber to Ravenna and had to listen to reproaches about their ignorance of Tacitus's *Germania*.[401] The Gautic king Roduulf left Scandinavia and went to the Amal court. Along with him came new tales from the Goths' "original homeland," tales that Cassiodorus added to the basic story of the Amal family tradition.[402]

While such relations increased Ravenna's prestige without demanding direct commitment, the first who needed real protection were the Alamanni.[403] When they were defeated and pursued by the Franks in 506, the border of Raetia and hence the borders of Italy as well seemed endangered. In 507 Theodoric demanded that Clovis respect the territory of the Goths.[404] The "Ostrogothic" Alamanni were divided into three groups. Perhaps this was the only way Theodoric could guarantee peace at his northwestern border, even though the Gothic king described those Alamanni as merely the rest (*reliqui*) of the once "enormous tribe" (*innumerabilis natio*) that the Frankish king had subjugated. In any case, the Alamannic refugees must have been settled within the border of Italy in such a way that Roman landed property suffered no damages,[405] something that was possible only in those territories where the Roman taxation system either no longer existed or was not called upon. This could have been the case both in modern Oberschwaben as well as south of Lake Constance in the Thurgau and the northern Vorarlberg.[406] But Alamanni were also marched through Noricum,[407] probably to Pannonia-Savia, where they took over, as they did north of the Alps, the function of border troops.[408] Accordingly, Theodoric's claim that he had "incorporated" the *generalitas Alamanniae* into his kingdom was no exaggeration, or only a slight one, if one also draws on the archaeological evidence of northern Italy.[409] It was merely the case that the Alamannic *generalitas* was settled not en masse but in dispersed groups. Institutionally it is possible, however, that the Alamanni in the region of the

Alps and the Alpine foothills differed from the southern groups. In the north they certainly had the status of federates; in Venetia and in Savia, that is to say, in the actual Italian prefecture, they appear to us like *dediticii*. When the Ostrogoths in 536/537 renounced the Raetian-Norican territories, the Alamanni who had settled there became Frankish. At the same time, however, the Suevic-Savian barbarians and probably their Italian fellow tribesmen as well were allowed to march against the Romans. Thereafter we hear nothing about the Savians for quite some time, until Vacho subjugated them to the Lombards.[410]

Following Euric's policy of encirclement, shortly before the beginning of the Frankish offensive against the Visigoths, Theodoric admonished the kings of the western Heruli, Varni, and Thuringians not to remain inactive in case Clovis should attack his southern neighbor. The Gothic king predicted to the non-Frankish Germanic peoples what in fact happened: namely, that they would be the next victims of Merovingian expansion. No action of any kind followed the exchange of letters, but none had been announced.[411] Ravenna had made much greater promises to the Danubian Heruli. Like the Rugians in lower Austria some time earlier, the Heruli had established a federate kingdom centered in the *barbaricum* but extending across the river into the Roman Empire.[412] The expansion of the Heruli, who were at first settled only along the March river, was made possible by the Ostrogothic departure from Pannonia in 473. Now Theodoric, as lord of Italy no less, returned "to the former homeland of the Goths."[413] At the latest from the time when the Gothic king had added to Gothic Pannonia the Sirmian province, he sought to establish good relations with the Herulian king Rodulf. The latter probably included in his sphere of influence the region north of Lake Balaton. Just as his father Thiudimir had done with the Suevic Hunimund,[414] Theodoric adopted Rodulf as his "son in arms" and, in keeping with the barbarian custom, sent him a horse, shield, and other weapons. The translator who rendered the accompanying letter to Rodulf "into German" told the king that from now on he "would hold the first rank among the peoples."[415] But that was of little use to the Heruli in 508 when they had to fight against the Lombards. The Heruli suffered a crushing defeat at the hands of their former slaves; on this occasion too Theodoric was not able to intervene in time. He only offered political asylum to part of the survivors, but his "son in arms" had been killed in battle.[416] The attempt of the Gothic king to thwart the Frankish-Lombard rapprochement with the help of the Danubian Heruli failed in the same way as the attempted mobilization of anti-Frankish Germanic peoples. Finally, Theodoric was also too late to help his son-in-law Alaric and the Visigoths.

Theodoric's barbarian policy had failed its first tests. The circle of protection that Theodoric had constructed of friendly and dependent peoples drawn around the borders of Italy collapsed in the years 506–508. It now remained to be seen what could be salvaged.

The second phase of Theodoric's barbarian policy is characterized by his friendship with the Thuringian kingdom.[417] As long as this relationship lasted the area between the Danube and the Alps remained closed to the Franks. Along with his Thuringian ally Theodoric was able to grant "his" Alamanni the necessary protection and to allow the emergence of a new people to the east. This is not to say that the Ostrogothic kingdom in the area between the Iller and the Enns rivers—the lower Austrian "wilderness" remained no doubt outside of the Gothic realm—extended up to a certain line on the other side of which Thuringian border guards kept watch. Rather, in the forefield of the two *regna*, but still well within their spheres of influence, there had existed since 510 at the latest the possibility of a Bavarian ethnogenesis. The Bavarians are considered the "foundlings of the *Völkerwanderung*."[418] This characterization is appropriate, for their appearance is sudden. But a foundling must first be born and then abandoned, and the question of who did this constitutes the Bavarian problem. For a long time it was considered old-fashioned to attribute the Bavarian ethnogenesis to Theodoric and his Thuringian ally; nevertheless this assumption is probably close to the truth.[419]

Around 510 Herminafrid, the king of the Thuringians, married Theodoric's niece, Amalaberga. In this way the Goths gained their strongest anti-Frankish ally, who ruled over a *regnum* that extended from modern lower Bavaria far into free Germania between the Rhine and the Elbe. Via the Thuringians it was also possible to come to an arrangement with the pro-Frankish and proimperial Lombards, who remained quiet during Theodoric's entire reign.[420] The Ostrogothic delegation that accompanied Amalaberga to the court of Herminafrid was instructed to convey thanks for the excellent "silver-colored" Thuringian horses. The alliance with the Ostrogoths was also in the interest of the northern neighbors, who had formally taken the initiative in concluding the arrangement.[421] Between 523 and 526 Theodoric had a letter written—probably for the king of the "Thuringian" Varni—in which he expressed his appreciation for valuable gifts, among them Damascened swords of excellent quality.[422] Until Theodoric's death the Ostrogothic-Thuringian alliance lived up to its promises. Then in 529 the Franks launched their first attack against the Thuringian kingdom. After five years of bloody battles Herminafrid fell victim to Frankish treachery, and his death completed in 534 the conquest of the

Thuringian kingdom. Amalaberga managed to escape to Ravenna with her children. Her daughter, who went to Byzantium with Vitigis in 540, would eventually become the second wife of the Lombard king Audoin, the father of Alboin.[423] Thus, through the Thuringians the "splendor of the Amal blood"[424] still reached and exalted the Lombards.

Of the original seven provinces of the western Illyrian-Pannonian diocese Odovacar ruled Dalmatia, which he occupied in 481/482 as the avenger of the murdered emperor Nepos and which he annexed to his Italian dominion. The question of whether Pannonia-Savia, Dalmatia's neighboring province to the north, was also under the rule of Odovacar cannot be directly answered. But the easy march of the royal armies into Noricum ripense in late fall 487 and early summer 488 and their victories suggest that Savia was included within the *regnum Italiae*. In 489, however, Odovacar awaited the Ostrogothic king at the Isonzo, that is, within the borders of *Italia annonaria*. The absence of any defenses at the upper reaches of the Sava suggests that the southwestern Pannonian region had been insufficiently occupied.[425] Instead, it was Theodoric who ruled over considerable portions of western Illyricum, which should be seen as the reconquest of Italian possessions. Theodoric had inherited Dalmatia from Odovacar and he united this large and wealthy province with Pannonia-Savia. A military *comes* of the highest rank became commander of this double province. The dates of the unification and appointment of the *comes* are uncertain but Theodoric's measures must have been taken before 504, that is to say, before the Ostrogoths launched their offensive from Savia. Between 507 and 511 an Osuin *vir inluster* governed the two provinces from his headquarters in Salona; after Theodoric's death King Athalaric renewed his appointment. Whether Savia, which was also called Siscia after its capital, ever formed a separate sphere of command seems questionable. The province was so strongly Suevicized that its name Savia could be read as "land of the Suevi," in which the Roman inhabitants were distinguished from the barbarian groups as Siscians, as the "people from the city and province of Siscia." The foreign element of "old barbarians" (*antiqui barbari*) had settled in that land before the arrival of the Goths and had even enjoyed intermarriage with the Roman population. In 523/527 agents of a Gothic *comes* were active in that area; but this does not mean that the latter was in charge only of Savia. The Fridibad who is attested in 507/511 had no title and was sent into Savia to exercise judicial authority exclusively. His special mission would therefore in no way mean that the Dalmatian-Savian sphere of command was ever dissolved, especially since both officials, Osuin and Fridibad, were probably active during the same period. Yet Pannonia II, taken from the

Gepids in 504/505, did form a separate *comitatus*; in the royal decrees it is called Pannonia Sirmiensis, or simply Pannonia. Its commander, attested in 509/510 and possibly appointed a little earlier, was the high-ranking *comes* Colosseus, a Goth with a non-Gothic name. The population structure was similar to that in Pannonia-Savia, but the number of barbarians must have been even greater.[426]

While things were mostly quiet along the Dalmatian rivers Drina and Neretva-Narenta, which for decades had formed the border between the Italian kingdom and the eastern empire, the situation at the confluence of the Drina and the Sava near Sirmium was far less stable. Here, in the "former homeland of the Goths," a Gepidic subtribe had spread out after the departure of the Goths in 473 and as early as 488 had obstructed Theodoric's trek to Italy.[427] In 504 the time had come: the Gothic king wanted to settle an old score and sent his army, led by the *comes* Pitzia, on the march downstream along the Sava. The stated motives of this expedition reveal imperial traditions. If Theodoric wanted to follow in the footsteps of "his ancestors," the Western Roman emperors,[428] he had to conquer Sirmium for two reasons. First, he had to free Roman imperial territory from the barbarians, and second, he had to reconquer from Constantinople a province that belonged to the Western empire. And, in fact, the Sirmian war did develop into an open, though regionally limited conflict between the Ostrogoths and the Byzantines.

Theodoric's Eastern policy was in the tradition of the century-long conflict between the Western and Eastern emperors over the boundaries of their respective *imperia*. This is how the Romans in East and West must have interpreted his policy, and this is also how it was presented to them.[429] But Ravenna's imperial propaganda served at the same time to justify a preventive strike against that very area of barbarian concentration where Theodoric himself had risen to power. The Sirmian conflict would remain the only offensive war the Gothic king waged as king of the Western empire. Since 488 and 489, when Theodoric himself had marched upstream along the Sava, much had changed in that region. In those days there were two Gepidic subtribes, of which one was settled north of the Danube outside the imperial territory and the other occupied Sirmium. Now both groups were making dangerous efforts to unite. If the Sirmian group of 488 had already been a formidable enemy, a greater Gepidic kingdom would have been strong enough to threaten Theodoric in Italy.[430] The years before 504 saw an ominous growth of self-confidence among the Gepids. The embassies to Ravenna were arrogant and are even said to have made territorial demands. Theodoric decided to take action.[431]

The events are quickly told. Pitzia took Sirmium, drove out the Gepidic king Thrasaric and captured his mother, the wife of that Thraustila who had once resisted Theodoric at the Vuka river. But the annexation of Pannonia Sirmiensis was not the end of the story. The victorious Goths had apparently taken a liking to marching and went farther, penetrating into the Margus-Morava valley and thus violating Byzantine territory. At the confluence of the Morava and the Danube the Hunnic-Gepidic robber-chieftain Mundo had set up his own kingdom. His base was the fortress Herta. Although even the *Origo Gothica* had nothing kind to say about this leader of "prowlers, robbers, murderers, and brigands," the Gothic commanders nevertheless had the order to enlist his services and to give him support. And the Goths were in desperate need of help, since Sabinianus the Younger, the son of the general of the same name who had nearly ended Theodoric's career in 479,[432] was approaching with a large Bulgarian army. But a Gothic force of twenty-five hundred men proved enough to defeat the Bulgarians near Horreum Margi-Cuprija. The Gothic army was four-fifths foot warriors, which was highly unusual.[433] Equally as unusual is the presence of a noble Roman—"with a Gothic heart," to be sure—and his brother in Pitzia's army.[434]

Initially Theodoric renounced none of his conquests, which stretched all the way into upper Moesia. As a result he was in a state of war with Anastasius, even though the emperor did not take direct military countermeasures. Nevertheless, the quick victories in the Sirmian war cost Theodoric dearly. Imperial diplomacy more than compensated for territorial losses by wrecking Theodoric's barbarian policy. During the five years before 510, when peace was formally concluded, the emperor prevented the Ostrogoths from coming to the aid of each of their allies. Thus in 507 the imperial fleet, unmolested by Theodoric's Vandal allies, ravaged the coast of southern Italy. It is true that the assault of Romans against Romans—only a few Gothic garrisons were located in the attacked areas[435]—was sharply criticized,[436] but Theodoric's help for Alaric II came too late. And then the Ostrogoths had to march to Gaul, where until 511 they were embroiled in ever new wars. The commitment of Theodoric's forces in the West kept him from saving his Herulian "son in arms" Rodulf, not to speak of Ravenna's inability to support its other Germanic allies against the Franks. The reception of Alamannic and Herulian refugees was thus the only remnant of great hopes and expectations, and, moreover, the disadvantageous result was that the Franks became neighbors of the Goths.

Probably in 510 Theodoric reached an agreement with Emperor Anastasius which ceded to Byzantium the *civitas* of Bassianae, that is, the eastern part of Pannonia Sirmiensis. Ravenna thus gave up former Gothic territory—the Huns had penetrated this far in their last attack against Valamir[437]—but good relations between East and West thereby seemed reestablished. The consuls for 511 and for the following years were appointed in traditional fashion and received mutual recognition. The cession of Bassianae meant the withdrawal of the Ostrogoths from the upper Moesian Morava valley as well as from the city of Singidunum-Belgrade.[438] With the defeat of their king Thrasaric the Gepidic groups had placed themselves under Theodoric's authority in order to hold their own settlements south of the Danube. In 523, at the earliest, a Gepidic contingent marched through Italy to Gaul to take part in the Burgundian war.[439] The Gepid who served with the royal bodyguards in 541 was certainly not the only one from his tribe who fought in the Gothic army of Hildebad.[440]

The Gepids had suffered defeat by Theodoric, but they had not been destroyed. Of course they kept quiet as long as the king of Italy was alive. In 512 the Lombard and Gepid royal houses established a marriage connection. Although this did not please Ravenna, the alliance was defensive in nature and not meant as a threat to Ravenna.[441] The first Gepidic attempt— probably with Herulian support—to regain what they had lost took place in 530 and was thwarted by a Gothic army led by the later king Vitigis. At the outbreak of the Byzantine-Gothic war, however, Ravenna withdrew also from Sirmium. In 537, at the latest, when the last Gothic offensive in Dalmatia petered out, the Gepids recaptured Sirmium, which now became their "capital." By that time, however, they had already long passed the height of their power. Thus the Gepids could not keep the emperor from opening Pannonia Sirmiensis to the Heruli as well.[442] Moreover, since 508 the Lombards had been advancing into the two northern Pannonian provinces. But they probably awaited Theodoric's death before they crossed the Danube in large numbers. This would also explain why Theodoric's chancery did not have any dealings with them.[443]

At what time the Ostrogoths gave up the provinces of Noricum ripense and Savia is uncertain. No later than 545 the Frankish king Theudebert stood at the borders of Pannonia, and in 547/548 southeastern Noricum and adjoining Savia were officially transferred to the Lombards as an imperial gift.[444] The strong contingents of Lombards in the army of Narses played an important role in the destruction of the Ostrogoths; and it was a Gepid who dealt Totila the death blow.[445] Eventually the Lombards became the heirs of the Ostrogoths in Italy.[446] Thus the year 568 confirmed the shrewdness of Theodoric's decision two generations earlier to fight the only preventive war while king of Italy in precisely that region from which Italy would be conquered during the next two centuries. Yet it was not the "multitude of Gepids"[447] who arrived but the "small Lombardic people."[448]

BARBARIAN TRADITIONS AND ETHNOGRAPHY

The Ostrogoths used their traditional language until the downfall of their Italian kingdom. They were probably Latinized later than the Visigoths or the Burgundians. The Roman Cyprianus, a member of the highest nobility whom Theodoric employed as *referendarius* and as an officer in the Pannonian war, had mastered the Gothic language and had it taught to his sons.[449] Two generations earlier Sidonius Apollinaris had criticized Syagrius-Burgundio for just such an attitude.[450] It is impossible to identify the linguistic effect of the strong Ostrogothic infiltration into the Visigothic kingdom between 508/511 and 526/531. For nearly the entire reign of Athalaric (526–534) Cassiodorus attests the vitality of the barbarian-Gothic traditions, the *carmina,* which he could draw upon as justification for certain political measures. Many names "from the distant past" and a barbarian *memoria* that reaches back into non-Mediterranean regions and pre-Roman times have survived even in a fragmentary form. The tribal tradition contains genuine names of many generations which are related to theogony and ethnogeneses. Yet we must be wary of synchronizing all too readily the tribal *memoria* with the accounts of the ancient ethnographers of the first centuries A.D. For especially those passages of the *Origo Gothica* which scholars like to use contain Cassiodorus's comment "still today." This is a clear reference to the sixth century and it separates such reports from classical ethnography by centuries. We must admit, however, that early medieval *origines gentium* are attested only for those Germanic peoples of the north and east who (1) are mentioned under the Principate as *vera et antiqua nomina,* (2) were small peoples at that time, and (3) have composite names of the Gutthiuda type. These observations give us something to think about. Theodoric's attitude toward the tribal tradition was not altogether positive. The king was selective. It goes without saying that he encouraged the ancestral cult that elevated the Amali to the rank of "heroes and demigods," thus placing them far above the "common people" (*puri homines*). Christianized and acceptable to the Roman nobility, the royal clan manifested itself as a second *gens Iulia,* which justified its dominion over Goths and Italians. But the custom of grave furnishings, the active expression of the old ancestor cult, was seen by Theodoric as outdated and above all as economically wrong. His Christian Goths needed neither gold nor silver in the hereafter.[451]

The *Origo Gothica* contains Gothic name material and Gothic terms, such as the word *belagines* for the tribal law. But the author claimed that this law had already been written down in the distant past. In like manner one has imagined a Gothic state correspondence and has postulated an "Amalatal," a saga of the Amali composed in the Gothic language, which Cassiodorus is said to have known and used.[452] But at this time we can prove only the existence of spoken Gothic, namely, in diplomatic relations, in the army,[453] and as the language of the court.[454]

As late as 551, more than a decade after the Goths had left Ravenna forever, some clerics of the Arian church Santa Anastasia used Gothic to sign their charters (*frabaúhtaboka*), which were written in Latin. Perhaps one of these men by the name of Wiljarith bokareis is identical with Uiliaric antiquarius. The latter may have been the head of the scriptorium in which the famous Codex Argenteus was produced. With the exception of one folio this magnificent manuscript is today kept in the university library at Uppsala. Ulfilas's Gothic translation of the Bible was written down in silver letters on purple-dyed parchment; for details such as the names of the evangelists the scribes even used gold ink. The letters are conspicuously regular, as if traced from a stencil.

Although this silver Bible with its 336 pages, 188 of which have been preserved, is not the only extant text in the Gothic language, it is by far the most comprehensive. It is probable that the Codex Argenteus was originally part of the royal treasure and that before 540 it was taken to safety in Pavia, from where Totila removed it to Cumae in southern Italy. At the capitulation of the fortress in 553 the silver Bible did not fall into the hands of the imperial troops but for unknown reasons remained in the south until it came to Carolingian Germany. The relatively well-known history of the Codex Argenteus is among the most fascinating chapters in the history of books: *habent sua fata libelli*.[455]

The *lex Gothica*,[456] the Gothic-Arian faith and law, experienced its greatest flowering in the kingdom of Theodoric the Great. The *lex* is as inconceivable without its Latin and especially Greek roots as it is without its opposition to Catholic-Roman Christianity.[457] Yet it was this dialectical relationship that allowed the transition from one religion to another. The *mutatio religionis* did not flow only in one direction, but it was undoubtedly undertaken more often by Goths than by Romans.[458] Nonetheless, the two Arian priests who affixed a Latin signature to the Ravennese papyrus mentioned above were probably Romans.[459] Theodoric professed the Arian faith and was active on its behalf without making much fuss about it. But the fruits of his efforts and the intellectual atmosphere he created are still today among the most beautiful and most valuable achievements of the European spirit: the Arian baptistry, the modern oratory of Santa Maria in Cosmedin, follows the example of the orthodox baptistry of San Giovanni in Fonte located near the cathedral. But the court church—today San Apollinare Nuovo—is probably the most magnificent testimony of an Arian sacred building, a generation older than the Catholic church of San Apollinare in Classe. In addition there are the Arian churches of Santa Andrea dei Goti, St. George, St. Anastasia, and also a church of St. Eusebius, whose builder is identified as Bishop Unimund. In Classis there was an Arian church of St. Zeno; the Goths also erected a church consecrated to St. Sergius in Caesarea, the third Ravenna city. Arian bishops resided in all three towns. In Ravenna proper the church of St. Theodorus, still preserved though without its mosaic decorations, was built by Theodoric, and it served as the see of the Gothic bishop. We owe it to the favor of the sources that we are so well-informed about Ravenna. The situation is different for the "provinces": we do know that there were two Arian churches in Rome; we can perhaps prove the existence of an episcopal church and a baptistry in Dalmatian Salona near modern Split. But no matter how great the achievements of Ostrogothic Arianism, they represent only a peripheral manifestation in a general flowering of late antique culture that Theodoric's reign made possible.[460]

The existence of Baltic and Scandinavian peoples who at the beginning of the sixth century were counted among the Goths is certainly no invention of Cassiodorus.[461] The Vistula island of Spesis-Gepedoios, which "is now supposedly inhabited by the Vidivarian *gens,*" was known at the time to Ravenna. But Ravenna knew also "about the creation of the Vidivarii in the delta of the Vistula out of remnants of Goths and Gepids as well as other refugees."[462] The report of the Scandinavian Goths or Gauts, regardless of whether they should be located in modern Gotland or in "Gothic" south Sweden, also seems contemporary. Cassiodorus mentions a long catalog of peoples. First he "improves" upon Ptolemy,[463] and the source of his knowledge might have been the Scandinavian king Roduulf, "who gave up his own kingdom, entrusted himself to the protection of the Gothic king Theodoric, and found what he was looking for."[464] The catalog contains three names in particular which sound Gothic and a fourth that is the product of a conjecture by Karl Müllenhoff: *Vagoth, Gauthigoth,* *Eva-Greotingi, Ostrogothae.* When Cassiodorus speaks of the Scandinavian Greutungi as "wild cliff dwellers," he is following a correct etymology. But since he based himself on Claudian, his testimony is somewhat suspect.[465]

Cassiodorus goes on to distinguish the Scandinavian Goths and their relatives from the Germanic peoples: they are supposedly "stronger in body and fight like wild animals."[466] And the younger contemporary Procopius knows the Thule Gauts as Ares worshippers and a people who engage in human sacrifice, something that was also said of the "older" Goths, the Getae.[467] The drawing of distinctions between peoples of such similar names seems more important to modern linguistics[468] than it was for the sixth century.[469] Roduulf's "contempt for his own kingship" and his flight to Ravenna prove his desire[470] to join a powerful relative, just as Theodoric had a lively interest in the Baltic-Scandinavian north;[471] the Gautic Amali had come from that region.[472] In the same way a Gutic-Scandinavian contribution to the Gutonic ethnogenesis is conceivable, a process linked with the names of the three-ship king Berig.[473] But the catalog of peoples that Cassiodorus prefaces to his Scandic history reflects not the situation during the first century B.C. or even in the fictional year 1490 B.C.; rather it is the history of Scandinavia at the beginning of the sixth century.[474] The remarkably high level of ethnographic efforts and knowledge at Theodoric's court is attested by the work of the Goth Aithanarid, who was probably active in Ravenna around 500 and who may have had two younger colleagues in Heldebald and Marcomir. The anonymous "cosmographer of Ravenna" names these three "Gothic philosophers" as his main sources.[475]

Theodoric's Roman Policy and the End of His Kingship, 526

"He ruled as one the two *gentes* of the Romans and Goths, and although he was an Arian, he took no measures against the Catholic faith." Theodoric's Roman policy and his policy toward the church were thus identical. The same Ravennese source reports that on the occasion of Theodoric's visit to Rome in 500 he "honored the apostolic prince [St. Peter] with deep reverence as if he himself had been a Catholic."[476] In fact Ereleuva, the king's mother, with whom Pope Gelasius exchanged letters was Catholic.[477]

The churches of the West and the East were split over many issues theological as well as personal. There was the theological controversy over the nature of Christ. Then Rome fought Constantinople's claim for primacy. The men who occupied the throne of St. Peter, such as the mighty Pope Gelasius, denied the emperor's right to be the final authority in questions of faith. Only on the advice of the young Justinian did his uncle, the Emperor Justin, seek reconciliation with Rome, its senatorial nobility, and the papacy.[478] Until then the majority of the Catholic leadership of Italy was to be found in Ravenna's camp. The tolerance of the Arian Gothic king was preferred to the caesaropapist claims of Constantinople. With the reconciliation between East and West this alternative disappeared. Although such a reconciliation was bound to hurt him politically, Theodoric had always taken the pope's side and had even accepted the consequences of a delay in his recognition by the emperor. The king must have known what opportunity the controversy between the two Catholic powers offered him. Nevertheless, he encouraged all efforts to put an end to the quarrel. Thus in 513 and the following years he even supported his former fellow tribesman and colleague Vitalianus. Since church matters were traditionally within a *magister militum*'s sphere of competence,[479] Vitalianus intended to reestablish church unity even by force and against the will of the emperor.[480] Religious unrest was part of the public life of the late antique state; it functioned as a release valve for the manifold pressures to which the masses were exposed. But such unrest could easily get out of control. It disturbed the domestic peace and affected mostly innocent people, as the Jews of Rome and Ravenna came to know.[481] Moreover, a "schismatic" emperor regained the political lever that Constantinople had possessed at the beginning of Theodoric's reign in Italy: Byzantium could deny the Ostrogothic kingdom future recognition by withholding the vital assent to the succession arrangements of the king.[482] Finally, between 499 and 514 the schism raged in Rome itself and intensified the already existing division within the church. Theodoric proceeded with the greatest caution in this protracted dispute. Again and again there was bloodshed and murder in the streets of Rome, but Theodoric held back. He placed himself at the service of the council of 502 and merely tried to treat the symptoms by charging Gothic *comites* with the task of reestablishing order.[483] The source of the disease itself, the quarrel between two popes over the legitimacy of their respective elections, he left untouched until the death of one settled the dispute.[484]

In 515 Theodoric married his daughter Amalasuintha to the Amal Eutharic, whom he had "found" among the Visigoths,[485] thus designating him as his successor.[486] After Justin had assumed imperial power he recognized Theodoric's arrangement for the succession, thus fulfilling a request Ravenna had already made of Anastasius. But in view of the schism nothing could have been expected from Anastasius. Now Eutharic was adopted by Justin "according to barbarian custom"[487] as the emperor's "son in arms"; he was given Roman citizenship and as Flavius Eutharicus Cilliga in 519 he assumed the consulship together with the emperor who had himself listed only as the second consul, thus conceding precedence to the Amal.[488] The legitimation of the succession was thus settled with an arrangement clearly understood by Goths and Romans alike. This arrangement included all the elements of Theodoric's own kingship: affiliation with the Amali, designation by the predecessor, adoption by the emperor, and the bestowal of Roman citizenship and the consulate. Eutharic arranged his entrance into the consulate as a great celebration. In Rome and Ravenna games were held for the people and the senators were showered with honors. Cassiodorus wrote on this occasion his *Chronica,* if not also his *Origo Gothica,* and at Eutharic's induction into the senate he delivered the customary panegyric. But Eutharic's popularity among the Romans must have declined quickly for during the unrest of 520 he advocated stern countermeasures. In the eyes of the Italian Catholics the Arians and Jews appeared to be forging an alliance.[489] Calm was soon restored, however, especially when the imperial government continued to demonstrate its willingness to make concessions: Constantinople in 519 all but ended the schism that had existed since 482 and made certain conciliatory gestures, as, for example, the bestowal of the consulship of 522 on the two sons of Boethius. In response the highly honored father delivered a panegyric on Theodoric and placed himself at the service of the royal government. But Eutharic subsequently died, and the succession arrangement, already confirmed by Constantinople, became null and void.[490]

At this point the senate felt entitled, if not actually obligated, to take action. Since the days of Stilicho the barbarian statesmen of Italy had pursued a policy of improving the status of this venerable institution. Odovacar had increased the rights of the senate, and Theodoric had imposed virtually no restrictions on it.[491] In a royal decree Theodoric's *intitulatio* was preceded by an address to the senate, which commenced: "To the conqueror of the world, the defender and renewer of republican liberty, the senate of the city of Rome."[492] What was there to keep the senators from taking this address seriously and from worrying about what would happen after Theodoric's death, especially as his star was setting? Simultaneous with Eutharic's death took place the murder of the Burgundian pretender to the throne, Theodoric's grandson Segeric, who was killed by his father. In 523 other important men of Theodoric's generation disappeared from the political scene: death claimed the allied Vandal king and the pope who was a supporter of Ravenna.[493]

The situation was precarious, but outward splendor masked the danger.[494] Men like Boethius and Symmachus, Ennodius and Cassiodorus, Probinus and his son Cethegus seem to have created the foundations of a general *civilitas* on which future generations could build. Compared to the elitist but by no means exclusive educational establishment of Italy, the Gaul Sidonius Apollinaris seems isolated. Despite the rhetorical tradition and the grossly exaggerated value attached to it, Italian civilization still possessed the knowledge, the skills, and especially the *iudicium* to keep alive the cultural tradition of antiquity.[495] The primary concern, however, was clearly the preservation and restoration of this tradition. A Benedict of Nursia probably read the signs of the times better than his classicistic contemporaries. The lessons he drew were lasting, and the Scythian monk Dionysius was also thinking and working toward the future. But even after the end of the Ostrogothic kingdom, Justinian accepted the measures that Theodoric had taken to promote higher education, and he took into imperial service those professors whom the Gothic king had appointed.[496] Among the Amali themselves Amalasuintha and her cousin Theodahad had enjoyed a superb education. Theodahad's sister Amalaberga, who was married off to the king of Thuringia, was probably also highly educated.[497] Yet the evidence for Theodoric's own attitude toward classical education is contradictory. The report that he was illiterate and had to use a stencil for his signature[498] has long been recognized as a doublet of the reproach brought against Justin, the Illyrian peasant on the imperial throne.[499] Someone who had, like Theodoric, spent the years of his later childhood and his youth at the imperial court can hardly have had such a glaring gap in his education.[500] Moreover, if he could say that he had learned in Constantinople "how to govern Romans,"[501] he must have possessed at least the rudiments of written administrative procedures. That he in fact knew a good deal about it Theodoric proved as a wandering general in the Balkans. Although the praise of the panegyrist Ennodius does not mean that the Gothic king was an accomplished rhetorician, it could have hardly been said of an illiterate.[502] Nevertheless, the Gothic magnates pointed to royal statements critical of education when they forced a change in the upbringing of Athalaric. In reality, however, they desired a change in the whole system of government, for the three tutors of the young king, who on Amalasuintha's request were to raise and educate him "after the model of Roman rulers," were also Goths.[503] At a time of political strife, when the old order was breaking down, a personality as deep and complex as Theodoric's could "disintegrate" after his death and serve as justification for opposing policies. Of course the image of the Gothic king as a persecutor of Romans, Catholics, and intellectuals was one that did become desperately real in 523.[504]

It is likely that the ex-consul and patrician Albinus circumvented the king and corresponded directly with the emperor on the question of the Amal succession. The letters were intercepted by Romans in Theodoric's entourage and delivered to Ravenna. Theodoric then summoned the *consisto-rium,* the highest court responsible for Roman affairs.[505] Boethius, recently appointed *magister officiorum* and hence a member ex officio of the *collegium,* tried to exonerate Albinus. But another ex-consul and patrician, Cyprianus, a faithful Roman follower of Theodoric's, insisted on a charge of high treason. Boethius's imprudent remark is well known: "The accusation brought by Cyprianus is false; if Albinus did anything, I myself and the entire senate are also guilty." Now the court party of Ravenna gained the upper hand over the Roman senators. Boethius not only failed to save his friends but became entangled in the affair himself. From the fall of 523 he spent more than a year in prison in Pavia, where he composed his famous work *The Consolation of Philosophy.* Without a chance to be heard by the king Boethius was sentenced to death and the loss of his property in the summer of 524 and was subsequently tortured and executed.[506] The *civilitas* so often preached by Ravenna[507] had vanished from the court itself. Constantinople interpreted Theodoric's actions as a persecution of Catholics and retaliated. In 524 after the execution of Boethius the emperor passed a law depriving the Arians—primarily the Goths who had remained behind in the East—of their religious freedom. Of course this did not stop the escalation of violence. In 525 the *princeps senatus* Symmachus shared the fate of his son-in-law Boethius.

These political blunders and misguided policies were not mitigated by the mission of 525 in which Theodoric pressed Pope John I into service as an envoy to the emperor. In the fall of that year a large number of secular and ecclesiastical dignitaries went from Italy to Byzantium in an effort to improve relations. From Theodoric's point of view the results of all these missions had to appear disastrous. The pope and his entourage remained in Constantinople far longer than anticipated or necessary. They were received in the imperial city with great honor and returned the favor to their hosts. On Easter Sunday Pope John performed the festive crowning of the emperor. Upon their return to Ravenna most of the envoys, including the pope, were sent to prison, where John died on May 18, 526. Now the "Greek" cause had found the best possible martyr. Although Theodoric promoted his own candidate to the vacant apostolic see, it was clear that a storm was brewing. When the king died on August 30, 526, like Arius, from dysentery,[508] most Catholics were convinced that the Gothic king had gone straight to hell. There were countless rumors and stories of the Amal's death; there is the vision of a pious hermit on the island of Lipari: "The king, barefoot, ungirt, and with his hands tied, was thrown into the crater of the neighboring volcano by Pope John and the patrician Symmachus."[509]

In other versions Theodoric is taken off by demonic horses or dies of typhoid fever brought on by fear and remorse over his misdeeds. Theodoric is said to have seen the look of the executed Symmachus in the eyes of a fish served at the royal table.[510] The horror of his contemporaries and posterity at the sinful, demonic end of the Amal bears pre-Christian features and damns his memory far beyond what was warranted by events. Nevertheless, it is clear that Theodoric's policy of accommodation between Romans and Goths, Catholics and Arians, Latin and barbarian culture, was a failure. In this lies the cause for the fall of the Ostrogothic kingdom and for the end of Italy as the heartland of late antiquity.

The architecture of the royal tomb, the famous mausoleum of Theodoric, symbolizes even beyond his death the program of a union of East and West, *Romanitas* and *gentilitas*. Is that why the tomb has been empty for so long? We cannot blame the medieval monks of the monastery of St. Mary (erected before the ninth century next to the tomb) for not having any use for the remains of the heretic king. But they were probably never faced with the problem of ridding themselves of the dreadful memorial: already in the ninth century the empty porphyry sarcophogus stood beside the monastery gate. Nobody knows who removed Theodoric from his final resting place.[511] Of course, in the eyes of the barbarian world the Gothic king had never died: fully armed he sat on his charger, ready to lead the demonic army of the dead or, as the god of war, to receive the sacrifices of the warriors.[512]

The Amal Successors of Theodoric, 526–536

The fall of the Italian kingdom of the Ostrogoths is often described in moralistic tones. Although the historian is not excused from the human obligation of rendering moral judgment, he, more than anyone else, must proceed with caution, conscious of his criteria. Because of the personal nature of the late antique and barbarian state, the ruler and his entourage could stand for broad political and socioeconomic developments, the emperor could embody the empire and the king the kingdom. To moralistically evaluate or condemn the dissolution and destruction of a state as a "wretched event"[513] characterizes the individuals involved in an event but says little about the event itself. Let us take as an example Theodahad: an unsympathetic *ramasseur des propriétées*, wily and perjurious, hated by Goths and Romans alike.[514] He murdered his cousin, who had made him king. He would have sold everything for a comfortable life in Constantinople. This portrait is certainly accurate; moreover, the list of Theodahad's sins could be expanded further. Yet even though he was for decades the only other male Amal among Thiudimir's offspring, Theodahad was systematically prevented from becoming a Gothic king. When he was still living in Tuscany, where his activities were arousing grave discontent, his sister had long since become queen of the Thuringians. When no male offspring appeared, Theodoric promoted the Visigoth Eutharic over his first nephew. And when this designated successor to the throne died, Theodahad knew that the child Athalaric and his mother Amalasuintha would become the leaders of the Amal clan and the rulers of the Gothic peoples. But like the royal child, about whose abilities and suitability there were justifiable doubts,[515] the Tuscan Platonist Theodahad was also descended from Gaut, Amal, and Ostrogotha.[516] Amal harmony was an illusion, a propagandistic fantasy. Theodoric's career had taught that only one Amal, namely, the most violent and most unscrupulous, could continue the tradition of the clan.[517] If the Ostrogoths had had a binding order of succession, such as existed among the Vandals, Theodahad would have automatically become king. Although there were Goths and Romans who could envisage such an order, it was suppressed by Theodoric.[518] Theodahad compensated himself by "acquiring" in Tuscany not only private estates but also the regional "patrimony," thus entering, if illegally, into part of Theodoric's inheritance.[519] For the distant Franks he was therefore the "king of Tuscany."[520] Of course Amalasuintha had to take measures against him and prevent the establishment of a state within the state.[521] Just how serious the situation was is revealed by Theodahad's plan, made during Athalaric's life-time, to relinquish his "kingdom" to the emperor. The purchase price would have been a financially secure life at Constantinople, with a yearly salary of twelve hundred pounds of gold, which was by no means an exaggerated demand. Theodahad would have had to live as a Roman senator at the imperial court for another thirty-three years to consume as much as Amalasuintha intended to take with her as a basic supply on her planned flight to the East.[522] Theodoric the Great himself and his "squinting" namesake too,[523] like many barbarian kings,[524] had expressed the desire to lead a quiet life in the imperial city. So this alone did not make Theodahad a *nithing*. Nonetheless, did Amalasuintha really believe that she could placate the enmity of this long neglected Amal by making a break with her own policy and with that of her father and appointing him coregent in 534?[525] By now he had already become the leader of a group hostile to Amalasuintha, and party strife, with Goths and Romans on both sides, tore apart the Ostrogothic kingdom when Justinian's great war of reconquest commenced in 535.

ATHALARIC (526–534)

At the death of his grandfather Theodoric, Athalaric was ten years old.[526] The seventy-five-year-old Amal had found time to arrange the succession with the Gothic magnates "the *comites* and the optimates of the people," but he had neglected to seek approval from Byzantium. So the matter was left at Theodoric's designation of Athalaric, just as Theodoric himself had once been presented to the Goths by his father Thiudimir. Cassiodorus praised the royal child as the seventeenth Ansic ruler since Gaut, who was said to have won the primordial victory over the Romans in 86/87. Since then 440 years had passed, whereupon there now began with Athalaric's kingship a παλιγγενεσία, a rebirth of the world.[527] Like a second Galla Placidia, and if possible better than the first one, Amalasuintha was to exercise the regency for the child Athalaric.[528] It was also her responsibility to carry out the political testament of the dead king: to seek accommodation with the senate and the Romans and to live in peace with the emperor.[529] Agents sent from Ravenna placed Romans as well as Goths under oath to the new king and promised in return the continuation, or rather the renewal, of harmonious relations between the two peoples.[530] Cassiodorus sent the appropriate letters to Constantinople and the senate; special pledges of protection were offered to the senate and it received once again the right of minting copper coins.[531] In a letter to the emperor Amalasuintha dissociated herself from the tough policy of Theodoric's last years.[532] At the same time the families of Symmachus and Boethius were given back their confiscated property.[533]

The death of Theodoric put an end to the personal link between the two Gothic kingdoms. His Visigothic grandson Amalaric now assumed independent rule for the next five years. This entailed a certain diminution of Ravenna's power: the Visigothic royal treasure was returned; the taxes from Spain had to be relinquished. Now that the Rhone formed a real border the joint defense of Gothic Gaul came to an end, which meant an additional burden for Ravenna. The Italian army was considerably weakened because every Goth was free to choose one of the Gothic kingdoms. Since far more Ostrogoths were stationed in western garrisons than vice versa, a large Ostrogothic group once again joined the Visigoths. This also explains why the Ostrogoth Theudis was able to succeed Amalaric, largely the result of support from fellow tribesmen who had gone west with him.[534]

In the first years after Theodoric's death there was peace at home and abroad.[535] The Ostrogothic army was sufficiently powerful, provided that it was led with determination and that the ruler dared to put it into action.

In 530 the attempt of the Gepids and Heruli to take Gothic Pannonia Sirmiensis failed. Vitigis, the future king, drove back the attackers, who were led by the old bandit Mundo. The Ostrogothic counteroffensive drove deep into East Roman territory, capturing the city of Gratiana in upper Moesia. The events of 504 and the following years seemed to be repeating themselves. And in fact this territorial violation in 530 was used by Justinian nearly half a decade later as a pretext for uttering powerful threats against Ravenna.[536] At the moment, however, Justinian was too busy with the Persian war.[537]

While the Ostrogothic troops were victorious along the northeastern frontier, Amalasuintha was striving to improve relations with the Burgundians. She ceded the territory north of the Durance and even entered into an alliance with the Burgundians. But when it became a matter of marching against the Franks, Ravenna was afraid of its own courage. Just as the Ostrogothic troops did not come to the aid of the Thuringian kingdom in 531 and 534, the Gothic army raised in 532/533 did not leave its own territory to support the Burgundians against the Franks. As a result the short Franco-Gothic border of Theodoric's time became a frontier nearly one thousand miles long. Any farther expansion along this line by the Franks was an immediate threat to Ostrogothic territory.[538]

Athalaric was a minor and stood under the tutelage of his mother. Thus Theodoric's successor had forfeited the main element of a Latin-barbarian kingship, namely, to be the king of the army. The supreme command of the *exercitus Gothorum* was vacant. The problem was solved in accordance with Roman practice, and the solution was justified by the saga of the Amali: Tuluin, who had proved himself in campaigns along the Sava and in Gaul, a faithful follower of Theodoric from the days of his youth, and husband to an Amal woman, assumed as *patricius praesentalis* the office of commander-in-chief, an office Theodoric himself had occupied until his royal elevation in 493 and had thereafter left vacant. The appointment of Tuluin, however, violated two principles of the dead king: first, it meant the restoration of the vice-imperial patriciate in the West, an office that competed keenly with the monarchy; second, without even asking the emperor Amalasuintha bestowed the patriciate on a Goth, who thereby automatically became a senator. It is not surprising that the quasi-king Tuluin had to be reminded of the example of Gesimund, who as an Amal "son in arms" could have become king but who nevertheless preserved the rule for the legitimate royal children.[539] Cassiodorus now began to invoke the tribal tradition with conspicuous frequency in an understandable attempt to emphasize Amal legitimacy to the Romans and the Goths.[540]

Despite initial signs of weakness the rule of Amalasuintha continued unchallenged for a time. Procopius praises her manly courage and her sagac-
ity,[541] virtues we can see reflected in her early attempt to improve relations
with her cousin Theodahad. Theodahad's mother's fortune had been confiscated after her death, but Amalasuintha agreed to a partial restitution
and held out the prospect of restoration of the remainder provided Theodahad acted loyally.[542] Although Theodahad had made himself thoroughly
hateful to the Roman and Gothic *possessores* of Tuscany, he must have
had excellent relations with the Gotho-Roman court party at Ravenna.[543]
The alliance between the Gothic hardliners who favored a hard course
toward Constantinople and the anti-imperial Romans around the brothers
Cyprianus and Opilio had lost nothing of its momentum. These men of
Theodoric's entourage were responsible for the disasters that befell Boethius
and Symmachus and for the vicious domestic policy during the last years
of Theodoric's rule. Immediately following his death the intransigent court
party had suffered a setback but was able to regain its former place as early
as 527/528.[544] There is no doubt that both Theodahad and Tuluin belonged
openly or secretly to this faction.[545] In late 532/early 533 this group thought
the time had come to seize power. To that end they realized that they had
to gain control of Athalaric, for the king had just turned sixteen and was
approaching his majority. The pretext for such an intervention was the
young Amal's allegedly un-Gothic upbringing, criticized as counter to the
principles established by Theodoric. The regent succumbed to the pressure,
and this precipitated a full-fledged crisis. Amalasuintha asked the emperor
for political asylum and sent a boat with the state treasure to Durazzo,
where Justinian had assigned her a palace. At the same time the emperor
invited the Gothic queen to come to Constantinople. The ship dropped
anchor in its port of destination; it was filled with forty thousand pounds
of gold, equivalent to approximately twice the annual budget of the Western
empire. But Amalasuintha herself remained in Ravenna and fought back.[546]
We can see that things were also getting too hot for her cousin Theodahad,
for he too sought to sell all of Tuscany to the emperor and emigrate to
Constantinople.[547] Tuluin must have been among the three nobles whom
Amalasuintha had removed from Ravenna and thereafter killed. In 532 the
Franks had attacked the Burgundians and had even occupied Gothic Arles
for some time,[548] so there was indeed no need for Amalasuintha to invent
a pretext for sending the three commanders to the front. The death of these
men struck like a bolt of lightning, preventing any countermoves. Amalasuintha's "golden ship" was able to sail home again across the Adriatic.[549]
The crisis had been mastered, and in 533 the regent made personnel changes
in the most important offices. At that time Liberius, the praetorian prefect

of troubled Gaul, took over the supreme command of the Gothic army in Gaul as *patricius praesentalis*. With this Theodoric's system had been completely turned on its head. At the same time Cyprianus lost his office and Cassiodorus became Italian praetorian prefect.[550] In the same letter in which Cassiodorus introduced the new *patricius praesentalis* to the senate, the propagandistic exploitation of the Amal genealogy reached its height.[551] In the euphoria of 533 the ruler Amalasuintha informed the senate of her achievements. Not a word was said about the domestic enemy; instead, real and alleged victories abroad were celebrated. Cassiodorus says that Amalasuintha corrected Galla Placidia's mistake, recovering Illyricum by "making the Danube Roman against the will of the Eastern ruler."[552] She also "defeated" the Franks—the opportunity for defeating the Franks was actually there but was carefully avoided—since "under this ruler [Amalasuintha], all of whose ancestors were kings, our army with God's help is putting the barbarians in their place."[553] Liberius is then presented as military *patricius* and Cassiodorus closes his letter with an Amal genealogy of nine generations, Amalasuintha's impressive legitimization.[554] Her ancestors, especially her father Theodoric but not her son the "glorious king,"[555] make Amalasuintha the commander of the Gothic army, indeed a Gothic "queen of the army."[556] Thus after the death of Athalaric in 534 his mother could step forward as queen and rule freely over the kingdom; the enormous increase in her power since 526 had given her all the means for acting thus.

On October 2, 534, Athalaric, the last of Theodoric's three grandsons, died without ever having been king in more than name. Even the edicts issued in his name reveal the policies of the royal mother and her advisers.[557] In one respect, at least, Athalaric was allowed to resemble his illustrious grandfather, namely, in royal appearance. Like Theodoric the Great and Alaric II before him, Athalaric wore "unparted hair that covered his forehead and flowed down on the sides over his ears." Ennodius had said of his king Theodoric: "The effect that in other rulers is achieved by the crown, God-inspired nature has produced for my king." Amalasuintha herself appeared with the "Phrygian" cap of the type worn by the queens of the Bosporans. The origins of the Ostrogoths had left traces not only in the tribal *memoria* but also in their insignia.[558]

THEODAHAD (534–536)

The death of Amalasuintha's son did not find the queen unprepared.[559] Her reactions were quick and courageous, indeed, even reckless, and they resemble a desperate flight forward. Amalasuintha's victory over her enemies at

home was barely a year old when she accepted her hostile relative Theodahad as coregent (*consors regni*)[560] and declared herself queen (*regina*).[561]
Theodahad had to swear to acknowledge her as the true ruler and to serve
merely as the figurehead of the Gothic military kingship.[562] He was allowed
to mint coins under his name[563] and to carry the royal title because he was
an Amal,[564] but his elevation to the kingship was based on the authoritative
word of the *domina rerum* Amalasuintha.[565] Elevated to the position of king
and coruler in November 534,[566] Theodahad, supported by Amalasuintha,
strove to gain Constantinople's recognition. The letters of the two Amali
to the emperor and the senate surpass each other in their professions of
harmonious relations and unanimity.[567] But Theodahad wasted little more
time; during the last weeks of 534 he arrested his cousin and removed her
from Ravenna to confinement on an island in Lake Bolsena.[568]

Amalasuintha's conflict with the opposition among her own nobility and
the Gothic hatred for the Carthaginian murderers of Theodoric's sister
Amalafrida had led her to take a stance of friendly neutrality toward
Constantinople in the war between the Romans and the Vandals. Belisarius
was allowed to use Sicily as a supply base for his operations against Carthage.[569] But the Gothic *comites* who commanded in Sicily and southern Italy
were little contented with this policy. The commander of Syracuse occupied
Lilybaeum, the Vandal-held section of southwestern Sicily, the dowry of
the dead Vandal queen. The *comes* of Naples sheltered deserters from
Belisarius's army and refused to turn them over. In the summer following
these events of winter 533/534 an imperial legate appeared in Ravenna to
complain about such behavior and about the apparently long-since forgotten events of 530.[570] Thereafter an intense shuttle diplomacy commenced
between East and West. The imperial legates, above all the historian Petrus
Patricius, became a permanent fixture in Ravenna, where they meddled
freely in the internal affairs of the Ostrogothic kingdom.[571] Their alleged
attempts to save the captive queen seem dubious. The empress Theodora
was supposedly so jealous of the beautiful and educated Amalasuintha that
she preferred to have her removed rather than see her resettled in Constantinople. Yet whether the nearly forty-year-old Amal lady represented a
serious threat to the former courtesan is questionable.[572] Whatever the gos-
sip of the two courts might mean, by April 30, 535, at the latest, the Ostrogothic queen was no longer alive; her personal enemies, the survivors of
that faction of nobles defeated by Amalasuintha in 532/533, were said to
have murdered her out of revenge. But Theodahad knew what was afoot
and was deeply involved in the plot.[573]

A delegation dispatched to Constantinople by Theodahad before the murder was committed to reassure Justinian, Amalasuintha's self-proclaimed protector, fell apart even while discharging its mission. One of the leaders of the delegation was the irreproachable Liberius, who had been employed on countless missions since the days of Odovacar. He remained faithful to his mistress beyond her death and probably went over to Justinian at this time. Thereafter he fought against the Goths in Italy and Spain. The other spokesman for the delegation was none other than the equally well-known Opilio, who, as was to be expected, had the nerve to claim that Theodahad was treating his coruler and cousin very well. Thus Opilio remained firm to the end in his hostility toward Amalasuintha.[574]

When the murder of the Gothic queen became known in the spring of 535, neither further "dissimulation" nor letters from Theodahad and his wife Gudeliva to the emperor and the empress were of any use.[575] The violent death of Amalasuintha constituted a casus belli and meant the declaration of an ἄσπονδος πόλεμος, a "war that could end only with unconditional surrender."[576] While Italy was in discord, while Romans and Goths were turning against the new regime and the Gothic army was needed more for the preservation of internal peace than for defense against an outside attack,[577] Justinian launched the war of reconquest on land and sea.[578] At first Justinian let loose the wild Mundo. Mundo had changed sides since the days of Theodoric and had already tried in 530 to expand along the Sava and the Danube at the expense of the Goths.[579] Now as the *magister militum* of Illyricum he opened the offensive in Dalmatia. Without encountering much opposition, by late 535 he had occupied the province along with its capital city of Salona. Belisarius, a specialist for combined naval-land operations, was sent into action to establish a second front. He was given the task of attacking Sicily with a small elite force of about nine thousand men.[580] The emperor's instructions to his general reveal caution and uncertainty about the expected resistance and the extent of Italo-Roman cooperation. Belisarius's naval mission was therefore declared a reinforcement for the Carthaginian garrison. When the ships of Belisarius were approaching Sicilian Catania in June 535, the attack could still have been called off and the fleet's appearance explained away as a stopover on the way to Africa.[581] It appears that the Byzantine leadership had taken into consideration the experiences of the naval campaign of 507 and the Vandal war of 533.[582]

The Roman militias of Sicily opened the gates of their cities, so even Syracuse, the seat of the Gothic *comes,* surrendered without a fight. Only the garrison of Palermo held out. But the otherwise strong city fortifications left the harbor itself unprotected, which allowed Belisarius's fleet to sail in and drop anchor. The ships' dinghies were then manned with archers and hoisted up the masts. Soon a shower of arrows rained down upon the Gothic garrison, forcing it to surrender. On the last day of the year 535, at the end of his consulship, Belisarius entered Syracuse in triumph, showering gold coins on the inhabitants. Justinian's general had taken his time on this "armed reconnaissance," but he had won a fine victory.[583]

While the war was already in full swing, imperial diplomacy continued its activities both inside and outside of Italy. In the name of Catholic solidarity a delegation tried to mobilize the Franks against the Arian Goths. Theodahad had just recently appeased the Merovingian kings' indignation at the shameful death of their beloved cousin with a wergild of fifty thousand solidi.[584] To incite the Franks to an invasion of Italy under these circumstances represents either a blatant blunder of imperial diplomacy or reveals a cynical readiness to allow the peninsula to become a barbarian battle ground in order to destroy the Gothic realm. At the same time Theodahad was haggling with Petrus Patricius about the conditions under which the Amal would be allowed to remain king. The first offer entailed the formal cession of Sicily, which had been lost militarily, and the definite renunciation of important rights. The Gothic king gave up (1) capital jurisdiction over senators and bishops, (2) the right of confiscating their fortunes, and (3) the right of appointing patricians and conferring all other senatorial dignities. In addition he had to accept restrictions on outward displays of august lordship. Thus the acclamation of Theodahad could only follow the proclamation of the imperial name. Likewise, when statues were erected the figure of the emperor was to be placed on the right and that of the Gothic king on the left. Moreover, Ravenna offered a yearly tribute in the form of a gold crown weighing three hundred pounds and promised to furnish the imperial army with a Gothic contingent of three thousand men.[585] In addition, however, in secret negotiations Theodahad declared himself willing to abdicate altogether and to renounce the Italo-Gothic kingdom in favor of Justinian. Amalasuintha is said to have made a similar offer when she was preparing her flight to Byzantium in 532/533. This time the negotiations were more serious. Theodahad also reactivated his plan of 533 when he had requested political asylum and had wanted to move to Constantinople as a senator. Now he again demanded the senatorial yearly income of twelve hundred pounds of gold. The emperor, clearly little interested in making the acquaintance of the Amal philosopher, offered in return the possession of the royal domains in Italy under imperial dominion.[586]

Winter passed in the course of these intensive but time-consuming exchanges of messages and the traditional campaigning season returned.[587]

The negotiations were still in full swing when on Easter 536 the imperial troops in Carthage rebelled[588] and the Goths simultaneously won their first victories. Mundo's bands were no match for Theodahad's Dalmatian army. The old bandit and his son were killed and the rest of his troops left the country. But the native Dalmatians, especially the inhabitants of Salona, had not the slightest intention of supporting the Goths.[589] The victory in 536 gave Theodahad new courage. He forgot the offers he and his wife had made to Constantinople and had affirmed on oath.[590] Indeed, the Gothic king even violated ambassadorial immunity by arresting Petrus Patricius, who subsequently spent four years in Gothic captivity.[591] But Theodahad was far from becoming a Gothic king of the army merely by grossly overestimating a minor victory in Dalmatia. Nor was anything changed because he was the first Italian *rex* who disregarded the imperial privilege and had himself depicted on coins as if *imperator*.[592] Soon an imperial fleet put to sea from Durazzo and conquered Dalmatia. Important cities such as Salona-Split and Epidaurus-Ragusa-Dubrovnik were occupied and the Gothic settlers were persuaded to join the imperial cause.[593] At the same time Belisarius, who had put down the African revolt,[594] received orders to resume the war immediately and to carry it into Italy. There he met Ebrimud, Theodahad's son-in-law and commander of Rhegium-Reggio Calabria. The Gothic general surrendered immediately, which is difficult to understand. Theodenanda's bond to her father was one of genuine love and affection.[595] Her husband Ebrimud enjoyed Theodahad's full confidence and had been sent by him to the southern tip of Italy. In keeping with the earlier plans for Theodahad's surrender to Belisarius,[596] Ebrimud was instructed to allow the imperial troops to cross into Italy without resistance in order to take the Gothic king and his family into protective custody as quickly as possible. Under these circumstances Ebrimud's surrender makes good sense. But after the Dalmatian victory Theodahad had wagered everything on war, as a result of which his son-in-law should have done everything in his power to prevent Belisarius from landing. That Ebrimud nevertheless laid down his arms reveals his profound understanding of the situation. Whoever belonged to the clan of the controversial Gothic king was safer in Roman custody than among the Goths; moreover he could count on a life as *patricius* in Constantinople after surrendering.[597]

Belisarius marched unopposed as far as Naples, where he met the first fierce resistance. The Gothic garrison rejected the call for surrender because their relatives were in Theodahad's hands.[598] Now the king knew that the situation was serious and that he would have to fight.[599] To counter Byzantine diplomacy, Theodahad also began negotiations with the Franks, but the talks were concluded only under Vitigis.[600] Meanwhile, after a tough struggle Naples fell, whereupon Belisarius made an example of the city. Theodahad now marched out of Ravenna and advanced toward the imperial general as far as Rome, in the vicinity of which he concentrated the greater part of the Gothic army. But a revolt took place among the Gothic troops at the end of November 536. Theodahad tried to escape to Ravenna but was murdered by a personal enemy on orders from the new king, Vitigis.[601]

The Non-Amal Kings and the Fall of the Ostrogothic Kingdom, 536–552

VITIGIS (536–540)

In the five years between 531 and 536 the last three kings who can be attested as members of the Amal clan died. All had been closely related: two grandsons of Theodoric and their uncle. Their own people were responsible for their deaths. Athalaric died on the "home front," a victim of the typical Gothic life-style focusing on wine and women. Amalaric and Theodahad were both deserted and killed by their own Goths because they proved failures in the battle for the survival of the *gens*.[602] The brilliant formula *reges ex nobilitate, duces ex virtute sumunt* [*Germani*] with which Tacitus summed up his analysis of barbarian kingship was once again proved.[603] The Gothic nobility was exhausted. No suitable Amal was still alive, and the non-Amal nobility could not fill the gap. The Gothic leading stratum had suffered severely in the preceding years. The execution of Odoin in 500—the year of great triumph—and the killing of Pitzia in 514—later regretted—had remained isolated measures by Theodoric against the high nobility. The leading Gothic magnates were therefore a considerable power with whom Amalasuintha had to contend. The unsuccessful court revolt of 532/533 provoked the victorious queen to a bloody reaction against the nobility, as a result of which the court party at least was numerically weakened. Subsequently Theodahad initiated the downfall of his coruler Amalasuintha by eliminating certain individuals from her entourage, presumably great nobles friendly to the Amal queen. Finally, those who had been defeated in 533—who "were still numerous and of high nobility"— killed her to satisfy the blood feud. This act must have compromised the entire nobility.[604] When Theodahad lost his kingship because he had proved "useless" (*inutilis*)[605] in the face of the enemy, thus disqualifying himself as king of the Goths, no one from among the nobility (*ex nobilitate*) could take his place. And so a proven commander (*dux ex virtute*)[606] was raised on the shield.[607] This was Vitigis, who was "of no illustrious family" but who did belong, along with his relatives, to the Gothic military "establishment."[608] Both the uncle and the nephew of the new Gothic king were high-ranking commanders.[609] Even during the last days of Theodoric Vitigis must have distinguished himself during the siege of an unknown city, for he became Athalaric's *comes spatharius,* his sword-bearer.[610] As such he served in Ravenna's "foreign office," and his duties even took him to Constantinople.[611] As an independent commander he successfully repulsed the attack of the Gepids and Heruli against Sirmium in 530.[612] Theodahad retained this capable warrior as his own sword-bearer and handed over to him the supreme command of the entire mobile Gothic army gathering in southern Latium. The army's revolt came at a time when the Gothic king was doing nothing to relieve Naples. Suspicions were voiced, there were rumors of treachery. Theodahad fled, and in late November 536 the Gothic army made Vitigis king.[613] The forces assembled at Regata northeast of Terracina constituted the Italian *exercitus* and thus had the right to choose the ruler over Goths and Romans. Although Justinian was still at war with the Goths, he accepted their decision. But Constantinople now had to use force of arms to compel the king, duly elected by the Gothic army, to submit himself and his kingdom to the emperor, thereby annuling Zeno's agreement with Theodoric. Fate would have it that Vitigis became this "king of the Goths and Italians" who had to fulfill the emperor's wishes.[614]

With great clarity Vitigis established his rule as that of a king of the army: he is the first Gothic king whose raising on the shield is recorded. It took place "with drawn swords according to ancestral custom." It is not surprising that Cassiodorus depicts the event as the election "of a *Martius rex* [war king] by the Getic people." Vitigis saw himself as Theodoric's relative because he was imitating his deeds. But his plan of clan association through personal suitability also demanded that as the new king he give up his advantageous position and move to Ravenna, seize the royal city, and marry Matasuntha, Theodoric's granddaughter.[615] This reminds us of the hasty departure of Thorismund, who immediately marched to Toulouse to secure his kingship after his father had died in battle on the Catalaunian Fields.[616] Theodahad had been killed in early December 536 on his flight from Rome to Ravenna.[617] Vitigis voiced his concern that the Franks might attack the Goths in the rear, and the army voted for the retreat to Ravenna. After reaching the city Vitigis concluded the long overdue treaty with the Franks.[618] The Ostrogoths paid an indemnity of two thousand pounds of gold, exactly five percent of the treasure with which Amalasuintha had intended to flee to Byzantium;[619] they gave up their protectorate over the

Alamanni and other Eastern Alpine peoples; and they relinquished south-eastern Gaul, from which they could now recall their troops.[620] Strengthened through the addition of the Gallic army, Vitigis was numerically superior to his Roman adversary.[621] Retreating to Ravenna, gathering the Gothic forces in northern Italy, reequipping them with offensive weapons and armor:[622] all this—in addition to the constitutional measures to secure the kingship—reveals the well-planned moves of the seasoned commander. Nor did Vitigis neglect to take his turn in attacking the Romans in Dalmatia. If we criticize Vitigis for incompetence and indecisiveness as early as 537 we are mistaking the king of the first hundred days for the king who withdrew defeated from Rome.[623]

Between the end of November 536 and February 537 Vitigis led the Gothic army from Terracina to Ravenna and back again to Rome.[624] It is true that within this short period the Eternal City was lost, contrary to the Gothic war plan; even the senatorial hostages whom the Goths had taken could not prevent this.[625] But Vitigis had strengthened his army, he had prevented a war on two fronts with a timely treaty, and he had won the royal city together with the royal child Matasuntha. The young girl, about eighteen years of age, was little pleased with the situation, but her displeasure probably had less to do with Vitigis's age—he was born around 500—than with his birth. Perhaps she was also annoyed because her royal consort had repudiated his first wife.[626] After the legally determinative act at the "barbarian fields" of Regata had been secured and extended by the equally important legitimization attained at Ravenna, Vitigis marched forth in great haste to face Belisarius. The Roman general had begun to entrench himself at Rome on December 9 or 10, 536.[627] Apart from the city militia, Belisarius had at his command only about five thousand imperial soldiers. In addition, there were sailors and camp followers, but they had little fighting ability and discipline. When in a dispatch to the emperor Belisarius lamented the thirtyfold superiority of the enemy, he was greatly exaggerating, but it was time for Constantinople to realize that the situation had changed since the death of Theodahad.[628] The *drôle de guerre* of the first eighteen months had turned into a full-scale Gothic war.

The situation of the Roman army now seemed so precarious that Vitigis was actually afraid he might not be able to force Belisarius to battle.[629] But even in this war there was no danger of arriving too late. Since Vitigis made a detour around Belisarius's advanced strongholds at Spoleto and Perugia he reached the Tiber city sooner than expected.[630] On February 21, 537, the Goths stood before the gates of Rome,[631] and for more than a year they would assault its walls, sustain defeats, and gain victories in splendid cavalry attacks.[632] But they suffered great losses. The heavy artillery as well as the mounted and armored archers wrought havoc among the Gothic lancers and foot warriors.[633] Moreover, with the arrival of Roman reinforcements the Goths' numerical superiority soon dwindled.[634] Nevertheless, the imperial troops struggled with many difficulties.

Belisarius had to send to Naples all the "useless eaters," such as women, children, and slaves. He even had to depose and exile the pope, who was the leader of a moderate party friendly to the Goths.[635] The large-scale assault on the eighteenth day of the siege nearly succeeded,[636] and this seemed to justify the decision of those who had deserted to the Goths at the very beginning because they had given up Belisarius's cause as lost.[637] But they were all proved wrong. Despite hunger and epidemics raging in the city, the Romans managed to hold out.[638] While still in Ravenna, Vitigis had commanded an army to cross to Dalmatia and recover Salona. Although the Goths had ships at their disposal, the expedition failed.[639] And at Rome too Vitigis was making no progress. His letters of reconciliation to the emperor and the high magistrates of Constantinople were still unanswered after a year,[640] and negotiations with the imperial general to divide Italy along the lines of the status quo were also unsuccessful. None the wiser for these experiences, the Gothic king arranged an armistice from which only Belisarius profited. It allowed the imperial general to reprovision Rome and then choose the next best opportunity to break the armistice once he had gathered enough troops to renew hostilities. In the first months of the winter of 538 a Roman cavalry force actually crossed the Apennines, laid waste to Gothic Picenum, led into slavery the women and children of the Gothic warriors besieging Rome, and finally advanced to Rimini where it entrenched itself dangerously close to Ravenna. Vitigis thus had no choice but to raise the siege in early March 538 and return to his royal city as quickly as possible.[641] The mountain fortress Auximum-Osimo south of Ancona was to stop the advance of the imperial forces: the "key to Ravenna" was thus placed in the hands of its strong Gothic garrison.[642]

When the siege of Auximum began a year later (spring 539) it tied down for seven months the main imperial army of eleven thousand soldiers under the command of Belisarius.[643] By that time Vitigis had already won his last, costly victories. The end was near. The murder of the senatorial hostages led if not to a break with Cassiodorus then to his resignation in 537/538.[644] In 538 a Byzantine fleet landed an army at Genoa, took Milan at the request of its population, and threatened Ticinum-Pavia, after Ravenna the most important fortified city of the Goths. Burgundian "volunteers" were therefore gratefully received by the Goths, and with their help Milan was retaken in March 539. But the Goths had to stand by and watch as the Burgundians, in return for their support, enslaved as many Milanese women as they needed. With such methods it was hardly possible to win the support of a city population already hostile to the Goths. Nevertheless, the expulsion of the imperial troops from Liguria was a success that the Goths owed to Vitigis's nephew Uraias;[645] but the Byzantine attack on Rimini had taken the life of the king's uncle.[646]

Perhaps the Goths could now get along with their northern neighbors, enter into treaties with them, and make use of their support. And it was certainly time, for just before the conclusion of the Gothic-Frankish alliance Alamannic raiders had ravaged upper Italy.[647] In 538, however, starvation was the dreaded enemy, afflicting friend and foe alike. Its horrors, from which, especially, the peasants of the lowlands suffered magnified the effects of increasingly brutal warfare, for which Belisarius's cavalry commanders bear much of the responsibility.[648]

The battles that spread across all of central Italy and into the valley of the Po had caused a dispersal of the forces on both sides. Leaving aside the scenes of minor engagements, we find in early 539 that large, even huge, imperial armies were fighting around Osimo near Ancona, around Fiesole near Florence, and around Milan.[649] On June 21, 538, Belisarius had set out from Rome. Shortly thereafter Narses together with seven thousand men went ashore in Picenum, probably at the port of Firmum-Fermo. The numerical superiority of the Goths was now a thing of the past. They could only hope that rivalries and disagreements among the Roman generals would prevent the successful operation of the imperial troops. This hope materialized as soon as the two armies united at Fermo. At times the quarrels between Narses and Belisarius completely paralyzed the imperial forces. The loss of Milan was in no small measure the result of unclear lines of command. The setbacks persuaded the emperor to intervene, and in the spring of 539 he ordered Narses to return to Constantinople.[650] The eunuch obeyed, but his two thousand Herulian troops, who felt bound to him personally, deserted the Roman army and planned to march home to Pannonia II through northern Italy. On the way they fraternized with the Goths, promised to stop fighting against them, and sold them slaves and captured cattle. They were not "apprehended" until they had reached northern Venetia, whereupon they were once again taken into Roman service; most, however, were sent off to the East.[651]

No sooner had Belisarius regained undisputed command over the imperial army than war resumed. The aim of the Roman operation was to eliminate the Gothic field armies through a broad offensive. By forcing them to defend strategically important sites the imperial forces would deprive the

Goths of their mobility; the result would be the eventual siege and capture of Ravenna. Although Procopius disliked Narses, he nevertheless gives a good description of the totally different strategies and tactics of Belisarius and Narses, who was Belisarius's rival in 538/539 and who more than a decade later brought the Gothic war to an end by doing what he had earlier demanded: attacking the Gothic army head-on and destroying it.[652] Belisarius's strategy against the Goths was substantially the same as that of Theodoric against Odovacar.[653] As early as the summer of 539 Uraias had to expect a reinforced imperial army in Liguria. It established its base at the fortress of Dertona and thwarted all attempts by Uraias to leave the Po Valley to relieve Gothic-held Fiesole.[654] As a result the garrison of this protective barrier to central Italy was soon in great distress.[655] But the main theater of war was on the Adriatic coast. There, with eleven thousand men, Belisarius assaulted the fortress of Auximum, defended by four thousand select Gothic warriors.[656] Vitigis, who had lost all faith in his fortunes of war during the siege of Rome,[657] sat in Ravenna, no longer participating in the fighting. But he was not completely inactive; nor was he as helpless as Procopius makes him out to be. It is more likely that the Gothic king had understood Belisarius's strategic superiority and had accordingly exchanged the role of general for that of statesman. Gothic envoys approached the Lombards, but the latter refused the request for assistance with reference to their own alliance with the empire.[658] Next Vitigis dispatched two Ligurian priests to the Persians with the intent of stirring them up against the empire. This threat was taken so seriously by Justinian that the Gothic delegation Vitigis had sent to Constantinople at the beginning of his reign was immediately returned with promises of peace. Belisarius, however, detained the envoys for some time, and eventually exchanged them for Petrus Patricius and his companions, who had been captured during the days of Theodahad.[659]

For the moment this was all that could be achieved, for in 539 King Theudebert led his Franks on a sudden raid into northern Italy. Like a tornado the barbarians first fell upon the Goths and then upon the imperial army. Before crossing the Po the Franks sacrificed Gothic women and children to the river god, who must have been surprised at this offering from the emperor's Catholic allies.[660] But when food shortages and epidemics afflicted the Franks, their advance came to a standstill. Theudebert soon withdrew from a large section of Italy. The Goths, however, had had enough of such help. From this time Vitigis rejected all Frankish offers of an alliance, preferring to submit to the emperor rather than deliver himself up to the "vultures" from the north.[661]

After the Frankish storm had blown over, the Goths and Romans in

Liguria resumed hostilities. While the situation there reached a stalemate, Fiesole and Auximum fell,[662] and in late 539 Belisarius led the combined Roman army to Ravenna. Thus began the siege of the royal city, which Vitigis would leave only as a captive. But at this time his nephew still commanded a considerable force of four thousand men and was drawing near to relieve the city. At this very moment the Gothic garrisons quartered in the Cottian Alps, in the province north of Genoa, surrendered. As a result the rear of the imperial forces was now secure, while the families of most of Uraias's warriors were helplessly exposed to the enemy. The Gothic relieving force dissolved, the warriors went home and submitted to the emperor. And so Uraias, "undefeated on the battlefield," had no choice but to shut himself up in Pavia with his remaining loyal followers:[663] exactly half a century earlier the great Theodoric had done the same.[664]

The first months of 540 had not yet passed when Theudebert's renewed offer of assistance reached Ravenna: the Frankish king asked for half of Italy in return for the expulsion of Belisarius. Vitigis declined, no doubt in part because the imperial general was eagerly negotiating with him and was promising an agreement acceptable to both sides.[665] Then one day the great granary at Ravenna burned down. The Goths cast suspicion on Queen Matasuntha,[666] who was said to have established treasonable contact with the Roman conqueror of Rimini as early as late winter of 538. It was claimed that she actually wanted to marry him, but this seems unlikely.[667] In any case, Theodoric's granddaughter had to wait patiently until 542 before she was allowed to contract a Roman marriage appropriate to her rank and celebrated in Constantinople.[668]

The reports from the Persian frontier worried the emperor. Justinian was now genuinely willing to make peace with the Goths. All of a sudden the Goths' offer to divide Italy between their kingdom and the *imperium* seemed a desirable solution. But since December 537 the situation had changed so decisively in the emperor's favor that he could now demand much more, namely, half of the rich royal treasure and all the territory up to the river Po. Although this would essentially have confined the Gothic kingdom to the two Italian provinces of Liguria and Venetia-Istria, from our point of view the solution would have been almost ideal for all parties. Italy would have been spared the really destructive phase of the Gothic war and a small but compact transpadane Gothic kingdom would have been the best protection for the peninsula. The *regnum* of the Goths and imperial Italy would have adjusted to each other peacefully: by no means would this arrangement have meant the actual division of the peninsula. Vitigis and his Goths as well as the advisers around the imperial general were in favor of accepting the offer from Constantinople. But Belisarius was a general, and generals prefer to fight until they have forced the enemy's unconditional surrender. He therefore declined to sign the treaty, whereupon the Goths withdrew their support for the agreement.[669]

It is also possible that the Goths misinterpreted the hesitation of the Roman *patricius* and supreme commander because it suited their hopes. Belisarius's appointment by the legitimate Roman authorities as well as his success over the Italian Gothic army had made him almost "automatically" king of the army and *rex* of the Western empire. Vitigis no longer dared wage the decisive battle and fight for the existence of the *gens*. The leaders of the *gens* now offered the kingship to the victorious enemy. But there must have been earlier negotiations concerning Belisarius's elevation to the emperorship of the West. Such negotiations are clearly mentioned before the offer of the kingship. Furthermore, Belisarius made a peculiar, and in light of the Gothic numerical superiority a nonsensical, decision before marching into Ravenna: he sent away four commanders and their units to distant places because these officers "had behaved in a hostile manner toward him." Moreover, he did the same with the new pretorian prefect who had just arrived from Byzantium with an appointment for Italy. Only then did Belisarius enter the capital of the Western Empire with the few contingents loyal and faithful to him. But in principle this army, as the *exercitus Romanorum,* had the right of proclaiming an emperor; mutatis mutandis Belisarius's soldiers would have taken over the role the Gallic army had played at the elevation of Avitus, while the Vitigis Goths would have been assigned the part played by the Visigothic army. But regardless of whether Belisarius was seriously thinking of accepting the elevation to the emperorship—his removal of the unreliable Roman troops and his cool reception by Justinian lend weight to such a notion—or whether he merely wanted to create the impression that he was prepared to do so, he succeeded in maneuvering Vitigis and his advisers into a position that gave them no choice but to surrender since they were already suffering a terrible famine.[670] The imperial army marched into Ravenna unopposed, took captive the Gothic king and his army, and thus seemed to have ended the conquest of the Western empire in May 540.[671] Procopius describes the scorn and horror of the Gothic women when they realized to whom their men had surrendered.[672] But the war was not over; as usual, a war fought with the aim of "total victory" had gambled away peace.

HILDEBAD AND ERARIC (540/541)

After the surrender, large numbers of cispadane Goths were dismissed to return to their *sortes.* Belisarius sent them home as imperial subjects, without forcing them to hand over any of their personal property, as the garrison of Auximum had had to do. This had formed part of the agreement and satisfied the general's wish to remove all these numerous Goths from Ravenna before they became dangerous. Moreover, Belisarius could afford to be generous since his army had captured rich booty in the royal city. That part of the Gothic treasure that Vitigis had not been able to transport to fortified Pavia or perhaps Verona fell into the hands of Belisarius, who took all the precious objects to his emperor in Constantinople. He also led before the emperor the Ostrogothic palace nobility and its retainers, a band of the very best troops, who were sent immediately to the Persian frontier. Among the deportees were the royal couple, supposedly Vitigis's son from his first marriage, the son and daughter of the former Thuringian queen Amalaberga, and the children of Hildebad.

Hildebad himself was a leader of those transpadane Goths who had not, or not yet, submitted and who in other ways too behaved atypically:[673] north of the Po some Goths continued fighting, despite the capitulation of their lawful king and despite the loss of the royal city and the royal treasure.[674] Thus Ticinum-Pavia was firmly in the hands of Uraias.[675] He had been successful against the Romans and had remained undefeated. Should he become the next king of the Gothic army? Uraias declined the honor: the hapless leadership of his uncle Vitigis had revealed that his family lacked τύχη—"royal fortune." As a result it fell to him to suggest a replacement: Uraias gave his support to Hildebad. Hildebad was a nephew of Theudis, the king of the Visigoths; in other words, he came from the same social stratum as Vitigis and his relatives. He was in command of the royal city of Verona, and like all the other leaders of the transpadane Goths he had established contact with Belisarius to negotiate the terms of surrender. Since his children were in the hands of Belisarius, Hildebad would have had an additional reason to submit. Nevertheless, he had himself elevated to the kingship. Perhaps this was only intended to put final pressure on Belisarius—the favorite candidate of all Italian Goths—to accept the imperial or royal dignity (βασιλεία) after all. To this end Hildebad's Goths sent an embassy to Ravenna which renewed the offer and at the same time scolded Belisarius for being a false slave who had broken his word and who had deprived himself and them of the independent dominion over the Goths and the Italians. But the Roman general still declined, bound as he was by a personal oath to his emperor Justinian never, during Justinian's lifetime, to seek dominion or imperial power.[676] With this final refusal the breach was complete; Belisarius sailed off for Constantinople and the war began anew.

Previously the *exercitus Gothorum* had possessed the right to elect the king of the Goths and Italians, but with the surrender of Vitigis in May 540 this right had expired. From that time those Goths who did not want to submit to the emperor had no choice but rebellion. The kings they proclaimed would be considered *tyranni,* usurpers. Their authority lacked all foundation in Roman law and to a large extent even in barbarian tradition. Like Vitigis they were elevated as pure kings of the army, but unlike Vitigis they gained no additional legitimacy through marriage into the Amal clan or possession of the royal city.[677] Only a part of the royal treasure—such as the Codex Argenteus and the royal insignia—must have reached Pavia and Verona in time, where it formed the core of a new treasure.[678] Jordanes's opinion that Gothic history extended only to 540 thus contains some truth as far as constitutional history is concerned.[679] But the Gothic kingship of the army of the last twelve years was not entirely without political roots. It was in the hands of the military establishment, a group of families whose prestige dated to the days of Theodoric and who combined traditionalist, barbarian beliefs[680] with the desire to rise out of the middle stratum. The office of sword-bearer, a position of special trust and one the Amal kings apparently did not fill with members of the high nobility, offered these families the chance they were seeking.[681] Theudis was the first among them who made the leap: he became king and set an example for Vitigis, thus qualifying his own family, which had stayed behind in Italy, for the royal dignity. The Visigothic king Theudis had the same importance for his Ostrogothic nephew Hildebad and his great-nephew Totila as Vitigis had for Uraias. The office of sword-bearer made possible a good career. But because of the holder's social background, he initially brought modest financial resources to the office. As Theodoric's governor in Spain, Theudis took the opportunity to marry a wealthy Roman woman, since he was able to ignore all marriage prohibitions and class distinctions.[682] Uraias, the nephew of the deposed king, must have gained similar wealth through marriage. As a result there arose between him and Hildebad, who had not yet "struck it rich," a life-and-death struggle in which Uraias lost his life. The confrontation arose from a meeting of their wives, which reminds us of the quarrel between the queens Brunhild and Kriemhild. The death of Uraias recalls the death of Siegfried of the heroic saga.[683]

At first the kingdom of Hildebad comprised just slightly more than the narrow strip of land between Pavia and Verona, and only one thousand Gothic warriors were in his following.[684] Nevertheless he achieved a swift victory. Tarbesium-Treviso was the strongest fortification in central Venetia. It was defended by the "imperial" Heruli, none other than the bands that had been so eager to return home the previous year. Among them was

Mundo's grandson, who was honoring the traditional ties of his family. Such loyalty very nearly cost him his life.

Hildebad struck hard and annihilated the only Roman troops stationed north of the Po. His nephew Totila took over the command in Treviso.[685] Now the number of Goths supporting Hildebad began to increase. Within a very short time he controlled the two provinces of Liguria and Venetia. Immediately after Belisarius had departed for Constantinople the imperial army suffered severely from desertion, and now the deserters had someone they could join. Dissension among the imperial commanders as well as strict, even ruinous, taxation—demands were made retroactive to the death of Theodoric—undermined the morale of the army and the civilian population. At the same time the imperial treasury reduced, if not halted altogether, the payments to the troops.[686] This explains why the Goths could indulge in bloody conflicts between their two leading families of sword-bearers without running the risk of a Roman attack. Hildebad also managed to maintain his position despite the failure of his uncle Theudis to send support. Only relatively late did the Visigoths try to establish something like a second front against Byzantium in Africa, but this attempt failed miserably.[687]

The war had reduced the Gothic *regnum* to a small kingdom with which the non-Gothic *gentes* of Italy now tried to compete. Just as Procopius frequently reduces his battle description to accounts of single combat,[688] he likes to "personalize" the causes of political events. For Procopius the fall of Hildebad—analogous to that of Uraias and Theodahad[689]—was caused by an affair with a woman. In reality the defeated Vitigis clan probably allied with non-Gothic barbarians—predominantly Rugians, but also Gepids—against the king. Hildebad was murdered at table by one of his personal retainers, whereupon the Rugians proclaimed their chieftain Eraric king, probably in May 541.[690] But the small tribe of the Rugians, which had been settled in Venetia since the days of Theodoric,[691] had assumed too heavy a burden. Eraric could not fulfill the expectations placed in him. His attempt to return to Justinian's offer to divide Italy, which Belisarius had sabotaged, is, however, noteworthy. To this end the new king sent an embassy to Constantinople. The Gothic kingdom north of the Po, in the original plan intended for Vitigis, had now survived for more than a year. Its existence was accepted by the imperial generals, who never crossed the Po, especially after the defeat of their colleague at Treviso. Yet Eraric did not even receive imperial recognition of the status quo. Since he let it be known privately that he just wanted to follow the example of his illustrious predecessors and lead a comfortable life in Byzantium, he was not taken seriously.

In the meantime a revolt had started among Eraric's Gothic enemies, and after a reign of five months he lost his power and his life. While Totila was negotiating with the imperial commander of Ravenna about the terms of surrender, just as his uncle had once done, the Goths of Pavia offered him the kingship. The man who had been commander at Treviso demanded that Eraric be killed before he would accept the royal authority. He fixed a day for the murder, probably sometime in October 541. His demand was met.[692]

TOTILA (541–552)

Like Alaric I,[693] the "heroic youth" Totila—he was in fact young when he became king[694]—is among the favorite figures in German historiography. As late as 1949 even Ernst Stein, who stood above all indulgence in Germanicism, shared the "real admiration" his Viennese teacher Ludo Moritz Hartmann—as "un-Germanic" as his student—felt for Totila.[695] By contrast, some authors to this day follow the judgment of contemporaries that Totila's "elevation was a disaster for Italy."[696] Both interpretations are quite unhistorical, since they exaggerate the range of Totila's motivations. The Goths declared him king so that he would recover for them the "dominion over the Italians."[697] This determined his choice of action, unless he wanted to share the fate of his predecessors. Together with Valamir and Theodoric, Totila is surely among the most capable commanders of the Ostrogoths. Yet one can neither blame him nor declare him a hero for fighting better and more skillfully than most other Gothic kings. To be sure, in the long run even Totila was no match for a general like Narses, and the catastrophe at Busta Gallorum does not show him in the best light. But in 541 he had before him a kingship of eleven years, the second-longest reign of a Gothic king in Italy after Theodoric.[698]

According to the evidence from coin inscriptions and some literary sources,[699] Totila's real name must have been Baduila-Badua. Although we do not know what "Totila" signifies, his original name means "the fighter" or "the warrior."[700] At the height of his kingship Totila controlled nearly all of Italy, a task for which he needed many Roman officials; nevertheless, hardly anything is known about these men or about the nature of Totila's administration.[701] Totila's kingship encompassed eleven years of war in Italy, on the Italian islands, and along the coast of Dalmatia and Epirus. If it is true that the king visited St. Benedict at Monte Cassino, the traditional accounts have distorted this event so much that we cannot say what the purpose of this visit might have been. According to the hagiographer Pope Gregory the Great, Benedict foretold his unexpected visitor the length of his rule and the hour of his death.[702]

The details of military operations—advances and retreats, cities selected for siege, length of siege, capitulation as a result of assault, starvation, or treachery—concern only the specialist. The military historian may be intrigued by these details, for at times a comparison between Procopius's *De bello Gothico* and World War II in Italy forces itself even upon the layman. The accounts of the cities and regions of the peninsula talk of destruction, decline, and misery. They are therefore also of great interest to a local historian investigating the fate of an Italian region during the period of transition from antiquity to the Middle Ages.[703] But the general historian can shorten Totila's reign by dividing it into three periods. The first phase of the war constitutes the short time from the elevation of Totila in the fall of 541 to the spring of 543. The second phase lasts somewhat longer, stretching from the capture of Naples in 543 to the year 550, when Germanus was appointed supreme commander for Italy and Justinian at the same time made possible the quick and successful conclusion of the war through a large-scale military effort. The third and last phase of Totila's reign begins in the spring of 550 and ends in the summer of 552 with the battle at Busta Gallorum. Teja's kingship until October of the same year is merely an epilogue to Totila's reign.

Phase 1: In the winter of 541/542 an authoritative command from the emperor aroused the quarreling generals enough for them to decide on a vigorous offensive against the Goths on the north side of the Po. Twelve thousand soldiers, the entire field army in Italy, left the area around Ravenna and marched north against Verona, where the collaboration of local nobles was firmly expected. While the generals were already dividing the spoils before they had won them, the campaign ground to a halt in a manner fit for a comedy show. The imperial army withdrew to the region between the river Reno and Faventia-Faenza, southwest of Ravenna.[704] Totila called up his entire army of five thousand men and went in pursuit. The speech that Procopius puts into his mouth before the crossing of the Po contains the creed of the king of the army: he must administer justice and win battles, "for only the victors can constantly increase their power and attraction."[705] Totila was in fact an inspiring leader: those Goths who were sitting on their estates and *sortes* as well as many Roman soldiers flocked to his banners. Barbarians of Gothic as well as non-Gothic descent joined Totila in masses; indeed, even one of Belisarius's high-ranking *buccellarii* abandoned the imperial cause.[706]

In the spring of 542 Totila won his great victory at Faenza. With a skillfull pincer movement in which three hundred Gothic lancers decided the battle, he routed a large Roman army, more than twice the size of his own. Within a short time the king once again commanded twenty thousand men.[707] Soon strong Gothic forces were besieging the city of Florence in order to open the Via Cassia to Rome. At the approach of the imperial relieving force the Goths withdrew a day's march north to the valley of Mugello, but there they inflicted a crushing defeat on the enemy. While the Roman army, shattered into small groups, was hiding behind the walls of the cities of northern and central Italy,[708] Totila broke through to southern Italy, where the imperial generals had least expected him. This region had so far been nearly completely spared; here the Goths had no trouble obtaining provisions, and here rich booty was waiting to be won. Beneventum was taken. Even Cumae fell into Totila's hand, and it remained an important Gothic stronghold beyond the end of the kingship. At the same time the king began the siege of Naples, where strong anti-imperial sentiments existed.[709] After Totila had conquered the south and had initiated his first attempt to break Byzantine control of the sea, in which attempt he was helped by surprise and the elements,[710] he cut off the most important supply lines of the imperial army and threatened Rome. In the spring of 543 Totila was able to move into Naples, where his treatment of the Roman garrison and the civilian population caused a tremendous stir.[711] Here it became clear, as it would later in Sicily,[712] that the Gothic king had a long memory. Depending on whether the Italians had remained loyal to the Gothic cause since 535 or had betrayed it, they were to be rewarded or punished. The Neapolitans had nothing to fear from Totila, but Tibur suffered a terrible fate when it was taken.[713]

Phase 2: During the seven years from 543 to 550 a war of attrition raged on Italian soil. Land and people suffered terribly. In November or December 544 Belisarius, who was crossing from Pola, went ashore at Ravenna. His appeal to Romans and Goths alike to desert Totila and rejoin the emperor met with no response. Indeed, it was virtually impossible to stop the disintegration of the Roman army. As early as the beginning of 545, for example, the Illyrians, who had just arrived, returned home because an invasion of Bulgarians was devastating their country. Soon Totila was able to capture Fermo, Ascoli, Spoleto, Assisi, Clusium-Chiusi, and probably also Auximum/Osimo; only Perusia-Perugia remained in Roman hands. As a result communications between Rome and Ravenna were cut, and in December of 545 Totila began his first siege of the Eternal City.[714]

The Gothic successes of 545, which were even surpassed by those in 546,[715] were possible in large measure because Totila's diplomacy had eliminated the Frankish threat. Theudebert was given Venetia, which allowed him to secure his conquest of the Alpine regions. The friendly neutrality of the most important Frankish king meant that the Gothic rear was secure and that an attack of the imperial army by way of the land route through Istria was unlikely. But this danger was contained only as long as the imperial forces were not commanded by a general like Narses.[716]

Although Belisarius had been supporting the defense of Rome since summer 546 from the port of Porto, Totila was able to enter the Eternal City on December 17. The Isaurian soldiers, who had not received any pay for some time, opened the gates to the Goths. Once again the captives were treated well, especially because there was still enough booty to be had in Rome;[717] some "inherited" from the Thracian Goth Bessas. This tough senior officer of Belisarius's had taken advantage of the food shortage in the city to enrich himself unashamedly. While he himself narrowly escaped to Porto, his treasure fell into the hands of the Goths.[718]

Totila opened negotiations with Constantinople from what he considered a position of strength. He wanted peace, but if his offer was refused he threatened to destroy Rome, kill the captive senators, and attack Illyricum. The emperor, however, was not ready to talk and referred the Gothic king to Belisarius, who had just recovered from a severe case of typhus.[719] And now Totila committed—or was he compelled to commit?—the momentous mistake of giving up Rome, even though the imperial general was in Porto. By April 547, while the Gothic army was marching to Ravenna, Belisarius had reestablished himself in Rome. It is not true that Totila abandoned the city carelessly; all attempts to secure and hold it must have failed because of the sheer size of Rome, which could not be "razed entirely to the ground."[720] Thus Totila lost his first "battle for Rome" and with it much of his prestige. As late as 549/550, just before his second capture of the city, his suit for the hand of one of the daughters of a Frankish king was rejected with reference to this debacle.[721] And from the years 546/547 come also the much quoted references to Totila's "revolutionary" policy concerning slaves. Former slaves had found their way into the Gothic army, thus gaining "Gothic freedom." Totila had not the slightest intention of returning them to their former masters. At the same time he succeeded in mobilizing the Italian lower classes in an organized fashion, but the Romans themselves were also trying to do that. For example, Tullianus, a patrician from southern Italy, called up the *coloni* from his estates and from the estates of his fellow senators. He then received from the Roman general a contingent of Antic rangers, and with this force he defeated a peasant army supporting the Goths. Subsequently Totila compelled the senators he held captive to promise their *coloni* free ownership of the land, whereupon the bands of Tullianus dissolved and returned home. But what Totila did was not revolutionary; rather, it was a shrewdly calculated, effective means of waging war.[722] The same holds true of Totila's readiness to protect the peasantry so that they could pursue their work in the fields. Totila could justify hope for victory only if he managed to mobilize the economic power of Italy against the emperor's nearly inexhaustible potential.[723] Yet it is clear that Totila found no real way of successfully approaching the Roman upper class, especially in the cities. On the whole, the Roman nobility remained loyal to the imperial cause, even if individual members, as, for example, Cethegus in 546, or some high ecclesiastical dignitaries strove for an accommodation or even a separate peace with the Goths.[724] Totila in return accused the senators of deserting the kingdom of the Goths and Italians. But ever since the days of Theodoric any basis for trust had been destroyed by arbitrary persecutions, the taking of hostages, forced manumission of slaves, even massacres among the senatorial nobility.[725]

In the spring of 547, probably in May, Totila returned to Latium and tried in vain to capture Rome. As a result of this setback the Gothic king suffered severe criticism from his leading nobles.[726] On the whole the military situation of the Goths had not deteriorated, but certainly a great victory had been gambled away. The year 547 had much worse in store for Totila's Visigothic great-uncle. Theudis wanted to profit from the success of his nephew by gaining a foothold in Septem, just as he had tried earlier during the Vandal war. His troops attacked the Romans in Mauritania, but the Visigothic king suffered such a devastating defeat that he lost the throne and his life in 548.[727] Meanwhile the war in Italy dragged on. Gothic successes alternated with defeats. Totila's attraction, however, had barely diminished; even Mauritanian and Isaurian deserters served in his army.[728] By the fall of 548—soon after the death of his patroness Theodora—Belisarius had been recalled by the emperor.[729] Eventually the Goths even possessed a fleet of their own which crossed the Adriatic in the summer of 549 and ravaged Dalmatia. It was commanded by Indulf, a deserter from the entourage of Belisarius. Just before Procopius reports this development he mentions an event that could have been decisive for the outcome of the war. Hildigis, the rightful heir to the Lombard kingdom, had been driven out by Vacho and had fought his way through to Italy with a large army. Apart from three hundred Lombards as personal retainers, he had in his following about seven thousand Gepids and Sclaveni. But after Hildigis had penetrated into Venetia and destroyed a Roman detachment, he returned to the Moesian Danube without ever joining Totila. The only explanation for this strange campaign is that the Lombard claimant was hoping for an immediate restoration to his throne. His decision to return proved wrong, and in the end he paid for it with his life. The Hildigis episode, however, is illustrative: the Gothic kingdom of Totila was still attractive to barbarian groups and individuals.[730]

From summer 549 to January 16, 550, Totila besieged Rome. For the second time the city fell because of the treachery of Isaurian soldiers who had not received their pay. This time the losses of the vanquished were more serious, and the survivors joined the Gothic army. Totila now saw himself as the ruler of Rome, where the old mint resumed its activities. Its coins competed with those of Pavia, Ravenna's successor as the Gothic royal city. The individual designs on the coins show a frontal portrait of the Gothic king wearing an imperial diadem. A new senate was created, its members drawn from Goths as well as Romans. For this purpose Totila brought the surviving senators back from Campania. Finally, another embassy was sent to Constantinople. This was the third legation since Totila's election but the first authorized to engage in serious negotiations. In the name of the king the embassy was to renounce Sicily and Dalmatia and offer an annual payment and a certain contingent of troops. Upon their arrival in Constantinople, the envoys were neither received by the emperor nor allowed to return home.[731] Justinian's answer was "total war." While Totila was plundering Sicily in May 550 and while another Gothic army captured Rimini in the north and inflicted a crushing defeat on the imperial forces near Ravenna, Justinian appointed his cousin Germanus—Matasuntha's second husband—as the new high commander of the Italian army.

Phase 3: The appointment of Germanus was preceded by imperial propaganda for Amal legitimacy; it was aimed at Italy as well as the Italian émigrés and the Belisarius followers in Constantinople.[732] It is possible that Jordanes wrote his extract of Cassiodorus's Gothic history at this time to support the hopes of the fugitive senators.[733] The Amali had always been "loyal to the emperor."[734] Now they had also joined themselves to the Anicii and had become in every respect high Roman nobility. From the traditions of these two families a new Western empire could arise—a *regnum Hesperium*—which would cast off all the "dregs" of its barbarian origins. Such hopes, if indeed they were nourished, remained political dreams.[735] Justinian had no intention of reestablishing an independent Western empire, but he did use the nostalgic ideology to win over Goths and Italians.

The name Germanus, as that of Matasuntha, had a particular impact on the many Roman deserters in the Gothic army, which itself was not too enthusiastic about fighting against Theodoric's granddaughter.[736] But it never came to that. Germanus died in the summer of 550 during his stay in

Serdica-Sofia where he was preparing the invasion of Italy.[737] It was probably his idea "to put on the boot from the top," that is, to conquer Italy with strong land forces via the Isonzo. In any case, this idea stood behind the strategy of Narses, who left Constantinople in April 551 as supreme commander and successor to Germanus. By the time the eunuch arrived in Salona in the summer of 551 the Roman fleet had won the naval victory of Senigallia near Ancona. As late as the spring of 551 three hundred Gothic ships had ravaged Corfu and Epirus. In the counterstrike the Goths were completely defeated by the Romans, who were using Ancona as their base. The weakness of Gothic naval warfare was clearly revealed, even though Totila's raid on the Greek mainland had a lasting effect on imperial strategy. At this time the long overdue Gothic embassy returned from Constantinople empty-handed. The morale of the Gothic army sank to its lowest point since 541. To provide some distraction and win a quick victory Totila occupied Sardinia and Corsica in the summer of 551, encountering no opposition. The evasion to the west was probably the worst possible response to the growing pressure from the east.[738]

In April 552 Narses left Salona and marched to Italy through Dalmatia and Istria.[739] Venetia was in the hands of the Franks, who denied the Roman army passage because Narses had in his following "mortal enemies" of the Franks: fifty-five hundred Lombards.[740] At the same time the *comes* Teja, who as governor of Verona also commanded a large Gothic army, had his men flood the Via Postumia, thus making all roads impassable. But neither the Franks nor the Goths paid any attention to the coastline, since they both considered it trackless because of its many estuaries and marshes. Yet the unimaginable happened: led by superb guides Narses moved with a gigantic army of close to thirty thousand men along the coast toward Ravenna. The water courses were crossed on portable pontoon bridges; in this way all Gothic defenses in the interior were circumvented.[741] While the Franco-Gothic "northeast wall" became useless, the Gothic position in southern Italy collapsed. Constantinople's strength at sea allowed the temporary transfer of the permanent garrison at Thermopylae to Bruttium-Calabria, where the Goths sustained a crushing defeat near Crotone.[742]

On June 6, 552, Narses entered Ravenna. Only nine days later he left the city again and with all available troops set out on the march to Rome. At first the imperial army moved along the coast as far as Fano, then it took the southern road parallel to the Via Flaminia and marched inland until it reached the central part of Umbria.[743] Before Narses could rejoin the Via Flaminia at Gualdo Tadina, there took place in late June/early July 552 on

the plateau of Busta Gallorum the memorable battle that put an end to Totila's kingship. Narses had arranged no less than eight thousand archers in a crescent-shaped formation well adapted to the broken ground. Behind them stood the "phalanx, the flower of the Roman army": the general with his officers surrounded by their *buccellarii* on the wings and in the center dismounted barbarians, primarily Lombards and Heruli. The reduced cavalry force of fifteen hundred men was placed at the extreme left wing behind Narses. It was to act as a tactical reserve: one third to back up those who were retreating before the enemy and two thirds to attack the Gothic infantry in the rear. An engagement that preceded the actual battle looks like a successful dress rehearsal. A small force of fifty Roman foot soldiers occupied a strategically important hill. There they formed a compact shield wall, bristling with lances, from which single soldiers armed with bows sallied forth and which repulsed every cavalry attack of the Goths.

Totila was aware of the numerical inferiority of his army. He therefore tried to distract the enemy and organize an unexpected strike. Clad in magnificent armor bearing the royal insignia and seated on his splendid charger, he performed the "djerid," the artistic lance-ride of the steppe nomads. He was displaying his skill, and friend and foe alike gazed spellbound upon the spectacle. Then finally two thousand cavalry, which Teja had wanted to bring to his king in Rome, arrived as the last reinforcement, and Totila signaled the attack. He gave the order to "use only the lance." The Goths were to ride the Romans down, since there was nothing else they could rely upon, least of all their infantry. The cavalry charge at the "Tomb of the Gauls" collapsed in a shower of arrows unleashed by the imperial archers, and it became the "Tomb of the Goths." Six thousand were killed, a figure that seems believable and that reveals an annihilating defeat for the Goths. We have two reports of Totila's death: one relates that he was struck and killed by an arrow at the very outset of the battle. The other version has him killed during his flight by Asbad, the leader of the Gepids under Narses. What is clear is that the retainers brought the mortally wounded king all the way to Caprae-Caprara, where he died and was hastily buried. Byzantine soldiers learned of the burial, opened the tomb, and made sure of the identity of the dead man before they sealed the grave again. According to a parallel tradition Narses is said to have sent Totila's bloodstained cloak to Constantinople. Later this report was elaborated and it was claimed that the general had also presented his emperor with the royal insignia of the dead king. This version contradicts Procopius's account; the author repeatedly stresses that at the start of the battle Totila took off his

resplendent gold armor and the insignia he had worn during the djerid and fought in the armor of a common soldier. It would therefore not have been possible to identify the king in flight. Be that as it may, Totila's death brought to a close the third phase of the war.[744]

THE EPILOGUE: TEJA (552)

The epilogue is both short and long: long if we count to the year 555, when the last Goths surrendered;[745] short if we stop with the end of Teja, whose kingship lasted not even three months.[746] The *comes* Teja was commander of Verona when Narses marched into Italy.[747] At the last moment he had come to the aid of his king.[748] After the catastrophe at Busta Gallorum Teja hastened to the royal city Ticinum-Pavia where he was declared king, took possession of the treasure, and made a pact with the Franks.[749] His father was Fritigern, namesake of the victor of Adrianople. Teja must have had several brothers, since Aligern is mentioned as the youngest.[750] During Teja's kingship the last battles of the Goths began with all the horrors of a lost war in its final convulsions: the murder of hostages, reprisals against innocent Romans, the march to the south and the withdrawal to the area around Naples, and finally the treason of the Gothic naval commander which rendered Teja's position untenable. In October 552 the last battle of the war was fought on Mons Lactarius—the "Milk Mountain" south of the Sarno River and thus closer to Salerno than to Naples. After the death of their king the Goths fought on until Narses guaranteed their return to their "proper land" (οἰκεία χώρα) if they promised to become faithful subjects of the emperor. On this assurance the remainder of the Gothic army surrendered and submitted, except for a band of a thousand warriors that Indulf, the former *buccellarius* of Belisarius, freed from the Roman pincer movement and led across Italy to Pavia. After reaching their capital city these Goths did not raise a new king. With this admission of weakness half a millennium of Gothic history came to an end.[751] Then began the "heroism after the final curtain," which individual Gothic commanders kept up for three years in the hope of a resurrection of their *gens*. The year 555 finally saw the capitulation of Compsa-Conza della Campania, which lies on the River Ofanto northeast of Salerno. But only a part of the seven thousand men penned up in this town were Goths. Many had been recruited from the "wreckage" of the Franco-Alamannic invasion that continued the Gothic war in 553/554 and at the same time brought it to an end.[752] The barbarian invasion caused a split among the Goths. Aligern surrendered the city of Cumae to the imperial forces and relinquished the royal insignia he had continued to guard even after the death of his brother.[753] Indulf and the Goths at Pavia—of whom nothing more is heard thereafter—probably joined the Franks. But the glory of the Franks soon came to an end. At Capua Narses destroyed one of their two detachments, while the other succumbed to an epidemic in Venetia. Thus the epilogue of the Roman war against the Ostrogoths closes with the final division of the Goths: some decided against a Franco-Gothic Italy, others for it. But in the end both the Frankish barbarian invaders and their Gothic supporters perished.[754]

Appendixes

Appendix 1. Roman Emperors

This list includes only those emperors and usurpers who appear in the text.

Augustus	31 (27) B.C.–A.D. 14
Tiberius	14–37
Caligula	37–41
Claudius	41–54
Nero	54–68
Galba	68–69
Otho, Vitellius	69
Vespasian	69–79
Titus	79–81
Domitian	81–96
Nerva	96–98
Trajan	98–117
Hadrian	117–138
Antoninus Pius	138–161
Marcus Aurelius	161–180 (161–169, dual principate with Lucius Verus)
Commodus	180–192
Septimius Severus	193–211
Caracalla	211–217
Opellius Macrinus	217–218
Elagabalus	218–222
Severus Alexander	222–235
Gordian III	238–244
Philip the Arab	244–249
Decius	249–251
(Priscus, usurper)	(250)
Trebonianus Gallus	251–253
Aemilianus	253
Valerian	253–260
Gallienus	253/260–268
Claudius II Gothicus	268–270
Aurelian	270–275
Probus	276–282

Diocletian	284–305		
Galerius	293–311		
Constantine I	306/324–337		
Licinius	308–324		
Constantine II	337–340		
Constans	337–350		
Constantius II	337/350–361		
Julian the Apostate	361–363 (as sole ruler)		
Jovian	363–364		

West		*East*	
Valentinian I	364–375	Valens	364–378
Gratian	367/375–383	(usurper Procopius)	(365/366)
		(usurper Marcellus)	(366)
Valentinian II	375–392	Theodosius I	379–395 (as sole ruler 392–395)
(usurper Maximus)	(383–388)		
Flavius Eugenius	392–394		
Honorius	395–423	Arcadius	395–408
(usurper Constantine)	(407–411)	Theodosius II	408–450
(usurper Iovinus)	(411–413)		
(usurper Attalus)	(409–410/416)		
Constantius III	421 coregent		
John	423–425		
Valentinian III	425–455	Marcian	450–457
Petronius Maximus	455		
Avitus	455–456		
Majorian	457–461	Leo I	457–474
Libius Severus	461–465		
Anthemius	467–472		
Olybrius	472		
Glycerius	473–474		
Julius Nepos	474–475	Zeno	474–491
Romulus Augustulus	475–476		
		Anastasius I	491–518
		Justin I	518–527
		Justinian I	527–565

Appendix 2.   A Survey of Gothic History

Gutones

7 B.C. to A.D. 17	Gutones in modern Pomerania–West Prussia first mentioned.
about 150	Guti recorded on the island of Scandia and Gutones east of the Vistula. Thereafter Gutonic migration into the Ukraine.

"The Scythians"

from 238	Repeated invasions of Gothic groups at the lower Danube.
242	Goths mentioned in the army of Gordian III during the campaign against the Persians.
251	Cniva's victory over the Roman army near Abrittus, death of the Emperor Decius and his son.
from 253	Repeated invasions of the Goths and of allied tribes as far as Greece and Asia Minor, and sometimes across the Black Sea.
268	Gothic advance into the Aegean Sea.
269	Triumph of Claudius II Gothicus over the Goths near Naissus–Nish.
271	Aurelian's victory over the Goths.
Spring 291	Tervingi mentioned for the first time; final division of the Gothic tribe.

Tervingi-Vesi   **Greutungi-Ostrogoths**

332	Foedus with Constantine the Great.
341	Ulfilas consecrated bishop.
365 to 376/381	Era of Athanaric.
365	Goths support the usurper Procopius.

Date	Tervingi-Vesi	Greutungi-Ostrogoths	Migrations of Gothic Groups
369		First mention of the Greutungi.	
367–369	War with Valens.		
375	Advance of the Huns.	Death of Ermanaric; division of the Ostrogoths.	
375/376		Most of the Ostrogoths subjected by the Huns.	
376	Crossing of the Danube River under the command of Alaviv and Fritigern.		
9 Aug. 378	Battle of Adrianople; death of Valens; decisive participation of Greutungi, Huns and Alans in the battle.		
380		Gratian settles Greutungi, Alans, and Huns in Pannonia as federates.	
3 Oct. 382	Foedus with Theodosius; settlement in the north of Thrace.		
391 to 401			The Goths of Alaric I in the Balkans.
394			Grave casualties among the Gothic federates in the battle of Frigidus.
395			Death of Theodosius; Alaric's elevation to king.
400			Catastrophe of the Goths in Constantinople; death of Gainas.

401 — Alaric's advance into Italy.

402 — Stilicho's victories over Alaric near Pollentia and Verona.

408 — Alaric's invasion of Italy.

24 Aug. 410 — Conquest of Rome by Alaric who dies in the same year.

410 to 415 — Athaulf.

412 — Expedition to Southern Gaul.

Jan. 414 — Athaulf's marriage to Galla Placidia.

414/415 — Expedition to Spain.

The New Visigoths: Regnum Tolosanum

418 — Settlement in Gaul.

418 to 451 — Theoderid; killed in the battle against the Huns on the Catalaunian Fields.

466 to 484 — Euric.

468/469 — Beginning of the war in Spain and Gaul.

405/406 — Radagaisus invades Italy.

The New Ostrogoths: Kingdom in Pannonia

451 — Defeat of the Amal Valamir Goths on the Catalaunian Fields.

454/455 — Battle fought at the river Nedao.

456/457 — Settlement of the Valamir Goths in Pannonia.

459 to ca. 469 — Theodoric the Great as hostage in Constantinople.

473		Theodoric Strabo's elevation to king in Thrace (d. 481); departure of the Valamir Goths from Pannonia to the Balkans.

The Migration of the Ostrogoths within the Balkans

474		Theodoric the Great's elevation to king in Macedonia.
475	Conclusion of a new treaty; recognition of Euric's conquests.	
about 475	Codex Euricianus?	
484		Theodoric the Great becomes consul.
484–507	Alaric II.	

The Italian Ostrogothic Kingdom

488		Theodoric's departure to Italy.
March 493		Conquest of Ravenna; murder of Odovacar.
497		Imperial recognition of Theodoric the Great as King of Italy.
probably 2 Feb. 506	Breviarium Alaricianum.	
10 Sept. 506	Synod of Agde.	
507	Battle of Vouillé; death of Alaric II.	
511	Death of Gesalec; Theodoric the Great also becomes King of the Visigoths.	
524		Death of Boethius.
525		Death of Symmachus.
30 Aug. 526		Death of Theodoric the Great.

| 526 to 531 | Amalaric. |
| 531 to 548 | Theudis (former sword-bearer of Theodoric the Great). |

526 to 534	Athalaric (Amalasuintha).
534 to 536	Theodahad.
535	Assassination of Amalasuintha; beginning of the war with Constantinople.
536 to 540	Vitigis.
536/537	Treaty with the Franks.
539	Franks invade Upper Italy.
541 to 552	Totila.
Dec. 546	First conquest of Rome.
Jan. 550	Second conquest of Rome.
June 552	Narses enters Ravenna.
end of June/beginning of July 552	Battle of Busta Gallorum; death of Totila.
552	Teja.
Oct. 552	Battle at Mount Lactarius; death of Teja.
555	Capitulation of the last Goths in Italy.

Kingdom of Toledo

568/569	Leovigild's assumption of the kingship; rebirth of the Visigothic kingdom.
589	The Visigothic kingdom becomes Catholic under Reccared.
711	Arab invasion ends the Visigothic kingdom.

Appendix 3. Genealogical Chart of the Balthi

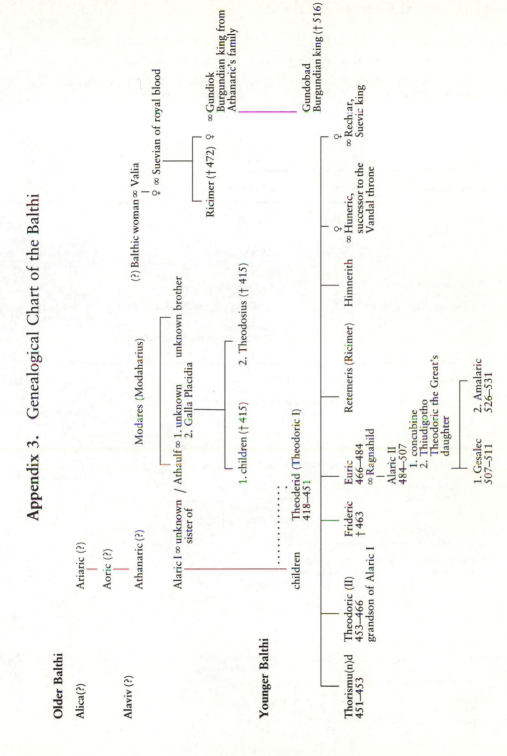

Older Balthi

Alica (?)

Ariaric (?)

Aoric (?)

Alaviv (?)

Athanaric (?)

(?) Balthic woman ∞ Valia
                    ♀ ∞ Suevian of royal blood

Ricimer († 472)   ♀
                  ∞ Gundiok
                  Burgundian king from
                  Athanaric's family

Gundobad
Burgundian king († 516)

Modares (Modaharius)   unknown brother

Alaric I ∞ unknown / Athaulf ∞ 1. unknown
         sister of   2. Galla Placidia

1. children († 415)   2. Theodosius († 415)

Younger Balthi

children

Theoderid (Theodoric I)
418–451

Thorismu(n)d
451–453

Theodoric (II)
453–466
grandson of Alaric I

Frideric
† 463

Euric
466–484
∞ Ragnahild

Alaric II
484–507
1. concubine
2. Thiudigotho
Theodoric the Great's
daughter

1. Gesalec
507–511

2. Amalaric
526–531

Retemeris (Ricimer)

Himnerith   ♀
             ∞ Huneric,
             successor to the
             Vandal throne

♀
∞ Rechiar,
Suevic king

Genealogical Chart of the Amali

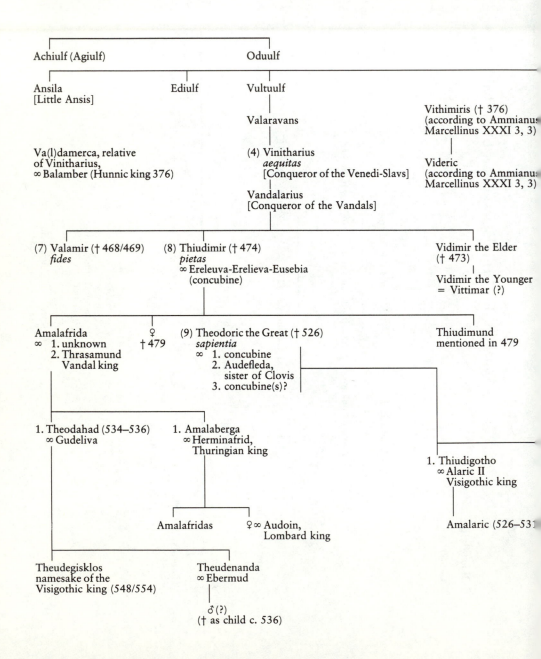

Gapt-Gaut [Father of the Gauti]
    (1) Amal [Father of the Amali], *felicitas*

Hulmul-Humli [Father of the Danes]
    Hisarna [The Iron One]

Augis-Avigis (see Wagner, "Personen-namen," pp. 27 ff.)
    (2) Ostrogotha [Father of the Ostrogoths], *patientia*, around 290

(3) Athal(a) [The Noble One], *mansuetudo*
    Hunuil [He who is immune to magic]

Achiulf (Agiulf)   Oduulf

Ansila [Little Ansis]   Ediulf   Vultuulf

Valaravans

Vithimiris († 376) (according to Ammianus Marcellinus XXXI 3, 3)

Va(l)damerca, relative of Vinitharius, ∞ Balamber (Hunnic king 376)

(4) Vinitharius *aequitas* [Conqueror of the Venedi-Slavs]

Videric (according to Ammianus Marcellinus XXXI 3, 3)

Vandalarius [Conqueror of the Vandals]

(7) Valamir († 468/469) *fides*

(8) Thiudimir († 474) *pietas* ∞ Ereleuva-Erelieva-Eusebia (concubine)

Vidimir the Elder († 473)

Vidimir the Younger = Vittimar (?)

Amalafrida ∞ 1. unknown 2. Thrasamund Vandal king

♀ † 479

(9) Theodoric the Great († 526) *sapientia* ∞ 1. concubine 2. Audefleda, sister of Clovis 3. concubine(s)?

Thiudimund mentioned in 479

1. Theodahad (534–536) ∞ Gudeliva

1. Amalaberga ∞ Herminafrid, Thuringian king

1. Thiudigotho ∞ Alaric II Visigothic king

Amalafridas   ♀ ∞ Audoin, Lombard king

Amalaric (526–531)

Theudegisklos namesake of the Visigothic king (548/554)

Theudenanda ∞ Ebermud

♂ (?) († as child c. 536)

This family tree is Theodoric's family tradition.
In it I have tried to present the schemes of the
Origo Gothica and Cassiodorus as well as historical
reality as far as we can recover it. The numbers (1)
to (9) identify those Amali who were represented in
Amalasuintha's genealogy. The virtues and qualities
attributed to them by Cassiodorus appear beside or
below the names in italics, my own interpretations
of the meaning of some names between brackets.
The placement of the individuals with the name
HUNIMUND follows from Jordanes, *Getica* 81,
p. 77, and 248–250, pp. 121 f.

Amali accepted by Theodoric

Hunimund the Elder

Gesimund
1 or 2 persons;
if two, second is
Amal son-in-arms

Hunimund
king of the Danubian Suevi
Amal son-in-arms

Amali rejected by Theodoric

Triarius

Theodoric Strabo   2 brothers   unknown sister
"The Squinter"   or aunt of
                                  Theodoric Strabo
                                  ∞ Aspar

Rekitach
"blood relative" of   Ermanaric
Theodoric the Great

Ermanaric (+375)

(5) Hunimu(n)d the Younger
forma
(according to Jordanes,
Getica 250, son of Ermanaric)

(6) Thorismu(n)d
castitas
40-year interregnum

Berimu(n)d

Videric
(Vetericus according to
Prosper a. 439)

Eutharic († 522/523)   Andela
husband of
Amalasuintha

Aidoingus (uncle of) ——▼   Giso   Andagis
comes domesticorum   ∞ Feletheus   ∞ sister of
                  Sidimund   king of the   the Alan Candac
                               Rugians (+487)

                               Frideric   Gunthigis-Baza

. Ostrogotho   2. Amalasuintha   3. ♀ (?)   3. ♀ (?)
∞ Sigismund   ∞ Eutharic   ∞ Tuluin   ∞ Flavius Maximus
  Burgundian king   ex gente Aniciorum

Sigeric († 522)   Athalaric (526–534)   Matasuntha
                                          ∞ 1. Vitigis
                                            2. Germanus
                                              cousin of Justinian

                                            2. Germanus (born 551)

Notes

Introduction

1. See especially Svennung, *Goticismus*, 1 ff., Messmer, *Hispania-Idee*, esp. 45 ff., Helbling, *Goten und Wandalen*, especially 53 ff. Wolfram, "Gothic History," 309 ff.

2. Zöllner, "Zusammenfassung: Noricum und Raetien I," 257. Klein, "Goten-Geten-Daken-Sachsengleichung," 84 ff. On Jan Sobieski as "Gothic Mars" see Wimmer, *Entsatz von Wien*, 273; cf. below, chap. 2, nn. 472 ff. and chap. 5, n. 615. (Mars). An early literary-topographical identification of a Slavic group with an East Germanic people occurs in the case of the lower Austrian Joseph Slavs who were still called Rugians around 900: see Wolfram, "Ethnogenesen," 123, n. 135. On the identification of Slavs and Avars as Vandals see Wolfram, *Conversio*, 102 with nn. 27–29.

3. This statement does not contradict the classification of Kienast, *Volks-stämme*, 87 and 155 (cf. chap. 4, n. 626 f.), according to whom the Goths of the Carolingian period formed a "French tribe." Apart from the terminology, which is open to debate, Kienast rightly refers here to the members of the Frankish Gotia, i.e., of a noble group that saw itself as a recognized community of Gothic law and whose contingents were levied in the royal army. Cf. below, n. 136.

4. Svennung, *Goticismus*, 34 ff. and 46 ff. Cf. Lhotsky, *Ebendorfer*, esp. 28 and 129.

5. Svennung, *Goticismus*, 51. Messmer, *Hispania-Idee*, 51 with n. 248.

6. Svennung, *Goticismus*, 91 ff. On the aftereffects of the theses of Rudbeck and of the ethnographic method of the humanists see, for example, Kraus, *Geschichtswissenschaft*, 190–192.

7. Svennung, *Goticismus,* 70 ff. and 101, after Montesquieu; 97 and 99.

8. Svennung, *Goticismus,* 99–103.

9. Jordanes, *Getica* 25, p. 60; cf. 19–24, pp. 58–60.

10. Svennung, *Goticismus,* 100.

11. Ibid., 103.

12. Svennung, *Goticismus,* 66 f. Gollwitzer, "Germanismus," 323 and 333.

13. Gollwitzer, "Germanismus," 349 ff., esp. 356.

14. Gruchmann, *Grossraumordnung,* 101. This work was kindly pointed out to me by Gerald Stourzh.

15. Messmer, *Hispania-Idee,* 49.

16. Ibid., 43 ff. (Italian position) and 48 ff. (reaction against Rome).

17. Ibid., 53 ff. Cf., for example, also Fichtenau, "Horizont," 227 ff.

18. On the genre of the *origo gentis* see the summary in Grundmann, *Geschichtsschreibung,* 12–17.

19. Bickerman, "Origines gentium," 65 ff.

20. For this expression see Tacitus, *Germania,* chap. 43. Cf. Much, *Germania,* 561, s.v. *interpretatio Romana.*

21. Cassiodorus, *Variae* IX 25.5, p. 292. Johann Weissensteiner (cf. n. 22) and Walter Goffart are preparing larger studies on the topic "Cassiodorus-Jordanes."

22. Wattenbach, Levison, Löwe, *Geschichtsquellen,* 1, 70 ff. and 75 ff. For the most recent discussion see Weissensteiner, *Abhandlungen,* 1 ff.

23. Wolfram, *Intitulatio I,* 56 ff. Wolfram, "Early Medieval Kingdom," 11 ff.

24. Wolfram, "Fortuna," 4 f. The joint transmission or even codification of the *origo gentis* and the *lex scripta* applies especially to the *Edictus Rothari* as attested by Paulus Diaconus, *Historia Langobardorum* I 21, p. 59 f.; cf. the transmission (ibid., p. 1 f.).

25. Grundmann, *Geschichtsschreibung,* 18 ff. Messmer, *Hispania-Idee,* 53 with n. 258.

26. Messmer, *Hispania-Idee,* 51 with n. 248.

27. Messmer, *Hispania-Idee,* 43 ff. Helbling, *Goten und Wandalen,* 73 ff. Graus, *Lebendige Vergangenheit,* 245 f. with n. 19.

28. Messmer, *Hispania-Idee,* 56 ff. Helbling, *Goten und Wandalen,* 85 with n. 169. For the myth of the young peoples see also Gollwitzer, "Germanismus," 317 ff. On the question of renewal see Ladner, *Idea of Reform* 1: 16 ff.

29. Hachmann, *Goten und Skandinavien,* 328 ff.

30. Wolfram, "Gothic History," 312.

31. See esp. Schlesinger, "Entstehung," 11–62, and Kahl, "Beobachtungen," 63–108. Cf. Wenskus, *Stammesbildung,* 175. The basis for the modern study of *gens* and *nationes* was established by Dove, "Studien," 1–98; the title, which—in this context—may seem strange today, should in no way keep the reader from consulting this important work.

32. Isidore of Seville, *Etymologiae* IX 2.1 and 4.4.

33. Cf., for example, Jordanes, *Getica* 26–28, p. 60 f.

34. Wenskus, *Stammesbildung,* 14 ff., 54 ff. (the tribe as a community of tradition) and 107 ff.; cf. 653, s.v. "Tradition." On the incompleteness of "entire" peoples see chap. 3, n. 97, and chap. 5, n. 162. On the polyethnicism of the Gothic peoples see below, n. 53 ff., chap. 2, n. 39 ff., chap. 4, n. 535 ff., and chap. 5, n. 259 ff. Barbarian peoples, such as the Huns, are σύγκλυδες: see Priscus, fr. 8 (FHG

4, 86). Characteristic also is Procopius, *De bello Gothico* III (VII) 21. 15 f., according to whom Totila called the Isaurians, who handed Rome over to him, φίλοι καὶ συγγενεῖς (friends and fellow tribesmen) and wanted to provide senatorial magistracies for them. Cf. ibid. 4. 10, the same address of Totila to the Gothic army. Yet membership in the Gothic army and Gothic nobility were not the same, at least among the Amali, as Maenchen-Helfen, *The Huns,* 199, following Ennodius, *Panegyricus* 20, p. 205, has discovered for the Bulgarians.

35. P. G. Schmidt, "Barbarus," 49.

36. On the barbarian mumbling of King Euric see Ennodius, *Vita Epifani* 69 f., p. 95.

37. Wolfram, "Ethnogenesen," 99, n. 15 f., esp. after Priscus, fr. 8 (FHG 4, 86).

38. See chap. 4, n. 311 ff. and nn. 504–513.

39. On the "Gothic" religion and the indifferent attitude of the believers cf. Gregory of Tours, *Historia Francorum* V 43, p. 251 f., and chap. 4, n. 203 ff.

40. Messmer, *Hispania-Idee,* 35 with n. 159, after Sozomenus, *Historia ecclesiastica* IX 6; cf. Claudianus, *De bello Gothico* vv. 544–549, p. 279. On the barbarian death wish see, for example, Ammianus Marcellinus XVI 5.17 and 12.50 as well as Libanius, *Oratio* XII 48 about the Alamanni. For the barbarians' fear of thunderstorms see chap. 3, n. 73; cf. chap. 2, n. 472. For the participation of barbarian women in battle see Ammianus Marcellinus XV 12.1, or Much, *Germania,* 165 f. On the Gothic Amazones see chap. 1, n. 87 and chap. 2, n. 104.

41. Wenskus, *Stammesbildung,* 38 ff., esp. 41–43 n. 182. Ladner, "On Roman Attitudes," 1 ff., esp. 3 n. 8 f. with extensive references. Messmer, *Hispania-Idee,* 32 ff. Straub, *Regeneratio Imperii,* 196 ff., 200, and 245. Lechner, "Byzanz und die Barbaren," 292 ff., esp. 297. On the barbarians' gold lust see Grönbech, *Kultur und Religion* 2:13–17. Claude, *Adel, Kirche und Königtum,* 202. Menandros Protector, fr. 48 (gold lust as a cause of war). Horn, "Gold," 902 f. The themes of "gold lust," "comparison to animals," and "rejection of the kingship" are discussed by Ammianus Marcellinus XXXI 2.7 and 11 (excursus on the Huns); cf. Maenchen-Helfen, *The Huns,* 12 f. with nn. 79 and 82.

42. On the appearance of the barbarians see Procopius, *De bello Gothico* I (III) 2.4 f.: the "Gothic peoples" are fair-skinned, blond, tall, handsome and all have the same laws and the same religion. On all these questions, but especially on habits of personal hygiene and sexual customs see Graf, *Orientalische Berichte* 43 ff. Cf. Ammianus Marcellinus XV 12.1: *De moribus Gallorum.*

43. See chap. 4, n. 312.

44. Ammianus Marcellinus XXXI 2.1 ff. Jordanes, *Getica* 127 f., p. 90 f.

45. Hachmann, *Goten und Skandinavien,* 94 f., as well as above nn. 7–9. Wolfram, "Ethnogenesen," 99 nn. 10–13, esp. after Synesius of Cyrene, *Oratio de regno ad Arcadium imperatorem,* chap. 15, on the question of barbarian continuity. Great procreative power was ascribed not only to the northern peoples. Tacitus, *Historiae* V 5.3 speaks of the *generandi amor* of the Jews. Cf. Jerome, *In Isaiam* 48.17.

46. See chap. 4, nn. 453–458, and chap. 5, n. 98. Cf. L. Schmidt, *Ostgermanen,* 50.

47. Hachmann, *Goten und Skandinavien,* 328 ff., esp. 382 ff., 402 ff., and 430 ff.

48. Graf, *Orientalische Berichte,* 43. Wolfram, "Gotische Studien I," 9, and II,

309 f. See, for example, the inventory of the treasure finds of Apahida and Somoşeni in Horedt and Protase, "Zweites Fürstengrab," 176 ff., and Horedt and Protase, "Völkerwanderungszeitlicher Schatzfund," 65 ff., esp. 96. On raw meat as a barbarian food see, for example, Ammianus Marcellinus XXXI 2.3 (excursus on the Huns) and Pomponius Mela 3.3.2 (the Germanic peoples); cf. Maenchen-Helfen, *The Huns*, 14 f. n. 91–96.

49. See above, n. 41 ("gold lust") and n. 47.

50. Wenskus, "Probleme," 34. Wolfram, "Gotische Studien II," 328 f. with n. 120. On Aligern see Agathias I 20.2–4, 6, as well as chap. 5, n. 333 and nn. 750 and 753.

51. Jordanes, *Getica*, p. 138.

52. Procopius, *De bello Gothico* III (VII) 2.1 f. Köpke, *Anfänge des Königthums*, 198 f. Wolfram, "Gotische Studien II," 311 f. with n. 101.

53. See chap. 2, n. 511.

54. See chap. 2, nn. 362 ff.

55. See chap. 4, nn. 494 ff.

56. See chap. 5, nn. 295 ff.

57. See chap. 2, nn. 73 and 76, as well as chap. 5, nn. 275–280.

58. Cf. Priscus, fr. 39 (Gothic peasants as slaves of the Huns). Eugippius, *Vita s. Severini*, ch. 8: the "evil" Giso enslaves Romans as well as barbarian goldsmiths.

59. Priscus fr. 8 (FHG 4: 85–88). Wirth, "Attila und Byzanz," 66 with nn. 126–128. Cf. Altheim, *Geschichte der Hunnen* 4:271 ff., esp. 302 f. Even if Doblhofer, *Byzantinische Diplomaten*, 80, is right that the story is a mere invention, it loses nothing of its significance as an example.

60. Wolfram, "Gotisches Königtum," 11 and 20 ff.

61. Jordanes, *Getica*, 251, p. 122; cf. Isidore of Seville, *Historia vel Origo Gothorum*, 1, p. 268 f., and 19, p. 275.

62. Cf. Borrscheuer, *Miseriae regum*, 22 f. and 68 ff.

63. Wolfram, *Intitulatio I*, 10 and 91 with n. 14.

64. Wenskus, *Stammesbildung*, 573 f.

65. *Concilium Toletanum* III 2, p. 19. Cf. Claude, *Westgoten*, 85 ff.

66. L. Schmidt, *Ostgermanen*, 360, n. 2. Ensslin, *Theoderich der Grosse*, 172 ff. See esp. Cassiodorus, *Variae* IX 24, 9, p. 290; cf. ibid. p. 505, s.v. "Italia."

67. Procopius, *De bello Gothico* III (VII) 1, 21.

68. See chap. 5, nn. 684, 692, 697, and n. 731. On the "tyrant" Totila cf. chap. 5, nn. 180 and 705, as well as Wolfram, "Gotisches Königtum," 23 f. with nn. 136–138.

69. Cf. Wolfram, "Gotisches Königtum," 24 f. with nn. 143–145.

70. On this expression see chap. 1, n. 67.

71. Procopius, *De bello Gothico* I (V) 13, 13.

72. Claude, *Westgoten*, 66 ff. See Wolfram, *Intitulatio I*, 217 ff. for the term "national peoples" (*Staatsvölker*) and its legal justification. Cf. esp. Kienast, *Volksstämme*, 75 ff., on the surrender of the Goths of Narbonne in 759 to Pepin I, who guaranteed them in return the use of their own law. Teillet, *Des Goths*, 421 ff., is especially good in discussing the later history of the Goths.

73. Cf. Brunner, *Land und Herrschaft*, 111–120.

74. Wolfram, "Ethnogenesen," 149, nn. 305–307. Wolfram, *Conversio*, 29 f. and 80 f.

75. Claude, *Westgoten,* 86, after *Leges Visigothorum* II 1.8, p. 53 f., and VI 1.7, p. 256; cf. p. 544, s.v. "patria." See also *Concilium Toletanum* VIII, p. 473, and XVI, p. 483.

76. Cf. on this Wolfram, "Ethnogenesen," 101, n. 24.

77. See above, n. 45.

78. Wolfram, "Ethnogenesen," 100, n. 17 f., esp. after Procopius, *De bello Vandalico* I (III) 2.2, 3.1, and Procopius, *De bello Gothico* I (V) 1.3. III (VII) 2.1. But *De bello Gothico* IV (VIII) 5.6 explains traditionally that the Gothic peoples were called Scythians "in the old days," "since all the nations who held these regions are called in general Scythians."

79. On the expression cf. above, n. 72. On the Goths in the Roman army of the sixth century see below, n. 130.

80. Brunner, *Land und Herrschaft,* 163; cf. 131 f. and 440.

81. Cf. Wolfram, "Ethnogenesen," 97, n. 2, and 99, n. 14.

82. See chap. 1, n. 24.

83. See chap. 1, n. 21, and chap. 2, n. 12.

84. On Jordanes, *Getica* 9, p. 55; 16–25, p. 57–60; 94, p. 82; and 121, p. 89, see esp. Hachmann, *Goten und Skandinavien,* 15 ff., as well as chap. 2, nn. 1 ff.

85. See chap. 1, nn. 17 ff. as well as chap. 2, nn. 11 ff.

86. Tacitus, *Germania,* chap. 2, grants the Vandili this name.

87. Pliny, *Historia Naturalis* IV 99, mentions the Gutones as the subgroup of the Vandili.

88. See chap. 2, nn. 37 ff. On the ideas of the Hippocratic ethnographers see chap. 2, n. 38.

89. Cf. Paulus Diaconus, *Historia Langobardorum* I 12 f., p. 53 f., and esp. I 17, p. 56. See esp. below, chap. 2, n. 39.

90. See chap. 2, nn. 23 ff.

91. See chap. 2, nn. 42 ff.

92. See chap. 2, nn. 94 ff.

93. Jordanes, *Getica* 21–24, p. 59 f. Cf. Hachmann, *Goten und Skandinavien,* 109 ff. Wagner, *Getica,* 103 ff. Svennung, *Jordanes und Scandia,* 32 ff. See also chap. 5, nn. 461 ff.

94. L. Schmidt, *Ostgermanen,* 398 f. Schwarz, "Krimgoten," 203–205.

95. The realization for the need of this work led me to suggest to Andreas Schwarcz the topic of his dissertation, *Reichsangehörige.*

96. Wolfram, *Intitulatio I,* 32 ff. Wolfram, "Early Medieval Kingdom," 1 ff. Wolfram, "Gotisches Königtum," 1 ff.

97. Wolfram, "Gotisches Königtum," 6 f., 19 ff., and 23 f.

98. See chap. 5, n. 195.

99. Claude, *Adel, Kirche und Königtum,* 61 ff.

100. See chap. 5, n. 183 f.

101. Cf. *Leges Visigothorum* III 1, 1, p. 121 f.

102. Ammianus Marcellinus XXVII 5.11–13. Orosius, *Historiae adversum paganos* VII 32, 12 f., cf. 32, 9 (Athanaric). Wolfram, "Gotische Studien III," 261 n. 5 (Burgundians-Romans). *Generatio regum Francorum,* pp. 851 and 854, cf. Goffart, "Table of Nations," 111 f. On the notion that the Romans were one *gens* among many see Wolfram, *Intitulatio I,* 34 ff. with n. 11; cf. 267, s.v. "Gentilismus."

103. See chap. 1, n. 102 as well as Sidonius Apollinaris, *Epistulae* VII 6.6, p. 109.

104. On the "splendor of the [Amal] clan" and the comparison of the royal clan with the senatorial nobility of Rome see Cassiodorus, *Variae* VIII 2, 3, p. 232. Cf. Wolfram, *Splendor Imperii*, 108 ff.

105. See chap. 5, n. 451.

106. See chap. 1, nn. 92 ff., and chap. 5, nn. 451.

107. See chap. 3, n. 233.

108. Wolfram, "Gotisches Königtum," 10 f. Characteristically enough Eunapius fr. 60 reports that the young Fravitta of the highest Gothic nobility was very welcome to his Roman father-in-law. The wedding must have taken place at the beginning of Fravitta's Roman career: see chap. 3, n. 180.

109. Cf. Jordanes, *Getica* 43, p. 65, with 315, p. 138.

110. See chap. 1, n. 100.

111. Cf. most recently Weissensteiner, 1 ff. and 21 ff.

112. Jordanes, *Getica* 78 and 80, pp. 76 and 78.

113. Jordanes, *Getica* 1, p. 53. Cf. chap. 2, n. 1.

114. Jordanes, *Getica* 314–316, p. 138.

115. Cf. Agathias I 20, 10, with Cassiodorus, *Variae* IV 39.2, p. 131, and X 31.5, p. 319: King Vitigis claims clan association to the Amali on the basis of his achievements; moreover, he was also married to an Amal woman.

116. Claude, *Adel, Kirche und Königtum*, 139 f. and 201 ff. Ewig, "Zum christlichen Königsgedanken," 21 ff.

117. Perhaps the best example for this is the formulary—composed in hexameter—of a Visigothic marriage certificate: see *Formulae Visigoticae* 20, pp. 583–585, esp. p. 583 lines 10–27, as well as p. 584 lines 10–13. The certificate is dated 615/616. Cf. also n. 119.

118. Nehlsen, "Aktualität und Effektivität," 493 ff.

119. Kienast, *Volksstämme*, 151–170, and esp. 196 f. L. Schmidt, "Die letzten Ostgoten," 94–103.

120. Isidore of Seville, *Institutionum disciplinae*, p. 557. Cf. chap. 1, n. 97.

121. See chap. 4, n. 307, and chap. 5, n. 456.

122. Jordanes, *Getica* 41, p. 64. Eunapius, as n. 123, fr. 55. Graf, *Orientalische Berichte*, 35 ff. Procopius, *De bello Gothico* II (VI) 15.24 f. as well as 25.9 (human sacrifices of the Gauts and Franks).

123. Eunapius fr. 60; cf. Ewig, "Probleme," 60, and Wolfram, "Gotische Studien III," 245 with n. 161.

124. Cf. Toynbee, *Study of History* 1:457 ff.

125. See chap. 2, nn. 239 ff., chap. 4, nn. 203 ff., esp. n. 307 and chap. 5, nn. 456 ff. On St. Ambrose and the cooperation between Romans and Gothic Arians see chap. 2, n. 465. On the support the Roman Arians received from the pagan Radagaisus Goths see chap. 3, n. 324. Cf. chap. 4, n. 227 and n. 503.

126. See chap. 2, nn. 192 ff., nn. 458 ff., and nn. 464 ff.

127. Schäferdiek, "Germanenmission," 501–504 and 523–527. An exception is probably indicated by Cassiodorus, *Variae* X 26, 3, p. 314.

128. Claude, *Westgoten*, 70 ff.

129. Schäferdiek, "Germanenmission," 517 f., esp. after *Epistolae Austrasicae* no. 8, p. 120 f. But this letter of Nicetius of Treves attests Gothic missionaries at the court of the Lombard king Alboin around 565, i.e., still in Pannonia.

130. *Codex Iustinianus* I 5, 12, 17. Jones, *Later Roman Empire*, 2:664 f. with nn. 132 and 135.

131. Salvianus of Marseille, *De gubernatione Dei* V 21, p. 59. On the "taming" of the Burgundians see chap. 5, n. 450 (Syagrius-Burgundio). But cf. still Ennodius CLXXXII (*Carmina* 2, 57–59), p. 157, who mocks a Roman who wears a beard in the Gothic fashion. In this context belongs also the fact that Isidore of Seville, *Etymologiae* XIX 23, 7, emphasizes especially the Goths' beards and hair style and that *cinnebar*-goatee is apparently the only Gothic word he knows. Cf. Wenskus, *Stammesbildung*, 262 n. 784.

132. See chap. 4, n. 299 f. (dress), and nn. 310–315 (language); cf. chap. 4, n. 507 (dress), and chap. 5, n. 453 f. (language).

133. In agreement with this is the fact that in the East Roman army of the sixth century the term *foederati* lost its old meaning, which had excluded the Roman element: Jones, *Later Roman Empire* 2:663 f.

134. See chap. 5, nn. 508–512.

135. See chap. 1, n. 79.

136. Among the possible approaches two in particular must be mentioned: either the later Goths are presented as a medieval *gens* or nation of the Frankish kingdom—as is done, for example, by Ewig, "Volkstum," 239 ff., and esp. by Kienast, *Volksstämme*, 74 ff.—or they are studied with the help of prosopographical studies in all regions of Europe where they are found, as Andreas Schwarcz plans to do as a continuation of his dissertation at the University of Vienna. The history of the Spanish Goths would have to be studied in the manner of Ewig or Kienast, since Thompson, *Goths in Spain*, did not accomplish this task. Presently Dietrich Claude is planning to fill the gap.

1: The Names

1. Wenskus, *Stammesbildung*, 255 ff. Much, *Germania*, 425 ff.

2. See Ammianus Marcellinus XXXI 2.12–17, esp. 17: . . . *Halani, quorum gentes varias nunc recensere non refert, licet dirempti spatiis longis per pagos ut Nomades vagantur immensos, aevi tamen progressu ad unum concessere vocabulum et summatim omnes Halani cognominantur ob mores et modum efferatum vivendi eandemque armaturam.* Cf. ibid. XVII 12.1: *mos et armatura.*

3. See below, n. 5

4. See below, nn. 83 ff. Cf., for example, Synesius of Cyrene, *De regno,* chap. 21. Philostorgius, *Historia ecclesiastica* XI 8: "Tribigild, a Scythian of the sort that is now called Goths." Procopius, *De bello Gothico* IV (VIII) 5.6: Scythians is the old name of the Goths and the other peoples of that area.

5. Procopius, *De bello Vandalico* I (III) 2.2, 3.1 and Procopius, *De bello Gothico* I (V) 1.3, III (VII) 2.1. Agathias I 3.3. Cf. Wenskus, *Stammesbildung*, 470, as well as P. Scardigli, *Goten*, 4.

6. See chap. 4, n. 307; cf. chap. 4, n. 190, and chap. 5, n. 456.

7. Although L. Schmidt, *Ostgermanen*, uses the name as the title of his book, he does not devote any thought to the name itself but uses it (cf. ibid. 45, 86, and 248 ff.) as if it were self-evident.

8. Jordanes, *Getica* 42, p. 64; 82, p. 78; 94 f., p. 82. The literature on the origin of the Goths would fill a library. Here I will only mention the following

works: the methodologically interesting study of Hachmann, *Goten und Skandinavien*. Wagner, *Getica*. The three works of Josef Svennung: *Jordanes and Scandia*; "Jordanes und die gotische Stammsage," 20 ff.; and *Skandinavien bei Plinius und Ptolemaios*. I originally intended to have the present work preceded by an historical study of the *Getica*. After initial preparatory work by Herbert Haupt, Johann Weissensteiner will take over this project. See currently Weissensteiner, *Abhandlungen*, 1 ff. and 120 ff. The best information on the older state of research on Jordanes-Cassiodorus can be found in Wattenbach-Levison-Löwe, *Geschichtsquellen*, 70–72.

9. Jordanes, *Getica* 97, p. 83.

10. Wenskus, *Stammesbildung*, 474 f.

11. For the terms *Visigoths* and *Ostrogoths* see below, n. 63.

12. The early reports about the Goths are conveniently compiled in Hachmann, *Goten und Skandinavien*, 498 f., but among these the last two passages, which come from the *Scriptores historiae Augustae*, must be excluded because they date from a period after 400: Wolfram, "Gotische Studien II," 300 f. n. 49. On the spelling of the tribal name see Schönfeld, *Wörterbuch*, 120 ff. The earliest reliable mentioning is found in Strabo, *Geographica* VII 1.3, where, however, we read Βούτωνας, which has been amended, no doubt correctly, to Γούτωνας. On this see most recently Strabo, *Geographica* 4:307 and 455. But there is no need for an emendation of the tribal name, for in "colloquial" Greek Β and Γ are interchangeable. As examples one might mention the spelling Βόλος and Γόλος, as well as Γασμοῦλος and Βασμοῦλος: cf. Hauschild, *Mistra*, 13 n. 5. Of course, if we can believe Pliny the Elder, *Historia naturalis* XXXVII 35, then Pytheas would have already attested Germanic Goths on the coast of the Baltic around 350 B.C. Strabo, *Geographica* 4:305–308 and 455, argues for a reading of *Gutonibus* as the *lectio difficilior*. Similarly Birkhan, *Germanen und Kelten*, 493 n. 1663. Ptolemy, *Geographica* II 11.16, is the first mention of the Γοῦται and III 5.8 the last mention of the Γύθωνες. The Ptolemaic Gutae are considered the forerunners of the Gauts in Procopius, *De bello Gothico* II (VI) 15.26: Wagner, *Getica*, 165 f. Hachmann, *Goten und Skandinavien*, 92, 115 f., 445, 572. Svennung, *Skandinavien bei Plinius und Ptolemaios*, 213. Wenskus, *Stammesbildung*, 297 with n. 160.

13. Bailey, "A Parthian Reference," 82 f., after *Res gestae Divi Saporis* 7, p. 307. The form Γούθθες used there also has, apart from the name Γουθθικᾶς, which is borne by one of the two presbyters who are named in the *Passio s. Sabae* 4, p. 281, early epigraphical counterparts. Schönfeld (as n. 12) in any case does not list this name form, as Bailey, "A Parthian Reference," 83 with n. 4, notes. But cf. Fiebiger, *Inschriftensammlung: Zweite Folge*, no. 16, p. 16: *Gude*; no. 20, pp. 19 ff.: Γούθθας υἱὸς Ἑρμιναρίου. The inscription is dated to February 21, 208.

14. Damerau, "Claudius II," 67 (coin inscriptions) and 105 (inscriptions). Fiebiger and Schmidt, *Inschriftensammlung*, nos. 149 and 151 f., p. 78 f. The monument reported by Alföldi, "Epigraphica," 101–103, which probably contains the Gothic name, cannot be dated with certainty before 270. Cf. Fiebiger-Schmidt, *Inschriftensammlung*, n. 157, p. 82. See also F. Stein, "Gothicus," 683–685. Cf. finally chap. 2, n. 100.

15. See chap. 2, n. 73.

16. Feist, *Wörterbuch*, 226 f. See above, nn. 12 f. and Wolfram, "Gotische Studien II," 302 f., 310 f., and 320 (Gutthiuda), as well as "Gotische Studien III," 243

(*Gutans). An asterisk (*) in front of a word indicates that this particular word-form is not attested but can be inferred.

17. For the point that the two tribal names belong together cf., Hachmann, *Goten und Skandinavien,* 454.

18. Meid, "Das Suffix -no," 72 ff., esp. 78 ff. Spitzer, "Das Suffix -one," 183 ff., esp. 193 ff. Spitzer tries to show that under Germanic influence *-one* can be both a diminutive as well as an augmentative suffix.

19. Tacitus, *Germania,* chap. 43. Cf. the interesting observation of Strabo, *Geographica,* 4:305 ff., according to whom the island Basilia mentioned in Pliny, *Historia naturalis* XXXVII 35, is actually called "land of the king" and may have something to do with the Gutones.

20. Strabo, *Geographica* VII 1.3, as well as Ptolemy, *Geographica* III 5.8.

21. Pliny, *Historia naturalis* IV 100. Solinus, *Collectanea rerum memorabilium* 20.2. Svennung, *Skandinavien bei Plinius und Ptolemaios,* 212–217, *Jordanes und Scandia,* 69–72, and "Jordanes und die gotische Stammsage," 20–22. It is interesting that neither Hachmann, *Goten und Skandinavien,* nor Wagner, *Getica,* addresses the Guthalus question. Krahe, "Einige Gruppen alter Gewässernamen," 109–112, sees Guthalus as the "pourer, water-course," not, in any case, as "river of the Goths." He identifies it with the Pregel.

22. Procopius, *De bello Gothico* II (VI) 15, 24–26. See also Jordanes, *Getica* 40 f., p. 64. Cf. Wolfram, "Gotische Studien II," 247–252.

23. Jordanes, *Getica* 22, p. 59. Wagner, *Getica,* 165 ff. and 207 ff.; Hachmann, *Goten und Skandinavien,* 117 ff.; Svennung, *Jordanes und Scandia,* 65–78, and *Skandinavien bei Plinius und Ptolemaios,* 212 ff.

24. Ranke, "Abstammungstraditionen," 29. Kuhn, "Gaut," 417–433. Wagner, *Getica,* 167 f. Svennung, *Jordanes und Scandia,* 69–72, 171–174, "Jordanes und die gotische Stammsage," 32 f. and 65. Feist, *Wörterbuch,* 226 f. Schönfeld, *Wörterbuch,* 123. Wolfram, "Theogonie," 92 nn. 76 f. On the self-description as "men" cf. Wenskus, *Stammesbildung,* 646 (index of sources). The Goths as "horse-people" are discussed below, n. 70.

25. Wolfram, "Theogonie," 90 ff. nn. 68 ff., esp. 94 n. 91.

26. Schwarz, *Goten, Nordgermanen, Angelsachsen,* 31–34, and *Stammeskunde,* 85. Hermann, "Gudden und Danzig," 207–291. Fraenkel, *Wörterbuch* 1, s.v. "Gudai," as well as Fraenkel, *Die baltischen Sprachen,* 64 f. But Max Vasmer in his review of the latter work (*Zeitschrift für Litauische Philologie* 22 [1953]: 216 f.) argues against a Slavic etymology. On Graudenz see below, n. 58.

27. See chap. 2, n. 274.

28. L. Schmidt, *Ostgermanen,* 549 f. Cf. Wenskus, *Stammesbildung,* 639, s.v. "Eudosen."

29. Procopius, *De bello Gothico* IV (VIII) 4, 9. Vasil'ev (as n. 27) and Höst, "Spuren der Goten im Osten," 62 ff., advocate the reading Τετραξΐται, whereas Gajdukevič, *Das bosporanische Reich,* 498 ff. with n. 9, decides for the emendation "Trapezites." See now the summary in Schäferdiek, "Germanenmission," 530 f.

30. Thompson, *Visigoths,* 64 ff. and 159 f., after *Passio s. Sabae* 1, p. 216, and 3, p. 217, as well as after the passio of the twenty-six martyrs, ibid. p. 279 f. Orosius, *Historiae adversum paganos* I 2.53; cf. VII 22.7. Wolfram, "Gotische Studien I," 1, n. 1. Bruun, *Roman Imperial Coinage* 7:215 n. 531.

31. Jordanes, *Getica* 73 f., p. 75. Cf. Svennung, *Goticismus,* 28.

32. Isidore of Seville, *Etymologiae* IX 2.89 f., XIV 4.3. Wolfram (as n. 30). Cf. below, n. 91.

33. See the compilation of sources in Høst, "Spuren der Goten," 56–58, among them esp. Walahfrid Strabo, *Libellus de exordiis*, p. 481. Cf. on this Schäferdiek, "Germanenmission," 506. The term *Gothi minores* is found in Jordanes, *Getica* 267, p. 127.

34. Wolfram, "Gotische Studien II," 302 with n. 54, after "Der Gotische Kalender," in Streitberg, *Die gotische Bibel* 1:472, or Stutz, *Gotische Literaturdenkmäler*, 70.

35. Jordanes, *Getica* 27, p. 60.

36. Ibid., 25 and 94, pp. 62 and 82. Hachmann, *Goten und Skandinavien*, 120 f. Wagner, *Getica*, 209. An etymology "Gothic coast" from *Gothisc-andza*, which seems linguistically questionable, would be supported by the Slavs' understanding of Pomerania as a "land by the sea": see Vasmer, *Wörterbuch*, 402 f. Cassiodorus reports the regional name by referring to both oral tradition and the otherwise unknown historian Ablabius. In the Ablabius controversy the fronts have just recently hardened again. Hachmann, *Goten und Skandinavien*, 569 (bibliography), sees in him the author of a detailed Visigothic history and transmitter of a likewise Visigothic Scandza tradition. See, in contrast, Wagner, *Getica*, esp. 62 ff., cf. 275 (list of sources), who considers the three instances where Ablabius is mentioned in Jordanes (*Getica* 28, p. 61; 82, p. 78; 117, p. 88) too weak a base on which to erect such a huge construct. Seeck, "Ablabius," 103 f. P. Scardigli, *Goten*, 197 ff., wavers between Ablabius as a pseudonym of Amalasuintha or as a personification of the Gothic tribal tradition. Helmut Birkhan in his review of Scardigli, 348 and 350, rightly comments that "this discussion does not reveal a well-developed sense of the probable."

37. Jordanes, *Getica* 36 and 96, pp. 63 and 82 f. Cf. Wenskus, *Stammesbildung*, 61, 435, and 449. Chambers, *Widsith*, 207–209 and 221 f. Much, "Vidivarii," 418. Kunkel, "Ostsee," 1812, 1816 f., 1847. Schönfeld, *Wörterbuch*, 264.

38. Cf. Jordanes, *Getica* 25, p. 60 and 94, p. 82, with 313, p. 138.

39. Cf., for example, Ammianus Marcellinus XXX 2.8, as well as Jordanes, *Getica* 26 f., p. 60.

40. L. Schmidt, *Ostgermanen*, 503.

41. Kienast, *Volksstämme*, 214, s.v. "Septimanien." Wolfram, *Intitulatio*, 70 f. Zöllner, *Völker*, 124 ff.

42. Høst, "Spuren der Goten," 58–60.

43. I am indebted to Thomas Bisson of the University of California, Berkeley, for kindly pointing out the excellent book by Bonnassié, *La Catalogne* 1:73 with n. 2, and especially 2:804 with n. 47.

44. Wenskus, *Stammesbildung*, 464 f. Svennung, *Jordanes und Scandia*, 184 ff. (Gotland), 169 ff. and 200 ff. (Västergötland), and 87 f. (Östergötland). Wagner, *Getica*, 165 ff. Cf. below, n. 45.

45. Svennung, *Goticismus*, 68 ff., esp. 71 and 87. Wolfram, "Ethnogenesen," 121 with n. 123, 124 n. 135, and 148 with n. 302.

46. See below, n. 58.

47. See n. 63 and chap. 5, nn. 461 ff.

48. XII *Panegyrici Latini* XI (III) 17, 1.

49. Wolfram, "Gotische Studien II," 300 f. n. 49. In the sequence of the appearances of the names given by Schönfeld, *Wörterbuch,* 39 f. (Austrogoti), 113 f. (Greutungi), 222 f. (Tervingi), and 267 f. (Vesi), a change must be made in the chronological place he assigns to the *Scriptores historiae Augustae* (SHA), which belongs to the period around 400. This entails, for example, that the SHA mentioning in the case of the Tervingi falls back from first to last place, and in the case of the Greutungi and Vesi it becomes the next to last mentioning. On the afterlife of the opposing pair Tervingi-Greutungi see below n. 58. The "correction" of Cassiodorus is treated extensively by Hachmann, *Goten und Skandinavien,* 121–125, with whom, apart from his great enthusiasm for Ablabius (see above n. 36), we can agree.

50. See n. 48.

51. *Notitia dignitatum or.* V 20 and 61, as well as VI 20 and 61. Straub, *Studien,* 29–31. Cf. Hoffmann, *Bewegungsheer,* part 2, 16 n. 157, and 46 n. 33. Cf. Wolfram (as in n. 49 above).

52. Wolfram, "Gotische Studien I," 2 with n. 8, after Ammianus Marcellinus XXXI 3.5. On the time of composition of the work see Seyfarth, *Ammianus Marcellinus* 1:26 f. Claudianus, *In Eutropium* II v. 158, p. 101: *Ostrogothis colitur mixtisque Gruthungis* (*sc. Phryx ager*). Cameron, *Claudian,* xv and 78 ff.

53. Jordanes, *Getica* 82 and 98, pp. 78 and 83. Wenskus, *Stammesbildung,* 472 f.

54. Wolfram, "Theogonie," 92 f. n. 84. Cf. chap. 2, n. 61.

55. Claudian (as n. 52). On the possibility that this passage was taken over by Jordanes, *Getica* 22 f., p. 59, cf. Hachmann, *Goten und Skandinavien,* 128 ff. Wagner, *Getica,* 171 ff. Kuhn, "Review of Wagner and Svennung," 152 f. On the meaning and equating of the two tribal names cf., for example, Walahfrid Strabo, *Vita s. Galli,* prologus, p. 281 f. Here the author mentions that his people are called either Alamanni or Suevi; the Latin-speaking neighbors use the first, the Germanic (barbarian)-speaking neighbors the second name. The land named accordingly is inhabited by *mixti Alamannis Suevi.* There is no indication that Walahfrid knew the passage in Claudian.

56. SHA 25 (Claud.) 6.2.

57. See above, nn. 49 and 51. Zosimus IV 38.1, who is here following Eunapius (see Paschoud, "Zosimos," 822), reports that a recently arrived Scythian people was given the name "Greutungi" by the barbarians north of the Ister, which can refer only to those Tervingi who after 376 were still living north of the Danube. Cf. below, chap. 3, nn. 107–109. Further evidence that the names were names given to "foreigners" is the fact that Ammianus Marcellinus, who had a Tervingian source, never uses the pair Vesi-Ostrogoths. Cf. n. 58.

58. On the etymology of the dual names see the basic discussion of Schönfeld (as n. 49), and similarly Bach, *Deutsche Namenkunde* 1, 1: 200 f. and 304 (Tervingi-Greutungi), and 199, 206, and 308 (Vesi-Ostrogoths).

I. The problem of Tervingi-Greutungi: in the controversy between Helmut Rosenfeld and Franz Altheim I follow the argument of Altheim, *Geschichte der Hunnen* 1:341–347, that the Gothic special names were not created before the end of the third century and not outside of the climatic belt of forest and steppe region. In that region Scythians had already appeared before the Goths and after them would come Hunno-Turkic as well as Slavic tribal pairs, who were named in accordance with the same "compelling law of geographical environment." To this we must add that the most famous, indeed the only hero of the Tervingi (see below, n. 77 f.) had the name Vidigoia, which means either "the man from the forest zone" (Much, "Vidivarii," 418, as well as Schönfeld, *Wörterbuch,* 263) or "the forest-barker/wolf": see Müller, "Studien," 211. Similar "forest names" are Veduco and Vidimir: see Wagner, *Getica,* 247 f. The Vidivarii are also "forest-people": Much, 418, Schönfeld, 263, and Kunkel, "Ostsee," 1812, 1816 f., and 1847. It must be mentioned, however, that the theory of the pre-Pontic origin of the name-pair continues to have important supporters, especially among the Germanists and Scandinavianists: see, for example, Svennung, *Skandinavien bei Plinius und Ptolemaios,* 205 (the Tervingi as Scandinavian "ox people"), *Jordanes und Scandia,* 117 ff. (the Greutungi as Swedish "rock people" west of the Gauts). In some instances the Greutungi are also linked to place-names that are today Polish, such as Grudziądz-Graudenz: Schwarz, *Goten, Nordgermanen, Angelsachsen,* 31–33 with n. 25. This idea, first advanced in 1927, was already opposed by Valentin Kiparsky, *Lehnwörter.*

II. The problem of Vesi-Ostrogoths: for the etymology of the two names one also starts with Jordanes, *Getica* 82, p. 78, and 130 f., p. 92. The interpretation of the Ostrogothic name causes virtually no problem, since a naming after the rising sun, that is, after the east, and a "boastful name" are not mutually exclusive: cf. Wolfram, *Splendor Imperii,* 108–113, as well as Jordanes, *Getica* 42, p. 64, where the Amali, in contrast to the Balthi, are singled out and praised through the adjective *praeclari.* Also, the name Hreidhgoths, the epic name of the people ruled over by the Ermanaric of legend, could mean "splendid Goths": Höfler, *Germanisches Sakralkönigtum,* 20 ff. Somewhat more difficult is the Vesian name, whereby it makes no difference, however, whether the boastful name was created as a euphemistic cover-up for the much maligned west or not; the name would in any case still mean "the good, the noble." Eunapius, next to Ammianus Marcellinus the leading expert on the Tervingi, calls their tribal warriors "the noble" (fr. 37), apparently without ulterior motives: Wolfram, "Gotische Studien II," 311 f. with n. 101. Although Svennung, *Jordanes und Scandia,* 122–127, is "of course," also able to find an eponymous Scandinavian river for the Vesi, one will no doubt adhere to the interpretation accepted by the majority of scholars: see Wenskus, *Stammesbildung,* 473. Rosenfeld, "Ost- und Westgoten," 247. Feist, *Wörterbuch,* 298, s.v. "iusiza." The boastful names became known to the Romans later than the names referring to geographical regions, possibly because the boastful names were as much subject to taboo as the tribal religion: see Wolfram, "Gotische Studien III," 240, after Eunapius fr. 55. On the afterlife of the Vesi name see n. 61.

59. See above, nn. 51 and 57. Straub, *Geschichtsapologetik,* 53 ff., and by the same author, *Studien,* 29 ff. The last mentioning of the Tervingi is in Ammianus Marcellinus XXXI 5. 8 (Fritigern with Lupicinus), which is at the same time the last appearance of a Gothic special name.

60. Ammianus Marcellinus XXXI 3.3 and 4.12 (Alatheus and Safrax are still considered Greutungian chieftains before the crossing of the Danube in 376), with XXXI 5.8 (the two men command the Gothic cavalry in 378). In XXXI 4.12 Farnobius is considered a Greutungian chieftain because he arrives with Alatheus

and Safrax, but in XXXI 9.3 he is a Gothic chieftain because he is already operating on Roman territory.

61. Sidonius Apollinaris, *Carmina* V vv. 476 f., p. 199 (Vesi and Ostrogoths); VII vv. 399 and 431, p. 213 f. (Vesi); II v. 377, p. 182. *Epistulae* VIII 9 v. 36, p. 137 (Ostrogoths). On this mention of the Ostrogoths see Wolfram, "Theogonie," 88 n. 53. For *Carmen* VII (Panegyric on Avitus of January 1, 456) see Loyen, *Recherches historiques,* 35 ff. On the other Vesi mentionings in Sidonius see the catalog of peoples in the Panegyric on Majorian (*Carmen* V, December 458), after Loyen, *Recherches historiques,* 59 ff.

62. Jordanes, *Getica* 98, p. 83.

63. Ibid., 82, p. 78, and 130 f., p. 92. Hachmann, *Goten und Skandinavien,* 122–124.

64. Cf. the explanation for the split of the Amal Goths in Jordanes, *Getica* 283 f., p. 131.

65. Wolfram, *Intitulatio I,* 77–79. Hachmann (as n. 63). Procopius, *De bello Gothico* I (V) 12, 12 ff. Cf. Procopius, *De bello Vandalico* I (III), 2, 2 ff.

66. Goffart, "Table of Nations," 111 (text), 115, and 120 ff. (commentary).

67. Ioannis Antiochenus fr. 206, 2. Wolfram, "Theogonie," 89 with n. 60, after Liberatus, *Breviarium,* chap. 18, col. 1028. Theodoric's grandson Athalaric is still called τοῦ Οὐαλεμεριακοῦ by Malalas, *Chronographia,* p. 460.

68. Jordanes, *Getica* 94 f., p. 82; cf. ibid. p. 160 as well as Wagner, *Getica,* 84 ff., Svennung, *Jordanes und Scandia,* 131 ff., and Goffart (as n. 66 above), 124 n. 111. On the politics of the Gepids in the sixth century, when the story was written down, see Pohl, "Gepiden," 288 ff., esp. 297 ff. Cf. Lakatos, *Quellenbuch,* 1 ff.

69. Jordanes, *Getica* 38, p. 63 f. Cf. Wagner, *Getica,* 89–96, as well as Kuhn, "Review of Wagner and Svennung," 151. Cf. Procopius, *De bello Gothico* II (VI) 6.28–30, according to whom Belisarius offered the Goths emigration to Britain, an island that was several times the size of Sicily. Unfortunately, the Gothic negotiators did not respond to the offer.

70. Wagner, *Getica,* 60 ff., 74 f., and 81 ff., esp. 82.

71. Wagner, *Getica,* 82 f., after Olympiodorus fr. 29. Much, "Völkernamen," 431. Thompson, *Visigoths,* 20 with n. 2.

72. Jordanes, *Getica* 22, p. 59. Cf. above, n. 55.

73. See above, n. 55.

74. See *Hervarasaga,* chap. 11 ff., pp. 51 ff. and 86 ff. (notes). Cf. below, nn. 104 f.

75. Gschwantler, *Heldensage,* 12 ff., 38 ff., esp. 57 ff. and 63 ff. Cf. Wolfram, "Theogonie," 82 n. 13 and n. 20. On Theodoric see chap. 5, nn. 508–512.

76. Cf. Chambers, *Widsith,* 47.

77. Jordanes, *Getica* 43, p. 65, and 178, p. 104. See above, n. 58.

78. Chambers, *Widsith,* 263 (index of passages). Jiriczek, *Deutsche Heldensage,* 292 ff. Heusler, "Amelunge," 77.

79. Heusler, "Amelunge," 88 f. Cf. n. 80. Much, "Völkernamen," 432.

80. Uiblein, *Studien,* 54 f. Höfler, *Germanisches Sakralkönigtum,* 9 ff. Heinzel, "Heldensage," 15 ff.

81. Cf. above, n. 71.

82. See above, nn. 29 and 42.

83. Wolfram, "Ethnogenesen," 99 nn. 10 f., after Synesius of Cyrene, *Oratio de regno,* chap. 15; cf. chap. 21. Harmatta, *Sarmatians,* 8 f.

84. FGrH 2 A: 452–480 no. 100, see esp. 20 (14): 465.

85. Petrus Patricius fr. 8. On the author see Stein, *Bas-Empire* 2:723–729.

86. See Orosius, *Historiae adversum paganos* VII 34, 5, followed, for example, by Marcellinus Comes, *Chronicon* a. 379, p. 60, or the Venerable Bede, *Chronica* a. 452, p. 298. Cf. Procopius, *De bello Gothico* IV (VIII) 5.6.

87. Procopius (as n. 86) and *De bello Vandalico* I (III) 2.2. Pliny, *Historia naturalis* IV 25 ff., as well as Herodotus IV 20 and 110 ff. On what are presumed to have been the Scythian-Pontic dwelling places of the Amazons see Graef, "Amazones," 1755 ff. The first equating of the Amazons and the Gothic women is attested by the SHA 26 (Aurelius) 34, 1; the date of this source is after 400: see above, nn. 49 and 51. Jordanes, *Getica,* 44–57, pp. 65–70, where Cassiodorus reports the story of the Amazons as belonging to Gothic prehistory. Ibid., 265, p. 126, appears also the first equating of Sauromates and Sarmates.

88. Svennung, *Goticismus,* 3–5.

89. Ibid., 5–10. Orosius, *Historiae adversum paganos* I 16.2. Cassiodorus prefixed to his *Origo Gothica* (i.e., Gothic *Getica*) the *Getica* of Dio Chrysostom, the history of the noblest Thracian people, the Getae (cf. Wiesner, *Thraker,* 11, after the Iliad II vv. 844 f., and Herodotus IV 93 [first mention of the Getae]): Jordanes, *Getica* p. xxx f. Jordanes, *Getica* 58, p. 70, attests the influence of Orosius on Cassiodorus.

90. Procopius, *De bello Gothico* I (V) 24.22–34. Cf. Procopius, *De bello Vandalico* I (III) 2. 3.

91. Jordanes, *Getica* 29, p. 61 and n. 1. Isidore of Seville, *Historia vel Origo Gothorum* 1 f. and 66, pp. 268 and 293, as well as *Additamentum* 1, p. 304, and *Etymologiae* IX 2.27 and esp. 89 f. Of interest is ibid. 62 f., where the Massagetae are called *quasi graves, id est fortes Getae.* See also XIV 3.31 and 4.3. For the derivation of the Dacians from the Getes-Goths see Justinus, *Epitoma historiarum Pompei Trogi* XXXII 3.16: *Daci quoque suboles Getarum sunt.* On Isidore's methodology, especially with reference to the history of Visigothic Spain, see Diesner, *Isidor* 1 ff., esp. 84 ff. Diesner shows (61 n. 1), following Isidore, *Etymologiae* IX 2, 118, that the Visigoths considered themselves related to the Mauri. Cf. in general Klinck, *Etymologie,* and Engels, "La portée," 99 ff. For the etymological method note the following example: Isidore finds in Augustine and St. Jerome the suggestion that Gog means *tectum* along with the rejection of the Ambrosian equation (as n. 88) *Gog iste Gothus.* Ignoring the latter, Isidore adopts Ambrose's dubious eschatology and turns *tectum*-house into the *Tecti*-Goths. In the Hebrew glossary of St. Jerome Gaza-*fortitudo* is listed alphabetically ahead of Gog-*tectum.* By joining the two entries Isidore gets the combination of *fortitudo* and *Goti.* On Gog-Magog-*tectum* see Augustine, *De civitate Dei* XX 11, and St. Jerome, *In Ezechielem* XI 38, as well as *Liber interpretationis Hebraicorum nominum* 51, 24; 57, 30 (Gog); 8, 11; 58, 7 (Magog). On the Frankish name see Libanius, *Oratio* LIX 127. Cf. Tiefenbach, *Studien,* 55. On the meaning of "free" see Köbler, "Die Freien," 39.

92. Isidore of Seville, *Historia vel Origo Gothorum* 2, p. 268 (cf. both versions).

93. Cassiodorus, *Variae* IX 25, 4, p. 291. Wenskus, "Sachsen-Angelsachsen-

Thüringer," 508 f. with n. 92, has rightly objected to the strange misinterpretation of this passage.

94. On the use of the oral Gothic tradition by Cassiodorus see Wagner, *Getica,* 64–70. This should be supplemented by, for example, Cassiodorus, *Variae* VIII 9, 8, p. 239. Much the same applies to Gothic laws, institutions, and social forms, which survived from the Istrian-Pontic period until the Italian kingdom of the sixth century: see Wolfram, "Gotische Studien I," 14 with pp. 63 f., and Wolfram, "Gotische Studien II," 304 ff. Cf. Wolfram, "Athanaric the Visigoth," 267.

95. Wenskus, "Amaler," 246–248. Wenskus, *Stammesbildung,* 653, s.v. "Traditionskern."

96. Isidore of Seville, *Historia vel Origo Gothorum,* p. 306.

97. *Institutionum disciplinae,* p. 557. Menéndez Pidal, "Los Godos," 296 ff. Wagner, *Getica,* 96 ff. But what was preserved in the Spanish kingdom from the pre-Toledan Gothic tradition were the names, as is shown by García Moreno, *Prosopografía.* Cf. Piel and Kremer, *Hispano-gotisches Namenbuch,* for which one must consult, however, Norbert Wagner's review, pp. 242–252.

98. Wenskus, "Amaler," 247. Cf. *Anecdoton Holderii* p. 4. Wolfram, "Theogonie," 87 ff. nn. 44 ff., and 90 n. 64.

99. Jordanes, *Getica* 42, p. 64.

100. Ibid., 146, p. 96. Cassiodorus, *Variae* VIII 10.2, p. 239; cf. IV 39.1 f., p. 131, and X 31.5, p. 319. Wolfram, *Splendor Imperii,* 108–113.

101. Wenskus, "Adel," 60 f. Wenskus, "Balthen," 13 f.

102. Jordanes, *Getica* 78 f., p. 76 (Amali). Merobaudes, *Carmina* IV vv. 16 ff., p. 5 ("younger" Balthi). For the family of the "younger" Balthi see Wenskus (as n. 101); cf. Wolfram, "Gotische Studien I," 11 f. On the quote taken from Mero-baudes see Loyen, *Recherches historiques,* 46 f., supplemented, however, with the correction given chap. 4, n. 42: the wife of Aëtius, whom Merobaudes honored with a descent from "kings and heroes," is not one of Theoderid's daughters but Pelagia, for whom a Visigothic descent can be traced.

103. Jordanes, *Getica* 246, p. 121.

104. Jordanes, *Getica* 78–81, pp. 76–78. Kuhn, "Amaler," 246. Kuhn, "Asen," 458. Höfler, "Abstammungstraditionen," 25. Wenskus, "Amaler," 246–248, with complete genealogical table. Ermanaric's oldest brother was called Ansila/little Ansis; however, there are also other individuals with this name: see Schönfeld, *Wörterbuch,* 23. Equally well-known is the Runic name *ansuz: see Klingenberg, *Runenschrift-Schriftdenken-Runeninschriften,* 190 f.

105. Wolfram, *Intitulatio I,* 99–104. On Cassiodorus, *Variae* IX 25.4, p. 291 f., and XI 1.10 ff., p. 329 f., see Weissensteiner, *Abhandlungen,* 2 ff. with nn. 17 ff. The expression *catalogus Amalorum* is found in Jordanes, *Getica* 174, p. 103. Cf. the genealogical table of the Amali (appendix). On Gapt-Gaut and the subsequent progenitors see chap. 2, nn. 6–8.

106. Wolfram, *Splendor Imperii,* 108–113. Cf. Wenskus, "Amaler," 248, and Wolfram, "Theogonie," 90 nn. 64–67. See Jordanes, *Getica* 270, p. 128; cf. 116, p. 88: *nobilissimus Amalorum.* Candidus Isaurus fr. 1: the son of Triarius had the name Ermanaric. Ioannis Antiochenus fr. 214, 3, calls Rekitach, Strabo's son, an ἀνεψιός of Theodoric the Great. Cf. the general term συγγενεῖς for the two Theodorics in Malchus fr. 15. See also chap. 5, n. 92.

107. Jordanes, *Getica* 209 and 265 f., pp. 111 and 126.

108. Malchus fr. 18 (FHG 4, 126): Ὁ δὲ Βαλαμήρου [sc. Theodoric] . . . πέμ-πει πρὸς Σιδιμοῆνδον ἐκ τῆς αὐτῆς φυλῆς τὸ ἀνέκαθεν ὄντα; cf. L. Schmidt, *Ostgermanen,* 271. Wagner, "Personennamen," 27 ff. Wagner, "Gausus und Harodus," 241 ff. On the Visigothic Amali see chap 4, n. 540. Cf. Chrysos, Ἱστορία τῆς Ἠπείρου, 56 ff.

109. Jordanes, *Getica* 146, p. 96 (as n. 100).

110. Pliny, *Historia naturalis* XXXVII 35 (as chap. 1, n. 19) and IV 956 (kindly pointed out to me by Reinhard Wenskus). Jordanes, *Getica* 117–119, p. 88 (the Herulian king Alaric). Ammianus Marcellinus XXXI 4.1 and 8, as well as 5.5 (Alaviv). Wenskus, "Balthen," 13 f. Wenskus, "Alarich (Erulerkönig)," 129. Wolfram, "Gotische Studien I," 10–12.

111. Wenskus, "Balthen," 14, after Sidonius Apollinaris, *Carmina* VII vv. 501–509, p. 215. Wenskus, however, thinks that "it is just as likely that Theoderid was a son of Alaric." Wenskus also gives a genealogical table of the "last Balthi."

112. Jordanes, *Getica* 245, p. 121. Other *magnus*-surnames are found ibid. 121 and 248, pp. 89 and 121. Cf. on this Kienast, "Magnus = der Ältere," 1 ff.

113. Martindale, *Prosopography* 2:64 f. On the higher status of the Amali see above n. 102.

114. Gregory of Tours, *Historia Francorum* II 4 and 28, pp. 43 and 73.

115. G. Schramm, "Namenbeziehung," 129 ff., esp. 135 ff., as well as Perrin, *Les Burgondes,* 405 ff., deny that the Nibelungs were totally exterminated in 436 or 437. For a contrary opinion see Stein, *Bas-Empire* 1:322 f., as well as L. Schmidt, *Ostgermanen,* 140 and 177. Cf. also Thompson, *Attila and the Huns,* 65 f. *Auctarium Havniense* a. 457, 3, p. 305, comes close to claiming that the Gundiok Burgundians were fully subject to the Theodoric Goths.

116. Martindale, *Prosopography* 2:524 f.

117. Claude, *Adel, Kirche und Königtum,* 29 f.

118. Cf. n. 112 above. Schönfeld, *Wörterbuch,* 188 and 189–192 shows that Retemeris, Theoderid's fifth son, was the namesake of Ricimer the son of Valia; it thus seems possible that the former was named after the latter, and hence that the Valia clan and the Theoderid clan were related.

119. Jones, *Prosopography* 1:605. Wolfram, "Gotische Studien I," 12 n. 51.

120. Sidonius Apollinaris, *Epistulae* VII 6.2, p. 108.

121. Zöllner, *Franken,* 85. See Wolfram, *Intitulatio I,* 106 n. 108, on the life of the Frankish Munderic. For the Tervingian Munderic see Schwarcz, *Reichsangehörige,* 154 f., after Ammianus Marcellinus XXXI 3, 2. Schönfeld, *Wörterbuch,* 169, knows only the second Munderic, which means that the name was originally not very common.

122. Buchner, *Provence,* 103 n. 31.

123. Stroheker, *Adel,* 144 n. 14. But Ewig, "Volkstum," 255 (623) n. 114, discovered East Germanic traditions in the environment around Aletheus.

124. Ammianus Marcellinus XXXI 3.3; 4.12; 12.12; and 17. Schönfeld, *Wörterbuch,* 11, also names only Alatheus. Cf. Jones, *Prosopography* 1:32.

125. Gschwantler, "Ermanarich," 187 ff.

126. Wagner, "Namengebung," 15, after Jordanes, *Getica* 129, p. 91. Gschwantler, "Ermanarich" (as n. 125).

127. Várady, *Pannonien,* esp. 217 f., cf. 601. Várady's theses are in general very

bold (cf., for example, Nagy, "Pannonia," 332 ff.) but his arguments about the Rosomoni are tacitly accepted by Wenskus, "Balthen," 14. See also Claude, *Adel, Kirche und Königtum,* 32 f. For the Alaric tradition, which reaches back to the Pontus, see above, n. 110. Diesner, "Buccellariertum," 327 ff. There is no evidence that Sarus was a relative of Alaric I. Maenchen-Helfen, *The Huns,* 21 ff., sees in Sarus an Alan. On Sarus see Martindale, *Prosopography* 2:978 f., and Schwarcz, *Reichsangehörige,* 162–167.

128. Gschwantler, "Rosomonen," 164–176.

129. Jordanes, *Getica,* 25 f. and 28, p. 60 f.; 39, p. 64; 94, p. 82; 121, p. 89. On the surname *Magnus*-the Elder see above, n. 112. The next namesake of Berig is found among the λογάδες (magnates) of Attila: see Maenchen-Helfen, *The Huns,* 406.

130. Jordanes, *Getica* 112 f., p. 87; cf. 43, p. 65. An Ostrogothic namesake of Geberic is the *vir spectabilis* to whom is addressed Cassiodorus, *Variae* IV 20, p. 123.

131. Jordanes, *Getica* 101–103, p. 83 f. Hachmann, *Goten und Skandinavien,* 112–114.

132. SHA 26 (Aurel.) 22, 2. Schönfeld, *Wörterbuch,* 65, and Hachmann, *Goten und Skandinavien,* 113.

133. Cf. Wolfram, "Gotische Studien I," 12 n. 51 with Wenskus, *Stammesbildung,* 409 ff., esp. 420 ff.

2: The Formation of the Gothic Tribes before the Invasion of the Huns

1. Jordanes, *Getica* 25 f., p. 60. On the term *memoria* cf. ibid. 28, p. 61, with Cassiodorus, *Variae* IX 25.4, p. 291, and Tacitus, *Germania,* chap. 2: . . . *carmini- bus antiquis, quod unum apud illos memoriae et annalium genus est* . . . Cf. chap. 1, nn. 93–95.

2. *Anecdoton Holderii,* p. 4. Cf. chap. 1, n. 98.

3. Hachmann's *Goten und Skandinavien* addresses this question. Cf. Schwarz, "Herkunftsfrage," 287 ff. Mildenberger, "Probleme der germanischen Frühge- schichte," 488 ff., esp. 492.

4. See chap. 1, n. 95.

5. Jordanes, *Getica* 82, p. 78, reveals the uncertainty of Cassiodorus on the question of who was named after whom. The naming of a people after its king, a popular theme of ancient literature, became so strongly suggestive that Karl Mül- lenhoff (Commentary, see Jordanes, *Getica,* p. 143 n. 6) felt the need to polemize against it. But just as the Amali are also the *Ostrogotharum genealogia* (see ibid. 246, p. 121) the Amal Ostrogotha presupposes the existence of the Ostrogothic people. Cf. chap. 1, n. 54, and below, n. 61.

6. Jordanes, *Getica* 79, p. 76.

7. On the Amal genealogy see ibid. 79 ff., p. 76 f. For the geography of the island of Scandia and of the Gothic names cf. Ptolemy II 11.16, and III 5. 8, with Jordanes, *Getica* 16–19, p. 57 ff. See also n. 12.

8. On the expression *gens Amalorum* see Jordanes, *Getica* 252, p. 123. Wol- fram, "Theogonie," 90 ff. with nn. 68 ff. On the derivation of Gaut from Gapt see ibid., 91 n. 72, which should be supplemented by Ewig, "Teilungen," 154 f., n. 215.

9. Cf. Jordanes, *Getica* 25 f., p. 60; 39–40, p. 64; and 79 ff., p. 76 f. See chap. 1, n. 104 ff. and n. 129.

10. Cf. Jordanes, *Getica* 25 f., p. 60 (first primordial deed); 43, p. 65 (*ante quos*); 76–78, p. 76 (second primordial deed); 101–103, p. 83 f. (kings of the third century); 313–315, p. 138 (the end of the history of the Amali and the Goths 2,030 years after it had begun).

11. Jordanes, *Getica* 25 f., p. 60. Cf. chap. 1, n. 12 and n. 36.

12. See chap. 1, n. 36, and below, n. 16 f. Hachmann, *Goten und Skandinavien,* 136–143, in contrast, assigns the Goths to the Przeworsk culture inland, but this culture was Vandalic.

13. Wolfram, "Aufnahme," 91 with n. 14. Jordanes, *Getica* 36, p. 63, and 94–96, p. 82 f.

14. Cf. Svennung, *Jordanes und Scandia,* 203 ff., as well as Chambers, *Widsith,* 219–221.

15. Strabo, *Geographica* VII 1.3. Pliny, *Historia naturalis* IV 99. Tacitus, *Germania,* chap. 44.1, and *Annales* II 62.2. See below, n. 23 ff.

16. Ptolemy, *Geographica* III 5.8. Hachmann, *Goten und Skandinavien,* 138 f. and 499. At the latest, from these decades of the second century (later period B2 and B2/C1), we can discern a comparably homogeneous culture group between eastern Pomerania in the west and the Passarge in the east. Its characteristics are mixed grave fields, occasionally combined with mound graves; among female finery snake-head bracelets of type B after E. Blume; in the male graves the absence of armor and—compared to female graves—usually less elaborate grave goods. Most recently Godlowski, *Chronology,* 31–44, gave this culture group the neutral name "East Pomeranian-Masovian culture." It did not cover the entire region of the Oder but is linked to it. Nonetheless, this region must be distinguished from eastern Pomerania—approximately in the area of the Persante—especially because of the difference in female costume; cf. most recently Leube, "Archäologische Formengruppen," 355 ff.

17. The "East Pomeranian-Masovian" or "Wielbark-Willenberg-culture" (as above, n. 16) largely breaks off—as far as the grave fields attest—around 200 but finds its chronological continuation in Masovia, Podlachia, and the region between the Bug and the Wieprz. The original region, however, was not entirely abandoned. We must therefore be dealing with a geographical shift or first expansion of the culture group. The evidence from burial customs, grave furnishings, costume, and general material culture would indicate that from the middle and second half of the third century the bearers of the original East Pomeranian-Masovian culture had direct contact in Wolhynia with the Cherniakhov culture of southern Russia and indirect contact via the Ukraine. From the perspective of the Cherniakhov culture of the third and fourth centuries there is therefore good reason to address also the East Pomeranian-Masovian culture as Gothic in its core. Hachmann (as n. 12) is therefore mistaken when he links to the Goths a regional group of the Przeworsk culture in Masovia before the end of the second century. Both cultures, the Przeworsk and the East Pomeranian-Masovian, can be clearly distinguished and they appear in Masovia in succession. This change of cultures goes back to a change in population and has nothing to do with a transformation of the culture against the background of continuous habitation. The change of culture can be well demon-

strated in Masovia in the late second century and around 200 even in smaller areas, such as the valley of the Wilga; see in the near future Ion Ioniţa in *Peregrinatio Gotica II* (Proceedings of the conference at Białe Błota, Poland, September 11–14, 1986).

18. Ptolemy, *Geographica* II 11.16, which is used by Jordanes, *Getica* 19–23, pp. 58–60, who, mildly reproachful, corrects it. For Cassiodorus knew of more than only seven Scandinavian tribes. Wenskus, *Stammesbildung*, 231 f.; see above, n. 6. Cf. Svennung, *Jordanes und Scandia*, 136 ff., and Svennung, *Skandinavien bei Plinius und Ptolemaios*, 198 ff. For Hachmann, *Goten und Skandinavien*, 81 ff., this information in the *Origo Gothica* about Scandinavia is, "of course," derived from Ablabius.

19. See the survey of scholarship on the issue in Wagner, *Getica*, 165–170. Cf. chap. 1, nn. 21–25.

20. Cf. chap. 1, and n. 129, as well as above, n. 5 and n. 17.

21. Cf. Hachmann, *Goten und Skandinavien*, 3–9.

22. Wolfram, "Theogonie," 95 f. nn. 100–105.

23. Tacitus, *Germania*, chap. 43. Cf. Much, *Germania*, 473–492.

24. Jordanes, *Getica* 26, p. 60; 89, p. 80; 113–115 and 161 f., p. 87 f. and 100 (cf. chap. 1, n. 130); 166 f., p. 101; 173, p. 103; 184, p. 106. Isidore of Seville, *Historia vel Origo Gothorum* 68, p. 294, also reports that the Vandals took to flight on the mere rumor that the Goths were coming. Even Sidonius Apollinaris had something similar to report: *Carmina* II vv. 368–370, p. 182. Loyen, *Recherches historiques*, 93.

25. Pliny, *Historia naturalis* IV 99. Hachmann's scepticism, *Goten und Skandinavien*, 131 f., concerning the equating of Vandals and Vandili is unfounded, as, for example, the Gothic personal name VVandil still reveals in the sixth century: see Cassiodorus, *Variae* III 38, p. 98. Cf. also Schönfeld, *Wörterbuch*, 253–256.

26. Strabo, *Geographica* VII 1.3. Cf. chap. 1, n. 12.

27. See above, n. 23.

28. Much, *Germania*, 478 f. and 564 (source index). Wenskus, *Stammesbildung*, 503 f. and 646 (source index). On the Przeworsk culture, which is considered Vandalic, see n. 12.

29. See Wolfram, "Gotische Studien I," 24 f., and Wolfram, "Gotische Studien II," 293 f. with n. 21. Cf. below, n. 486 and Wenskus, *Stammesbildung*, 227 f.

30. See above n. 25 f. and below, n. 32.

31. Ptolemy, *Geographica* III 5.8. On the burial custom see below, n. 442 and chap. 5, n. 451.

32. Strabo, *Geographica* VII 1.3.

33. Tacitus, *Annales* II 62.2. Much, *Germania*, 463 and 471.

34. Tacitus, *Annales* II 44–46, and 63. XII 30.

35. Cf. Jordanes, *Getica* 25, p. 60, with 315, p. 138.

36. Tacitus, *Germania*, chap. 43, 1. Much, *Germania*, 486–492. See von Uslar, *Germanische Sachkultur*, 26–36.

37. Much, *Germania*, 486–492.

38. Jordanes, *Getica* 26, p. 60. According to the view of the Hippocratic ethnographers, kingship and barbarian wildness are mutually exclusive: see Maenchen-Helfen, *The Huns*, 12 f. with nn. 79 and 82. Cf. above, Introduction n. 88.

39. Ostrogotha: see Jordanes, *Getica* 90 f., p. 81. But something similar is re-ported about Alaric I and Totila. On the polyethnicism of the Gothic armies see below, n. 511, chap. 4, nn. 498 ff., and chap. 5, nn. 259 ff. But, it is likely that the Gutones were joined by Balto-Prussian Galindi, as the Visigothic personal name Galindus(o) still attests in the ninth century: see L. Schmidt, *Ostgermanen*, 198. Kiessling, "Galindai," 1815–1820. Zöllner, *Völker,* 129. Kienast, *Volksstämme,* 87 with n. 43.

40. Thus in Ptolemy, *Geographica* II 3.5 ff. we would expect to find mention of Hadrian's Wall, which at the time Ptolemy wrote was already a generation old; cf. Polaschek, "Ptolemaios als Geograph," 753 ff., esp. 758 f. On the anachronistic account of Ptolemy see also Demougeot, *La formation* 1:322.

41. See below, nn. 504 and 509 f.

42. Jordanes, *Getica* 26–28, p. 60 f.

43. Hachmann, *Goten und Skandinavien,* esp. 328 ff.

44. Jordanes, *Getica* 42, p. 64; 82, p. 78; 98, p. 83; 130, p. 91: these are the most important, frequently contradictory accounts on the split of the Gothic peoples.

45. L. Schmidt, *Ostgermanen*, 199. On the state of archaeological research see above, n. 17 (Ioniţa). On the Frankish analogy see Zöllner, *Franken,* 29 ff. For the terminology Gutones-Goths see chap. 1, n. 58. The time frame in which the Gutonic emigration occurred can be more closely defined with the help of archaeology. In accordance with the views expressed above, n. 17, the emigration from the region, which is circumscribed by the spread of the East Pomeranian-Masovian culture, probably took place sometime in the late second century or around 200. Of course this was not a wholesale emigration, as is also attested by the fact that not all grave fields were abandoned. The early phase of the Cherniakhov culture can be attested in Wolhynia, but also in the Ukraine, no earlier than the middle of the third century.

46. Cf. above, nn. 12, 17, 28.

47. Jordanes, *Getica* 28, p. 61.

48. Vasmer, *Wörterbuch* 1:489, s.v. "Ispolín"; cf. 3:515.

49. Cf. chap. 1, n. 71.

50. Alföldi, *Weltkrise* (book-title).

51. Cassius Dio, *Historia Romana,* 72.8.1.

52. Alföldi, *Weltkrise,* 325 f. For the borders of Trajan's Dacia see Kirsten, "Dacia," 560 f., as well as Kirsten and Lippold, "Donauprovinzen," 150 (map).

53. Bichir, *Carpi,* esp. 145 ff. Cf. also Harmatta, *Sarmatians,* 41–49. Patsch, "Carpi," 1608–1610. Stein, "Carpicus," 1610.

54. Wenskus, "Bastarnen," 88 ff. Wolfram, "Gotische Studien I," 25. Much, *Germania,* 522–530. L. Schmidt, *Ostgermanen,* 94 and 200. Harmatta, *Sarmatians,* 48 f.

55. Dexippus fr. 20 (14). Yet the two consecratory inscriptions in a Buddhist temple near Junnar in the district of Poona near Bombay are not evidence for the southeastward migration of the Goths: see Wüst, "Goten in Indien?" 141 ff. On the events cf. Schönfeld, "Goti," 802. Lippold, "Goti," 858 f. L. Schmidt, *Ostger-manen,* 200 ff., is only of limited usefulness because of the author's uncritical dependence on the SHA for the third century. Cf. Wolfram, "Gotische Studien II," 300 f. n. 49. Real problems are created by the name Gouththas, the son of Her-minarius, who in 208 commanded a barbarian unit in Syria (as chap. 1, n. 13). It

is difficult *not* to link father and son to the Goths. The date of the monument, however, is surprisingly early: see Schwarcz, *Reichsangehörige,* 141 and 143 f.

56. Petrus Patricius, fr. 8.

57. Jordanes, *Getica* 91, p. 81.

58. Wenskus, *Stammesbildung,* 469–471. See chap. 1, nn. 83 ff. But the philologist St. Jerome must have known that the Goths spoke a Germanic language, as can be seen from his correspondence with Sunnia and Fretela (see n. 241).

59. See chap. 1, n. 13. On what is possibly the first treaty between the Goths and the Roman Empire see Masur, *Verträge,* 1 n. 1. Cf. Classen, "Kaiserreskript," 112 with n. 52. See Chrysos, "Gothia Romana," 65 f. n. 33.

60. Alföldi, *Weltkrise,* 316 ff., esp. after Jordanes, *Getica* 101–104, p. 83 f., and 89–100, pp. 80–83 (Ostrogotha). Cf. below, n. 61.

61. The participation in the Gothic campaign of the peoples and Roman troops mentioned in the text is reported by Jordanes, *Getica* 90 f., p. 81, for the time of King Ostrogotha, the alleged predecessor of Cniva (cf. ibid. 101, p. 83). Ostrogotha (cf. Jordanes, *Getica* p. 143 n. 6) is linked by the *Origo Gothica* (cf. chap. 1, n. 54, and above, nn. 5 ff.) primarily to three events:

1. Ostrogotha was either the last king to rule over both Gothic peoples (see Jordanes, *Getica* 98, p. 83) or the first Ostrogothic king: see ibid. 82, p. 78, which in principle seems more likely: see Wenskus, *Stammesbildung,* 471 f.

2. Ostrogotha was also supposedly a contemporary of the emperor Philip the Arab (244–249): see Jordanes, *Getica* 90, p. 81. From this period comes a report of a large-scale attack by the king against the Romans, but the offensive was conducted by Ostrogotha's generals Argaith and Gunteric: see Jordanes, *Getica* 91, p. 81. We recognize in this a pattern of behavior that runs counter to the concept of military kingship but that clearly characterized the Tervingian judgeship: see Wolfram, "Gotische Studien I," 18 with n. 87 and 26 with n. 118. The SHA reports the invasion of the Scythian king Argunt, which is supposed to have taken place at the time of Philip's usurpation, i.e., in 244. This chronology cannot be maintained, even though Alföldi, *Weltkrise,* 316 with n. 19, argues for the historicity of the date. The identification of Argunt as "king of the Scythians" indicates that the information was borrowed from Dexippus, which increases the value of the account: see SHA 20 (Gord.) 31. 1. L. Schmidt, *Ostgermanen,* 205 with n. 6, explains "Argunt" as a contraction of Argaith and Gunteric, which is plausible not least because the SHA is entirely capable of such creations: see Straub, *Studien,* 29. Moreover, because the operations of the two chieftains correspond to the task assigned to the third army unit that Cniva sent to Moesia, Argaith and Gunteric could have indeed been Cniva's subordinate commanders. This finds support in the mention of the Bastarni based on the Danubian island of Peuke as comrades in arms (Jordanes, *Getica* 91, p. 81, as well as above, n. 54). Cniva's southern forces must have passed by Peuke if they marched through the Dobrudja to Thrace. The unsuccessful siege of Marcianopolis attributed to the two chieftains is also possible. Carpi are attested in 250 as allies of Cniva, while the Romans who had gone over to Ostrogotha resemble the unreliable Thracian army under Priscus, which committed treason during the siege of Philippopolis (Alföldi, *Weltkrise,* 319 and 344). Finally, as far as the participation of the Hasdingian Vandals is concerned, they can be attested at the Danube and Tisza at the latest in 270 (see Dexippus fr. 6 [24]). Parts of the story of the conflict

between Aurelian and the Vandals was translated by Capelle, *Germanien*, 245 f. The large-scale campaign of Ostrogotha had practically no results; historically and chronologically it is suspended in mid-air. For this reason alone one is inclined to regard the events mentioned here and attributed to Ostrogotha as a doublet of the story of Cniva. This assumption is confirmed by the explanation for the retreat of the allegedly three hundred thousand warriors of Ostrogotha (Jordanes, *Getica* 91 and 94, p. 81 f.).

3. The Gepids attack: Jordanes, *Getica* 95–100, p. 82 f. Under pressure from the Gepidic king Fastida, Ostrogotha himself undoubtedly takes up arms and drives back the attacker. But the chronological framework of these events is not around 250, and even less so before 250, but dates to around 290 and thus dates also the existence of Ostrogotha: see *XII Panegyrici Latini* XI (III) 17. 1. L. Schmidt, *Ostgermanen*, 223 and 530.

62. See above, nn. 36 ff.

63. Alföldi, *Weltkrise*, 317.

64. Fiebiger-Schmidt, *Inschriftensammlung*, n. 138, p. 72 f. Kirsten and Lippold, "Donauprovinzen," 153; Kirsten, "Dacia," 560.

65. See n. 61, no. 2.

66. Alföldi, *Weltkrise*, 319–321, and Hanslik, "Gallus," 1984–1994, esp. 1986. Paschoud, *Zosime* 1:146 ff., n. 50 ff.

67. Alföldi, *Weltkrise*, 322.

68. On barbarian ruthlessness and death wish see above, Introduction, n. 40. My discussion follows largely the version of Alföldi, *Weltkrise*, 321–325 and 436–439, which Straub, *Studien*, 40–74, corrects in a few details. When in doubt I have more often than not agreed with Straub. Paschoud (as n. 66) is an excellent guide through the maze of Zosimus passages of interest here. Cf. Zosimus I 34. 1 f. on the Gothic strategy.

69. See esp. Zosimus I 28, as well as Jordanes, *Getica* 105 f., p. 86. Paschoud, *Zosime* 1:28 and 150.

70. Dexippus fr. 22 (16). Straub, *Studien*, 48.

71. Apart from Goths, Carpi, and Borani, Urugundi are also mentioned: see Paschoud, *Zosime* 1:148 f., n. 53. Alföldi, *Weltkrise*, 221 with n. 44.

72. Gajdukevič, *Das bosporanische Reich*, 462 ff., esp. after Zosimus I 31 ff. Cf. Vasil'ev, *Goths in the Crimea*, 3 ff. The chronology of the two authors is to be corrected following Straub (as n. 68).

73. Gregorios Thaumaturgos, *Epistola canonica*, 1019–1048, esp. 1038 f. L. Schmidt, *Ostgermanen*, 213.

74. Alföldi, *Weltkrise*, 285 ff. Vogt, "Christenverfolgung," 1184–1188, esp. 1186 f. On the issue of tasting sacrificial meat cf. I Cor. 8. 1–13.

75. Herter, "Dirne," 1204 ff., esp. 1208.

76. Gregorios Thaumaturgos (as n. 73) 1038 f. Cf. Rostovtzeff, *Social and Economic History* 1:477 f. Cf. *Codex Iustinianus* XII 35, 9 (collaborators are threatened with death at the stake); IX 5 (against private prisons); XII 35, 15 (against the use of soldiers for private purposes); IX 12, 10 (against the maintaining of armed retainers, here called *buccellarii*). *Codex Theodosianus* V 6, 2 (demand for the restitution of captured booty and of liberated prisoners); XII 14 (against the

"peacemakers" who act on their own initiative), as well as *Digesta* IL 15, 1–30, and *Codex Iustinianus* VIII 50, 1–20, esp. 20.

77. Zosimus I 34, 1 ff. Straub, *Studien,* 47 ff., esp. 59. Paschoud, *Zosime* 1:153 f. n. 62. Cf. Wenskus, *Stammesbildung,* 455 n. 154, after Tacitus, *Historia* IV 23, 3 f.: prisoners and deserters pass on to the Germans new military techniques.

78. Gajdukevič, *Das bosporanische Reich,* 462 ff. The spread of the Cherniakhov culture, whose salient group is Gothic, covers the region between Wolhynia in the north, the Dnieper in the east, and the Prut/Dniester in the west. At the middle reaches of the Dnieper it reaches eastward across the river, but the steppe zone in the south, unlike the forest steppe, remains outside its sphere. Its continuation in the west is the Sîntana-de-Mureş culture; it comprises parts of Romania, namely, mainly Moldavia and Muntenia as well Transylvania; the river Olt to the west is only rarely crossed: Ioniţă, "Probleme," 95 ff. with map 1, and the same author (as above, n. 17).

79. Paschoud, *Zosime* 1:148 f. n. 53, after Zosimus I 31, 1. Cf. Alföldi, *Weltkrise,* 321 with n. 44, after L. Schmidt, *Ostgermanen,* 130 f.

80. Cf. what is believed to have been the contemporary conflict between the Gepids and Burgundians in Jordanes, *Getica* 97, p. 83. See above, n. 61 no. 3.

81. Jordanes, *Getica* 23 and 117–118, p. 59 and 88. The Gothic-Herulian conflict of the time of Ermanaric is thus already assumed for the third century. See also Straub, *Studien,* 29 f.; cf. 172, s.v. "Heruler." Paschoud, *Zosime* 1:159 ff. nn. 70 ff., after Zosimus I 42 ff. Wolfram, "Theogonie," 95 n. 100. L. Schmidt, *Ostgermanen,* 210, 215 f., and 550. On the "Scythian" unrest at the beginning of the century see above, n. 51 ff.

82. L. Schmidt, *Ostgermanen,* 215, and Schäferdiek, "Germanenmission," 502. Alföldi, *Weltkrise,* 324. Straub, *Studien,* 51–59.

83. Synkellos p. 716, 16–22. Cf. SHA 23 (Gall.) 12, 6.

84. Jordanes, *Getica* 107 f., p. 85 f.

85. Alföldi, *Weltkrise,* 436–439. Paschoud, *Zosime* 1:159 n. 70. But see esp. below, n. 250.

86. Alföldi, *Weltkrise,* 436 ff.; Straub, *Studien,* 59 ff.; Paschoud, *Zosime* 1:159 ff.

87. Zosimus I 42.

88. Jordanes, *Getica* 117, p. 88 after Dexippus fr. 5 (8).

89. See n. 84.

90. Zosimus I 43, 2. Dexippus fr. 20 f. and 29 (23).

91. Straub, *Studien,* 59.

92. Thompson, *Early Germans,* 148. For the heavily armed cavalry see Hoffmann, *Bewegungsheer,* 1 ff. and 247–257. Simon, "Reform," 435 ff., esp. 439.

93. Alföldi, *Weltkrise,* 325. L. Schmidt, *Ostgermanen,* 216 f. with n. 7. On the size of a tribal army see Wolfram, "Gotische Studien II," 313 with n. 103.

94. Straub, *Studien,* 65, does not venture "to make a decision." Alföldi, *Weltkrise,* 438 n. 6, shows the problems inherent in the attempt to keep both battles.

95. Zosimus I 45, 2. SHA 25 (Claud.) 11, 6–9. Stallknecht, *Untersuchungen,* 14 n. 59.

96. L. Schmidt, *Ostgermanen,* 220.

97. Jordanes, *Getica* 108 f., p. 86.

98. Alföldi, *Weltkrise,* 439. Damerau, "Claudius II," 74 f.

99. Straub, *Studien,* 72 f. Damerau, "Claudius II," 73 f.

100. Damerau, "Claudius II," 99 and 105; cf. Fiebiger-Schmidt, *Inschriften-sammlung,* no. 151, p. 79. Stein, "Gothicus," 1683–1685. Ever since the tetrarchy, victory titles of all sorts could also be bequeathed and inherited: Kneissl, "Die Siegestitulatur," 174 ff. Habicht, "Zur Geschichte Kaiser Konstantins," 371. On Probus and Tacitus see Straub, *Studien,* 52, and Paschoud, *Zosime* 1:172 f. n. 92 f., after Zosimus I 63 f. Fiebiger-Schmidt, *Inschriftensammlung,* nos. 155 f., p. 81 f.

101. Damerau, *Claudius II,* 81–91.

102. Alföldi, *Weltkrise,* 326–329.

103. SHA 26 (Aurel.) 22, 2. See chap. 1, nn. 130–133. On the significance of the loss of five thousand warriors see Wolfram, "Gotische Studien II," 313 with n. 103. It is true that *Cannabas* goes back to a Greek derivation of *Cannabaudes.* The accusative Cannaban used here points to a Greek source, which could be Dexippus. But a *rex Cannabas* is dangerously close to *cannabis,* and the Latin author turns the great Gothic prince for his readers into a "king hempstalk." Such inventions—even with tacit reference to Dexippus—are not only perfectly possible in the SHA but have already been proved: see Straub, *Studien,* 29.

104. The successful Gothic war of 271 was celebrated with a magnificent triumph in Rome, but not until 274. First Syrian Palmyra had to be defeated and the Gallic separatist state eliminated. Aurelian is said to have used a chariot drawn by four deer for his triumphal trip to the capitol and to have sacrificed the animals to Jupiter Optimus Maximus on the capitol: see SHA 26 (Aurel.) 33.3. For a discussion of the problems of this passage see most recently Scheibelreiter, *Tiernamen,* 33, n. 84; cf. 140 (source index). Moreover, a Gothic royal clan is mentioned from which Aurelian is said to have chosen a certain Hunila as wife for a General Bonosus. Furthermore, the emperor supposedly kept such noble Gothic women in groups of seven in Perinthus-Heraclea (Eski Eregi). The rich dowry of Hunila is described in detail: see SHA 29 (Firmus) 15, 3 ff. Schönfeld, *Wörterbuch,* 142 f. The predilection of the author of the SHA for such little stories, which date to around 400, is as noticeable as it is revealing. This applies also to another "Gothic" detail of the triumph. It is said that in the procession were ten Gothic women who as they walked along were preceded by a sign with the word "Amazons," just like the procession of nations opening modern Olympic games. These Gothic women were allegedly the survivors of an entire division of women who fought against the Romans alongside their menfolk and who were captured in battle: see SHA 29 (Firmus) 34, 1. For the notion of the Gothic women as Amazons see chap. 1, n. 87. It is also possible that at this time the Gothic word for bride, girl, or young woman—*brutes-bruta*—came as a loanword into the Latin language: see Feist, *Wörterbuch,* 110 f.

105. Ammianus Marcellinus XXXI 5.17.

106. Alföldi, *Weltkrise,* 328 f. Iliescu, "Räumung Dakiens," 5 ff. Bodor, "Emperor Aurelian," 41 ff. Horedt, "Räumung Dakiens," 135 ff.

107. Eutropius, *Breviarium* VIII 2, 2, p. 136. Cf. above, n. 53 f. and n. 61. See also *XII Panegyrici Latini* XI (III) 17, 1.

108. L. Schmidt, *Ostgermanen,* 95, after SHA 28 (Probus) 18, 1, and Zosimus

I 71, 1. The settlement of Gepids, Greutungi, and Vandals reported by the SHA is an anachronism: see Straub, *Studien,* 29 f.

109. Patsch, "Völkerbewegungen," 7 ff.

110. *XII Panegyrici Latini* XI (III) 17, 1. See chap. 1, nn. 48 ff.

111. Courtois, *Les Vandales,* 32 ff. Miltner, "Vandalen," 302 f.

112. See n. 100 on Tacitus and Probus. L. Schmidt, *Ostgermanen,* 222 f. Patsch (as n. 109). Vetters, *Dacia ripensis,* 5 with n. 14, assumes a contractual arrangement between the empire and the Goths.

113. See n. 110.

114. *XII Panegyrici Latini* XI (III) 17.1. *Laterculus Veronensis* 13, 35 f., where for the period 303/314 Taifali and Goths are attested in succession, attests both the social interpenetration of both peoples as well as their location at the lower Danube. On the dating see Demougeot, *La formation* 2:229 ff. and 395 f. Cf. also chap. 1, n. 48.

115. See chap. 1, n. 48 and n. 58.

116. See, for example, Zosimus IV 25, 1. The polyethnicism of the Gothic land is archaeologically reflected in the Sîntana-de-Mureş-Chernjachov culture, which is named after both a Romanian and a Ukrainian site: see above n. 17 and Ioniţă, "Probleme," 95 ff. Mitrea, "Goten an der unteren Donau," 81 ff. Tudor, "Preuves archéologiques," 149 ff.

117. Eutropius VIII 2, 2, p. 136. Mitrea, "Goten an der unteren Donau," 92. Miltner, "Vandalen," 303, Courtois, *Les Vandales,* 32 ff. Patsch, "Völkerbewegungen," 16 ff. Harmatta, *Sarmatians,* 48 f. and 53 ff. Eutropius composed his work as *magister memoriae* of the Emperor Valens in the 360s: Matthews, *Aristocracies,* 96 f.

118. See chap. 1, n. 30.

119. See above, n. 114.

120. Steinhauser, "Kultische Stammesnamen," 13 ff. Patsch, "Völkerbewegungen," 28 ff., and Patsch, "Sarmaten," 181 ff. Ammianus Marcellinus XVII 12.17 ff. See, however, Harmatta, *Sarmatians,* 55 ff., and Courtois, *Les Vandales,* 26 with n. 6.

121. Jordanes, *Getica* 113 f., p. 87, with whom Courtois, *Les Vandales,* 32–34, rightly agrees against L. Schmidt, *Ostgermanen,* 106. The expansion of the Vandals as described geographically by Jordanes apparently does not match the archaeological finds or their interpretation: see Bóna, "Bemerkungen," 367 f. But Bóna's attempt to find an explanation for this discrepancy seems at least as "desperate" as the suggestions of other archaeologists, whom he opposes. For Bóna enters the field of philological-historical textual criticism, a field that must remain fundamentally alien to him as an archaeologist. Cf. below, nn. 124 ff.

122. Jordanes, *Getica* 94–100, p. 82 f. Cf. Feist, *Wörterbuch,* 18 f. (Auha) and 189 (Galtis).

123. See above, n. 61 no. 1.

124. Horedt-Protase, "Zweites Fürstengrab," 216. Horedt, "Frühe Gepiden," 705 ff. Bóna, "Bemerkungen," 365 ff., does not agree with them. Bóna is correct in taking Jordanes, *Getica* 98, p. 83, as evidence that the Gepidic-Gothic conflict cannot have occurred east of the Carpathians: see below, n. 125.

125. Cf. Jordanes (as n. 124) with *XII Panegyrici Latini* XI (III) 17, 1. Cf. also above, n. 114 and n. 119 as well as below, n. 151 (second Gothic-Vandal conflict).

126. Bóna, "Bemerkungen," 366 f. The information that Taifali, Victu(f)ali, and Tervingi were occupying the former Roman province of Dacia comes from the 360s: see n. 117. Cf. below, n. 186, chap. 3, n. 29, n. 62, and n. 89 f.

127. L. Schmidt, *Ostgermanen,* 223 f., and Patsch, "Völkerbewegungen," 7–13, esp. after Jordanes, *Getica* 110–112, p. 86 f. See Stallknecht (as n. 128).

128. Stallknecht, *Untersuchungen,* 5 ff., esp. 15 and 97 n. 67. On the Gothic *foedera* of the early period cf. above, n. 59, and below, nn. 144–146 (list of *foedera*).

129. Schwarcz, *Reichsangehörige,* 13 f., according to Lactantius, *De mortibus persecutorum,* chaps. 13 and 28, pp. 187 and 218 f.

130. Among the sources see esp. Anonymus Valesianus 5, 12; cf. 35 (*ripa Gothica*), as well as Zosimus II 21, 1 ff., and Fiebiger-Schmidt, *Inschriftensammlung,* no. 160, p. 83 f. On this and for the chronology of the events cf. Habicht, *Geschichte,* 370–372. Stallknecht, *Untersuchungen,* 34 with n. 19 f. Schwarcz, *Reichsangehörige,* 16 ff. Rausimod, who is mentioned only by Zosimus, is frequently not considered to have been a Goth: see most recently Jones, *Prosopography* 1:762 (Sarmatian chieftain); but Paschoud, *Zosime* 1:213 n. 31, returns, no doubt correctly, to the older scholarly opinion—see, for example, L. Schmidt, *Ostgermanen,* 225—and calls him a Goth.

131. *Codex Theodosianus* VII 1, 1. Zosimus (as n. 130) as well as Stallknecht and Schwarcz (as n. 130).

132. L. Schmidt, *Ostgermanen,* 226, esp. after Anonymus Valesianus 5, 27. On the name of the mountain range cf. Ammianus Marcellinus XXVII 5, 3. See also above, n. 128.

133. Jordanes, *Getica* 111, p. 87.

134. Stallknecht, *Untersuchungen,* 34.

135. Anonymus Valesianus I 35, p. 11.

136. Stein, *Bas-Empire* 1:131 ff.

137. Vetters, *Dacia ripensis,* 22 f. Chrysos, "Gothia Romana," 59. On the tribal territories of the Tervingi and Taifali cf. below, nn. 362 ff. and nn. 408–411.

138. Ioniţă, "Probleme," 973, and Ioniţă (as above, n. 17). L. Schmidt, *Ostgermanen,* 226–228. Patsch, "Sarmaten," 181 ff. Harmatta, *Sarmatians,* 55 ff. Thompson, *Visigoths,* 11 ff.

139. Wolfram, "Gotische Studien I," 7 with n. 31 f., after Jordanes, *Getica* 43 and 178, pp. 65 and 104. The second passage refers to Priscus fr. 8 (FHG 4, 83), whose name of the river—Tigas—the *Origo Gothica* misreads as Tisza, but in doing so it offers a good location for the Gothic-Sarmatian confrontation: Fluss, "Tisia," 1469–1478 (with an excellent compilation of the names of the left tributaries of the Tisza), as well as Fluss, "Tigas," 941.

140. Stallknecht, *Untersuchungen,* 34 ff.

141. Zosimus II 31, 3; a report that Fluss, "Taifali," 2027, and Paschoud, *Zosime* 1:229 n. 43, describe as an anti-Constantinian invention of the author. But there is no reason to deny a partial Taifalian victory. In actuality the Taifali must have suffered severely, as Paschoud rightly points out. Cf. L. Schmidt, *Ostgermanen,* 546.

142. Cf. Anonymus Valesianus I 31, p. 10, with Jordanes, *Getica* 112, p. 87. For

the mention of Gothic chiefs in ancient sources other than the *Origo Gothica* see n. 61 no. 2 (Argaith and Gunteric). Stein, *Bas-Empire* 1:129. Chrysos, Βυζάντιον, 55 n. 2 (source index), who also discusses the question of whether the battle was fought on April 20 (*Consularia Constantinopolitana* a. 332, p. 234) or on February 18, as the quote from Anonymus Valesianus would indicate: on this see Seeck, *Untergang* 4:382.

143. Wolfram, "Gotische Studien I," 4 f. and 11 f. Stallknecht, *Untersuchungen* 18 f. and 34 f. Patsch, "Völkerbewegungen," 32 (flow of trade). The economic dependence of the Tervingi on the trade with the Roman Empire is still given by Ammianus Marcellinus XXVII 5.7 as the main reason why they had to make peace in 369.

144. See n. 59 (238), n. 66 (251), nn. 111–113 (271 and 295/297), and n. 127 f. (295/297).

145. See above, n. 129 and n. 132 f. (Licinius).

146. Anonymus Valesianus I 31, p. 10. Stallknecht, *Untersuchungen,* 18 f. and esp. 34 f. Evangelos Chrysos argues, against Stallknecht, that this treaty established the "Reichsangehörigkeit" of the Danubian Goths: "Gothia Romana," 52 ff., see esp. 53 n. 6., 57 (*annonae foederaticae*), and 61 ff. (Tervingian "Reichsangehörigkeit" from 332 to 376). Chrysos, ibid., 54–76, esp. 61 n. 2, follows Theodor Mommsen in distinguishing a type of "post-Diocletian" *foedus* from the treaty provisions of the early period. Accordingly, the treaty of 332 would have indeed been a great innovation and in a sense would have anticipated by fifty years the treaty of 382 (see chap. 3, n. 102). This *foedus* of 332 is said to have consisted of the following points: pacification, obligatory military service in return for yearly payments (*annonae foederaticae*), and land allotments on imperial territory accompanied by tribal autonomy.

147. Fiebiger-Schmidt, *Inschriftensammlung,* no. 164, p. 86.

148. Ibid., no. 163, p. 85.

149. Wolfram, "Gotische Studien I," 4–12.

150. Ibid., 9. Cf. below, nn. 170 ff.

151. Ammianus Marcellinus XVII 12 f. Jordanes, *Getica* 112–116, p. 87, and 162, p. 100. See Courtois, *Les Vandales,* 32 f., against Miltner, "Vandalen," 303. Cf. Wolfram, "Gotische Studien I," 7, as well as above, n. 120 f. On Geberic's ancestors see chap. 1, nn. 130 ff. On the unlikelihood of Vandal settlement areas along the rivers mentioned cf. Bóna, "Bemerkungen," 367 f. The remainder of Bóna's polemical comments here are an irresponsible misrepresentation of the sources.

152. Ammianus Marcellinus XVII 12.19.

153. R. Werner, "Anten," 587 ff. Harmatta, *Sarmatians,* 48–57. Jordanes, *Getica* 265 f., p. 126, and esp. Ammianus Marcellinus XVII 12 f. and XIX 11.

154. On the problems relating to the Taifalian tribal territory see Paschoud, *Zosime* 1:229 n. 43, as well as Fluss, "Taifali," 2027 f. Cf. below, nn. 366 ff.

155. Thompson, *Visigoths,* 16 f.; but his accurate observations suffer from the faulty premise that in 332 Constantine did not conclude a treaty with the Goths: cf. above, n. 146 and L. Schmidt, *Ostgermanen,* 229.

156. Wolfram, "Gotische Studien I," 7 f. Cf. Schäferdiek, "Germanenmission," 499 f.

157. Epiphanius, *Adversus haereses* III 1.15 (= 70.15.4), still explains the persecution of the Christian in 369/372 as revenge against the "Roman emperors."

158. Jordanes, *Getica* 267, p. 127. Auxentius (Max. diss. 63); Streitberg, *Die gotische Bibel* 1:xviii.

159. Wolfram, "Gotische Studien II," 296 n. 28 and 302 f.

160. Ibid., 318 f. with n. 120, esp. after Ammianus Marcellinus XXVII 7.8. Cf., in contrast, Eunapius fr. 22.1, where Julian is credited with the premonition that the "Scythians" would no longer keep quiet. L. Schmidt, *Ostgermanen*, 229.

161. To the sources discussed by Wolfram, "Gotische Studien I," 1 ff., one might also add Gregory of Tours, *Historia Francorum* II 4 and 28, pp. 43 and 73 (as chap. 1, n. 114).

162. Zosimus IV 34.3. Wolfram, "Gotische Studien I," n. 51.

163. See chap. 1, n. 109 f. Wenskus, "Balthen," 14.

164. Wolfram, "Gotische Studien I," 10–12.

165. Ammianus Marcellinus XXVI 5.1 ff. Before Ammianus describes these events he lists the problems of the Romans after the death of Julian: on all sides the empire was threatened by invasion, with hardship, devastation, and plundering by dangerous marauders everywhere. The last in the list of Rome's enemies are the Goths (ibid. 4.5). They are preceded by the Alamanni, but the latter did not attack until the winter of 365, after first negotiating with Valentinian I. The negotiations are mentioned (ibid., 5.7–9), i.e., after the events at Nish. An absolutely accurate chronology of the events is necessary, however, because on it depends the question of whether or not the Goths were planning an offensive war in 364/365.

166. Hoffmann, *Bewegungsheer* 1:122 ff.

167. *Codex Theodosianus* XV 1.13. On the dating of this decree see Seeck, *Regesten*, 71 and 224.

168. The panegyrics in 369 which celebrate the success of Valens against the Goths claim incorrectly that the emperor at his assumption of the imperial throne found the defensive works on the Danube in an absolutely disastrous state of disrepair: Straub, *Regeneratio Imperii*, 204. Patsch, "Völkerbewegungen," 41 with n. 1, after Themistius, *Oratio* X 135d ff. On the actual activities of Valens see Nagl, "Valens," 2106 and 2131, after CIL III 6159 and 7494.

169. Ammianus Marcellinus XXVI 6.11. Seeck, *Regesten*, 224–227.

170. Ammianus Marcellinus XXVI 6.12–7.9. Hoffmann, *Bewegungsheer* 1:120.

171. Ammianus Marcellinus XXVI 6.1 and 7.10, as well as XXVII and 5.1 (correspondence between Procopius and the Goths). On Athanaric cf. XXVI 6.10 f., 10.3 and XXXI 3.4. Eunapius fr. 37; Zosimus IV 7. Wolfram, "Gotische Studien I," 8 f. and 16. Stein, *Bas-Empire* 1:175 f.

172. The troop strength given by Ammianus Marcellinus XXVI 10.3 should be given preference over the ten thousand men reported by Zosimus IV 7.2: on the strength of a barbarian army cf. Wolfram, "Gotische Studien II," 311–313.

173. Cf. Eunapius fr. 37.

174. Ibid.; Nagl, "Valens," 2107; Patsch, "Völkerbewegungen," 42 f. On the correspondence between the usurper and Athanaric see above, n. 171.

175. Stein, *Bas-Empire* 1:176 with n. 98; Zosimus IV 8.

176. One could possibly identify the Colias-Sueridus group mentioned by Ammianus Marcellinus (XXXI 6.1 ff.) with these Goths. But Schwarcz, *Reichsangehörige*, 109 f., shows that this is untenable. The report of Ammianus Marcellinus that the

Colias-Sueridus Goths were *longe ante suscepti* makes it impossible to assume (as does Hoffmann, *Bewegungsheer* 1:440) that they crossed the Danube as a sort of vanguard of Fritigern. Yet it is just as impossible to see the "admission of the Goths" as a result of a forced internment. Schwarcz is probably right in placing the arrival of this group in the empire "at some unknown date between 369 and 376" and making either the persecution of the Christians by Athanaric or recruitment by the Romans responsible.

177. Ammianus Marcellinus XXVII 4.1 and 5.2.

178. See n. 160.

179. A similar conclusion is reached by Stallknecht, *Untersuchungen,* 71 with n. 125.

180. Stein, *Bas-Empire* 1:169 f. and 186. Patsch, "Völkerbewegungen," 39 f. Cf. Ammianus Marcellinus XXVII 7.7 f., and Eunapius fr. 22.1: Julian and the Goths before Julian's expedition against the Persians. Wolfram, "Gotische Studien I," 8 ff. and 18 ff. On the institutional aspect see also below, nn. 391 ff.

181. Stallknecht, *Untersuchungen,* 61 ff. and 71 with n. 125. Thompson, *Visigoths,* 17 ff. Nagl, "Valens," 2106 ff. Patsch, "Völkerbewegungen," 43 ff. The most important source for this is Ammianus Marcellinus XXVII 5.2 ff. Cf. Chrysos, Βυζάντιον, 94–103, esp. 100.

182. Ammianus Marcellinus XXVII 5.4.

183. Ibid., 5.5. Cf. Vetters, *Dacia ripensis,* 27 f.

184. While Thompson, *Visigoths,* 25 ff., has freely invented his discussion of the material culture and life-style of the Ostrogoths, his description of the economic system of the Tervingi, ibid., 27 ff., and their dependence on trade with the Romans, ibid., 34 ff., esp. 38, is excellent. Wolfram, "Gotische Studien I," 4, n. 12. Straub, *Regeneratio Imperii,* 208 ff. Dahn, *Könige der Germanen,* 14 ff. Priscus fr. 39. *Passio s. Sabae,* chaps. 3 ff., pp. 217–220.

185. On the holiness of the Gothic Danube see, for example, Claudianus, *Carmina,* p. 434, s.v. "Danubius," and 442, s.v. "Hister." Claudianus, *De bello Gothico* vv. 81 f., p. 263 (cf. n. 471), speaks of an oath of the Goths to the *patrii numen Histri.* The Virgil-imitator Claudian certainly knew the relevant passage—see esp. Servius, *Vergilii Georg.* II 497—according to which "the Dacians used to swear [by the Hister]." It is, however, a one-sided philological notion that the proof of literary borrowing robs a report of its value as historical testimony. For if that were the case, one could—to take things to the extreme—forget about writing medieval history. Rather, in each case one has to examine the relationship between *inventio* and *imitatio.* See also Brandis, "Danuvius," 2133, as well as the remotely comparable mention in the panegyric on Avitus of Sidonius Apollinaris, *Carmina* VII vv. 40–44, p. 204, where the assembly of the gods is already attended by the "old" rivers Rhine and Danube as representatives of the barbarian peoples. Wolfram, "Gotische Studien I," 5 with n. 19.

186. Cf. Ammianus Marcellinus XXVII 5.6 with XXXI 3.1 ff. Wolfram, "Gotische Studien I," 8 with nn. 36 and 38.

187. Wolfram, "Gotische Studien I," 3 with n. 10; Schäferdiek, "Arianismus," 76 f. n. 3.

188. Wolfram, "Gotische Studien I," 10 n. 42, after Thompson, *Early Germans,* 146–149.

189. Ammianus Marcellinus XXVII 5.6 f.

190. L. Schmidt, *Ostgermanen,* 232 f. Themistius, *Oratio* 10.132a ff. Zosimus IV 11. Ammianus Marcellinus XXVII 5.9 and XXXI 4.13. Cf. Wolfram, "Gotische Studien I," 12 ff. Stallknecht, *Untersuchungen,* 62 ff. He points out (61) that Valentinian I had to negotiate on the Rhine with the Alamannic prince Macrianus in the fall of 374, a piece of information that also comes from Ammianus Marcellinus (XXX 3.4 f.). For the restrictions on trading cf., for example, Priscus fr. 36, according to whom in 468/469 Attila's sons "according to ancient custom" request a trading site on the Danube but the request is turned down by Constantinople.

191. Wolfram, "Gotische Studien I," 9 f. with n. 42 and 13 with n. 54 ff. as well as 16–18. Matthews, *Aristocracies,* 116 ff., esp. after Dagron, *L'Empire romain.* Chrysos, Βυζάντιον, 103–108.

192. Schäferdiek, "Germanenmission," 501 ff. Gschwantler, "Bekehrung," 176 f. On the persecution in the mid-fourth century cf. above, n. 156 f., as well as below, nn. 282 ff. On the second persecution (369–372) and its causes see also Chrysos, Βυζάντιον, 109–120, who analyses the most important sources, Socrates and Sozomenus. Sozomenus corrects his predecessor Socrates to the effect that the Gothic martyrs were not Arians but Catholics. Cf. Heather, "Gothic Conversion," 298–304.

193. *Passio s. Sabae,* chap. 3, p. 217. Thompson, *Visigoths,* 94 ff.

194. Wolfram, "Gotische Studien I," 9 with n. 40, and "Gotische Studien II," 302 ff.; "Gotische Studien III," 240 with n. 140 and 255 with n. 190. Perhaps the ἄρχων τῆς ἀνομίας in the *Passio s. Sabae* chap. 3, p. 218, was Athanaric. As the persecutor this source names the subking Atharid: ibid. chap. 4, p. 219 ff. Another persecutor was Winguric: see Delehaye, *Saints de Thrace,* 279. Thompson, *Visigoths,* 48.

195. Socrates IV 33.7. Sozomenus VI 37.12. Cf. Thompson, *Visigoths,* 98 f.

196. Sozomenus VI 37.13 f. Cf. Wolfram, "Gotische Studien III," 240 with n. 140.

197. Ibid., 239 with nn. 135–141, as well as 259 with n. 201. Apart from burning at the stake, drowning is also attested as a form of religious punishment. Cf. the rule in the "law book of Gulathing," section 23, according to which "serious criminals, traitors to the king, murderers, violators of penance, thieves, and those people who take their own lives . . . are to be buried at the level of the ocean tide, where the sea and the green pastures meet": see *Norwegisches Recht,* transl. Rudolf Meissner, *Germanenrechte* 6:21. 1935. On the possibility of linking the Aesir with a stake cult, see Kuhn, "Asen," 458.

198. Epiphanius, *Adversus haereses* III 1.15 (=70.15.4). Wolfram, "Gotische Studien III," 244 f.

199. See above, n. 195.

200. The title of the work of Klein, "Frithigern, Athanarich und die Spaltung," 34 ff., is entirely justified; the chronology of the events offered there must be corrected with Schäferdiek, "Der germanische Arianismus," 76 with n. 3, as well as "Germanenmission," 504 f.

201. See below, nn. 278–280, n. 305 f., and chap. 3, n. 2 f.

202. Wolfram, "Gotische Studien I," 10 f., 22 with n. 74 and 26 with n. 101.

203. Wolfram, "Gotische Studien I," 26: there was the similar concern of Caesar and his allies, the Celtic aristocrats, that the kingdom of the Haedui might be reestablished.

204. Schäferdiek (as n. 200).

205. Ammianus Marcellinus XXXI 3.4.

206. Cf. the praise for the Roman way of constructing a camp and the lament over the decay of this art by Vegetius, *Epitoma rei militaris* I 21 ff.

207. See above, nn. 182 and 185 ff.

208. Otherwise Munderic could not have been Ammianus's source: see Wolfram, "Gotische Studien I," 2 n. 8.

209. Ammianus Marcellinus XXXI 3.1 ff. Vulpe, *Le vallum*, 25 ff. Vulpe, 27 with n. 4, uses the emendation of Petschenig in order to look for a Greutungian "wall" in Bessarabia. But the difficult passage in question (Ammianus Marcellinus XXXI 3.5) reads as follows: *agere ut ungoru vallem*. This could easily be turned into *a greutungorum vallem,* whereby *a* with the accusative could be explained in a number of ways: Altheim, *Geschichte der Hunnen* 1:352 n. 33. The no doubt untenable conjecture therefore seems to be the work of a modern emendator, who was motivated to make this "improvement" by the report about the building of the Athanaric wall: Ammianus Marcellinus XXXI 3.7. With the planned erection of "his" wall between the Prut and the Siret Athanaric took exactly the sort of measures one would expect from the leader of a "forest people" threatened by nomadic horsemen. Yet his "well-planned work" cannot have progressed far enough to allow us today to locate its archaeological remains in the countryside. In a conversation Ion Ioniţă raised the question of whether Munderic and Lagariman actually crossed the Dniester or whether they did not rather advance downstream along a Roman road as far as a "twentieth milestone" (see Ammianus Marcellinus XXXI 3.5) from the Black Sea coast. Ammianus's account is indeed not entirely clear. But the Huns, against whom the Gothic vanguard was sent out and which they allowed to advance within sight, circled around the Goths and then crossed the Dniester. For that reason I would prefer to adhere to the old interpretation. On the innertribal tensions in the Gothic land caused by the Hunnic invasion see Wolfram, "Gotische Studien II," 320 f. n. 126.

210. Ammianus Marcellinus XXXI 3.7.

211. Ibid., 3.8, where the *Gothorum reliquae gentes* are mentioned, who find out about the appearance of a new enemy after the defeat of Athanaric.

212. See n. 189.

213. Ammianus Marcellinus XXX 3.8.

214. While Athanaric in 367 withdrew to Muntenia in the face of a Roman attack (see n. 182) he put up resistance in 369 when the emperor invaded Moldavia via Bessarabia: see n. 186.

215. See above, nn. 200 ff.

216. Following Sozomenus VI 37.6–8, one may assume that Fritigern was contractually bound to the emperor. Schäferdiek, "Germanenmission," 504, and "Der germanische Arianismus," 76 n. 3. Ammianus Marcellinus XXXI 4.1 and 8, as well as 5.5, and Eunapius fr. 55, also reveal a "special relationship" between the Fritigern Goths and Valens. On the Tervingi who after 376 remained behind north of the Danube see chap. 1, n. 57, and chap. 3, n. 109.

217. Wolfram, "Gotische Studien I," 10 and 30.

218. Ammianus Marcellinus XXXI 5.5: last mention of Alaviv, whose name always preceded that of Fritigern. On the bond by treaty see Sozomenus (as n. 216).

219. Jordanes, *Getica* 134 f., p. 93, is undoubtedly a variation upon Ammianus Marcellinus XXXI 4.8, 4.12, and 5.3.

220. That the classical sources, indeed even Jordanes himself, despite his explicit statement (as n. 219), assign to Fritigern (and incidentally also to Athanaric [cf. below, n. 233]) the royal title is no contradiction: Jones, *Prosopography* 1:120 f. (Athanaric) and 374 (Fritigern). L. Schmidt, *Ostgermanen,* 244–246. Köpke, *Anfänge des Königthums,* 113. Wolfram, "Gotische Studien I," 5–7, 17 f., and "Gotische Studien II," 302 f. Wenskus, *Stammesbildung,* 307.

221. See chap. 3, n. 29 (concluding of an alliance with Alatheus and Safrax) and nn. 56–60 (Fritigern's negotiations with Valens prior to the battle of Adrianople).

222. Ammianus Marcellinus XXXI 4.11 ff. Eunapius fr. 42. Seeck, *Regesten,* 249.

223. Ammianus Marcellinus XXXI 4.7 and 12 f.; cf. 5.3 f.

224. Vulpe, *Le vallum,* 54–57; L. Schmidt, *Ostgermanen,* 404; Patsch, "Völkerbewegungen," 64 ff. Cf. Wolfram, "Gotische Studien II," 320 with n. 126. But Athanaric can no longer be linked to the treasure of Pietroasa: Harhoiu, *Treasure from Pietroasa,* 23 ff. and 29 ff. Harhoiu, "Das norddonauländische Gebiet," 101 ff.

225. Ambrose, *Expositio in Lucam* X 10. Ammianus Marcellinus XXXI 3.7: Athanaric excluded the Taifalian tribal territory from his defensive preparations against the Huns. Wolfram, "Gotische Studien II," 320 f. n. 126; Vulpe, *Le vallum,* 53 ff.

226. Zosimus IV 25.1.

227. Ammianus Marcellinus XXXI 9.3, cf. ibid. 4.12.

228. Schäferdiek, "Germanenmission," 503 f., saves the Gaatha story for historical interpretation.

229. Ammianus Marcellinus XXVII 5.10. Zosimus IV 34.1–4. Ambrose, *De Spiritu Sancto* I prol. 17. Wolfram, "Gotische Studien I," 3 with n. 9 f., 12 with n. 51, and 19 with n. 91. On the dating of Athanaric's entrance see n. 231 below.

230. Straub, *Regeneratio Imperii,* 203 and 207. L. Schmidt, *Ostgermanen,* 417. Wolfram, "Gotische Studien I," 12 ff.

231. *Consularia Constantinopolitana* a. 381, p. 243.

232. Zosimus IV 34.1–4. Ammianus Marcellinus XXVII 5.10 says that Athanaric was buried *ritu nostro.* That involved the *laudatio funebris,* in which the deeds and the titles of the deceased were honored. Hence, if it is said, ibid. 9, that Athanaric had been a *iudex gentis,* his judgeship was an institution in the eyes of the Romans: Wolfram, "Gotische Studien I," 1 ff.

233. Wolfram, "Gotische Studien I," 2 with n. 4 and 19 with n. 93, after Jordanes, *Getica* 142–145, p. 95 f. Cf. Orosius, *Historiarum adversum paganos* VII 34.6 f.

234. See below, n. 251 and nn. 330–332.

235. Thus reports Prosper Tiro, *Epitoma Chronicon* a. 382, p. 461, even if he is the only one who does. The sources closer in time to the events know nothing of this: see Wolfram, "Gotische Studien I," 2 n. 7.

236. See below, n. 251.

237. Jordanes, *Getica* 145, p. 96, does not say that Athanaric's retainers (L. Schmidt, *Ostgermanen,* 418 with n. 2) were alone sufficient to form the two Roman auxiliary units. Cf. on this Hoffmann, *Bewegungsheer* 1:241 and 467, 2:273, s.v. "Tervingi," together with the modification suggested by Schwarcz, *Reichsange-*

hörige, 47; see also chap. 1, nn. 48 ff., on the chronology and origin of the Gothic names mentioned. The emigration of the Tervingi occurs parallel with the abandonment of the grave fields of the Sîntana-de-Mureș culture. Cf. the similar findings on the Cherniakhov culture in southern Russia (as chap. 5, n. 51). On the term "Visigoths" see chap. 1, n. 63.

238. Hodgkin, *Italy and Her Invaders* 1:70.

239. Ulfilas and the Christianization of the Goths has been discussed most recently by Schwarcz, *Reichsangehörige,* 208–211, Lippold, "Ulfila," 512–531, as well as Schäferdiek, "Germanenmission," 497 ff. See Auxentius (Max. diss. 63), Streitberg, *Die gotische Bibel* 1:xviii; Stutz, *Gotische Literaturdenkmäler,* 9 ff.; Heather, "Gothic Conversion," 289 ff.

240. Stutz, *Gotische Literaturdenkmäler,* 74 ff. Wolfram, "Gotische Studien II," 289 ff. and III, 244 ff.

241. Stutz, *Gotische Literaturdenkmäler,* 43 ff. Sunnia and Fretela; cf. Jerome, *Epistula* 106, p. 247 ff. Schäferdiek, "Germanenmission," 500 f., 506, 522 f.

242. Krause, *Handbuch,* 16 ff. Stutz, *Gotische Literaturdenkmäler,* 28 f.: of the Old Testament only Nehemiah 5–7 survived.

243. Philostorgius II 5. Streitberg, *Die gotische Bibel* 1:xx.

244. Wolfram, "Gotische Studien II," 298–300.

245. Jordanes, *Getica* 132, p. 92, and 267, p. 127.

246. Philostorgius II 5.

247. L. Schmidt, *Ostgermanen,* 215. Schäferdiek, "Germanenmission," 502.

248. Straub, *Studien,* 58 f. Cf. above, nn. 82–85.

249. Alföldi, *Weltkrise,* 146 f. See n. 250.

250. See the dating of the emperors' rule in Philostorgius II 5, where the origin of the Scythians/Goths is also placed in the transdanubian region but the route of their invasion is then said to be Asia-Galatia; cf. above, nn. 82 and 85.

251. According to Auxentius (Max. diss. 53–59); Streitberg, *Die gotische Bibel* 1:xvi, Ulfilas was bishop for forty years and gained the bishopric at the age of thirty. Since his death (see n. 330) occurred in 382/383, this calculation points to the time around 311 as the year of his birth. But these numbers also have a symbolic significance; cf. below, n. 265.

252. Krause, *Handbuch,* 15 f. Lippold, "Ulfila," 512 f. The vulgar Greek and Moesian-Gothic dialect form Οὐρφίλας is attested by a bronze stamp from Corfu, which probably belonged to Ulfilas. Schäferdiek, "Germanenmission," 500, after Fiebiger-Schmidt, *Inschriftensammlung,* no. 169, p. 89 (with illustration), and Fiebiger, *Inschriftensammlung,* no. 31, p. 23 (with a defense of the identification).

253. Schwarcz, *Reichsangehörige,* 168 f. Thompson, *Visigoths,* 82 with n. 1. Schäferdiek, "Germanenmission," 505.

254. Jordanes, *Getica* 267; p. 127.

255. Philostorgius II 5. Auxentius (*Max. diss.* 62); Streitberg, *Die gotische Bibel* 1:xvii.

256. Wolfram, "Gotische Studien I," 3–8.

257. Auxentius (Max. diss. 53 f.); Streitberg, *Die gotische Bibel* 1:xvi.

258. Cf. Ammianus Marcellinus XXXI 12.8.

259. Schäferdiek, "Germanenmission," 498 f. Cf. above, n. 257. See Socrates I 18.4.

260. This is probably what Philostorgius II 5 means when he describes Ulfilas's appointment by Eusebius with the words ἐν τῇ Γετικῇ.

261. Wolfram, "Gotische Studien II," 307 f. and 314 f.

262. *Passio s. Sabae,* chap. 3, p. 218.

263. Schäferdiek, "Arianismus," 79 ff. Lippold, "Ulfila," 514 f. On the terminology of social rank see below, n. 456.

264. As n. 251, as well as Schwarcz, *Reichsangehörige,* 44 f. and 150.

265. Klein, "Auxentiusbrief," 116 f. On number symbolism cf. in general Meyer, *Zahlensymbolik,* 133 ff. (seven), 155 ff. (thirty), 158 (thirty-three), and 160 (forty).

266. Philostorgius II 5. Thompson, *Visigoths,* p. xiv f.

267. As n. 251. Chrysos, Βυζάντιον, 85–93 as well as 121–123, shows that in admitting Ulfilas and his group in the middle of the century Constantius II had anticipated the Christianization, or rather the Arianization, of the Goths, as it was later undertaken by Valens with the help of Eudoxius of Constantinople. Thus in Antioch Ulfilas was ordained not by the local bishop but by the bishop of the imperial capital, whose authority over the church *in barbaricis* was established by the second canon of the ecumenical council of Constantinople in 381 and explicitly laid down in the canon of Chalcedon in 451: Hefele-Leclercq, *Histoire des conciles* 2 1, 21 ff., and 2 2, 815 ff. On this Chrysos in a forthcoming publication.

268. See n. 267. Schwarcz, *Reichsangehörige,* 208–211. Thompson, *Visigoths,* p. xv ff., after Philostorgius II 5. Klein, "Gotenprimas Wulfila," 94 f. Lippold, "Ulfila," 515 f. On the quote see n. 260.

269. Auxentius (*Max. diss.* 55); Streitberg, *Die gotische Bibel* 1:xvi. Lippold, "Ulfila," 519. Schwarcz (as n. 264). Cf. above, n. 267 (ecumenical council).

270. Gschwantler, "Bekehrung," 175 f. Stutz, *Gotische Literaturdenkmäler,* 4 f. Fridh, "Bekehrung," 130 ff. Schäferdiek, "Germanenmission," 497 ff., esp. 503.

271. Basil the Great, *Epistola* 164. Cf. nn. 259 and 270.

272. Gschwantler, "Bekehrung," 175, after Basil (as n. 271).

273. See above, nn. 71 ff.

274. Socrates II 41. Schäferdiek, "Germanenmission," 498 and 530 f., assigns Theophilus to the Dacian Gothia. Cf., in contrast, the testimony of Philostorgius (as n. 255), according to whom Ulfilas was "their [the Goths'] first bishop." Chrysos, "Gothia Romana," 63 sees in Theophilus the teacher of Ulfilas. Cf. Gschwantler, "Bekehrung," 175 f. Cf. Thompson, *Visigoths,* 82 and 164. Vasil'ev, *Goths in the Crimea,* 10 ff. Gajdukevič, *Das bosporanische Reich,* 482 ff. Hóst, "Spuren der Goten," 67 ff. Karlsson, "Goten im Osten," 165 f.

275. Gajdukevič, *Das bosporanische Reich,* 511 ff. with nn. 43 and 48. On John Chrysostom see Schäferdiek, "Germanenmission," 506, and Schwarcz, *Reichsangehörige,* 56–58.

276. Procopius, *De bello Gothico* IV (VIII) 4.9–13 (on the year 548), and Procopius, *De aedificiis* III 7.10–17 (on the year 488 and the dependent status of the Crimean Goths in the time of Procopius). Stein, *Bas-Empire* 2, 62 f.

277. Hóst, "Spuren der Goten," 70 ff.

278. Auxentius (*Max. diss.* 44–48); Streitberg, *Die gotische Bibel* 1:xiv f. Thompson, *Visigoths,* p. xix f. Schäferdiek, "Germanenmission," 522 ff., esp. 523 f.

279. See n. 276.

280. Lippold, "Ulfila," 524–526. Cf. Sozomenus VI 37.8 f. Theodoret IV 33.

281. Gschwantler, "Bekehrung," 176. Thompson, *Visigoths,* 62 f. and 167. Cf. Vasil'ev, *Goths in the Crimea,* 9 f., and Zeiller, *Les origines chrétiennes,* 419 f. and 601, but these two authors start from the assumption that Audaios was driven out by Constantine the Great. See esp. Epiphanius, *Adversus haereses* III 1.14 f. (= 70.14 f.). Schäferdick, "Germanenmission," 502.

282. See above, n. 156.

283. Auxentius (*Max. diss.* 63); Streitberg, *Die gotische Bibel* 1:xviii.

284. Auxentius (*Max. diss.* 58 f.) as well as Streitberg, *Die gotische Bibel* 1:xvii. Cf. Gschwantler, "Bekehrung," 176.

285. *Passio ss. Innae, Rhimae et Pinae,* p. 215 f. The placement of the *passio* in the first persecution is argued by Gschwantler, "Bekehrung," 176, and by Thompson, *Visigoths,* 161–165. Schäferdiek, "Germanenmission," 499 and 501.

286. Cf. Thompson, *Visigoths,* 159 f.

287. Kirsten, "Chorbischof," 1105 ff. Cf. Kirsten, "Cappadocia," 882. Schäferdiek, "Germanenmission," 500, states cautiously: ". . . presumably Ulfilas acted from that time also as bishop of Nicopolis."

288. Klein, "Gotenprimas Wulfila," 87 ff., unjustly polemizes (ibid., 89) against Patsch, "Völkerbewegungen," 35 f. In this context the signature of the seal attributed to Ulfilas is also of significance: cf. Klein, 85, and above n. 252, and n. 287. Chrysos, Βυζάντιον, 85–93, rightly notes that the Goths who were admitted were forbidden to settle in the cities.

289. Jordanes, *Getica* 267, p. 127. Thompson, *Visigoths,* 103 and 110 f.

290. Kirsten (as n. 287), esp. "Cappadocia," 872 f., 882, 887.

291. Auxentius (*Max. diss.* 53–55, 60); Streitberg, *Die gotische Bibel* 1:xvi f., cf. Lippold, "Ulfila," 516–519 and 527–529.

292. Krause, *Handbuch,* 63 ff.

293. Ibid., 18 after Stutz, *Gotische Literaturdenkmäler,* 28 ff.

294. Stutz, *Gotische Literaturdenkmäler,* 31–47.

295. Stutz, *Gotische Literaturdenkmäler,* 48.

296. Auxentius (*Max. diss.* 46); Streitberg, *Die gotische Bibel* 1:xv.

297. Lippold, "Ulfila," 518. Schäferdiek, "Germanenmission," 523 f.

298. Socrates IV 33.7.

299. Lippold, "Ulfila," 530; cf. above, n. 254.

300. Høst, "Spuren der Goten," 56–58. But it remains doubtful whether the Goths of Tomis mentioned in Walahfrid Strabo, *Libellus de exordiis* 7, p. 481, were in fact contemporaries of the author: see Schäferdiek, "Germanenmission," 506. Cf. chap. 1, nn. 89–91.

301. Schäferdiek, "Germanenmission," 505.

302. Schäferdiek, "Germanenmission," 504, corrects Thompson, *Visigoths,* 103 f., who takes Isidore of Seville, *Historia vel Origo Gothorum,* chap. 10, p. 271, at his word and must therefore assume next to the Arian Ulfilas Goths the existence of Catholic Goths who also lived in the mountains. Here, however, we are probably dealing with a clash between Arian Goths, which Isidore could only explain by making one group Catholics.

303. See below, nn. 460 ff.

304. Jordanes, *Getica* 267, p. 127. Evangelos Chrysos has suggested in a conver-

sation that traditional geographers added the adjective *minor* only to those geographical and ethnic units considered Roman.

305. Lippold, "Ulfila," 519 f. Thompson, *Visigoths,* 157 f. Schäferdiek, "Arianismus," 76 f. with n. 3, and Schäferdiek, "Germanenmission," 504 f. Cf. below, n. 330.

306. Schäferdiek (as n. 305).

307. As n. 305 (Schäferdiek).

308. *De civitate Dei* XVIII 52.56 ff. Sozomenus VI 37.12–14.

309. Socrates IV 33.7. Chrysos (as n. 192).

310. Gschwantler, "Bekehrung," 176. Thompson, *Visigoths,* 94 ff. Schönfeld, "Goti," 812 f.

311. Delehaye, *Saints de Thrace,* 215–221.

312. Ibid., 209–215. Cf. Thompson, *Visigoths,* 82 with n. 3.

313. As n. 302.

314. Delehaye, *Saints de Thrace,* 276 ff., esp. 279, as well as Sozomenus VI 37.14. On the Gothic calendar see Schwab, "*bilaif* im Gotischen Kalender (29. Oktober)," 357 ff., esp. 366 f. and 393 f. (summary); Streitberg, *Die gotische Bibel* 1:472–474, or Stutz, *Gotische Literaturdenkmäler,* 69–72, who also offers a good interpretation of this difficult source. The calendar reveals that an accommodation took place between native traditions and the traditions of the Moesian Goths. The fragment of the calendar was not written before 419, but it does go back to Ulfilas's community. This community remembered the Arian emperor Constantius II, who admitted Ulfilas and is said to have called him Moses (Philostorgius II 5), probably also Fritigern, and certainly the twenty-six martyrs of whom a few are named both here and in the Greek menologies. Moreover, the name of Beroea-Stara Zagora is mentioned, i.e., a city situated in the vicinity of the settlement area of the *Gothi minores.* See also Thompson, *Visigoths,* 100 and 159 f., as well as Zeiller, *Les origines chrétiennes,* 434 ff. On the Gaatha story see Claude, *Adel, Kirche und Königtum,* 16 f. Schäferdiek, "Germanenmission," 503 f., has also paved the way for a better historical and constitutional interpretation of this source.

315. Klein, "Ambrosius," 14 ff.

316. L. Schmidt, *Ostgermanen,* 234 ff. Schäferdiek, "Arianismus," 80 with n. 2. Schäferdiek, "Germanenmission," 502 f.

317. Thompson, *Visigoths,* 173.

318. Ibid., 84 f. Stutz, *Gotische Literaturdenkmäler,* 71.

319. *Passio ss. Innae, Rhimae et Pinae,* p. 215 f. *Passio s. Sabae,* chaps. 4–7, pp. 218–220, esp. chap. 7, p. 220: Sansalas is set free, Saba is drowned.

320. Eunapius fr. 55.

321. Ammianus Marcellinus XXXI 12.8 f.

322. Schwarcz, *Reichsangehörige,* 138. Thompson, *Visigoths,* 161 ff. *Passio ss. Innae, Rhimae et Pinae,* p. 215 f.

323. *Passio s. Sabae* chap. 3, p. 218.

324. Whereas Epiphanius, *Adversus haereses* III 1.15 (=70.15.4), who wrote immediately after the persecution, explains Athanaric's actions as arising from his enmity against Rome and the Roman emperor, Socrates IV 33.7 and Sozomenus VI 37.12 see the cause in Athanaric's concern for the preservation of the religious and social order of the tribe.

325. Thompson, *Visigoths,* 106 ff., underestimates the extent of the Christianization of the Danubian Goths before 376. Cf. Gschwantler, "Bekehrung," 178 f., and Schäferdiek, "Arianismus," 74 ff., as well as "Germanenmission," 504 ff.

326. Cf. above, n. 320.

327. Jordanes, *Getica* 132 f., p. 92. Schäferdiek, "Germanenmission," 506–519.

328. Schäferdiek, "Arianismus," 80.

329. As n. 302 and n. 304.

330. Lippold, "Ulfila," 520–524. On the connection between Ulfilas and Fritigern see above, n. 305 as well as n. 328 f. On the standing of the bishop of the imperial capital since 381 see above, n. 267.

331. Auxentius (*Max. diss.* 63); Streitberg, *Die gotische Bibel* 1:xvii. Cf. Lippold, "Ulfila," 524–526.

332. Auxentius (*Max. diss.* 62); Streitberg, *Die gotische Bibel* 1:xvii.

333. Hefele-Leclercq, *Histoire des conciles* 2:22 and 24. Cf. *Codex Theodosianus,* XVI 1.4. Schäferdiek, *Die Kirchen der Westgoten,* 9. *Codex Iustinianus* I 5.12.17 (section 527).

334. The Arians of Bourges mentioned by Sidonius Apollinaris, *Epistulae* VII 8.3, p. 112, were not Goths. Cf. below, chap. 4, n. 230.

335. Gschwantler, "Bekehrung," 179. Thompson, *Visigoths,* 133 ff. Zöllner, *Franken,* 64. Schäferdiek, "Germanenmission," 511 (Franks) and 519 ff., is sceptical about the possibility that the East Germanic peoples reached Germania with a real Arian mission.

336. *XII Panegyrici Latini* XI (III) 17.1, cf. chap. 1, n. 48 and 50, as well as above, n. 114. Zosimus I 27.1 and 31.1 says the Goths of the second half of the third century were related to a tribal group he called Οὐρουγοῦνδοι. Modern scholars compare them to the Βουρουγοῦνδοι in Agathias V 11.2 and 4, who considers them, however, Hunnic peoples: see Paschoud, *Zosime* 1:148 n. 53. Nevertheless, Perrin, *Burgondes, 95,* still does not think it impossible that this refers to East Burgundians. Cf. L. Schmidt, *Ostgermanen,* 130 f. and 223. As allies of the Burgundians the panegyrist names the Alamanni, but this can be easily corrected to read Alans. Cf. the same mix-up in Gregory of Tours, *Historia Francorum* II 9 and 19; Zöllner, *Franken,* 39 f. n. 10.

337. See above, n. 274.

338. Ammianus Marcellinus XXVII 5.6. Cf. above, n. 186. That the Greutungi were Goths follows from Ammianus XXXI 4.12 and 12.17.

339. See Wolfram, "Gotische Studien I," 2 n. 8.

340. Ammianus Marcellinus XXXI 3.3–5. Cf. above, nn. 205 ff.

341. See n. 338.

342. Jordanes, *Getica* 78 f., p. 76 f., and 82, p. 78. See above, n. 61.

343. See above, nn. 122–125.

344. Thus the royal Scythians of Herodotus, Pomponius Mela, and Pliny the Elder reappeared under a different name: see Kretschmer, "Scythae," 930, after Herodotus IV 19. Zosimus IV 20, 3, has the Scythians reappear as the Huns.

345. Ammianus Marcellinus XXVII 5.6 and XXXI 3.1, and Jordanes, *Getica* 116–120, p. 88 f.

346. G. Schramm, "Eroberungen," 3 ff., after Jordanes, *Getica* 116–120, p. 88 f. Cf. L. Schmidt, *Ostgermanen,* 240 f., and Maenchen-Helfen, *The Huns,* 24.

347. Schramm, "Eroberungen," 13.
348. Ibid., 4 and 5. Altheim, *Geschichte der Hunnen* 1:306 ff.
349. Cf. Wenskus, *Stammesbildung*, 469 f.
350. Schramm, "Eroberungen," 13 f. with n. 40.
351. Jordanes, *Getica* 120, p. 89.
352. *Variae* V 2, p. 143 f. Jordanes, *Getica* 36 and 96, pp. 63 and 82 f. Cf. Chambers, *Widsith*, 252 ff. Höfler, *Germanisches Sakralkönigtum*, 20 ff. and 289. Schwarz, "Urheimat der Goten." See chap. 1, n. 37 and *Hervarasaga* and "The Battle of the Goths and the Huns" (as chap. 1, n. 74).
353. Cf. above, n. 16 f., as well as n. 45 on the northwestern boundary of the Cherniakhov culture.
354. Jordanes, *Getica* 129 f., p. 91 f. Gschwantler, "Heldensage," 12 ff., esp. 114 ff. See chap. 1, nn. 125 ff. Cf. Wolfram, "Theogonie," 81 ff.
355. Gschwantler, "Rosomonen," 174 ff., esp. after Jordanes, *Getica* 129, p. 91.
356. Procopius, *De bello Gothico* III (VII) 2.1 ff.
357. See n. 354.
358. Ammianus Marcellinus XXXI 3.2.
359. Gschwantler, "Heldensage," 65. Jordanes, *Getica* 129 f., p. 91 f. See below, n. 481.
360. Ammianus Marcellinus XXXI 3.3 and 4.12. Jordanes, *Getica* 246–249, p. 121; cf. 119, p. 89. See chap. 5, nn. 23 ff.
361. This chapter follows Wolfram, "Gotische Studien" I, II, and III. Additions and changes are mentioned in the notes. See esp. "Gotische Studien II," 289 ff. and 295.
362. Wolfram, "Gotische Studien II," 302 and 320. On the *genitales terrae* see 106 n. 18; on the fixed borders in "Roman fashion" see chap. 4, n. 615, chap. 5, n. 388. On the settlement of Oltenia cf. below, n. 366. On the question of the Gothic conquest of Transylvania see above, nn. 117 f. and 151. On the settlement areas of Athanaric, Fritigern, and the other chieftains see below, nn. 408 ff.
363. On the Taifali in general see L. Schmidt, *Ostgermanen*, 546–548, as well as Fluss, "Taifali," 2026–2028. The two peoples are mentioned together from the first references (*XII Panegyrici Latini* XI [III] 17.1) and *Laterculus Veronensis* 13.26 and 35 [cf. above, n. 114]) right up to the last passage (Zosimus IV 25.1, who still attests the union of the Tervingians and the Taifali).
364. Ammianus Marcellinus XXXI 3.7.
365. Ibid., XVII 13.19 f.
366. See the maps of the finds in Mitrea, "Goten an der unteren Donau," 81, as well as Ioniţă, "Probleme," 97. The Taifali, however, cannot be archaeologically defined. Despite the absence of finds Chrysos, "Gothia Romana," 61 with n. 43, still maintains that the Tervingi also settled in the old province Dacia inferior, i.e., Oltenia.
367. Zosimus II 31.3. Wenskus, *Stammesbildung*, 561 with n. 851, points out (after Tacitus, *Annales* XII 29.3) that Vannius the king of the Quadi led his infantry together with Sarmatian horsemen into battle.
368. Ammianus Marcellinus XXXI 9.3 f., cf. ibid., 4.12. On Farnobius and his ethnic identification see chap. 1, n. 60.
369. Hoffmann, *Bewegungsheer* 1:278; cf. 2:260, s.v. "Taifalen" and "Ter-

wingen." *Notitia dignitatum oc.* VI 16 and 59, VII 172, as well as *Notitia dignitatum or.* V 20 and 61 (*Visi*), and VI 20 and 61 (*Tervingi*).

370. Cf. Vulpe, *Le vallum,* 51–54, and the map between pp. 32 and 33.

371. Steinhauser, "Kultische Stammesnamen," 8 ff. Diculescu, *Wandalen und Goten,* 11–14.

372. Ammianus Marcellinus XXXI 9.4.

373. L. Schmidt, *Ostgermanen,* 547 with n. 4.

374. *Notitia dignitatum oc.* XLII 65. On this see chap. 4, nn. 552–564.

375. Cf. above, nn. 107–109, as well as n. 128.

376. Cf. Mitrea, "Goten an der unteren Donau," 92 f., as well as Ioniţă, "Probleme," 95 ff.

377. Wenskus, "Alanen," 122–124. According to Harmatta, *Sarmatians,* 48 f. and 52, the Alans penetrated into what is modern Hungary only in the fourth century. On the identification of the Alans as a "Gothic people" that joined the likewise "Gothic people" of the Vandals, see Procopius, *De bello Vandalico* I (III) 2.2 and 3.1.

378. See above, nn. 223–227.

379. Wolfram, "Gotische Studien II," 320 f. with n. 126, 322 with n. 126, as well as III, 240 with n. 141 (Sansalas). Mitrea, "Goten an der unteren Donau," 81 ff., Ioniţă, "Probleme," 95 ff. On the Gothic as well as non-Gothic minorities see above, n. 253 and nn. 270–272, as well as some of the names of the twenty-six martyrs (as above, n. 314).

380. See the strategy of Athanaric in the years 367 and 369, as well as 376: see above, nn. 181 ff. and nn. 206 ff.

381. See above, nn. 138 ff. (Sarmatians) and n. 151 (Vandals).

382. See Bach, *Namenkunde* 2:182 ff.

383. Vulpe, *Le vallum,* 47 with n. 50, whose discussion I have followed, except for his incorrect "improvement" of Ammianus Marcellinus XXXI 3.4; cf. XXVII 5.6; cf. above, n. 209.

384. See the map of Ioniţă (as n. 366).

385. The Tervingian southern border was the *ripa Gothica*: see Anonymus Valesianus 5.35. On the Roman-type fixed borders cf. chap. 4, n. 615, and chap. 5, nn. 388 ff.

386. Wolfram, "Gotische Studien II," 297 ff. and 319 f. with n. 121. Eunapius fr. 55 (φυλαί), Philostorgius II 5 (ἔθνη) and Ammianus Marcellinus XXXI 3.8 (*gentes*). The Gothic term was *kuni*: see Feist, *Wörterbuch,* 316.

387. Ammianus Marcellinus XXVI 6.11.

388. On *thiudans* see Wolfram, "Gotische Studien II," 295–300, as well as 302 f. with n. 56. N.B.: since references for the following discussion will be mostly to Wolfram, "Gotische Studien" I, II, and III, they will be cited only as GS I, II, or III.

389. On the Greek and Latin names for the Tervingian petty kings see GS II, 303 ff. Cf. below, n. 400.

390. GS I, 8 with nn. 36–38, and 12 ff.

391. Ibid., 319 f. and 323.

392. Cf. 1 Cor. 1.24. In this case, however, δύναμις does not mean might but power (*virtus*).

393. GS I, 17. N.B.: *rex,* ῥήξ, and *reiks* all read *rēx.*

394. Ibid., 16 with n. 72. Ambrose, *De Spiritu Sancto* I prol. 17. Ammianus Marcellinus XXVII 5.9: *iudex gentis*; cf. above, n. 232.

395. GS I, 20 ff. GS II, 295 f. with n. 26, and 297.

396. The Roman emperor is called *thiudans* in the Gothic calendar: Streitberg, *Die gotische Bibel* 1:472 ff., as well as Stutz, *Gotische Literaturdenkmäler,* 69 ff. Yet an apparently barbarian, "Gothic"-speaking craftsman created the legend *regis* [for *reges*] *Romanorum* on an imitative Valens medallion that no doubt also comes from the treasure of Şimleul Silvaniei-Szilágy Somlyó: see GS III, 245 f. with n. 162. Cf. GS II, 295 ff., esp. 302 f. Alföldi, "Nachahmungen," 10 ff.

397. GS I, 4–12 and 17 f. On the archaic titles that used the "leader-suffix" see GS II, 297–300, where I have also tried to infer a Gothic *drauhtins.*

398. GS II, 303 ff., esp. 305 with n. 74 and 319 with n. 121.

399. GS I, 7 f. and 9 f.

400. Ibid., 9 f. *Passio s. Sabae,* chap. 3, p. 217 (κατὰ τὴν Γοτθίαν μεγιστᾶνες) and p. 218 (ἄρχων τῆς ἀνομίας).

401. Jordanes, *Getica* 43, p. 65; 178, p. 104 (Vidigoia); 112–116, p. 87 f. (Geberic). GS I, 5–7 and 25–31.

402. Cf. Ammianus Marcellinus XXXI 3.8–4.1, with Jordanes, *Getica* 134, p. 93, who was dependent on Ammianus. On the term *universa gens Gothorum* see *Consularia Constantinopolitana* a. 382, 2, p. 243.

403. See GS I, 6 with nn. 24–26.

404. GS I, 21 and GS II, 299 f.

405. GS II, 303 ff. (*reiks* and other titles). Ammianus Marcellinus XXVI 6.11. Cf. above, nn. 389 and 400.

406. *Passio s. Sabae* 3 f., p. 218 f., and 7, p. 220. On the terminology of retainership see GS II, 314–317. Cf. below, n. 453 (*siponeis*).

407. Wenskus, "Adel," 60 f. Jordanes, *Getica* 146, p. 96, compares the nobleness of the Balths with the higher ranking nobility of the Amali.

408. *Passio s. Sabae* 6 f., p. 220; cf. n. 406.

409. See above, nn. 223–227 as well as nn. 378 and 380.

410. This suggested location follows the tribal conflict between Athanaric and Fritigern. Fritigern would have never taken on his much more powerful opponent unless he had direct access to the Romans: cf. above, nn. 201–204.

411. See above, n. 314 (Schäferdiek and Claude).

412. GS III, 240 f., 246 and 269 f. Ammianus Marcellinus XXVIII 5.11–13.

413. GS I, 10 and 31. See also chap. 1, nn. 49 and 59 (Gothic special names), as well as chap. 3, nn. 158 ff. (displacement of the *kunja* in favor of the Balthic kingship).

414. Ammianus Marcellinus XXX 2.8 uses the expression *tota Gothia* for the entire Gothic army on Thracian soil. On the identity of Gothic army and Gothic people see, for example, Jordanes, *Getica* 26, p. 60. On the notion that the army is a "people in arms" see Schlesinger, "Heerkönigtum," 56 (108) with n. 11, and GS II, 311 f. with n. 101.

415. Schlesinger, "Heerkönigtum," 56 (109) with n. 11a: "in Lombardic law 4 men constitute an army, in Danish law 5, in Anglo-Saxon law 35, in Bavarian law 42."

416. Both Eunapius fr. 37 and Olympiodorus fr. 9 call Gothic (i.e. Visigothic)

warriors nobles, even though they were talking about large groups (once three thousand and then twelve thousand men). Cf. Wenskus, "Adel," 63 ff.

417. GS II, 312 f. with n. 103. Jones, *The Later Roman Empire* 2:680 f.: the new Roman legion around 350 had about three thousand men.

418. GS II, 313 with n. 104.

419. The passages listed in GS II, 313 n. 103 could be easily expanded: Cassius Dio 71.21: three thousand Naristi are admitted by Rome; Theodahad offers the emperor an army of three thousand men as a condition for a peace agreement: Procopius, *De bello Gothico* I (V) 6.2; Clovis has himself baptized along with three thousand men: Zöllner, *Franken*, 61; Cf. Acts. 2.41: baptism of the three thousand men after the sermon of Petrus; three thousand Burgundians destroy a Hunnic army three times that size: Maenchen-Helfen, *The Huns*, 83; three thousand Heruli, the "nationalist party," crossed "the Danube and joined the Gepids (around 545)": Procopius, *De bello Gothico* III (VII) 34.43. See also other sources as diverse as Eunapius fr. 13 and *Annales regni Francorum* a. 819, p. 151, to say nothing of the virtual canonization of the figure 3,000 because of its use in the Bible, esp. Acts 2.41.

420. Olympiodorus fr. 9 calls the elite troops of Radagaisus the "optimates." Eunapius fr. 37. Cf. GS II, 311 f. with n. 101, as well as Altheim, *Geschichte der Hunnen* 5:207; cf. 2:52 and 4:55 f. The wasplike waistline was also the ideal of beauty for the Gothic women, as Synesius of Cyrene, *Epistulae* 5.1, p. 25, observed. Zosimus IV 40.1, reports about Goths whom the emperor Theodosius is said to have handpicked for their ability and physical size.

421. Cf. above, n. 182 and n. 188.

422. Ammianus Marcellinus XXII 7.8. Cf. GS II, 318 f. with n. 120.

423. See n. 414.

424. GS I, 6 n. 25.

425. GS II, 318 with n. 120. Similar "peaceful" conditions are attested for Roman Africa by St. Augustine, *Epistolae in lucem prolatae* 10, pp. 46–51.

426. Thus Ammianus Marcellinus XXVI 4, 5 speaks of the *praedatorii globi Gothorum* before he reports about the confederation of the Goths: see ibid., 6.11. Cf. chap. 5, n. 111.

427. GS I, 8–11, and 26 with n. 118. Thompson, "Visigoths from Fritigern to Euric," 105 with n. 2, after Mommsen, "Militärwesen," 229.

428. Ammianus Marcellinus XXXI 3.5.

429. Ammianus Marcellinus XXXI 6.1. Cf. above, n. 176.

430. Cf. above, n. 61.

431. GS II, 312 f. with n. 103, and 313 f. with nn. 105–107.

432. Ibid., 313 with n. 105. Cf. chap. 1, n. 74.

433. Priscus fr. 39; cf. chap. 5, n. 125.

434. See chap. 3, n. 62 (the course of the battle of Adrianople) and above, n. 369: the Tervingi and the Visi were, unlike the Taifali, infantry units of the Roman army around 400. Cf. Ammianus Marcellinus XXXI 8.9.

435. See above, nn. 367–369.

436. Ammianus Marcellinus XXXI 8.4, 12.7–13, 12.18; cf. 16.3. Jordanes, *Getica* 130, p. 91, and 246, p. 121. Cf. chap. 3, n. 29.

437. See above, nn. 182, 189, 213.

438. Ammianus Marcellinus XXXI 3.7 and 9.3 f.

439. See chap. 5, n. 312.

440. Straub, *Studien,* 11 f., 20–28, 36 f., and 74, esp. after Ammianus Marcellinus XXXI 7.7 and 12.11.

441. Wenskus, "Bewaffnung," 458.

442. GS II, 312 n. 101 should be supplemented by, for example, J. Werner, "Zeugnisse der Goten," 127 ff., as well as Bierbrauer, *Grab- und Schatzfunde,* 63. The absence of arms in the graves of Gothic men can be attested for the late Roman Empire (East Pomeranian-Masovian culture), where the graves did contain riding equipment but no weapons, right up to the fifth century, and even still in Visigothic Spain and Ostrogothic Italy: see Raddatz, "Bewaffnung," 425 ff.

443. GS II, 311 f. For the quote see Birkhan, "Review of P. Scardigli," 346. Wenskus, "Bewaffnung," 461, and Feist, *Wörterbuch,* 411.

444. Johanek, "Bewaffnung," 465, as well as Wenskus, "Bewaffnung," 461 f. For the quote see Birkhan (as n. 443).

445. Johanek, "Bewaffnung," 465, and Altheim, *Geschichte der Hunnen* 1:200 ff. Werner, *Archäologie des Attila-Reiches,* 38–45.

446. See also the battle accounts in Ammianus Marcellinus XXXI 12.17, and 13.1 ff., as well as Jordanes, *Getica* 261, p. 125, and Procopius, *De bello Persico* II 18.24. According to Claudianus, *De consulatu Stilichonis* I v. 111, p. 193, the *contus* was the weapon of the "Sarmatians."

447. On Ammianus Marcellinus XXXI 7.12 see Wenskus "Bewaffnung," and Johanek, "Bewaffnung," 458 and 464.

448. Wenskus "Bewaffnung," and Johanek, "Bewaffnung," 459 f. and 465. Cf. chap. 5, n. 283 and n. 307.

449. Feist, *Wörterbuch,* 56, on *arhvaznos funiskos* (Gothic: fire arrows).

450. Dunareanu-Vulpe, *Schatz von Pietroasa,* 20 (D) and 23 (N). Cf. Wenskus, "Bewaffnung," and Johanek, "Bewaffnung," 458 and 465. Von Heland, "Golden Bowl from Pietroasa," 58 ff., examines the warrior (plate 38) on the bowl of Pietroasa. She thinks that he represents most likely the Thraco-Phrygian god Sabazius. There are no objections against this or against her thorough interpretation of the decorative program of this unique bowl. The same goes for her identification of Antioch as the bowl's city of origin (96 ff.). Nevertheless, it is likely that the Goths of the late fourth/early fifth centuries (on the burying of the treasure of Pietroasa see Harhoiu, as n. 472) subjected the depicted gods to an *interpretatio Gothica,* whereby similarities were sought out and equated. For the dating of the treasure see also above, n. 224.

451. Altheim, *Geschichte der Hunnen* 2:52, 4:55 f., and 5:207. See also above, n. 420.

452. GS II, 321 with n. 127. Petrus Patricius fr. 9.2 (FHG 4:196). According to the *Passio s. Sabae* chap. 4, p. 218, Saba originally intended to spend Easter in a ἑτέρα πόλις, where he would be safe and where the presbyter Guththikas lived.

453. GS II, 314–317. According to Zosimus V 34.5, Stilicho's entourage was composed of both free and unfree armed retainers. Diesner, "Buccellariertum," 331 f.; cf. 329. On *asneis* see Feist, *Wörterbuch,* 60. On *siponeis* see Birkhan, "Altgermanistische Miszellen," 19 f.

454. GS I, 17 with n. 78, and 19 with n. 92, as well as GS II, 303 ff. with nn.

67–71, 314–316, and 317 with n. 115. *Passio s. Sabae,* chap. 6, p. 220. On *siponeis/siponjos* see n. 453.

455. GS II, 298 n. 34, 304 f. and 316 f., as well as GS III, 260. Harhoiu, *Treasure from Pietroasa,* 23 ff., considers the social differentiation of Attila's time far more pronounced than that of the Sîntana-de-Mureş culture. It must be pointed out, however, that the appropriate sociological studies have not yet been done. The presumed difference could very well go back to changes in burial customs and grave furnishings. In the fourth century there were large grave fields, whereas the Danubian region of the fifth century is characterized by single graves or small grave clusters as far as the East Germanic finds are concerned. Thus it is difficult to compare the richly furnished graves of the Cherniakhov and Sîntana-de-Mureş cultures with the richly furnished graves from the Danubian region of the fifth century.

456. GS I, 14 and GS II, 304 as well as 307 f. The reports about the Getic-Thracian nobility and the "less" long/curly-haired, which go back to Dio Chrysostom, *Getica,* are found in fragments of Chrysostom, *Oratio* 72.3; cf. ibid., 2:V–VII, as well as Petrus Patricius fr. 5. For the depiction of the warrior on the bowl of Pietroasa see above, n. 450 f. On the *capillati* of the sixth century see chap. 5, n. 274. On the *pilleati* see also Hauck, "Halsring und Ahnenstab," 176 with n. 158.

457. GS II, 310 f. with n. 100. Olympiodorus frs. 17 and 26. On the dissolution of the kuni by the retainer groups cf. Wolfram, *Intitulatio I,* 191 ff. Theodoric, however, justified at least one, if not two, political murders as blood vengeance: see chap. 5, n. 151 (Rekitach), and chap. 5, nn. 168–170 (Odovacar). To what extent there also existed among the Goths, apart from the traditional blood vengeance, blood magic is hard to say; see GS III, 252 with n. 180. On Euphemia and the Goths see chap. 3, n. 103 and 107.

458. For this phrase from the *Codex Euricianus* cf. chap. 4, n. 570 and n. 588. On the terms in the Gothic Bible for retainership see GS II, 314 and 317.

459. For this and the entire chapter see GS II, 311 with n. 100 and 321–324.

460. Straub, *Regeneratio Imperii,* 208 ff.; cf. Priscus fr. 39. Dahn, *Könige der Germanen* 6:14 ff. Mitrea, "Die Goten an der unteren Donau," 88 ff., and Ioniţă, "Probleme," 88 ff. Cf. above, n. 376.

461. *Passio s. Sabae,* chap. 7, p. 221.

462. It is difficult to suggest a biblical Gothic name for the notables of Saba's village because in the villages of the New Testament no one is mentioned who holds a position of leadership. The speakers of the village assembly might have been called *faúramathljos* (sing., *–eis*), since this word describes one or more "speakers" of a group, an entire village (2 Cor. 11.32), a synagogue (Luke 8.49), or the tax collector (Luke 19.2) as representatives of a higher authority. Another possibility might be *faúrstasseis,* "Vorsteher" (leader) in the true sense of the word, especially since it is used in I Thess. 5.12. For the village assembly itself scholars have suggested the biblical Gothic term *gaimainths* (Neh. 5.13) and *gagumths* (Math. 5.22).

463. I wish to express my gratitude to Volker Bierbrauer (cf. above, n. 17) for the following survey: Like the material culture, the settlements and economic organization in the Sîntana-de-Mureş-Cherniakhov culture had not been closely examined, largely because larger segments have been unearthed in only a handful (about twelve) of the numerous settlement sites (well over three hundred). And the results

of those studies have not been published comprehensively, especially not those of the comparatively large-scale excavations of the settlements of Lepesovka and Ripnev II in the Wolhynian group of the Cherniakhov culture. Preliminary reports for Lepesovka have been published by the excavator, Maria I. Tichanova. In general we can say: (1) The settlements are always unfortified and are usually situated halfway up terraces that slope down more or less steeply to a river below. (2) For the reasons given above we cannot say anything definite about the village types or the size of the settlements; the fragmentary plans of Lepesovka and Ripnev II or Nežvisko so far published do not reveal the arrangement of the houses, storage ditches, ovens, etc., not even in the sense of defined economic units. (3) As to the types of houses, we know of sunken huts and ditch dwellings (usually 5–16 m²), but also in part much larger dwellings at ground level (up to 80 m²); the side walls were a compact wattle-and-daub construction or wood covered with mud. (4) Economic system: the primary means of support were agriculture and cattle breeding. At this time we cannot say to what extent a limited "commercial" production existed which satisfied the domestic needs of one or more villages or whether there was even large-scale "industrial" production that was displacing agricultural activities. In any case, evidence for "industrial" activity exists in Cherniakhov and Sîntana-de-Mureş settlements: pottery and metalworking, glass production, leather and wool working; also comb making workshops and bone working are attested.

464. GS III, 239 f. To this we should add Claudian, *De bello Gothico* vv. 528 f., p. 278, where the Getic gods and the spirits of Alaric I's ancestors are equated. The veneration of "stake idols" as ancestor worship might even be reflected in the etymology of the word "Aesir-Ansis": Kuhn, "Asen," 458. In Gaul of around 450 primitive ancestor worship was considered Alanic: see Courcelle, *Histoire littéraire,* 81 n. 3, after Claudius Marius Victor, *Alethia* III. vv. 189 ff., p. 413.

465. GS II, 254 f., esp. after Eunapius fr. 55.

466. GS III, 255–257. On the Gothic witches see chap. 5, n. 78 f. and Altheim, *Geschichte der Hunnen* 1:336 ff.

467. To Ammianus Marcellinus XXXI 9.5, cf. Procopius, *De bello Persico* II 25.27 f., and *De bello Gothico* II (VI) 14.26. Thurnwald, *Die menschliche Gesellschaft* 2:285. L. Schmidt, *Ostgermanen,* 548 n. 4. Ranke, "Bär," 47. Cf. Svennung, *Goticismus,* 42 and 82 f.

468. GS III, 258 with n. 197 f.; cf. 252.

469. GS III, 252 f. nn. 179–181 should be supplemented by Claudian, *De bello Gothico* vv. 544–551, p. 279, concerning Alaric I's "drivenness." On the Gothic word *hailags see also GS III, 244 with n. 159.

470. To GS III, 258, should be added the oath for the destruction of the Roman Empire (as chap. 3, nn. 178 ff.) as well as the anti-Hunnic oath of the Goths according to Priscus fr. 39. On the Saba story cf. GS II, 323.

471. See Claudian, *De bello Gothico* vv. 81 f., p. 263, as well as above, n. 185. The Goths had given the Danube their own name: see chap. 5, n. 52. On the sacrifice of people who did not belong to the tribe see below, n. 490. GS I, 5, and GS III, 259 with n. 201.

472. GS III, 241–252. On Fravitta see Schwarcz, *Reichsangehörige,* 120–122. Harhoiu, *Treasure from Pietroasa,* 13 with nn. 85–98. The assumption of a Gothic Jupiter finds support in the "clubs of Hercules," which are "already attested in the

fourth century both in Germanic northern Germany of the Elbe region as well as in the East Germanic Cherniakhov culture": J. Werner, "Herkuleskeule," 176 ff., esp. 182 f. Ibid., 182: "The god of vegetation Hercules, who in the *interpretatio Romana* in place of the lightning-hurling Jupiter could be equated with the Germanic Donar-Thor, apparently had many qualities very similar to the latter." Cf. also J. Werner, "Zwei prismatische Knochenanhänger," 133 ff. For the quotes and evidence listed in GS III, 241–252, see (Maximinus) *Contra paganos,* in *Journal of Theological Studies* 17: 327. 1916: *Nam de Marte quid dicam, qui aput Tracias natus ibi est defunctus . . .* For the Celtic influence on the Goths see GS I, 24 f. with nn. 107–114, and GS II, 293 f. with n. 2 f. For the reading of the runic inscription of Pietroasa—which most German Germanists (for example, Elfriede Stutz) consider most unlikely (Krause, *Handbuch,* 22 f., omits the reading altogether)—see, for example, Bonfante, *Latini e Germani,* 13 f. with n. 5; Kabell, "Baugi," 39 f. n. 36. Many thanks to Klaus Düwel for calling my attention to the work of Kabell. Düwell has also pointed out a possible parallel, the still unpublished disk fibula of Cherey (Ardennes). On the problem of the Latinization of the Danubian Goths see, for example, Gamillscheg, *Romania Germanica* 1:300, 353, 358, and 363. These additions belong especially to GS III, 243 with n. 154. The possibly bilingual runic inscription corresponds with the designation of the Roman emperors by a Goth as *regis Romanorum,* as the imitative Valens medallion, probably also from Szilágy-Somlyó, attests. On this see GS III, 245 f. with n. 162, as well as above, n. 396. On Eunapius's interest in the Gothic pagan Fravitta cf. Ewig, "Probleme," 60: "As conscious adherents to paganism [the Frankish generals] were like-minded individuals, whereby we should think of late antique Neoplatonism rather than the religion of Woden." But this undoubtedly correct observation applies only in part to Fravitta and his ancestors. Cf. chap. 3, nn. 178 ff. On Týrfingr see chap. 1, n. 74, on the *Hervarasaga* as bearer of authentic Gothic traditions see GS II, 313 with n. 105, after Kuhn, "Das römische Kriegswesen," 36.

473. See chap. 1, nn. 99 ff.

474. See chap. 1, n. 74 and n. 104 f. Wolfram, "Theogonie," 91 f. GS III, 254 with n. 185. On the Aesir-Ansis worship cf. above, n. 464.

475. GS III, 252 with n. 178 (Helmut Birkhan).

476. Snorri Sturluson, *Sagas of the Norse Kings: Heimskringla II,* chaps. 1 and 4, pp. 7 and 8 f.

477. See esp. Jordanes, *Getica* 78 ff., pp. 76 ff. Cf. GS III, 252 n. 178.

478. Snorri Sturluson, *Sagas of the Norse Kings: Heimskringla II,* chap. 32, p. 109. On the phrase "reduced custom of grave furnishings" and its significance in Gothic tradition see Bierbrauer, *Grab- und Schatzfunde,* 63 ff.

479. See above, n. 442.

480. Cf. Höfler, "Sakralcharakter," 85–88. Höfler, *Germanisches Sakralkönigtum,* 2 ff.

481. GS III, 250 n. 174 and 252 n. 178. Gschwantler, *Ermanarich,* 195 ff.: the assumption of a self-sacrifice is not refuted by the fact that Ammianus's report of Ermanaric's suicide (as above, n. 358) might have literary models in the deed of King Midas at the invasion of the Cimerians (Eitrem, "Midas," 1534 f. and 1539) or in that of Catuvolcus (Caesar, *De bello Gallico* VI 31.5). Ammianus's information came from Gothic sources (as above, n. 208), even if his account is reminiscent

of known stories such as the Midas legend. Feist, *Wörterbuch*, 132, s.v, "enguz" and "Ermeniricus." On **ingwaz*, the god of the fertile year, see esp. Klingenberg, *Runenschrift-Schriftdenken-Runeninschriften*, 190 f. But I think the equating of **ansuz, anse, ase* with Woden (see n. 480) is questionable. Helm, *Altgermanische Religionsgeschichte* 2, 1, 31 ff., is a reliable guide through the dangerous terrain. I take his rejection (ibid., 43 f.) of a Gothic Woden seriously. Likewise his command "Thou shall not invent new Gods": see Helm, "Erfundene Götter?" 1 ff., where he objects esp. to *Irmin*. On the Gothic Dioscuri see GS I, 5 ff.

482. Cf. n. 481.

483. GS III, 254 with n. 184 f.

484. On the Tervingian stake idols see GS III, 240 with n. 140. On the deification of the Danube see above, n. 185, n. 468, and below, n. 490.

485. GS III, 254 with n. 186, and 259 with n. 200.

486. GS I, 24 with nn. 107–111, as well as II, 292–294. Cf. chap. 2, n. 29, chap. 3, n. 73, as well as n. 242, but also Wenskus, *Stammesbildung*, 227 f.

487. GS II, 294 with n. 23 and III, 244 f. nn. 160–162. Ammianus Marcellinus XXVII 5.1 and XXXI 12.8 f. speaks of the Latin correspondence between Gothic princes and Romans.

488. GS II, 310 with n. 99; cf. GS III, 244 with n. 160.

489. GS III, 258 with n. 197.

490. GS III, 244 f. with n. 160 f. In this context belongs also the report of Zosimus V 21.9: Gainas had the Romans in his following killed before he crossed or wanted to cross the Danube and return to the northern Danubian region.

491. GS II, 310 with n. 98.

492. See above, n. 456.

493. See the rich list in P. Scardigli, *Goten*, 75–86.

494. Thompson, *Visigoths*, 28 f. and 161 f., interprets the village settlement (called Haliskon) by the sea which is mentioned in the *Passio ss. Innae, Rhimae et Pinae*, p. 216, as a Gothic port on the Pontus in the Danubian region. This is not supported by the source itself. Yet one could place Haliskon at the Cappadocian river Halys-Kizilirmak, despite the basic linguistic difficulty, and assume that the village was located where the river flows into the Black Sea. The strong ties between the Cappadocian Christians and the north Danubian Gothic mission would support such an interpretation: see Schwarcz, *Reichsangehörige*, 138.

495. See the still useful list in Dahn, *Könige der Germanen* 6:12 ff.

496. Birkhan, "Review of P. Scardigli," 248.

497. Feist, *Wörterbuch*, 35 f.

498. Ibid., 73 f.

499. Ibid., 251.

500. Ibid., 59 f. and 515 f.

501. P. Scardigli, *Goten*, 54 and 84 f. Feist, *Wörterbuch*, 328 (*lein*) and 329 (*lekeis*). Dahn, *Könige der Germanen* 6:17. Cf. the remark in Ammianus Marcellinus XXXI 16.1, according to whom the Goths after the unsuccessful assault on Adrianople used the short summer night *ad vulnerum curas artesque medendi gentiles*.

502. Dahn, *Könige der Germanen* 6:19 f. On the place-name Mautern see Bach, *Namenkunde* 2:427; on the Slavic loanword *plinsjan* see GS III, 257 n. 196.

503. Jordanes, *Getica* 78 ff., p. 76 ff. Wolfram, "*Intitulatio I,*" 99 ff. See also above, n. 60 f., and chap. 5, n. 451 f.

504. Schlesinger, "Heerkönigtum," 139 with n. 166. Cf. Wolfram, *Intitulatio I,* 43 with n. 60 and 55 with n. 104.

505. Altheim, *Geschichte der Hunnen* 1:314 ff. Birkhan, "Beizjagd," 171–173; Werner, *Archäologie des Attila-Reiches,* esp. 90 ff.; Werner, "Zeugnisse der Goten," 127 ff. Wenskus, *Stammesbildung,* 469 ff. with n. 244: the Gothic duel on horseback probably also goes back to this time. For the distances the Gothic lance-riders covered see above, nn. 347 ff.

506. Jordanes, *Getica* 116, p. 88.

507. See chap. 1, n. 105 and chap. 5, nn. 10 ff. Gschwantler, "Ermanarich," 187 ff., esp. 195 ff. Cf. above, nn. 358–360 and n. 481.

508. According to Schlesinger, "Heerkönigtum," 137 with n. 156, a *dux* was elected only in kingless tribes. Ammianus Marcellinus XXXI 3.3 says of Vithimiris that he was *rex creatus,* but he does not say the same for Alatheus and Safrax, who were *duces exerciti et firmitate pectorum noti.* Claude, "Die ostgotischen Königserhebungen," 151 n. 12, thinks that election of Vithimiris is *not* securely attested. On **drauhtins* see above, n. 397. On Ermanaric's suicide see above, n. 358 f. and n. 481.

509. Cf. Wenskus, *Stammesbildung,* 411: "The unbroken tradition of the Gothic king is also suggested by the preservation of the old word for king (*thiudans*), which in the West was replaced by a new word."

510. Wolfram, *Intitulatio I,* 40–43.

511. Jordanes, *Getica* 116–120, p. 88 f. On "Greutungian" Huns and Alans see Ammianus Marcellinus XXXI 3.3, 8.4. Cf. G. Schramm, "Eroberungen," 1 ff. On the Aesti (cf. Cassiodorus, *Variae* V 2. 1–3) see W. P. Schmid, "Aisten," 116 ff.

3: The Forty-year Migration and the Formation of the Visigoths (376/378 to 416/418)

1. Claude, *Geschichte der Westgoten,* 27. Cf. chap. 1, n. 49.

2. The most important source for the events is Ammianus Marcellinus XXXI 4.1 ff.; cf. the evaluation by Stallknecht, *Untersuchungen,* 24 ff., 65 f., as well as 103 nn. 136 and 143. Schwarcz, *Reichsangehörige,* 36 f. Cesa, "Romani e Barbari," 69 f. Very important also are Eunapius fr. 42 f. and Zosimus IV 20.5–7, who used him. In addition one must mention *Consularia Constantinopolitana* a. 376, p. 242, Orosius, *Historiae adversum paganos* VII 33.0 (*sine ulla foederis pactione ne arma quidem . . . tradidere Romanis*), Jordanes, *Getica* 131–133, p. 92 (with a list of the intended settlement areas: *Dacia ripensis, Moesia Thraciaeque*), Prosper, *Epitoma chronicon* 1161, p. 460 (*sine armorum depositione suscepti*), Isidore of Seville, *Historia vel Origo Gothorum* 9, p. 271 (follows essentially Orosius), Hieronymus, *Chronicon* a. 377, Socrates IV 34 f., Sozomenus VI 37.15 ff., Philostorgius IX 17. Chrysos, Βυζάντιον, 124–128 (admission of the Visigoths to Thrace; ibid. 127: the admitted Goths were investigated regarding their Christianity), and 129–134 (Gothic rebellion and battle of Adrianople). Eunapius fr. 55

thinks the conspicuously displayed Christianity of the Goths was meant to
the Romans.

3. Cesa, Stallknecht and Schwarcz (as above, n. 2). Cf. Demougeot, "
dalités," 174 f. and 146 n. 20. See esp. Ammianus Marcellinus XVII 12 f. and X
11.6 f. (cf. chap. 2, nn. 153 f. and n. 190, where Ammianus describes similar events),
XXXI 3.8; 4.5 and 8 (assignment of Thrace, distribution of foodstuffs and actual
settlement); 4.4 (recruits and monetary redemption); 6 ff. (huge mass of Goths,
calamity for the empire, incompetence of the officials); XXX 2.6 (recruitment of
Goths-Scythians for the Persian campaign); see also Socrates and Jordanes (as n. 2).
Orosius and Prosper (as n. 2) mention explicitly that the Romans did without the
signing of a formal treaty and neglected to disarm the Goths.

4. On a possible treaty between Fritigern and the emperor see chap. 2, n. 216
f. Cf. the fundamental study of Stallknecht, *Untersuchungen,* 9 on the question of
who could act as a partner in a treaty with the Romans.

5. Burns, "Adrianople," 336, claims—against Eunapius fr. 42, Orosius and
Prosper (as n. 2), and Zosimus IV 20.6—that the Goths were in fact disarmed.

6. Eunapius frs. 42 and 55. Ladner, "On Roman Attitudes," 1 ff.

7. Ladner (as n. 6), Ammianus Marcellinus XXXI 4.5 and 8–11; 5.1 f., 6.5.
Wolfram, "Gotische Studien II," 318. Hoffman, *Bewegungsheer* 1:440 f.

8. Ammianus Marcellinus XXXI 5.1–4. The importance of the three-tribe
confederation was rightly understood by Várady, *Pannonien,* 20–26, 31 ff., but his
conclusions are sometimes too far-reaching, which is why Nagy, "Pannonia," 306
ff. should be consulted as a corrective. In the eyes of Jordanes, *Getica* 134 f., p. 93,
Alatheus, Safrax, and Fritigern were *duces* of equal rank who ruled the Goths "in
place of kings." On Lupicinus see Jones, *Prosopography* 1:519 f. n. 3.

9. See chap. 1, n. 60, esp. after Ammianus Marcellinus XXXI 4.12 and 9.3.
Cf. Várady, *Pannonien,* 21 f. and 597 s.v. "Farnobius," as well as Nagy, "Pannonia," 307. On the Taifali see chap. 2, nn. 363 ff.

10. Ammianus Marcellinus XXXI 9.3 ff.

11. Ammianus Marcellinus XXXI 5.4. Joint actions are also attested ibid. 8.4,
12.12 and 12.17.

12. Cf. ibid., 3.5 with 5.3 f. On the possible crossing places see Vetters, *Dacia
ripensis,* 29 (map); on the first Tervingian moves on imperial soil, ibid. and Hoffmann, *Bewegungsheer* 1:440 ff.

13. Against Várady, *Pannonien,* 29–33, see Nagy, "Pannonia," 300 and ibid.,
"Reoccupation," 169 with n. 2. Mócsy, "Review of Várady," 348.

14. Ammianus Marcellinus XXXI 4.13.

15. Ibid., 5.4–9; cf. Jordanes, *Getica* 135 f., p. 93.

16. Ammianus Marcellinus XXXI 5.5 and 7. On the Tervingian name see chap.
1, n. 58 f.

17. Ibid., 6.1–7; cf. 16.8. On Sueridus and Colias see chap. 2, n. 176 and n. 429.

18. As chap. 2, n. 302.

19. Ammianus Marcellinus XXXI 6.7.

20. Ibid., 5.5 and 9, and 6.3. On the supplying of the Goths with weapons from
Roman weapons factories cf. below, n. 145 (Alaric I in Epirus), and chap. 5, n. 295
(Theodoric the Great).

21. Ammianus Marcellinus XXXI 7.12. Cf. chap. 2, n. 447.

22. L. Schmidt, *Ostgermanen,* 402 with n. 4. See above, nn. 2 and 5.

23. See chap. 2, nn. 181 ff. Cf. Stallknecht, *Untersuchungen,* 71 with n. 125.

24. Stallknecht, *Untersuchungen,* 25 with n. 150 and 65 ff., after Ammianus Marcellinus XXX 2.6 and 8.

25. Ibid. XXXI 7.1–3. Hoffmann, *Bewegungsheer* 1:441. On Frigeridus (cf. Schwarcz, *Reichsangehörige,* 124–127, esp. 124 f.), Profuturus, and Traianus see Jones, *Prosopography* 1:373 f., 749 n. 2, 921 f. n. 2. Demandt, "Magister militum," 600 f., 705 ff.

26. Ammianus Marcellinus XXXI 7.5. Demandt, "Magister militum," 604 f. Cf. Hoffmann, *Bewegungsheer* 1:436 f. and 441 ff. On Richomeres see Jones, *Prosopography* 1:765 f., and Demandt, "Magister Militum," 718 f. Ewig, "Probleme," 58 ff.

27. Ammianus Marcellinus XXXI 7.4–10.

28. Ibid., 7.11–8.1; cf. 6.4 and 16.7. On the dating of the events see 8.2. On the word *barritus* cf. Demougeot, *De l'unité,* 25 with n. 142.

29. Ammianus Marcellinus XXXI 8.2–4. But Ammianus speaks here only of the Huns and Alans. Although it is possible that the three-tribe confederation of Alatheus and Safrax split up temporarily, one should not take Ammianus too literally, as does, for example, Várady, *Pannonien,* 32 f. with n. 61. Ammianus mentions in 3.3 Greutungi and Huns still fighting the Alans, in 4.12 the Greutungi under Videric, Alatheus, and Safrax; in 5.3 he speaks only of the Greutungi, and in 5.4 of their mighty "kings" (cf. above, n. 8). In 11.6 appear only the Alans, and in 12.12 and 17 only Alatheus and Safrax, in 12.17 Goths and Alans; in 16.4 we find once again all three peoples united. One is thus led to believe that we are basically always dealing with the same group or parts of it whenever Ammianus mentions at least one of the relevant tribal names. Fritigern's important role in bringing about the Tervingian-Greutungian alliance, which is mentioned in 5.3 f., is emphasized in 16.3. For this discussion it also seems significant that Jordanes, *Getica* 134, p. 93, mentions Fritigern, Alatheus, and Safrax together as *duces* of the Goths *regum vice,* while ibid. 140, p. 95, he talks of the dissolution of this union (*diviso exercitu*) in such a way that Fritigern splits off from the other two.

30. See above, nn. 11–13.

31. Ammianus Marcellinus XXXI 8.4–8.

32. Eunapius fr. 60.

33. Ammianus Marcellinus XXXI 8.9.

34. See ibid., 5.15–17, Ammianus's comparisons with the terrible and glorious Gothic wars of the third century.

35. Ibid., 8.9 f. Hoffmann, *Bewegungsheer* 1:443. Oberhummer, "Develtos," 260.

36. Ammianus Marcellinus XXXI 9.1–5.

37. See chap. 2, n. 66.

38. See chap. 2, nn. 363 ff., esp. n. 372; cf. above, n. 9.

39. Hoffmann (as n. 35). Ammianus Marcellinus XXXI 10.1–17. 20.

40. Hoffmann, *Bewegungsheer* 1:437.

41. Ibid., 416 with n. 235. Ammianus Marcellinus XX 4.18 and XXXI 10.21 f.

42. Jones, *Prosopography* 1:812 f. and Demandt, "Magister militum," 706 (Sebastianus): cf. Jones, *Prosopography* 1:922 (Traianus) and Klein, "Valens," 56.

43. Hoffmann, *Bewegungsheer* 1:443.

44. Eunapius fr. 46.

45. Hoffmann, *Bewegungsheer* 1:444. L. Schmidt, *Ostgermanen*, 408.

46. Hoffmann, *Bewegungsheer* 1:445 f. Nagl, "Valens," 2122. Cf. above, n. 42. Ammianus Marcellinus XXXI 11.1 f. On the bad omens that Valens encountered see ibid., XXXI 1.1–5. Zosimus IV 21.2 f.

47. Klein, "Valens," 58 ff.; cf. 56 and 63, after Ammianus Marcellinus XXXI 11.2.

48. Ammianus Marcellinus XXXI 11.2–5. Cf. above, n. 31.

49. Vetters, *Dacia ripensis,* 29 (map).

50. Hoffmann, *Bewegungsheer* 1:446; Nagl, "Valens," 2133: "approximately in the first half of July. . . ." Yet Klein, "Valens," 63, has the army set out from Melanthias during the last days of July, for which he cites Ammianus Marcellinus XXXI 12.1 as insufficient evidence.

51. Ammianus Marcellinus XXXI 11.6–12. On the location of Castra Martis see Mócsy, "Review of Várady," 348. Sozomenus IX 5.1 even calls Castra Martis a "Moesian city"; L. Schmidt, *Ostgermanen*, 409 n. 5, however, thinks this refers to upper Moesia, which is no doubt wrong. Ammianus Marcellinus XXXI 12.3 (numerical strength of the Goths).

52. Hoffmann, *Bewegungsheer* 1:446 f. Ammianus Marcellinus XXXI 12.7.

53. Ammianus Marcellinus XXXI 12.4 f. The arrival of Richomeres follows from the account of the events up to XXXI 12.10, where the day of the battle is fixed on August 9. Cf. L. Schmidt, *Ostgermanen,* 410 n. 1.

54. Ammianus Marcellinus XXXI 11.6.

55. Ibid., 12.5–7. On Victor see Jones, *Prosopography* 1:957 ff. n. 4. Demandt, "Magister militum," 703 ff.

56. Ammianus Marcellinus XXXI 12.7–9. L. Schmidt, *Ostgermanen,* 410 f. n. 3. Stallknecht, *Untersuchungen,* 26 with n. 160: "The emperors (382) therefore returned to a suggestion that Fritigern had made shortly before the battle of Adrianople, namely, the contractual handing over to the Goths of large territory with everything it produced."

57. Cf. Jordanes, *Getica* 152, p. 94 (Alaric). Sidonius Apollinaris, *Carmina* VII vv. 489 to 519, p. 215 f. (Theodoric II). Jordanes, *Getica* 290–292, p. 133 (Theodoric the Great). Procopius, *De bello Gothico* I (V) 6.1–5 (Theodahad).

58. Thompson, "Visigoths from Fritigern to Euric," 106 f., L. Schmidt, *Ostgermanen,* 410 f., and Seeck, *Untergang* 5:117 f., take Fritigern's offer seriously. Likewise Klein, "Valens," 66 ff., who gives a survey of the interpretations of this passage.

59. Ammianus Marcellinus XXXI 12.8 f. and 12.13; cf. above, n. 56. Ladner, "On Roman Attitudes," 3.

60. Ammianus Marcellinus XXXI 12.12–14.

61. Ibid., 12.10–17. Hoffmann, *Bewegungsheer* 1:447 ff.

62. Ammianus Marcellinus XXXI 12.10–13. 10, 13.18 (losses), 15.1. Hoffmann, *Bewegungsheer* 1:448 ff. and 454 ff. On the Gothic style of fighting on horseback and the impossibility of repulsing a lightning-fast attack if one's own troops were stationary, see chap. 5, nn. 284 ff.

63. Hoffmann, *Bewegungsheer* 1:472, after Ammianus Marcellinus XXXI 13.12.

64. Ibid., 13.14–16.

65. Seeck, *Untergang* 5:476 to n. 27; Hoffmann, *Bewegungsheer* 2:186 to n. 168; L. Schmidt, *Ostgermanen*, 412 n. 2. Straub, *Regeneratio Imperii*, 196 ff. and 245, esp. after Orosius, *Historiae adversum paganos* VII 33.15–19.

66. Straub, *Regeneratio Imperii*, 196 f.

67. Ammianus Marcellinus XXXI 13.12 f., and 17, where Valens and Scipio are compared. See chap. 2, n. 66.

68. Ammianus Marcellinus XXXI 13.18 f. Cf. Cameron, *Claudian*, 351 with n. 1.

69. See chap. 2, nn. 100–110.

70. Straub, *Regeneratio Imperii*, 195 ff. Rufinus, *Eusebii historia ecclesiastica* 11.13.

71. Ammianus Marcellinus XXXI 6.3 f. (first assault on Adrianople); 15.2 (treasures in Adrianople in 378); 15.1–15 (second assault on Adrianople, against the will of Fritigern, esp. 13–15; repulsed with heavy losses to the Goths); 15.5–9 (attempted use of a fifth column).

72. Ibid., 16.1 f. as well as 16.3 f. and 7. Eunapius fr. 50 (Nicopolis).

73. Ammianus Marcellinus XXXI 15.12 f., and 15.5 (storm; cf. Wolfram, "Gotische Studien I," 25 with n. 110, and III, 246 with n. 163, as well as chap. 1, n. 486).

74. Ammianus Marcellinus XXXI 16.5 ff. Cf. Wellhausen, *Reste*, 125 with n. 6.

75. This follows directly from Ammianus Marcellinus XXXI 16.2.

76. L. Schmidt, *Ostgermanen*, 413 with nn. 3 and 6. According to Ammianus Marcellinus XXXI 16.7, after Adrianople the Goths advanced as far as the Julian Alps. Cf. Courcelle, *Histoire littéraire*, 25 f. Hoffmann, *Bewegungsheer* 1:458 f.

77. Cf. the attempts described by Ammianus Marcellinus XXXI 15.13.

78. See chap. 2, n. 90.

79. Ammianus Marcellinus XXXI 16.7.

80. Ibid., 16.1; cf. 8.1.

81. Cf. ibid., 8.6 ff. (situation after *Ad Salices*), with 16.1–7. L. Schmidt, *Ostgermanen*, 413. Hoffmann, *Bewegungsheer* 1:461.

82. Ammianus Marcellinus XXXI 16.8. Eunapius fr. 42. Zosimus IV 26.2 ff. Demandt, "Magister militum," 710 f. See chap. 2, n. 160 and above, n. 17.

83. See above, nn. 26 and 53. Cf. Wolfram, "Fortuna," 23.

84. This effect of the battle of Adrianople follows clearly from the source list and interpretation in Paschoud, *Zosime*, 2, 2:474 ff.

85. Jordanes, *Getica* 146, p. 96. Lippold, *Theodosius der Grosse*, 122. Beninger, *Der westgotisch-alanische Zug*, esp. 128 f. A new study of the East Germanic Danubian material of the fifth century has not yet been made. Beninger's work was based on an erroneous interpretation of the finds; cf. the reviews by L. Schmidt, p. 216 f., and Zeiss, p. 249 ff. For a map of the distribution of the richly furnished East Germanic women's graves of the fifth century with costume accessories of precious metals, which might indicate that these grave inventories of the Danube region are identical, cf. Tejral, "Mähren im fünften Jahrhundert." 74 ff. with map 3,

p. 76. J. Werner, "Studien, 422 ff. Kovrig, "Nouvelles trouvailles," 209 ff., esp. ill. 3 on p. 213. Bierbrauer, *Ostgotische Grab- und Schatzfunde,* 65 f. with ill. 8. Harhoiu, *Treasure from Pietroasa,* 24–26. Friesinger, "Funde," 62 ff.

86. Lippold, "Theodosius I," 838 ff.; cf. Lippold, *Theodosius der Grosse,* 9 ff. Jones, *Prosopography* 1:904 n. 4; cf. 902 ff. n. 3 (father of the emperor). Hoffmann, *Bewegungsheer* 1:458 f. Demandt, "Magister militum," 601 f.

87. Lippold, "Theodosius I," 844 f. Hoffmann, *Bewegungsheer* 1:460 f. On Modares see Schwarcz, *Reichsangehörige,* 37 ff. and 152 ff.

88. Cf. Zosimus IV 25.2 with 24.3. Wolfram, "Gotische Studien I," 12 with n. 51. Jones, *Prosopography* 1:605. Demandt, "Magister militum," 713 f., but he calls Modares an "eastern Goth," which is not supported by Zosimus.

89. Lippold, "Theodosius I," 844 f. Hoffmann, *Bewegungsheer* 1:461. On the position of Modares cf. Demandt (as n. 88). On the proclamation of the victories in the imperial city see *Consularia Constantinopolitana* a. 379, 3, p. 243. On the low social origins of the *magistri militum* cf. Demandt, "Magister militum," 566 f.

90. Wolfram, *Mitteleuropa,* 474 f. n. 15. Ammianus Marcellinus XXXI 11.6 shows that groups of the three-tribe confederation had already left the Thracian area proper before the battle of Adrianople. But according to ibid. XXXI 16.7 the groups invaded the whole of Illyricum only after Adrianople. See chap. 5, n. 60 f.

91. This is probably what Ammianus Marcellinus XXXI 16.7 refers to. Jordanes, *Getica* 140, p. 95, speaks of a division of the Gothic army; Fritigern led one half to Thessaly, Epirus, and Achaea, the others went with Alatheus and Safrax to Pannonia.

92. Schwarcz, *Reichsangehörige,* 40. Lippold, "Theodosius I," 850 ff., and *Theodosius der Grosse,* 24 ff. Hoffmann, *Bewegungsheer* 1:464. Várady, *Pannonien,* 36 and 522 ff., who builds on the study of Egger, "Historisch-epigraphische Studien," 57–67. The decision whether to include Valeria among the settlement areas of the federates depends on where one assigns the bishopric of Amantius; on this see chap. 5, n. 25. Demandt, "Magister militum," 602 f., on Vitalianus and on the return of Illyricum to Gratian. See esp. Nagy, "Pannonia," 319 f. against Várady. Stallknecht, *Untersuchungen,* 76 nn. 18–22.

93. Lippold (as n. 92). Hoffmann, *Bewegungsheer* 1:461 ff. and 465. Ewig, "Probleme," 59 ff., on Arbogast and Bauto.

94. Lippold, "Theodosius I," 851.

95. See chap. 2, nn. 229 ff., and Schwarcz, *Reichsangehörige,* 40 f. and 103.

96. Hoffmann, *Bewegungsheer* 1:465 ff. Demandt, "Magister militum," 717 f. Cf. L. Schmidt, *Ostgermanen,* 417 n. 6, on the mood in the months leading up to the concluding of the *foedus.* Lippold, "Theodosius I," 861 f., and *Theodosius der Grosse,* 26.

97. *Consularia Constantinopolitana* a. 382, p. 243. See on this Hoffmann, *Bewegungsheer* 2:193 to n. 290, who describes and explains how soon after 382 Fritigern was mistaken for Athanaric. L. Schmidt, *Ostgermanen,* 419 n. 3. On the meaning of "an entire *gens*" see above, Introduction n. 34, and chap. 5, n. 162.

98. See above, n. 92.

99. Wolfram, "Gotische Studien II," 319 with n. 121.

100. See above, n. 97.

101. Jordanes, *Getica* 134 f., p. 93. Wolfram, "Gotische Studien I," 5–7, 17 f., and 25–31. Cf. chap. 2, n. 220.

102. Schwarcz, *Reichsangehörige,* 41 f. Wolfram, "Ansiedlung," 28 f. Lippold, "Theodosius I," 861 f., *Theodosius der Grosse,* 26 f. and 123. Stallknecht, *Untersuchungen,* 26 ff. and 75 ff. Gaupp, *Ansiedlungen,* 372 ff. From the list of sources in Jones, *The Later Roman Empire* 3:29 n. 46, see esp. Themistius, *Oratio* XXXIV 24: "under the same roof," ὁμορόφιοι; Synesius, *De regno,* chaps. 14 f. and 21. From the point of view of Synesius, bishop of Cyrene, "[Emperor Theodosius] made federates of the barbarians, thought them worthy of belonging to the empire, granted them honorary offices and gave the murderers Roman land." Jordanes, *Getica* 146, p. 96, reports annual payments, which from the perspective of the sixth century could be anachronistic but this is not necessarily so. On the question of the "Goths who had been admitted earlier" see chap. 2, n. 160, and above, n. 17. For additional literature see Demougeot, "Modalités," 143 ff.; *De l'unité,* 15 with n. 78 and 23 f.; *La formation,* vol. 2, part 1, 152 f.; Ewig, "Probleme," 51 ff., esp. 53; Chrysos, Βυζάντιον, 138–166, esp. 160–164, emphasized especially the Goths' renunciation of their own command of their units.

103. See Claudianus, *De VI consulatu Honorii* vv. 218–222, p. 243, and Orosius VII 37.1 and 3, as well as the legend of "Euphemia and the Goth," after Burkitt, *Euphemia and the Goth,* chap. 24, p. 140 f., even though the Goth came from the Greutungian settlement area of Phrygia (Schwarcz, *Reichsangehörige,* 54 f.). Cf. Hoffmann, *Bewegungsheer* 1:466, on the situation in Thrace. On tribal conflicts see chap. 3, nn. 178 ff.

104. Schwarcz, *Reichsangehörige,* 47 f. Jones, *Prosopography* 1:393 f. nn. 4 and 6, after Zosimus IV 40.1–8. Cf. Ammianus Marcellinus on *magister militum* Julius (as above, n. 82).

105. See below, n. 178.

106. Philostorgius X 6. Cf. L. Schmidt, *Ostgermanen,* 263.

107. Zosimus IV 35.1 and 38 f. Claudian, *De IV consulatu Honorii* vv. 626–636, p. 173. *Consularia Constantinopolitana* a. 386, p. 244. Demandt, "Magister militum," 714 f. Jones, *Prosopography* 1:750. A good commentary can be found in Paschoud, *Zosime* 2, 2:426 ff. and 177. Cf. Schwarcz, *Reichsangehörige,* 48.

108. As above, n. 92.

109. Rosenfeld, "Ost- und Westgoten," 250, after Ammianus Marcellinus XXVII 5.10, from which follows that the majority of the Athanaric Goths stayed "at home" (cf. XXXI 4.13); see also chap. 2, n. 229. Furthermore, the northern Danubian barbarians, who according to Zosimus IV 38.1 (cf. chap. 1, n. 57) called the Odotheus group Greutungi, must have been Tervingi. The Arimir Goths also remained behind north of the river: see chap. 2, n. 314 and n. 411. On the fall of Gainas see below, nn. 191–193.

110. See chap. 2, n. 314 and n. 411. On the general Gothicization see Schwarcz, *Reichsangehörige,* 46–50. Demandt, "Magister militum," 726. Straub, *Regeneratio Imperii,* 214 ff. Claude, *Westgoten,* 15 with n. 9. Stein, *Bas-Empire* 1:194. L. Schmidt, *Ostgermanen,* 421 ff. Dahn, *Könige des Germanen,* 5:26 with n. 4.

111. Várady, *Pannonien,* 58 ff. Nagy, "Pannonia," 313 f. and 323. Hoffmann, *Bewegungsheer* 2:196 to n. 47, after *XII Panegyrici Latini* (Pacatus) II (XII) 32.4

f. and 33.4 f.; cf. 11.4. For the army of Theodosius see Hoffmann, *Bewegungsheer* 2:196 f. to n. 50. On the end of Maximus see Hoffmann, *Bewegungsheer* 1:479.

112. Zosimus IV 45.4 f. and 48 f. Hoffmann, *Bewegungsheer* 1:481. Cf. L. Schmidt, *Ostgermanen*, 424 with n. 2, who tries, though not entirely consistently, to correct the contamination of Zosimus IV 49. Paschoud, *Zosime* 2, 2:446 f. and 196.

113. This might be inferred from the contamination of Zosimus IV 49 (see n. 112).

114. Hoffmann, *Bewegungsheer* 1:517, 2:204 to n. 194 f. See above, nn. 93 and 107, as well as below, n. 178.

115. Claudian, *De VI consulatu Honorii* vv. 105–108, p. 239; *De bello Gothico* v. 524, p. 278; *De consulatu Stilichonis* I vv. 94–96 and 106–111, p. 192 f.; *In Rufinum I* vv. 309–353, p. 30 f. Hoffmann, *Bewegungsheer* 2:204 to n. 195. Demandt, "Magister militum," 714–716; cf. 790. L. Schmidt, *Ostgermanen*, 424.

116. L. Schmidt, *Ostgermanen*, 428. Demougeot, *De l'unité*, 153 f. Cameron, *Claudian*, 156 ff., esp. 168 ff.

117. L. Schmidt, *Ostgermanen*, 431, Demougeot, *De l'unité*, 170 f., Cameron (as n. 116).

118. L. Schmidt, *Ostgermanen*, 439 f.; however, Schmidt dates the battle not until 403, as is commonly done in the older literature. Demougeot, *De l'unité*, 274–281, gives a detailed justification for dating it to the summer of 402. Cameron, *Claudian*, 180–188. On Stilicho see Jones, *Prosopography* 1:853–858.

119. Demougeot, *De l'unité*, 119 ff. Cameron, *Claudian*, 171 f. Cf. the passages cited in n. 115, esp. *In Rufinum* I vv. 309 ff., p. 30 f.

120. Orosius VII 57.1.

121. Zosimus V 7.2. Cameron, *Claudian*, 169–171. Claudian, *De bello Gothico* vv. 87–89, p. 263.

122. Hoffmann, *Bewegungsheer* 1:479 and 2:198 to nn. 64–66.

123. Characteristic is the "excuse" in Claudian, *De VI consulatu Honorii* vv. 127–129, p. 240, that after Pollentia Alaric's life had been spared for reasons of "high politics."

124. Cf. the policy of Constantius toward the Visigoths (as below, nn. 341 ff., and chap. 4, nn. 5 ff.).

125. These phrases are found in Claudian, *Epithalamium Palladii* (carm. XXV) vv. 88 f., p. 305 (*saevi Getae* outside of the *ripa Sarmatica*), as well as In *Rufinum* II vv. 270 f., p. 44 (*turpes Hunni* and their *famuli,* the *impacati Alani*—a notion that is probably derived from Ammianus Marcellinus XXXI 2 f., cf. Várady, *Pannonien*, 445 to n. 297). Várady, *Pannonien*, 189–193, thought they referred to the tribal groups outside the empire, and he distinguished those from the Pannonian and Moesian federates. Although we welcome once again Nagy's corrections, ("Pannonia," 334) of Várady's grandiose inferences, Várady nevertheless correctly interpreted the basic distinctions in the terminology of Claudian. This is also supported by Orosius's description of Radagaisus VII 37.5 and 9 as opposed to Alaric. But it goes too far to infer specific tribes from Claudian's general differentiation of internal and external barbarians.

126. See above, n. 107 (Odotheus), and below, nn. 321 ff. (Radagaisus) as well as chap. 4, nn. 51 ff. (Catalaunian Fields).

127. Straub, *Regeneratio Imperii,* 214 ff. and 246 ff. Pavan, *La politica gotica,* 39 ff. L. Schmidt, *Ostgermanen,* 436. Courcelle, *Histoire littéraire,* 26–28, esp. 26 n. 5. See, for example, the demand of Synesius, *De regno* chap. 19, that no "Scythians" (Goths and Huns) be employed in the army; instead, philosophers, craftsmen, merchants, and the lazy circus spectators should be sent to the front.

128. Claudian, *De consulatu Stilichonis I* vv. 94–96 and 109–111, p. 192 f., is the somewhat murky source. This raises the general question (cf. chap. 5, n. 113) of what one should think of poetic catalogs of peoples: see Loyen, *L'esprit précieux,* 20 ff., esp. 25, on Sidonius Apollinaris; *Carmina* V vv. 474–477, p. 199, as well as Loyen, *Recherches historiques,* 43, 51 f., on Sidonius Apollinaris; *Carmina* VII vv. 233–237 and vv. 321–328, pp. 209 and 211, where nearly identical wording is used. Claudian himself could be based on Ammianus Marcellinus (as n. 125). On the question of the Bastarni see Maenchen-Helfen, *The Huns,* 47 f. and 50 with n. 165, as well as 266 ff. (Bastarni still existed in the sixth century); cf. 447 ff. Wenskus, "Bastarnen," 90, also adheres to the sources. Hoffmann, *Bewegungsheer* 2:204 f. to n. 194 f. and 197, and Nagy, "Pannonia," 323 f. and 327, reject the authenticity of the Claudian passage, and we should follow them. Finally, one should consider that Alaric I supposedly came from the Danubian island of Peuke (Claudian, *De VI consulatu Honorii* vv. 105 f., p. 239; cf. below, n. 150) but that the Bastarni are considered Peukini (see chap. 2, n. 54). Peuke as a general name for the barbarian land on the lower Danube, which is at the same time a border region of the Roman Empire (see, for example, Claudian, *De IV consulatu Honorii* v. 630, p. 173) lives on in literature and can be applied to the most diverse tribal groups.

129. Jones, *Prosopography* 1:379 f., and Demandt, "Magister militum," 732–736, on Gainas. For the beginnings of Alaric I see Demougeot, *De l'unité,* 236 ff., and L. Schmidt, *Ostgermanen,* 424 f. Zosimus V 5.4 f. reports that Alaric was angry that Theodosius had slighted him: he wanted a Roman office and not merely the position of leader of the federates. On Alaric's age cf. Claudian, *De bello Gothico* vv. 493–495, p. 277. Chrysos (as above, n. 102) assumes that Theodosius was merely adhering to the provisions of the treaty of 382 when he ignored Alaric in the appointment to the supreme command of the Gothic federate army. Martindale, *Prosopography* 2:43–48 (Alaricus 1).

130. The best account of the events is by Demougeot, *De l'unité,* 107 ff., as well as Stein, *Bas-Empire* 1:216 ff. Cf. also Demandt, "Magister militum," 612 ff. Of great value among the older works because of their examination of the sources are Seeck, *Untergang,* 5:253 ff., esp. 272, 542 and 548 f., and L. Schmidt, *Ostgermanen,* 425. Nagy, "Pannonia," 326 f., should be used in addition to Várady, *Pannonien,* 86 ff. Zosimus V 4.2 attests that Stilicho for a time commanded both armies. Hoffmann, *Bewegungsheer* 1:520 ff. On the intended weakening of the Goths see esp. Orosius VII 35.19 and IV 58.3. On Arbogast see Jones, *Prosopography* 1:95 ff., and Ewig, "Probleme," 59.

131. Demougeot, *De l'unité,* esp. 589 f. s.v. "Alaric." Cameron, *Claudian,* 474 ff. Nagy, "Pannonia," 326 f. Demougeot, "Modalités d'établissement," 150 f. and 160. Stein, *Bas-Empire* 1:228 f. with n. 48. Vetters, *Dacia ripensis,* 37 f. L. Schmidt, *Ostgermanen,* 427. Seeck, *Untergang* 5:273–275 and 548 f. Hoffmann, *Bewegungsheer* 1:520, attests two armies in Venetia in 394/395. On Stilicho's departure from

Italy see Claudian, *In Rufinum II* vv. 100–105, p. 37 f. On the devastation in Dalmatia see Wilkes, *Dalmatia*, 419. Martindale, *Prosopography* 2:43 ff. (Alaricus). Jones, *Prosopography* 1:379 (Gainas) and 1:853 ff. (Stilicho).

132. Várady, *Pannonien*, 88 and 436. Thompson, *Attila and the Huns*, 26 f. Maenchen-Helfen, *The Huns*, 51 ff. L. Schmidt, *Ostgermanen*, 425 n. 5, wants to infer from Claudian, *In Rufinum II* vv. 26 ff., p. 35, that the rest of the former Athanaric Goths switched sides. See also the literature listed in n. 131.

133. See above, n. 106. On the motif of the frozen Danube see chap. 5, n. 129.

134. See above, n. 128.

135. Philostorgius XI 8 (beginning). Cf. Maenchen-Helfen, *The Huns*, 40 and 59.

136. Hieronymus, *Epistulae* 77.8.

137. See below, n. 289. Courtois, "Les politiques navales," 254 ff.

138. Claude, *Westgoten*, 16. Wenskus, *Stammesbildung*, 477. But it is nowhere stated that Taifalian contingents also followed Alaric. Cf. above, n. 9 f., and L. Schmidt, *Ostgermanen*, 126.

139. Jones, *Prosopography* 1:778 ff. n. 18. Martindale, *Prosopography* 2:44. On the treaty of 382 see above, n. 102. Claudian, *In Rufinum II* vv. 70–85, p. 36 f. Ibid. v. 75, p. 37, Rufinus is called *foederis auctor*. Schwarcz, *Reichsangehörige*, 53 f. and 87. On the wearing of Gothic clothes by Roman dignitaries see Wolfram, "Gotische Studien III," 255 n. 189, and Wenskus, *Stammesbildung*, 103 with n. 543.

140. On the question of when the dioceses of Dacia and Macedonia became part of the Eastern empire see Hoffmann, *Bewegungsheer* 2:207–215, esp. 208 ff. and 213 f., against, for example, Stein, *Bas-Empire* 1:229.

141. L. Schmidt, *Ostgermanen*, 428 n. 2.

142. Stein (as n. 140). Cf. Chrysos, "Βησιγότθοι," 181 ff., esp. 187 (type of booty: jewelry for the Gothic women, statues, mixing bowls, etc.) and 190 f. (the destruction caused was so severe that it was still noticeable after thirty years). Among the sources for the Goths' stay in Greece see esp. Claudian, *In Rufinum II*, praefatio vv. 1–20, p. 33 f., as well as II vv. 22–53, p. 35 f.

143. Cf. Courtois, "Les politiques navales," 254.

144. Schwarcz, *Reichsangehörige*, 178 f. Cameron, *Claudian*, 168 ff., 173 ff., cf. 93 ff. Demougeot, *De l'unité*, 143 ff. and 170 ff. Stein, *Bas-Empire* 1:231. L. Schmidt, *Ostgermanen*, 431 f.

145. Chrysos, Ἱστορία τῆς Ἠπείρου, 43–50, shows that the Alaric Goths were settled in Macedonia (cf. chap. 5, n. 145: East Gothic settlement). The former assumption of an Alaric kingdom in Epirus goes back to a corruption of the events of 397 and 406/407 by Zosimus V 26.1 and V 48.2 f. (cf. below, nn. 222 and 226). Chrysos, Ἱστορία τῆς Ἠπείρου, esp. 44 f. and 49, takes seriously the statement of Claudian that Alaric was appointed *dux Illyrici* and was made commander of Illyricum only in 406/407. Demandt, "Magister militum," 730 ff., cf. 639 ff., sticks to the traditional notion that Alaric became *magister militum per Illyricum* in 397. Schwarcz, *Reichsangehörige*, 54 f., 88 f., and 177 f., not only gives good reasons why he agrees but he even thinks that Alaric was already considered for the Illyrian magisterium in 395 (as above, n. 139). Of the sources see esp. Claudian, *In Eutropium II* vv. 214–218, p. 104: . . . *[Alaricus] praesidet Illyrico . . . illis responsa daturus, quorum coniugibus potitur natosque peremit.* Claudian, *De bello Gothico* vv. 535–544, p. 279: . . . *Illyrici postquam mihi tradita iura meque (Alaricum) suum*

fecere ducem . . . inque meos usus vectigal vertere ferri oppida legitimo iussu Romana coegi. The formula *provinciam praesidere* refers also in Cassiodorus primarily to military commanders: Wolfram, "Ethnogenesen," 113 n. 73. According to the *Codex Theodosianus* XI 14.3 and 9 (July 9, 397) and VI 28.6 (November 12, 399), an Illyrian praetorian prefect exercised his constitutional functions during the time in question. Cf. Demougeot, *De l'unité,* 267 with n. 187, as well as Hoffmann (as n. 140). On the Illyrian weapons factories see Vetters, *Dacia ripensis,* 38.

146. Wenskus, *Stammesbildung,* 322 f. and 477; cf. Wolfram, *Intitulatio I,* 42 f. and 77. Claude, *Adel, Kirche und Königtum,* 21 ff., and *Westgoten,* 25, as well as L. Schmidt, *Ostgermanen,* 426. Köpke, *Anfänge des Königthums,* 129, stated: "Alaric resurrected the kingship among the Visigoths and tried to place it on a firm footing, but the most important thing was to pass on the emerging authority to a successor, for on this depended the possibility of keeping the tribe together."

147. Ioannis Antiochenus fr. 206.2; cf. chap. 1, n. 67.

148. Formulas similar to the ones used by Jordanes, *Getica* 146, p. 96, and Isidore, *Historia vel Origo Gothorum* 12, p. 272, are found in Ammianus Marcellinus XXXI 3.3. Wenskus, *Stammesbildung,* 478 f. emphasizes that Ammianus was used by the *Origo Gothica.*

149. See chap. 1, n. 109 f. On the term *Peukinian* see n. 150.

150. Claudian, *De VI consulatu Honorii* v. 105, p. 239; cf. *De IV consulatu Honorii* v. 630, p. 173. See also above, n. 128.

151. See chap. 1, n. 110.

152. Claude (*Adel, Kirche und Königtum,* 24) notices that the sources ascribed monarchical traits to the Balth without drawing the full consequences (cf. n. 146) from this observation. Alaric is compared to Brennus and the giants. He is the "lord and victor over the Thracians" and their mythical king Rhesus, and he has "put many emperors to flight"; all these are distinctive features of the kingship of the army: Wolfram, *Intitulatio I,* 43. Claudian, *De bello Gothico* vv. 430–432 (Brennus), vv. 524 f., p. 278 (defeated emperors); *De VI consulatu Honorii* vv. 185 f., p. 242 (comparison to the giants), vv. 471–483, p. 252 (Thracians).

153. Jordanes, *Getica* 147, p. 96: the departure from Thrace is jointly decided upon; cf. Ammianus Marcellinus XXXI 15.13–15: the assault on Adrianople was carried out by the magnates against the advice of Fritigern. In contrast, in Claudian, *De bello Gothico* vv. 479–487, p. 277, "[Alaric] orders the magnates among his people" to assemble for a war council, which ends in a revealing way (as n. 154).

154. Alaric listens impatiently to the warning of an old warrior, who was some kind of foster-father to Alaric, and then rebukes him in a threatening manner. Thereafter Alaric's orders are carried out: Claudian, *De bello Gothico* vv. 488–551, pp. 277–279. This passage should be interpreted against Claude, *Adel, Kirche und Königtum,* 31 f.

155. Olympiodorus fr. 18 (Hunnic *rhiges,* among whom one is the highest); fr. 26 (a Gothic *rhix* of a subtribe). On the Gothic *rhix* see Wolfram, "Gotische Studien II," 303 to 306; cf. chap. 2, n. 405. John Chrysostom, *Epistula* 14.5, col. 618, cf. Maenchen-Helfen, *The Huns,* 196, also speaks of a *rhix* of the Gothic Crimea.

156. Olympiodorus fr. 3 (Alaric is *phylarchos* of the Goths), fr. 10 (Athaulf succeeds Alaric), fr. 26 (Sigeric succeeds Athaulf; Valia—*hegemon* of the Goths—succeeds Sigeric; on the meaning of *hegemon* see Wolfram, "Gotische Studien I," 26),

fr. 35 (the *phylarchos* Valia dies; Theoderid takes over the ἀρχή). Note 158 shows that *hegemon* and *phylarchos* underwent an analogous semantic change.

157. Olympiodorus fr. 17. On *hendinos* see Wenskus, *Stammesbildung*, 576 ff., after Ammianus Marcellinus XXVIII 5.14.

158. Wolfram, "Gotische Studien II," 319 f. with nn. 121 and 125. Claude, *Adel, Kirche und Königtum*, 16–18. One should compare Eunapius frs. 55 and 60 with Luke 2.36 and Phil. 3.5. Eunapius fr. 60 speaks of the *hegemones* of the Gothic *phylai*, thus presupposing a number of them.

159. Claude, *Adel, Kirche und Königtum*, 31–36.

160. Wolfram, "Gotische Studien II," 310, 316 n. 110, and 320 n. 124.

161. On the structure according to the decimal system see ibid., 313 with n. 105. On the expression "Alaric Goths" see chap. 1, n. 67, and above, n. 147. The following of Alaric's competitors, however, declined drastically: Claude (as n. 159).

162. Olympiodorus frs. 3 and 26. Claude, *Adel, Kirche und Königtum*, 33 ff. Cf. above n. 153 f. On Sarus cf. Schwarcz, *Reichsangehörige*, 162–167, and chap. 1, nn. 126 ff. Similar processes of political displacement took place among the Franks, as the story of Munderic reveals: Wolfram, *Intitulatio I*, 106 with n. 108.

163. John 19.12 and 15.

164. Wolfram, "Gotische Studien II," 296 with n. 28, 302 with n. 56, 303 with n. 58, and "Gotische Studien III," 245 f. with n. 162.

165. Orosius VII 34.7. The expression "emperor of the army" is found, for example, in Synesius, *De regno* chap. 21: Arcadius should be a βασιλεὺς πολεμικός.

166. Prudentius, *Contra Symmachum II*, 695 f. Cf. Claudian, p. 596. See also the designation of Theodoric the Great as tyrant by Procopius, *De bello Gothico* I (V) 1.29, which refers to a greater barbarian king. The Romans also definitely noticed Alaric's unusual exercise of authority: see above, n. 145. Demandt, "Magister militum," 693 ff. and 730 ff. Wolfram, *Intitulatio I*, 39 ff. and 99 ff.

167. Hartke, *Kinderkaiser*, 92 ff. Stein, *Bas-Empire* 1:662 f., s.v. "usurpation." Demougeot, *De l'unité*, 173 ff. (Gildo), 387 f. (Constantine III), 389 (Jovinus), 448 ff. (Attalus).

168. Wolfram, *Intitulatio I*, 34 f.

169. Ibid., 40 ff. Wolfram, "Early Medieval Kingdom," 3–9 and 18. Wolfram, "Gotische Studien II," 305 with nn. 68 ff., shows after Mark 14.42, and Romans 15.12 the connection of *reiks* and *thiuda*.

170. See the events immediately following the battle of Adrianople, as above, nn. 87 ff.

171. The phrase is found in Zosimus IV 25.2 (Modares). Procopius, *De bello Gothico* III (VII) 1.41 reports as one reason for the downfall of Uraias that King Hildebad claimed he was planning to join the Romans. Cf. the Arminius-Flavus controversy in Tacitus, *Annales* II 10: *gentis suae desertor et proditor*.

172. The best known examples from this period are Modares and Fravitta, who fought above all against their former tribesmen: see Schwarcz, *Reichsangehörige*, 120–122, as well as 152–154, and Jones, *Prosopography* 1:372 f. and 605. Cf. above, n. 171.

173. See Prudentius (as n. 166). Cf. esp. the comment the Malchus fr. 14 ascribes to Theodoric Strabo. Raised to the kingship Theodoric Strabo feels obligated toward his electorate; he is no longer a private individual and must take care of all Gothic warriors.

174. According to Zosimus V 40.2 and 48.2, some Romans already began to cooperate with Alaric I in Macedonia. Cf. below, n. 292, and chap. 4, n. 517.

175. See above, nn. 56–60.

176. Jordanes, *Getica* 152, p. 97 (Alaric's offer to Honorius), prefigured by ibid. 145, p. 96 (Gothic federates and Roman soldiers form a *corpus*). Sozomenus IX 7.5 (cf. IX 9.2): Alaric demands from the emperor enough grain and settlement area, in which case he would be at the service of the empire as a federate without laying claim to Roman offices.

177. See chap. 4, nn. 241 ff.

178. Demandt, "Magister militum," 728 and 736. Jones, *Prosopography* 1:372 f. Eunapius fr. 60 and Zosimus IV 56 as well as 57.1. Cf. on this Paschoud, *Zosime,* 2, 2:460 ff., esp. 460: "ne pas . . . trop longtemps avant 395." Schwarcz, *Reichsangehörige,* 120–122. Thompson, "Visigoths from Fritigern to Euric," 107 with n. 7. L. Schmidt, *Ostgermanen,* 422 f.

179. Wolfram, "Gotische Studien I," 6 f. On Alaric's rebellion of 391 see above, nn. 113 ff.

180. Eunapius fr. 80 and 82. Zosimus V 20.1 and 21.5. On Modares and Munderic see Jones, *Prosopography* 1:605 and 610, and Wolfram, "Gotische Studien I," 2 n. 8 and 12 n. 51. Cf. Thompson, "Visigoths from Fritigern to Euric," 108, as well as chap. 2, n. 472.

181. Goffart, "Zosimos," 412 ff., esp. 418 ff. Paschoud, "Zosimos," 810 ff.

182. See most recently Albert, *Goten in Konstantinopel,* esp. 66 ff. Cf. Demandt, "Magister militum," 733–736. Jones, *Prosopography* 1:379 f. (Gainas). The kinship of Tribigild and Gainas is inferred from Sozomenus VIII 4.2, but Sozomenus may have meant merely that they were of the same tribe. Cf. Schwarcz, *Reichsangehörige,* 129 f., on Gainas 128–136, on Tribigild 202–205.

183. Cf. Claudian, *In Eutropium II* vv. 194 ff., p. 103.

184. Hoffmann, *Bewegungsheer* 1:82 f., and 2:16 to n. 57, 2:46 to n. 33, and 2:194 to n. 310; Hoffmann, however, has left out Claudian, *In Eutropium II* vv. 576–583, p. 117. Cf. Seeck, *Untergang* 5:563 to n. 28, and below, n. 185.

185. That we are dealing with Greutungian horsemen follows from Zosimus V 15.8; Claudian, *In Eutropium II* vv. 176 f., p. 102; cf. Claudian, *De bello Gothico* vv. 473 f., p. 277, and not least from the fact that Tribigild's units were employed against the Huns and were successful (as n. 182).

186. Zosimus V 15 f. For a correction of Zosimus see Fiebiger and Schmidt, *Inschriftensammlung,* no. 241, p. 117.

187. Cf. Zosimus V 17. Cameron, *Claudian,* 183 f.

188. See the speech that Bellona in the shape of his wife addresses to Tribigild: Claudian, *In Eutropium II* vv. 160–229, pp. 102–104, esp. vv. 198–201, p. 103, and vv. 213–218, p. 104. Cf. chap. 3, n. 103 (Euphemia and the Goth).

189. Schwarcz, *Reichsangehörige,* 128–136. Cf. Demougeot, *De l'unité,* 225 and 229.

190. Schwarcz, *Reichsangehörige,* 134–136. Martindale, *Prosopography* 2:1126, after Philostorgius XI 8: Tribigild is killed in action in Thrace. Zosimus V 21.5. Eunapius fr. 82. Because Fravitta had to let his enemy get away, he was also accused of treason. Schäferdiek, "Germanenmission," 506.

191. Zosimus V 21.6. Cf. Schwarcz (as n. 190).

192. Zosimus V 22.1. Maenchen-Helfen, *The Huns,* 59 ff. Thompson, *Attila and*

the Huns, 29. Yet Lippold, "Uldin," 511 f., thinks that the Huns, and especially their leader Uldin (Martindale, *Prosopography* 2:1180), were interested only in the reward.

193. Demougeot, *De l'unité,* 261 n. 153. Stein, *Bas-Empire* 1:237. In the *Chronicon paschale* of the seventh century the sea battle in the straits takes place only on this day, while the head of Gainas arrives in Constantinople on January 3, 401. Marcellinus Comes, *Chronicon* aa. 400 and 401, p. 66, however, does not have Gainas killed until February. See on this Schwarcz, *Reichsangehörige,* 134–136.

194. Cf. Schwarcz, *Reichsangehörige,* 58 f. and 134–136. Albert, *Goten in Konstantinopel,* 25 f. and 181 f. On Fravitta see above, n. 178.

195. Maenchen-Helfen and Thompson (as n. 192). But Várady, *Pannonien,* 206, probably does not do justice to Uldin and his emerging Hunnic state. See esp. Lippold, "Uldin," 511 f.

196. On Illyricum as *patria Gothorum* see St. Ambrose, *Expositio in Lucam* X 10. Cf. Egger, "Historisch-epigraphische Studien," 64 f.

197. Cameron, *Claudian,* 156 ff., esp. 178 ff. Demougeot, *De l'unité,* 267 ff., esp. 268 with n. 191. Courtois, *Les Vandales,* 39 f. Miltner, "Vandalen," 303 f. See also Seeck, *Untergang* 5:572, and Claudian, *Carmina,* pp. XLVII ff.

198. Jordanes, *Getica* 147, p. 96. Cf. Várady, *Pannonien,* 179 ff.

199. *Fasti Vindobonenses priores* a. 401, p. 299.

200. L. Schmidt, *Ostgermanen,* 437 n. 4; cf. Claudian, *Carmina,* p. 460, s.v. "Timavus." Since Claudian thinks that the karst river Reka, which under the name Timao flows into the sea at Duino, has nine estuaries, he assumed that the Isonzo is also connected to it. This might explain the equation Isonzo-Timao. *Dizionario corografico dell'Italia* 6:819 (Recca), and 8:254 f. (Timavo). On the barriers at the Hrušica cf. most recently Šašel, "Iulisch-alpische Militärzone," 255–262. Šašel and Petru, *Claustra,* 27–45 (sources from the later period), 51 f. (on the state of archaeological research); the barriers at the Hrušica forest pass at the fortress Ad Pirum-Hrušica: ibid., 93 ff. Excavations at the Hrušica by German and Slovenian archaeologists have so far yielded no conclusive results, but the Slovenian scholars seem to be arriving at the opinion that the barriers still existed at the beginning of the fifth century. Of course it cannot be archaeologically proved whether they were manned when Alaric marched to Italy: this information was kindly provided by Jaro Šašel.

201. From Jerome, *In Rufinum III* 21, we learn of the siege of Aquileia, but not that it was actually taken, as Demougeot, *De l'unité,* 269 f., thinks.

202. Seeck, *Untergang* 5:572.

203. Claudian, *De bello Gothico* vv. 233–266, p. 268 f.

204. Cameron, *Claudian,* 183 f. Fiebiger-Schmidt, *Inschriftensammlung,* no. 23, p. 25.

205. Nagy, "Pannonia," 325 and 330 ff., against Várady, *Pannonien,* 182 f. According to Bachrach, *Alans,* 34 ff., Stilicho's Alanic troops were recruited from among Italian settlers.

206. Claudian, *De VI consulatu Honorii* vv. 456–469, p. 251 f. Cf. Schwarcz, *Reichsangehörige,* 181 ff.

207. Stein, *Bas-Empire* 1:249.

208. Prudentius, *Contra Symmachum* II 702. Claudian, *De bello Gothico* vv. 430 ff., p. 275; cf. vv. 531 ff., p. 279.

209. Ibid., vv. 416–429, p. 274 f.

210. Ibid., vv. 554–557, p. 279. Claudian, *De VI consulatu Honorii* v. 204, p. 242. L. Schmidt, *Ostgermanen*, 438 f. *Dizionario corografico dell'Italia* 5:715 (Orba) and 6:359 and 360 ff. (Pollentia-Pollenzo). But an active imagination is needed to connect the Orba with Pollentia, since the river flows only east of Alessandria into a right tributary of the Tanaro. Thus Schwarcz, *Reichsangehörige*, 183 f., can say that "all around the battle of Pollentia there probably took place a number of minor and major engagements. Known and clearly located are the unsuccessful siege of Hasta by the Goths and the fighting at the Orba."

211. Orosius, *Historiae adversum paganos* VII 37.2. Nagy, "Pannonia," 325. Cf. above, n. 205.

212. Claudian, *De VI consulatu Honorii* vv. 274 ff., p. 245 f.; Claudian, *De bello Gothico* vv. 565–597, p. 280 f., vv. 605 ff., 624 ff., pp. 281 ff. On Saul see Jones, *Prosopography* 1:809, and Martindale, *Prosopography* 2:981. Schwarcz, *Reichsangehörige*, 167 f. Maenchen-Helfen, *The Huns*, 49 and 71 with n. 281. The frequently assumed capture of Alaric's wife is refuted by Schwarcz, 183.

213. Cameron, *Claudian*, 181 ff.

214. See above, n. 123.

215. Claudian, *De VI consulatu Honorii* vv. 230–233, p. 243: Alaric was prevented from undertaking his planned trek to Gaul.

216. Ibid., v. 223 f.

217. On the dating and the events of the battle of Verona cf. Maenchen-Helfen, *The Huns*, 67 with n. 258. Cameron, *Claudian*, 184 with n. 3. Demougeot, *De l'unité*, 278 to 281. Schwarcz, *Reichsangehörige*, 184 f.

218. Claudian, *De VI consulatu Honorii* vv. 224–264, p. 243 f.

219. Ibid., vv. 219 f., p. 240. Cf. Wolfram, *Intitulatio I*, 43.

220. L. Schmidt, *Ostgermanen*, 440 with n. 6; cf. Demandt, "Magister militum," 637–639 and 643 f. On Sarus see chap. 1, nn. 126 ff. On Ulfilas see Martindale, *Prosopography* 2:1181.

221. L. Schmidt, *Ostgermanen*, 439 with n. 4, after Claudian, *De bello Gothico* vv. 83–85, p. 263, and vv. 623–628, p. 282, as well as *De VI consulatu Honorii* vv. 297–300, p. 246.

222. Sozomenus IX 4.4. On the Alaric Goths in Dalmatia see Wilkes, *Dalmatia*, 419 esp. after Zosimus V 48.3. Cf. above, n. 145.

223. *Collectio Avellana* no. 38, p. 85.

224. Demandt, "Magister militum," 731 f. and 739 f. Maenchen-Helfen, *The Huns*, 67 ff. Cameron, *Claudian*, 157 ff. and 184 ff. Demougeot, *De l'unité*, 365–375. Hoffmann, *Bewegungsheer* 2:214 f. Schwarcz, *Reichsangehörige*, 89 f., 187, 190.

225. Zosimus V 26.2 ff. See below, n. 329 (Radagaisus). Cf. Schwarcz, *Reichsangehörige*, 187–190.

226. As above, nn. 222 and 224.

227. Zosimus V 27. Stein, *Bas-Empire* 1:250.

228. Demougeot, *De l'unité*, 375 ff. Stroheker, *Adel*, 45.

229. Zosimus V 27.2 ff.

230. Stein, *Bas-Empire* 1:251. Not until December 10, 408—i.e., several months after the fall of Stilicho—were the barriers between the two empires taken down again: *Codex Theodosianus* VII 16.1.

231. Demougeot, *De l'unité,* 365 f. with nn. 74 and 78; cf. 375.

232. Zosimus V 29.4–6. Maenchen-Helfen, *The Huns,* 63 and 68 f. Várady, *Pannonien,* 241 ff. Demougeot, *De l'unité,* 402 ff. L. Schmidt, *Ostgermanen,* 441 f. Egger, *Hermagoras,* 57 ff. Wirth, "Anmerkungen," 229 n. 20.

233. Zosimus V 29.9; cf. 31.5. Stein, *Bas-Empire* 1:253 with n. 174. The yearly incomes of senators are reported by Olympiodorus fr. 44. Maenchen-Helfen, *The Huns,* 459, radically doubts all figures given by Olympiodorus. Cf., however, Jones, *The Later Roman Empire* 2:554 ff. Matthews, *Aristocracies,* 384.

234. Zosimus V 31.4–6. Demandt, "Magister militum," 641 f.

235. Zosimus VI 2. Demandt, "Magister militum," 638.

236. Demandt, "Magister militum," 641.

237. But Zosimus V 42.1 and 44.1, as well as 50.3, contradict one another, while one could infer from Olympiodorus fr. 5, Zosimus's source, the payment of the stipulated sum, if we knew exactly which demand he refers to: see Demougeot, *De l'unité,* 409 with n. 286.

238. Cf. the differentiation in Orosius VII 37.9 between Alaric *Christianus propiorque Romano* and Radagaisus *paganus barbarus et vere Scytha.*

239. Zosimus V 35.6 and 37.4. Cf. above, n. 233. On the "Twelve thousand optimates" of Radagaisus see chap. 2, n. 420 after Olympiodorus fr. 9.

240. Demandt, "Magister militum," 627 and 638. Stein, *Bas-Empire* 1:253 f. and 555 with n. 6 f. Demougeot, *De l'unité,* 409. Zosimus V 34.1, 36.2 ff., and 37.1.

241. Zosimus V 36 f., esp. 37.2. Seeck, *Untergang* 5:391. Stein, *Bas-Empire* 1:555. On Athaulf see below, n. 248 and n. 293.

242. Zosimus V 39, and 41.1–3. Sozomenus IX 6.3–5. Demougeot (as n. 248), 31. Cf. chap. 2, n. 486.

243. Socrates VII 10.8 f. Sozomenus IX 6.6. Claudian, *De bello Gothico* vv. 544 to 551, p. 279. See chap. 2, n. 469 and Demougeot, *De l'unité,* 478 with n. 211.

244. Zosimus V 40, 41.3–7, and 42.1 f. For criticism of the figures see above, n. 233.

245. Zosimus V 42. On the handing over of the contributions cf. n. 237.

246. Wolfram, "Gotische Studien II," 309 f. Loyen, *Recherches historiques,* 35 f., shows that even the often disappointed Gallic nobility remained loyal to the house of Theodosius.

247. Stein, *Bas-Empire* 1:256 ff., esp. 262. L. Schmidt, *Ostgermanen,* 444 ff. Zosimus V 50.3, and VI 6; cf. V 42.1. Jordanes, *Getica* 152, p. 97. On the problem of Romania-Gothica see below, n. 284.

248. Zosimus V 44.1 f., and 45.1 f., as well as 4–6. Sozomenus IX 7.1. Cf. Demougeot, "Interventions du pape Innocent Ier," 32. On Generidus see Martindale, *Prosopography* 2:500 f., Demandt, "Magister militum," 646 f.

249. Zosimus V 48.1–4. Sozomenus IX 7.5; cf. above, n. 176. Schwarcz, *Reichsangehörige,* 92 f., shows, against Demandt ("Magister militum," 628 f., esp. 732), that Alaric—as hitherto claimed in the literature—laid claim to the highest military command.

250. Zosimus V 48.4–51.1. Maenchen-Helfen, *The Huns,* 69 with n. 269.

251. Prosper, *Epitoma chronicon* 1238, p. 466. Zosimus VI 6 f. and 12.1. De-mandt, "Magister militum," 627. Seeck, *Untergang* 5:596. On the personnel deci-sions of Attalus see L. Schmidt, *Ostgermanen,* 445 f. On Sigesar see Sozomenus IX 9.1, and Olympiodorus fr. 26.

252. Zosimus VI 7.5 f. Ibid. VI 8.1–2 shows that Honorius was at first ready to make extreme concessions to Attalus but that he gained new courage through the arrival in Ravenna of fresh troops and the loyalty of the governor of Africa. Ibid. 9.1 reports the failure of Attalus's expedition against Africa; 11 describes the outbreak of famine in Rome.

253. Sozomenus IX 8.4 ff., and Zosimus VI 9.3 (Alaric before Rome) and 10 (Alaric in northern Italy).

254. Zosimus VI 12.2. Olympiodorus fr. 13. Martindale, *Prosopography* 2:180 f. (Priscus Attalus 2).

255. Sozomenus IX 9.2; cf. L. Schmidt, *Ostgermanen,* 447 with n. 2.

256. Zosimus VI 13.2: Athaulf attacks Sarus in Picenum, whereupon the latter goes to Honorius in Ravenna. Sozomenus IX 9.3. Philostorgius XII 3. Olympiodorus fr. 3. On the figures of Olympiodorus cf. above, nn. 38 and 49. On Sarus see chap. 1, n. 127.

257. Demougeot, *De l'unité,* 463 ff., esp. 468 f. L. Schmidt, *Ostgermanen,* 448 ff. Courcelle, *Histoire littéraire,* 49 ff., Jones, *The Later Roman Empire* 1:185 ff.

258. Claude, "Frühmittelalterliche Königsschätze," 8 f. But Procopius, *De bello Vandalico* II (IV) 9.5–9 (Vandals rob the treasure in 455) and *De bello Gothico* I (V) 12.42 (the Goths rob the treasure in 410), contradicts himself. On the basis of other considerations Claude is right in choosing 410 as the date. On the Visigothic treasure cf. for example Gregory of Tours, *Historia Francorum* III 10, p. 107.

259. Orosius VII 40.2. Philostorgius XII 4 has a lacuna at a critical passage. According to Zosimus (as n. 256) Placidia would have fallen into the hands of the Goths before the capture of Rome: Demougeot, *De l'unité,* 461 n. 114 and 474. Oost, *Galla Placidia,* 94 n. 23.

260. St. Jerome, *Epistulae* 123, 16.4. Cf. the historical reminiscences of Cas-siodorus in the year 536: *Variae* XII 20.4, p. 344. See Straub, *Regeneratio Imperii,* 249 ff.; 488 (source index). Stein, *Bas-Empire* 1:259 ff. Demougeot, *De l'unité,* 481 ff.

261. Demougeot, *De l'unité,* 471 ff. Oost, *Galla Placidia,* 96 f. with nn. 32 and 34. Courcelle, *Histoire littéraire,* 52 ff., rightly criticizes German historiography, which from contemporary discussions of the event derives the justification to down-play the capture of Rome.

262. Demougeot, *De l'unité,* 478 f.

263. Ibid., 479 ff. L. Schmidt, *Ostgermanen,* 451 ff. Courtois, "Les politiques navales," 254. The abandoning of the expedition because of bad weather is indicated by Orosius's comparison of the two Gothic attempts to cross straits: VII 43.11 f. Oost, *Galla Placidia,* 102 with nn. 53 and 55, after Olympiodorus fr. 15: a miracle-working statue had stopped the Goths, or so the pagans believed.

264. Düwel, "Alarich," 128.

265. L. Schmidt, *Ostgermanen,* 452.

266. Jordanes, *Getica* 158, p. 99.

267. Düwel (as n. 264) against L. Schmidt (as n. 265). In the *Origo Gothica* the Goths' mourning over the death of Thorismund is followed suspiciously soon by the mourning of the Huns after the death of Attila: cf. Jordanes, *Getica* 251, p. 122, with 254–258, pp. 123–125. On the combining of heroic saga and sacral kingship cf. Wolfram, "Gotische Studien III," 253 with n. 182.

268. Demougeot, *De l'unité,* 480 f. Stein, *Bas-Empire* 1:262. Cf. Cassius Dio LXVIII 14.4 f.: death and burial of the Dacian king Decebalus.

269. See above, n. 243. The anger of Alaric is described by Zosimus V 49.1.

270. Wolfram, "Gotisches Königtum," 1 ff., esp. 7 ff. Thompson, "Visigoths from Fritigern to Euric," 105 ff.

271. Zosimus V 36 f., esp. 37.2, and Jordanes (as n. 266). Claude, *Adel, Kirche und Königtum,* 29 f. It was probably only after the death of Athaulf that several pretenders appeared: Prosper, *Epitoma chronicon* 1257, a. 415, p. 467 f. Cf. L. Schmidt, *Ostgermanen,* 459 n. 5. On Athaulf see Martindale, *Prosopography* 2:176–178.

272. Jordanes, *Getica* 159, p. 99, reports that Athaulf had wrought havoc "like locusts." Cf. *Codex Theodosianus* XI 28.7 (May 8, 413). Cf. L. Schmidt, *Ostgermanen,* 453 f. Claudius Rutilius Namatianus, *De reditu suo sive* 1:21.

273. Demougeot, *De l'unité,* 483 ff.

274. Matthews, *Aristocracies,* 314 ff. Stroheker, *Adel,* 45 ff., 185 ff. n. 204. Loyen, *Recherches historiques,* 38 f., after Gregory of Tours, *Historia Francorum* II 9, p. 57. Martindale, *Prosopography* 2:621 (Iovinus 2). The most important source for the events is Olympiodorus fr. 17.

275. Stroheker, *Adel,* 152 ff. n. 58; cf. chap. 4, nn. 65 ff. Martindale, *Prosopography* 2:196–198 (Eparchius Avitus).

276. See above, n. 215.

277. *Codex Theodosianus* (as n. 272). Prosper, *Epitoma chronicon* 1246, a. 412, p. 466. *Chronica Gallica* 67, a. 411, p. 654.

278. Olympiodorus fr. 17. Schwarcz, *Reichsangehörige,* 165 f.

279. Olympiodorus fr. 19. Stroheker, *Adel,* 51 and 162 f. n. 99. Courcelle, *Histoire littéraire,* 90 and 92 ff. On the presumed Gothic settlement in Aquitaine before 418 see *Chronica Gallica* 73 (as n. 277). Paulinus of Pella, *Eucharisticos,* vv. 283–290, p. 302. Cf. ibid., v. 312, p. 303, on the admission of the Goths into Bordeaux. See also Matthews, *Aristocracies* (as n. 274), 315, and Goffart, *Barbarians and Romans,* 104 with n. 3.

280. Olympiodorus fr. 20 f. Narbonne was captured during the wine harvest; Dahn, *Könige der Germanen* 5:58, builds on Hydatius 55, a. 413; cf. L. Schmidt, *Ostgermanen,* 455 n. 8 (a nice but unhistorical legend). Toulouse probably also became Gothic at that time; however, it follows from Claudius Rutilius Namatianus, *De reditu suo* I v. 496, only that the city was captured before 416/417.

281. *Chronica Gallica* 72, a. 414, p. 654.

282. Hydatius 57, a. 414. Cf. Isidore, *Historia vel Origo Gothorum* 19, p. 275.

283. Olympiodorus fr. 24; cf. fr. 46. Honorius had Constantius fight on: ibid., frs. 22 and 26. Matthews, *Aristocracies,* 316 f. and 380. Stein, *Bas-Empire* 1:266.

284. Orosius VII 43.2–8. Matthews, *Aristocracies,* 316 f. Straub, *Regeneratio Imperii,* 212 f. Claude, *Adel, Kirche und Königtum,* 29 f. Courcelle, *Histoire lit-*

téraire, 91. For the identification of the honorable citizen of Narbonne see Matthews, *Aristocracies,* 322. An interesting comparison of the similar statements in the sources by Athaulf, Eriulf, and Uldin is in Lippold, "Uldin," 512. For additional thoughts see Suerbaum, *Staatsbegriff,* 222–228.

285. Jordanes, *Getica* 146, p. 96. Cf. above, n. 85.

286. Olympiodorus fr. 26; cf. n. 283. Claude (as n. 284). Cf. Loyen (as n. 246) on Theodosian legitimism in Gaul. Martindale, *Prosopography* 2:1100 (Theodosius 5).

287. Olympiodorus fr. 34. Demandt, "Magister militum," 629–633. Seeck, *Untergang* 6:64 ff.

288. Orosius (as n. 284). Claude, *Westgoten,* 7–27, treats Gothic history before the settlement as a prologue. Nehlsen, *Sklavenrecht,* 248 f., emphasizes the new beginning "after the settlement of the Visigoths in Gaul and Spain."

289. Orosius VII 43.1 *Chronica Gallica* 72, a. 411, p. 654.

290. Matthews, *Aristocracies,* 317 f. Cf. L. Schmidt, *Ostgermanen,* 457 n. 4. Paulinus, *Eucharisticos* vv. 292–398, pp. 302–306, esp. vv. 303–313 and 346–351, pp. 303 and 304. Prosper, *Epitoma chronicon* 1254 ff., aa. 414 f., p. 467. Orosius VII 42.7. The identity of the Alanic king was clarified by Levison, "Bischof Germanus," 135. Martindale, *Prosopography* 2:514 f. (Goar).

291. Olympiodorus (as n. 286). Demandt, "Magister militum," 631. L. Schmidt, *Ostgermanen,* 458 n. 4 and 459 n. 4 (after *Chronicon paschale* a. 415, p. 72: the death of Athaulf).

292. Claude, *Adel, Kirche und Königtum,* 28 f., should be supplemented with Zosimus V 48.2; cf. 40.2.

293. Zosimus V 37.2. Martindale, *Prosopography* 2:176 ff. Though the Gothic-Hunnic unit is not explicitly described as cavalry, this is indicated by its ethnic composition and by the fact that Athaulf became one of the first *comites domesticorum equitum* that we know of; Sozomenus IX 8.2. Martindale *Prosopography* 2:1239 (Fasti). Schwarcz, *Reichsangehörige,* 104. On the death of Athaulf see nn. 291 and 302.

294. See chap. 3, nn. 29–31 and n. 89 f.

295. Várady, *Pannonien,* 213 ff. and 458 f. with n. 639, would be a good start, were it not for the inextricable intertwining of "Dichtung und Wahrheit." Nagy, "Pannonia," 334, is only of limited use as a corrective, although he is certainly right in rejecting the Ostrogothic infantry discovered by Várady. The fantastic story that Várady tells of the two Ostrogothic divisions is based on Orosius VII 37.3, who mentions tribal confrontations of two Gothic *cunei* (units), the Alans and the Huns. The two Gothic units appear a little later (8) as the peoples of Radagaisus and Alaric, while a few lines later *Uldin et Sarus Hunorum et Gothorum duces* are mentioned as supporters of the Romans against the Radagaisus Goths (12). Thus there are two possible ways of interpreting the tribal conflicts in the sense of Orosius without having to invent anything. Cf. L. Schmidt, *Ostgermanen,* 266 n. 4. On the withdrawal of the Vandals and Alans in the year 401 and on the Pannonian Ostrogoths see chap. 5, n. 25.

296. Zosimus V 37.2 (brother-in-law). Jordanes, *Getica* 158, p. 99 (blood relative). Regarding the second passage, one must, however, consider that blood kinship

can also mean a contractual bond, as was the terminological custom since the days of Caesar and Cicero for the relationship between the Romans and the Haedui (this was kindly pointed out to me by Gerhard Dobesch).

297. Thus most recently Nagy, "Pannonia," 332 ff. This is contradicted by Jordanes, *Getica* 98, p. 83: *Ostrogothae quam Vesegothae, id est utrique eiusdem gentes populi.* Thus Theodoric the Great became king of the Visigoths around 510/511: see Claude, *Westgoten,* 55.

298. See above, nn. 211 and 218.

299. Diesner, "Buccellariertum," 327 ff. Olympiodorus fr. 26 (Dubius) and Jordanes, *Getica* 163, p. 100 (Evervulf), are the only ones who report the name of the assassin and his personal motive. See Claude, *Adel, Kirche und Königtum,* 32 with n. 59, against L. Schmidt, *Ostgermanen,* 458 f. Cf. Oost, *Galla Placidia,* 134–137. It was also known that at his murder Athaulf was engaged in a confidential discussion, *inter familiares fabulas:* Hydatius 60, a. 416. Orosius, *Historiae adversum paganos* VII 43, 8 f. treats Athaulf's murder, Sigeric, and the election of Valia from the perspective of friendship/enmity toward Rome. On Olympiodorus's institutional terminology see above, nn. 155–162.

300. Olympiodorus fr. 26. See above, n. 162.

301. See chap. 5, nn. 33 ff.

302. Olympiodorus fr. 26. Oost, *Galla Placidia,* 136 f. L. Schmidt, *Ostgermanen,* 459 n. 6, wonders how Dahn knows that Athaulf had six children. The explanation lies in the Latin translation that FHG 4:63 included with the Greek text. It reads: *Adaulphi e priore coniuge liberos vi* [read by Dahn as VI] . . . *occidit* (Sigeric). Because of an incomplete source, however, there grew up the story that Athaulf's first wife had been Sarmatian: Philostorgius XII 4. Cf. above, nn. 291 and 293. Martindale, *Prosopography* 2:987 (Segericus).

303. Cf. chap. 1, n. 126 f.

304. Orosius VII 37.12. Toward the middle of 400 Sarus still had three hundred men, in 412/413 only thirteen: Claude, *Adel, Kirche und Königtum,* 33, on Zosimus VI 13.2, and Olympiodorus fr. 17.

305. Olympiodorus fr. 17. See Schwarcz, *Reichsangehörige,* 162–167, as well as above, n. 285.

306. See above, nn. 241 and 248.

307. See above, n. 293. Cf. Demandt, "Magister militum," 568 ff., 637, and 648 f.: Alaric's later colleague Valens rose from *comes domesticorum peditum* to the position of supreme commander.

308. See above, n. 256.

309. Demandt (as n. 307). Claude, *Adel, Kirche und Königtum,* 29 f. Wolfram, *Intitulatio I,* 45 ff.

310. Sánchez-Albornoz, "La caballería visigoda," 92 ff., or by the same author, *Feudalismo* 3:83 ff. On the primarily unmounted Tervingian-Vesian predecessor of the Visigoths see chap. 2, n. 434 f.

311. Claudian, *De bello Gothico* vv. 191–193 and 213–217, p. 267. Cf. above, nn. 60 ff. (Adrianople).

312. Claudian, *De VI consulatu Honorii* vv. 283–285, p. 245.

313. Cf. above, nn. 218–221.

314. See chap. 4, n. 540, chap. 5, n. 11 f., n. 18, and nn. 63 ff.

315. See above, n. 299. Olympiodorus fr. 26.

316. On Adrianople see above, n. 62, on Sisak n. 111. In general cf. chap. 4, n. 376 (Toulouse), and chap. 5, nn. 284 ff. (Ostrogoths).

317. Jordanes, *Getica* 199, p. 109; 209, p. 111; 265 f., p. 126.

318. Gregory of Tours, *Historia Francorum* II 37, p. 87 f.

319. Isidore, *Historia vel Origo Gothorum* 69, p. 294.

320. Wenskus, *Stammesbildung,* 469 with n. 244. The significance of this later report is explained by Kienast, *Volksstämme,* 170 with n. 45.

321. Orosius VII 37.5 and 9. Martindale, *Prosopography* 2:934.

322. Zosimus V 26.3. Rosenfeld, *Ost- und Westgoten,* 250 f. Wenskus, *Stammesbildung,* 481; cf. 449 (index of sources). L. Schmidt, *Ostgermanen,* 265–267. Demougeot, *De l'unité,* 354 ff. In general one has inferred from the paganism of Radagaisus and most of his followers that they were Ostrogothic. Maenchen-Helfen, *The Huns,* 60 ff., esp. 61, had expressed his doubts about this, basing himself on *Chronica Gallica* 50–52, a. 405, p. 652. But it does not follow directly from this source that there were Arians among the Radagaisus Goths. Rather, it is stated (ibid. 51) that in consequence of the invasion of Radagaisus the Arians, who had already disappeared from the Roman world, regained strength with support from the barbarian peoples whom they are said to have joined. Schäferdiek, "Germanenmission," 512, calls the Radagaisus group "purely pagan." Schwarcz, *Reichsangehörige,* 188 thinks it possible that Arian retainers of Alaric joined the Radagaisus Goths. In any case, the army of the newcomer was significantly larger than that of Alaric who still suffered from the losses of 402.

323. Among the sources listed by L. Schmidt, *Ostgermanen,* 267 n. 3, see esp. Orosius VII 37.4 f., 8 and 16, as well as St. Augustine, *De civitate Dei* V 23, and *Chronica Gallica* (as n. 322).

324. Maenchen-Helfen and Schäferdiek (as n. 322). On Odotheus see above, n. 107. Cf. Wolfram, "Gotische Studien III," 243 f.

325. L. Schmidt, *Ostgermanen,* 265 n. 2. Demougeot (as n. 322). Rosenfeld, "Ost- und Westgoten," 249–251. Wenskus, *Stammesbildung,* 477 f.

326. For the chronology see Seeck, *Untergang* 5:587.

327. *Codex Theodosianus* X 10.25 (December 10, 408). The location that Zosimus reports, V 26.3 f., is nullified by his mention also of the Rhine (apart from the Danube) as the marshaling zone of the Radagaisus Goths.

328. Cf. L. Schmidt, *Ostgermanen,* 265. Nagy, "Pannonia," 333 f. Egger, *Hermagoras,* 56 with n. 9. (Flavia Solva). Hudeczek, "Flavia Solva," 467 with n. 280, speaks of the "fictive character" of the date for the destruction of the city. According to Alzinger, "Das Municipium Claudium Aguntum," 380–413, esp. 403, Aguntum was destroyed around 406 by a catastrophic fire.

329. Cameron, *Claudian,* 157–188. Zosimus V 26.2–4: Alaric remains quiet because Stilicho has placed him and the "peoples of Illyricum" under contract for his Eastern policy. The arrangement had been made because of Radagaisus. Stilicho is said to have raised 30 *numeri* (at most thirty thousand men; cf. Stein, *Bas-Empire* 1:425 n. 173), for which provincials and slaves were recruited: *Codex Theodosianus* VII 13.16 and 17 (April 17 and 19, 406). On Uldin and Sarus see Lippold, "Uldin," 511 f., and above, n. 295.

330. Isidore, *Historia vel Origo Gothorum,* 13–15, p. 272 f., after Orosius VII 37.8 f.

331. See above, nn. 182 ff. (Gainas and Tribigild).

332. L. Schmidt, *Ostgermanen,* 267, after *Auctarium Havniense* a. 405, p. 299. Schwarcz, *Reichsangehörige,* 187–190.

333. Cf. St. Augustine, *Sermo* CV 10 (sacrificing of the Romans by Radagaisus), with Ammianus Marcellinus XXVIII 5.13 f. (killing of the Romans by the Burgundian *hendinos*-kings. Wolfram (as n. 324). Wenskus, *Stammesbildung,* 576 ff. See chap. 2, n. 490 (Gainas sacrifices the Romans before his return to Transdanubia).

334. Cf. above, n. 109, and chap. 5, nn. 7 ff.

335. Orosius VII 37.16. Zosimus V 26.4. Cf. n. 329 above.

336. See chap. 3, nn. 233, 239 and 244.

337. Zosimus V 26.3: Radagaisus arrives with 400,000 Goths. Ibid. V 35.6: 30,000 Goths join Alaric. Ibid. V 42.3: 40,000 slaves join Alaric. All these figures probably come from Olympiodorus: Paschoud, "Zosimos," 822–824. Olympiodorus fr. 9: 12,000 "optimates" are left over from the army of Radagaisus.

338. Among the inscriptions from Rome celebrating the victory of Stilicho (see Fiebiger-Schmidt, *Inschriftensammlung,* nos. 24 f., p. 25 f.) the first even claims that the Goths had been "wiped out" forever. Cf. Zosimus V 26.5 with 35.6.

339. Orosius VII 43.10 ff. The time of his election follows from two pieces of chronological information: on September 24, 415, the death of Athaulf became known in Constantinople: see *Chronicon paschale* a. 415, p. 72. Athaulf's successor Sigeric could maintain his rule for only one week: see Olympiodorus fr. 26. Martindale, *Prosopography* 2:1147 f. (Valia). Matthews *Aristocracies,* 318 ff. Jones, *The Later Roman Empire* 1:188. Reinhart, *Historia de los Suevos,* 34 ff., as well as Menéndez-Pidal, *Historia de España* 3:59 ff. Courtois, *Les Vandales,* 54, and Miltner, "Vandalen," 308 f., describe the events from the Vandals' perspective.

340. Olympiodorus fr. 29. See chap. 1, n. 71.

341. For Orosius VII 43.11, the distance is "twelve thousand paces." Jordanes, *Getica* 167, p. 102, speaks of the seven-mile-wide strait of Gibraltar. Olympiodorus fr. 31 reports the 600,000 *modii* of grain, which corresponds approximately to the yearly ration of the indicated number of warriors: see Jones, *The Later Roman Empire* 3:39 to n. 65, and 3:191 ff. to n. 44 ff. Rouche, *L'Aquitaine,* 163, would feed over 20,000 federate warriors and their families and followers with this amount. The number of warriors should be multiplied by about a factor of five in order to arrive at the size of the tribe; cf. L. Schmidt, *Ostgermanen,* 50, as well as chap. 4, n. 453. Schwarcz, *Nachrichten,* 21, discusses Gothic groups who joined the Vandals.

342. Orosius VII 43.11. Ibid. 14 recounts an anecdote that reminds one of Theodoric's words to Zeno (as chap. 5, n. 158): see Suerbaum, *Staatsbegriff,* 230 and 275 f. Hydatius 60 ff., aa. 416 ff.

343. See above, n. 290 (Alans). The inferiority of the Vandals to the Goths is a popular theme of both Jordanes, *Getica* 162 ff., pp. 100 ff., as well as Isidore, *Historia vel Origo Gothorum* 68, p. 294. But both authors have an interesting predecessor in Sidonius Apollinaris, *Carmina* II vv. 348–370, p. 182: Valia is a hero "at whose sight the Vandals always turn to flight like cowards." It almost seems as if both Cassiodorus and Isidore knew this passage.

344. Cf. Sidonius Apollinaris (as n. 343).

345. Wolfram, *Intitulatio I,* 79 ff., esp. 85.

346. Hydatius 63, a. 417.

347. Martindale, *Prosopography* 2:1148.

4: The Kingdom of Toulouse

1. *Chronica Caesaraugustana* a. 507, p. 223. Hydatius 69, a. 418. Isidore of Seville, *Historia vel Origo Gothorum* 23, p. 277. Cf. below, n. 273.

2. See chap. 2, nn. 414 and 423.

3. See chap. 3, n. 284.

4. For this phrase see L. White (ed.), *The Transformation of the Roman World.* According to *Novellae Valentiniani* 6.3, p. 89 (499 VII 14), the late Roman imperial government spent each year 30 solidi for one recruit. An army of 30,000 soldiers would thus have cost at least 900,000 solidi, a sum that according to Stein, *Bas-Empire* 1:383, would have used up nearly the entire yearly budget of the Western Roman Empire in the middle of the fifth century.

5. Hydatius 69, a. 418. Prosper, *Epitoma chronicon* 1271, a. 419, p. 469.

6. Philostorgius XII 4; cf. Wolfram, "Ansiedlung," 31 ff. See below, nn. 420 ff.; cf. chap. 5, nn. 240 ff.

7. Salvianus of Marseille, *De gubernatione Dei* VII 8, p. 85.

8. Matthews, *Aristocracies,* 334. Stein, *Bas-Empire* 1:270 f., esp. after *Epistolae Arelatenses* 8, pp. 13–15. The sending of delegates was not limited to the provinces; representatives of the *civitates* were also invited, and even senatorial nobles (on this see Stroheker, *Adel,* 40 with n. 176).

9. See Prosper, *Epitoma chronicon* 1271, a. 419, p. 469. Matthews, *Aristocracies,* 336. Courcelle, *Histoire littéraire,* 143 ff. See the picture that Sidonius Apollinaris, *Carmina* VII vv. 210–215, p. 208, paints of Constantius, for which one should consult Loyen, *Recherches historiques,* 37.

10. This is how even Ensslin, "Vallia," 285, explains the withdrawal of the Goths; cf. L. Schmidt, *Ostgermanen,* 461, and Courcelle, *Histoire littéraire,* 143 n. 1.

11. Jones, *The Later Roman Empire* 1:189 f. Matthews, *Aristocracies,* 332. Stroheker, *Germanentum,* 74 ff.

12. Ewig, "Probleme," 52 f. Demougeot, "Modalités d'établissement," 148 ff. Thompson, "Settlement of the Barbarians," 69.

13. Reinhart, *Historia de los Suevos,* 36–54. Stroheker, *Germanentum,* 97.

14. Sidonius Apollinaris, *Epistulae* VIII 6.13–16, p. 132 f. This letter is addressed to Namatius, the Visigothic "admiral." On Namatius see Stroheker, *Adel,* 194 n. 253. Sidonius reveals that the recipient of the letter performed his "half-military, half-maritime" tasks without direct support from the Visigoths. Cf. Courcelle, *Histoire littéraire,* 236 with n. 1, as well as L. Schmidt, *Ostgermanen,* 494 and 518. On the unseaworthiness of the later Goths see Maenchen-Helfen, *The Huns,* 75.

15. See chap. 3, n. 290.

16. Matthews, *Aristocracies,* 336 ff. Thompson, "Settlement of the Barbarians," 69 ff. Stroheker, *Adel,* 50. Loyen, *Recherches historiques,* 65 f.

17. Cf. Wolfram, "Ansiedlung," 5 ff., and Goffart, *Barbarians and Romans,* esp. 95 ff., with Jones, *The Later Roman Empire* 1:249 ff. and 3:45ff. to nn. 26 ff. On Theoderid see Martindale, *Prosopography* 2:1070 f. (Theodoricus 2).

18. For these expressions see the later *Leges Visigothorum* VIII 5.5, p. 347; cf. *Codex Euricianus* (CE), chap. 276.3 and 5, as well as below, n. 59. On the "burden" of the term *hospes* see Courcelle, *Histoire littéraire,* 144 with n. 2, as well as Goffart, *Barbarians and Romans,* 165 ff.

19. If one compares Prosper, *Epitoma chronicon* 1259, a. 416, with 1271, a. 419, p. 468 f., and with this Orosius VII 43.12, treaties were concluded in 416 as well as 418, since Orosius finished his work in 417 (Wattenbach-Levison-Löwe, *Geschichtsquellen,* 82 f.). On the giving of hostages by the Romans in 418 see Loyen, *Recherches historiques,* 39 ff., after Sidonius Apollinaris, *Carmina* VII vv. 214 ff., p. 208 f.

20. Olympiodorus fr. 35. Cf. chap. 3, n. 156.

21. Hydatius 77, a. 421.

22. Cf. Olympiodorus frs. 34 and 41. Stein, *Bas-Empire* 1:274 f.

23. On the role of Arles in the first half of the fifth century: Matthews, *Aristocracies,* 334 ff. Brühl, *Palatium* 1:234 ff. Ewig, "Résidence," 28. On the economic significance of Arles, Narbonne, and Marseille, see Vercauteren, *Civitates,* 440.

24. See n. 23 and below, nn. 34 and 77. On the relatively small size of Narbonne see Büttner, "Frühmittelalterliches Städtewesen." 153.

25. See below, nn. 35 ff.

26. Prosper, *Epitoma chronicon* 1290, a. 425, p. 471. Loyen, *Recherches historiques,* 40 f. Martindale, *Prosopography* 2:21–29 (Fl. Aëtius 7).

27. Dahlheim, "Aetius," 1:91 f. Demandt, "Magister militum," 654–667.

28. See chap. 3, n. 280.

29. Possidius, *Vita s. Augustini,* chap. 28.4, mentions that Goths also came to Africa with the Vandals and Alans, but these Goths must have been a group that had split off from the main tribe in 415. L. Schmidt, *Ostgermanen,* 465 n. 3. Martindale, *Prosopography* 2:237–240 (Bonifatius 3). Schwarcz, *Nachrichten,* 21. Prosper, *Epitoma chronicon* 1294, a. 427, p. 471 f.

30. Hydatius 92 f., a. 430, as well as 95, a. 431. Loyen, *Recherches historiques,* 41 f.

31. Hydatius 97, a. 431.

32. Olympiodorus fr. 40. *Chronica Gallica* 111–113, aa. 432 f., p. 658. Demandt, "Magister militum," 656 f. Maenchen-Helfen, *The Huns,* 91; cf. 77. Oost, *Galla Placidia,* 142.

33. Prosper, *Epitoma chronicon* 1322–1326, aa. 435 ff., p. 475. *Chronica Gallica* 117–119, aa. 435 ff., p. 660. Hydatius 107 and 112, aa. 436 and 438. Loyen, *Recherches historiques,* 44 ff. Perrin, *Les Burgondes,* 263 ff. On the quote after Merobaudes, *Carmina: Panegyricus* I fr. II B v. 18, p. 10: *rei publicae venena,* see Rouche, *L'Aquitaine,* 32.

34. Rouche, *L'Aquitaine,* 31 f., after Sidonius Apollinaris, *Carmina* VII vv. 300 f., p. 210. Prosper, *Epitoma chronicon* 1324, p. 475. Martindale, *Prosopography* 2:684 f.

35. Prosper, *Epitoma chronicon* 1326, 1333, and 1335, p. 475 f.

36. See chap. 3, n. 248.

37. Prosper, *Epitoma chronicon* 1335, p. 476. Hydatius 116, a. 439.

38. Salvianus of Marseille, *De gubernatione Dei* VII 39, p. 90 f. Cf. nn. 37 and 39, as well as Demandt, "Magister militum," 666 f., and Lotter, "Zwangsbekehrung," 315 ff.

39. *Vita Orientii,* chaps. 3 and 5, p. 61f. Courcelle, *Histoire littéraire,* 98–100, 145 f. and 347 with n. 1; cf. 420 (index of sources). Rouche, *L'Aquitaine,* 31.

40. This differentiation is already indicated in Salvian (as n. 38), and it is

terminologically supported by Sidonius Apollinaris, who calls the Huns Scythians and the Goths Getae: cf., for example, *Carmina* VII vv. 246 f., p. 209. See Loyen, *Recherches historiques,* 45.

41. Prosper, *Epitoma chronicon* 1337, a. 439, p. 477. See chap. 5, n. 66 f.

42. Sidonius Apollinaris, *Carmina* VII vv. 295 ff., p. 210, as well as V vv. 126 ff., p. 191. Loyen, *Recherches historiques,* 47 ff. and 67 with n. 1, supported most recently by Demandt, "Militäradel," 621 with n. 57, thinks that Aëtius married another daughter of Theoderid in 439 in order to strengthen the peace treaty. But according to Martindale, *Prosopography* 2:21 and 856 f. n. 1, Aëtius did not marry a third time after his marriage to Pelagia, the widow of Bonifatius, in or after 432. Schwarcz, *Nachrichten,* 21, considers Pelagia a Goth (Visigoth), so that consequently the "royal-heroic" descent (as above, chap. 1 with n. 102) of Aëtius's wife would have to refer to her. On Avitus see Martindale, *Prosopography* 2:197 f. Rouche, *L'Aquitaine,* 3: it is possible that the Goths received Novempopulana at that time; however, this does not follow from the quotes that Rouche lists; cf. the map ibid. 25.

43. Prosper, *Epitoma chronicon* 1348, a. 442, p. 479. Jordanes, *Getica* 184, p. 106. Schwarcz, *Nachrichten,* 21. Miltner, "Vandalen," 320 f. Diesner, "Vandalen," 957 f. See chap. 3, nn. 343–345, as well as above, n. 29: Gothic-Vandal hostilities.

44. Hydatius 129 and 132, aa. 444 and 445, and 144, a. 450. Cf. Demandt, "Magister militum," 657. Martindale, *Prosopography* 2:983 f. (Sebastianus 3).

45. Hydatius 134, a. 446.

46. Ibid., 137, 140, 142, aa. 448 f.

47. Jordanes, *Getica* 204, p. 110.

48. Ibid. 185 ff., p. 106 f. Priscus fr. 15. Miltner, "Vandalen," 321. Prosper, *Epitoma chronicon* 1364, a. 451, p. 481. A short survey of the sources is offered by L. Schmidt, *Ostgermanen,* 471 f. Clover, "Geiseric and Attila," 104 ff.

49. Jordanes, *Getica* 191 ff., pp. 107 ff., esp. 194 f., p. 108; 197, p. 109; 205, p. 110; 210, p. 111. Zöllner, *Franken,* 30 f., esp. 31 with n. 1. On Aëtius cf. above, n. 26 f.

50. Sidonius Apollinaris, *Carmina* VII vv. 316 ff., p. 211 f. Loyen, *Recherches historiques,* 50–52.

51. Jordanes, *Getica* 190, p. 107.

52. Ibid., 192, p. 108. Maenchen-Helfen, *The Huns,* 131 n. 620.

53. *Auctarium Havniense* a. 451, p. 302. Jordanes, *Getica* 115 f., p. 87 f. Fredegar, *Chronicon* II 53, p. 74, emphasizes and greatly embellishes the see-saw policy of Aëtius.

54. Jordanes, *Getica* 209, p. 111; 211–219, p. 112–114.

55. Ibid., 199 f., p. 109 f.; 217, p. 113. See also Fredegar (as n. 53).

56. Jordanes, *Getica* 199 f., p. 109; 209, p. 111. On Andagis see Wagner, *Getica,* 6 f. and 29 f., and Martindale, *Prosopography* 2:86.

57. Jordanes, *Getica* 284, p. 131.

58. Ibid., 190, p. 107.

59. *Auctarium Havniense* aa. 451 and 453, p. 302. *Chronica Gallica* 621, p. 663. Gregory of Tours, *Historia Francorum* II 7, pp. 48–50. Fredegar, *Chronicon* II 53, p. 74 f., and IV 73, p. 157; contrary to what is stated here, however, Aëtius

could not have been the giver of the keys. Sidonius Apollinaris, *Epistulae* VII 12.3, p. 118 f., who calls Thorismund *Rhodanus hospes*. Cf. Stein, *Bas-Empire* 1:336 f. But to reach the Rhone had already been the stated goal of his father, Theoderid: see Sidonius Apollinaris, *Carmina* VII vv. 300 f., p. 210. In general see Rouche, *L'Aquitaine*, 32 f. nn. 126 and 136. Rouche, however, has Aëtius die in 453; cf. Martindale, *Prosopography* 2:29. On Thorismund see ibid. 1115 f. (Thorismodus).

60. Zöllner, *Franken*, 39.

61. Loyen, "Les débuts," 413 ff. Rouche, *L'Aquitaine*, 32 f. Martindale, *Prosopography* 2:1071–1073 (Theodericus 3).

62. Hydatius 158, a. 454. On Frideric, who is once even called a Gothic king and who then again acts like a commander of Gaul, see Demandt, "Magister militum," 690, and L. Schmidt, *Ostgermanen*, 479 with nn. 2 and 5. Martindale, *Prosopography* 2:484 (Fredericus 1).

63. Demandt, "Magister militum," 681 f.

64. Sidonius Apollinaris, *Carmina* VII vv. 391–519, pp. 213–216. Loyen, *Recherches historiques*, 53 ff., cf. 35 ff. The detailed Sidonius passage attests that Frideric had vice-royal rank. On the entrance into Toulouse see Sidonius Apollinaris, *Carmina* VII vv. 435 f., p. 214.

65. Sidonius Apollinaris, *Carmina* VII vv. 519 ff., p. 216. Loyen, *Recherches historiques*, 55 ff. On Theodoric's suggestion to Avitus see vv. 441 ff. and 508 ff. See Hydatius 163, a. 455, who describes the Avitus elevation in an interesting abbreviation (cf. below, n. 99). Marius of Avenches, *Chronica* a. 455, p. 232, Ioannis Antiochenus fr. 202. Isidore, *Historia vel Origo Gothorum* 31, p. 279. Rouche, *L'Aquitaine*, 29, f. The interpretation I have offered in the text does not clash with the notion that the Aquitanians were holding on to an illusion if they believed that in the long run they could use the Visigoths for their own purposes.

66. Loyen, *Recherches historiques*, 55 ff. Stroheker, *Adel*, 152 ff. n. 58. On Valia cf. chap. 3, nn. 339 ff. Hydatius 183, a. 457: *Avitus tertio anno, posteaquam a Gallis et a Gothis factus fuerat imperator, caret imperio Gothorum promisso destitutus auxilio, caret et vita.*

67. Schäferdiek, *Die Kirchen der Westgoten*, 106 ff. Reinhart, *Historia de los Suevos*, 46 ff., esp. after Hydatius 169 ff., esp. 175 and 178, a. 456—the quote *cum voluntate et ordinatione Aviti imperatoris* can be found ibid. 173, a. 455, as well as Jordanes, *Getica* 229 ff., pp. 116 ff. On Gundiok see above, chap. 1, nn. 114–118. On Ag(r)iwulf see Claude, "Prosopographie," 654 n. 3, and Martindale, *Prosopography* 2:39 f. (Aioulfus).

68. Hydatius 168, a. 457. Cf. 201, a. 460.

69. Ibid., 187, a. 457.

70. Ibid., 213, a. 461; cf. 230, a. 465. Demandt, "Magister militum," 683 f. Claude, "Prosopographie," 667 n. 68.

71. Loyen, *Recherches historiques*, 59 ff., esp. 74 ff., on Sidonius Apollinaris, *Carmina* V vv. 510 ff., pp. 200 ff. On Majorian see Martindale, *Prosopography* 2:702 f.

72. Demandt, "Magister militum," 691 ff. Zöllner, *Franken*, 39 ff. Lippold, "Chlodovechus," 143. Stroheker, *Adel*, 141 f. n. 1. On Aegidius see Martindale, *Prosopography* 1:11–13, and on Childeric ibid. 285 f.

73. Demandt, "Magister militum," 689.

74. Priscus fr. 27. Hydatius 197, a. 459. Paulinus of Périgueux, *De vita Martini* VI, 111 ff., p. 143; Gregory of Tours, *De virtutibus s. Martini* I 2, p. 587. Brühl, *Palatium,* 236 with n. 16.

75. Paulinus and Gregory (as n. 74). Courcelle, *Histoire littéraire,* 173 and 239.

76. Hydatius 192, 200 f., and 209 f., aa. 458, 460, and 461. Priscus fr. 27. Ioannis Antiochenus fr. 203. Sidonius (as n. 71). Miltner, "Vandalen," 324 f.

77. Demandt, "Magister militum," 673 ff., 689 ff. Among the sources see esp. Hydatius 217, 218, 224, and 228, aa. 461 and 465. *Epistolae Arelatenses* 15, p. 22 f. *Chronica Gallica* 638, p. 664. Cf. Schäferdiek, *Die Kirchen der Westgoten,* 11 f. Zöllner, *Franken,* 39. Martindale, *Prosopography* 2:942–945 (Fl. Ricimer 2).

78. Hydatius 220, 223, 226, 230–232; aa. 461, 465, and 466. Cf. below, n. 247 as well as Claude, "Prosopographie," 655 n. 5 (Aiax).

79. Hydatius 237 f., a. 467. Marius of Avenches, *Chronica* a. 467, p. 233. *Chronica Gallica* 643, p. 664. *Chronica Caesaraugustana* a. 466, p. 222. Jordanes, *Getica* 235, p. 118. Martindale, *Prosopography* 2:427 f.

80. Rouche, *L'Aquitaine,* 27 ff. and 161 ff.

81. Stroheker, *Eurich,* 9 and 89. Claude, *Westgoten,* 33.

82. See chap. 3, n. 1.

83. Loyen, *Recherches historiques,* 94. See above, nn. 62, 67, and 77.

84. We may recall Arborius, his predecessor Nepotianus, possibly also Cyrila (cf. Schönfeld, *Wörterbuch,* 68) under King Theodoric: see Hydatius, 192, 197, 201, 213; aa. 458, 459, 461. Better known and more certain than these Roman-Gothic officers, whose unclear position (cf. Hydatius 271, a. 461, on Agrippinus) stems from the policy introduced by Avitus and Theodoric (cf. Hydatius 170 and 173, a. 455), are the two *duces* Vincentius and Victorius under Euric: see Claude, *Adel, Kirche und Königtum,* 43. Schäferdiek, *Die Kirchen der Westgoten,* 25. Stroheker, *Eurich,* 20 and 29.

85. Wolfram, *Intitulatio I,* 43, after Procopius, *De bello Gothico* III (VII) 4.10 ff.

86. Jordanes, *Getica* 237, p. 118.

87. See above, n. 77.

88. Hydatius 238 and 240, a. 467.

89. Stroheker, *Eurich,* 9 ff. Claude, *Westgoten,* 31 f.

90. Hydatius 240, a. 467.

91. Sidonius Apollinaris, *Epistulae* VI 6.1; p. 98, and VII 6.4, p. 109. Stroheker, *Eurich,* 11 f. n. 26.

92. Ibid., 11 n. 25.

93. Ibid., 19 ff. Loyen, *Recherches historiques,* 85 ff. Martindale, *Prosopography* 2:96–98 (Anthemius 3).

94. Stroheker, *Eurich,* 28 with n. 83. Loyen, *Recherches historiques,* 88. See the insulting name *Graecus imperator* which was supposedly given to him by Arvandus: Sidonius Apollinaris, *Epistulae* I 7.5, p. 11. Cf. Procopius, *De bello Gothico* I (V) 18.40 and 29.11. Procopius, *Anecdota* 24.7, attests the word "Greek" as a term of abuse for "weaklings" and "cowards."

95. Stroheker, *Eurich,* 19 ff. and 28 ff. Stroheker, *Adel,* 221 n. 370. Zöllner, *Franken,* 39 ff. Demandt, "Magister militum," 691 f. Wolfram, *Intitulatio I,* 44. Stein, *Bas-Empire* 1:389. On the battles of Anthemius against the Pannonian Ostrogoths see chap. 5, n. 117.

96. Stroheker, *Germanentum,* 76, esp. after Hydatius 246 and 251, a. 469.

97. Stein, *Bas-Empire* 1:389 ff. Miltner, "Vandalen," 327 ff. Courtois, *Les Vandales,* 200 ff.

98. Hydatius 245 f., a. 469.

99. Sidonius Apollinaris (as n. 94). Stroheker, *Adel,* 80 and 148 n. 37. When Hydatius 163, a. 455, has Avitus proclaimed emperor *ab exercitu Gallicano et ab honoratis primum Tolosa, dehinc apud Arelatum,* this shortening of the events (cf. above, n. 65) should be understood entirely in the spirit of the Arvandus suggestion.

100. Cf. Sidonius Apollinaris, *Epistulae* VIII 9.5 vv. 42–44, p. 137, with *Carmina* II v. 378, and V vv. 238–253, p. 193 f. Loyen, *Recherches historiques,* 94, and Courcelle, *Histoire littéraire,* 238. But I do not find the depiction of the Frankish warriors as positive as Courcelle does.

101. Sidonius Apollinaris, *Epistulae* III 9, p. 46.

102. Jordanes, *Getica* 237 f., p. 118. Gregory of Tours, *Historia Francorum* II 18, p. 65. Stroheker, *Eurich,* 31 with n. 94.

103. Zöllner, *Franken,* 39.

104. Schäferdiek, *Die Kirchen der Westgoten,* 13 f.

105. Zöllner, *Franken,* 39.

106. Stein, *Bas-Empire* 1:393 f.

107. *Chronica Gallica* 649, p. 664.

108. Stein, *Bas-Empire* 1:394.

109. Stroheker, *Eurich,* 34 f., esp. after Sidonius Apollinaris, *Epistulae* VI 12.5, p. 101 f.

110. Stroheker, *Eurich,* 64–82. Stroheker, *Adel,* 81 ff.

111. Sidonius Apollinaris, *Epistulae* III 3.2 f., p. 41. Stroheker, *Eurich,* 64 with n. 11. *Scriptores historiae Augustae* 18 (Alex. Severus) 60.6, has a female druid prophesy *Gallico sermone.* On the dating of the SHA to around 400 see chap. 1, n. 49.

112. Sidonius Apollinaris, *Epistulae* VII 7.1 f., p. 110 picks up the old notion of a kinship between the Romans and the Auvergnians that was first developed by Lucanus, *Pharsalia* I v. 427.

113. Stroheker, *Eurich,* 65 with n. 17, after Caesar, *De bello Gallico* VI 13.1 f.

114. Sidonius Apollinaris, *Epistulae* III 2.2.1 f., p. 40. Stroheker, *Eurich,* 72 f.

115. Sidonius Apollinaris, *Epistulae* III 3.3 ff., p. 41 f. Stroheker, *Eurich,* 69 f. Demandt, "Magister militum," 680. See Martindale, *Prosopography* 2:383 f. (Ecdicius 3).

116. Sidonius Apollinaris, *Epistulae* III 4.1, p. 43; 8.2, p. 45. Stroheker, *Eurich,* 73 f. and 76.

117. Sidonius Apollinaris was related to the *dux* Victorius: see below, n. 140.

118. Sidonius Apollinaris, *Epistulae* II 1.4, p. 22: the complete impotence of the empire and of the emperor Anthemius was forcing the Auvergnian nobility "to lose either their homeland or their locks."

119. Stroheker, *Eurich,* 79 f. Sidonius Apollinaris, *Epistulae* VII 7.1 ff., p. 110 f. Cf., however, the slightly changed chronology of events in Loyen, *Sidoine Apollinaire* 2:xx.

120. Sidonius Apollinaris, *Epistulae* III 2.4 f., p. 40.

121. Stroheker, *Germanentum,* 76, and *Eurich,* 22 ff. and 25 ff., after Hydatius 245 f. and 251, a. 469 (as n. 96). Rouche, *L'Aquitaine,* 35 ff. The quote comes

from the title of the chapter.

122. Stroheker, *Eurich,* 69 f.

123. Ibid., 70 ff., esp. after *Chronica Gallica* 651 f., and Isidore, *Historia vel Origo Gothorum* 34, p. 281. Martindale, *Prosopography* 2:1168 (Vincentius 3).

124. Sidonius Apollinaris, *Epistulae* III 1.5, p. 40, and VII 1.1, p. 102. Cf. the Arvandus suggestion ibid. I 7.5, p. 11, and above, n. 59.

125. Loyen, *Sidoine Apollinaire* 2:xv ff.

126. *Chronica Caesaraugustana* a. 473, p. 222. *Chronica Gallica* 653, p. 665, cannot be combined with it. Cf. below, n. 144 and n. 153: the end of Vincentius, as well as n. 152: the capture of Arles in 476/477.

127. *Notitia Galliarum* 12, p. 270.

128. Martindale, *Prosopography* 2:1162–1164 (Victorius 4). Ensslin, "Victorius," 2086 n. 5. Victorius was surely not brought down because of his conflict with Euric; cf. below, n. 140. On the date of his appointment see Gregory of Tours, *Historia Francorum* II 20, pp. 65–67. The chronology given there is obviously wrong if one adds up the dates given. But if one counts backward, then it would have been four years before the death of Euric, i.e., in about 480, that Victorius was driven out of Clermont, where he had been in office for nine years, which means he had been appointed in about 471. Cf. Stroheker, *Adel,* 86 f. and 146 n. 22, according to whom Apollinaris, the son of Sidonius Apollinaris, "went to Italy with the Visigothic *dux* Victorius around 479." See below, n. 140.

129. Stroheker, *Eurich,* 68–70. Loyen, *Sidoine Apollinaire* 2:xviii-xx. Cf. Sidonius Apollinaris, *Epistulae* III 2.1 ff., p. 40 f. A Roman in Visigothic services was the *dux* Salla (Stroheker, *Germanentum,* 125 n. 3) who is already attested in 466 as an envoy of Theodoric: Vives, *Inscripciones cristianas,* n. 363. Vives, "Inschrift," 57 ff. But while Salla was active in Spain, Calminius, perhaps an ancestor of the sixth century Aquitanian *dux* of same name (Stroheker, *Adel,* 159 n. 81) was fighting against his own countrymen, even if he supposedly did so reluctantly: see Sidonius Apollinaris, *Epistulae* V 12, p. 86.

130. Stroheker, *Eurich,* 35, and *Adel,* 148 n. 37 and 215 n. 352. Cf. Schäferdiek, *Die Kirchen der Westgoten,* 25, and Stein, *Bas-Empire* 1:392 with n. 163, as well as Ensslin (as n. 128). See finally the hidden reproach for Agrippinus right after the well-known praise of Theodoric in Sidonius Apollinaris, *Carmina* XXIII vv. 69 ff., p. 251 f. Sidonius also made a clear distinction between Arvandus (cf. *Epistulae* I 7.1 ff., pp. 10–13) and Seronatus, whom he hated: ibid. II 1.1 ff., p. 21 f.; V 13.1 ff., p. 86 f., and VII 7.2, p. 111.

131. See below, n. 140. The harshness of the conflict—even during the winter—is reported by Sidonius Apollinaris, *Epistulae* III 1.4, and III 2.3, p. 40.

132. See above, n. 128.

133. Ennodius, *Vita Epifani* 79–91, p. 94 f. Cf. the somewhat different account of Loyen, *Sidoine Apollinaire* 2:xx. Stroheker, *Adel,* 165 n. 110. Stroheker, *Eurich,* 80 ff. Rouche, *L'Aquitaine,* 41–43. On Ecdicius see Jordanes, *Getica* 241, p. 120. Cf. Procopius (as below, n. 154).

134. Sidonius Apollinaris, *Epistulae* VII 17.1, p. 123. On the description of Victorius as both *dux* and *comes* see below, n. 379.

135. *Notitia Galliarum* (as n. 127). Cf. Claude, *Bourges and Poitiers,* 49 with n. 413.

136. Stroheker, *Adel,* 218 n. 358.

137. Sidonius Apollinaris, *Epistulae* VIII 3.1, p. 127.

138. Ibid., 1 f. Cf. ibid. II 2.10 and 9.8, pp. 24 and 32.

139. Ibid., VII 17.1 ff., p. 123 f.

140. Stroheker, *Adel,* 86 f. On the *dux*'s namesake who died in 469 see Loyen, *L'esprit précieux,* 70 f. For Sidonius's son Apollinaris see Stroheker, 146 n. 22, and Martindale, *Prosopography* 2:114 (Apollinaris 3). Cf. in general Stroheker, *Eurich,* 50, 59, 62 f., 81, 113 f.

141. Stroheker, *Adel,* 168 n. 121. Cf. Sidonius Apollinaris, *Epistulae* III 8.1 f., p. 45, with VII 9.18, p. 116. On Bourges see above, n. 127 and 135 as well as Schäferdiek, *Die Kirchen der Westgoten,* 21 ff. For the suggestion that the inner conflicts in Auvergne could date back to the time of Iovinus see Matthews, *Aristocracies,* 315. Lotter, "Lauriacum-Lorch," 40 f., rightly sees in Odovacar's Rugian war of 487/488 a conflict not only between barbarians but also between Romans: cf. *Consularia Italica* a. 487, p. 312 f.

142. Victorius (as nn. 128 and 140).

143. Salla (as n. 129).

144. *Chronica Gallica* 653, p. 665, has Vincentius fight and die for Euric in Italy. The dating of these events causes the greatest difficulties. Loyen, *Sidoine Apollinaire* 2:xvi with n. 1, places the report under the year 473, which has much to recommend it. But we would have to advance the date from 473 to at least 474, since in 473 Vincentius was still fighting in Spain. Cf. above, n. 123. But in that case the Visigothic advance into Italy and the fall of Arles and Marseille in 473 (as n. 126) could not be connected for chronological reasons. Thus, nothing stands in the way of detaching the event from its context and linking it to the Visigothic-Italian tensions following Odovacar's takeover, as was suggested by L. Schmidt, *Ostgermanen,* 328 and 493. Ensslin, "Vincentius," 2189 n. 8. Martindale, *Prosopography* 2:114 (Apollinaris 3).

145. Jordanes, *Getica* 283 f.; cf. 199, 252 f., 268, 270, and 278, pp. 131, 169, 123, 127 f. and 130. Jordanes, *Romana* 347, p. 45, calls Thiudimir and Vidimir *utrique reges.* Cf. Claude, "Königserhebungen," 153. See Martindale, *Prosopography* 2:1164 f. (Vidimir 1 and 2), and below 334 n. 61. Cf. Claude, "Königserhebungen," 153, on the institutional position of Vidimir.

146. Jordanes, *Romana* 347, p. 45. See esp.: *Vidimer (sc. filius) ab Italis proeliis victus ad partes Galliae Spaniaeque omissa Italia tendit,* and *Getica* 284, p. 131. Wenskus, *Stammesbildung,* 481.

147. Stroheker, *Eurich,* 74 with n. 57, on the question of whether Vidimir could have formed "a counterweight against the Visigoths in Gaul." Cf. chap. 5, n. 63 ff.

148. Cf. Sidonius Apollinaris, *Epistulae* VIII 9.5 vv. 36 f., p. 137.

149. On the Amal names see below, n. 530.

150. Jordanes (as n. 146). Ruricius of Limoges, *Epistulae* II 60 (61) and 62 (63), p. 349 (439 f.). Martindale, *Prosopography* 2:1165 and 1178. On Ruricius see Stroheker, *Adel,* 209 f. n. 327, as well as Schäferdiek, *Die Kirchen der Westgoten,* 57.

151. Cf. Jordanes, *Getica* 277, p. 130, and Priscus fr. 8, against Maenchen-Helfen, *The Huns,* 388. In Priscus fr. 8 we also find the father and father-in-law (Romulus) of Orestes. Cf. Lotter, *Severinus,* 200 and 248 f., as well as chap. 5, n. 120 and n. 128. Martindale, *Prosopography* 2, 811 f. (Orestes 2) and ibid., 791–793 (Odovacar).

152. Stroheker, *Eurich*, 83 ff. Loyen, *Sidoine Apollinaire* 2, XVI and XXI. Stein, *Bas-Empire* 2:152. As Wolfgang Hahn has kindly informed me, solidi coins minted in Arles (AR) are known from the emperors Julius Nepos and Romulus Augustulus, which means that aside from a temporary occupation (see n. 126) the Visigoths probably captured the city only after the end of the Western empire: Ulrich-Bansa, *Moneta Mediolanensis*, pl. O/m and n. as well as p. 322 n. Cohen, *Description* 8:239 no. 6 and 8:243 no. 6. See Jordanes, *Getica* 244, p. 120 f. *Auctarium Havniense* a. 476, p. 309. *Chronica Gallica* 657, cf. 653, p. 665.

153. L. Schmidt, *Ostgermanen*, 493: see above, nn. 144 and 151. On Alla and Sindila see Martindale, *Prosopography* 2:60 f. and 1016.

154. On Euric's acquisition of *totae Spaniae Galliaeque* see Jordanes, *Getica* 244, p. 121. Procopius, *De bello Gothico* I (V) 12.20, reveals that the emperor did *not* consent to these arrangements. Odovacar is here called a usurper. Cf., in contrast, Stroheker, *Eurich*, 85 f. There is also no evidence that the Senate gave its consent.

155. Ibid., 88 f. with n. 2. Schäferdiek, *Die Kirchen der Westgoten*, 243 ff.: the list of signatories at the Council of Agde. Fiebiger-Schmidt, *Inschriftensammlung*, 120 f. n. 249.

156. *Chronica Caesaraugustana* aa. 494 and 497, p. 222, mentions the first Gothic settlement in the Iberian peninsula. Claude, *Westgoten*, 59.

157. Stroheker, *Eurich*, 89 with n. 4.

158. Cf. chap. 3, n. 284.

159. Sidonius Apollinaris, *Epistulae* VIII 9.5 vv. 1 ff., p. 136 f. (panegyric for Euric). Wolfram, *Intitulatio I*, 267 s.v.

160. Cf. Sidonius Apollinaris, *Epistulae* VIII 3.3, p. 128. On the topos *arma et leges* we find there, see Fichtenau, *Arenga*, 26 ff. Wolfram, *Splendor Imperii* 114.

161. Sidonius Apollinaris, *Epistulae* IX 3.2, p. 151. Courcelle, *Histoire littéraire*, 237 f.

162. Sidonius Apollinaris, *Epistulae* VIII 3.3, p. 128; VIII 8.5 vv. 28–33, p. 136. Zöllner, *Franken*, 41 f. Stroheker, *Eurich*, 86. On the dating of the two letters see Loyen, *Sidoine Apollinaire* 3:216 n. 3 and 3:217 n. 3. L. Schmidt, *Ostgermanen*, 494 with n. 4, still dates both to "about 478." Claude, "Politik Theoderichs," 34 n. 108, revises for good reasons the widespread notion that there was a kingdom of Rhenish Thuringians separate from the kingdom in central Germany.

163. See above, n. 67 (Agriwulf).

164. Cassiodorus, *Variae* III 3.3, p. 80.

165. Sidonius Apollinaris, *Epistulae* VIII 6.13 ff., p. 132 f. On the dating of the letters see Loyen, *Sidoine Apollinaire* 3:216 n. 6. The date he suggests, 466, is convincing.

166. *Auctarium Havniense* a. 486, p. 313: *Euricus rex Gothorum penes Arelas urbem, quam ipse ceperat, moritur locoque eius Alaricus filius eius confirmatur V Kal. Ian. - Chronica Gallica* 666, p. 665: *Mortuus est Euricus Arelate et ordinatur filius suus Alaricus Tolosa.* On the other reports see n. 167.

167. L. Schmidt, *Ostgermanen*, 495–497. Stroheker, *Eurich*, 128 with n. 176.

168. As n. 166 and Claude, *Westgoten*, 34, after Cassiodorus, *Variae* III 2.2, and 4.2, p. 79 f. (Theodoric to Clovis about Alaric): *ambo aetate florentes.* From Sidonius Apollinaris, *Epistulae* IV 8.5 vv. 7 f., p. 60, from the year 466/467, it follows that at the time the letter was written Euric's wife Ragnahild had already

given birth to Alaric II but that he must have still been a small child. Martindale, *Prosopography* 2:288–290 (Chlodovechus).

169. Ennodius, *Vita Epifani* 80, p. 94.

170. Isidore, *Historia vel Origo Gothorum* 36, p. 281 f. Cf. Schäferdiek, *Die Kirchen der Westgoten,* 32, against, for example, L. Schmidt, *Ostgermanen,* 497, or Dahn, *Könige der Germanen,* 5, 102. Zöllner, *Franken,* 48 with n. 3. Düwel, "Alaric II," 128 f. The negative judgment on Alaric II hardly gains credibility just because to this day it has been passed from one author to the next. See Messmer, *Hispania-Idee,* 66 ff., esp. on Gregory of Tours, and Martindale, *Prosopography* 2:49 (Alaricus 3).

171. L. Schmidt (as n. 170). On Syagrius see Martindale, *Prosopography* 2:1041 f.

172. Zöllner, *Franken,* 48–51.

173. Anonymus Valesianus II 11.53 and 12.63. Cf. Stein, *Bas-Empire* 2:56 with n. 5. Zöllner, *Franken,* 54 with n. 2.

174. As above, n. 156. Claude, *Westgoten,* 35 and 59. See Reinhart and Schäferdiek (as n. 176).

175. *Auctarium Havniense* aa. 496 and 498, p. 331. Claude, *Westgoten,* 34. Zöllner, *Franken,* 54 and 64.

176. *Chronica Caesaraugustana* aa. 496, 497, and 506, p. 222. Claude, *Westgoten,* 35 and 59. Schäferdiek, *Die Kirchen der Westgoten,* 68 with n. 2, after Reinhart, "Asentamiento," 124 ff. Menéndez Pidal, *Historia de España* 3:82 f. Cf. below, n. 529.

177. See above, n. 16.

178. Cf. Zöllner, *Franken,* 54.

179. Ibid., 60 with n. 2 f. On the question of the alleged loss of Tours in 496/498 to the Franks and the supposed baptismal promise of Clovis in Tours in 498 see Lippold, "Chlodovechus," 155 f. Cf. Zöllner, "Review of Weiss," 173–177. Cassiodorus, *Variae* III 1.1, p. 78 (military weakness of the Visigoths; a statement as introduction-*prooemium*). See below, n. 412 on the increase of revenues by debasing the coinage.

180. Zöllner, *Franken,* 64 f., esp. after Marius of Avenches, *Chronicon* a. 500, p. 234, and Gregory of Tours, *Historia Francorum* II 32 f., pp. 78–81.

181. See chap. 2, n. 190. Claude, *Westgoten,* 34. Uwe Eckhardt, "Untersuchungen," 75 with n. 192. Lippold, "Chlodovechus," 160 f.

182. Cassiodorus, *Variae* III 1–4, pp. 78–81. See above, n. 162.

183. Ibid., III 1.3, p. 78 (Theodoric to Alaric II), according to which neither the death of *parentes* nor the loss of Visigothic territory had to be mourned, which is why the letter should be dated to the time before the beginning of the Frankish invasion.

184. Ibid., III 4.5, p. 81.

185. Marcellinus Comes, *Chronicon* a. 508, p. 97. Cassiodorus, *Variae* I 16, and II 38, pp. 22 f and 67.

186. Procopius, *De bello Gothico* I (V) 12.33–40.

187. Ibid., II (VI) 25.2 f. it is reported that only the immediate entourage of a Frankish king was mounted. The battle itself is reported esp. by Gregory of Tours, *Historia Francorum* II 37, pp. 85–88. See Lippold, "Chlodovechus," 160–164.

Zöllner, *Franken,* 64–66. Claude, *Westgoten,* 35 f. Cf. also chap. 3, n. 318, chap. 4, n. 1 and n. 377.

188. On this and what follows see Nehlsen, "Codex Euricianus," 42–47, Nehlsen, "Lex Visigothorum," 1966–1979, Nehlsen, *Sklavenrecht,* 62 ff. (Breviarium Alaricianum), as well as 153 ff. (Codex Euricianus), and Nehlsen "Review of Vismara," 246 ff. Siems, "Lex Romana Visigothorum," 1910 1949. Nehlsen takes a position opposite to that of Vismara, *Scritti, Edictum Theoderici,* "Romani e Goti," and "El 'edictum Theoderici.'" The fundamental work on this topic was done by the editor of the *Monumenta Germaniae Historica* edition, Zeumer, "Westgothische Gesetzgebung." Important also is Wohlhaupter, "Das germanische Element," 135–264. A survey can be found in Buchner, *Rechtsquellen,* 6–10. For the edition of the *Breviarium Alaricianum* (BA) see *Lex Romana Visigothorum.* For the *Codex Euricianus* (CE) one now uses the edition of d'Ors, *Código,* 20 ff. For the palingenesis see ibid., 1 ff., and Beyerle, "Frühgeschichte," 1 ff. The proper assessment of the BA and CE in the context of the history of Roman law we owe to the work of Wieacker, *Zustände,* as well as "Kommentare," 259 ff., and *Recht und Gesellschaft.* Building on this foundation and largely in agreement with Wieacker's views are the works of Claude, *Westgoten,* 39 f. and 44 f., Stroheker, *Eurich,* 94 ff., and *Germanentum,* 119 ff., and finally Schäferdiek, *Die Kirchen der Westgoten,* 27 ff. and 42 ff. I have followed the evaluation of Visigothic legislation and ecclesiastical policy which Schäferdiek presents in a balanced exposition, in explicit opposition to the views of Bruck, *Caesarius von Arles,* 146 ff., although certain valuable observations of Bruck will of course be given recognition. The same goes for Rouche, *L'Aquitaine,* 40 f., 48, esp. 169 ff. as well as 387 ff. (the legal and ecclesiastical policy of the last two Visigothic kings). On my position cf. Nehlsen, *Sklavenrecht,* 64 with n. 134 f. On the impact and aftereffect of the *Leges Visigothorum* see Nehlsen, "Aktualität und Effektivität," 483 ff. with nn. 169–173.

189. Demandt, "Magister militum," 690 f.; cf. Schäferdiek, *Die Kirchen der Westgoten,* 11 f.

190. On the expression cf. below, n. 307. On the topic see Schäferdiek, *Die Kirchen der Westgoten,* 8 ff. Stroheker, *Eurich,* 36 ff. On the designation of the Gothic king as lord of the Romans see below, n. 266. The examples for the rule of the Gothic king over the Arian church and its dignitaries, though not numerous, are nevertheless unambiguous. Fritigern sends a Gothic-Arian dignitary to negotiate with Valens before the battle (Ammianus Marcellinus XXXI 12.8 f.). Revealing is also the misunderstanding of an act of cooperation between Fritigern and Ulfilas in Sozomenus VI 37.6 ff. Sigesar, "the bishop of the Goths," baptized the usurper Attalus and thereby makes him "beloved by everyone and by Alaric" (Sozomenus IX 9.1.). The same bishop tries—if in vain—to protect Athaulf's children against Sigeric. The new king forces him to hand them over (Olympiodorus fr. 26). Theodoric (II) sends the Arian missionary Ajax to the Suevi (Hydatius 232, a. 466). The same Gothic king and "his priests" *(sacerdotes sui),* probably the Arian court priests, are described by Sidonius Apollinaris, *Epistulae* I 2.4, p. 3. Yet *Modaharius, civis Gothus, haereseos Arianae iacula vibrans,* (ibid. VII 6.2, p. 108), was probably not an envoy of Euric (cf. Schäferdiek, *Die Kirchen der Westgoten,* 29). For Euric's general rule over the church, i.e., over both the Gothic as well as the Roman church, one cites esp. CE 306 and 335; cf. Schäferdiek, *Die Kirchen der Westgoten,* 16 f.

191. Cf. Claude, "Königs- und Untertaneneid," 360–371.

192. Beck and Nehlsen, "belagines," after Jordanes, *Getica* 69, p. 74. Nehlsen, however, seems to relate the *belagines* exclusively to the Ostrogoths; although this seems entirely plausible, it does not exclude similar Visigothic traditions, since the *Dekaineos* tradition, no matter how literary it may be, points to Dacia (Wolfram, "Gotische Studien I," 14 and II, 304).

193. Claude, *Adel, Kirche und Königtum,* 198 ff. with n. 205. Kienast, *Volksstämme,* 151 ff., esp. 170. Nehlsen, "Aktualität und Effektivität," 449 ff., esp. 483 ff.

194. CE 277.3; 305; 327.

195. Nehlsen, *Sklavenrecht,* 155 f. n. 18. Sidonius Apollinaris, *Epistulae* II 1.3, p. 21 f., and VIII 3.2, p. 128. On the dating of the two letters cf. Loyen, *Sidoine Apollinaire* 2:246 n. 1, and 3:216 n. 3. Stroheker, *Eurich,* 97 with n. 25 and 27. Sidonius (first quote) describes Seronatus as *leges Theudosianas calcans Theudoricianasque proponens.* This passage is the foremost evidence for Vismara (see most recently *Scritti,* 297 ff.) to assume that the *Edictum Theoderici* is of Visigothic origin. Cf. on this Nehlsen (as n. 188). On the question of assigning the CE to the time of Alaric II see Nehlsen, *Sklavenrecht,* 154 ff. with n. 11 and 16–20, and "Aktualität und Effektivität," 488 ff.

196. Nehlsen, *Sklavenrecht,* 44 ff. and 63 ff., esp. after Wieacker, *Vulgarismus.* Among the Roman lawyers who helped Euric one has, with good reason, looked for the *consiliarius* Leo: see Loyen, *Sidoine Apollinaire* 3:197 n. 7, after Sidonius Apollinaris, *Epistulae* VIII 3.3, p. 128, as well as Stroheker, *Adel,* 187 n. 212, and Claude, *Westgoten,* 45 f. with n. 108.

197. Nehlsen, "Aktualität und Effektivität," 488 ff., and *Sklavenrecht,* 154 ff. (possible contribution of Alaric to the CE), as well as 159 ff., especially on d'Ors, *Código,* 50 ff., and Stroheker, *Eurich,* 96 with n. 24. See also Claude, *Westgoten,* 39 f.

198. CE 310.1 and 3 f. (*buccellarius*); 286.1 f.; 307.1 f. (*scriptura*). See Nehlsen, *Sklavenrecht,* 154. Claude, *Westgoten,* 39, and "Königs- und Untertaneneid," 371. On Gothic, esp. Visigothic use of charters: Classen, "Fortleben," 20 ff., and Nehlsen, "Aktualität und Effektivität," 491 ff. On *frabaúhtaboka* see Feist, *Wörterbuch,* 160, and P. Scardigli, *Goten,* 269 ff., following Tjäder, *Papyri,* vol. 2, Pap. Marini 118 l. 47, p. 45.

199. See n. 196 (Leo).

200. Schäferdiek, *Die Kirchen der Westgoten,* 15 f. with n. 35 and 42 ff. with n. 122, as well as 44 with n. 128. Claude, *Westgoten,* 135 f. with n. 70 and 74. Nehlsen, *Sklavenrecht,* 63 f. with nn. 125–135, discusses also the date of the promulgation of the *Breviarium Alaricianum.* On the question of the personality and territoriality of the law see the incisive statement by Nehlsen, *Sklavenrecht,* 63 n. 125.

201. Sidonius Apollinaris, *Epistulae* VIII 3.3, p. 128. Cf. above, n. 195 f.

202. Nehlsen, *Sklavenrecht,* 63–65 with n. 126. On Goiaricus see Martindale, *Prosopography* 2:517. On the quotes see *Lex Romana Visigothorum* (Haenel), pp. 2–4, and *Codex Theodosianus* (Mommsen), p. xxxiii f. Ladner, "Justinian's Theory," 195 ff. Soliva, "Lex Romana Curiensis," 73 ff.

203. Gregory of Tours, *Historia Francorum* V 43, p. 251 f. Schäferdiek, "Germanenmission," 525 f. Giesecke, *Ostgermanen und der Arianismus,* 87 f., cites

passages from Salvian according to which Arianism and paganism existed side by side among the Visigoths. These passages do not refer only to the Goths but to all barbarian tribes; indeed, it is striking that in the catalog of peoples (Salvianus of Marseille, *De gubernatione Dei* IV 67, p. 48 f.) the Goths are explicitly omitted. Moreover, the contemporary and countryman of Salvian, Claudius Marius Victor (*Alethia* III vv. 190 ff., p. 113), mentions as an example of ancestor worship only the Alans in his native southern Gaul. Cf. Courcelle, *Histoire littéraire*, 81 with n. 3.

204. See Schwarcz, *Reichsangehörige*, 44–46 and 57 f., as well as Schäferdiek, *Die Kirchen der Westgoten*, 9, 27 ff., and esp. 45 f. n. 129 and 92 f. with n. 66, contra Rouche, *L'Aquitaine*, 40 f.

205. Schwarcz, *Reichsangehörige*, 122–124 (Fretela), and 198 f. (Sunnia). Stutz, *Gotische Literaturdenkmäler*, 43–47. Claude, *Westgoten*, 27 with n. 65. Thompson, *Visigoths*, 138 ff.

206. Schäferdiek, *Die Kirchen der Westgoten*, 10 f. with n. 17, after Fiebiger, *Inschriftensammlung*, no. 55, p. 35 f.

207. Schäferdiek, *Die Kirchen der Westgoten*, 12 with n. 23, after Hydatius 174 and 186; aa. 455 and 457.

208. Schäferdiek, *Die Kirchen der Westgoten*, 11 f.; cf. Demandt, "Magister militum," 690 f. See also above, n. 189.

209. Sidonius Apollinaris, *Epistulae* VII 6.0, p. 110.

210. See above, n. 38 f.

211. Stroheker, *Adel*, 64 ff. with n. 127, after Sidonius Apollinaris, *Epistulae* V 16.4, p. 89. On the dating of the letter see Loyen, *Sidoine Apollinaire* 2:256 n. 16.

212. Stroheker, *Adel*, 74, after Salvianus of Marseille, *De gubernatione Dei* IV 32 f., p. 41 f. Cf. Jones, *The Later Roman Empire* 2:923 ff.

213. Sidonius Apollinaris, *Epistulae* VII 12.1–4, esp. 4, addressed to Tonantius Ferreolus, the *praefectus praetorio* of 451, who shortly thereafter turned Thorismund away from Arles; Tonantius Ferreolus should now seek to become bishop. Cf. Stroheker, *Adel*, 74 and 173 n. 149.

214. Sidonius Apollinaris, *Epistulae* II 1.4, p. 22.

215. Zöllner, *Völker*, 91.

216. Sidonius Apollinaris, *Epistulae* VII 8 and 9, pp. 111–117. Schäferdiek, *Die Kirchen der Westgoten*, 22. Courcelle, *Histoire littéraire*, 176. Stroheker, *Adel*, 119 n. 363.

217. Sidonius Apollinaris, *Epistulae* VII 9.19 f., p. 116.

218. Schäferdiek, *Die Kirchen der Westgoten*, 22 f.

219. Sidonius Apollinaris, *Epistulae* IV 22.2 f., p. 72 f. Stroheker, *Adel*, 187 n. 12 and 218 n. 358.

220. Sidonius Apollinaris, *Epistulae* I 2, pp. 2–4, and VIII 9.5 vv. 1–59, p. 136 f. Martindale, *Prosopography* 2:115–118 (Apollinaris 6).

221. Ennodius, *Vita Epifani* 89, p. 95. Cf. chap. 4, n. 321.

222. Sidonius Apollinaris, *Epistulae* VII 6.4 ff., p. 109 f. On the dating of the letter see Loyen, *Sidoine Apollinaire* 2:xx, and 3:214 n. 6. Cf. Wolfram, "Fortuna," 5 f. with n. 22.

223. See chap. 3, nn. 248 and 250 (Alaric I), above, n. 38 f. (Theodoric) and n. 133 (Euric).

224. Schäferdiek, *Die Kirchen der Westgoten*, 18 ff.

225. See n. 222 and n. 224.

226. Schäferdiek, *Die Kirchen der Westgoten,* 110 f. See above, n. 78.

227. Schäferdiek, *Die Kirchen der Westgoten,* 20 ff., after Sidonius Apollinaris, *Epistulae* VII 8.3, p. 112. On the dating of the letter see Loyen, *Sidoine Apollinaire* 3:214 n. 8.

228. Schäferdiek, *Die Kirchen der Westgoten,* 27.

229. Cf., for example, Rouche, *L'Aquitaine,* 40 f.

230. Schäferdiek, *Die Kirchen der Westgoten,* 26 ff., esp. 26 and 28 f.

231. Ibid., 30 ff.

232. These conflicts went back to the beginning of the century. Matthews, *Aristocracies,* 313 (Ecdicius, who is not mentioned in Stroheker, *Adel*) and 320 with n. 4. Schäferdiek, *Die Kirchen der Westgoten,* 24.

233. Matthews, *Aristocracies,* 344 ff. and Schäferdiek, *Die Kirchen der Westgoten,* 25 ff.

234. Schäferdiek, *Die Kirchen der Westgoten,* 31.

235. The view of Schäferdiek, *Die Kirchen der Westgoten,* 42 ff., has been taken over by Nehlsen, *Sklavenrecht,* 64 with n. 134 f. Cf. Eckardt, "Treueidleistungen," 75 f.

236. Rouche, *L'Aquitaine,* 43.

237. *Lex Romana Visigothorum* (Haenel), pp. 2–4. *Codex Theodosianus* (Mommsen), p. xxxiii f. On the constitutional significance of the term *utilitas* see Ewig, "Zum christlichen Königsgedanken," 30 ff. (33 ff.), and below, n. 239.

238. Schäferdiek, *Die Kirchen der Westgoten,* 55 ff., esp. 56 with n. 171, and 243 ff., after *Concilium Agathense,* chaps. 48 f., pp. 122 and 213 ff. (list of signatories).

239. *Concilium Agathense,* p. 192. See for this most recently Ewig, "Gebetsklausel," 87 ff. Cassiodorus, *Variae* IV 17.2, p. 122, mentions Narbonne's favorable treatment by Alaric.

240. Schäferdiek, *Die Kirchen der Westgoten,* 32–42, esp. 35 ff. and 40. On Caesarius of Arles see esp. Stroheker, *Adel,* 58 f. n. 80.

241. Wenskus, "Balthen," 13. Schäferdiek, *Die Kirchen der Westgoten,* 8, and Sidonius Apollinaris, *Carmina* VII v. 202, p. 211, (Theoderid). The Sidonius tradition is all the more significant because it is preserved in a panegyric on Avitus, i.e., a song of praise for the man who was a friend of Theoderid's and the teacher of Theodoric. Cf. ibid. vv. 470 and 495 ff., p. 214 f. This agrees with Jordanes, *Getica* 229, pp. 116 ff., who (ibid. 190, p. 104) lists the names of Theodoric's six sons. Cf. Schönfeld, *Wörterbuch,* 226 f. On the Balthi in general see chap. 1, nn. 101–113.

242. On Loyen's assumption, *Recherches historiques,* 67 with n. 1, that there was a marriage between a third daughter of Theoderid and Aëtius in 439, see above, n. 42. On Retemeris-Ricimer see chap. 1, nn. 116 and 118.

243. Jordanes, *Getica* 184, p. 106.

244. Hydatius 140, a. 449. Claude, "Prosopographie," 666 n. 66.

245. Schäferdiek, *Die Kirchen der Westgoten,* 108 f. Kampers, "Genealogie," 50 ff., esp. 55 ff.

246. Wolfram, "Theogonie," 83–88, esp. 84 with n. 28 and 86 with n. 41, following suggestions of Eckhardt considers the highly improbable possibility that Berimund was the daughter of Thorismund.

247. Hydatius 226, a. 465. Claude, "Prosopographie," 667 n. 69.

248. Ragnahild is known only through Sidonius Apollinaris, *Epistulae* IV 8.5, p. 60. The second Sidonius quote mentioned by Seeck, "Ragnahilda," 127, does not refer to her. Cf. Loyen, *Sidoine Apollinaire* 3:187 n. 32. On Ragnahild see also Martindale, *Prosopography* 2:935.

249. Loyen, *Sidoine Apollinaire*, 2:252 n. 8.

250. Stroheker, *Eurich*, 5 with n. 3.

251. Cf. Konecny, *Frauen*, esp. 21, 24, and 71 ff.

252. Claude, *Adel, Kirche und Königtum*, 36 f.

253. Claude, "Probleme," 329 ff.

254. Claude, *Adel, Kirche und Königtum*, 36 f. and 47 ff. On the position of Frideric, who is even called *rex Gothorum* (Marius of Avenches, *Chronica* a. 463; cf. a. 455 p. 232): L. Schmidt, *Ostgermanen*, 479 n. 5, Loyen, *Recherches historiques*, 55 with n. 2. On the death of Euric cf. above, n. 166.

255. Loyen, *Recherches historiques*, 66 f.: Sidonius Apollinaris, *Carmina* V vv. 126 ff., esp. 203–206, pp. 191–193. Merobaudes, *Carmina* IV vv. 15–17, p. 5. Cf. chap. 1, n. 102.

256. See above, nn. 222 and 224.

257. The spelling of the names follows Jordanes, *Getica* 297, p. 134. Cf. Schönfeld, *Wörterbuch*, 230. See also Procopius, *De bello Gothico* I (V) 12.22. The approximate date of the marriage can be inferred from Anonymus Valesianus II 63, even though the source confuses Thiudigoto with her sister. On this error cf. Anonymus Valesianus II 58. On Thiudigoto see Martindale, *Prosopography* 2:1068 (Theodegotha). On the "higher nobility" of the Amali cf. Jordanes, *Getica* 146, p. 96. See chap. 1, n. 100 f.

258. An examination of the admittedly scanty accounts (as above, n. 133) shows—as Evangelos Chrysos has pointed out—that contrary to the most widely held assumption the sovereignty of the Visigothic kingdom was not recognized de jure in 475.

259. Courcelle, *Histoire littéraire*, 145 n. 1. Loyen, "Les débuts," 406 ff., esp. 414 n. 1 and 415 with n. 6. Cf. L. Schmidt, *Ostgermanen*, 487 f. Stroheker, *Eurich*, 11 f., and Stroheker, *Adel*, 79 ff. Sidonius Apollinaris, *Epistulae* VII 6.10, p. 110 (from the year 475 but before the conclusion of the new treaty; cf. Loyen, *Sidoine Apollinaire* 3:189 n. 20). *Epistulae* IX 3.3, p. 151 (from the year 476); IX 5.1, p. 153 (from the year 476/477; cf. Loyen 2:xxi n. 2, and 3:140 n. 17. There is a widespread consensus in the literature that the *regna* of the last two passages of Sidonius refer to the kingdoms of the Visigoths and the Burgundians. But since Loyen (*Sidoine Apollinaire* 3:46), in agreement with Dalton (*The Letters of Sidonius* 2:242 to 109 n. 2) interprets the phrase *regnum utrumque* used in Sidonius, *Epistulae* VII 6.10, p. 110 as referring to the Roman Empire and the Gothic kingdom, we must ask whether the *regna* of the other two passages should not also be understood in this sense. On the *regna* terminology of the Visigothic kingdom cf. the compilation, though not complete, in L. Schmidt, *Ostgermanen*, 503 n. 1 ff.

260. *Codex Euricianus* 277.

261. Schäferdiek, *Die Kirchen der Westgoten*, 43. Courcelle, *Histoire littéraire*, 339–344. Stroheker, *Eurich*, 38 f. As can be inferred from Sidonius Apollinaris (as above, n. 209), Aquitaine was considered Roman imperial territory with all the

consequences entailed for the public and private life of that region until the break of the *foedus* by Euric. See Sidonius (as below, n. 272).

262. Matthews, *Aristocracies,* 333 and 338 ff. Stein, *Bas-Empire* 1:270 ff., 283, 382 ff., and cf. 653 (index of sources). Goffart, *Barbarians and Romans,* 115. Cf. below, n. 350.

263. Although the assumption of a division of the land between Goths and Romans (Gaupp, *Ansiedlungen,* 394 ff., or, for example, Rothenhöfer, *Untersuchungen,* 14 f.) must be rejected, one can, with Goffart (*Barbarians and Romans,* 113 ff., 160 f., 206 ff., but esp. 123 f. n. 34) give reasons for a change around 425 in the original arrangement.

264. See the passages cited in n. 259 and n. 263, as well as above, n. 39, esp. Sidonius Apollinaris, *Epistulae* VII 6.10, p. 110, and VIII 3.3 (Euric's kingdom), from the years 475 and 476/477, respectively (Loyen, *Sidoine Apollinaire* 3:43 and 86). Cf. Goffart, *Barbarians and Romans,* 173 f.

265. Characteristically enough in the "Gothic" CE sections 276, 3.277, 1.301, 304, and 312, the provincials are called Romans in contrast to the Goths. By comparison, the "Roman" *Breviarium Alaricianum* uses the conventional term *provinciales* in addition to *leges Romanae.* L. Schmidt, *Ostgermanen,* 504 with n. 3. Demandt, "Magister militum," 673 ff. See also the list of *Gothus, Romanus, Sirus, Grecus vel Iudeus* in the *Concilium Narbonense,* chap. 4, p. 254 f., a. 589.

266. Fichtenau, "'Politische' Datierungen," 465, on Fiebiger-Schmidt, *Inschriftensammlung,* 119 f. no. 146. Wolfram, *Intitulatio I,* 46 with n. 75 and 59 with n. 23. See also *Breviarium Alaricianum* (as n. 265).

267. Wolfram, *Intitulatio I,* 63 with n. 46 and 69 with n. 77. L. Schmidt, *Ostgermanen,* 510.

268. Olympiodorus, fr. 35. See chap. 3, n. 156. Claude, *Adel, Kirche und Königtum,* 31.

269. Cf. Demandt, "Magister militum," 631.

270. This "inaccurate equivalence" became clearly visible under Theodoric and his brother Frideric. Cf. Demandt, "Magister militum," 690 f. with 694 f. and 697–699.

271. See chap. 3, nn. 341 ff.

272. Sidonius Apollinaris, *Epistulae* VII 12.3, p. 118, looking back in 476, thinks that fifteen years earlier Gaul was still "largely unscathed." Loyen, *Sidoine Apollinaire* 3:193 n. 69, and Loyen, "Les débuts," 406. Stroheker, *Adel,* 64. It is, however, advisable to consult Sidonius (p. 442, index) in order to compare the author's various comments on the theme "Gaul." In this way one can quickly correct the optimistic picture of the later period. On the phrase "patrimonial official" see below, n. 332.

273. Brühl, *Palatium,* 189 f. L. Schmidt, *Ostgermanen,* 503 with n. 5. See the index in Stevens, "Tolosa," 1689.

274. Sidonius Apollinaris, *Epistulae* VIII 9.1, p. 135. Higounet, *Bordeaux,* 14 f., and Étienne, *Bordeaux,* esp. 213 ff. Gregory of Tours, *Gloria martyrum* 91, p. 549. Schäferdiek, *Die Kirchen der Westgoten,* 45 n. 129. Bordeaux was the capital of Aquitania II, Narbonne the capital of Narbonensis I: *Notitia Galliarum* XIII 2 and XV 2, pp. 270 and 272. Euric died in Arles, where the palace of the abolished prefecture was probably taken over by the king: *Chronica Gallica* 666, p. 665.

275. Brühl, *Palatium,* 192 f. Cf. Ewig, "Résidence," 29 f. On the size of late antique cities cf. Zöllner, *Franken,* 210. Büttner, *Frühmittelalterliches Städtewesen,* 152 ff.

276. Cf. Claude, *Westgoten,* 50 with n. 127.

277. Brühl, *Palatium,* 196–200.

278. Hydatius 69 and 116, aa. 418 and 439. See the portent of the downfall reported ibid. 244, a. 468. Cf. the passages listed in L. Schmidt, *Ostgermanen,* 461 n. 2 and 468 n. 1.

279. Jordanes, *Getica* 216, p. 113. Claude, *Kirche, Adel und Königtum,* 36 f.

280. Claude, *Kirche, Adel und Königtum,* 36 with n. 1. Claude, "Frühmittelalter-liche Königsschätze," 5 ff., esp. 8 f. See *Breviarium Alaricianum* (as n. 265): the treasure was also the place where the documents were kept.

281. Claude, *Westgoten,* 51. See below, n. 289 and p. 207 no. 4 (end).

282. *Chronica Gallica* 666, p. 665.

283. Claude, *Westgoten,* 37 f. See below, nn. 467 ff.

284. On the question of the Gothic language cf. below, n. 310.

285. Wolfram, *Intitulatio I,* 77–89. Cf. ibid., 40 ff., 69 n. 78 and 148 ff.

286. See above, nn. 64 f.

287. Loyen, *Sidoine Apollinaire* 2:245 n. 2. Cf. below, n. 295.

288. Wolfram, "Mittelalterliche Politik," 9 f.

289. Sidonius Apollinaris, *Epistulae* I 2, pp. 2–4. Claude, *Westgoten,* 51 f.

290. Here already appears the famous term *civilitas,* which then comes to repre-sent something of a maxim of Theodoric's rule in the *Variae* of Cassiodorus. See *Variae,* p. 521, s.v. "civilitas," cf. "civilis" and "civiliter." Sidonius Apollinaris, *Carmina* XXIII vv. 69–72, p. 251 f., celebrates Theodoric (II) as *Martius rector atque magno patre prior, decus Getarum, Romanae columen salusque gentis.* On the dating of this passage to 463–66 see Loyen, *Sidoine Apollinaire* 1:196.

291. Wolfram, "Fortuna," 29–31.

292. Sidonius Apollinaris probably saw in the hands of the Gothic king the curved bow of the mounted nomads: see Maenchen-Helfen, *The Huns,* 221–232. J. Werner, *Archäologie des Attila-Reiches,* 46 ff. The reports about the Gothic skills as archers are contradictory. Jordanes, *Getica* 43, p. 65, repeats Lucanus, *Pharsalia* VIII v. 221, and refers to the Getes of Dacia. For Vegetius, *Epitoma rei militaris* I 20, the use of long-range weapons is typically Gothic. But a closer reading reveals that we are dealing in this case with the military techniques of the three-tribe confederation of Ostrogoths, Huns, and Alans. It appears that in the sixth century the Ostrogoths did not know how to use the bow as a major weapon: see chap. 5, nn. 307–318. Much the same probably also applies to the Visigoths, insofar as we can say from the brief account of the battle of Vouillé: see above, n. 187.

293. Sidonius Apollinaris probably saw the king's moderation as "un-Gothic" or "unbarbarian": see below, n. 508.

294. Cf. Grönbech, *Kultur und Religion* 2:189 ff. See also Tacitus, *Germania,* chap. 24, Much, *Germania,* 322 ff.

295. At this time Sidonius Apollinaris must have moved freely within the court at Toulouse: Courcelle, *Histoire littéraire,* 166 f. Loyen, *Sidoine Apollinaire* 2:245 n. 2.

296. On the theme of "ridicule at the banquet" see Grönbech (as n. 294), 105

ff. and 197. Cf., for example, Paul the Deacon, *Historia Langobardorum* I 23 f., p. 61 f.

297. In the eyes of Sidonius all Goths, including the kings, wore the Scythian fur dress: *Epistulae* I 2.4, p. 3; VII 9.16, p. 116; as well as *Carmina* VII vv. 453–457, p. 214. Claudius Rutilius Namatianus writes much the same: *De reditu suo sive iter Gallicum* II vv. 49 f. See also the illustrations of the Scythians in the catalog *From the Lands of the Scythians,* Metropolitan Museum of Art Bulletin XXXII 5 (1975). Cf. below, n. 507.

298. James, *Merovingian Archaeology* 1:36 f., 61 and 239. See esp. ibid., 196 ff. on the question of a Visigothic archaeology in Gaul as well as for the useful catalog of all archaeological sites concentrated in Septimania: ibid. 2; 404 ff. Cf. Ioniţă, "Probleme," 98. See below, n. 300.

299. See n. 297.

300. Gamillscheg, *Romania Germanica* 1:397. Claude, *Westgoten,* 60 and 138 n. 37 (bibliographical references). James (as n. 298) could not identify a single cemetery that would with certainty be attributed to the Toulousan Goths of the fifth century. This is all the more surprising since from the Spanish finds from the later fifth and early sixth centuries we know of Gothic dress that was worn at least by members of the Visigothic middle stratum. The archaeological layman may be permitted to ask whether this phenomenon is not connected to the appearance of the use of row graves. This type of burial would have then offered the possibility of giving new and visible expression to cultural behavior that was in fact never interrupted.

301. On falconry see chap. 2, n. 505. On the story of the chasing away of the game and the hunting party see *Vita Caesarii* I 48, p. 475. L. Schmidt, *Ostgermanen,* 597 with n. 5.

302. L. Schmidt, *Ostgermanen,* 514 n. 9, after Sidonius Apollinaris, *Epistulae* I 2.4, p. 514. Ennodius, *Vita Epifani* 92, p. 95.

303. Sidonius Apollinaris (as n. 302).

304. Stutz, *Gotische Literaturdenkmäler,* 21 ff. Cf. Gregory of Tours, *Historia Francorum* III 10, p. 107. Schäferdiek, *Die Kirchen der Westgoten,* 160 f. n. 97.

305. Schäferdiek, *Die Kirchen der Westgoten,* 29 with n. 83 and 92 f. with n. 66.

306. See chap. 3, nn. 87–89.

307. On the term *lex Gothica*: Tjäder, *Papyri,* vol. 2, no. 34, pp. 91 ff., esp. 102, lines 98, 108, 122; cf. 130–135. Cf. below, n. 309 and n. 503, and *Codex Theodosianus* VII 8.2: relieving the *synagoga Judaicae legis* from the billeting of soldiers.

308. See above, n. 78.

309. According to the *Passio sancti Sigismundi,* chap. 4, p. 335, the Burgundians were of the Gothic faith.

310. Kienast, *Volksstämme,* 44 f. with n. 7, essentially after Gamillscheg, *Romania Germanica* 1:354 ff. Wartburg, *Entstehung,* 89 ff. Claude, *Westgoten,* 42 f., Schäferdiek (as n. 304). Cf. below, n. 326.

311. Krause, *Handbuch,* 21 f.

312. *Carmina* XII vv. 1–22, p. 230 f.

313. *Anthologia Latina* I no. 285, vv. 1 f. See above, n. 311. P. Scardigli, "Das

gotische Epigramm," 16 ff. attempts a different interpretation of the passage, referring it to the Gothic-Arian cult.

314. See above, n. 289.

315. Jordanes, *Getica* 214, p. 112 f., where the "nonmusical" nature of the presentation is explicitly noted. On the cultic ancestor worship see chap. 2, n. 464.

316. *Institutionum disciplinae,* p. 557. Cf. Claude, *Westgoten* (as n. 310).

317. See above, n. 286 and n. 295.

318. See esp. Sidonius Apollinaris, *Epistulae* VIII 9.1 ff., esp. 3 and 5, vv. 4 ff., p. 135 f., as well as VIII 11.3 ff., esp. 11, pp. 139–142.

319. Sidonius Apollinaris, *Epistulae* VIII 9.5 vv. 1–59, p. 136 f., produces the panegyric on Euric which turned out to be somewhat short. But for Theodoric (II) (see above, n. 289: end of the letter) Sidonius does not want to write a *historia*. It was probably Leo (cf. Stroheker, *Adel,* 187 n. 212), to whom Sidonius owed his release and who directly addressed to Sidonius the request to write a history. But Sidonius turned the tables on him, compared Leo to Tacitus, and flatly refused to engage in any historical writing: *Epistulae* IV 22.3–5, p. 73. On the dating of the letter (476 or 477) see Loyen, *Sidoine Apollinaire* 1:254.

320. Sidonius Apollinaris, *Epistulae* IV 8.5 vv. 1–12, p. 60. The friend for whom Sidonius composed these verses was a Roman who on orders from the king (see ibid. IV 8.1, p. 59) had to go to Toulouse and who was for that purpose preparing a silver bowl with an appropriate dedication as a gift. Cf. Claude, *Westgoten,* 52 f.

321. Ennodius, *Vita Epifani* 89 f., p. 95. Claude (as n. 320). Cf., in contrast, Stroheker, *Eurich,* 6 f. n. 10, or Kienast (as n. 310).

322. Procopius, *De bello Gothico* I (V) 10.10 and 16.2, shows that the Gothic general in Roman services, Bessa, spoke Gothic and could also converse with Ostrogothic warriors in their language.

323. On the survival of the Gothic language in the Balkans cf. the late testimony of Walahfrid Strabo, *Libellus de exordiis,* chap. 7, p. 481, which has been criticized, however, by Schäferdiek, "Germanenmission," 506.

324. Procopius, *De bello Gothico* I (VI) 12.44–49 and 13.7 f.

325. Kienast (as n. 310) seems to assume something similar.

326. See the survey in Gamillscheg, *Romania Germanica* 1:356 ff. Cf. Claude, *Westgoten,* 53. On the passages see esp. *Leges Visigothorum,* p. 522, s.v. "gardingus"; 564, s.v. "thiufa, thiufadus"; as well as ibid., p. 485 f. See below, n. 380 (*thiufadus*) and n. 593 (*gardingus*). On *morgingeba* see *Formulae Visigothicae* 20, p. 584 vv. 10–13; cf. Sánchez-Albornoz, "Caballería visigoda," 95 n. 43. On the *comes scanciarum* see below, nn. 392, 396, and 401. The (nick)name Wamba (king, 672–680), "Big Paunch," is no sufficient proof for a Gothic language in use after the year 600. Cf. the Lombard Paulus Diaconus's interest in "the old language" (Wolfram, *Intitulatio I,* 190 f. n. 28) although he certainly spoke a Romance dialect.

327. Wolfram, *Intitulatio I,* 43 ff.

328. Wolfram, "Gotische Studien II," 311. See chap. 2, n. 414.

329. Cf. the words of Alaric I according to Claudian, *De bello Gothico* vv. 535–539, p. 279. Wolfram, "Early Medieval Kingdom," 7 ff. See chap. 3, n. 176 and n. 255.

330. See above, nn. 81–87.

331. See above, nn. 8 f., and nn. 261–263. Matthews, *Aristocracies,* 336.

332. Cf. Weber, *Wirtschaft und Gesellschaft* 2:549 ff.

333. See above, n. 194 f., and below, nn. 350 and 431 ff.

334. Wolfram, "Gotische Studien I," 10 n. 44 and 21 f.; II, 322 ff. and III, 255 with n. 190, esp. after *Passio s. Sabae,* chaps. 1 ff., pp. 216 ff., Socrates IV 33 f., and Sozomenus VI 37.6 ff. Cf. above, n. 190 and n. 307.

335. See above, n. 189.

336. L. Schmidt, *Ostgermanen,* 511 f.

337. Wolfram, "Gotische Studien II," 319 f. and 323. Cf. chap. 3, n. 153 f. on the changes in the tribal council during the period of migration.

338. Claude, *Adel, Kirche und Königtum,* 38. Procopius, *De bello Gothico* I (V) 12.33–40. Cf. below, n. 379.

339. L. Schmidt, *Ostgermanen,* 512. See above, n. 254 (confirmation of the succession) and Jordanes (as n. 344) (declaration of war).

340. When Avitus succeeded in 455 in Toulouse in preserving and reaffirming the *foedus,* the Gothic "senate" was summoned: Sidonius Apollinaris, *Carmina* VII vv. 452–488, p. 214 f. Cf. above, n. 64.

341. See above, n. 202.

342. Hydatius 243, a. 467.

343. Sidonius Apollinaris, *Carmina* VII vv. 452–519, pp. 214–216. Loyen, *Recherches historiques,* 55 f.

344. Jordanes, *Getica* 189, p. 107. Cf. Tacitus, *Germania,* chaps. 13.2 f. and 14.1, as well as Ammianus Marcellinus XVI 12.60, after Timpe, "Comes," 65.

345. Timpe, "Comes," 63 ff. Claude, "Comes," 65 ff. Seeck, "Dux," 869 ff., and Seeck, "Comites," 622 ff. Cf. Jones, *The Later Roman Empire* 1:366 ff.

346. *Notitia dignitatum,* p. 302 f., s.v. "comes limitis, comes rei militaris," and p. 304, s.v. "dux." See esp. below, nn. 362 ff. On the quotes see Timpe, "Comes," 64.

347. *Leges Visigothorum,* p. 485 f. *Concilios visigoticos,* pp. 289, 307, 434 f., 474, and 521.

348. Cf. below, n. 379 (*Theoderici Italiae regis dux*). See also chap. 5, nn. 215 ff. For the king as highest-ranking *dux* in theory see Schlesinger, "Heerkönigtum," 77 (131) with n. 125.

349. On the differentiated development in the Frankish kingdom see esp. Ewig, "Ribuarien," 452 ff. (4 ff.). Cf. Wolfram, *Intitulatio I,* 145 f. n. 27, 188, 193 f. with n. 38.

350. On this and the following see above, n. 209, n. 262, n. 271, and below, n. 519 f. (Arvandus and Seronatus); cf. the good compilation in Jones, *The Later Roman Empire* 1:257 ff., as well as 3:50 f. Cf. Rouche, *L'Aquitaine,* 27 f. and 31 with n. 116, after Prosper, *Epitoma chronicon* 1324 a. 436, p. 475, and 1338 a. 439, p. 477.

351. See above, n. 99 and below, n. 519 f. (Arvandus and Seronatus cooperate with Euric). See Rouche, *L'Aquitaine,* 33 with n. 136, as well as above, n. 59 (a praetorian prefect prevails upon Thorismund to abandon the siege of Arles in 453). On the curiales see below, n. 430 f.

352. Ewig, "Ribuarien," 451 ff. (2 ff.) with n. 5, after *Codex Euricianus* 322.2. See also Jones, *The Later Roman Empire* 1:258, and 3:51 n. 50. To this one should

add Sidonius Apollinaris, *Epistulae* VII 2.5, p. 105 (around 470 according to Loyen, *Sidoine Apollinaire* 2:189 n. 9 and 214 n. 2). *Vita Caesarii,* chap. 48, p. 475. *Concilium Narbonense,* sections 4 and 9 (589 IX 1), p. 254 f.

353. Rouche, *L'Aquitaine,* 23 f., after *Notitia Galliarum* XIII–XV, pp. 270–272, assumes for the original extent of the federate kingdom nine *civitates,* a figure that by 466 probably increased to nineteen, since the two Aquitanian provinces together with Toulouse in Narbonensis added up to this figure.

354. Hydatius 92, a. 430, as well as 192 ff., aa. 458 ff.

355. This statement does not contradict the fact that the Visigoths did not take over the positions either of the imperial *comitatus* or of the Gallic prefecture as such. See Jones, *The Later Roman Empire* 1:257 and 366 ff.

356. Ewig, "Résidence," 31.

357. Jones, *The Later Roman Empire* 1:499 ff. Timpe, "Comes," 64.

358. See the well-selected survey of passages in Jones, *The Later Roman Empire* 3:50 f. n. 50. Cf. esp. *Codex Theodosianus* I 29.6–8, or *Breviarium Alaricianum* I 10.1–3.

359. Jones, *The Later Roman Empire* 257 f., and 3:50 nn. 47 and 49. The mention of the *comes patrimonii* dates the passage to 500 at the earliest, for it was only then that this Italian innovation was adopted in East and West: see below, n. 399, and chap. 5, n. 227. Later Visigothic legislation still adheres to the basic equality of the two officials, whereby the *numerarius* is chosen by the bishops and the *defensor* by the "people": *Leges Visigothorum* II 1.27, p. 75, and XII 1.2, p. 407. Closer to the original situation is a document from the year 592: *Consensus de fisco Barcinonensi,* 473. On the definition of *numerarius* cf. Isidore of Seville, *Etymologiae* IX 4.119.

360. Demandt, "Magister militum," 683 f.

361. Hydatius, 192–201, aa. 458–460. Cf. Hoffmann, *Bewegungsheer* 1:314. See above, n. 345, and chap. 5, n. 216.

362. See above, n. 346. Jones, *The Later Roman Empire* 2:609 f., as well as Grosse, *Römische Militärgeschichte,* esp. 154 ff. On the image of a "cancerlike" expansion of the Visigothic kingdom see Rouche, *L'Aquitaine,* 32 n. 133, after Merobaudes, *Carmina: Panegyricus* I fr. II B vv. 11 ff., p. 10; II B vv. 150 f., p. 17; and II B vv. 189, p. 18. Ibid. I fr. II B v. 18, p. 10, the Goths are called *rei publicae venena.*

363. *Notitia dignitatum* oc. 36–41, esp. 37.24–29, on the expansion of the *tractus (ducatus) Armoricanus et Nervicanus,* to which belonged nearly three-quarters of Gaul, see Stein, *Bas-Empire* 1:268 f. Rouche, *L'Aquitaine,* 24 n. 53. Cf. Wolfram, *Intitulatio I,* 193.

364. Stein, *Bas-Empire* 1:269. A *comes Gothorum per Hispanias* who in Spain was placed in command and operated in Zaragoza, Pamplona, and the "neighboring *civitates*" is distinguished from *Vincentius dux Hispaniarum:* see *Chronica Gallica* 651 f., p. 664 f.

365. Stroheker, *Adel,* 90 n. 35. Cf. below, n. 379: list of passages.

366. Jordanes, *Getica* 240, p. 119. Cf. Stroheker, *Adel,* 82 and 185 n. 110.

367. Gregory of Tours, *Historia Francorum* II 20, p. 65 f. Cf. Stroheker, *Adel,* 86 f., 90 n. 35 and 146 n. 22.

368. See above, n. 363.

369. Jones, *The Later Roman Empire* 3:51 n. 52. Cf. below, n. 373. The *vir illustris* Vincentius in 464 is already described by the bishops of Tarraconensis as *dux provinciae nostrae.* Jones, however, sees in him an agent of Theodoric II, but this is contradicted by Stroheker (as n. 365), and esp. by the other title given to the functionaries of Euric (as n. 364).

370. On the designation *dux provinciae* and *rector provinciae* see *Leges Visigothorum,* p. 515, s.v. "dux" and p. 553, s.v. "rector." Especially significant in this context is *Concilium Toletanum* XII (681 I), p. 476. With this later source one should compare the *Breviarium Alaricianum,* which according to *Codex Theodosianus* I 16.7 still speaks of the *comites provinciarum;* cf. I 16.9–12 and 14. This entire section is devoted to the *officium rectoris provinciae* and most of it was taken over into the BA.

371. L. Schmidt, *Ostgermanen,* 515 n. 6. Stroheker, *Germanentum,* 125 n. 3. Cf. Jones (as n. 369).

372. As above, n. 363.

373. Victorius is called both *dux* and *comes.* But it is striking that the contemporary Sidonius Apollinaris (*Epistulae* VII 17.1, p. 123) assigns the correct title *comes* to his relative, whereas Gregory of Tours (as n. 367), from the perspective of the sixth century, calls Victorius *dux.* See in general K. Brunner, "Fürstentitel," 192 ff. and 211 ff. Cf. below, n. 379, as well as Ewig, "Ribuarien," 457 (10).

374. This is confirmed by a brief look at the modest dissertation of Oldenburg, *Kriegsverfassung,* 21 ff.

375. See chap. 3, nn. 310 ff.

376. See above, nn. 34 ff. (439), n. 56 (451), nn. 59 f. (Alans, 452/453), and n. 102 (Bretons, 469). Rouche, *L'Aquitaine,* 150 ff., and esp. 358 ff. The Visigothic preference for mounted combat is still mentioned by Isidore of Seville, *Historia vel Origo Gothorum* 69, p. 294. Cf. L. Schmidt, *Ostgermanen,* 518 n. 2.

377. Cassiodorus, *Variae* III 1.1, p. 79. On the battle of Vouillé see Gregory of Tours, *Historia Francorum* II 37, p. 87 f., according to whom the Goths "as usual" fled. This is correctly described as a tactical maneuver of feigned flight, which Byzantine military writers also recommended in fighting the Franks and which the Visigoths later used several times successfully: see Bodmer, *Der Krieger der Merowingerzeit,* 124 f., esp. Gregory of Tours VIII 45, p. 411, and IX 31, p. 450. On Gothic cowardice cf. ibid. II 27, p. 71. Examples for feigned flight as a tactical maneuver are given by Bachrach, *Alans,* 88 f. The difference in the manner of fighting Gregory of Tours (III 37, p. 88) expresses by using *comminus* for the Frankish foot soldiers and *eminus* for the Gothic horsemen.

378. Cf. L. Schmidt, *Ostgermanen,* 518 f. On imperial legislation that prohibited Roman provincials from bearing arms see chap. 5, n. 264. On the Roman generals in the Gothic army see below, n. 379. Isidore, *Historia vel Origo Gothorum* 70, p. 294 f., claims a late "Visigothic eminence at sea." For the crew of the fleet of Toulouse cf. Cassiodorus, *Variae* V 16.4 f., p. 152 f. A Roman who was forced into military service in the Gothic army is mentioned by Sidonius Apollinaris, *Epistulae* V 12, p. 86. On the Roman volunteers cf., in contrast, below, n. 525.

379. On the king's replacement as leader of the army cf. above, n. 354. On the adoption of the late antique territorial divisions as organizational units of the

kingdom of Toulouse see above, nn. 351 f. and nn. 363 ff.; cf. nn. 346 and 380. The first authorized commander is known from the time of Theodoric (II): *Nepotianus magister militum (comes)*. On *Sunericus comes,* who as *comes* served under Nepotianus, a properly appointed Roman commander whom Theodoric dismissed, see Demandt, "Magister militum," 683 f. Sunericus later replaced a certain Cyrila. As fully authorized agents acting in place of the king and as generals both of them received the title *dux*. Eventually Cyrila returned to Spain: Hydatius 192, 193, 197, 201, 212, 220, aa. 458, 459, 460, 461. On Nepotianus see Martindale, *Prosopography* 2:778 (Nepotianus 2), on Sunericus ibid. 1040, on Cyrila ibid. 334. As Euric's generals are mentioned esp.: *Gauterit comes Gothorum per Hispanias,* who was responsible for the capture of Zaragoza, Pamplona, and the surrounding territory; a Heldefredus, who together with *Vincentius Hispaniarum dux* captured Tarragona and the coastal cities. Vincentius is then immediately called *quasi magister militum*: *Chronica Gallica* 651–653, p. 664 f.; finally, we hear of a certain Salla in Mérida (Stroheker, *Germanentum,* 125 n. 3) and of Victorius of Auvergne: as above, nn. 369 and 373. A certain Namatius acted as Euric's "admiral": Stroheker, *Adel,* 194 n. 253. Under Alaric II a certain *Suatrius Gothorum dux* was in charge of Bordeaux: *Auctarium Havniense* a. 498, p. 331. We do not know whether the *magnificus et inluster Goiaricus comes* (cf. below, n. 405), who was responsible for the redaction of the *Breviarium Alaricianum,* also had military functions. He is probably identical with the Goiaricus who was killed by Gesalec: *Chronica Caesaraugustana,* chap. 510, p. 223. Ibid. the commander of the Ostrogothic expeditionary force is aptly called *Theodorici Italiae regis dux.* Cf. Claude, *Westgoten,* 54 with n. 3.

380. Claude, "*millenarius* und *thiuphadus,*" 181 ff., is against equating the *millenarius* and the *thiuphadus*; see esp. 187: "With the settlement in Aquitaine, the unit of one thousand warriors could have become the basis of the Visigothic administration, but the development took a different course. The administrative structure followed the existing Roman institutions, the *civitates.* For that reason the commander of the unit of one thousand had to hand over part of his authority to the officials who stood at the head of the Roman administrative units that the Visigoths had taken over, to the *comites* and the *duces.*" Subsequently, Claude argues, the Visigothic *millenarius* disappeared, whereupon the position that had thus become vacant was filled by the *thiuphadus.* This argument is attacked by Diesner, *Isidor,* 55 f., whose arguments are worth noting. He points to Isidore of Seville, who in his own days knew the *millenarius* as the military leader of a unit of one thousand. Diesner cannot believe that Isidore, "who was acquainted better than anyone else with the tasks of ecclesiastical and civil administration, and who, moreover, attached such great importance to the judgeship, did not also know about the administrative and judicial tasks of the *millenarius.* We simply once again detect in Isidore a large gap of factual knowledge, which was perhaps a result in part of the Latin term's being increasingly replaced in Visigothic law by the Gothic word *thiufadus*" (p. 56). See on this *Leges Visigothorum* II 1.27, p. 75, where the *thiufadus* and the *millenarius* still appear side by side, whereas ibid. IX 2.1 ff., pp. 366–369, the latter already seems to have been replaced by the *thiufadus.* On the organization of the Gothic army according to the decimal system see *Leges Visigothorum* II 1.27,

p. 75; IX 2.1–5, pp. 366–369. Sisebut, *De libro rotarum* vv. 4 f.: *At nos congeries obnubit turbida rerum/Ferrataeque praemunt milleno milite curae;* cf. Diesner, *Isidor,* 29 f. with nn. 6 and 32. On Sisebut see Manitius, *Lateinische Literatur* 1:188.

381. Claude (as n. 380), 182, and Jones, *The Later Roman Empire* 3:49 nn. 45 and 51 n. 55.

382. See above, n. 379.

383. *Codex Euricianus* 322; cf. Claude, *"millenarius* und *thiuphadus,"* 183, and Ewig, "Ribuarien," 451 ff. (2 ff.).

384. Feist, *Wörterbuch, 555.* Gamillscheg, *Romania Germanica* 1:357, and Dahn, *Könige der Germanen* 6:209. Claude, *"millenarius* und *thiuphadus,"* 182 f. (as above, n. 380).

385. On the question of when the Visigoths gave up their traditional language see above, n. 326.

386. *Leges Visigothorum* IX 2.1 ff., pp. 366 ff. Cf. Claude, *"millenarius* und *thiuphadus,"* 184 ff. (as above, n. 380).

387. See esp. Claude (as n. 380), 189 f., after Gamillscheg (as n. 384).

388. The widespread belief that in the later Visigothic kingdom of Spain there were only "masters and slaves" is attacked esp. by Diesner, "König Wamba," 16 ff. and 22 ff. with powerful arguments.

389. On the legal regulations (as n. 380) cf. Diesner, "König Wamba," 16 with n. 37, and Claude (as n. 380), 185. On the expression *exercitales* see *Leges Visigothorum* IX 2.9, p. 378.

390. Cf. the Herulian δοῦλοι in Procopius, *De bello Persico* II 25.28 (Wenskus, *Stammesbildung,* 336 n. 446, with special reference to the Germanic warrior names ending in *-theuaz,* "servant/slave"), as well as chap. 5, n. 346 (Amalafrida's military entourage). On the "lord over the multitude" see Feist (as n. 384). We can agree with Claude (as n. 380), 189, that the *thiufa* did not comprise exactly one thousand men. But this probably also applies already to the Toulousan *millena.*

391. Cf. the survey above, n. 326 as well as below, n. 593 (*gardingus*).

392. See *Leges Visigothorum,* p. 485 f., or *Concilios visigóticos,* pp. 289, 307, 434 f., 474, and 521. On *comes patrimonii* see above, n. 359 and below, n. 399.

393. This term is actually used (as n. 392); cf. Claude, *Adel, Kirche und Königtum,* p. 212, s.v. "Hofadel."

394. See above, nn. 367 and 369.

395. Stroheker, *Germanentum,* 137 ff. Claude, *Adel, Kirche und Königtum,* 55 ff., esp. 61 ff.

396. Claude, *Adel, Kirche und Königtum,* 67 ff. Stroheker, *Germanentum,* 231 ff.

397. As n. 396; cf. above, n. 289 and p. 207 no. 4.

398. Claude, *Adel, Kirche und Königtum,* (as chap. 3, n. 258). L. Schmidt, *Ostgermanen,* 523 n. 1 (list of passages in which the treasure is mentioned).

399. As n. 396. According to Procopius, *De bello Gothico* I (V) 4.1, the institution of the *patrimonium* was before its adoption by Constantinople considered a Western (Gothic) administrative unit: see Jones, *The Later Roman Empire* 1:255, and 258. This innovation, however, probably came too late for the kingdom of Toulouse. Cf. chap. 5, n. 227 on the establishment of the *patrimonium* under Odovacar and Theodoric the Great.

400. Claude, *Adel, Kirche und Königtum,* 68 n. 71.

401. Claude, 68 n. 72; cf. above, 260 n. 86. Gregory the Great, *Dialogi* I 9, p. 56: *biberunt ut Gothi.* Thus in Spanish the Gothic *exscaniar* has been preserved: Schmidt-Wiegand, "Die volkssprachigen Wörter," 74 n. 103.

402. Stroheker, *Adel,* 90 f., where 91 n. 42 additional Romans are named who were active in the administration of West Gothic Gaul. See ibid., 187 n. 212. Leo is called *consiliarius.* Martindale, *Prosopography* 2:662 f. (Leo 5).

403. Stroheker, *Adel,* 145 n. 18.

404. Ibid., 91 n. 42 and 168 f. n. 122, assumed that Eudomius became Leo's successor. On Anianus see Martindale, *Prosopography* 2:90 (Anianus 2).

405. *Auctoritas Alarici regis* (*Lex Romana Visigothorum,* pp. 2–4, or *Codex Theodosianus,* pp. xxxii–xxxv). See also L. Schmidt, *Ostgermanen,* 514 f., and *Leges Visigothorum,* p. 466 f.

406. As above, n. 404.

407. Jones, *The Later Roman Empire* 3:50 nn. 47–49. See also 1:257 ff.

408. See above, n. 399.

409. *Leges Visigothorum* X 1.16, p. 389, where *villici* and *praepositi* are already mentioned, has the greatest probability of dating back to the time of Euric. Cf. *Codex Euricianus* 276 f. On the *actores* (*fiscales*) and *numerarii* (cf. above, n. 359), see the corresponding entries in the index to the *Leges Visigothorum. Villici* are called oppressors and are abolished: Cassiodorus, *Variae* V 39.15, p. 166.

410. See chap. 3, n. 258. On the bowl that a Roman presented to Queen Ragnahild, see above, n. 320. Cf. L. Schmidt, *Ostgermanen,* 523.

411. The *Breviarium Alaricianum* was to be kept "in our treasure": see above, n. 405.

412. Claude, "Frühmittelalterliche Königsschätze," 6–13. L. Schmidt, *Ostgermanen,* 521 f. For the notion that the treasure, the capital, and the kingdom are one and the same see Jordanes, *Getica,* 215–218, p. 113. On the income from the minting or debasing of coins see L. Schmidt, *Ostgermanen,* 501 n. 2. Rouche, *L'Aquitaine,* 302 with n. 371, after Avitus, *Epistulae* 78, p. 96 f., and *Leges Burgundionum, Constitutiones extravagantes* XXI 7, p. 120 f.

413. Cassiodorus, *Variae* V 39.1–15, pp. 164–166: the tax collectors did not take the *polyptycha publica* into consideration but proceeded arbitrarily: ibid. 2, p. 164, whereas 13, p. 166, the level of taxation for the time of Alaric II and Euric is laid down. See chap. 5, n. 358.

414. On the treaty of 475 see above, nn. 151 and 258 f. The Goths' exemption from taxation follows from *Leges Visigothorum* X 1.16, p. 389. On the relief for the budget through the use of federates see Wolfram, "Gotisches Königtum," 14 ff. According to the *Vita s. Bibiani,* chap. 4, p. 96, Theoderid taxed the Romans. Goffart, *Barbarians and Romans,* 96 f. and 125 assigns this source to the time of Theodoric II between 456 and 466. Cf. Courcelle, *Histoire littéraire,* 146 ff. and 339 ff. On the image of a barbarian "tax paradise" see Salvian of Marseille (as below, n. 513). Cf. Claude, *Westgoten,* 43.

415. L. Schmidt, *Ostgermanen,* 522. Reinhart, "Münzen," 107 ff. Cf. Rouche, *L'Aquitaine,* 300 ff., esp. 303 (map of the mints), 301 f. and 306, as well as the literature cited above, n. 412. See also Barral i Altet, *La circulation,* 168 ff., as well as a review of this work by Wilfried Hartmann in *Deutsches Archiv* 34:619. 1978.

416. L. Schmidt, *Ostgermanen,* 521 f., after *Codex Theodosianus* X 1.2 (*Bre-*

viarium Alaricianum X 1.1) on *fiscus noster* and *domus dominicae*. See also *Leges Visigothorum*, p. 521, s.v. "fiscus." The expression *domus regiae* is used by Cassiodorus, *Variae* V 39.6, p. 165. Claude, *Adel, Kirche und Königtum*, 214, s.v. "Reichsgut." The administrators of the royal estates are given in n. 409. A good survey can be found in Jones, *The Later Roman Empire* 1:257 f. and 3:50 n. 49 (abundant citation of sources).

417. Claude, *Adel, Kirche und Königtum*, 38.

418. Claude, *Westgoten*, 84 n. 25 and 95 n. 65; cf. Nehlsen, *Sklavenrecht*, 164 n. 72.

419. Nehlsen, *Sklavenrecht*, 164–167. Jones, *The Later Roman Empire* 1:417–420 and 3:424, s.v. "emphyteutic leases." On the term *possessores* cf. *Leges Visigothorum* II 4.10, p. 103 and IX 1.21, p. 364.

420. Gaupp, *Ansiedlungen*, 394 ff. Goffart, *Barbarians and Romans*, 37 f., 206–208, and 272, s.v. Dahn, *Könige der Germanen* 6:55 f. Lot, "Régime de l'hospitalité," 1007 ff. Nehlsen, *Sklavenrecht*, 182 f. with n. 57. Rothenhöfer, *Untersuchungen*, 13 f. L. Schmidt, *Ostgermanen*, 505. Stein, *Bas-Empire* 1:266 ff. Courcelle, *Histoire littéraire*, 144 f. Matthews, *Aristocracies*, 343 with n. 5.

421. From the different terms of limitation in the *Codex Euricianus* 277.1–5 (cf. *Leges Visigothorum* X 1.16, p. 389), where a fifty-year period is provided for (in contrast to the usual thirty-year term), Gaupp, *Ansiedlungen*, 402, inferred that the original agreements of 418 were changed around 425 in the Goths' favor. He started from the assumption that the decrees of the *Codex Euricianus* were promulgated around 475 (cf. above, nn. 188 and 201). Cf. most recently Goffart, *Barbarians and Romans*, 123 f. with n. 34, and Rothenhöfer, *Untersuchungen*, 14 f. On the death of Honorius in the year 423 see above, n. 22.

422. *Codex Euricianus* 277.1; but the expression *sors Gothica* also refers to the entire kingdom of Toulouse: Sidonius Apollinaris, *Epistulae* VII 6.10, p. 110; VIII 3.3, p. 128. Cf. *Leges Visigothorum* X 1.16, p. 389 (*tertia Romanorum*).

423. *Codex Theodosianus* VII 8.5, p. 328.

424. Wirth, "Review of Wolfram," 698.

425. See chap. 5, n. 243 (Jean Durliat and Walter Goffart).

426. For the agreement between Constantius and the Aquitanian magnates see above, n. 9. On the very different reaction to the settlement of the Burgundians and Alans and on the silence about the modalities of the Visigothic settlement, see Wolfram, "Ansiedlung," 8 with n. 11, following Goffart, *Barbarians and Romans*, 111 ff., after *Chronica Gallica* 126–129 aa. 441–444, p. 660.

427. *Codex Theodosianus* VII 8, 1–9, 4; pp. 327–333. Cf. Goffart, *Barbarians and Romans*, 40 ff., 103 ff. and 162 ff. Wolfram, "Ansiedlung," 11.

428. Goffart, *Barbarians and Romans*, 124 and 162 ff.

429. This modification as against the view of Goffart is developed in the works mentioned below, (chap. 5, n. 243), especially by Jean Durliat. On the expressions *sortes Gothicae* and *tertia Romanorum* see above, n. 422; on the royal protection of the latter see *Leges Visigothorum* X 1, 8 and 16, pp. 385 f. and 389.

430. Durliat and Goffart (as chap. 5, n. 243). On the division of the kingdom of Toulouse into *civitates* see above, nn. 352 f.

431. Ammianus Marcellinus shows that the maintenance of the army and its Gothic members was traditionally the task of the curiales (XXI 6.2 f., revolt of the

units of Sueridus and Colias). Even at the "supposed abolition of the urban curias by the Emperor Anastasius" it was said that the curiales "governed the cities, maintained the soldiers, and with good right exercised administrative functions": see Chrysos, "Abschaffung," 97 f. Bandy's translation of τὸν στρατιώτην in Ioannes Lydus III 46, p. 204, as "civil servant," for which he bases himself on the usage in III 30, p. 178, probably rests on a false analogy, for the latter passage, in contrast to the one mentioning the curiales, uses the plural. Be that as it may, Ioannes Lydus also describes the curiales as the "sinews of the state" (see chap. 5, n. 252). His choice of words resembles that of Cassiodorus (see chap. 5, n. 212: *militia Romana*), and his division into "administration of the cities, maintenance of the army, exercising the functions of state" corresponds to the traditional order (see chap. 5, n. 252), and everything is tied in with the question of taxation. For the region of the kingdom of Toulouse the *Vita s. Bibiani*, chap. 4, p. 96, probably mentions the curiales and their tasks, even if indirectly. Cf. below, n. 433.

432. *Codex Euricianus* 323 mentions the use of slaves *in expeditione*. On the *buccellarii* and the *saiones* as well as on the different states of dependence of the free and the unfree see below, nn. 570 ff. Cf. Goffart, *Barbarians and Romans,* 172 f., 252 ff., as well as Wolfram, "Ansiedlung," 14 f.

433. Goffart, *Barbarians and Romans,* 95 ff. and 124 ff., esp. following the *Vita s. Bibiani,* chap. 4, p. 96; this source describes events in the time of Theodoric II between 456 and 466. Cf. Courcelle, *Histoire littéraire,* 146 ff. and 339 ff.

434. See, for example, Paulinus of Pella, *Eucharisticos* v. 570, p. 313 (purchase), and *Codex Euricianus* 305 (gift). For the possible taxation of Visigothic *possessores* (cf. Wolfram, "Ansiedlung," 18, on the Italian Ostrogoths), there is no evidence.

435. Courcelle, *Histoire littéraire,* 144 n. 2. Goffart, *Barbarians and Romans,* 165 ff.

436. Paulinus of Pella, *Eucharisticos* vv. 302–314, p. 303. See chap. 3, n. 290.

437. Cf. above, nn. 7 ff. on the question of senatorial input in the case of the Gothic settlement of the year 418. See Goffart, *Barbarians and Romans,* 110–113, esp. after *Chronica Gallica* a. 442, p. 660, on the encroachments of the Alans in *Gallia ulterior.*

438. Ausonius, *Epistolae* XXV vv. 115 f., p. 193. Stroheker, *Adel,* 41 with n. 182 and 78 with n. 201, as well as 39–41 and 85 f. with n. 11. Matthews, *Aristocracies,* 343. See Procopius, *De bello Gothico* I (V) 12.50 f., as well as below, n. 620 on Theudis.

439. Sidonius Apollinaris, *Epistulae* III 3.7, p. 42. Cf. Stroheker, *Adel,* 81.

440. See above, n. 435. On the expression *thesaurus publicus,* which was common at the latest in the Visigothic kingdom of Spain, see *Leges Visigothorum* VII 2.10, p. 292; XII 1.3, p. 409; and *Concilium Toletanum* XIII, p. 479, 20–30, or *Concilios visigóticos* no. 32, p. 26. On the escape into the woods of the provincials of Gaul, i.e., their joining the "Goths, Bagaudae, and other barbarians," see Salvianus of Marseille, *De gubernatione Dei* V 5.22 and 6.24–26, p. 59 f. On the expression "escape into the forest" see Sidonius Apollinaris, *Epistulae* II 1.3, p. 21. Cf. Courcelle, *Histoire littéraire,* 146 ff., esp. 149. One aspect of the traditional doctrine about the settlement of the Visigoths is also the assumption that the estates of the curiales were not divided at all: see Jones, *The Later Roman Empire* 1:253, and cf. 2:737 ff. Thompson, "The Settlement of Barbarians," 48 with n. 25 f.; cf.

Thompson, "Visigoths from Fritigern to Euric," 119 with n. 53. Lot, "Régime de l'hospitalité," 989–993. Delbrück, *Geschichte der Kriegskunst* 2:328 ff. Cf. Goffart, *Barbarians and Romans,* 206 f.

441. Sidonius Apollinaris, *Epistulae* III 5.2, p. 43. On the dating of the letter see Loyen, *Sidoine Apollinaire* 2:249.

442. *Codex Euricianus* 277.3, 280.6 (*legum statuta*), 305.1. Stroheker, *Eurich,* 98 f. Cf. above, n. 194. On the date that was set see *Leges Visigothorum* X 3.5, p. 398, but this provision was probably in the lost part of the *Codex Euricianus* 276.1 ff. See, however, on this Goffart, *Barbarians and Romans,* 235 ff. On the date set by the Ostrogoths see chap. 5, n. 256. On the division in front of "relatives and neighbors" see *Leges Visigothorum* X 1.8 f., p. 386 f.

443. *Leges Visigothorum* VIII 5.6, p. 348. Cf. Claude, *Adel, Kirche und König-tum,* 44 with n. 40.

444. Cf. ibid., 20 and 44 with Wolfram, "Gotische Studien II," 310 f. n. 100. On the term "functional comparison" see Wolfram, "Gotische Studien I," 24 and 31 f., and Wolfram, "Athanaric," 261.

445. *Leges Visigothorum* X 1.16, p. 389. On the titles of the managers of the domains see above, n. 409.

446. *Codex Euricianus* 276.3 ff.

447. Ibid., 286.1 f. and 307.1 f.

448. Paulinus of Pella, *Eucharisticos* vv. 570 ff., p. 313. Goffart, *Barbarians and Romans,* 105 n. 3. Courcelle, *Histoire littéraire,* 95. Matthews, *Aristocracies,* 344 n. 2. Cf. chap. 3, n. 290, and above, n. 15.

449. On the terms used here cf. Sidonius Apollinaris, *Epistulae* VII 6.10, p. 110; VIII 3.3, p. 128.

450. On the *gesta municipalia* see in general Fichtenau, *Urkundenwesen,* 77 ff.

451. To Rouche, *L'Aquitaine,* 136 ff., we owe the best discussion on this topic. Cf. James, *Merovingian Archaeology* 1:194 ff., and Matthews, *Aristocracies,* 343 with n. 4 f. Cf. above, n. 300.

452. Zöllner, *Franken,* 190 ff., esp. 197 f.

453. Ibid., 209–212. L. Schmidt, *Ostgermanen,* 49–51 and 453. The numerical strength of the Vandals is reported by Victor of Vita, *Historia persecutionis* I 1.2, p. 2. Cf. Claude, *Westgoten,* 37 f., and Goffart, *Barbarians and Romans,* 231–234, who doubts the authenticity of the figures in our sources.

454. See chap. 5, n. 144 (list of quotes).

455. Cf. Zöllner, *Franken,* 209 ff., unlike, for example, Altheim, *Geschichte der Hunnen* 1:366–368, even though there too one can find some interesting observations.

456. Garaud, "Peuplement," 98 with n. 2

457. Cf. Steinbach, *Studien,* 44 ff. See below, n. 467.

458. See chap. 3, n. 129 and n. 341. Rouche, *L'Aquitaine,* 163, follows Stein, *Bas-Empire* 1:267, and still calculates twenty thousand Gothic warriors, a figure that is still entirely possible.

459. Zöllner, *Franken,* 210.

460. Hachmann, *Goten und Skandinavien,* 473, has rightly denounced this methodological error.

461. Steinbach, *Studien,* 9 f. and 44 ff.

462. See below, n. 530 f. Cf. below, n. 488 (Walchen toponyms).

463. Bierbrauer, *Grab- und Schatzfunde*, 61–69. Cf. chap. 2, nn. 478 f.

464. Bierbrauer, *Grab- und Schatzfunde*, 53–56, after Cassiodorus, *Variae* IV 34.1–3, p. 129.

465. Bierbrauer, *Grab- und Schatzfunde*, 63 f., cf. 61.

466. On the problems of the archaeology of the Toulousan period cf. also the survey in Broëns, "Peuplement," 23 ff., but esp. Rouche, *L'Aquitaine,* 146 ff., as well as James, *Merovingian Archaeology* 1:196 ff. Cf. above, n. 451.

467. Gamillscheg, *Romania Germanica,* vols. 1–3 (1934–1936). Of the new edition, which will also be in three volumes, only the first volume has appeared (ibid. 11, 1 [1970]), but unlike the first edition this one does not contain the chapter "The Visigoths" which is of particular interest here. Gamillscheg is supported to a large extent by von Wartburg, *Entstehung,* 86 ff. An opposing position has been taken by Ferdinand Lot in several essays, esp. "Que nous apprennent," 289 ff., esp. 294–296. Cf. Lot, "De l'origine," 199 ff. Broëns, "Peuplement," 18 ff. and 29 ff., works in Lot's tradition, though in a very differentiated way. French scholars are above all concerned to trace back to Ligurian a word-ending that Gamillscheg spoke of as being a Germanic–*ingôz* suffix. A good survey of the discussion can be found in Kienast, *Volksstämme,* 43 f. n. 4 f. Cf. Claude, *Kirche, Adel und Königtum,* 43 f., and above, n. 451 (Rouche) and n. 457. Rouche, *L'Aquitaine,* 137, offers a good critique of Broën's work. See in general also above, n. 310.

468. Gamillscheg, *Romania Germanica* 1:vii f. (v. f.).

469. Ibid., 300–302. On Gothic bilingualism cf. chap. 2, nn. 487–490. Cf. Rouche, *L'Aquitaine,* 138 ff. with n. 15 (map of Gothic toponyms and index of Gothic places).

470. *Scriptores historiae Augustae* 25 (Claud.) 9.3-6. The Gallic *laeti* and barbarian settlements of the *Notitia dignitatum* oc. 42.65 ff., contain no reference to Goths. But such references do exist for Syria (or. XXXIII 32), but there every soldier was called "Goth": Jones, *The Later Roman Empire* 3:193 n. 53.

471. Gamillscheg, *Romania Gemanica* 1:302 ff., esp. 303 f. On Gothic bilingualism see n. 469, as well as chap. 2, nn. 487–490. On the Frankish forms that were created by way of analogy see Zöllner, *Franken,* 195 ff., esp. 199 f. See esp. Rouche, *L'Aquitaine,* 136 ff.

472. Gamillscheg, *Romania Germanica* 1:330–336 and 336 ff. (index of names). Rouche (as n. 471).

473. See Lot and Broëns (as n. 467). Cf. Gamillscheg, *Romania Germanica* 1:334–336.

474. Claude, *Adel, Kirche und Königtum,* 43 f.

475. Zöllner, *Franken,* 195 ff.

476. Gamillscheg, *Romania Germanica* 1:346 f.

477. Ibid., 140 and 346 f. (place-names along the border), 303 and 307 (place-names in the interior). Cf. Claude, *Westgoten,* 38. On *haims* and *villa* see Gamillscheg, *Romania Germanica* 1:302, 347, and 352.

478. Gamillscheg, *Romania Germanica* 1:347 ff.

479. Lechner, *Babenberger,* 96 f. Cf. Bach, *Namenkunde* 2, 1:233 ff.

480. See above, n. 77 and n. 109. Cf. Broëns, "Peuplement," 28 and 30 f.

481. Ibid., 21–23. Kienast, *Volksstämme,* 44. Rouche, *L'Aquitaine,* 142 n. 26,

rightly calls attention to the important "mark"-*gastald* places, which probably indicate an early colonization in the Toulousan heartland.

482. Kienast, *Volksstämme,* 74–95.

483. Ibid., 151–160, esp. 155 ff. and 168.

484. Ibid., 85 n. 38.

485. Ibid., 81 n. 26; cf. 17 n. 13, 19 f. n. 15a and 88.

486. Claude, *Westgoten,* 135 n. 66, on Gamillscheg, *Romania Germanica* 1:304, who hints (334 f.) at similar thoughts.

487. Gamillscheg, *Romania Germanica* 1:122 and 301. Cf. the maps of Gamillscheg (facing 304) and Broëns, "Peuplement," 38.

488. On the Walchen toponyms in general see Bach, *Namenkunde* 2, 2:180 f. For the special examples from Salzburg see Hörburger, "Ortsnamen," 14 and 38.

489. Gamillscheg, *Romania Germanica* 1:325 and 343.

490. Ibid., 303 and 307. On the *buccellarii* see below, nn. 573 ff.

491. Gamillscheg, *Romania Germanica* 1:318 and 328. On the Italian parallel see *Romania Germanica* 2:16 and 77. Cf. Battisti, "L'elemento gotico," 638 and 647 (on the low level Ostrogothic Latinization).

492. Bach, *Namenkunde* 2, 1:345 ff.

493. Gamillscheg, *Romania Germanica* 1:340 f.

494. Cf. Wolfram, *Intitulatio I,* 34 with n. 11.

495. Rostovtzeff, *Social and Economic History* 1:496 ff.

496. Salvianus of Marseille (as above, n. 440). Even when the Ostrogothic army moved into Visigothic Gaul in 508, it was joined by many runaway slaves, whom Theodoric explicitly ordered returned to their masters: Cassiodorus, *Variae* III 43.2, p. 100. Cf. Rothenhöfer, *Untersuchungen,* 108.

497. See chap. 2, nn. 73 ff. Cf. Wenskus, *Stammesbildung,* 471 and 476 f.

498. Thus the prohibition of marriage was felt to be a social injustice, as is revealed for the reasons of its abolishment: *Leges Visigothorum* III 1.1, p. 121 f. Cf. King, *Law and Society,* 12 f. On the later polarization of Hispano-Gothic society see Thompson, *The Goths in Spain,* 262–274. Stroheker, *Germanentum,* 161. Diesner (as below, n. 515). Cf. Goffart (as below, n. 519).

499. L. Schmidt, *Ostgermanen,* 504, after *Codex Euricianus* 276.3, 304, 312.1 f. *Leges Visigothorum* X 1.8 f., p. 385, and 16, p. 389.

500. This expression from imperial legislation still appears in Alaric's letter that accompanied his *Breviarium: Lex Romana Visigothorum,* pp. 2–4. Cf. *Codex Theodosianus* 1, p. xxxiv.

501. Ewig, "Volkstum und Volksbewusstsein," 246 (610) ff.

502. King, *Law and Society,* 14 with nn. 1–3, after *Lex Romana Visigothorum (Codex Theodosianus)* III 14.1. Cf. Stroheker (as n. 498). *Leges Visigothorum* III 1.1, p. 121 f. Cf. chap. 5, n. 106 and n. 241: a list of selected examples of "mixed marriages" among the Romano-barbarian upper stratum.

503. Stroheker, *Adel,* 91 f. Schäferdiek, *Die Kirchen der Westgoten,* 32 ff. Cf. L. Schmidt, *Ostgermanen,* 504, after Dahn, *Könige der Germanen,* 6, 71 f., as well as Ewig (as n. 501), 246 (610) f. n. 68, and Rouche, *L'Aquitaine,* 4, after Gregory of Tours, *Liber in gloria martyrum,* chap. 24, p. 502: *Romanos enim vocitant [Gothi] nostrae homines relegionis* [!].

504. *Epistulae* VII 14.10, p. 121 f. Ibid., V 13. 4, p. 87 (Seronatus).

505. Ibid., V 5.3 f., p. 81. Cf. Stroheker, *Adel,* 157 n. 74 and 221 n. 369.

506. Ennodius, *Vita Epifani* 89, p. 95.

507. See above, nn. 297 and 299 f., but this "hideous" costume was imitated by the Roman upstarts: Sidonius Apollinaris, *Epistulae* V 7.4, p. 82. Salvianus of Marseille, *De gubernatione Dei* V 21, p. 99. Stein, *Bas-Empire* 1:344–347, esp. 345 n. 152.

508. Sidonius Apollinaris VIII 3.2, p. 127 f. Cf. Courcelle, *Histoire littéraire,* 236. *Anthologia Latina,* vol. 1, no. 285, and Krause, *Handbuch,* 21 f.: *Inter eils Goticum scapia matzia ia drincan / non audet quisquam dignos educere versus. Vita Orientii,* chap. 5, p. 62 (in keeping with barbarian custom the king's table is set with an overabundance of food).

509. Sidonius Apollinaris, *Epistulae* VIII 9 v. 34, p. 136, and *Carmina* XII vv. 10 f., p. 231, on the seven-foot-tall Burgundians.

510. *Epistulae* IV 20.1 f., on the appearance and dress of the young Frankish prince Sigismer. Cf. on this Zöllner, *Franken,* 33 n. 4 and 276 (Sigismer).

511. Stroheker, *Adel,* 91 f., after Paulinus of Pella, *Eucharisticos* vv. 280–290, p. 302, and v. 514, p. 311, as well as Sidonius Apollinaris, *Epistulae* III 3.9, p. 42, and Avitus of Vienne, *Epistulae* 51, p. 79 f.

512. Courcelle, *Histoire littéraire,* 92–96, and 146, esp. after Paulinus of Pella, *Eucharisticos* v. 500, p. 310.

513. Courcelle, *Histoire littéraire,* 146–154, esp. 147 n. 6. The best known criticism of the late antique empire comes from Salvianus of Marseille, *De gubernatione Dei* V 15–58, esp. 21–23, 26, 28, 34–44. Cf. Orosius, *Historiarum adversum paganos* VII 41.7. But the story that Salvian's contemporary Priscus (fr. 8 [FHG 4, 86 ff.]) relates strikes the same note. One cannot therefore explain Salvian's criticism as a mere literary topos. Cf. Jones, *The Later Roman Empire* 2:767 ff., esp. 808 ff.

514. Cf. the expression *Romani tributarii(ales)* in the early medieval sources: Wolfram, "Zeit der Agilolfinger," 153. Nehlsen, *Sklavenrecht,* 166 n. 83. Goffart, *Barbarians and Romans,* esp. 93–99.

515. See the good bibliographical survey in Nehlsen, *Sklavenrecht,* 160–167, esp. 166 with nn. 80–82. Cf. below, n. 516. But Diesner, "König Wamba," 16 n. 37, rightly points out that there must have been a middle stratum, even if a thin one, in the Visigothic kingdom to the very end. Cf. above, nn. 388 and 498.

516. Claude, *Westgoten,* 111–115. Cf. the corresponding sections in Jones, *The Later Roman Empire* 2:712 ff. (The Cities), and 767 ff. (The Land). King, *Law and Society,* 159 ff. Dahn, *Könige der Germanen* 6:300 ff. Diesner, "König Wamba," 19. Cf. Cassiodorus, *Variae* V 39.5, p. 166: *vilicorum genus volumus amoveri.*

517. Zosimus V 40.2 Cf. chap. 3, n. 244 and n. 292. See Claude, *Adel, Kirche und Königtum,* 28 f. One of the most famous collaborators was without doubt the later emperor Avitus: see Loyen, *Recherches historiques,* 39 ff.

518. Paulinus of Pella, *Eucharisticos* vv. 303–310, p. 303, and vv. 498–502, p. 310: the sons of Paulinus went to Gothic Bordeaux "out of love of freedom." See Courcelle, *Histoire littéraire,* 93–96 and 167.

519. Wolfram, "Gotisches Königtum," esp. 4–12. Goffart, *Barbarians and Romans,* 125 n. 28 and 140 with n. 25. See chap. 3, n. 244, n. 292, and above, n. 99, n. 129 f., and n. 350. Cf. Stroheker, *Adel,* 159 n. 81; but the Calminius mentioned

there probably belongs to the Frankish period, while Sidonius's friend Calminius (cf. Sidonius, *Epistulae* V 12, p. 86) did in fact fight against the Auvergne *ad arbitrium terroris alieni.*

520. Stroheker, *Adel,* 145 n. 18 and 187 n. 212. Rouche, *L'Aquitaine,* 42 f.

521. Sidonius Apollinaris, *Epistulae* VIII 9.1 ff., esp. 5 vv. 1 ff., p. 135 ff., esp. 136 f. Cf. above, nn. 295 ff., and Courcelle, *Histoire littéraire,* 166.

522. Sidonius Apollinaris, *Epistulae* VIII 6.13 ff., esp. 16, p. 132 f. Cf. Stroheker, *Adel,* 194 n. 253.

523. Sidonius Apollinaris, *Carmina* VII vv. 215 ff., p. 208 f.; vv. 469 ff., p. 214; vv. 481 and 495–498, p. 215. Loyen, *Recherches historiques,* 39 ff. Courcelle, *Histoire littéraire,* 146, cf. 166 f.

524. Courcelle, *Histoire littéraire,* 95, after Paulinus of Pella, *Eucharisticos* vv. 498–515, p. 310.

525. Stroheker, *Adel,* 145 f. n. 22; cf. above, n. 140. See Gregory of Tours, *Historia Francorum* II 37, p. 88.

526. Rouche, *L'Aquitaine,* 52–57. Stroheker, *Adel,* 81.

527. *Concilium Narbonense,* chap. 4, p. 254 f. (p. 147). Rouche, *L'Aquitaine,* 160 and 300 f.

528. King, *Law and Society,* 133–145. D'Ors, *Código,* 130 f. See, for example, Sidonius Apollinaris, *Epistulae* III 4.1, p. 43; IV 5.1, p. 57; VI 11, p. 100 f. (letter of recommendation for a Jew); VIII 13.3 f., p. 145 (the conversion of a Jew to Christianity is celebrated). Cf. Procopius, *De bello Gothico* I (V) 8.41, and 10.24–26: the Jews of Naples supported the Ostrogoths against Belisarius. Cassiodorus, *Variae* V 37, p. 163 f.: "The Jew, since he 'cannot find eternal rest,' shall at least be given 'earthly rest.'" See in general Ladner, "Aspects of Patristic Anti-Judaism," 355 ff.

529. Rouche, *L'Aquitaine,* 150 ff. and 358 ff. On the revitalization of the Celtic language see, for example, Sidonius Apollinaris, *Epistulae* III 3.2 f.; p. 41, and above, n. 111. On King Riothimus see *Epistulae* III 9, p. 46, and Martindale, *Prosopography* 2:945 (Riothamus). Cf. Loyen, *Sidoine Apollinaire* 2:249 f. n. 9. On the Bagaudae in general see MacMullen, *Enemies,* 192 ff., esp. 211–213. Szádeczky-Kardoss, "Bagaudae," 346–354. Von Ungern-Sternberg, "Bagaudes," 1344 f. Wolfram, "Ethnogenesen," 115 n. 81 f.

530. Rouche, *L'Aquitaine,* 135 ff., offers the best discussion of the problem. Ibid., 139 includes a carefully prepared map of the Gothic toponyms in Aquitaine and Septimania. The index of the *-villa* places that are included on the map is confined to "un minimum, mais un minimum sûr" (ibid., 143). The corresponding indices of names are found in ibid., 532–534 n. 12 (*-ingôz*), n. 15 (*villa Gothorum*), n. 19 (Taifali), n. 26 ("mark"-*gastald*), n. 31 (*-villa*) and ibid., 554–562. Cf. on this Gamillscheg, *Romania Germanica* 1:72, 140, 307, 326, 346 f.

531. Gamillscheg, *Romania Germanica* 1:338, and Rouche, *L'Aquitaine,* 138 n. 12 (list of places). Cf. with this Bessas, a Gothic general under Belisarius, who did not join Theoderic the Great in his trek to the West: Procopius, *De bello Gothico* I (V) 16.2 as well as Jordanes, *Getica* 265, p. 126. On the Bessi see Wiesner, *Thraker,* 13, 19 f., and 164. On the Galindi see Gamillscheg, *Romania Germanica* 1:315, as well as Kienast, *Volksstämme,* 87 n. 43, and Zöllner, *Völker,* 129 n. 29. See also Kunkel, "Ostsee," 1820.

532. Gamillscheg, *Romania Germanica* 1:315 and 327. Cf. chap. 3, nn. 182 ff. (Gainas), and nn. 300 ff. (Sarus).

533. Rouche, *L'Aquitaine,* 140 n. 19 f. (Taifali), 148 n. 47 (Vandals), n. 48 (Burgundians), n. 49 (Alans) (after Bachrach, *Alans,* 30 and 137), 148 n. 53 f. (Sarmatians).

534. Ibid., 140 with n. 19 f. The list of names given in n. 19 is currently unsurpassed. On the Taifali see chap. 2, nn. 372–374 and below, n. 560.

535. Sidonius Apollinaris, *Carmina* VII vv. 341 f., p. 211.

536. See chap. 3, n. 128, esp. Claudian, *De consulatu Stilichonis* I, as well as *In Rufinum* I. Cf. Sidonius Apollinaris, *Carmina* V vv. 474–477, p. 199; II vv. 321–328, p. 211. Loyen, *Recherches historiques,* 51 f. Loyen, *L'esprit précieux,* 20 ff., esp. 25.

537. Sidonius Apollinaris, *Carmina* V v. 476, p. 199; VII vv. 399 and 403, p. 213 f. See chap. 1, n. 61.

538. See chap. 3, nn. 90–92.

539. See chap. 3, nn. 293 ff. (Athaulf), nn. 302 ff. (Sarus), and nn. 321 ff. (Radagaisus), n. 239 f. (Alaric I and Sarus).

540. Wolfram, "Theogonie," 88 with nn. 49 and 53. The passages in question are Sidonius Apollinaris, *Epistulae* VIII 9.5 vv. 36–37, p. 137 as well as Jordanes, *Getica* 166, p. 101; 173 f., p. 103; 283 f., p. 131. Jordanes, *Romana* 347, p. 44 f., cf. above, with nn. 145 ff. and 150 (Ruricius letter).

541. As above, n. 530.

542. Perhaps this is how Jordanes, *Getica* 284, p. 131, is best to be understood.

543. Sidonius Apollinaris (as n. 540).

544. Courtois, *Les Vandales,* 46.

545. Cassiodorus, *Variae* III 3.3, p. 80. Cf. above, nn. 162 ff.

546. *Epistulae* VIII 9.5 vv. 31–32, p. 136.

547. See above, n. 67. Jordanes, *Getica* 233, p. 117.

548. Procopius, *De bello Gothico* I (V) 12.50 ff. Cf. Jordanes, *Getica* 302, p. 135 f. Claude, *Adel, Kirche und Königtum,* 48. On Theudis see Martindale, *Prosopography* 2:1112 f.

549. See above, n. 522. Cf. Sidonius Apollinaris, *Epistulae* VIII 9.5 vv. 21–27, p. 136. *Carmina* VII vv. 369–371, p. 212, and v. 390, p. 213. Courcelle, *Histoire littéraire,* 235 f.

550. Ewig, "Volkstum," 233 (590) f., 235 (593) f., as well as 239 n. 39 (599 n. 37) and 254 n. 110 (621 n. 97).

551. Sidonius Apollinaris, *Epistulae* VIII 3.3, p. 128.

552. Ewig, "Probleme," 47 ff. Böhme, *Germanische Grabfunde,* 195 ff., whose assumption of the existence of federates on the left bank of the Rhine in the fourth century is deprived of its historical basis by Ewig, "Probleme," 53. Hoffmann, *Bewegungsheer* 1:139 f. Jones, *The Later Roman Empire* 2:611 ff., esp. 614 with nn. 12 and 620.

553. *Notitia dignitatum oc.* XLII 44.65; cf. Ewig (as n. 552), 47 f. n. 4.

554. As above, n. 533 f.

555. Jordanes, *Getica* 194 f. and 197, p. 108 f., as well as 226–228, p. 115 f. Cf. Wenskus, "Alanen," 123. See above, n. 59 f.

556. As above, n. 533.

557. Courtois, *Les Vandales,* 51 ff. Miltner, "Vandalen," 305–307. Wenskus (as n. 555). Ammianus Marcellinus XXXI 2.17: beginning of the famous excursus on the Alans, remarks on the splitting up of the Alans before they entered the Roman Empire.

558. See chap. 3, n. 290. Cf. Hoffmann, *Bewegungsheer* 1:143 nn. 96, and 105 as well as 194 n. 663.

559. Claudius Marius Victor, *Alethia* III vv. 189–194, p. 413. Cf. Courcelle, *Histoire littéraire,* 81 n. 3. On Gothic ancestor worship see chap. 2, n. 464.

560. Rouche, *L'Aquitaine* (as n. 533 f.), and 358 ff. Cf. Hoffmann, *Bewegungsheer* 1:198: "The Taifalian horsemen were probably recruited from the former Taifalian prisoners of war who had been settled as *gentiles* in northern Italy and Gaul to cultivate the soil." Cf. chap. 2, nn. 372–374. See esp. *Notitia dignitatum oc.* XLII 65–70 on the Sarmatian-Taifalian settlements of *gentiles in Gallia.*

561. *Historia Francorum* V 7, p. 204. Ewig, "Volkstum," 234 (591) ff. Cf. Rouche, *L'Aquitaine,* 140. Broëns, "Peuplement," 33. Garaud, "Peuplement," 96 f.

562. Ewig, "Volkstum," 235 f. (592–594). In this context it should be mentioned that the *Equites Taifali Honoriani,* which were established between 395 and 398, were employed in Gaul and Britain at the beginning of the fifth century and were no doubt recruited from the Taifali of northern Italy and Gaul: Hoffmann, *Bewegungsheer* 1:198, and 2:6 n. 161.

563. Stein, *Bas-Empire* 1:328 f. Schäferdiek, *Die Kirchen der Westgoten,* 107 ff.

564. *Codex Theodosianus* XIII 11.10 (399 IV 5). Cf. Ammianus Marcellinus XX 8.13. Hoffmann (as n. 560) on the Taifali and Alans. Cf. *Notitia dignitatum oc.* (as n. 560).

565. Cf. the name given to Ag(r)iwulf (as n. 547).

566. See above, n. 59 f. and n. 533 f., esp. Rouche, *L'Aquitaine,* 140.

567. Ewig, "Volkstum," 233 f. (591) n. 12 f., after the reconstruction of a charter of Sigibert III by Levison, "Metz und Südfrankreich," 144 f.

568. Cf. above, nn. 420 ff.

569. Wolfram "Gotische Studien II," 311 and 322–324.

570. Claude, *Adel, Kirche und Königtum,* 40 with n. 17, after *Codex Euricianus* 323. On the levying of slaves for military purposes by the Roman government see *Codex Theodosianus* VII 13.16 f. (406 IV 17/19). The unfree, however, are promised freedom in return for military service. *Codex Theodosianus* VII 13.16 (406 IV 17), also presupposes the slaves of the barbarians as fellow warriors.

571. Cf. Wolfram, *Splendor Imperii* 108 ff.

572. Grosse, *Römische Militärgeschichte,* 86 f. 194, and 280 ff.

573. Olympiodorus fr. 7. See Constantinus Porphyrogenitus, *De thematibus orientis,* chap. 6 (11), on the etymology of *buccellarius.*

574. Wirth, "Buc(c)ellarii," 802. Stein, *Bas-Empire* 1:239 with n. 103. Grosse, *Römische Militärgeschichte,* 287 ff. Jones, *The Later Roman Empire* 2:665–667. Diesner, "König Wamba," 22 ff. Diesner, "Das Buccellariertum," 321 ff.

575. *Codex Iustinianus* IX 12.10 (468 VIII 28). On Euric's legislation of 475 see above, n. 188 and n. 200 f.

576. *Codex Euricianus* 310 f.

577. On what follows see Claude, *Adel, Kirche und Königtum,* 40 ff. King, *Law*

and Society, 187 f. Cf. *Leges Visigothorum* V 3.4, p. 217. The Roman precursor to the Gothic buccellariate is discussed by Diesner (as n. 574).

578. *Codex Euricianus* 310.1–6. Cf. *Leges Visigothorum* V 3.1, p. 217.

579. Claude, *Adel, Kirche und Königtum,* 43.

580. As above, n. 573.

581. Caesar, *De bello Gallico* VI 23.7 f. Claude, *Adel, Kirche und Königtum,* 41 f. King, *Law and Society,* 187–189. See esp. *Leges Visigothorum* V 3.1–4, p. 216 f. Diesner, "König Wamba," 24 n. 71, 25 n. 74, and esp. 26: "Up to now it has not been realized that among those who owed the *patrocinium* the *buccellarii* . . . formed an elite."

582. *Codex Euricianus* 311. D'Ors, *Codigo,* 242–245 with n. 825. Claude, *Adel, Kirche und Königtum,* 40 ff. Zeumer, "Gesetze I," 102 f. Cf. King (as n. 581). Wrede, *Sprache der Ostgoten,* 109–111. Gamillscheg, *Romania Germanica* 1:358.

583. See chap. 2, n. 453.

584. D'Ors, *Código,* 243 n. 829. *Leges Visigothorum* V 3.3, p. 217.

585. Jones, *The Later Roman Empire* 1:254 ff. and 265. Stein, *Bas-Empire* 2:122 f. See chap. 5, nn. 229 ff.

586. Zeumer (as n. 582).

587. Claude, *Adel, Kirche und Königtum,* 42 f. should be modified a little in view of Isidore of Seville, *Etymologiae* X 263; cf. King, *Law and Society,* 188, after *Leges Visigothorum* V 3.3, p. 217, and p. 556, s.v. "saio." On the term "patrimonial official" see above, n. 332.

588. Cf. D'Ors, *Código,* 287, s.v. "dominus"; with 290, s.v. "patronus," esp. *Codex Euricianus* 310 f. with 323. See also Nehlsen, *Sklavenrecht,* 168 ff. and Rothenhöfer, *Untersuchungen,* 37.

589. Claude, *Adel, Kirche und Königtum,* 39, after CE 276.7 and 284.2.

590. Nehlsen, *Sklavenrecht,* 168 f.

591. Thus the *comes civitatis* of the later period can have the *iudex* whipped if he is guilty of an offense: *Leges Visigothorum* III 4.17, p. 157. Claude, *Westgoten,* 115 has some general comments. Cf., in contrast, Nehlsen, *Sklavenrecht,* 169 ff., who speaks explicitly of Chindasuintha's "legislation that was favorable to the slaves." See finally the index (as n. 587) for "saio," as well as *Leges Visigothorum,* p. 558 f. on *servus* and *servitium.* Above all, in this context reference should be made to the *servi fisci* (*fiscales*); cf. Claude, *Adel, Kirche und Königtum,* 214, s.v. 'Unfreie des Königs.' See Diesner, "König Wamba," 12 f., and below, n. 592.

592. As n. 587: *saio.* See Diesner, "König Wamba," 16 n. 37. Concerning corporal punishment cf. above, n. 591.

593. The fundamental study of Sánchez-Albornoz, *Feudalismo* 1:77 ff., sees in the *gardingus* the *fidelis regis,* the king's retainer, and neglects somewhat the late occurrences of the term. Claude, *Adel, Kirche und Königtum,* 15 with n. 29 and esp. 73 n. 93. King, *Law and Society,* 56 ff. Thompson, *Goths in Spain,* 252 f. Diesner, "König Wamba," 16 n. 36, who also discusses the most recent literature on the topic. L. Schmidt, *Ostgermanen,* 515. Cf. above, n. 310 and n. 325 f. on the problem of the switch in languages. On the equating of *gardingus* and *domesticus* see the description of a Gothic retainer as δομέστικος in Olympiodorus fr. 17. Diesner, "protectores (domestici)," 1113 ff.

594. See above, n. 1.

595. Düwel, *Alarich II,* 128 f., or L. Schmidt, *Ostgermanen,* 497. The bad press Alaric II has received goes back to a comment of Isidore of Seville, *Historia vel Origo Gothorum* 36, p. 281 f. The events themselves are described in L. Schmidt, *Ostgermanen,* 342 ff., as well as Stein, *Bas-Empire,* 2:152 ff. and in 2:153 n. 1, see the survey of the sources, esp. Procopius, *De bello Gothico* I (V) 12.43–48. Cf. also above, n. 169 f., Claude, *Westgoten,* 36 f.

596. See chap. 5, nn. 751 ff.; cf. above, n. 377 (Vouillé).

597. See above, n. 179.

598. Claude, *Westgoten,* 54 ff. Zöllner, *Franken,* 83 ff., cf. 67. Rouche, *L'Aquitaine,* 51 ff.

599. The description as a "narrow strip of land" is a stereotype in the literature: see, for example, L. Schmidt, *Ostgermanen,* 502.

600. Narbonne replaced Toulouse as the Visigothic capital, until another defeat in 531 forced the transfer of the royal court south of the Pyrenees, namely, to Barcelona: see *Chronica Caesaraugustana* a. 531, p. 223, and Isidore of Seville, *Historia vel Origo Gothorum* 40, p. 283. Cf. Rouche, *L'Aquitaine,* 56 with n. 19.

601. After *Concilium Toletanum* XVII (694 XI 9), p. 525 (*Leges Visigothorum,* p. 485), the *Gallia provincia* was a *ducatus.*

602. Wolfram, *Intitulatio I,* 70 f.

603. On the age of Alaric II cf. n. 168. For a general discussion of the situation after the king's death see Claude, *Adel, Kirche und Königtum,* 47 f., and Claude, *Westgoten,* 36 f. esp. after *Chronica Caesaraugustana* a. 508, p. 223. Gesalec was born *ex concubina,* but on principle that by no means disqualified him from the succession: see chap. 5, n. 105. Martindale, *Prosopography* 2:509 f. (Gesalicus).

604. Claude, *Adel, Kirche und Königtum,* 47 f.

605. Claude, *Westgoten,* 55, assumes that Amalaric was born around 502. This view, with which I agree, probably finds support in the marriage of Amalaric after 526 to the daughter of Clovis: see ibid., 56 with n. 9. Cf. Zöllner, *Franken,* 84 with n. 3.

606. Cf. Jordanes, *Getica* 146, p. 96. Martindale *Prosopography* 2:64 f. (Amalaricus).

607. Cf. Cassiodorus, *Variae* V 43.1, p. 170. Cf. Wolfram, *Splendor Imperii,* 108 ff.

608. Claude (as n. 598).

609. Cf. Cassiodorus, *Variae* V 43.2, p. 170. Cf. chap. 5, n. 105.

610. Isidore of Seville, *Historia vel Origo Gothorum* 37, p. 282. *Chronica Gallica* 690, p. 665.

611. Procopius, *De bello Gothico* I (V) 12.41–43, where it is claimed, however, that Gesalec was not made king until after the loss of Carcassonne.

612. *Chronica Caesaraugustana* a. 510, p. 223 (cf. Martindale, *Prosopography,* 2: 517, and above, n. 202 and n. 405, Goiaricus), as well as ibid. a. 511: the murder of the *comes* Veila, who probably belonged, however, to the party of Gesalec.

613. L. Schmidt, *Ostgermanen,* 344 f., esp. after Procopius, *De bello Gothico* I (V) 12.43 ff.

614. On the designation of the Franks and Burgundians as barbarians see Cassiodorus, *Variae* III 43.1, p. 100. The reestablishment of the prefecture of Gaul

cannot be precisely dated, but it probably took place in 509 at the earliest, if not actually in 510: L. Schmidt, *Ostgermanen,* 347; cf. Ensslin, *Theoderich,* 146 ff., as well as chap. 5, n. 227.

615. *Chronica Caesaraugustana* aa. 510–513, p. 223. Isidore of Seville, *Historia vel Origo Gothorum* 38, p. 282. Cassiodorus, *Variae* V 43 f., p. 170 f. Zöllner, *Franken,* 66 with n. 3 f. Ewig, "Teilungen," 125 (663) with n. 57, realizes that Gesalec met his death on Burgundian territory (cf. chap. 5, n. 373); but Isidore does not tell us whether Burgundians or Ostrogothic guards captured and killed the luckless Visigothic king. Ewig, "Teilungen," 124–127 (663–666) gives one of the best accounts of Gesalec. Ibid., 125 n. 61, after Agnellus, *Liber pontificalis ecclesiae Ravennatis,* chap. 39, p. 304 (331), assumed fighting in Sicily in 513/514, but the editor Oswald Holder-Egger (ibid. 304 n. 3) does not accept this. On the exodus of the Gothic upper stratum cf. Claude, *Westgoten,* 59. On the emigration of the Goths from Gaul see Procopius, *De bello Gothico* I (V) 13.13.

616. Claude, *Westgoten,* 55, after *Laterculus regum Visigothorum,* nos. 17 f., p. 465 f. It is claimed here, however, that Theodoric exercised the "monarchy in Spain" as the guardian of Amalaric. Cf. *Chronica Caesaraugustana* a. 513.2, p. 223. On Theodoric's elevation to the kingship see chap. 5, n. 145, n. 173 f., as well as n. 192 f. On this and what follows see also chap. 5, nn. 352 ff.

617. Ewig, "Teilungen," 127 f. (666 f.). Procopius, *De bello Gothico* I (V) 12.44–54. On the treasure cf. also above, nn. 410–412.

618. See chap. 5, n. 358.

619. *Laterculus regum Visigothorum,* no. 19, p. 466. Procopius, *De bello Gothico* I (V) 13.4–13.

620. Isidore, *Historia vel Origo Gothorum* 40, p. 283, reports the killing of Amalaric "by the army," but it is not quite clear whether this occurred in or near Narbonne or in Barcelona. *Chronica Caesaraugustana* a. 531, p. 223, reports the slaying of the king in Barcelona by a Frank called Besso. This Besso could have been a retainer of Amalaric's Frankish wife. As Gregory of Tours (*Historia Francorum* III 10, p. 107) has it, the deed was committed by an unknown Frank right after the battle of Narbonne. Cf. Ewig, "Teilungen," 129 (669) n. 79. See also Wolfram, *Intitulatio I,* 60.

621. It is characteristic that Gregory of Tours (*Historia Francorum* III 30, p. 126) gives the first description of the "Gothic disease" right after the defeat of Amalaric. The expression *morbus Gotorum,* however, comes from Fredegar, *Chronicon* IV 82, p. 163. Cf. Messmer, *Hispania-Idee,* 68 and 73. Claude, *Adel, Kirche und Königtum,* 48: after the death of Amalaric there existed in 531 "no legitimate member of the family of Theodoric I (recte: Theoderid)." Theudis thereupon reigned until his assassination in the year 548. He was followed by Theudegisel (548/549). That he has the same name as Theodahad's son Theudegisklos (Procopius, *De bello Gothico* I [V] 11.10; Wenskus, "Amaler," following p. 247 [appendix]) raises the problem of identification. Isidore, *Historia vel Origo Gothorum,* chap. 43, p. 285, reports that Theudis was killed in a blood feud. At the point of death King Theudis prohibited the persecution of his murderer, *quod et ipse privatus ducem suum sollicitatum occiderit.* If we identify this *dux* of the Ostrogothic governor Theudis (see Assunta Nagl, "Theudis," RE II 11 [1936], 246–249) as King Amalaric, for whose death Theudis was certainly not without guilt, we would be dealing here with

a case of blood vengeance, behind which may have been Amalaric's cousin Theudegisel. For a rather positive assessment of this proposed identification see Wenskus, "Amaler," 248, genealogical chart of the Amali, and Wolfram, "Gotisches Königtum," 25 n. 148. But since the successor of Theudis is nowhere called an Amal, not even by Jordanes (*Getica* 303, p. 126), this scenario is rather unlikely; cf. Claude, *Adel, Kirche und Königtum,* 48 with n. 9. Finally, if Zimmermann, "Grabstein," 330 ff., esp. 343 ff., 349 f., and 352 f., is correct in reading *frater* instead of *parvulus,* then the Amal Theudegisel must have died by 537 and the discussion becomes pointless. Cf. chap. 5, n. 362 and n. 497.

622. Claude, *Adel, Kirche und Königtum,* 55 ff.; Claude, *Westgoten,* 66 ff.; Stroheker, *Germanentum,* 134–191 (Leovigild).

623. Cf. Claude, *Westgoten,* 83 f.

624. Kienast, *Volksstämme,* 75 ff., esp. 88.

625. See above, Introduction, n. 102 (Goffart).

626. Kienast, *Volksstämme,* 87 and 155.

627. Ibid., 75 and 84 ff.

5: The Ostrogoths

1. On the name "Ostrogoths" cf. chap. 1, nn. 62 ff. Two peculiar works on the Ostrogoths were written by Thomas Burns, *The Ostrogoths;* cf. the reviews by Claude and Pohl. Burns's book *A History of the Ostrogoths* is not much better; he proceeds from the false premise that the Ostrogoths before the invasion of the Huns are identical with the Ostrogoths after the fall of the Hunnic empire. See also Goffart's review.

2. Jordanes, *Getica,* 199 f. and 253, pp. 109 f. and 123.

3. Procopius, *De bello Gothico* IV (VIII) 35.15–30.

4. L. Schmidt, "Die letzten Ostgoten," 92 (5) ff. Wenskus, *Stammesbildung,* 485 and 494. Wolfram, *Intitulatio I,* 96 n. 47.

5. Wenskus, "Amaler," 247. Cf. chap. 1, n. 98.

6. On Odovacar see Jordanes, *Romana* 344–349, p. 44 f., and Isidore, *Historia vel Origo Gothorum* 39, p. 283, who even sees him as Ostrogothic king.

7. Priscus fr. 8 does mention among Attila's *logades* (magnates) some clearly Gothic names, though none from the Amal family tradition—see Maenchen-Helfen, *The Huns,* 192 f.; nevertheless, Theodoric the Great's tradition, which claims that the generation of his father held such a position at Attila's court, seems credible: see Jordanes, *Getica* 199 f., p. 109 f.; 209, p. 111; 252 f., p. 123.

8. Jordanes, *Getica* 246–251, p. 121 f. On the forty-year interregnum mentioned ibid. 251, p. 122, see Wenskus, *Stammesbildung,* 481. L. Schmidt, *Ostgermanen,* 257. Wagner, "Namengebung," 5 and 15. On the kingless Alatheus group see below, n. 42.

9. Jordanes, *Getica* 252, p. 123, states explicitly that Valamir "as the successor to his forefathers" attained the kingship at a time when the Huns "ruled over the Goths, among other peoples." Fröhlich, *Studien,* 44. On the lengthy process of the consolidation of Hunnic power, until it finally reached its height and at the same time came to an end under Attila, see the historical accounts in Maenchen-Helfen,

The Huns, 59 ff.; Thompson, *Attila and the Huns,* 24 ff.; Altheim, *Geschichte der Hunnen* 1:338 ff., 4:271 ff., 5:265 ff.

10. Jordanes, *Getica* 246–250 (esp. 248), p. 121 f.

11. Ibid., 174 f., p. 103; 251, p. 122 f.

12. As chap. 4, nn. 538–543 esp. n. 540. Cf. Wolfram, "Theogonie," 88.

13. See the list as in chap. 3, n. 109.

14. On the chaos of the Hunnic invasion see St. Ambrose, *Expositio in Lucam* X 10. Zosimus IV 25.1 Cf. Ammianus Marcellinus XXXI 3.7 (Athanaric excluded the Taifalian tribal territory from his defensive measures). See in general Altheim, *Geschichte der Hunnen* 1:338 ff. Cf. chap. 2, n. 225 f.

15. Schäferdiek, "Germanenmission," 503.

16. Zosimus IV 38 f. Ibid. IV 38.1 speaks of the large number of Greutungi, their good weapons, and their strange appearance.

17. Maenchen-Helfen, *The Huns,* 59, esp. after Zosimus V 21 f. (Gainas). But see the literature given in chap. 3, n. 193 f. on the various versions of the death of Gainas. Orosius, *Historiae adversum paganos* VII 37.12 f. (Radagaisus). Cf. chap. 3, n. 192 f. and nn. 321 ff., esp. 331.

18. Jordanes, *Getica* 166, p. 101; 174 f., p. 103; 250 f., p. 122. Cf. on this Wolfram, "Theogonie," 85 f. with nn. 32–36.

19. See below, nn. 87–93. Thus it is characteristic that the Andagis-Andela Amali, who in 451 fought under Valamir on the side of the Huns, split off from the Valamir Goths after the disintegration of the Hunnic realm: Cf. Jordanes, *Getica* 209, p. 111 with 266, p. 126.

20. On this quote cf. Jordanes, *Getica* 315, p. 138.

21. The Tervingian Munderic is considered one of the best sources of information: see Wolfram, "Gotische Studien I," 2 n. 8.

22. Wenskus, *Stammesbildung,* 479 ff. with nn. 310 ff., and "Amaler," 247, has rightly pointed out this observation of the editor Theodor Mommsen: See Jordanes, *Getica,* p. xxxiii f.

23. Jones, *Prosopography* 1:965.

24. Ammianus Marcellinus XXXI 3.3; 4.12, 5.3 f., 8.4; 12.12 and 17; 16.3. Cf. chap. 3, n. 29. See Wolfram, "Schlacht von Adrianopel," 243 and 249.

25. See the account of the events by Nagy, "Pannonia," 306–321. Cf. on this chap. 3, n. 92 and n. 111. Mócsy, "Pannonia," 578–582. Egger, "Historisch-epigraphische Studien," 57 ff. L. Schmidt, *Ostgermanen,* 261. Miltner, "Vandalen," 303 f. Courtois, *Les Vandales,* 39. Stein, *Bas-Empire* 1:202. The last mention of this Videric occurs in Ammianus Marcellinus XXXI 5.12, where the arrival of the Greutungi in 376 at the left back of the lower Danube is reported. See also below, nn. 55 ff. St. Ambrose, *Epistulae* LXXIII 21, p. 46, comments on the abundant harvest of the year 383 in Pannonia and Raetia; on the use of Huns and Alans in Raetia see ibid., XXX 4 and 8, pp. 209 and 212.

26. Jordanes, *Getica* 246–253, p. 122 f. See R. Werner, "Anten," 590. L. Schmidt, *Ostgermanen,* 268, compares this structured form of joint rule to that of the Burgundian kings (see ibid., 177–180). Yet the question arises whether we should in this case also assume a Hunnic model: Prosper, *Epitoma chronicon* a. 445, 1353, p. 480. Jordanes, *Getica* 180 f., p. 105. Cf. Thompson, *Attila and the Huns,* 56 ff. and 73 ff. Unfortunately Maenchen-Helfen, *The Huns,* 195–198, is

much truncated and burdened with a polemic, which is why it is better to also consult Thompson, *Attila and the Huns,* 81 ff. (account of the historical events) for aspects of institutional history. Yet the *hendinos*-kings of the fourth century (Ammianus Marcellinus XXVIII 5.14; Wenskus, *Stammesbildung,* 576 ff.) can hardly still be compared to the Burgundian kings of the fifth and sixth centuries.

27. Wolfram, "Theogonie," 82 f. with n. 21 f. For a glaring contradiction see ibid., 85 n. 34.

28. Ammianus Marcellinus XXXI 3.3. Wenskus, *Stammesbildung,* 479. Claude, "Die ostgotischen Königserhebungen," 151 with nn. 11 ff.

29. Jordanes, *Getica* 116, p. 88. Here also Ermanaric is compared to Alexander the Great.

30. Wolfram, "Theogonie," 82 with nn. 17–20.

31. Ibid., 83 ff.

32. Jordanes, *Getica* 130 f., p. 191; and 246, p. 121.

33. See above, n. 24 (Ammianus) and 26 (Jordanes). Although Wenskus, *Stammesbildung,* 479, assumes a division of the Ostrogoths, he does not think that Vithimiris and Videric were Amali but speaks instead of a change of dynasties. In "Amaler," 247 f., Wenskus has changed his opinion and now wants to assume, against H. Rosenfeld, that the Gothic princes named by Ammianus Marcellinus were also Amali.

34. Jordanes, *Getica* 119, p. 89. Cf. most recently Godłowski, "Aufhören," 225 ff., and Szydłowski, "Anwesenheit," 233 ff.

35. Jordanes, *Romana* 388, p. 52: Bulgarians, Antes, and Sclaveni. Jordanes, *Getica* 34 f., p. 62 f.: Venethi, Sclaveni, and Antes. Ibid. 119, p. 89: Venethi, Antes, and Sclaveni. All these references differ from ibid. 247, p. 121; not only in that here the Antes are mentioned alone but also that the spelling is different. Here we read *Anti,* everywhere else *Antes,* which points to the different sources used by the *Origo Gothica.* Vinitharius is actually an Anticus, who can be a victor over the Venethi-Slavs only from the perspective of the sixth century. See most recently R. Werner, "Anten," 594 n. 42.

36. Altheim, *Geschichte der Hunnen* 1:71–77, 320 f.; cf. 451.

37. Ammianus Marcellinus XXXI 3.3.

38. See chap. 3, n. 29. Cf. Altheim, *Geschichte der Hunnen* 1:352–354.

39. Cf. Ammianus Marcellinus XXXI 4.12 f., where first the retreat of the Videric Greutungi and then the conquest of the Caucaland are reported.

40. Jordanes, *Getica* 249, p. 122, with reference of the editor to Constantinus Porphyrogenitus, *De administrando imperio,* chap. 45. Altheim, *Geschichte der Hunnen* 1:76 f. and 351.

41. See chap. 1, n. 29. L. Schmidt, "Krimgoten," 322 ff.; Karlsson, "Goten im Osten," 165 ff.; from the archaeological point of view most recently summarized by A. K. Ambroz, "Danubian elements," 10–23 (in Russian); see also the older work of de Baye (not cited by Ambroz), *Les tombeaux.*

42. On the Alatheus group see Jordanes, *Getica* 134, p. 93; on Videric below, nn. 55 ff. K. A. Eckhardt, "Nachbenennung," 41 ff. For Altheim, *Geschichte der Hunnen* 1:76 f., 320, 351 f., and 361, this identification is so self-evident that he no longer thinks about it, which is certainly not without danger. According to Wenskus, "Amaler," 247, the case for this identification has become considerably

stronger by Eckhardt's suggestion that Theodoric's uncle Vidimir could be named after his grandfather Vithimiris-Vinitharius. But in the meantime Wenskus has in discussion clearly dissociated himself from this identification.

43. Jordanes, *Getica* 245 with 248. Kienast, "Magnus," 1 ff. Cf. Wolfram, "Theogonie," 80 n. 5.

44. Karl Müllenhoff considered this for Jordanes, *Getica*, pp. 142 and 143 f. n. 16., but wanted to emend *Hun(n)imundus magnus* to *Ermanaricus magnus*. Wenskus, "Amaler," 247.

45. Jordanes, *Getica* 79, p. 77; 248 f., p. 122.

46. Cassiodorus, *Variae* VIII 9.8, p. 239.

47. L. Schmidt, *Ostgermanen*, 254 f. and 267 f.

48. Ibid., 255. A cautious identification is attempted by Martindale, *Prosopography* 2:510 (Gesimund).

49. Wolfram, "Theogonie," 89, esp. after Eckhardt, "Nachbenennung," 45. Schönfeld, *Wörterbuch*, 249 (Vadamerca). Maenchen-Helfen, *The Huns*, 414, and Demougeot, *La formation* 2:384 f. (Balamber-Balimber).

50. The *Origo Gothica* emphasizes that the Ostrogoths continued to exist in Scythia: Jordanes, *Getica* 174, p. 103; 246, p. 121; 253, p. 123. Cf. Wenskus, *Stammesbildung*, 480.

51. Zosimus IV 38.1 emphasizes explicitly that at the lower Danube the Greutungi were unknown strangers, even though the barbarians who lived there, apparently Tervingi, knew their name. Rosenfeld, "Ost- und Westgoten," 250 f., with whom Wenskus, *Stammesbildung*, 481 agrees. As with the Tervingi (cf. chap. 2, n. 237), the abandonment of the old settlement areas by the Greutungi is reflected in the discontinuance of burials in nearly all burial grounds of the Cherniakhov culture.

52. Jordanes, *Getica* 226, p. 116, as well as 174, p. 103; 178, p. 104; 246, p. 121; 254, p. 123; 257, p. 124; and other passages. Ibid. 263, p. 116, Jordanes states only that the Goths had been settled "previously on the shores of the Black Sea," a comment that already appears, if anachronistically, in 38, p. 63: after their stay *in Scythiae solo iuxta paludem Meotidem* they stayed in the Roman provinces of Moesia, Thrace, and Dacia, and afterward again *supra mare Ponticum . . . in Scythia*. Thus Jordanes distinguishes here two Scythiae; cf. 63, p. 71. Jordanes, *Romana* 331, p. 42, resembles the catalog of provinces given above, but it states emphatically that Attila with the Gepids under Ardaric, the Goths under Valamir, and many other peoples and their kings settled in all of Illyricum, Thrace, Dacia I and II, Moesia, and Scythia. From Priscus fr. 8 (FHG 4, 89 f.) follows the identification of Scythia with the land of the Huns. Cf. Wolfram, "Theogonie," 89 n. 60. Evidence for a strong Gothic continuity in the Danube region, esp. along the lower reaches of the Danube, can be found in the river's Gothic name Δούναβις, which the Slavs took over: G. Schramm, *Nordpontische Ströme*, 37 ff. and 173, after Pseudo-Caesarius of Nazianzus, *Dialogus* I, quaestio 68, col. 935 f.

53. Priscus fr. 8 (FHG 4, 86, and 92). Jordanes, *Getica* 199 f., p. 109 f.

54. The location of the Ostrogoths and Gepids at the time of Attila follows from Jordanes, *Getica* 74, p. 75; 264, p. 126. Compared to the subjugated Germanic tribes the Black Sea peoples have greater autonomy: see Priscus fr. 8 (FHG 4, 82 f. and 89). Cf. Altheim, *Geschichte der Hunnen* 4:274 ff. and 295. Thompson, *Attila*

and the Huns, 95 ff. Horedt and Protase, "Völkerwanderungszeitlicher Schatzfund," 87–89, and "Zweites Fürstengrab," 174–220. Horedt, "Neue Goldschätze," 105 ff. Harhoiu, *Treasure from Pietroasa,* 23–36. The uncertainty concerning the ethnic interpretation exists not only for the Transylvanian material of the fifth century—i.e., before the appearance of the row graves—but for the entire East Germanic material from this period from the Danube region. This applies especially to the richly furnished graves of women—mostly single graves or grave clusters—with costume accessories of precious metals. Archaeological clues that would indicate continuous Gothic settlement under Hunnic rule outside of Muntenia and the Carpathian mountains do not exist, if we leave aside the Crimean Goths and a few finds along the northern and northeastern periphery of the old settlement areas.

55. Wolfram, "Theogonie," 87.

56. Rosenfeld, "Ost- und Westgoten," 250. Eckhardt, "Nachbenennung," 43 f. Neither Miltner, "Vandalen," 303 f., nor Courtois, *Les Vandales,* 34 f., can detect any Hunnic pressure that forced the Vandals in 401 to leave the Danube-Tisza region. Yet there were relations between the Goths and the Vandals which were not only warlike. On Hunimund and Thorismund see Cassiodorus, *Variae* IX 1.19, p. 330, and Jordanes, *Getica,* esp. 250–252, p. 122 f. Cf. L. Schmidt, *Ostgermanen,* 252–255.

57. Várady, *Pannonien,* 231 ff., cf. 601, bases himself on the authority of Egger, "Historisch-epigraphische Studien," 64, after Olympiodorus fr. 26. But Nagy, "Pannonia," 334, has Videric disappear altogether. Cf. chap. 3, nn. 299 ff. Wenskus, *Stammesbildung,* 478. The last mention of Videric is in Ammianus Marcellinus XXXI 4.12; cf. Jones, *Prosopography* 1:965, and above, n. 42. On Alatheus and Safrax see ibid. 1:32 and 802, esp. after Jordanes, *Getica* 134, p. 93, and 140, p. 95. On Amantius see above, n. 25.

58. Mócsy, "Pannonia," 581 f. and 630. Demandt, "Magister militum," 646 f. On Generidus see Martindale, *Prosopography* 2:500 f.

59. Maenchen-Helfen, *The Huns,* 76 f.

60. Marcellinus Comes, *Chronicon,* a. 427, p. 76. See below, n. 61.

61. Wolfram, *Mitteleuropa,* 32 with n. 15. Ammianus Marcellinus XXXI 16.7. Cf. chap. 3, n. 90 f.

62. Maenchen-Helfen, *The Huns,* 77 ff. The modification of the basic thesis of Várady, *Pannonien,* 278 ff., esp. 280 ff., which I have offered follows the stimulating criticism by Nagy, "Pannonia," 330 f., and "Reoccupation," 159 ff.

63. Jordanes, *Getica* 174 f., p. 103; 252, p. 122. Theophanes, a. 5931, also reports a Gothic exodus from Pannonia in the year 427. Though we can agree with Alföldi, *Pannonien,* 95, and Maenchen-Helfen, *The Huns,* 78 n. 328, that Theophanes here combined Marcellinus Comes with Procopius; nevertheless, such combinations are not necessarily a priori meaningless. Cf. Wolfram, "Theogonie," 85 ff. nn. 36 and 48 f.

64. Prosper, *Epitoma chronicon* a. 439, 1337, p. 477. Wenskus, "Amaler," 247. Martindale, *Prosopography* 2:1157 (Vetericus) has a different interpretation.

65. See above, n. 57.

66. As chap. 4, n. 540, and above, n. 42 and n. 57. Wolfram, "Theogonie," 85 ff. was a deliberate and unsuccessful attempt to turn reflections drawn purely from the study of names into history, thus reducing them ad absurdum. The historian is

again and again tempted to turn Cassiodorus's Amal genealogy into a narrative account, but any such attempt fails quickly. Cf., for example, Wenskus, *Stammesbildung*, 479 n. 310, who in 1961 reserved for himself such a study, which he has wisely never written.

67. As n. 64. Cf. chap. 4, n. 41.

68. In general on the attraction of Attila's realm for the optimates on both sides of the *limes* see the report of the envoy Priscus fr. 8. Cf. Maenchen-Helfen, *The Huns*, 94 ff. and 192 ff. *Chronica Gallica* 133, a. 448, p. 662, reports the escape of the Bagaudian doctor Eudoxius to the Huns.

69. Jordanes, *Getica* 185, p. 106: Attila claims to be attacking only the Visigothic king Theoderid. Ibid. 197–200, p. 109 f.: the Amal Ostrogoths face the Visigoths; the royal brothers "outrank in nobility even the king [Attila] whom they were at that time still serving, because the charisma of the Amal race shone brightly upon them." Cf. Wolfram, *Splendor Imperii*, 109 with n. 13. Jordanes, *Getica* 209, p. 111: the Amal Andagis kills King Theoderid. Ibid. 253, p. 123: the battle is considered a *parricidium*. The Ostrogoths cannot resist the command of the Hunnic king Attila to fight against their *parentes Vesegothae*. See also Priscus fr. 15: Attila attacks the Visigoths to do Gaiseric a favor. Clover, "Geiseric and Attila," 104 ff.

70. Cf. L. Schmidt, *Ostgermanen*, 268.

71. Theodoric's father Thiudimir adopted the Suevic king Hunimund: Jordanes, *Getica* 274, p. 129, and Theodoric himself adopted in the same manner the Herulian king Rodulf: Cassiodorus, *Variae* IV 2, p. 114 f.; VIII 9.8, p. 239.

72. As chap. 1, nn. 62 ff.

73. Altheim, *Geschichte der Hunnen* 4:142 ff. and 337 f. Jordanes, *Getica* 268, p. 127, attests that the Huns regarded the Ostrogoths as their slaves (*mancipia*).

74. Maenchen-Helfen, *The Huns*, 386 ff.; cf. Jordanes, *Getica* 58, p. 70. Schönfeld, *Wörterbuch*, 51 (Bleda) and 274 f. (Attila). Cf. Fröhlich, *Studien*, 44.

75. J. Werner, *Archäologie des Attila-Reiches*, 90 ff. On the Scythian fraternal kiss see Priscus fr. 8 (FHG 4, 93).

76. Wolfram, "Theogonie," 87 n. 47 f., after Jordanes, *Getica* 174, p. 103; 251, p. 122; 284, p. 131. On the longing to be freed from the yoke of Attila see ibid. 253, p. 123. On the notion that the Amali were of higher nobility than Attila see ibid. 199, p. 109; cf. Wolfram, *Splendor Imperii*, 109 n. 13. The high esteem for the Amali has, however, a counterpart in the praise of the Balthi: Theoderid is compared to Aëtius the *summus ductor*—even in Hydatius 150; a. 451, he is a *rex* next to the *dux* Aëtius; Visigoths and Romans are first among the peoples of the world: Jordanes, *Getica* 181, p. 105, and 196, p. 108 f. On the nobility see Priscus fr. 12. Cf. Maenchen-Helfen, *The Huns*, 198 f. Priscus frs. 1–8.

77. Cf. Jordanes, *Getica* 248, p. 121 f., with Priscus fr. 39. On the latter cf. below, n. 125.

78. Ammianus Marcellinus XXXI 2.1 ff. (excursus on the Huns) was of course known to Cassiodorus: see Jordanes, *Getica* 127 f., p. 90 f.

79. Wolfram, "Gotische Studien III," 255 f., where, however, only two periods are distinguished in the saga of the Haliurun(n)ae.

80. Maenchen-Helfen, *The Huns*, 81 ff. Wolfram, "Gotische Studien I," 5 ff. L. Schmidt, *Ostgermanen*, 179 and 268. Cf. above, 26. That Valamir's younger brothers were subordinate to him is attested, in strong words even, by Jordanes,

Getica 253, p. 123. Cf. ibid. 199, p. 109. See Claude, "Die ostgotischen Königs-erhebungen," 152 f.

81. Jordanes, *Getica* 197–200, p. 109 f.; 217, p. 113; 252, p. 123. Cf. Zöllner, *Franken,* 30 f. Martindale, *Prosopography* 2:1135 f. (Valamer), 1164 (Videmer), and 1069 f. (Theodemer 2).

82. Jordanes, *Getica* 209 and 265 f., pp. 111 and 126.

83. See on this Pohl, "Gepiden," 252–266, esp. 254 ff. (analysis of the battle report), 258 f. (role of the Ostrogoths), 259 f. (location and date of the battle of Nedao). On the Gepid king Ardaric see Martindale, *Prosopography* 2:138. As esp. Maenchen-Helfen, *The Huns,* 143 ff., has pointed out, a comparison of Jordanes, *Getica* 240–264, p. 125 f., with Jordanes, *Romana* 386, p. 52, should allow us to locate the battle. The passage in the *Romana* compares two conflicts, which occurred during Jordanes' time, with what is probably the battle of Nedao. Since this compari-son refers to events that Procopius (*De bello Gothico* I [V] 7.1–4, and III [VII] 33.8) locates in Dalmatia, one could think of the Savia, which during the period of Ostrogothic rule was part of Dalmatia: see below, n. 214, n. 227, and n. 425 f.

84. Jordanes, *Getica* 74 and 264, pp. 75 and 126. Horedt, in his publications (as above, n. 54) but also in private conversations, has expressed the opinion that the archaeological material does not exclude the possibility that Ostrogoths also remained behind in Transylvania after the middle of the fifth century. To the historian this suggests that some Ostrogothic groups did not participate in the westward trek of the Valamir Goths to Pannonia, fell under Gepid domination, and, insofar as they did not become Gepids, penetrated into the Roman Empire during the second half of the fifth century, as, for example, the group of 469 (see below, n. 125).

85. Wolfram, *Mitteleuropa,* 37 f. with n. 5. Pohl, "Gepiden," 268–280. Lotter, "Stammesverbände," 29 ff.

86. On the obfuscating account of the battle of Nedao by Jordanes, *Getica* 260–263, see Pohl, "Gepiden," 254–259.

87. Despite, or precisely because of, Paulus Diaconus, *Romana* XV 11, p. 211 f., according to whom Valamir led the uprising of the tribes against the Huns, there is a widespread notion that the Ostrogoths did not participate in the battle of Nedao at all: see Maenchen-Helfen, *The Huns,* 144 with n. 202 and 147 ff. In contrast, Altheim, *Geschichte der Hunnen* 4:340 ff., expresses the opinion that the Ostrogoths certainly did fight with the Gepids and the other peoples against the Huns. Martin-dale, *Prosopography* 2:1135 (Valamer), supports Altheim's argument. But Rosen-feld, "Ost- und Westgoten," 252 f. (cf. Altheim, 344 f. n. 4), got it right when he has the Ostrogoths march alongside the Huns until the battle of Nedao, which the heroic saga supports: see Rosenfeld, "Dietrichdichtung," 431. This interpretation is also supported by Theophanes, a. 5977 (cf. Alföldi, *Pannonien,* 100 with n. 4) but esp. by the pleas for admission into the Roman Empire by all defeated tribes, whereas the victors remained outside. Jordanes (as n. 84) says explicitly that the Goths could not maintain themselves in their old settlements and fled into the Roman Empire.

88. Priscus fr. 39. Maenchen-Helfen, *The Huns,* 144. See below, nn. 125–127.

89. Stein, *Bas-Empire* 1:336.

90. Jordanes, *Getica* 263–269, pp. 125–128. Maenchen-Helfen, *The Huns,*

149–152. Cf. Várady, *Pannonien,* 327 f. and 332 ff. For the Sadagares see Harmatta, *Sarmatians,* 57 with n. 220 and 101. Cf. in general Altheim, *Geschichte der Hunnen* 4:338 ff., as well as L. Schmidt, *Ostgermanen* 98 and 271.

91. Jordanes, *Romana* 336, p. 43. Ardabur was put into action in Thrace in the sixties: Demandt, "Magister militum," 764 f., after Priscus fr. 20. In Priscus frs. 7 ff. a namesake of the Gothic king Bigelis is mentioned as a Hunnic-Greek interpreter. Cf. Wagner, "Personennamen," 19 ff. On the mention of Tuldila in Sidonius Apollinaris, *Carmina* V vv. 458–503, p. 199 f., see Martindale, *Prosopography* 2:1131.

92. Ensslin, *Theoderich,* 12. Demandt, "Magister militum," 769–773 and 775 f. Cf. Nagl, "Theoderich Strabo," 1771 ff., esp. after Jordanes, *Getica* 270, p. 128. On the kinship of the two Theodorics see chap. 1, n. 107 esp. after Ioannis Antiochenus fr. 214.3. What Nagl, "Theoderich Strabo," 1771, has to say about his non-noble descent is without foundation in the sources. Moreover, some disorder must have gotten into the author's notes while she was writing the article because many of the references are incorrect. The conflict between the two Theodorics (cf. Stein, *Bas-Empire* 2:10 ff.) is reported to us, esp. in the fragments of Malchus, from which we can infer that the two opponents were of equal rank. Esp. fr. 15 can be thus interpreted. On the name Ermanaric in the clan of Aspar see Candidus Isaurus fr. 1; cf. Wenskus, "Amaler," 248, but the quote from Ioannis Antiochenus given there should be replaced by Candidus Isaurus fr. 1. See also Martindale, *Prosopography* 2:1073–1076 (Theodericus Strabo n. 5).

93. Malchus fr. 18. Wolfram, "Ansiedlung," 32; cf. chap. 1, n. 108 and below, n. 148. Martindale, *Prosopography* 2:1007 (Sidimundus), and ibid. 503 (Gento 2). On Fravitta see chap. 3, nn. 178 ff.

94. Stein, *Bas-Empire* 1:369 with n. 21. Loyen, *Recherches historiques,* 57 f. The starting point for the discussion is less than two and a half verses in the Avitus panegyric of Sidonius Apollinaris, *Carmina* VII vv. 589 ff., p. 217. Maenchen-Helfen, *The Huns,* 144–147, considers the *revocatio Pannoniarum* as an exaggerated report of victory. In contrast, Mócsy, "Pannonia," 582, and Lotter, "Donausueben," 284 f., take the statement of Sidonius much more seriously. With some justification they point to the report of the *Fasti Vindobonenses priores* a. 577 (= 455), p. 304, according to which Savaria-Steinamanger was destroyed by an earthquake on September 7 of that year, a Friday. The fact that a Western source would report an event in Pannonia I seems to indicate that there was a continuing link between the province and the central government. What seems to be such a well-documented event, however, raises a chronological puzzle: September 7 does not fall on a Friday until the year 456, while the other date that has been suggested, September 10, also does not fall *die Veneris* in 455, contrary to what one often reads. Cf. Lotter, "Donausueben," 284 n. 32. Of course Várady, *Pannonien,* 331 ff. and 506 n. 815 f., knows it better than everyone else, but he does discuss the other points of view thoroughly. The connection Várady claims existed between Avitus and the Pannonian Goths is in itself plausible, but it cannot be substantiated by a single source of any kind. Jordanes, *Getica* 263 and 270, pp. 126 and 128, merely reports that the Pannonian Goths became the federates of Marcian. On this see Stein, *Bas-Empire* 1:353 with n. 22, as well as Alföldi, *Pannonien,* 100 ff.

95. Perhaps we could gather as much from Eugippius, *Vita s. Severini,* chap.

5.1–4, and Jordanes, *Getica* 282, p. 130 f. The first passage contains the complaint of the Rugian king that the Goths did not let him move to Italy, along with the warning of St. Severin not to cross a large river (*amnis*) while chasing "plunderers" (Ostrogoths). Noll, *Eugippius,* 125, identifies this river—no doubt correctly—as the Danube. See ibid., 124, according to which the Ostrogoths extended their influence far into Noricum ripense. Cf. Lotter, *Severinus,* 201 ff., who assumes the "Wiener-wald" as the western boundary of Ostrogothic territory. On the east of the Enns section of Noricum ripense see Zibermayr, *Noricum,* 7 ff., after *Notitia dignitatum oc.* 34.31 ff. Cf. Csendes, "Flaccitheus," 289 ff. The Jordanes passage, however, reveals that the Goths considered a Sarmatian attack on Eastern Roman Singidunum-Belgrade as a casus belli. Jordanes, *Getica* 264, p. 126, describes the part of Pannonia that traditionally belonged to the Goths as lying between Sirmium and Vindobona-Vindomina. Cf. Mirković, "Ostgoten in Pannonien," 119 ff., esp. 127 f. (summary in German), with an original interpretation of Scarniunga, the eastern boundary of the Ostrogothic settlement area.

96. Csendes, "Flaccitheus," 289 with n. 5. Stein, *Bas-Empire* 1:356. Ensslin, *Theoderich,* 32, after Priscus fr. 35. Loyen, *Recherches historiques,* 94, after Sidonius Apollinaris, *Carmina* II v. 377, p. 182. Exactly the opposite has often been mistakenly read into this passage, as, for example, by L. Schmidt, *Ostgermanen,* 273 f., which has been pointed out most recently by Lotter, *Severinus,* 213, n. 135.

97. Várady, *Pannonien,* 336 f., Alföldi, *Pannonien,* 101–104, Jordanes, *Getica* 268, p. 127. Cf. Claude, "Die ostgotischen Königserhebungen," 153.

98. This figure is reached if we start from the assumption that the six thousand warriors with whom Theodoric the Great captured Singidunum were Valamir's portion of the tribal forces. This assumption is supported by Jordanes, *Romana* 347, p. 44, and by the direction of attack of Valamir's first military action: cf. Jordanes, *Getica* 282, p. 130 f. Since the military strength of the three Amal brothers did not differ much, though it was not equal, one could multiply the number of Valamir-Theodoric Goths by three and thus arrive at the strength of the Pannonian Ostrogoths. Also, during the Epirean interlude Theodoric's forces comprised six thousand elite troops: see Malchus fr. 18 (FHG 4, 129); cf. below, n. 148.

99. See above, n. 94. There is unnecessary confusion over the chronology of the Gothic exodus from Pannonia. Jordanes, *Getica* 283, p. 131, dates it to the reign of the Western emperor Glycerius, who was proclaimed emperor on March 3, 473 and who renounced the imperial power in June 474: Seeck, *Untergang* 6:375. For an account of the events see Stein, *Bas-Empire* 1:353 f., 356 f., as well as Hartmann, *Geschichte Italiens* 1:62 ff., after Jordanes, *Getica* 272–283, pp. 128–131.

100. Priscus fr. 39. Cf. below, nn. 125–127.

101. See chap. 4, nn. 429 ff., and below, nn. 243 ff.

102. Cf. Jordanes, *Getica* 270, p. 128, with 283, p. 131. See also Priscus fr. 28.

103. Jordanes, *Getica* 268 f., p. 127. Cf. Priscus fr. 39. Várady, *Pannonien,* 337.

104. Procopius, *De bello Gothico* IV (VIII) 5.15 ff. Schwarz, "Krimgoten," 204 (157) ff.

105. On the conversion of the Ostrogoths to the "faith of Ulfilas" see (after Jordanes, *Getica* 132 f., p. 92) Schäferdiek, "Germanenmission," 511–513. On Ereleuva see Jordanes, *Getica* 269, p. 128. Anonymus Valesianus II 58. Ensslin, *Theoderich* 10 f. Martindale, *Prosopography* 2:400 (*Erelieva quae et Eusebia*)

considers her a Catholic Goth. Ibid., 1077–1084 (Fl. Theodericus 7). Benjamin, "Erelieva," RE 11 (1907): 412. On the salutation of Ereleuva as queen see, for example, the two letters of Pope Gelasius from 495/496: *Epistulae Theodericianae* 4 f., p. 390 f. On the origin of the name see Schönfeld, *Wörterbuch*, 75, and Wrede, *Sprache der Ostgoten*, 61 f., but he interprets Ereleuva as "Schwertlieb." Only Anonymus Valesianus describes the mother of Theodoric explicitly as a Goth, but he knows so little about his youth that he follows the Byzantine model in naming Valamir as the father of the king. Cf. L. Schmidt, *Ostgermanen*, 272 with n. 2. Assunta Nagl, "Theoderich der Grosse," 1746. On this problem cf. Konecny, *Frauen*, 9 ff. and 24 ff.

106. Cf. Sidonius Apollinaris, *Carmina* II v. 358, p. 182, and V v. 57, p. 189. Procopius, *De bello Vandalico* I (III) 3.23. Other mixed marriages were contracted by Fravitta (see chap. 3, n. 180), Gento (Malchus fr. 18), and Theudis: see below, n. 357, while the marriage between Athaulf and Placidia became best known: chap. 3, n. 282 f.

107. Ensslin, *Theoderich*, 10, after Jordanes, *Getica* 271 and 282, pp. 128 and 131. Cf. Wenskus, *Stammesbildung*, 482.

108. Chrysos, Βυζάντιον, 55 f. Stein, *Bas-Empire* 1:356 f., and Ensslin, *Theoderich*, 13, after Priscus fr. 28, Jordanes, *Getica*, 270 f., p. 128, and Prosper, *Epitoma chronicon* a. 459, p. 492. On the revolts of the Visigothic federates cf. chap. 4, n. 23.

109. Ensslin, *Theoderich*, 14 ff., is absolutely right in devoting a separate chapter to the stay of the king's small son in Constantinople. Although no details are known about this period, the Gothic child must have witnessed many events we know from history.

110. Jordanes, *Getica* 271, p. 128. See chap. 1, n. 8.

111. Cf. Jordanes, *Getica* 283, p. 131, with Procopius, *De bello Gothico* III (VII) 33.10–12 (Lombards in Pannonia and Noricum), as well as with the Turkish definition of armistice and peace: see Wolfram, "Gegenstände," 100 f. Important in this context seems the definition of Ulpian: see *Digesta* IL 15.24: *Hostes sunt, quibus bellum publice populus Romanus decrevit vel ipsi populo Romano; ceteri latrunculi vel praedones appellantur.* Cf. Lotter, *Severinus*, 321, s.v. "Räuber."

112. The earthquake of Savaria in the year 456 (see n. 94) was also felt in Comagenis-Tulln: Eugippius, *Vita s. Severini*, chap. 2. In this city were stationed unnamed federates who were driven out in the open by the earthquake because they felt encircled by mighty barbarian enemies—no doubt those who had shortly before destroyed Asturis (ibid. chap. 1.5). Although their fear was groundless they fell into such a panic that they killed each other. Perhaps they thought that the heavens were collapsing: see chap. 2, n. 486. The federates of Comagenis may be described as Germanic peoples from the Danube and their enemies can be seen as the Pannonian Goths. See most recently Lotter, "Endphase," 73 f. In contrast, the conclusion of Lotter, *Severinus*, 156 ff., is not compelling enough to divide up the chronology of the earthquake and the revolt of the federates in Comagenis and assign the former event to 456 and the latter to 467.

113. Sidonius Apollinaris, *Carmina* V vv. 474–479, p. 199, esp. vv. 553 ff., p. 201: *magister militiae*. Loyen, *Recherches historiques*, 78 n. 3. Demandt, "Magister militum," 683 f. Both Várady, *Pannonien*, 341, and his critic Lotter, *Severinus*,

242 ff., esp. 243 n. 221, succumb to overinterpretation. The description of the army of Majorian by Priscus fr. 27 sounds, at any rate, much more sober and down-to-earth. See most recently Lotter, "Endphase," 73 with n. 219, and Wirth, "Anmerkungen," 254 n. 51. On Tuldila, who is mentioned right after the army of Majorian, see above, n. 91.

114. Cf. the "motto" of Jordanes, Getica 315, p. 318. Várady, Pannonien, 337 ff.

115. According to Priscus fr. 28 in 459/460 the Ostrogoths received three hundred pounds of gold a year. Cf. fr. 1 according to which Constantinople paid the Attila Huns at first three hundred fifty and then seven hundred pounds of gold. The annual payments increased enormously during the forties and in 447 reached the sum of six thousand pounds of gold, which was, however, only slightly more than a top senatorial income: see Maenchen-Helfen, The Huns, 180 ff., and Jones, The Later Roman Empire 2:554 ff.

116. See chap. 4, n. 94.

117. Loyen, Recherches historiques, 90 f. Demandt, "Magister militum," 777. Stein, Bas-Empire 1:356 f. See Sidonius Apollinaris, Carmina II vv. 223–242, p. 179, as well as Priscus fr. 36.

118. Jordanes, Getica 272 f., p. 128. On the Sadagares see above, n. 90. On Bassianae see Dušanić, "Bassianae," 74; on the embattled Noricum, Wolfram, Mitteleuropa, 39 with n. 10.

119. On the adoption of a "son in arms" according to the "barbarian custom" see Procopius, De bello Persico I 11.22. On the "Amal" Hunimund see Wolfram, "Theogonie," 83 f. nn. 23–27. The foundation in the sources is provided by Jordanes, Getica 273–275, p. 128 f. On Hunimund cf. Lotter, Severinus, 202 ff., and "Donausueben," 275 ff., esp. 295 ff. Also, one must consider the "Suevicization" of Pannonia-Savia attested by Procopius, De bello Gothico I (V), 15.26 f., as well as 16.9 and 12; but it is not said when the Suevi arrived there. I would therefore locate the Suevic kingdom of Hunimund in northern Pannonia.

120. Jordanes, Getica 275 ff., p. 129 f. Cf. Claude, "Die ostgotischen Königserhebungen," 153 with n. 31 f. The chronology of the last campaign of Valamir and the first campaign of Thiudimir is in a poor state. Precise dates are usually the result of circular reasoning. But a genuinely reliable terminus ante quem is offered by Ioannis Antiochenus fr. 206.2, who dates both the beginning of the war of Euric and the transfer of the kingship from Valamir to Thiudimir to the consular year of Zeno, i.e., to 469: see Stein, Bas-Empire 1:360 with n. 55. A second possibility of dating is offered by the panegyric on Anthemius by Sidonius Apollinaris, Carmina II v. 377, p. 182, cf. Loyen, Recherches historiques, 94, according to whom Sidonius knew on January 1, 468 that at that very time the Ostrogoths were trying, if unsuccessfully, to establish themselves in Noricum (Wolfram, Mitteleuropa, 39 with n. 10). This passage can certainly be used to provide an approximate date for Eugippus, Vita s. Severini, chap. 5, according to which the Goths prevented the lower Austrian Rugians from marching off to Italy. Cf. Várady, Pannonien, 338 f., and 508 n. 839 f., as well as Lotter, Severinus, 201 f.

121. Ioannis Antiochenus (as n. 120), as well as Jordanes, Getica 244, p. 120 f. Cf. chap. 4, nn. 95 ff.

122. Jordanes, Getica 277–279, p. 129 f. Priscus fr. 35; cf. 39. L. Schmidt, Ostgermanen 274 ff., esp. 275 n. 3 (Alaric is identified as king of the Heruli), as

well as Lotter, "Stammesverbände," 38 f. Lotter, *Severinus,* 200 f., and "Donau-sueben," 287 ff. Martindale, *Prosopography* 2:49 (Suevic King).

123. Cf. the boundaries of the Ostrogothic settlement areas (as n. 97).

124. Jordanes, *Getica,* 281, p. 130. Ensslin, *Theoderich,* 35 with n. 37. Hartmann, *Geschichte Italiens* 1:64, explains Theodoric's being sent home as a result of the emperor's desire to win over the Pannonian Ostrogoths in his conflict with the Thracian Ostrogoths; this interpretation, however, raises chronological problems. On Flavius Ardabur Aspar see Martindale, *Prosopography* 2:164–169.

125. Demandt, "Magister militum," 768, after Priscus fr. 39. Among the other works, which all date the event to 467, see esp. Maenchen-Helfen, *The Huns,* 167 f. and L. Schmidt, *Ostgermanen,* 274. Cf. Stein, *Bas-Empire* 1:357.

126. Fredegar, *Chronicon* IV 48, p. 144.

127. Marcellinus Comes, *Chronicon* a. 469, p. 90. *Codex Iustinianus* IX 12.10. My interpretation follows that of Stein, *Bas-Empire* 1:360. On the equating of *buccellarii* and Goths see Olympiodorus fr. 7. On Dengizich see Martindale, *Prosopography* 2:354 f.

128. Martindale, *Prosopography* 2:791 (Odovacar) and 806 (Hunulf). Jordanes, *Romana* 344, p. 44, even calls Odovacar a Rugian who invaded Italy with Turcilin-gian, Scirian, and Herulian troops. Cf. *Getica* 291, p. 133. See also Anonymus Valesianus II 37, according to which Odovacar came to Italy with "the Scirian people," while in the *Auctarium Havniense,* ordo prior a. 476.2, p. 309, the Heruli proclaimed Odovacar king. See Wolfram, *Intitulatio I,* 58 ff. Cf. above, n. 120 and chap. 4 n. 151.

129. Jordanes, *Getica* 280 f., p. 130. Eugippius, *Vita s. Severini,* chap. 22.4. The suggestion of Lotter, *Severinus,* 203 with n. 99, and "Donausueben," 291 ff., to identify Jordanes' Hunimund with the Hunumund of the *Vita s. Severini* can be entirely accepted. On Hunimund see Martindale, *Prosopography* 2:574 (Huni-mundus). On the image of the attack across the frozen Danube see the study of Hornstein, "ΙΣΤΡΟΣ," 154 ff., esp. 160 f., which deals both with the literary topos and the reality.

130. Stein, *Bas-Empire* 1:394. See chap. 4, nn. 106–108.

131. Procopius, *De bello Gothico* II (VI) 14.1–25. See below, n. 413 ff.

132. See above, nn. 119 f. as well as 129.

133. Eugippius, *Vita s. Severini,* chap. 8.1, attests Feletheus-Feva as the son of Flaccitheus and the husband of Giso. From Ioannis Antiochenus fr. 214a and Ennodius, *Panegyricus* 25, p. 206, has been inferred that Giso was a relative (cousin?) of Theodoric's: see Wenskus, "Amaler," genealogical table to p. 248. L. Schmidt, *Ostgermanen,* 120, assumes that Feva's accession to the throne took place around 475, i.e., after the departure of the Ostrogoths from Pannonia. On Feva see Martindale, *Prosopography* 2:457 (*Feletheus qui et Feba*).

134. Stein's assumption (*Bas-Empire* 1:356 f.) that Theodoric was coregent with his father and uncle Vidimir follows from Jordanes, *Romana* 347, p. 44 f.

135. Jordanes, *Getica* 282, p. 130 f. According to this passage Theodoric under-took the campaign at the age of eighteen, which would take us to the year 469 (cf. above, n. 107). But since Theodoric celebrated the thirtieth year of his reign in 500, one has rightly placed its beginning into the period around 470/471: Claude, Die ostgotischen Königserhebungen," 153, as well as Claude, "Zur Königserhebung

Theoderichs." 1 ff. Cf. on this also Martindale, *Prosopography* 2:1078; Wenskus, *Stammesbildung,* 482; and Ensslin, *Theoderich,* 350 n. 13, who all start from the assumption that Theodoric was elevated to kingship in 471.

136. Malchus fr. 2.

137. See above, n. 125.

138. Jordanes, *Getica* 283, p. 131.

139. See chap. 3, n. 138.

140. Jordanes, *Getica* 283 f., p. 131. Cf. above, n. 128.

141. Wolfram, *Mitteleuropa,* 39 with n. 10 (cf. above, n. 120). The identification of the army commander Bilimer with Vidimir, which Stein, *Bas-Empire* 1:394 f., suggested and which was taken over by Lotter, *Severinus,* 204, 249, and 276, has been rejected by Demandt, "Magister militum," 695–697. Martindale, *Prosopography* 2:230 considers Bilimer a Goth. On the possible abduction of Saint Leonian from Savaria to Gaul by the Goths of Vidimir see Tóth, "Obere Wart," 89.

142. See chap. 4, nn. 145–147 and 150, as well as n. 540 and above, n. 99.

143. The departure from Pannonia is dated by the reign of the emperor Glycerius (see above, n. 99). If the report of Eugippius, *Vita s. Severini,* chap. 17.3–4, cf. chap. 21.2, refers to 473 (which is rather unlikely: see above, n. 120 and Wolfram, *Mitteleuropa,* 39 with n. 10), it would follow that the Vidimir Goths passed by Teurnia during the cold season and there received the donation of clothing that had actually been collected for Noricum ripense. Theodoric set out from Moesia also in the late summer of 489: see below, n. 165. The collection of clothes for the Goths which Eugippius mentions corresponds to Jordanes, *Getica* 283, p. 131, who explicitly speaks of a general shortage of clothes among the Goths.

144. Of the sources mentioned by Martindale, *Prosopography* 2:1073, see esp. Ioannis Antiochenus fr. 206.2, and Candidus fr. 1, as well as Malchus fr. 2 (Theodoric Strabo becomes Gothic king in Thrace), fr. 4 (the Goths in Thrace), fr. 10 (Odovacar's elevation, cf. Wolfram, "Gotisches Königtum," 3 ff. and 18 ff.), fr. 11 (the Thracian Goths are called federates), fr. 14 (a Gothic king, in contrast to a federate general, is no longer a "private person"). On the demands of the Huns to hand over the deserters see above, n. 76: Priscus frs. 1–8. On the theoretical possibility of Theodoric Strabo's hiring more than twenty-five thousand federate warriors with two thousand pounds of gold see Ensslin, *Theoderich,* 190; but cf. below, n. 254. On the Goths' "sea-worthiness" see Maenchen-Helfen, *The Huns,* 75, as well as chap. 3, n. 191 (catastrophe at the Bosporus), n. 263 (catastrophe in the Straits of Messina), n. 341 (catastrophe in the Straits of Gibraltar), chap. 4, n. 378, and below, nn. 319 ff.

145. Ensslin, *Theoderich,* 36–38. Wenskus, *Stammesbildung,* 482 f. See esp. Jordanes, *Getica* 285–288, p. 131 f. Cf. chap. 3, n. 145. Chrysos, Ἰστορία τῆς Ἠπείρου, 48. On the death of Thiudimir see Stein, *Bas Empire* 1:357 with n. 38, after Hartmann, *Geschichte Italiens* 1:79 n. 9.

146. Malchus fr. 18. Ensslin, "Theodimund," 1773. Martindale, *Prosopography* 2:1084.

147. Wenskus (as above, n. 145). On the expression *Valameriaci* see chap. 1, n. 67.

148. Chrysos, Ἰστορία τῆς Ἠπείρου, 56–63. Lippold, "Zenon," 158 f. Ensslin,

Theoderich, 39–54. Stein, *Bas-Empire* 2:10–18. L. Schmidt, *Ostgermanen,* 278–287. The main sources are Malchus frs. 11, 14, 15 (confrontation between the two Theodorics), 16 (peace treaty between the Theodorics and joint negotiations with Constantinople), 17 (Theodoric Thiudimirson falls into disfavor, Strabo takes his place and receives pay for thirteen thousand warriors), 18 (Theodoric Thiudimirson leaves Thrace and marches via Macedon to Epirus; on the Sidimund story see Martindale, *Prosopography* 2:1007; cf. below, n. 250 ff; negotiations with Adamantius, Theodoric demands the office of *magister militum,* citizenship, and "admission into the city"; an attempt to settle in Pautalia fails: see on this Danov, "Pautalia," 800–824, esp. 801 and 824). Ioannis Antiochenus fr. 211.4 and 5 (Theodoric Strabo has thirty thousand warriors, battle against the Bulgars: cf. L. Schmidt, *Ostgermanen,* 286 n. 4; death of "the Squinter," dissipation of his inheritance by Rekitach who kills his uncles). On the death of Theodoric Strabo see also Eustathius fr. 3. Ioannis Antiochenus fr. 214.3: slaying of Rekitach by Theodoric (the Great). On Rekitach see Martindale, *Prosopography* 2:936 and chap. 1, n. 106. Theodoric (the Great) became Zenon's son-in-arms in 476/478: see Martindale, *Prosopography* 2:1079, according to Jordanes, *Getica* 289, p. 132, and Malchus fr. 17. On the adoption of a barbarian as the "son-in-arms" of the emperor, "according to the barbarian custom," see Procopius, *De bello Persico* I 11.6 ff., esp. 22. On Apahida II see Horedt, "Apahida II," 366 f. About ill. XXVI included there, note that the treasures of Apahida are today no longer in the museum of Cluj-Napoca but in the National Museum in Bucharest. Cf. Horedt and Protase, "Zweites Fürstengrab," 174 ff. On the barbarian "summit meetings" at or on rivers see chap. 2, n. 190 (Athanaric and Valens), and chap. 4, n. 180 f. (Alaric II and Clovis), or the best known example in Tacitus, *Annales* 11.9 f. (Arminius and his brother Flavus). On Theodoric the Great's comment that he had learned in the East how to rule over Romans, see below, n. 195. On Sidimund see chap. 1, n. 108, and above, n. 93.

149. Ensslin, *Theoderich,* 53 ff. Stein, *Bas-Empire* 2:18 ff. L. Schmidt, *Ostgermanen* 287 ff. See esp. Marcellinus Comes, *Chronicon* aa. 482 and 483, pp. 92 f.

150. Malchus, fr. 18 (FHG 4, 128).

151. Ensslin, *Theoderich,* 54–56, after Ioannis Antiochenus fr. 214.3 Cf. Wolfram, *Intitulatio I,* 58, and chap. 1, n. 106. Theodoric may have exacted blood vengeance because Rekitach had murdered his uncles, i.e., two Amali: cf. above, n. 148. But behind the murder of Rekitach was also the political interest of the emperor: see Martindale, *Prosopography* 2:936.

152. This idea starts from the assumption that Theodoric was born in 451: see above, n. 107. On the minimum age for the appointment to the consulate, which was, however, often circumvented during the empire, see Mommsen, *Staatsrecht* 1:574.

153. Ioannis Antiochenus fr. 214.4. Lippold, "Zenon," 186 f. and 189.

154. As chap. 1, n. 106. On Ermanaric see Martindale, *Prosopography* 2:549.

155. L. Schmidt, *Ostgermanen,* 199, after Jordanes, *Getica* 266, p. 126 f.

156. Jordanes, *Getica* 289, p. 132. Lippold (as n. 153).

157. Lippold, "Zenon," 190. Ensslin, *Theoderich,* 56–61. Stein, *Bas-Empire* 2:28–31. L. Schmidt, *Ostgermanen,* 287 ff. The sources are esp. Ioannis Antiochenus fr. 214.4.6 and 8 f., as well as Eustathius fr. 4. Ennodius, *Panegyricus* 19, p. 205,

even celebrates the success of Theodoric in a one-on-one fight against the khan of the Bulgarians. Marcellinus Comes, *Chronicon* a. 487, p. 93. Martindale, *Prosopography* 2:63 f. (Amalafrida).

158. Best known is the alleged speech of Theodoric in Jordanes, *Getica* 291, p. 133, which reminds us of Orosius, *Historiae adversum paganos* VII 43.14 (as chap. 3, n. 342). Cf., in contrast, Eustathius fr. 4, and Lippold, "Zenon," 190–192.

159. Stein, *Bas-Empire* 2:52 ff.; but Stein does not want to believe Ioannis Antiochenus fr. 214.2 and 7, according to which Odovacar and Illus had established contact with each other. Furthermore, the emperor supposedly encouraged the Rugians to invade Italy. L. Schmidt, *Ostgermanen,* 119 ff., esp. 122, considers the Byzantine source trustworthy; similarly Ensslin, *Theoderich,* 58 ff. The main source on the Rugians is Eugippius, *Vita s. Severini,* chap. 5.1 (the Rugians want to move to Italy), chap. 8.1 f. (Feletheus and his evil wife Giso), chaps. 30 f. (the provincials at the Danube are gathered together by Severin and are placed under Rugian protection), chap. 44 (destruction of the Rugian kingdom, flight of Frideric to Theodoric, expulsion of the provincials). For the Rugian battle at the Danube see *Fasti Vindobonenses priores* 635 a. 487, p. 312, and *Auctarium Havniense* a. 487 n. 1 (2), p. 313, as well as Lotter, "Lauriacum-Lorch," 40 f. Theodoric's kinship with Giso can probably be inferred from Ennodius, *Panegyricus* 25, p. 206, as well as Ioannis Antiochenus fr. 214a. On Hunulf see Malchus fr. 18. That Odovacar's measures were successful is shown by the Herulian inability to support themselves in the land of the Rugians because it was a "wasteland": see Procopius, *De bello Gothico* II (VI) 14.23–25. Cf. L. Schmidt, *Ostgermanen,* 553. On the end of Italy's rule over Gaul in the year 471 see chap. 4, nn. 106–108. McCormick, "Odoacer," 212 ff.

160. Anonymus Valesianus II 49. Evangelos Chrysos has been able to find evidence in Syrian sources that both Odovacar in the initial stages of his rule and Theodoric in Italy were considered legitimate representatives of the emperor: see Chrysos, "Ἀντικαῖσαρ," 73 ff.

161. On this and what follows see esp. Ensslin, *Theoderich,* 62 ff.

162. Jordanes, *Getica* 292, p. 133: "the entire Gothic people [or better: "an entire Gothic people" (see chap. 3 with n. 97)], who had nevertheless given their consent, he [Theodoric] led to the West." The Amal Andela-Andagis clan and also the family to which Jordanes himself belonged almost certainly remained in the East; cf. Jordanes, *Getica* 266, p. 126. The two "battle-proven and noble Goths" Godigisclus and Bessas also stayed behind: Procopius, *De bello Gothico* I (V) 8.3 and 16.1 f. Procopius, *De aedificiis* III 7.13.

163. See Cassiodorus, *Variae* I 42–44, pp. 37–39, esp. 43.2, p. 38. It is probable that the doctor Anthimus, who is mentioned in Malchus fr. 11 and who in 477/478 joined the Gothic cause, went to the West with Theodoric, who sent him to the Frankish kingdom as a medical adviser: see Zöllner, *Franken,* 249–252; cf. 269.

164. Eustathius fr. 4.

165. Ensslin, *Theoderich,* 62 ff., after Ennodius, *Panegyricus* 26–47, pp. 206–209, who gives an especially lively description of Theodoric's departure and his battles. On the expansion of the Gepids in Pannonia, see Pohl, "Gepiden," 291 f. and L. Schmidt, *Ostgermanen,* 533 f. On the alleged or actual negotiations with

Odovacar see Ennodius, *Vita Epifani* 109, p. 97; cf. L. Schmidt, *Ostgermanen*, 289 with n. 5. On the justification of Odovacar's murder by Theodoric see Ioannis Antiochenus fr. 214a. When Procopius, *De bello Gothico* I (V) 1.13 reports that Theodoric and his people originally intended to travel from Epirus to Italy by boat, this might be his misunderstanding of Malchus fr. 18 (FHG 4, 127 and 129), according to which the imperial government, on the one hand, feared that Theodoric, who had invaded Epirus in 479, might seize the fleet stationed there, and, on the other hand, rejected Theodoric's offer to lead Nepos from Dalmatia back to Italy. Cf. Chrysos, Ἱστορία τῆς Ἠπείρου, 58 ff. An accurate account of Theodoric's trek to Italy is given by Löwe, "Theoderichs Gepidensieg," esp. 2–10 (Gepids) and 10–12 (Sarmatians and the joining of the Rugians). On the Pannonian road network see Mócsy, "Pannonia," 659.

166. On Caesar Thela see Classen, "Der erste Römerzug," 336 and 339 f., as well as Wolfram, "Gotisches Königtum," 21 f., and Martindale, *Prosopography* 2:1064. On Tufa see Martindale, 2:1131, and Cassiodorus, *Variae* IV 32, p. 128, as well as Martindale, 2:484 f. (Frideric), after *Auctarium Havniense* a. 493.2, p. 321, and Anonymus Valesianus II 51 f. From Ennodius, *Panegyricus 55*, p. 209, one could infer equally the death of Frideric or his elimination through defeat and subjection. For the events see L. Schmidt, *Ostgermanen*, 296 f.

167. MGH *Auctores antiquissimi* 9:318 f.

168. Ioannis Antiochenus fr. 214a.

169. Ibid., and esp. Ennodius, *Panegyricus* 50–52, p. 209. Cassiodorus, *Chronicon* a. 493, p. 159. See also L. Schmidt, *Ostgermanen*, 300 with n. 2.

170. See above, n. 168 as well as Anonymus Valesianus II 54.

171. For the preceding section see Ensslin, *Theoderich*, 66–73. L. Schmidt, *Ostgermanen*, 291–301.

172. Anonymus Valesianus II 57.

173. Avellana 113.4, p. 507, dates only from July 28, 516, but the source bases itself on the conclusion of a peace and a treaty that Anonymus Valesianus II 64 reports for the year 498. For the year 493 see Anonymus Valesianus II 57. The expression *vestis regia* is found ibid. II 53. Ibid. II 64 we read: . . . *et omnia ornamenta palatii, quae Odoacar Constantinopolim transmiserat, remittit.*" Jordanes, *Getica* 295, p. 134, speaks in connection with the same event of *regius amictus*. On this and for this chapter in general see Ensslin, *Theoderich*, 74–79, 156, and L. Schmidt, *Ostgermanen*, 337 ff. and 371 ff. Altheim, *Geschichte der Hunnen* 1:322 ff., also speculates on the appearance of the "Ostrogothic royal insignia." See the summary of Hauck (as below, n. 204). Cf. Wolfram *Intitulatio I*, 54 f. with n. 103. Wolfram, "Gotisches Königtum," esp. 22 f.

174. Anonymus Valesianus II 49 (cf. above, n. 160), II 57. According to Agathias I 5.4–10, esp. 6 f., Theodoric had the emperor's permission to establish a kingdom in Italy. This is why the Goths of King Teja complained to the Franks about the injustice of the Romans and asked for help against them. Malalas, *Chronographia* pp. 383–385 and 459 f., also follows a tradition that recognized Theodoric's legitimate rule as ῥὴξ Ῥώμης. The "ex-consul and magister militum" had once been a "tyrant," but that was in Thrace, before he had marched to Rome on imperial orders. Theodoric's successor Athalaric (ibid. 459 f.) had the same rights as his

grandfather, rights that the "kings of the Africans," the legitimate Vandal kings, also called their own. Only Gelimer was a tyrant, which is why Justinian urged Athalaric not to receive his envoys or recognize his title ῥήξ.

175. Procopius, *De bello Gothico* II (VI) 6.23.

176. Ibid. I (V) 1.25 ff. Cf. Eustathius fr. 4.

177. Wolfram, *Intitulatio I*, 70 with n. 82, after *Anagnosticum regis* (*Acta synhodorum habitarum Romae* 14), 425. Quoted by Löwe, "Von Theoderich dem Grossen," 33 with n. 2.

178. Procopius, *De bello Gothico* I (V) 1.29, cf. 26 f.

179. Wolfram, *Intitulatio I*, 54 f. with n. 103: titles and offices of Odovacar and Theodoric the Great, esp. after Avellana 113.4, p. 507; 114.1, p. 508; 199.2, p. 658.

180. Wolfram, *Intitulatio I*, 47 f., after Procopius, *De bello Gothico* II (VI) 29.17–27. Cf. also I (V) 11.5 (Vitigis's elevation to the kingship), 2.10 and 3.12 (Amalasuintha disposes over the kingship); 20.11 (Vitigis is introduced to Belisarius as such a king); II (VI) 30.26 (Belisarius is to become Vitigis's successor: see below, n. 670); see also III (VII) 9.13 (Totila invokes the memory of this kingship—last mention). The political vocabulary of the *Sanctio pragmatica*, chaps. 1 f., 6, esp. 8, but also 15 and 22, agrees with this terminology.

181. Jordanes, *Romana* 349, p. 45: . . . *regnum gentis sui et Romani populi principatum . . . continuit.* Cf. the well-known formulation of Anonymus Valesianus II 60: . . ." thus he [Theodoric] ruled the two peoples of the Romans and the Goths as one, and *militiam Romanis sicut sub principes* [!] *esse praecepit.*" On *militia Romana* cf. Cassiodorus, *Variae* p. 559 (index). Cf. below, n. 212. On the question of the role of the Romans in the kingdom of Theodoric see Claude, "Universale und partikulare Züge," 19 ff., esp. 42 ff.

182. See the excellent assessment of the events and their significance by Stein, *Bas-Empire* 2:107 ff. Wolfram, *Intitulatio I*, 45 ff., tries in particular to fit the events into institutional history. On this and the following see Wolfram, "Gotisches Königtum." 1 ff. Claude, "Universale und partikulare Züge," esp. 42 ff. Important passages on this are Cassiodorus, *Variae* I 18, p. 24, II 41.3, p. 73; and IX 24.9, p. 290 (cf. above, Introduction with n. 66).

183. On this and the following see Wolfram, *Intitulatio I*, 54 ff. Ensslin, *Theoderich*, 152 ff. Stein, *Bas-Empire* 2:116 ff.

184. Stengel, "Der Heerkaiser," esp. 15 f.

185. Ensslin, *Theoderich*, 42, after Malchus fr. 11. Characteristically enough this demand was raised by Theodoric Strabo after he had been proclaimed τῶν Γότθων αὐτοκράτωρ by a Gothic army (see ibid. fr. 2 and above, n. 144). That a yielding to barbarian legal idea with simultaneous adherence to Roman legal institutions could threaten the existence of the *imperium* was discussed in a most illuminating way by Procopius, *De bello Persico* I 11.10 ff., esp. 16–18 and 22. On the legal status of the federates and on their ethnic composition see Grosse, *Militärgeschichte*, 280 ff.

186. Jordanes, *Romana* 344, p. 44.

187. See below, nn. 212 ff.

188. See above, n. 181. Cf. n. 173. What is meant here is the imperial *iussio*, which the Goths did not await. But there was no question about their right to

proclaim a king, even if it was done on royal orders. On the royal insignia see below, n. 204.

189. On this and the following see Wolfram, "Gotisches Königtum," 1 ff. and 22 f. Cf. chap. 2, n. 389, chap. 3, n. 169, and above, nn. 174, 176.

190. Anonymus Valesianus II 64.

191. Demandt, "Magister militum," 627. Ensslin, Theoderich, 97 ff. Stein, Bas-Empire 2:41 ff. Stengel, "Heerkaiser," 14 f.

192. See above, n. 145 (Kyrrhos), n. 135 (Theodoric's elevation to the leadership of the army in 471), n. 148 (adoption as son-in-arms in 476/478), n. 149 (Flavius Theodericus, consul and patricius-magister militum).

193. Cassiodorus, Variae III 16.3, p. 88. Cf. Ensslin, Theoderich, 158. See Procopius (as n. 178): Theodoric was a true emperor. On the clause of praeregnare see above, n. 160 and n. 173 f.

194. Ensslin, Theoderich, 154, after Cassiodorus, Variae V 14.7, p. 151.

195. Ibid., I 1.2–5, p. 10. Cf. Wolfram, Intitulatio I, 54 n. 103. Ennodius, Panegyricus 11, p. 204: Educavit te in gremio civilitatis Graecia praesaga venturi. See below, n. 206, as well as Suerbaum, Staatsbegriff, 247 ff.

196. Anonymus Valesianus II 60, 67, 71. On the comparison of rulers see Wolfram, "Constantin," 226 ff. Hahn, Moneta Imperii Byzantini I, 83 with n. 25, 128 and 36 n. 1 (tables). Hauck (as below, n. 204).

197. Ensslin, Theoderich, 154 f. with nn. 13 and 20, as well as Chrysos, "Amaler-Herrschaft," 450, 462–469, esp. 468, who corrects Ensslin on a few points.

198. Chrysos, "Amaler-Herrschaft," 452–462. Cf. below, n. 585.

199. Chrysos, "Amaler-Herrschaft," 446, 450–452. Ensslin, Theoderich, 76 and 93 ff.

200. Hartmann, Geschichte Italiens 1:128 n. 20, esp. after Cassiodorus, Variae X 27, p. 314; XII 27, p. 383; 28.8, p. 385: emergency measures to combat rising prices. See also Hahn, Moneta Imperii Byzantini, I, 77–91; cf. Hahn, "Moneta Imperii Byzantini II, 25–32, which contains an excellent discussion of the Ostrogothic monetary system. On the economic policies of Theodoric in general see Ensslin, Theoderich, 237 ff. A rich mine of quotations can be found in the little-known Heidelberg dissertation of Heerklotz, Variae, esp. 44 ff. Grain was on occasion brought from Bruttium (Cassiodorus, Variae IX 3.4, p. 270) and Sicily (IV 7.1 f., p. 117 f.) to the areas that needed it, for example, Ostrogothic Gaul after the war of 507/511. On the movement of grain, on trade in general, and on the type of ships used, see the excellent discussion of Claude, Handel, esp. 71 ff. An attempt to bring grain from Spain (V 35, p. 162 f.) to Rome was something of a failure. A small shipload of grain did not arrive in Ostia but, of all places, in a port of Vandal Africa. Cf. Ruggini, Economia, 292 ff. Hannestad, L'évolution, esp. 28–41. Special attention was also paid to deep-sea fishing (Cassiodorus, Variae XII 24,5, p. 380) as an important source of protein for the Italian population. For that reason Theodoric did not allow the fishermen to be recruited during the naval buildup against the Vandals: see Cassiodorus, Variae V 16.5, p. 153. Similar reasoning was probably behind the prohibition against the export of laridum, bacon: see ibid. II 12.1, p. 52, and XII 14.6, p. 372. Of course Theodoric's economic policy did not differ from that of the late antique Roman state and had the same problems:

see Cracco-Ruggini, "Vicende," 261 ff., esp. 268 ff. The royal treasure amassed by Theodoric around 533 contained, apart from other precious objects of great value, gold worth forty thousand pounds, which according to the estimate of Stein, *Bas-Empire* 1:343, corresponded to about twice the yearly budget of the Western Roman empire after the middle of the fifth century. At that time, however, the empire had approximately the same dimensions as the later Ostrogothic kingdom. For the significance of the royal treasure in general see Claude, "Frühmittelalterliche Königsschätze," 5 ff.

201. Ensslin, *Theoderich*, 220 ff. On the most recent discussion of who issued the *Edictum Theoderici* see chap. 4, nn. 188 and 195 as well as Nehlsen, *Sklavenrecht*, 120 ff. Cf. Procopius, *De bello Gothico* II (VI) 6.17, as well as I (V) 1.27–39.

202. Nehlsen, "belagines," 206 f., after Jordanes, *Getica* 69, p. 74. Cf. Procopius, *De bello Gothico* IV (VIII) 35.33, where the Ostrogoths ready to depart prefer an "autonomous life with other barbarians" to any form of subordination. Apart from the chronological correction of this report (see below, nn. 751 ff.), the phrase αὐτόνομοι βιοτεύσοντες should be translated as "living under their own laws." Also, the law that the Goths in Italy did not give up until the eleventh century must have come from the kingdom of Theodoric: see L. Schmidt, "Die letzten Ostgoten," 87 ff., and Wenskus, *Stammesbildung*, 485.

203. Ensslin, *Theoderich*, 244–262. On Ravenna see the monumental work of Deichmann, *Ravenna* 1. 1969. See, for example, also the volume of illustrations by von Matt, *Ravenna*. 1971. Heerklotz, *Varien*, 41 ff., evaluates his source regarding the question of building activity. The visit to Rome of the African Fulgentius of Ruspe is described by Ferrandus, *Vita s. Fulgentii*, chap. 9, p. 55 f. Cf. Martindale, *Prosopography* 2:487 f. On the construction of fortifications see Cassiodorus, *Variae* I 17.1 ff., p. 23 f., as well as III 48.1 ff., p. 103 f. The foundation of a city near Trent is decreed in Cassiodorus, *Variae* V 9, p. 148 f. On The(o)doricopolis see Ensslin, *Theoderich*, 142 n. 1., Wolfram, "Gotisches Königtum," 16 with n. 97, and Clavadetscher, "Churrätien," 164. See below, n. 396. On the building activity cf. Anonymus Valesianus II 71, p. 324. Fiebiger, *Inschriftensammlung Zweite Folge*, n. 7, p. 9 f.

204. See Hahn, *Moneta Imperii Byzantini* I, 79 f., on the question of jurisdiction over the minting of coins. Ensslin, *Theoderich*, 156 f., thinks that Theodoric, "unlike Odovacar," probably did wear the purple. On the ruler image of Theodoric see Hauck, "Brustbilder von Königen," 219–231, esp. 128 ff. (Gothic crowns) and 148 ff. (Germanic ruler insignia). According to Procopius, *De bello Gothico* I (V) 1.29, Theodoric "was in name a tyrant, in his acts a true emperor." According to II (VI) 6.17, οἱ νόμοι καὶ ἡ πολιτεία were preserved. See the similar judgment in Anonymus Valesianus (as n. 181); cf. also n. 176 f., n. 200 f., and below, n. 339.

205. On the kingdom of Toulouse see chap. 4, nn. 273–283. On the role of Pavia before the capture of Ravenna see, for example, MGH *Auctores antiquissimi* 9:318 f., as well as Ensslin, *Theoderich*, 66 and 70, cf. 142 f. and 405, s.v. "Ticinum." Bierbrauer, *Die Grab- und Schatzfunde*, 33 with n. 94 as well as 34 with n. 104. In Pavia Hildebad (see below, n. 675 f.), Totila (see below, n. 692), and Teja (see below, n. 749) were elevated to the kingship. Totila's attempts to make Rome his residence can be inferred directly from the resumption of coinage at the Roman mint between 549 and 552 after a long break: see Hahn, *Moneta Imperii Byzantini*

I, 78 f. Cf. Stein, *Bas-Empire* 2:593 ff. To what extent Rome was actually considered Totila's residence and capital in the eyes of "foreigners" is revealed by the rejection of his suit for a Frankish princess. The Frankish king, when asked for the hand of his daughter, did not consider Totila the king of Italy because he had lost Rome to Belisarius: see Procopius, *De bello Gothico* III (VII) 37.1 f. On Cumae see below, n. 332 f. The Gothic royal throne is called *sedes regni* and is attested both at the crowning as "a custom whose roots lie in the legal sphere of the Germanic house, and as an additional formal act at the Ostrogothic elevation of a king." Claude, "Die ostgotischen Königserhebungen," 180 with n. 293. Cassiodorus, *Variae* VIII 6.2 and 8.2, p. 236 f.

206. See Anonymus Valesianus II 61, and above, n. 195. On *civilitas* see Cassiodorus, *Variae,* p. 521 (index). Ennodius, *Panegyricus* 11, p. 204, or, for example, also Cassiodorus, *Variae* IV 16.1, p. 121. Ensslin, *Theoderich,* 217 ff., and esp. 231. On the Goths as the chosen among the "peoples" see, for example, Cassiodorus, *Variae* VII 25.1, p. 216. The dual position of Theodoric's rule follows from Jordanes (as n. 181) and Procopius (as n. 180).

207. On the equality before the law of all *subiecti* of Theodoric and their subjection to taxation, see Ensslin, *Theoderich,* 158, 198 ff., and 220 ff., together with the reservations expressed by Goffart, *Barbarians and Romans,* 77 ff. and 91 ff. This policy is defended by Cassiodorus, *Variae* IV 14.2, p. 120 f., in characteristic fashion. See, for example, ibid. I 27.1, p. 29: *Si exterarum gentium mores sub lege moderamur, si iuri Romano servit quicquid sociatur Italiae, quanto magis decet ipsam civilitatis sedem legum reverentiam plus habere.* Ibid. VII 3.1, p. 203: . . . *ut unicuique [sc. Gotho vel Romano] sua iura serventur et sub diversitate iudicum una iustitia complectatur universos,* does not contradict the previous statement.

208. Wolfram, *Splendor Imperii,* 108 f. Cassiodorus, *Variae,* p. 468, s.v. "Amali." See chap. 1, nn. 87 ff. The Amal identity was "returned" to Eutharic: see chap. 1, n. 108; cf. n. 106 f. One of the *saiones* of Theodoric was called Candac (cf. below, n. 261) and thus had the same name as one member of the Andela-Andagis clan. On Vidimir the Younger see above, nn. 140 ff.

209. Stein, *Bas-Empire* 2:108.

210. In the discussion that follows I have omitted a detailed description of the bureaucratic structure of the Ostrogothic kingdom. For that see Ensslin, *Theoderich,* 152 ff., Stein, *Bas-Empire* 2:119 ff., Jones, *The Later Roman Empire* 1:253 ff. On the former prefecture of Italy-Illyricum-Africa see Stein, *Bas-Empire* 1:132.

211. See chap. 4, nn. 344 ff., esp. 29, and below, nn. 213–215.

212. Anonymus Valesianus II 60 uses this term and emphasizes specifically that Theodoric had not made any changes. Of great importance in this context is Cassiodorus, *Variae* VII 25, p. 216, a formulary that announces to a Gothic *comes* that Roman officials have been assigned to him. It emphatically stresses that "this is something the other *gentes* could not have." Cf. ibid. 559, s.v. "militia."

213. See above, n. 212. Cassiodorus, *Variae* VII 3, p. 202 f.: *Formula comitivae Gothorum per singulas civitates.*

214. On the Gothic-barbarian settlers see below, n. 221. On the *comes Dalmatiae et Saviae* see Seeck, "Comites," 646, and Martindale, *Prosopography* 2:815 (Osuin), after Cassiodorus, *Variae* I 40, p. 36 f.; III 26, p. 92 f.; IV 9, p. 118; as well as after the formularies VII 1 and 24 f., pp. 201 f. and 215 f.; and finally after IX 8

f., pp. 274–276. From the formularies follows the assignment of the *comes provinciae* to Dalmatia. On the other commanders see in general the list in Cassiodorus, *Variae*, p. 523, s.v. "comitiva rei militaris," especially on Arigern, ibid. IV 16.1, p. 121. On the *comes* of Sirmium cf. Martindale, *Prosopography* 2:305. The undivided military-civilian authority of the Sirmian provincial *comes* follows from Cassiodorus, Variae III 23.2, and 24.2, p. 91. Yet ibid. V 24, p. 157, mentions a Dalmatian civilian governor who was possibly also in charge of Savia. We have evidence in Savia for a special civilian envoy of Theodoric: see ibid. V 14, p. 150 f.

215. Ensslin, *Theoderich*, 168 f. L. Schmidt, *Ostgermanen*, 380 f.

216. Cf. chap. 4, nn. 361 and 379. Ensslin, *Theoderich*, 192. Cassiodorus, *Variae*, p. 537, s.v. "dux exercitus Gothorum."

217. L. Schmidt, *Ostgermanen*, 344 and 380. Ensslin, *Theoderich*, 142 f.

218. Ensslin, *Theoderich*, 168 and 192. Cf. Cassiodorus, *Variae* I 11, p. 20, and VII 4, p. 203 f.

219. Ensslin, *Theoderich*, 169. See below, nn. 680–683.

220. Cf. Jordanes, *Getica* 304, p. 136, with Procopius, *De bello Gothico* II (VI) 29.18 and 24. See below, n. 670.

221. Cassiodorus, *Variae* V 26.1, p. 158. Wolfram, "Ansiedlung," 15 f. See below, n. 250 f. (*millenarii*) and n. 274 (*capillati*).

222. Cassiodorus, *Variae* III 22.1, p. 90, invites Artemidorus (see above, n. 163) to come to Ravenna and join Theodoric's *comitatus* with these words: *Congruit comitatum nostrum viris nos decorare nobilibus.* Cf. ibid. X 29.1, p. 315, where Theodahad assigns Pavia to a Gothic *comes,* both on account of the man's proven loyalty and his nobility. The best example for that is Tuluin: see ibid. VIII 9.1–8, as well as 10.3, pp. 237–239. Tuluin was probably a son-in-law of Theodoric: L. Schmidt, *Ostgermanen,* 361. On Tuluin see Martindale, *Prosopography* 2:1131–1133. The Anician Flavius Maximus, of the highest nobility, also received an Amal princess as wife, though only under Theodahad: see Cassiodorus, *Variae* X 11.1 f., and 12.2 f., p. 304 f. See also Stein, *Bas-Empire* 2:343 n. 1. Jordanes, *Getica,* 314, p. 138, is perhaps based on a misunderstood report about this marriage. On the creation of a stratum of Gothic subjects see below, n. 274. Maximus, who in Procopius, *De bello Gothico* I (V) 25.15, is persecuted as a friend of the Goths, possibly also appears in *Sanctio pragmatica,* chap. 1, for there a Maximus is specifically mentioned as the recipient of a gift from Theodahad. In that case he would have been the brother of Marcianus: see Cassiodorus, *Variae* IV 42.2, p. 133.

223. In the triumphal year 500 Odoin, a namesake of the Lombard king Audoin, was beheaded in the Sessorio palace in Rome: Anonymus Valesianus II 68 f., p. 324. Cf. *Auctarium Havniense,* a. 504, p. 331, but the event should be placed in the year 500, as reveals Marius of Avenches, *Chronica,* a. 500.3, p. 234. On June 7, 514, Theodoric went to Milan in person where he had the *comes* Pitz(i)a—who was apparently in command there—arrested and executed: *Auctarium Havniense,* a. 514, p. 331. Cf. on this Cassiodorus, *Variae,* p. 498, s.v. "Pitzia," as well as p. 497, s.v. "Patza." Pitzia, highly celebrated in 504 as the victor at the Sava, had several namesakes, one of whom commanded in Samnium and surrendered to Belisarius in 536/537 after the latter had captured Rome. One could see the surrender as a strategic necessity. Calabria and Apulia, where no Goths were in the field, had just gone over to the imperial troops. Moreover, the Gothic commander of the

Eternal City had abandoned his retreating army and had surrendered to Belisarius, after he had been prevented, principally by the Roman population, from mounting a meaningful defense. But the Pitzia in Samnium gained a following only from among those Goths who were settled as far as the river Biferno or, at most, the river Sangro, in other words, those who were still settled south of the Pescara-Rome line. But these Goths were just as threatened by Belisarius as their northern neighbors. It is therefore conceivable that the Gothic *comes* Pitzia went over to the emperor's side because he wanted to protest the elevation of Vitigis to the kingship but waited to do so until the southern Gothic army had left southern Italy and Belisarius was protecting his flank. The imperial general in fact dispatched a protective force to Samnium and placed it under the command of Pitzia. If this Pitzia was related to the older Pitzia, his decision probably was not brought about by the latter's execution twenty years earlier, which Theodoric very much regretted: see Cassiodorus, *Variae* V 29.2 f., p. 159. The Pitzia who was killed in 514 was, in any case, a *nobilissimus:* see Ennodius, *Panegyricus* 62, p. 210. Cf. L. Schmidt, *Ostgermanen* 374, as well as Ensslin, *Theoderich*, 111 and 339 (Oduin), and 130, 168, and 192 (Pitzia). Martindale, *Prosopography* 2:886 f., overlooks the execution of Pitzia in 514 and has him live on until 523/526 or maybe even until 537.

224. Ensslin, *Theoderich*, 170. L. Schmidt, *Ostgermanen*, 378. On the *maiores domus* known by name from Cassiodorus see *Variae*, p. 558. Tuluin (as n. 222) was one of them.

225. Ensslin, *Theoderich*, 168–170. A non-Gothic member of the *comitatus* was Artemidorus (as n. 222); cf. Ensslin, *Theoderich*, 392.

226. *Epistulae Theodericianae* 5–8, p. 390 f. Cassiodorus, *Variae* IX 15.7, p. 280. (Athalaric to the pope concerning the negotiations of the *comitatus* about the appointment of bishops). Ibid. VII 34, p. 220 (formula for summoning the *comitatus*); cf. III 22, p. 90 f. On the legal status of the clerics see Pfeilschifter, *Theoderich*, 234 ff. But the primary function of the *comitatus* was that of a palace court: see Ensslin, *Theoderich*, 167 and 210. Stein, *Bas-Empire* 2:120 f. Cassiodorus, *Variae*, p. 523, s.v. "comitatus."

227. Ensslin, *Theoderich* 169 f. (*cubiculum*), 172 ff. (prefecture and provincial administration), and 164–167 (patrimony and other top financial agencies). Stein, *Bas-Empire* 2:51 f. (patrimony-Odovacar), 124 (Theodoric), 206 (Anastasius), as well as 152 (prefecture of Gaul), as well as Stein, *Untersuchungen*, 384–387 (Sirmium; cf. above, n. 214). Jones, *The Later Roman Empire* 1:255. Cassiodorus, *Variae*, p. 523, s.v. "comes patrimonii," lists the men who held this office. On the quote (patrimony) see Procopius, *De bello Gothico* I (V) 4.1 On the capture of Sirmium, see below, nn. 432 ff. On the recognition of the Visigothic kingdom and the abolition of the prefecture of Gaul, see chap. 4, n. 133 and n. 153 f.

228. Diesner, "protectores," 1121. Ensslin, *Theoderich*, 160 f. On the *magister officiorum* see Jones, *The Later Roman Empire* 1:369, and now Clauss, *Magister officiorum*, 15 ff., esp. 53 f. n. 139 (supervision of the weapons factories, *fabricae*). Cf. below, n. 295.

229. Ensslin, *Theoderich*, 161 f. The *saiones* known from Cassiodorus are listed in *Variae*, p. 582, s.v. "saio." On the Visigothic *saio* see chap. 4, nn. 582 ff. On the Italian *praefectus praetorio* see Ensslin, *Theoderich*, 172 ff. As concerns the distinctions of rank I have assumed, one could imagine, for example, that a man

like Duda (Cassiodor, *Variae* IV 34, p. 129) needed personal clout for his delicate task and could not have been a mere lackey. It is highly probable that he later rose to the office of *comes,* something that was usually denied the *saiones:* see Cassiodorus, *Variae,* p. 492 (index). On the authority of the *saiones* as the deliverers of the royal orders cf. ibid. IV 47.2, p. 135: . . . *ut nullum Gothorum vel Romanorum . . . egredi patiaris . . . cuiuslibet nationis fuerit vel honoris.*

230. Ensslin, *Theoderich,* 162 and esp. 215 ff. On *civilitas* see above, n. 206. Cf., for example, Cassiodorus, *Variae* I 37.5, p. 35.

231. See above, n. 202.

232. See below, nn. 256 and 258. The illegal acts of the powerful were especially denounced in the *Edictum Athalarici.* Cassiodorus, *Variae* IX 18.1 ff., pp. 282 ff. On this edict cf. Nehlsen, *Sklavenrecht,* 123.

233. Cassiodorus, *Variae* V 32 f., p. 160 f.

234. Ibid., V 29 f., p. 159 f.

235. See below, nn. 256 and 258.

236. See above, n. 234.

237. Cassiodorus, *Variae* II 20, p. 57 f., and IV 47, p. 135 f. Cf. above, n. 229.

238. Cassiodorus, *Variae* III 42.3, p. 100: *duces et praepositi.* The commanding officer Patza who was put into action in the Gallic war (cf. below, n. 262) is also called *dux:* see ibid. V 33, p. 161—See Goffart, *Barbarians and Romans,* 61, 80–88, 172, after Cassiodorus, *Variae* V 27, p. 159, on *millena* or *iugum* (cf. Cassiodorus *Variae,* p. 559 s.v.). Durliat, "Polyptyque d'Irminon," 196. On the Visigothic *millenarius* see chap. 4, nn. 380–391. Cassiodorus, *Historia tripartita* VI 35.1, was familiar with the military meaning of *millenarius.* Cf. Claude, "millenarius," 17 ff.

239. Cassiodorus, *Variae* V 11, p. 149. Cf. ibid. V 10. Goffart, *Barbarians and Romans,* 47 f. and 219.

240. Procopius, *De bello Gothico* I (V) 1, 4–8 and 28.

241. Cassiodorus, *Variae* II 16.5, pp. 55 f. Cf. *Variae* II 15, p. 54, and VII 3.1 and 3, pp. 202 f. Ennodius, *Epistulae* IX 23.5, p. 307, also speaks of the *larga praediorum conlatio* that the *innumerae Gothorum catervae* were provided with. The reason the Gothic settlement could not have begun earlier than 493 is that it was carried out by Liberius, who was named praetorian prefect only in 493 at the earliest: see Martindale, *Prosopography* 2:677.

242. Cf., for example, Wolfram, "Ansiedlung," 12 ff., esp. 17. A good example that even a lifelong study of diplomatic texts, which in fact contain clear statements contrary to the traditional interpretation, does not protect against making the same mistake is Tjäder, *Papyri* 2, p. 31, l. 6 f., pp. 68 f., and 261 n. 7.

243. Wolfram, "Ansiedlung," 5 ff., (cf. still Claude, "Ansiedlung," 13 ff.) received the theses presented by Goffart in his *Barbarians and Romans* with a good deal of scepticism, even resisted them, since they contained many inconsistencies. I was, however, well aware that the last word on the subject had not been spoken. Following a suggestion of Martin Heinzelmann (Paris), I contacted Jean Durliat (Toulouse) and held a "Zwettler-Symposium" on this topic between May 7 and 9, 1986. See Wolfram and Schwarcz (Ed.), *Anerkennung und Integration,* 1 ff., esp. Durliat, "Le salaire," 21 ff., 45 ff. (Italy), 55 ff. (Visigoths) and 61 ff., as well as Goffart, "After the Zwettl Conference," 73 ff.

244. Martindale, *Prosopography* 2:677 f., esp. after Ennodius, *Epistolae* IX 23,

pp. 307 ff., and Cassiodorus, *Variae* II 16, 2–5, pp. 55 f. O'Donnell, "Liberius," 38 ff.—When Theodoric received the *generalitas Alamanniae* into his kingdom, their settlement took place *sine detrimento Romanae possessionis*. (Ennodius as below, n. 405). Since the *curiales* are the *possessores*—Durliat, "Le salaire," 31 with n. 46—this may mean that they were not enlisted for the settlement of the Alamanni. Cf. Procopius, *De bello Vandalico* I (III) 3.2 f.: this passage is undoubtedly anachronistic: see Goffart, *Barbarians and Romans,* 66 f. n. 18 and 68 n. 20. Miltner, "Vandalen," 307 f. Even though Procopius gets a number of things all jumbled up, what is of interest is his remark that the Vandals were to settle in Spain "without damage to the [taxable] land."

245. Cassiodorus, *Variae* X 29.4, p. 316. *Variae* VIII 26.3 f., p. 257, thinks that the Goths behaved differently than the *gentes*; III 17, p. 88, celebrates in 508 the reestablishment of the prefecture of Gaul and the replacement of the Visigothic by the Ostrogothic regime as the vanquishing of the *barbaries*; III 43.1, p. 100, calls the peoples driven out of what was formerly the Visigothic Provence and is now Ostrogothic Gaul *barbari confusi*. To be sure, Cassiodorus, *Variae* V 39.13–15, p. 166, has to admit that the Spanish provincials longed for the days of Alaric II and Euric.

246. Goffart, *Barbarians and Romans,* 220; cf. 173 with n. 24.

247. Durliat, "Caput," 70 with n. 24, reports a Syrian source according to which one *iugum* had the tax value of 5 *iugera* of vineyards, 20 *iugera* of good, 40 *iugera* of average, and 60 *iugera* of poor farmland. Of course the tax unit *iugum* varied considerably over time and from place to place.—Cassiodorus, *Variae* XII 22.1 f., p. 378, in his capacity as praetorian prefect orders the provincials of Istria to use a certain amount of their tax revenues to purchase wine, grain, and oil and send these provisions to Ravenna. The remaining money is to be used to defray the yearly expenses in Istria itself. Cf. ibid. XII 23 f., pp. 379 f. *Codex Theodosianus* XI 28.2, p. 617: the taxpayers of Campania are remitted a certain number of *iugera. Novellae Maioriani* VII 16, p. 171 f.: instead of one and a half solidi, two solidi are collected *per iugum vel millenam,* and the distribution of the additional income *inter diversa officia* is ordered. Cassiodorus, *Variae* II 37, p. 67: the Spoletans are to use for the maintenance of their baths *supra consuetudinem aliam millenam. Variae* IV 20, p. 123: a bishop complains that *unum iugum,* which earlier emperors had allotted to him, is being illegally withheld. In this context the reference is not to the church's property but its income, *ecclesiae compendia.* Goffart, *Barbarians and Romans,* esp. 80 ff.

248. Cassiodorus, *Variae,* p. 516, s.v. *annona,* and 559, s.vv. *miles, militare, militaris, militia.* Anonymus Valesianus II 60. Goffart, *Barbarians and Romans,* 46 f.

249. See above, n. 240.

250. For the expression *Gothi deputati* see Cassiodorus, *Variae* IX 29.9, p. 292. Goffart, *Barbarians and Romans,* had not yet been able to use Tjäder, *Papyri* 2, n. 31, l. 6 f., p. 68 f. and 261 n. 7, where the seller declares to the buyer that the property for sale is free of all obligations to the treasury and of all other possible burdens, among them *a sorte barbari* (derived from a nominative *barbaris*). The deed of sale was drawn up in January 540 in Ravenna still under the Gothic king Vitigis. It is a matter of opinion whether Cassiodorus, *Variae* II 17, p. 56, is talking about landed property or an allocated taxshare. Likewise, VIII 26.4, p. 257, reveals

only that the Goths were to live from their *sortes propriae* and would be enriched through royal gifts. But the deed of sale from Ravenna can mean *only* a tax or a tax share to be allotted, depending on one's point of view. My thanks go to Jean Durliat for pointing this out. For the meaning of *millena* and *millenarius* according to Cassiodorus, *Variae* V 27, p. 159, see Goffart, "After the Zwettl Conference," 79 ff. as well as above, n. 238.—On the tax-exempt status of the Ostrogothic *sors* see Wolfram, "Ansiedlung," 12 f., after Goffart, *Barbarians and Romans*, 91: Cassiodorus, *Variae* II 17, p. 56, and VI 24.1, p. 196, contrasts the Goths, "who follow our commands," to the Romans, "who pay yearly taxes."

251. Wolfram, "Ansiedlung," unjustly opposes Goffart, *Barbarians and Romans*, 84 f. n. 52, who realized (following Cassiodorus, *Variae* V 27, p. 159; cf. V 26, p. 158) that one cannot say that the donatives were paid out every year. Instead, the *nostrae mansuetudinis praemia* (given) *annis singulis* are the annual intake from the *millenae* or the *sortes*, an interpretation that agrees with VIII 26.4, p. 257. The yearly sums of money sent to the Gothic troops in Spain as reported by Procopius, *De bello Gothico* I (V) 12.48, is specially justified. Cf. Goffart, *Barbarians and Romans*, 85 n. 52, as well as below, n. 254.

252. Cf. above, chap. 4, n. 431 (tasks of the curiales). Cassiodorus, *Variae* IX 25.9, p. 292 (about himself around 527: Martindale, *Prosopography* 2:267); I 4.17, p. 16 (about his father). On the praise of the curiales and the distribution of the land tax see *Novellae Maioriani* VII 1 and 16, pp. 167 and 171 f. Tjäder, *Payri* 2, nn. 47 f., l. 26, p. 192: the note of indebtedness for the arrears of *de titulus* (sic) *tertiarum* is kept in the *arca* of the praetorian prefect. Cf. Tjäder p. 188 as well as above, n. 242. For the regional disposal of the *tertia* see *Codex Theodosianus* IV 13.7, p. 193, and *Codex Iustinianus* IV 61.13, p. 187. Cf. Cassiodorus, *Variae* XII 22.2, p. 378 (as above, n. 243). On the *annona* see n. 253, on the curiales' concern with the Gothic *sors* see Cassiodorus, *Variae* II 17, p. 56. Ibid. I 14, p. 22, refutes the assumption that the *tertia* was an additional tax; this passage also speaks of the *suspectum tertiarum nomen*. For the *patrimonium regis* see above, n. 227 and below, n. 256 f. For the *fiscus Gothorum* see Durliat, "Le salaire," 67 f. with n. 250.

253. On the distribution of the Gothic settlers see Bierbrauer, *Grab- und Schatzfunde*, 25–41, with very instructive maps on pp. 29 and 40 ff.; cf. Ensslin, *Theoderich*, 91–93. Heuberger, *Rätien*, 134 ff. and 162 ff. Vinski, "Archäologische Spuren," 33 ff. For the Gothic garrisons see the list in Bierbrauer, 52. For the expression *vicini et consortes* applied to the Goths and the Roman landowners in the individual *civitates*, see Cassiodorus, *Variae* VII 3.1 and 3, p. 202 f. On the Gothic *milites* who were quartered in barracks and who received the *annona*, cf., for example, St. Ambrose, *Epistulae* 30 (Maur. 24) 4, p. 209, see Cassiodorus, *Variae*, p. 516 s.v., esp. I 40, p. 36 f. (Salona-Dalmatia). Variae II 5, p. 49 f. (Aosta-valley); III 40–42, p. 99 f. (Gaul); IV 13, p. 120 (cf. III 23.2, p. 91 [*quondam sedes Gothorum*]) and VI 22.3, p. 195 (Pannonia Sirmiensis and Syracuse-Sicily, for which the *comitiva patrimonii* is responsible—see above, n. 227); VI 23.3, p. 195 (Naples and probably all of southern Italy). In Spain the Visigothic garrisons are still mentioned as recipients of the *annona* in Lex Visigothorum IX 2.6, p. 369, cf. Jones, *The Later Roman Empire* 1:258. See on this also Procopius, *De bello Gothico* I (V) 12.48. Cf., however, Cassiodorus, *Variae* V 39.15, p. 166 (Spain—*Gothi in civitate positi*). The simple *annona* was set in the Western empire of the mid-fifth

century at 4 solidi a year. See Jones, *The Later Roman Empire* 2:630 and 3:192 n. 49. On the local militias that were also called *milites* see above, n. 218.

254. For exemption from military service as well as the dangers in case of illness or unfitness, see Cassiodorus, *Variae* V 29 and 36, pp. 159 and 163. For the economic policy see above, n. 200. As regards the great purchasing power of one solidus see Anonymus Valesianus II 73. Ensslin, *Theoderich*, 190, infers from Cassiodorus, *Variae* V 16.4, p. 152 (donatives to the free sailors), that 5 solidi were distributed as donatives. This sum agrees with Procopius, *Anecdota* 24.27–29, where it is also explicitly said that such an amount was paid out only every fifth year. See above, n. 251. The Italian Ostrogoths too received only extraordinary donatives, a fact that also explains why these gifts had to be picked up in Ravenna. A yearly payment of the *munera* would have meant that the Goths had been on the march constantly. Goffart, *Barbarians and Romans*, 83 f. n. 50, unjustly opposes the notion that the recipients of the donatives called to Ravenna (see Cassiodorus, *Variae* V 26.2, p. 158) received *exercituales expensae* that were not *annona*. The use of words, however, is completely identical with that in V 13, p. 150.

255. Cassiodorus, *Variae* V 13, p. 150, and V 23, p. 157 (allocation of the *annona*). Compensation: *Variae* II 8, p. 50 f. (payment of 1,500 solidi to a bishop for distribution among the provincials after an army had marched through). *Variae* III 38, p. 98; III 42 f., p. 100; IV 36, p. 130 (on the Gallic war of 508/509 and its consequences); V 10 f., p. 149 (522/523: Gepids march through northern Italy to Gaul); IV 45, p. 134 f. (Heruli on the march to Ravenna receive for a certain length of time the *annona*); V 16.4, p. 152 (the sailors of the planned Ostrogothic fleet receive in 526 the *annona*); X 18.2, p. 309 (Theodahad's Gothic garrison in Rome receives money in order to buy supplies on the market); cf. III 42.2 f., p. 100 (*exercituales expensae* are sent from Italy to the Provence, conquered in 508, to enable the Gothic commanders to buy there enough food supplies). Cf. Procopius, *De bello Vandalico* I (III) 21.10. Cassiodorus, *Variae* XII 5.3, p. 364 (the oppressed rural population of southern Italy fights back with armed force when Belisarius is already in Sicily).

256. On the taxation of the Gothic landowners see esp. Cassiodorus, *Variae* IV 14.1 f., p. 120, and V 14.6, as well as 15.3, p. 151 f.; cf. Goffart, *Barbarians and Romans*, 91–93. Cassiodorus, *Variae* I 18.2, p. 24 (effective date). For *pittacium* see Tjäder, *Papyri* 2:356 s.v., and Cassiodorus, *Variae*, p. 568 s.v., esp. III 35, p. 97: Theodoric tells a certain Romulus, probably the deposed emperor, that he should rely on the *pittacium* that had been allocated to him and to his mother on royal orders by the patricius Liberius. *Variae* VIII 28, p. 257 f. (Tanca-affair); a decree that is ironically directed at the same Cunigast whom Boethius, *Consolatio philosophiae* I 4.9–15, describes as an expropriator in the grand manner. See also Ennodius CCLXXXI (*Epist.* 6.14), p. 222, as well as above, n. 234. On Theodahad see Cassiodorus, *Variae* IV 39.4 f., p. 131, as well as V 12, p. 149 f. and X 3.5, p. 299. Cf. Procopius, *De bello Gothico* I (V) 3.1 f., and 4.1 f., as well as 6.16 and 26. Gregory of Tours, *Historia Francorum* III 31, p. 127. On the *patrimonium regis* see Cassiodorus, *Variae*, p. 566 s.v., esp. IV 37, p. 130 f. as well as VIII 23.2 f., p. 254. For the expression *comites et primates gentis* see above, n. 220.

257. On the *patrimonium regis* see above, n. 227, and esp. Jones, *The Later Roman Empire* 1:255, and 3:48 f. n. 44. See also Cassiodorus, *Variae*, p. 523 s. vv.

comitiva patrimonii and *comitiva privatarum*. Procopius, *De bello Gothico* I (V) 4.1; cf. 3.3 f., and 4.6, as well as 6.26. On the royal fiscal estates see Cassiodorus, *Variae* V 6, p. 147 f., and IX 3.2, p. 270, as well as XII 5.7, p. 364 (southern Italy, the last-named estates have to pay taxes since the hardships of the war are pressing); V 9, p. 148 f. (the royal estates around Feltre and Trent have to share the burden); V 18, p. 154 (Po Valley). See in general Hannestad, *L'évolution*, 29.

258. Procopius, *De bello Gothico* I (V) 12.48: δῶρον ἐπέτειον. Cassiodorus, *Variae* V 14.6, p. 151: tax liability for property "no matter under what title acquired." Although there was in Italy no legislation comparable to the Visigothic (as chap. 4, n. 432), different types of mobile retainer groups are attested: Procopius, *De bello Vandalico* I (III) 8.12; cf. below, n. 346. The attempts—frequently rebuked by Ravenna—of Gothic magnates, among them Theodahad, to force free Goths into dependency and thus deprive them of their freedom, presupposes the existence of unfree retainers: see above, nn. 234 and 256.

259. Cf. above, n. 163. See the revealing words of Procopius, *De bello Gothico* III (VII) 2.1: " . . . in the Gothic army there was a certain Eraric who was by descent a Rugian," as well as ibid. 2.2: "Theodoric had earlier prevailed upon them [the Rugians] and other peoples to form a confederation, so that they were received into the Gothic people and together with them fought against all enemies." Downright classic is the formulation of Ennodius, *Panegyricus* 26, p. 206: *Tunc a te conmonitis longe lateque viribus innumeros diffusa per populos gens una contrahitur.*

260. Wenskus, *Stammesbildung*, 20, 483 f., and 497 with n. 449, after Procopius, *De bello Gothico* III (VII) 2.1–5.

261. Cassiodorus, *Variae* III 38, p. 98, and I 37.5, p. 35; cf. Jordanes, *Getica* 265 f., p. 126. Cassiodorus, *Variae* V 25, p. 158. The telling name Vandil does not necessarily point to a Vandal, since Ostrogotha, for example, was also a Gepidic personal name: see L. Schmidt, *Ostgermanen*, 662. Candac, in contrast, is either an Alanic or a Hunnic name; in any case, it appears in an Amal family that was closely related to the Alans: see above, n. 208. According to Jordanes, *Getica* 58, p. 70, the ethnic identification of names is problematic. Cf. Wagner, *Getica*, 6–9. The influx of other peoples is also reported by Anonymus Valesianus II 72; cf. Wenskus, *Stammesbildung*, 484 with n. 351.

262. According to Jordanes (*Romana* 344, p. 44), Rugian, Herulian, Scirian, and Turcilingian groups formed the retainers of Odovacar. According to *Notitia dignitatum oc.* Suevic, Sarmatian, and Taifalian *gentiles* were settled in Italy. See Ensslin, *Theoderich*, 91, and L. Schmidt, *Ostgermanen*, 328. On the desertion of the troops of Odovacar see above, n. 166. Lotter, "Donausueben," 277 f., proves the existence of a strong Suevic minority in Pannonia-Savia; cf. below, n. 267 f. On the Sava barbarians see Šašel, "Antiqui barbari," 134 ff., esp. after Cassiodorus, *Variae* V 14.6, p. 151. On Brandila and Patza see ibid. V 32 f., p. 162 f.

263. Of Cyprianus (see Martindale, *Prosopography* 2:332 f.) we know for certain that he did military service in the field army: see Cassiodorus, *Variae* V 40 f., pp. 166–168 (ibid. 41.5, p. 168, it is said that already Opilio, Cyprianus's father, was an "old warrior"), as well as VIII 21 f., p. 252 f., esp. 21.3 f. and 6 f., p. 252 f., from which follows that the entire family was engaged in the military profession. The expression "with a Gothic heart" is not attested in this way; it was formed as a counterpart to *cor Latinum* by Sidonius Apollinaris, *Epistulae* V 5.3, p. 81, where

it is said that the Burgundians had learned from Syagrius (as below, n. 450) their own language, *sermo patrius,* and had taken over from him a "Latin heart." Since Ensslin, *Theoderich,* 188 ff., clings all too stubbornly to the notion that the Romans were barred from serving in the army, he does not know what to make of Cyprianus, and he even wants to turn the Raetian Servatus into a non-Roman: see ibid., 373 n. 25. Cassiodorus, *Variae* I 7.2, p. 17, calls a Roman *miles noster.* The person referred to, a child under age, had been deprived of his rights to a royal gift which he was supposed to inherit; cf. I 8, p. 17 f. Cassiodorus, *Variae,* p. 559 (index), lists him under the *saiones* for which there is no indication whatsoever. *Milites* could be Roman civil officials, but that also is nowhere indicated. Cf. above, n. 181. See esp. Liberius (as below, n. 357), who even became *patricius praesentalis.* On Romans in the Vandal army see Diesner, "Auswirkungen," 15 with n. 55 and 21 f. with n. 83; on Romans in the Visigothic army see chap. 4, n. 378 and with n. 519.

264. Procopius, *De bello Gothico* III (VII) 8.41, and 10.24–26 (Jews in Naples). Cassiodorus, *Variae* III 48, p. 103 f. (Verruca); III (VII) 16.16 ff. (Sicily); I 17 (Dertona: Goths and Romans are to build for themselves houses within the fortress and lay in supplies). In doing this the Ostrogothic administration was only continuing the late antique practice of granting the right of arms to the population in exceptional cases: Ensslin, *Theoderich,* 189 n. 9, after *Novellae Valentiniani* IX of June 24, 440 (an attack threatens from Gaiseric).

265. See above, n. 218, cf. Bierbrauer, *Grab- und Schatzfunde,* 36. Ensslin, *Theoderich,* 188 and 217. On Noricum see below, nn. 390 ff. The ability of Roman federate groups "which once had been Roman soldiers"—cf. Jordanes, *Getica* 191, p. 108, and Procopius, *De bello Gothico* I (V) 12.8–19 (Arborychi); on this see Zöllner, *Franken,* 30 f. and 51 f.—to join a barbarian federate army was legally not in question.

266. Cf. Procopius (as n. 259). L. Schmidt, *Ostgermanen,* 360 f.

267. Cassiodorus, *Variae* III 23.2, p. 91. From D.O III 221 (966 VIII 1), after D.O I 274 (965 I 3), which follows verbatim D. Hugo and Lothar 30 (932 IV 28), a Gepidic place in Italy is attested. For these citations see Wolfram, *Intitulatio II,* 163 f. These Gepids, however, could have also been the descendants of the members of the Lombardic army: see Paulus Diaconus, *Historia Langobardorum* II 26, p. 87, which does seem more plausible. On the relations between the Ostrogoths and the Lombards see below, nn. 430 ff. and 439 ff.

268. On the Suevi of Pannonia-Savia see Lotter (as nn. 262 and 274), who rightly saw that Theodor Mommsen was wrong in ignoring the popular etymology Savia-Suavia, after Cassiodorus, *Variae* IV 49, p. 136, and esp. V 14 f., pp. 150–152. The term *antiqui barbari* is found in V 14.6, p. 151. See Šašel, "Antiqui barbari," 125 ff.

269. See below, nn. 408–410.

270. See below, n. 416.

271. Cassiodorus, *Variae* V 29 f., p. 159 f.

272. Ibid., I 38, p. 35 f. Cf. Ensslin, *Theoderich,* 189. See also the stipulations of the *Leges Visigothorum* IV 5.5, p. 201, according to which a son, during his father's lifetime, might dispose of over two-thirds of all the goods he (the son) had acquired during military service.

273. Cassiodorus, *Variae* V 33.1, p. 161.

274. Wolfram, "Gotische Studien II," 307 f., after Jordanes, *Getica* 72, p. 74 f.,

as well as Cassiodorus, *Variae* IV 49, p. 136, which should be compared with III 24, p. 91 f. The same analogy exists between *Edictum Theoderici,* sections 32, 34, 43 f., and 145.3 *(capillati).* On this see most recently Nehlsen, *Sklavenrecht,* 122; cf. chap. 4, n. 188. We can agree with Lotter (as nn. 262 and 268) but not in his assumption that the *capillati* were the native nobility of non-Gothic Germanic peoples. Instead, the exact opposite is the case; the nobility of all barbarian units as well as the units themselves should be subsumed under this term, which describes the Gothic freemen. On the appearance of a Gothic *Untertanenverband* (class of subjects) see Claude, "Königs- und Untertaneneid," 371–373, which should also be compared with Ensslin, *Theoderich,* 158. In general on the concept of *Gemeinfreie* as an element of the *Untertanenverband* see Dilcher, "Gemeinfreie," 1513–1516, as well as the good survey in Schulze, "Mediävistik und Begriffsgeschichte," 400 f.

275. Cf. Wenskus, *Stammesbildung,* 490.

276. See L. Schmidt, *Ostgermanen,* 364.

277. Cassiodorus, *Variae* III 43, p. 100. Cf. chap. 4, n. 496 and n. 570.

278. Procopius, *De bello Gothico* III (VII) 16.15, and 22.20 ff. Nehlsen, *Sklaven-recht,* 127 ff. Rothenhöfer, *Untersuchungen,* 110–114.

279. Hartmann, *Geschichte Italiens* 1:297 f.

280. Cf. above chap. 2, nn. 73 and 76.

281. See chap. 2, n. 505 (Greutungi) and chap. 3, nn. 310 ff. (Visigoths).

282. Malchus fr. 15. Cf. above, n. 148.

283. Toward the end of Theodoric's era, freshly trained *sagittarii* were supposed to reinforce the troops of General Viliaris, who was possibly at that time already commanding in Naples. If that was the case the archers would have been intended as a garrison for the city: see Cassiodorus, *Variae* V 23, p. 157, as well as p. 501. Cf. Procopius, *De bello Gothico* I (V) 3.15, as well as III (VII) 5.1. In the battle outside the gates of Rome in 537 the Gothic infantry stopped their retreating cavalry and made possible a renewed attack of the horsemen: see ibid. I (V) 18.16 f.

284. Ibid. I (V) 18.17 ff., and 29.13–50. Cf. above, n. 283 as well as Isidore of Seville, *Historia vel Origo Gothorum* 69, p. 294, who explicitly credits the Goths with the ability to fight both types of warfare, adding, however, that they "nevertheless relied more on the flying speed of the horses."

285. For this and what follows see the fundamental works of Gamber, "Dakische und sarmatische Waffen," 22. Cf. Gamber, "Schutzwaffen," 47ff., and "Kataphrakten," 47 ff., where esp. the tactics of the heavily armed cavalry are discussed, after Heliodorus, *Aethiopica* IX 15. On the problem of the "cavalrization" cf. Wenskus, *Stammesbildung,* 442 and 469, as well as chap. 4, nn. 310 ff.

286. Gajdukevič, *Das bosporanische Reich,* plate 94 to p. 356.

287. Bóna, *Anbruch des Mittelalters,* 98. Cf. Paulus Diaconus, *Historia Langobardorum* V 10, p. 149. Johanek, "Bewaffnung," 464 and plate 42.

288. Gamber, "Dakische und sarmatische Waffen," 30. Noll, *Vom Altertum zum Mittelalter* 1:plate 61.

289. Bierbrauer, *Grab- und Schatzfunde,* 194–198. Gamber, "Dakische und sarmatische Waffen," 32 f.

290. Gamber (as n. 289): the flexible armor of the Roxolani on the column of Trajan apparently reaches down to the ankles (p. 28), while the horseman on the golden jug of Nagyszentmiklós is wearing a sort of knickerbockers (p. 30); as Falko

Daim has kindly pointed out, the latter can probably also be archaeologically attested for the Avars. On the type of material used cf. Ammianus Marcellinus XVII 12.1 f., who speaks of the *hastae longiores et loricae ex cornibus rasis et laevigatis plumarum specie linteis indumentis innexae*; in other words, Ammianus is describing the *contus* pole and the scale armor made of horn. See also Procopius, *De bello Persico* I 1.12.

291. Maenchen-Helfen, *The Huns*, 238 f. White, *Medieval Technology*, 8 f. On the term *contus* see, for example, Jordanes, *Getica* 261, p. 125. Cf. Ammianus Marcellinus (as n. 290).

292. Procopius, *De bello Gothico* I (V) 18.11, and 27.27 f.; *De bello Persico* I 1.12 f.

293. Procopius, *De bello Gothico* I (V) 16.11: "most" of the horsemen whom Vitigis put into the field against Belisarius were armored, as were their horses.

294. Procopius, *De bello Persico* II 18.24.

295. Ensslin, *Theoderich* 191. For armaments (on the supervision of the *fabricae* see above, n. 228) and for the supply of horses, Theodoric also enlisted private individuals, such as Cassiodorus himself: see *Variae* I 4.17, p. 16, and IX 25.9, p. 292. In the winter of 536/537 Vitigis could make use of the northern Italian "armories" (see Procopius *De bello Gothico* I [V] 11.16) and stables to arm his troops (ibid. 11.28 and III (VII) 8.20). For the value placed on the silver-colored horses that the Thuringians raised see below, nn. 417 and 421. On the effectiveness in war of the "white-spotted horse" cf. Procopius, *De bello Gothico* I (V) 18.6, who transmits for the animal the probably Gothic word **bala*-"Blässel" (horse with a blaze): Feist, *Wörterbuch*, 77 f. Moravcsik, *Byzantino-Turcica* 2:85, introduces into the discussion a Turkish etymology.

296. Procopius, *De bello Gothico* I (V) 18.9 ff. (cavalry engagement outside of Rome) as well as IV (VIII) 32.7 ff. (Busta Gallorum).

297. See chap. 3, nn. 62 ff. (Adrianople) and chap. 4, n. 187 (Vouillé).

298. Procopius, *De bello Gothico* III (VII) 4.21–26, as well as IV (VIII) 31.14–16. At Busta Gallorum as well Totila at first wanted to use the same strategy as Narses: cf. ibid. 31.7 f., and 32.5, where the failure of the original plan is described. On the Roman strategy see Grosse, *Militärgeschichte*, 254–256.

299. It follows from Eustathius fr. 3 that the Goths knew how to stay on the horse merely by means of pressure from the thighs.

300. Procopius, *De bello Gothico* III (VII) 5.7 (Romans against Goths), 4.19 and 31 f. (Totila against the Romans). See esp. I (V) 29.33–38.

301. Ibid., IV (VIII) 32.2 and 8.

302. Ibid., I (V) 18.17 ff., as well as 29.13, and IV (VIII) 32.6.

303. Ensslin, *Theoderich,* 189, after Ennodius, *Panegyricus* 83, p. 213. See above, n. 298: the tactics of the Goths differ hardly at all from those of the "Romans."

304. Cf. Procopius, *De bello Gothico* III (VII) 5.5.

305. Jordanes, *Getica* 118 and 261, pp. 88 and 125.

306. As above, n. 294. Thus the Romans successfully used Antic and Slavic "mountain troops": see Procopius, *De bello Gothico* III (VII) 22.3 and 5.

307. Ibid., III (VII) 27.15 and 26–29.

308. As above, n. 296. On the terminology see Procopius, *De bello Persico* I 1.8 ff.

309. Ibid., I 1.8 ff.

310. See above, n. 283 and n. 307.

311. See above, n. 283 f. and n. 302.

312. Procopius, *De bello Gothico* IV (VIII) 5.18 f.

313. Jordanes, *Getica* 280, p. 130, and 300, p. 135.

314. See above, nn. 295 and 303.

315. Procopius, *De bello Gothico* IV (VIII) 32.17 f. (Busta Gallorum). Ibid. I (V) 18.16 f. (before Rome).

316. Vetters, "Der Vogel auf der Stange," 145 f. Berges and Gauert, "Die eiserne 'Standarte,'" 240–242. Cf. Gamber, "Kataphrakten," 43, which shows that the military dress discussed above, the origins of which Vetters has rightly seen in the "caftan of the [mounted] peoples of Central Asia," was no longer necessarily worn only by a horseman. Bóna, *Anbruch des Mittelalters,* 98, therefore interprets the figure also as a Lombard infantryman. In that case the *contus* (cf. above, n. 290 f.) should be postulated as part of the standard panoply instead of the banner that is depicted.

317. Vegetius, *Epitomae rei militaris* I 20 and III 26. On the three-tribe confederation see chap. 3, n. 8.

318. Jordanes, *Getica* 261, p. 125.

319. See chap. 2, nn. 77 ff. and 86 ff.

320. See the survey of the sources above, n. 144.

321. Malchus fr. 18 (FHG 4, 127).

322. Bierbrauer, *Grab- und Schatzfunde,* 49 f. Ensslin, *Theoderich,* 141, 144 f., 190, and 307. L. Schmidt, *Ostgermanen,* 383. See Cassiodorus, *Variae* V 16–20, pp. 152–155.

323. See below, n. 546 and n. 549.

324. Cassiodorus, *Variae* V 16.5, p. 153. Cf. above, n. 200.

325. Stein, *Bas-Empire* 2:592 and 598, after Procopius, *De bello Gothico* III (VII) 35.23–30, as well as IV (VIII) 22.17 ff.

326. Stein, *Bas-Empire* 2:604, after Procopius, *De bello Gothico* IV (VIII) 35.12 ff.

327. Ibid., 35.9.

328. Ibid., 26.21 ff.

329. Delbrück, *Kriegskunst* 2:392 f. Procopius, *De bello Gothico* I (V) 21.3 ff., and 23.33: construction and easy destruction of Gothic siege towers before Rome.

330. Stein, *Bas-Empire* 2:351. Procopius, *De bello Gothico* I (V) 19.13–19 (destruction of the aqueducts in Rome). Ibid. 14.16, and 24.13 on the difficulties in defending Rome.

331. Cf. ibid., III (VII) 37.1 f. Zöllner, *Franken,* 97 n. 3.

332. Bierbrauer, *Grab- und Schatzfunde,* 34 f. with nn. 104–106. Cf. Ensslin, *Theoderich,* 260 and 309. Procopius, *De bello Gothico* IV (VIII) 33.7 and 34.19, does not say that Totila had the treasures taken to Pavia only in 552 but that Teja found them there.

333. Agathias I 8.4–6 and 20.1–9. Procopius, *De bello Gothico* IV (VIII) 34.19, on the division of the treasure between Pavia and Cumae. Cf. n. 332.

334. Bierbrauer, *Grab- und Schatzfunde,* 33–35. L. Schmidt, *Ostgermanen,* 381–383. Ensslin, *Theoderich,* 142 and 146. Cf. above, n. 203. Löhlein, *Alpen- und Italienpolitik,* 27. As to the sources see esp. Cassiodorus, *Variae* I 17, p. 23 f.

(Dertona); II 5, p. 49 f. (a garrison of sixty men in the barricade of the valley of Aosta); III 48, p. 103 f. (Verruca in the valley of the Adige); VII 16, p. 212 f. (fortifications on the islands of Krk and Cres); XI 14.1, p. 342 f. (Como); II 19, p. 57 (directed in general at Goths and Romans, ordering the guarding of ports and fortresses). Ennodius, *Vita Epifani* 171, p. 105 (possibly Susa, at the foot of the Alpes Cotticae). Procopius, *De bello Gothico* II (VI) 28.28 ff. (Alpes Cotticae).

335. Cf. above, n. 227.

336. Stein, *Bas-Empire* 2:107 f.

337. Cf. above, n. 196.

338. McCormick, *Eternal Victory*, 270 f. and 282. Wolfram, *Intitulatio I*, 69 f. Cf. Bierbrauer, *Grab- und Schatzfunde*, 125 and 292 f. plate 26.2 (gold coin from Morro d'Alba, province of Ancona, reworked into fibula. This artifact appears in the literature incorrectly under the name of Senigallia, the place of its alleged discovery).

339. McCormick (as n. 338). Ensslin, *Theoderich*, 56 complemented and confirmed by Hauck, "Brustbilder von Königen," 219 ff., esp. 229 n. 1. See also above, n. 173 as well as n. 196 and n. 204.

340. On one occasion he also had himself called augustus: see McCormick, *Eternal Victory*, 277 ff., and above, n. 197.

341. See above, n. 196.

342. Ennodius, *Panegyricus* 81, p. 213; cf. 72 f., p. 212. Cf. above, n. 340, and McCormick (as n. 340).

343. Wolfram, "Gotische Studien I," 13 ff., after Straub, *Regeneratio Imperii*, 204 f.

344. On this and for what follows see Bierbrauer, *Grab- und Schatzfunde*, 49 f. Diesner, "Auswirkungen," 3 ff., and "Vandalen," 964–970. Courtois, *Les Vandales*, 192 f. On the expulsion of the Vandals from Sicily by the Ostrogoths cf. above, n. 166.

345. Cf. Wolfram, "Theogonie," 87 ff. with nn. 47 ff.

346. For the quote see Ennodius, *Panegyricus* 70, p. 211. Amalafrida's dowry as well as the number and quality of her escort are reported by Procopius, *De bello Vandalico* I (III) 8.12. Diesner, "Auswirkungen," 5 n. 10.

347. Cf. chap. 4, n. 615. Within Theodoric's system of marriage policy the tie to the Vandals was the most important: see Cassiodorus (as n. 363). Cf. Diesner, "Auswirkungen," 3 with n. 2, 5 with n. 9, 9 with n. 32, as well as 19, who emphasizes the weakness of the Vandal fleet in the later period. Ibid., 11 with n. 40 and Martindale, *Prosopography* 2:509 f., on Gesalech.

348. Cassiodorus, *Variae* V 43 f., p. 170 f., esp. 44.3, p. 171.

349. Cassiodorus, *Chronica* 1364, chap. 519, p. 161.

350. See above, n. 322. Ensslin, *Theoderich*, 326 n. 5. Stein, *Bas-Empire* 2:264. Cassiodorus, *Variae* IX 1, p. 267 f.

351. Procopius, *De bello Gothico* I (V) 3.17–24, and 4.19. See below, n. 583. Diesner, "Auswirkungen," 20 f.

352. See chap. 4, n. 153 f.

353. On this and the following see Bierbrauer, *Grab- und Schatzfunde*, 47–49. Ensslin, *Theoderich*, 80 ff. Claude, *Westgoten*, 34 ff. Cf. above, n. 166.

354. Cf. chap. 4, nn. 66 and 68.

355. See below, nn. 434–438. On Thiudigotho see Martindale, *Prosopography* 2:1068.

356. Procopius, *De bello Gothico* I (V) 12.33–40. Cf. chap. 4, n. 184 ff.

357. Procopius, *De bello Gothico* I (V) 12, 50–54 (Theudis; his marriage). Cassiodorus, *Variae* III 40–42, pp. 99 f.: tax relief for the Provence. On the reestablishment of the prefecture of Gaul see above, chap. 4, n. 614. On the judgment of the Gallic *gentes* as barbarians see Cassiodorus, *Variae* III 17.1, p. 88; cf.. p. 504, s.v. "Galli." On Liberius see O'Donnell, "Liberius," 44, 48, and 60; Martindale, *Prosopography* 2:677 ff., esp. 678 f. Cassiodorus, *Variae* IX 1.16, p. 330, speaks already in 533 of Liberius as prefect of Gaul and *exercitualis vir* before he had received the *praesentanea dignitas*. Liberius is also praised as *vulneribus pulchrior,* which is probably a reference to the events at the Durance. On this see *Vita Caesarii* II 10, p. 487. Cf. also below, n. 365 and n. 550.

358. Procopius, *De bello Gothico* I (V) 12.48 f., and 13.6 Cassiodorus, *Variae* IV 14, p. 122, and V 39.1–13 ff., pp. 164–166.

359. See chap. 1, n. 108, and below, n. 485 f. Wolfram, "Theogonie," 83–87, esp. 86 with n. 37. On Eutharic see Martindale, *Prosopography* 2:438 (Fl. Eutharicus Cilliga), and on Amalasuintha ibid. 2:65.

360. Procopius, *De bello Gothico* I (V) 13.4 ff. Claude, *Westgoten,* 56 ff. Zöllner, *Franken,* 83–86, 92 and 96.

361. Procopius, *De bello Gothico* II (VI) 30.15, and II (VI) 2.7.

362. Diesner, "Vandalen," 971, as well as Stein, *Bas-Empire* 2:315 and 560 ff. Thompson, *The Goths in Spain,* 15 ff. Claude, *Westgoten,* 56–59. See chap. 4, n. 621.

363. On this and the following see Bierbrauer, *Grab- und Schatzfunde,* 18 f. and 46 f. L. Schmidt, *Ostgermanen,* 150 and 156–158. Ensslin, *Theoderich,* 83 f. On the invasion of the Burgundians in 490/491 see above, n. 166. On the situation after the independent Burgundian kingdom ceased to exist: see Procopius, *De bello Gothico* I (V) 13.15 f. On Theodoric's marriage policy cf. Cassiodorus, *Variae* V 43.1, p. 170: *Quamvis a diversis regibus expetiti pro solidanda concordia aut neptes dedimus aut filias deo nobis inspirante coniunximus,* but most important is his sister Amalafrida, whom he married to the Vandal king. On Areagne see Martindale, *Prosopography* 2:138 f.

364. Cf. Procopius, *De bello Gothico* I (V) 13.14 f. and 16.7.

365. Cf. Cassiodorus, *Variae* III 41, p. 99. Cf. above, n. 357 (Liberius wounded at the Durance).

366. Wolfram, *Intitulatio I,* 51 and 87–89. On Theodoric's countermeasures see esp. L. Schmidt, *Ostgermanen,* 161 f. On Sigismund see Martindale, *Prosopography* 2:1009 f.

367. L. Schmidt, *Ostgermanen,* 162 f., and Bierbrauer, *Grab- und Schatzfunde,* 18. On Tuluin's relationship to the Amali as son-in-law see above, n. 222. On Theodoric's cases of blood revenge see above, n. 151 (Rekitach) as well as nn. 168–170 (Odovacar); cf. chap. 2, n. 457.

368. Cassiodorus, *Variae* XI 1.10–13, p. 329. Cf. Zöllner, *Franken,* 84–87. Stein, *Bas-Empire* 2:332 f. In the year 532 the Franks occupied Arles but soon after withdrew again: Zöllner, *Franken,* 85 n. 6.

369. Cassiodorus, *Variae* I 45 f., pp. 39 ff. For the dating of this event see

L. Schmidt, *Ostgermanen,* 397, whom Ensslin, *Theoderich,* 132 f., is right in correcting. Cf. Stein, *Bas-Empire* 2:147 f. n. 1, where the chronology of the source is described. Cf. below, n. 379.

370. Ensslin, *Theoderich,* 284 f., L. Schmidt, *Ostgermanen,* 158 ff.

371. Ibid., 347; cf. chap. 4, n. 240.

372. L. Schmidt, *Ostgermanen,* 343.

373. See chap. 4, n. 615.

374. On this and the following see Bierbrauer, *Grab- und Schatzfunde,* 18–23 and 43–45. Ensslin, *Theoderich,* 82 f. L. Schmidt, *Ostgermanen,* 339 f. See esp. Zöllner, *Franken,* 54 f., 66 f., 88–91, and 231. On Audofleda see Martindale, *Prosopography* 2:185.

375. Zöllner, *Franken,* 67–69. Hauck, "Randkultur," 20–56. Wolfram, *Intitulatio I,* 54 n. 103.

376. Cassiodorus, *Variae* VII 4.2, p. 203.

377. Ibid., II 41.1 ff., p. 73. Ennodius, *Panegyricus* 72 f., p. 212. Zöllner, *Franken,* 57 with n. 1. On the Burgundian expansion see L. Schmidt, *Ostgermanen,* 153 f. Keller, "Spätantike," 10 f. Ensslin, *Theoderich,* 131. Behr, *Das alemannische Herzogtum,* 50–52. See below, n. 386 f. and nn. 403 ff.

378. Cassiodorus, *Variae* II 41.3, p. 73.

379. Ibid., 40.17, p. 72.

380. See above, n. 369.

381. See chap. 4, nn. 182–187.

382. See chap. 4, n. 615.

383. See chap. 4, n. 615 to n. 620, as well as Zöllner, *Franken,* 82 ff. Cf. n. 360 (Visigoths), n. 368 (Burgundians), and nn. 417 ff. (kingdom of the Thuringians).

384. Procopius, *De bello Gothico* I (V) 13.14–28. Agathias I 6.3–6.

385. For further developments see below, n. 715 f., n. 740, and nn. 752–754.

386. Behr, *Das alemannische Herzogtum,* 45–67, esp. 62.

387. Bierbrauer, *Grab- und Schatzfunde,* 19 ff. Cf. Behr, *Das alemannische Herzogtum,* 45–51, Ensslin, *Theoderich,* 131 f., and below, n. 403.

388. Cf. above, n. 373. See also chap. 4, n. 615.

389. See above, n. 334.

390. Cassiodorus, *Variae* I 11, p. 20, and VII 5, p. 203 f. (Raetia), as well as III 50, p. 104 f. (Noricum). The memory of Theodoric's rule even favored the creation of forgeries: see Heuberger, "Ein angebliches Edikt," 201 ff.

391. Heuberger, *Rätien,* 126 ff. and 300 ff. Sandberger, "Bistum Chur," 723 f.

392. Wolfram, "Die Zeit der Agilolfinger," 152.

393. Wolfram, *Mitteleuropa,* 73 f. Cf. Eugippius, *Vita s. Severini,* edited by Theodor Mommsen, p. 60, s.v. "Noricum" with Cassiodorus, *Variae* III 50, p. 104: *Provincialibus Noricis Theodericus rex.* But this terminology seems to be older than hitherto believed: see Vetters, "Virunum," 350.

394. Cassiodorus (as n. 393), as well as *Variae* VII 4.3, p. 203.

395. From *Variae* I 11.2, p. 20, one has inferred Bretonic federates, which is no doubt correct: cf. Heuberger (as n. 391).

396. Cassiodorus (as n. 390), on Raetia. Heuberger (as n. 391), and above, n. 218 and n. 265. Wolfram, "Ethnogenesen," 112 ff. with nn. 73 and 80 (Raetia), as well as 119 ff. with nn. 108 ff. (Breones). On *civilitas* see above, n. 206. It remains an

open question where the Raetian *dux* Servatus resided. Chur-Curia comes to mind, but it can hardly be identical with a "founder-city" The(o)doricopolis (cf. above, n. 203). Clavadetscher, "Churrätien," 159–165. On the border of the Ostrogothic settlement see above, n. 253. Geldner, "Frühgeschichte," 30 f.

397. Cf. above, n. 218, on the question of his origins. *Notitia dignitatum oc.* 1, 88 f. and 92 f., lists for each of the two Norican as well as the two Raetian provinces a *praesides* (civil provincial governor). Ensslin, *Theoderich,* 177, shows, however, that *praeses* under Theodoric did not have the rank of a *spectabilis.* Only the higher provincial governor held this rank. Wolfram, "Ethnogenesen," 112 ff.: If one describes *Ursus vir spectabilis* as a civil functionary, he must have been equal in rank to the governor of Dalmatia and Pannonia-Savia. Yet all difficulties disappear if one accepts Ursus as a *dux,* since it is, after all, also said of Servatus: . . . *ut per provinciam cui praesides* (Cassiodorus, *Variae* I 11.1, p. 20). See above, n. 396. Finally, Theodoric's order to the provincials of Noricum to exchange their own livestock for that of the Alamanni who were passing through (Cassiodorus [as nn. 393 and 396]) is not unusual, even if neither a *dux* nor a civil governor is mentioned. In keeping with the legal maxim *quod tangit omnes, et iure omnes comprobent,* in matters that concern all, all have to be addressed, regardless of whether there is an authorized official where the order is to be carried out: Cassiodorus, *Variae,* p. 595 f., s.v. "universitas, universus." First signs of a comparison between Ursus and Servatus are found already in Zeiss, "Nordgrenze," 29 and 33. See on this also Heuberger, *Rätien,* 81 f. with nn. 3–8. An interesting analogy appears in the cathedral of Trent. A tomb inscription, which dates most likely to the sixth century, honors the memory of the *v(ir) s(pectabilis) Censorius:* See Rogger, "La basilica paleocristiana" VII 20–22. If this testimony goes back to the Gothic period, the Roman Censorius could have been a section *comes* of the *tractus Italiae:* see above, n. 264, after Cassiodorus, *Variae* III 48, p. 103 f. Perhaps one could compare Censorius with Marcianus of Verona: see Procopius, *De bello Gothico* III (VII) 3.6 ff.

398. Eugippius, *Vita s. Severini* 21.1; cf. 17.4. Cf. above, n. 143.

399. Wolfram, *Mitteleuropa,* 74 with n. 26.

400. Wolfram, "Libellus Virgilii," 191 f. with n. 64. Cf. Forstner, *Verbrüderungsbuch,* 30 n. 108. Of course the name Ursus appears also in Eugippius, *Vita s. Severini* 38.1. Heuberger, *Rätien,* 134 ff. For the sake of completeness, however, it should be mentioned that García Moreno, *Prosopografía,* 37 n. 28, attests a certain Bera (Bear), who in 673 supported the rival king Paulus (cf. Wolfram, *Intitulatio I,* 70 ff.).

401. Cassiodorus, *Variae* V 2, p. 143 f.

402. Jordanes, *Getica* 24, p. 60. Cf. Wagner, *Getica* 193 ff., and Hachmann, *Goten und Skandinavien,* 85 ff. See also chap. 2, nn. 5 ff.

403. See above, nn. 376 f. and 386 f. Keller, "Spätantike und Frühmittelalter," 10 f. Cf. by the same author, "Fränkische Herrschaft und alemannisches Herzogtum," 8 with n. 41.

404. Cassiodorus, *Variae* II 41, p. 73. Cf. Ensslin, *Theoderich,* 142, after L. Schmidt, *Ostgermanen,* 343. On the Bavarian problem see below, n. 418 f.

405. Cassiodorus, *Variae* II 41.2, p. 73. Ennodius, *Panegyricus* 72 f., p. 212. It is also reported there that the fugitives were resettled from marshy areas to solid ground. But to infer specific areas from this report seems risky, since Germania as such was considered marshy: see Much, *Germania,* 108 ff. and 380.

406. Wolfram, *Mitteleuropa,* 74 f. with n. 28. Clavadetscher, "Churrätien," 163 f. Cf. Behr, *Das alemannische Herzogtum,* 54 f.

407. As above, nn. 393 and 397.

408. Lotter, "Donausueben," 277 f., and Ensslin, *Theoderich,* 131 f. See esp. Procopius, *De bello Gothico* I (V) 15.26 and 16.9. Stein, *Bas-Empire* 2:349 n. 1, is commendably thorough in his survey of the sources and the literature, but his interpretation is not quite right. Cf. Ennodius (as n. 405), and Bierbrauer (as n. 409).

409. As above, n. 405. Bierbrauer, "Alamannische Funde," 559 ff., esp. 573 ff., and Bierbrauer, "Zu den Vorkommen ostgotischer Bügelfibeln," 131 ff., esp. 156 f. (map of finds) and 160–165 (historical interpretation).

410. Procopius, *De bello Gothico* I (V) 13.14–28; 15.16; 16.9. Agathias I 6.3–6. Cf. below, n. 444 as well as n. 620, and above, n. 268 f.

411. Cassiodorus, *Variae* III 3, p. 78 f. Cf. chap. 4, n. 162 and n. 182. Zöllner, *Franken,* 72.

412. See above, n. 85.

413. Cassiodorus, *Variae* III 23.2, p. 91.

414. See above, n. 119.

415. Cassiodorus, *Variae* IV 2, p. 114 f. Procopius, *De bello Persico* I 11.10–30, esp. 22.

416. Ensslin, *Theoderich,* 140 f. and 148, as well as 365 n. 4. Cf. Cassiodorus, *Variae* IV 45, p. 134 f. For the general events see esp. Procopius, *De bello Gothico* II (VI), 14.8 ff., as well as Paulus Diaconus, *Historia Langobardorum* I 20, pp. 57–59. Stein, *Bas-Empire* 2:150 f.

417. Cassiodorus, *Variae* IV 1, p. 114.

418. Wolfram, "Ethnogenesen," 105 ff., and Wolfram, *Mitteleuropa,* 69 ff. On the lower Austrian "desert" see Procopius, *De bello Gothico* II (VI) 14.23–25. Cf. above, n. 159. Stein, *Bas-Empire* 2:151. L. Schmidt, *Ostgermanen,* 578 f., shows that the Lombards would have prevented an Ostrogothic expansion into lower Austria.

419. The question is whether Jordanes, *Getica* 280, p. 130, was written around 551 by Jordanes or before 526 by Cassiodorus (see chap. 1, n. 105). In both cases the first mention of the Bavarians presupposes that they had already existed for about a generation: Wolfram, "Ethnogenesen," 105 ff. with nn. 50 ff., and Wolfram, *Mitteleuropa,* 319 ff.

420. Anonymus Valesianus II 70. Jordanes, *Getica* 299, p. 135. Procopius, *De bello Gothico* I (V) 12.22. See esp. Ensslin, *Theoderich,* 147. On the simultaneous marriage connection with the Thuringians and the Lombards see L. Schmidt (as n. 418), after Paulus Diaconus, *Historia Langobardorum* I 21, p. 60. Cassiodorus never had to mention the Lombards, which may indicate at least acceptable relations with them. On Amalaberga see Martindale, *Prosopography* 2:63.

421. As n. 417. Cf. Wolfram, *Splendor Imperii,* 109 with n. 12. On the importance of Thuringian horse breeding see, for example, Jordanes, *Getica* 21, p. 59, as well as L. Schmidt, *Westgermanen,* 119.

422. Cassiodorus, *Variae* V 1, p. 143. Cf. Bierbrauer, *Grab- und Schatzfunde,* 46.

423. Zöllner, *Franken,* 82 ff. Ensslin, *Theoderich,* 327. Procopius, *De bello Gothico* I (V) 13.1 f., and IV (VIII) 25.11 f.

424. Wolfram, *Splendor Imperii,* 108 f., after Cassiodorus, *Variae* IV 1.1, p. 114.

425. Ensslin, "Praefectus praetorio," 2439–2443. Kornemann, "Dioecesis,"

727–732. Mommsen, "Ostgothische Studien," 461 f. On the division of Illyricum in 396 see Hoffmann, *Bewegungsheer* 2:207 ff. *Notitia dignitatum oc.* II 5–8 lists the praetorian prefect of Italy and the three dioceses under his command: Italy, Illyricum, and Africa. Ibid. 28–34 describes Illyricum and its six provinces, whereby the east Pannonian Valeria as the seventh province has already dropped out. On the west Illyrian capital Sirmium see *Laterculus Polemii Silvii* V 3, p. 257. On Emperor Nepos and his end see Martindale, *Prosopography* 2:777 f., as well as Stein, *Bas-Empire* 2:51 f. On Odovacar's Rugian war see above, n. 159, on his defense against Theodoric n. 165, on Raetia and Noricum see Lotter "Endphase," 76 ff.

426. Wolfram, *Mitteleuropa,* 72 with nn. 16–27. See above, n. 397 (organization of Noricum and Raetia). Cassiodorus, *Variae* IV 49, p. 36, has Siscia and Savia side by side in a manner similar to the way Procopius, *De bello Gothico* I (V) 15.26, distinguishes the Siscian and Suevic peoples "who are not subject to the Franks"; instead, he counts both peoples (ibid. 28) explicitly among those who were Gothic until the outbreak of the war. Ibid. 16.9, he reports that King Vitigis tried to reconquer Dalmatia with the help of these Suevi. Cassiodorus, *Variae* V 14.6, p. 151, mentions the "old barbarians" who are married to Roman women and who are of the mistaken belief that their property was exempt from taxation: see above, n. 258. On Fridibad and Osuin see further Cassiodorus, *Variae* IV 49, p. 136, and V 14.8, p. 151, as well as Martindale, *Prosopography* 2:485 and 815. Fridibad might have been subordinated to Osuin in the same way as the *comes* of the Dalmatian island, who was also active as a judge, and who is mentioned by Cassiodorus, *Variae* VII 16, p. 212. Cf. on this Wilkes, *Dalmatia,* 427, and in general Wozniak, "East Rome," 351 ff.

427. On the quote see Cassiodorus, *Variae* III 23.2, p. 91, and in general above, n. 165, as well as Pohl, "Gepiden," 291 ff.

428. See above, n. 194, as well as Pohl, "Gepiden," 293 ff..

429. See esp. Ennodius, *Panegyricus* 60 ff., p. 210 f. Ensslin, *Theoderich,* 129; cf. ibid. 320, after Cassiodorus, *Variae* XI 1.9, p. 328 f.

430. See above, n. 165.

431. Ennodius (as n. 429), and Pohl, "Gepiden," 294.

432. Cf. above, n. 148.

433. See esp. Jordanes, *Getica* 300 f., p. 135. Cf. above, n. 313. On Mundo see most recently Pohl, "Gepiden," 290 f. and 292 f., as well as Martindale, *Prosopography* 2:767 f. On the *scamarae,* his followers, see Wolfram, "Ethnogenesen," 115, n. 82.

434. See above, n. 263.

435. See above, n. 253.

436. Marcellinus Comes, *Chronicon* a. 508, p. 97.

437. See above, n. 118.

438. Ensslin, *Theoderich,* 149–151. Cf., for example, Cassiodorus, *Variae* II 6, p. 50. L. Schmidt, *Ostgermanen,* 249 f. Dušanić, "Bassianae," 74 f.

439. Cassiodorus, *Variae* V 10 f., p. 149, esp. 10.2. Cf. above, n. 367.

440. Procopius, *De bello Gothico* III (VII) 1.43 ff.

441. Paulus Diaconus (as n. 420). Cf. Werner, *Langobarden in Pannonien,* 133.

442. Stein, *Bas-Empire* 2:306–309. See esp. 306 n. 1. Cf. Cassiodorus, *Variae*

IX 1.9 f., p. 328 f. Procopius, *De bello Gothico* I (V) 3.15 and 11.5, confuses, however, the war of 504 with that of 530. See Procopius (as n. 444), as well as below, n. 623 and n. 639.

443. Cf. J. Werner, *Langobarden in Pannonien*, 136 f.

444. Zöllner, *Franken*, 91 ff. J. Werner, *Langobarden in Pannonien*, 11 and 140. Procopius, *De bello Gothico* III (VII) 33.7–14.

445. Procopius, *De bello Gothico* IV (VIII) 26.12 (Lombards), and 32 (a Gepid slays Totila). L. Schmidt, *Ostgermanen*, 539 and 582.

446. L. Schmidt, *Ostgermanen*, 585 ff.

447. Cf. Cassiodorus, *Variae* V 10.2, p. 149.

448. Wenskus, *Stammesbildung*, 490 f. Reports about numerical weakness of the Lombards extend from Tacitus, *Germania* 40.1 to Procopius, *De bello Gothico* III (VII) 34.3 and 28 and Paulus Diaconus, *Historia Langobardorum* I 11, p. 53.

449. Cassiodorus, *Variae* V 40.5, p. 167, and VIII 21.3 and 6 f., p. 252 f. Ensslin, *Theoderich*, 281 f. See above, n. 263. On the Visigoths cf. chap. 4, nn. 310 and 322. Martindale, *Prosopography* 2:332 f. (Cyprianus n. 2).

450. Stroheker, *Adel*, nos. 74 and 369, pp. 157 and 221. Sidonius Apollinaris, *Epistulae* V 5.3, p. 81.

451. Wolfram, "Aufnahme," 90 f. nn. 10–15. Moisl, "Genealogies," 215 ff., esp. 219 ff. For criticism of the barbarian *memoria* see most recently Goffart, *Barbarians and Romans*, esp. 21 ff. Cf. chap. 1, nn. 93 ff., and chap. 2, nn. 1 ff. Bierbrauer, *Grab- und Schatzfunde*, 53–55, after Cassiodorus, *Variae* IV 34, p. 129, on the prohibition of the custom of grave goods. Cf. chap. 2, n. 478 f. That the Ostrogoths became accustomed to the Roman burial customs is attested by numerous inscriptions from gravestones: Fiebiger-Schmidt, *Inschriftensammlung*, nos. 183 f., p. 94; no. 204, p. 103; nos. 220–235, pp. 111–115. Fiebiger, *Inschriftensammlung*, nos. 42–51, pp. 29–33; Fiebiger, *Inschriftensammlung: Zweite Folge*, nos. 10–12, p. 11 f. On the Amal tradition see Wolfram, "Theogonie," 90 nn. 69 ff.; *Intitulatio I*, 99–104; *Splendor Imperii*, 108 ff.: an allusion to the *gens Iulia* is contained in the comparison of Athalaric with Romulus; both are the seventeenth kings in the line, the Goth after the founding king Gaut, Romulus after Aeneas; cf. Cassiodorus, *Variae* IX 25.4, p. 292. See also below, n. 527. Gothic history is linked to Troy because the Amazons/Gothic women (see chap. 1, n. 87) came to the aid of the besieged: see Jordanes, *Getica* 55–60, pp. 69–71. But the Goths themselves also passed by Troy: see ibid. 108, p. 86. Cf. in general chap. 1, nn. 90 ff., and above, n. 208.

452. Ensslin, *Theoderich*, 281 f., cannot "believe in a Gothic section of the royal chancery," and he is no doubt right. The most important justification for the existence of the *Amalatal* is deprived of its precondition by Wolfram, "Theogonie," 91 n. 72; cf. 84 n. 29. On the *belagines* see Beck, "belagines," 205 f., as well as Nehlsen, "belagines," 206 f. Cf. above, n. 202.

453. Cassiodorus, *Variae* IV 2.4, p. 115 (language of the envoys). Procopius, *De bello Gothico* I (V) 10.10 and 18.6 (language of the army).

454. Amalasuintha spoke both the classical languages as well as Gothic: Cassiodorus, *Variae* XI 1.6, p. 328. Cf. above, n. 449, where the same is said of Cyprianus.

455. Tjäder, "Codex Argenteus," 144 ff. Stutz, *Gotische Literaturdenkmäler*, 16

ff., and "Codices Gotici," 52 ff., esp. 53 ff. P. Scardigli, *Goten,* 269 ff. Krause, *Handbuch,* 16 ff. Until recently only 187 of the 336 pages of the Codex Argenteus were known. In 1970 its last page was rediscovered in the cathedral treasury in Speyer, a "find of the century" which made scholarly history as the "Haffner folio." See Stutz, "Fragmentum Spirense-Recto," 85 ff., and Stutz, "Fragmentum Spirense-Verso," 1 ff. On the possible transfer of the Codex Argenteus to southern Italy see above, n. 332 f.

456. See chap. 4, n. 307.

457. Ensslin, *Theoderich,* 279–281. P. Scardigli, *Goten,* 330 ff.

458. Cf. Procopius, *De bello Gothico* II (VI) 6.18 ff. But, Goths who went over to the Catholic faith must have sometimes encountered difficulties: see Cassiodorus, *Variae* V 26.3, p. 314 (Theodahad to Justinian a. 535): *De Ranildae quoque causa, unde vestra serenitas me commonere dignata est, quamvis ante longum tempus sub parentum nostrorum regno contigerit, tamen necesse nobis fuit negotium de propria largitate componere, ut tali facto eam non paeniteret mutata religio.*

459. Tjäder, "Codex Argenteus," 148–153.

460. Ensslin, *Theoderich,* 254–259. Cf. Scardigli, *Goten,* 330 ff. Cf. Agnellus, *Liber pontificalis ecclesiae Ravennatis,* chaps. 85–92, pp. 334–336. Cf. above, n. 203. Cortesi, *La zona.* Breschi, *La cattedrale.* On Salona cf. Fiebiger, *Inschriftensammlung,* Zweite Folge, no. 12, p. 12 (Ariver tombstone).

461. Entire libraries exist on Jordanes, *Getica* 21–24, pp. 59 f. Wagner, *Getica,* 103 ff., esp. 156 ff., has the most comprehensive discussion of the state of scholarship on the question "Scandinavian Goths—original homeland of the Goths." Svennung, *Jordanes und Scandia,* 32 ff., is only the most important work of a scholar who has spent a lifetime on this topic; cf. most recently *Skandinavien bei Plinius und Ptolemaios,* esp. 198 ff. Critical comments by Hachmann, *Goten und Skandinavien,* 109 ff., who realized that the term "original homeland" is untenable; this, however, was a consequence of Wenskus, *Stammesbildung,* 654 (index).

462. Jordanes, *Getica* 36, p. 63, and 96, p. 82 f. Wenskus, *Stammesbildung,* 449; cf. 61 and 435. See chap. 2, n. 13 f.

463. Jordanes, *Getica* 19 ff., p. 58 ff., on Ptolemy, *Geographica* II 11.35.

464. Jordanes, *Getica* 24, p. 60. Cf., however, L. Schmidt, *Ostgermanen,* 28 n. 2, who sees Cassiodorus's Scandza excursus as a mere literary compilation. On Rodulf see also ibid., 549 n. 2, and, with outdated identification, Martindale, *Prosopography* 2:946 f.

465. Jordanes, *Getica* 22, p. 59. Wagner, *Getica,* 171 ff., esp. 183 ff., on Claudian, *In Eutropium* II v. 154, p. 101.

466. As above, n. 464.

467. Procopius, *De bello Gothico* II (VI) 15.23–26. Jordanes, *Getica* 40 f., p. 64. Wolfram, "Gotische Studien II," 249 ff.

468. Cf. Wagner, *Getica,* 168.

469. Cf. Wolfram, "Theogonie," 96.

470. As above, n. 464.

471. Since Theodoric commissioned the writing of the Gothic history but was also exchanging letters with the Aisti-Aesti, Cassiodorus can be held responsible for the form but not solely for the content of the work; cf. chap. 1, n. 98, and Wolfram, "Theogonie," 90 with n. 65, as well as above, n. 401 (Aesti).

472. See chap. 2, nn. 1 ff.

473. Cf. Wagner, *Getica*, 160 and 184.

474. Jordanes, *Getica* 313, p. 138; cf. ibid., p. xxi. Wolfram, "Aufnahme," 91 n. 14 and 117 n. 68.

475. Staab, "Ostrogothic Geographers," esp. 54 ff.

476. Anonymus Valesianus II 60. Ibid. II 65. See the fundamental study of Pfeilschifter, *Theoderich*, 47–54 and passim. Vismara, "Romani e Goti," 409 ff. Ensslin, "Beweise der Romverbundenheit," 509 ff. See also Fulgentius of Ruspe in Rome (as above, n. 203).

477. Anonymus Valesianus II 58. *Epistulae Theodericianae* 4 f., p. 390 f. Ennodius, *Panegyricus* 80, p. 212 f. Schäferdiek, "Germanenmission," 513.

478. On this and the following see Beck, "Frühbyzantinische Kirche," 3–19.

479. Demandt, "Magister militum," 566 and 691.

480. Stein, *Bas-Empire* 2:179 and 224 f. Cf. 897. Ensslin, *Theoderich*, 288 f.; cf. 406. Martindale, *Prosopography* 2:1171 ff.

481. Ensslin, *Theoderich*, 302. Cf. below, n. 483.

482. Ensslin, *Theoderich*, 295.

483. Cassiodorus, *Variae* III 45, p. 101, and IV 23, p. 124.

484. Ensslin, *Theoderich*, 113 ff.

485. Jordanes, *Getica* 298, p. 134 f. Cf. chap. 1, n. 108.

486. On this and the following see Ensslin, *Theoderich*, 293 and 296 ff.

487. Cf. Procopius, *De bello Persico* I 11.9 ff., esp. 22.

488. On the name see Fiebiger-Schmidt, *Inschriftensammlung*, no. 188, p. 96. The cognomen has still not been adequately explained. For the events see esp. Ensslin, *Theoderich*, 298 and 300 f. See also Cassiodorus, *Chronica* 1362–1364, aa. 518 f.; p. 160 f. On the significance of the chronicle see Wattenbach, Levison, and Löwe, *Geschichtsquellen* 1:70.

489. Ensslin, *Theoderich*, 302 f. Cf. above, n. 481. For a comparison of the position of Eutharic with that of Theodoric see above, n. 192 (survey).

490. Ensslin, *Theoderich*, 304 f. and 307: the death of Eutharic cannot be dated, but it should probably be placed in 522/523. Cf. L. Schmidt, *Ostgermanen*, 352 ff. Anonymus Valesianus II 80–82: . . . *qui Eutharicus nimis asper fuit et contra fidem catholicam inimicus*. For the events in general see Sundwall, *Abhandlungen*, 230 ff., and Beck, "Frühbyzantinische Kirche," 14–18.

491. See above, n. 191.

492. *Epistulae Theodericianae* 9, p. 392.

493. Ensslin, *Theoderich*, 305 and 306 f. On the murder of Sigeric see above, n. 367.

494. Ensslin, *Theoderich*, 308 ff.

495. Ibid., 263–279. Cf., for example, above, nn. 369 and 379 f. (techniques and skills). On *civilitas* see above, n. 205. Cf. also Wolfram, "Gotisches Königtum," 23 n. 135, after Cassiodorus, *Variae* III 9.1, p. 84. See also Ennodius, *Panegyricus* 56, p. 210, who tells Theodoric that it means more to stop the downfall than to begin anew.

496. Ensslin, *Theoderich*, 264 with n. 6, after *Sanctio pragmatica*, chap. 22. The appreciation of this measure, however, depends on the general appreciation of the Amal kingdom.

497. Ensslin, *Theoderich*, 263 f. Cf. above, n. 420 (Amalaberga). Amalafrida Theodenanda's high qualities of mind and soul are indicated by the eloquent inscription she dedicated to the memory of a small son or her brother Theudegisel and to that of her deceased father Theodahad: Fiebiger-Schmidt, *Inschriftensammlung*, no. 204, p. 103. Zimmermann, "Grabstein" (as chap. 4, n. 621).

498. Anonymus Valesianus II 79.

499. Ensslin, *Theoderich*, 263 and 296.

500. Ensslin, *Theoderich*, 21. Malalas, *Chronographia*, p. 383, makes a causal connection between Theodoric's education in Constantinople and his literary training (he was ἀναγνούς).

501. Cassiodorus, *Variae* I 1.2, p. 10.

502. Ensslin, *Theoderich*, 21 f. and 45; cf. Ennodius, *Panegyricus* 11, p. 204, and Malchus fr. 16.

503. Procopius, *De bello Gothico* I (V) 2.6–67, esp. 6 f. and 14 f. Cf. below, n. 546.

504. Cf. Anonymus Valesianus II 83 ff.

505. On this and the following Ensslin, *Theoderich*, 308–316. Martindale, *Prosopography* 2:51 f., n. 9, and 332 f.

506. Anonymus Valesianus II 85 ff.

507. Cf. above, n. 205. On Boethius see Martindale, *Prosopography* 2:233–237 (Boethius 5), on Cyprianus see ibid., 2:332 f.

508. Anonymus Valesianus II 83–95, esp. 94 f. Cf. Cassiodorus, *Historia ecclesiastica tripartita* III 10.9 f., p. 151, after Socrates I 38.

509. On this and the following see Ensslin, *Theoderich*, 318–324 and 332 ff. Stein, *Bas-Empire* 2:262. L. Schmidt, *Ostgermanen*, 358 ff. Hartmann, *Geschichte Italiens* 1:222 and 240. Graus, *Lebendige Vergangenheit*, 39 ff. *Vita Willibaldi*, chap. 3, p. 101: Willibald of Eichstätt on his trip to southern Italy in 720 went to see the crater, known as *infernus Theoderici*.

510. Procopius, *De bello Gothico* I (V) 1.35–39. Höfler, *Germanisches Sakralkönigtum*, 285 f. (Theodoric's descent into hell).

511. Ensslin, *Theoderich*, 321–324. The "armor of Odovacar" that was found in 1854 near the tomb of Theodoric is in fact a saddle decoration from an Ostrogothic "prince's grave": Bierbrauer, *Grab- und Schatzfunde*, 193 and 300 as well as ill. 30 f.

512. Höfler, *Germanisches Sakralkönigtum*, 9 ff. and 257 ff., esp. 271 ff. Cf. Graus (as n. 509). In the thirteenth century a Saxon described to his Norwegian audience King Thidrek as the new Constantine: Wolfram, "Constantin," 241 f. A different aspect of the legendary afterlife is discussed by Wagner, "Ich armer Dietrîch," 209 ff.

513. Cf. Hartmann, *Geschichte Italiens* 1:225.

514. Wolfram, *Splendor Imperii*, 108 f. Cf. above, nn. 235, 256 and 258. Procopius, *De bello Gothico* I (V) 4.6: " . . . Goths as well as Italians had a low opinion of him."

515. Procopius, *De bello Gothico* I (V) 2.18–20; 3.10 f.; 4.4.

516. See chap. 1, nn. 102 ff. Cf. Procopius, *De bello Gothico* I (V) 6.15 ff. Martindale, *Prosopography* 2:1067 f.

517. Cf. above, n. 140.

518. Claude, "Probleme," 329 ff., esp. 340. But he shows (340 ff.) how Huneric tried to circumvent his father's succession arrangement. To be sure, Theodahad was not popular, at least among the majority of the Goths: see Procopius (as n. 514).

519. Procopius, *De bello Gothico* I (V) 3.1 f., and 4.1 f.

520. See above, n. 256. (Gregory of Tours, *Historia Francorum* III 31, p. 127.)

521. Procopius, *De bello Gothico* I (V) 3.3 and 4.2 f.

522. Procopius, *De bello Gothico* I (V) 3.4 and 9 as well as 29; 16.19 f. (the offer to renounce his kingship for twelve hundred pounds of gold was not made, however, until 535). On the "small flight luggage" of Amalasuintha in the amount of forty thousand pounds of gold see ibid. 2.26. Yet the basis for the evaluation of Theodahad's demands is Olympiodorus fr. 44 on the annual senatorial income: according to him four thousand pounds would have been a high income and fifteen hundred pounds a medium one. Cf. Matthews, *Aristocracies,* 384.

523. Malchus frs. 11 and 18.

524. Eraric also wanted to sell his kingship: Procopius, *De bello Gothico* III (VII) 2.17.

525. Ibid., I (V) 4.4 Cf. above, n. 521.

526. On this and the following see Ensslin, *Theoderich,* 301 and 324 ff. Stein, *Bas-Empire* 2:262 ff. Hartmann, *Geschichte Italiens* 1:224 ff. On Athalaric see Martindale, *Prosopography* 2:175 f.

527. Jordanes, *Getica* 304, p. 136. Cf. above, n. 145. On Athalaric as the seventeenth king see Wagner, "Bemerkungen," 28 ff., building on Wolfram, *Intitulatio I,* 99–104.

528. Cassiodorus, *Variae* XI 1.9, p. 328 f. Cf. Ensslin, *Theoderich,* 320. Procopius, *De bello Gothico* I (V) 2.1–5.

529. Jordanes, *Getica* 304 f., p. 136.

530. Claude, "Königs- und Untertaneneid," 371–373, after Cassiodorus, *Variae* VIII 2–8, pp. 232–237.

531. Cassiodorus, *Variae* VIII 1 f., pp. 231–233. See esp. 2.10, p. 233, where the senators are asked to demand special pledges for their safety. On the senatorial minting of coins see Stein, *Bas-Empire* 2:264 with n. 2.

532. Ensslin, *Theoderich,* 325, after Cassiodorus, *Variae* VIII 1.2, p. 231.

533. Ensslin, *Theoderich,* 325, after Procopius, *De bello Gothico* I (V) 2.5.

534. Procopius, *De bello Gothico* I (V) 12.49 and 13.4–8. Stein, *Bas-Empire* 2:332.

535. Cf. Procopius, *De bello Gothico* I (V) 2.3 f.

536. Ibid., 3.15–17. Cf. above, n. 442.

537. Stein, *Bas-Empire* 2:287 ff., esp. 291 ff.

538. See above, n. 368 and n. 423.

539. Wolfram, *Intitulatio I,* 47 and 51, and *Splendor Imperii,* 112 f., after Cassiodorus, *Variae* VIII 9–10, pp. 237–241. On Martindale, *Prosopography* 2:679, see O'Donnell, "Liberius," 61. On Gesimund see above, nn. 43 ff.

540. Jordanes, *Getica* XX f. and XXX f. Cf. Wiesner, *Thraker,* 55–59 (Troy and the Amazons), 84–86 (Zalmoxis), 116 ff. (Sitalkes), 158 ff. (Burvista), 176 ff. (Dorpaneus and Decebalus). See also Sybel, *Entstehung,* 196 f.

541. Procopius, *De bello Gothico* I (V) 2.3.

542. Cassiodorus, *Variae* VIII 23.2, p. 254.

543. One would like to infer this from the comparison of Procopius, *De bello Gothico* I (V) 4.6 and 12 f. Cf. below, n. 547. Jordanes, *Getica* 306, p. 136, states explicitly that Theodahad had Amalasuintha murdered by his retainers (*satellites*).

544. Ensslin, *Theoderich,* 318. Stein, *Bas-Empire* 2:328 f.

545. On Tuluin see Wolfram, *Intitulatio I,* 47. On Theodahad cf. above, n. 543 and below, n. 547.

546. Procopius, *De bello Gothico* I (V) 2.19–26. There is a similar story about Gelimer who—in case of a defeat against Belisarius—wanted to send his "golden ship" to the Visigothic king Theudis: see *De bello Vandalico* II (IV) 4.33–41.

547. Procopius, *De bello Gothico* I (V) 3.3 f. But Procopius states that the reason for the renunciation of Tuscany was merely the quarrel between Amalasuintha and Theodahad over the latter's "greediness." But the way the story unfolds also allows for the interpretation I have offered.

548. See above, n. 368.

549. Procopius, *De bello Gothico* I (V) 2.27–29.

550. O'Donnell (as n. 539). Cf. above, n. 357.

551. See chap. 1, n. 105.

552. Cassiodorus, *Variae* XI 1.9 f., p. 328 f. See above, n. 442.

553. Cassiodorus, *Variae* XI 1.10 and 12, p. 329.

554. Ibid., 16–19, p. 329 f. On Amalasuintha's family tree see Wolfram, "Theogonie," 82 ff. nn. 15 ff., and "Gotische Studien," 14.

555. Cassiodorus (as n. 552) 14, p. 329.

556. See above, n. 553 f.

557. Agnellus, *Liber pontificalis ecclesiae Ravennatis,* chap. 62, p. 322 (333). Stein, *Bas-Empire* 2:334 f. and 337 f. with n. 2. Nehlsen, *Sklavenrecht,* 123. See Cassiodorus, *Variae* IX 18–20, pp. 282–285: *Edictum Athalarici.*

558. Altheim, *Geschichte der Hunnen* 1:322 n. 1 and 328. Hauck, "Brustbilder von Königen," 229 f. Fiebiger, *Inschriftensammlung,* no. 39, p. 28. Ennodius, *Panegyricus* 91, p. 214. Piltz, "Kamelaukion," 86 f. Cf. below, n. 592.

559. Procopius, *De bello Gothico* I (V) 4.4 f.

560. Cassiodorus, *Variae* X 3.2, p. 298; cf. X 2.2. On Theodahad's involvement in the conspiracy of the nobility see above, nn. 543, 545, and 547. Cf. *Continuator Marcellini* a. 534, p. 104: Amalasuintha is the *creatrix* of Theodahad. Claude, "Die ostgotischen Königserhebungen," 162 ff.

561. See the *superscriptiones* of Cassiodorus, *Variae* X 1 and 3, p. 297 f.

562. Procopius, *De bello Gothico* I (V) 4.8 f. Jordanes, *Getica* 306, p. 136.

563. Hahn, *Moneta Imperii Byzantini I* I, 80 and 90.

564. See Cassiodorus, *Variae* X 3.3, p. 299.

565. Ibid., 4.1, p. 299. Cf. Schneider, *Königswahl,* 27 ff.

566. Stein, *Bas-Empire* 2:337 f. with n. 2.

567. Cassiodorus, *Variae* X 1–4, pp. 297–301. Procopius, *De bello Gothico* I (V) 4.11.

568. Procopius, *De bello Gothico* I (V) 4.12 ff.

569. See above, n. 351.

570. Procopius, *De bello Vandalico* II (IV) 5.11 ff., and *De bello Gothico* I (V) 3.15 ff.

571. Stein, *Bas-Empire* 2:723–729. Clauss, *Magister officiorum,* 181 f. Chrysos, "Amaler-Herrschaft," 430 ff.

572. Procopius, *Anecdota* 16.1 ff. Cf. ibid. 9.8 ff., esp. 15, as well as 24, 23. Amalasuintha's age at her death follows from the marriage of her parents in either 493 or 494: see above, n. 374.

573. Stein, *Bas-Empire* 2:338 f., and esp. 341 f. n. 2. See, for example, Procopius, *De bello Gothico* I (V) 4.13 and 26 f.

574. Ibid., 4.15; 21; 23–25. On Liberius see O'Donnell, "Liberius," 62 ff., Martindale, *Prosopography* 2:679 ff., as well as Stein, *Bas-Empire* 2:562; cf. 882, s.v. "Libère." On Liberius cf. above, n. 357. On Opilio see Martindale, *Prosopography* 2:808 (Opilio 4).

575. Cassiodorus, *Variae* X 19–26, pp. 309–314.

576. On this and the following see the excellent account of Stein, *Bas-Empire* 2:339–347, esp. after Procopius, *De bello Gothico* I (V) 4.30.

577. Cassiodorus, *Variae* X 13 f. and 16–18, pp. 306 f. and 308 f.; XII 5, esp. 5.2 f. and 5.6 f., p. 363 f. Into this period also falls Theodahad's attempt to establish family ties with the Anicii: see above, n. 222, and below *Genealogical Chart of the Amali.*

578. The main source is Procopius, *De bello Gothico* I (V) 5.1 ff., 11 ff.

579. See above, nn. 433 and 442. Procopius, *De bello Gothico* I (V) 5.2 and 11.

580. See Hannestad, "La guerre gothique," 139–141.

581. Procopius, *De bello Gothico* I (V) 5.6 f. and 12.

582. See above, nn. 347 and 351 as well as n. 435 f.

583. Procopius, *De bello Gothico* I (V) 5.12–19.

584. Ibid., 5.8–10. Irsigler, *Untersuchungen,* 179, after Gregory of Tours, *Historia Francorum* III 41, p. 127, on the compensation to the Frankish kings for the death of their cousin Amalasuintha.

585. We are indebted to Chrysos, "Amaler-Herrschaft," 430 ff., after Procopius, *De bello Gothico* I (V) 6.2–5, for the best assessment of the planned treaty. Cf. above, n. 198 f.

586. Procopius, *De bello Gothico* I (V) 6.6–27, esp. 10, 19, 24, and 26. Cf. above, n. 522.

587. Procopius, *De bello Gothico* I (V) 7.1 ff.

588. Stein, *Bas-Empire* 2:322 ff., and 344 f. Hartmann, *Geschichte Italiens* 1:249 f.

589. Procopius, *De bello Gothico* I (V) 7.10 and 31. See above, n. 433.

590. Procopius, *De bello Gothico* I (V) 6.11 f.

591. Stein, *Bas-Empire* 2:724 f.

592. Hahn, *Moneta Imperii Byzantini I,* 90. Hauck, "Brustbilder von Königen," 230 f. Stein, *Bas-Empire* 2:345. Altheim, *Geschichte der Hunnen* 1:322 f. Piltz, "Kamelaukion," 60 and 80 ff.: according to the coin portraits Theodahad and Totila wore a καμηλαύκιον, whereas according to ibid., 86 f., the head covering worn by Athalaric and Amalasuintha was a πῖλος. The work of Piltz, which shows little knowledge of the institutional position of the Gothic kings, should be corrected by Ladner, "Ursprung der päpstlichen Tiara," 449 ff., esp. 452 f. n. 18. See also below, n. 744 on the reliability of the tradition that Totila wore a kamelaukion.

593. Procopius, *De bello Gothico* I (V) 7.26–37, esp. 37.

594. See above, n. 588.

595. Zimmermann, "Grabstein" (as chap. 4, n. 621, and above, n. 497). Assunta Nagl, "Theodenanda-Theodenantha," 1735, esp. Fiebiger-Schmidt, *Inschriften-sammlung,* no. 204, p. 103, and Procopius, *De bello Gothico* I (V) 8.1 ff.

596. Ibid., 6.25–27.

597. Stein, *Bas-Empire* 2:346 f., as well as Procopius (as n. 595). Jordanes, *Getica* 309, p. 137, on the one hand, explains Ebrimud's desertion by saying that he "realized that the cause of his people was lost," and, on the other hand, he explains the abandoning of Theodahad with just this desertion. Cf., however, *Continuator Marcellini* a. 536, p. 104, where both events are still reported without connection.

598. Procopius, *De bello Gothico* I (V) 8.8.

599. Cf. ibid., 6.9.

600. See above, n. 384.

601. Procopius, *De bello Gothico* I (V) 9.1 ff. to 11.10. Again and again Theodahad is accused of having betrayed his people, which even Stein, *Bas-Empire* 2:346 f., seems to assume. Theodahad's inaction, which seems especially incomprehensible in the case of Naples, can probably be explained by indecision and poor generalship. Yet we must not forget that Vitigis after his withdrawal from Rome also avoided military action: see below, n. 656 f.

602. On Theudegisel's possible Amal identity see chap. 4, n. 621. On Amalaric see chap. 4, n. 619 f., and above, n. 383.

603. Tacitus, *Germania,* chap. 7.1. Cf. Schlesinger, "Heerkönigtum," 131. See below, n. 615.

604. Procopius, *De bello Gothico* I (V) 2.21 f., 25–29; 4.13, 26–30. See above, n. 223.

605. Irsigler, *Untersuchungen,* 239 ff. See Vitigis to all the Goths: Cassiodorus, *Variae* V 31.4, p. 319: . . . *Ad gentis utilitatem respiciet omne quod agimus: privatim nec nos amabimus: hoc sequi promittimus quod ornet regium nomen. . .*

606. Cf. above, n. 603.

607. According to Cassiodorus, *Variae* X 31.1, p. 318, Vitigis was elevated on the shield *more maiorum.* This type of elevation to the kingship is not attested among the Goths before this, but we must take seriously the statement that it took place "according to the custom of the ancestors." Vitigis was addressing "all the Goths," and he could not tell them any invented stories. Ensslin, "Witigis," 395 ff. Stengel, "Heerkaiser," 16. Claude, "Die ostgotischen Königserhebungen," 166 f. and 180, also discusses the other non-Amal Ostrogothic kings, apart from Vitigis.

608. Procopius, *De bello Gothico* I (V) 11.5.

609. Cf. ibid., II (VI) 10.2 and 12.37.

610. Cf. Cassiodorus, *Orationum reliquiae,* p. 474, vv. 20 f., with p. 476, vv. 6–21. From this follows a course of events delimited, on the one hand, by the last days of Theodoric and, on the other, by the hostilities at the Sava in 530. The key passage is ibid. p. 476, vv. 6–9. For that reason also the *Unigis spatharius* who is mentioned in Cassiodorus, *Variae* III 43, p. 100, cannot be identical with Vitigis. Moreover, the chronology of the early Vitigis given by Hartmann, *Geschichte*

Italiens 1:287 n. 13, is only partially correct. On the court position of the sword-bearer see above, n. 219, and below, nn. 680–683.

611. Cassiodorus, *Variae* X 32.3, p. 319. But Vitigis was also a leading figure in negotiations with foreign envoys under Athalaric: see Cassiodorus, *Orationum reliquiae,* p. 476, vv. 16 f.

612. See ibid., v. 21. Procopius, *De bello Gothico* I (V) 11.5. Cf. above, n. 442.

613. Stein, *Bas-Empire* 2:346 f. Among the sources should be emphasized Procopius, *De bello Gothico* I (V) 11.1 f. and 5–9, Jordanes, *Romana* 371 f., p. 48 f., as well as *Getica* 309 f., p. 137.

614. See above, n. 180.

615. Cassiodorus, *Variae* X 31.1 ff., p. 318 f.: Vitigis announces his elevation to the kingship by "our Gothic brothers" by first giving thanks to the Lord. The translation of *Martius Rex* is backed by Cassiodorus, *Orationum reliquiae* p. 474, vv. 15 f. (*aperto . . . marte*). See above, n. 607, and Wolfram, "Gotische Studien III," 251 with n. 176 f. On the marriage to Matasuntha see esp. Procopius, *De bello Gothico* I (V) 11.27, Jordanes, *Romana* 373, p. 49, as well as *Getica* 311, p. 137, based on *Continuator Marcellini* a. 536, p. 105. Cf. Stengel, "Heerkaiser," 16. See finally Cassiodorus, *Orationum reliquiae,* p. 479, vv. 17–19: *. . . non potuissent [Gothi] eligere, nisi qui probetur saepius bella peregisse,* as well as ibid. p. 463 n. 3. In contrast it is said of Matasuntha (ibid. p. 480, vv. 14 f.): *. . . quae tantorum regum posteritas potuit inveniri.* On the imperial recognition of the Amal kingship see above, n. 180.

616. See chap. 4, n. 54 as well as nn. 278 ff.

617. Stein, *Bas-Empire* 2:347 n. 1.

618. Procopius, *De bello Gothico* I (V) 11.11 ff.; 13.15 ff.

619. See above, n. 546.

620. Procopius, *De bello Gothico* I (V) 13.14 ff. Agathias I 6.4 f. See above, n. 410.

621. Pertusi, "Ordinamenti militari," 631 ff., esp. 636. Hannestad, "La guerre gothique," 180 f. Procopius, *De bello Gothico* I (V) 19.12; however, the Gallic troops of Markias joined Vitigis's main force only before Rome.

622. Procopius, *De bello Gothico* I (V) 11.28. Cf. above, n. 295.

623. Hannestad, "La guerre gothique," 180 f. On this and the following see the superb study of Pertusi, "Ordinamenti militari," 638–643, with an excellent map following p. 638. On the events and their chronology see esp. Stein, *Bas-Empire* 2:347–353. On the resumed Dalmatian war see Procopius, *De bello Gothico* I (V) 16.9 and 12. Cf. below, n. 639.

624. Stein, *Bas-Empire* 2:347 (retreat of Vitigis to Ravenna), and *Liber pontificalis* 98 (Vita Silverii, chap. 4), p. 291 (Vitigis once again before Rome).

625. Procopius, *De bello Gothico* I (V) 11.26 and 14.12 ff.

626. The age difference of the royal couple has been generally exaggerated. Cf. Stein, *Bas-Empire* 2:348, cf. Ensslin, "Matasuntha," 2180. Procopius, *De bello Gothico* I (V) 11.27, calls her a παρθένος ὡραία, which should indicate an eighteen-year-old girl. Thus she would have been about two years younger than her brother Athalaric, which also seems likely. Cf. above, n. 526. But the career of Vitigis did not begin until around 526; the idea that he already participated in the Sirmian war

of 504 is a mistake of Procopius, *De bello Gothico* I (V) 11.5; cf. above, n. 442. Since one cannot assume that Vitigis performed his first military exploits as a thirty-year-old (or even older "veteran"), he can hardly have been born before 500. The non-noble descent of Vitigis (cf. above, n. 608) probably caused problems for Cassiodorus. Cf. his *Orationum reliquiae*, p. 479, vv. 8 f. and 17 ff., which is followed immediately (vv. 20 ff.) by the praise of Matasuntha, which culminates (p. 480 vv. 14 f.) in the allusion to her illustrious line of ancestors. For the expulsion of his *privata coniunx* see Jordanes, *Romana* 373, p. 49. Vitigis is said to have had a son by her (see below, n. 673).

627. *Liber pontificalis* 98 (Vita Silverii, chap. 4), p. 290 f. Hartmann, *Geschichte Italiens* 1:287 n. 15.

628. Pertusi, "Ordinamenti militari," 639. Hannestad, "La guerre gothique," 140. See Procopius, *De bello Gothico* I (V) 22.17 and 24.1–3. On the militia of Rome and its lack of fighting ability see ibid., 18.34 and 20.5 ff. Likewise the ναῦται καί οἰκέται, who participated in the battles, were no help: ibid., 29.26–29.

629. Ibid., 16.20 f.

630. Ibid., 17.7.

631. See n. 627.

632. Pertusi, "Ordinamenti militari," 643. Stein, *Bas-Empire* 2:350 ff. Hartmann, *Geschichte Italiens* 1:261 ff. The siege lasted exactly one year and nine days, as reports Procopius, *De bello Gothico* II (VI) 10.13. Ibid., I (V) 28 f. to II (VI) 1.1, is devoted to the great battle between the two armies, which the Goths won, whereupon the Romans undertook no more large-scale attacks. On the Gothic defeats see, for example, ibid., I (V) 27.6–14 and 27.15–23 but also II (VI) 2.19 ff.

633. See above, nn. 307 ff. On the Roman artillery cf., for example, Procopius, *De bello Gothico* I (V) 21.14 ff.

634. Stein, *Bas-Empire* 2:350 with n. 6, esp. after Procopius, *De bello Gothico* I (V) 27.1

635. Ibid., 25.1–4 and 10–16. Cf. Stein, *Bas-Empire* 2:350 f. *Liber pontificalis* 100 f. (Vita Silverii, chaps. 7 f.), p. 292 f. Procopius, *De bello Gothico* I (V) 20.5 ff.

636. Stein, *Bas-Empire* 2:351. Procopius, *De bello Gothico* I (V) 22 f.

637. Ibid., 17.17 and 18.7.

638. Ibid., II (VI) 3.1 ff.; however, the Goths were soon plagued by the same problems: see ibid., IV (VIII) 16 f. Cf. also *Liber pontificalis* 100 (Vita Silverii, chap. 5), p. 291.

639. Procopius, *De bello Gothico* I (V) 16.8–18 and II (VI) 28.2. See Stein, *Bas-Empire* 2:349 and 360. Cf. above, n. 623.

640. Cf. Cassiodorus, *Variae* X 32–35, pp. 319–321.

641. Stein, *Bas-Empire* 2:352–355, esp. Procopius, *De bello Gothico* II (VI) 6 f. and 9 f.

642. See esp. ibid., 24.7 and 10 as well as 26.13. On the significance of the fortress see Hannestad, "La guerre gothique," 145 n. 54 and the Italian literature listed there.

643. Procopius, *De bello Gothico* II (VI) 23.1 and 5 to 24.17, 26.2 to 27.24, and 27–34. Stein, *Bas-Empire* 2:360 and 362.

644. Ibid., 353 f. with n. 6, esp. after Procopius, *De bello Gothico* I (V) 26.1.

O'Donnell, *Cassiodorus,* 104 f., advances good arguments against the generally assumed break.

645. Stein, *Bas-Empire* 2:354 f., 359 f. Zöllner, *Franken,* 89. Löhlein, *Alpen- und Italienpolitik,* 31–33.

646. Procopius, *De bello Gothico* II (VI) 10.2.

647. Schwarcz, *Nachrichten,* 40, is probably right in placing Cassiodorus, *Variae* XII 7, p. 365 f., before the conclusion of the Gothic-Frankish alliance, against, for example, Zöllner (as n. 645).

648. Stein, *Bas-Empire* 2:353 f.

649. See n. 643 (Osimo) and n. 645 (Milan), as well as Procopius, *De bello Gothico* II (VI) 24.18 ff. (Fiesole).

650. Stein, *Bas-Empire* 2:356–360, esp. 358 f. Pertusi, "Ordinamenti militari," 636. Hannestad, "La guerre gothique," 141 f. Lippold, "Narses," 871–874.

651. Procopius, *De bello Gothico* II (VI) 22.5–8. On the Herulian homeland at that time see above, n. 442. On the Heruli who stayed behind in Venetia see below, n. 685.

652. Stein, *Bas-Empire* 2:355 n. 5, as well as Hartmann, *Geschichte Italiens* 1:270, after Procopius, *De bello Gothico* II (VI) 18.12–27.

653. Cf. above, nn. 165 ff.

654. Procopius, *De bello Gothico* II (VI) 23.5 and 24.18–24.

655. The surrender of the city immediately preceded that of Osimo: Procopius, *De bello Gothico* II (VI) 27.25–27.

656. See above, n. 643.

657. Cf. Procopius, *De bello Gothico* II (VI) 30.12.

658. Ibid., 22.9–12.

659. Ibid., 22.13–25. Cf. *De bello Persico* II 2.1 f. Cf. above, n. 571.

660. Löhlein, *Alpen- und Italienpolitik,* 33 f., after Procopius, *De bello Gothico* II (VI) 25.9 f.

661. Ibid., 25.1 to 26.2, and 28.9–23. Cf. 22.9 f. See esp. Zöllner, *Franken,* 90 f. Stein, *Bas-Empire* 2:365 ff.

662. See above, n. 643 (surrender of Osimo) and n. 655 (surrender of Fiesole).

663. Stein, *Bas-Empire* 2:365 f.

664. See above, n. 166.

665. Procopius, *De bello Gothico* II (VI) 28.7 ff. Cf. above, n. 661.

666. Stein, *Bas-Empire* 2:365 f. Procopius, *De bello Gothico* II (VI) 28.25–27.

667. Ibid., 10.11.

668. See below, nn. 732–736.

669. Stein, *Bas-Empire* 2:280 f., and 366 f. Cf. above, n. 641 on the first offer of Vitigis to divide Italy between the empire and the Goths. Chrysos, "Reichsideologie," 42 ff.

670. Procopius, *De bello Gothico* II (VI) 29.17 ff.; 30.3, 24, 36 ff. The question of whether Belisarius was offered the Western emperorship or the Gothic-Italian kingship is discussed by Claude, "Die ostgotischen Königserhebungen," 168 f., and he decides—as does Wolfram, *Intitulatio I,* 47 f.—for the kingship. But now Evangelos Chrysos (cf. Chrysos, "Reichsideologie," 48 n. 41) has in a conversation expressed his doubts about this interpretation, whereupon another careful examina-

tion of the sources, esp. Procopius, *De bello Gothico* II (VI) 29.17, 20, 26–31, allowed the interpretation given in the text. On the barbarian-Latin kingship of the army of the Goths and Italians see above, nn. 188 ff., and below, n. 676. On the elevation of Avitus see chap. 4, n. 65. For a similar situation in the year 411 when Iovinus usurped the emperorship, cf. chap. 3, n. 274 and n. 290. Not without interest in this context is Procopius, *De bello Vandalico* I (III) 20.21, according to whom Belisarius, after entering Carthage, seated himself on the Vandal royal throne and dispensed justice.

671. Stein, *Bas-Empire* 2:367 f. Cf. Procopius, *De bello Gothico* III (VII) 1.20 f.

672. Ibid., II (VI) 29.34.

673. Ibid., II (VI) 29.35–41; 30.7. II (VII) 1.1–7. IV (VIII) 25.11 f. (the Thuringian Amali). Cf. *De bello Persico* II 14.10 f. Ioannis Malalas, *Chronicon,* p. 480, speaks of a son of Vitigis from his first (?) marriage. On the division of the property after the capture of Auximum-Osimo see Procopius, *De bello Gothico* II (VI) 27.31 f. The children of Hildebad are mentioned ibid. 29.41.

674. Cf. *Continuator Marcellini* a. 540.5, p. 106. On the treasure see n. 678.

675. Bierbrauer, *Grab- und Schatzfunde,* 34 with n. 105 and the Italian literature listed there.

676. Procopius, *De bello Gothico* II (VI) 30.3–30; see esp. 3.22–30 (pressure of Belisarius) as well as 5 and 12 (lucklessness of Vitigis and his clan); cf. Wolfram, "Fortuna," 13 f. On the negotiations of the leaders of the transpadane Goths and on the children of Hildebad see Procopius, *De bello Gothico* II (VI) 29.39–41; cf. above, n. 673. On Belisarius's bond to his countryman Justinian by oath see ibid. 29.20, as well as Stein, *Bas-Empire* 2:284 ff.

677. See above, n. 615. *Continuator Marcellini* a. 540.5, p. 106.

678. Agathias I 20.7–10. Cf. above, n. 332 f. and n. 455.

679. *Getica* 313–316, p. 138.

680. See, for example, the idea of royal charisma (as n. 676), the "Gothicizing tendencies" on the coins, which did begin under Athalaric but which became much stronger under Totila (see Hahn, *Moneta Imperii Byzantini I,* 78 ff., Wolfram, *Intitulatio I,* 41 f. with n. 53), possibly also Totila's name Baduila (see below, n. 699 f.), and not least Totila's lance-ride (djerid) at the beginning of the battle of Busta Gallorum (see below, n. 744). On the barbarian traditions in the Ostrogothic kingdom of Theodoric cf. above, nn. 451 ff.

681. Perhaps this statement, which is confirmed by this single instance, can be read into Cassiodorus, *Orationum reliquiae,* p. 476, vv. 14 f., even though the passage corresponds to a standard type: see Wolfram, *Splendor Imperii,* 50 f.

682. Procopius, *De bello Gothico* II (VI) 30.4–15 (Uraias-Vitigis and Hildebad-Theudis) as well as III (VII) 2.7 and 10–12 (Totila-Hildebad). On Theudis among the Visigoths of Spain see above, n. 357. On the prohibition of *connubium* between Visigoths and Romans see chap. 4, n. 502, and above, n. 106.

683. Procopius, *De bello Gothico* III (VII) 1.37–42. See on this Altheim, *Geschichte der Hunnen* 4:204 f., and the literature discussed there.

684. Wolfram, *Intitulatio I,* 43, after Procopius, *De bello Gothico* II (VII) 4.12.

685. Ibid., 1.34–36 and 2.7. On the Heruli see above, n. 442 and n. 651.

686. Procopius, *De bello Gothico* III (VII) 1.22–33.

687. See below, n. 727.

688. Cf., for example, Procopius, *De bello Gothico* III (VII) 4.21 ff., IV (VIII) 31.11–16.

689. See above, n. 683 (Uraias) as well as Procopius, *De bello Gothico* I (V) 11.6–9.

690. Ibid., III (VII) 1.42 to 2.18. Ibid., 2.5 and 11 f., probably indicates that the "Gothic" Hildebad party regained the upper hand. On the non-Gothic barbarians see 2.1 f.

691. See above, n. 260.

692. Procopius, *De bello Gothico* III (VII) 2 to 3.1. On Hildebad's negotiations for surrender see above, n. 676. At one time even Theodoric the Great expressed the sole desire to live the good life in Constantinople: see above, n. 523 (Malchus fr. 18).

693. See chap. 3, n. 264 f.

694. Jordanes, *Romana* 379, p. 50. Cf. Procopius, *De bello Gothico* III (VII) 9.15. Stein, *Bas-Empire* 2:568.

695. Stein (as n. 694), after Hartmann, *Geschichte Italiens* 1:296. Cf., for example, also Pepe, *Il medio evo barbarico,* 71. Nagl, "Totila," 1828–1838, esp. 1837 f., as well as Roisl, "Totila," 808 f. A positive assessment of Totila, based on his behavior at the capture of Rome, is given by *Liber pontificalis* 107 (Vita Vigilii, chap. 7), p. 298. Cf. Stein, *Bas-Empire* 2:569.

696. Jordanes (as n. 694). Cf. Stein, *Bas-Empire* 2:569.

697. This phrase, coined for Hildebad (see Procopius, *De bello Gothico* III (VII) 1.26), applies also to Totila, who is considered a real successor of his uncle and one whom "the Goths trusted": ibid., 2.11.

698. The best account of Totila is in Stein, *Bas-Empire* 2:568–602.

699. A list of the sources is given by Nagl, "Totila," 1828. See esp. *Liber pontificalis* (as n. 695).

700. Schönfeld, *Wörterbuch,* 41 and 240 f.; cf. Birkhan, *Germanen und Kelten,* 506 n. 1527.

701. Stein, *Bas-Empire* 2:570 f. Procopius, *De bello Gothico* III (VII) 40.20–29, gives the name of a Roman who as quaestor enjoyed the king's confidence but who did not serve the king entirely faithfully when his own life seemed at stake.

702. Stein, *Bas-Empire* 2:574 n. 1, after Gregory the Great, *Dialogi* II 14 f., where Totila is prophesied the capture of the city, a nine-year reign, and his death in the tenth year. If one takes this *prophetia ex eventu* seriously and if one starts from the assumption that Totila's elevation to the kingship probably took place in October 541 (see above, n. 692) and that the battle of Busta Gallorum took place in summer 552 (see below, n. 744), the king must have visited St. Benedict in 542.

703. Thus the destruction of Rome's aqueducts by Vitigis in 537 has affected the history of the Eternal City to this day, more so than the unsuccessful attempt of Totila to destroy Rome in 547: cf. Stein, *Bas-Empire* 2:351 and 585.

704. Hannestad, "La guerre gothique," 148. Procopius, *De bello Gothico* III (VII) 3.1–22.

705. Ibid., 4.1 ff., esp. 14; cf. ibid., 8.12–25. See also Ensslin, *Theoderich,* 207 n. 40, as well as Wolfram, *Intitulatio I,* 43.

706. Hannestad, "La guerre gothique," 152 f. and 164 ff. The Goth Indulf, a former *buccellarius* of Belisarius's went over to Totila before the spring of 549: see Procopius, *De bello Gothico* III (VII) 35.23. Cf. also below, nn. 730 and 751.

707. Procopius, *De bello Gothico* III (VII) 4.31. Cf. Hannestad, "La guerre gothique," 151. Stein, *Bas-Empire* 2:572 ff.

708. Procopius, *De bello Gothico* III (VII) 5.18 and 6.8.

709. Ibid., 6.1–3. On Naples cf. above, n. 601.

710. Procopius, *De bello Gothico* III (VII) 7.4–7.

711. Ibid., 7.11–8.9.

712. Ibid., 16.14–21 and 31.

713. Ibid., 10.19–22.

714. Stein, *Bas-Empire* 2:576–578. On the disintegration within the imperial army see Procopius, *De bello Gothico* III (VII) 12.8.

715. Cf. Stein, *Bas-Empire* 2:584.

716. Zöllner, *Franken,* 91, after Procopius, *De bello Gothico* III (VII) 31.1 ff. and 7. On Narses see below, nn. 738 ff.

717. Stein, *Bas-Empire* 2:578–584.

718. Procopius, *De bello Gothico* III (VII) 20.1 and 16 f.

719. Stein, *Bas-Empire* 2:584 f. On Belisarius's typhoid fever see Procopius, *De bello Gothico* III (VII) 19.30 ff. On the embassy see ibid., 21.18–25, esp. 23, where the challenging passage should be read ὧνπερ μνημεῖά τε καὶ παραδείγματα κάλλιστα ἔχομεν Ἀναστάσιόν τε καὶ Θευδέριχον, οἳ βεβασιλεύκασι μὲν οὐ πολλῷ πρότερον, εἰρήνης δὲ καὶ ἀγαθῶν πραγμάτων ἅπαντα ἐνεπλήσαντο τὸν κατ᾽ αὐτοὺς χρόνον, which reminds one semantically of Luke 3.1; a passage on the rule of Tiberius and Pilate which was even too strong for Ulfilas: see Wolfram, "Gotische Studien III," 296 with n. 27. The "good old days" represented by Anastasius and Theodoric is also invoked on Totila's coins: Hahn, *Moneta Imperii Byzantini I,* 79–85.

720. Stein, *Bas-Empire* 2:584 f. Procopius, *De bello Gothico* III (VII) 21.18–22.

721. Zöllner, *Franken,* 97, and Stein, *Bas-Empire* 2:587.

722. Nehlsen, *Sklavenrecht,* 127. Rothenhöfer, *Untersuchungen* 110–114. Cf. above, nn. 275–280. See esp. Procopius, *De bello Gothico* III (VII) 16.14 f. and 25 (former slaves in the Gothic army) and 22.2–6 and 20–24 (the episode with Tullianus). The number of slaves who in some way or another gained their freedom under Totila was probably not small, since the *Sanctio pragmatica,* chap. 15, deals with these slaves, to their disadvantage. That the Ostrogothic government basically supported the preservation of the late Roman social structure is shown, for example, by Cassiodorus, *Variae* XII 5.4, p. 364. The use of poorly armed warriors, who could not afford defensive arms, was of course a somewhat questionable practice: see Procopius, *De bello Gothico* I (V) 29.26.

723. Procopius, *De bello Gothico* III (VII) 13.1 and 22.20. Stein, *Bas-Empire* 2:570 f. Cf. Russell, "Plague," 174–184.

724. Stein, *Bas-Empire* 2:570 n. 1 and 580 ff. Procopius, *De bello Gothico* III (VII) 15.15, reports the maltreatment of a Roman bishop by Totila himself.

725. Ibid., 21.12–17, cf. esp. 15 f.

726. Ibid., 24.8–27, esp. 27. The reproach of ἀβουλία, "lack of wisdom," is of

course serious. Cf. Wolfram, "Gotische Studien I," 13 ff., and Wolfram, "Athanaric," 267.

727. Stein, *Bas-Empire* 2:560 f., and Claude, *Westgoten*, 57.

728. Procopius, *De bello Gothico* III (VII) 18.26 and 28 (Mauri), and 20.14 f. and 21.15 f. (Isaurians).

729. Stein, *Bas-Empire* 2:589 ff.

730. Procopius, *De bello Gothico* III (VII) 35.16–30; cf. IV (VIII) 27.12–29 (death of Hildigis). On this see L. Schmidt, *Ostgermanen*, 539 and 581 f. For the events in general see Stein, *Bas-Empire* 2:592 f.

731. Stein, *Bas-Empire* 2:593 f. On the coins see Hahn, *Moneta Imperii Byzantini I*, 78–80, 85, 88, and 90 f. The minting was done in the name of "the long since deceased pro-Gothic Anastasius," on which one should compare Procopius, *De bello Gothico* III (VII) 21.23 (Totila's letter to Justinian after the first capture of Rome, cf. above, n. 719). The tenor of the letter is as follows: "when Anastasius and Theodoric were kings (βεβασιλεύκασιν), there was peace and prosperity all the time."

732. Stein, *Bas-Empire* 2:594–597. See below, n. 735. On Germanus and his kinship with Justinian see Martindale *Prosopography* 2:505 ff., no. 4.

733. Wes, *Ende des Kaisertums*, 185–192. See Weissensteiner as chap. 1, n. 8.

734. Cassiodorus, *Variae* X 2.3, p. 298; 22.2, p. 312; XI 13.4, p. 342.

735. Such a connection is attested by ibid. X 11 f., pp. 304–306, esp. 12.2 f., p. 305. It is greatly emphasized in the famous closing chapter of Jordanes, *Getica* 314, p. 138. Cf. Wes, *Ende des Kaisertums*, 189–193. Stein, *Bas-Empire* 2:596. On the barbarian origins of the *regnum Hesperium* since 476 see above, nn. 184–191.

736. How the news of the appointment of Germanus raised the morale of the imperial army and lowered that of its enemies is described well by Procopius, *De bello Gothico* III (VII) 39.9–28, esp. 15, 21 f., and 25–27.

737. Martindale, *Prosopography* 2:507.

738. Stein, *Bas-Empire* 2:597–599. Chrysos, Ἱστορία τῆς Ἠπείρου, 65 ff.

739. Lippold, "Narses," 874 ff.

740. Procopius, *De bello Gothico* IV (VIII) 26.18 f. Wolfram, *Mitteleuropa* 80 with n. 9 f.

741. Procopius, *De bello Gothico* IV (VIII) 26.20–25. Ibid. III (VII) 39.15 ff., and IV (VIII) 26.5, on the enormous troop strength of the Roman army. On the troop strength cf. Pertusi, "Ordinamenti militari," 636, who is thinking of a total of 29,000–30,000 men, as well as Hannestad, "La guerre gothique," 153 f., who counts a total of 25,000 men.

742. Stein, *Bas-Empire* 2:599.

743. Ibid., 601. Lippold, "Narses," 876 f.

744. Lippold, "Narses," 847–879, esp. 877 f., who agrees largely with Roisl, "Tadinae," 749 ff., but who should be corrected with Roisl, "Totila," cols. 805–808 on one point. Cf. most recently Roisl, "Totila und die Schlacht," 44 ff., esp. 47 f. n. 56. An interesting if outdated account of the events is given by Pertusi, "Ordinamenti militari," 643 ff. See also Stein, *Bas-Empire* 2:601 f. The source on which the modern accounts are based is Procopius, *De bello Gothico* IV (VIII) 29–32. Ibid. 29.11–21 (battle for the hill), 31.1–7 (disposition of the Roman army), 31.17–

21 (Totila's djerid), 29.1, 31.17, 32.1 (arrival of the last 2,000 reinforcements), 32.6 ff. (attack of the Gothic lancers without regard for or confidence in their own infantry, 8 f., which then of course fails, 16 f., 6,000 Gothic dead, 20, Totila's death 22–28). What an "annihilating battle" meant in barbarian terms cf. chap. 1, n. 133. On the term *djerid* see Roisl, "Totila," 807. As an aside it might be mentioned that Theodoric Strabo also rode up and down in front of his rival's Goths wearing splendid armor—Malchus fr. 15; cf. above, n. 148; likewise one should recall that the "Greutungian Warrior" of the "Battle of the Huns and the Goths" (see chap. 1, n. 74) searched out the enemies in order to consecrate them with his spear to the god of war and hence to destruction. On Totila's kamelaukion cf. Piltz, "Kamelaukion," 19 f., 27, 60, and 80 ff. See above, n. 592.

745. Lippold, "Narses," 884. Stein, *Bas-Empire* 2:609.

746. Lippold, "Narses," 878 f. Stein, *Bas-Empire* 2:604.

747. See above, n. 741.

748. Procopius, *De bello Gothico* IV (VIII) 29.1 f., 31.17, and 32.1.

749. Ibid., 33.6 f., 34.9, and 17.

750. Agathias, *Historiarum praefatio* 31 and I 8.6. Cf. Nagl, "Theia," 1602–1604.

751. Lippold, "Narses," 878 f. Stein, *Bas-Empire* 2:602–604. On the dating problem ibid., 604 n. 1. Cf. Pertusi, "Ordinamenti militari," 648. But Agathias II 2.1 says that the Goths were thinking of making Butilin, the prince of the "Frankish" Alamanni, their king. Cf. Löhlein, *Alpen- und Italienpolitik,* 46 ff., Claude, "Die ostgotischen Königserhebungen," 172 f. For the Goths and other barbarians who owned property in Italy see Durliat, "Le salaire," 69 with n. 258 f.

752. Lippold, "Narses," 884. Stein, *Bas-Empire* 2:609. Agathias II 13.1 ff., the Goths of Compsa had supported the Franks.

753. Agathias I 8.4–6 and 20.1–10.

754. Lippold, "Narses," 882–884. Stein, *Bas-Empire* 2:605–609. Zöllner, *Franken,* 98–101. See L. Schmidt, "Die letzten Ostgoten," 87 ff., who corrects (with Agathias I 1.1) the notion spread by Procopius, *De bello Gothico* IV (VIII) 35.33, that the defeated Goths marched off. For the battle of Capua cf. Pertusi, "Ordinamenti militari," 650 ff. Agathias II 13.1 ff.

List of Abbreviations

BA – *Breviarium Alaricianum*. See Sources

BAR – *British Archaeological Reports*

CC Ser. Lat. – *Corpus christianorum: Series Latina*. Turnhout (Belgium), 1953 ff.

CE – *Codex Euricianus*. See Sources

CFHB – Corpus fontium historiae Byzantinae. Washington, 1967 ff.; Berlin–New York, 1967 ff.; Vienna, 1975 ff.; Rome, 1975 ff.; Brussels, 1975 ff.

CIL – *Corpus inscriptionum Latinarum*. Berlin, 1873 ff.

CSEL – *Corpus scriptorum ecclesiasticorum Latinorum*. Vienna, 1866 ff.

CT – *Codex Theodosianus*. See Sources

FGrH – *Fragmente der griechischen Historiker,* ed. Felix Jacoby. Berlin, Leyden, 1923 ff.

FHG – *Fragmenta historicorum Graecorum*. Ed. C. et Th. Müller. Vols. 4 and 5, Paris, 1883/1885.

fr(s) – fragment(s)

Germ. Abt. – Germanistische Abteilung

GS – Wolfram, "Gotische Studien I–III." See Literature

ill(s). – illustration(s)

Mansi – (ed.) Mansi, Joannes Dominicus. *Sacrorum conciliorum nova et amplissima collectio*. Vols. 1–53. Reprint Graz, 1960.

MGH – *Monumenta Germaniae historica,* 1826 ff.

Migne PG – (ed.) Migne, Jacques Paul. *Patrologia Graeca.* Paris, 1857 ff.

Migne PL – (ed.) Migne, Jacques Paul. *Patrologia Latina.* Paris, 1844 ff.

MIÖG – *Mitteilungen des Instituts für Österreichische Geschichtsforschung.* Vienna, 1880 ff.

MIÖG suppl. vols. – *Mitteilungen des Instituts für Österreichische Geschichtsforschung. Ergänzungsbände.* Vienna, 1885 ff.

n.s. – nova series. Neue Folge

PG – See Migne PG

PL – See Migne PL

Phil.-hist. Kl. – Philosophisch-historische Klasse

Philolog.-hist. Kl. – Philologisch-historische Klasse

RE – *Realencyclopädie der classischen Altertumswissenschaften.* Stuttgart, Munich, 1893 ff.

SHA – *Scriptores historiae Augustae:* See Sources.

Bibliography

Sources

Agathias of Myrina. *Historiarum libri V.* Edited by Rudolf Keydell. CFHB 2. 1967.

Agnellus qui et Andreas. *Liber pontificalis ecclesiae Ravennatis.* Edited by Oswald Holder-Egger. MGH Scriptores rerum Langobardicarum, 265 ff. 1878. Or: *Excerpta.* Edited by Theodor Mommsen. MGH Auctores antiquissimi 9:273 ff. 1892.

Ambrose. *De spiritu sancto libri III.* Edited by Otto Faller. CSEL 79. 1964.

————. *Epistulae* nn. 1–35. Edited by Otto Faller. CSEL 82, 1. 1968. *Epistulae* nn. 70–77. *Epistulae extra collectionem* nn. 1–15. Edited by Michaela Zelzer. CSEL 82, 3. 1982.

————. *Expositio in Lucam.* Edited by M. Adriaen. CC Ser. Lat. 14. 1957.

Ps. Ambrose. *De trinitate.* Migne, PL 17:537 ff. 1889.

Ammianus Marcellinus. *Rerum gestarum libri XXXI.* Edited by Wolfgang Seyfarth. Vols. 1 and 2. Leipzig, 1978.

Anagnosticum regis (*Acta synhodorum habitarum Romae* 14); see Cassiodorus, *Variae,* p. 425 f.

Anecdoton Holderii. Edited by Hermann Usener. Bonn, 1877.

Anonymus Valesianus. *Pars prior* (I). Edited by Theodor Mommsen. MGH Auctores antiquissimi 9:1–11. 1892.

————. *Pars posterior* (II). Edited by Theodor Mommsen. MGH Auctores antiquissimi 9:314 ff. 1892. Or: *Excerpta Valesiana.* Edited by Jacques Moreau and Velizar Velkov. Leipzig, 1968.

Anthologia Latina. Edited by Alexander Riese. Vol. 1. Leipzig, 1894.

Auctarium Havniense. See *Consularia Italica.*

Auctoritas Alarici regis. See *Lex Romana Visigothorum.*

Augustine. *De civitate Dei libri XXII.* Edited by Bernhard Dombart and Alphons Kalb. CC Ser. Lat. 47 and 48. 5th ed. 1981.

———. *Epistolae nuper in lucem prolatae.* Edited by Johannes Divjak. CSEL 88. 1978.

———. *Sermo* CV. Migne, PL 38:618–625. 1841.

Ausonius. *Epistolae.* Edited by Karl Schenkl. MGH Auctores antiquissimi 5, 2. 1883.

Auxentius. In *Dissertatio Maximini contra Ambrosium* 41–73. Edited by Friedrich Kaufmann. *Aus der Schule des Wulfila,* 73–77. Strasbourg, 1899. Or: *Bible, the Gothic,* 1:xiv–xix.

Avellana. *Collectio, Epistulae imperatorum, pontificum, aliorum: 376–553.* Edited by Otto Guenther. CSEL 35, 1 and 2. 1895/1898.

Avitus of Vienne. *Epistulae.* Edited by Rudolf Peiper. MGH Auctores antiquissimi 6, 2:29 ff. 1883.

Basil the Great. *Epistola* 164. Migne, PG 32:634 ff.

Bede, the Venerable. *Chronica.* Edited by Theodor Mommsen. MGH Auctores antiquissimi 13:223 ff. 1898.

Bible, the Gothic. Edited by Wilhelm Streitberg. Vols. 1 and 2. 6th ed. Darmstadt, 1971.

Boethius. *De consolatione philosophiae.* Edited by Wilhelm Weinberger. CSEL 67. 1934.

Breviarium Alaricianum. See *Lex Romana Visigothorum.*

Caesar. *De bello Gallico libri VII.* Edited by Otto Seel, *C. Iulii Caesaris commentarii.* Vol. 1. 1961.

Pseudo-Caesarius of Nazianus. *Dialogi IV.* Migne, PG 38:851 ff.

Candidus Isaurus. *Historiarum fragmenta.* In FHG 4:135 ff.

Cassiodorus. *Chronica.* Edited by Theodor Mommsen. MGH Auctores antiquissimi 11:109 ff. 1894.

———. *Historia ecclesiastica tripartita.* Edited by Rudolf Hanslik. CSEL 71. 1952.

———. *Orationum reliquiae.* Edited by Ludwig Traube. MGH Auctores antiquissimi 12:457 ff. 1894.

———. *Variae epistolae.* Edited by Theodor Mommsen. MGH Auctores antiquissimi 12. 1894. Or: Edited by Åke J. Fridh. CC Ser. Lat. 96. 1973.

Cassius Dio. *Historia Romana.* Edited by U. P. Boissevain. 2d ed. Berlin, 1969.

Chronica Caesaraugustana. Edited by Theodor Mommsen. MGH Auctores antiquissimi 11:221 ff. 1894.

Chronica Gallica. Edited by Theodor Mommsen. MGH Auctores antiquissimi 9:615 ff. 1892.

Chronicon paschale aa. 395–469. See Marcellinus Comes.

Claudius Claudianus. *Carmina.* Edited by Theodor Birt. MGH Auctores antiquissimi 10. 1892.

    De bello Gothico, 259 ff.

    De IV consulatu Honorii, 150 ff.

    De VI consulatu Honorii, 234 ff.

    De consulatu Stilichonis liber I, 189 ff.

    Epithalamium Palladii (carm. XXV), 301 ff.

    In Eutropium liber II, 96 ff.

    In Rufinum libri I et II, 17 ff.

Claudius Marius Victor. *Alethia*. Edited by Karl Schenkl. CSEL 16, 1:335 ff. 1888.

Codex Euricianus. Edited by Alvaro d'Ors. *Estudios Visigóticos II*. Cuadernos del Instituto Juridico Español 12. Rome, Madrid, 1960.

Codex Iustinianus. See *Corpus iuris civilis* 2.

Codex Theodosianus. Edited by Theodor Mommsen. Reprint of the 2d ed. Vol. 1. Berlin, 1954.

Collectio Avellana. See *Avellana*.

Concilios Visigóticos. Edited by José Vives. *España Cristiana*. Vol. 1. Barcelona, Madrid, 1963.

Concilium Agathense (Agde). Edited by C. Munier. *Conciliae Galliae I, 314–506*. CC Ser. Lat. 148 A:189 ff. 1963.

Concilium Narbonense. Edited by Carl de Clercq. *Concilia Galliae II, 511–695*. CC Ser. Lat. 148 A:253 ff. 1963.

Concilium Toletanum III. See *Concilios Visigóticos* no. 12.

Concilium Toletanum XII. See *Concilios Visigóticos* no. 31 or *Leges Visigothorum*, 475 ff.

Concilium Toletanum XVII. See *Concilios Visigóticos* no. 37 or *Leges Visigothorum*, 484 ff.

Consensus de fisco Barcinonensi. Edited by Mansi. 10:473 f.

Constantinus Porphyrogenitus. *De administrando imperio*. Edited by Gyula Moravcsik and translated by Rouilly J. H. Jenkins. CFHB 1, 1 and 2. 1949/1962.

———. *De thematibus Orientis*. Migne, PG 113:63 ff. 1864.

Consularia Constantinopolitana. Edited by Theodor Mommsen. MGH Auctores antiquissimi 9:197 ff. 1892.

Consularia Italica. Edited by Theodor Mommsen. MGH Auctores antiquissimi 9:249 ff. 1892.

Continuatio Prosperi Havniensis. Edited by Theodor Mommsen. MGH Auctores antiquissimi 9:266 ff. 1892.

Continuator Marcellini. Edited by Theodor Mommsen. MGH Auctores antiquissimi 11:104 ff. 1894.

Corpus iuris civilis. Edited by Paul Krüger and Theodor Mommsen. Vol. 1, Berlin, 1902; vol. 2, Berlin, 1900.

Damascius. *Vitae Isidoris reliquiae*. Edited by Clemens Zintzen. Hildesheim, 1967.

Dexippus. *Chronica*. FGrH II A. 1926.

———. *Scythica*. FGrH II A. 1926.

Digesta. See *Corpus iuris civilis*.

Dion Chrysostomus. *Quae exstant omnia*. Edited by Johann von Arnim. 2:IV–IX. Berlin, 1896.

Edictum Theoderici. Edited by Friedrich Bluhme. MGH Leges 5:145 ff. 1868.

Ennodius. *Opera*. Edited by Friedrich Vogel. MGH Auctores antiquissimi 7. 1885.

———. 355. *Carmina* 2, 136, p. 256 f.

———. 281. *Epistulae* 6, 14, p. 222.

———. *Panegyricus dictus Theoderico regi*, 203 ff.

———. *Vita Epifani*, 84 ff.

Epiphanius. *Adversus haereses*. Edited by Karl Holl. *Die griechischen christlichen Schriftsteller der ersten drei Jahrhunderte* 37. Leipzig, 1933.

Epistolae Arelatenses genuinae. Edited by Wilhelm Gundlach. MGH Epistolae 3:1 ff. 1892.

Epistolae Austrasicae. Edited by Wilhelm Gundlach. MGH Epistolae 3:110 ff. 1892.

Epistulae Theodericianae. Edited by Theodor Mommsen. MGH Auctores antiquissimi 12:387 ff. 1894.

Eugippius. *Vita s. Severini.* Edited by Theodor Mommsen. MGH Scriptores rerum Germanicarum, 1898. Edited by Pius Knoell. CSEL 9, 2. 1886. Edited by Hermann Sauppe. MGH Auctores antiquissimi 1, 2, 1877.

Eunapius. *Historiarum fragmenta.* In FHG 4:7 ff. 1885.

Eustathius. *Historiarum fragmenta.* In FHG 4:138 ff. 1885.

Eutropius. *Breviarium ab urbe condita.* Edited by Hermann Droysen. MGH Auctores antiquissimi 2:8 ff. 1879.

Excerpta Valesiana. See Anonymus Valesianus.

Fasti Vindobonenses priores. Edited by Theodor Mommsen. MGH Auctores antiquissimi 9:274 ff. 1892.

Ferrandus. *Vita s. Fulgentii.* Edited and translated by G. G. Lapeyre. Paris, 1929.

Formulae Visigothicae. Edited by Karl Zeumer. MGH Formulae, 572 ff. 1886.

Fragmente der griechischen Historiker. Edited by Felix Jacoby. Vol. II A. 1926.

Fragmenta Historicorum Graecorum. Edited by Karl Müller. Vols. 4 and 5, Paris 1885 and 1883. Note: The FHG were used in preference to other, more modern editions (see Hunger, *Die hochsprachliche profane Literatur* 1:279 ff.) because they add Latin translations to the sometimes difficult texts, which probably makes them more useful for many readers of this book.

Fredegar. *Chronicon.* Edited by Bruno Krusch. MGH Scriptores rerum Merovingicarum 2. 1888.

Generatio regum Francorum. Edited by Bruno Krusch and Wilhelm Levison. MGH Scriptores rerum Merovingicarum 7:851. 1920.

Generatio regum Romanorum. MGH Scriptores rerum Merovingicarum 7:854. 1920.

Georgios Synkellos. *Chronographia.* Edited by Ludwig Dindorf. Vols. 1 and 2. Berlin, 1829.

Gregorios Thaumaturgos. *Epistola canonica.* Migne PG 10:1019–1048. Or: Johannes Dräseke. „Der kanonische Brief des Gregorios von Neocäsarea," *Jahrbücher für protestantische Theologie* 7:730 ff. 1881.

Gregory the Great. *Dialogi.* Edited by Umberto Moricca. Fonti per la storia d'Italia 57. 1924.

Gregory of Tours. *Historia Francorum.* Edited by Bruno Krusch and Wilhelm Levison. MGH Scriptores rerum Merovingicarum 1, 1. 2d ed. 1951.

———. *Liber de passione et virtutibus s. Iuliani martyris.* Edited by Bruno Krusch. MGH Scriptores rerum Merovingicarum 1, 2:562 ff. 1885, repr. 1969.

———. *Liber in gloria martyrum,* 484 ff.

———. *Liber in gloria confessorum,* 744 ff.

———. *Liber vitae patrum,* 661 ff.

———. *Miraculorum libri VIII,* 451 ff.

———. *De virtutibus s. Martini libri IV,* 584 ff.

Gulathing. See *Norwegisches Recht.*

Heliodorus. *Aethiopica.* Edited by R. M. Rattenbury and T. W. Lumb. Paris, 1960.

Herodotus. *Historiae.* Edited by Carolus Hude. 3d ed. 2 vols. Oxford, 1960.

Hervarar Saga. Edited by Gabriel Turville-Peter; with an introduction by Christopher Tolkien. Viking Society for Northern Research: University College, London, 1956.

Homer. *Iliad*. Edited by M. M. Willcock. London, 1978.

Hydatius Lemicus. *Continuatio chronicorum Hieronymianorum*. Edited by Theodor Mommsen. MGH Auctores antiquissimi 11:1 ff. 1894. Or: *Sources chrétiennes* 218/219. Edited by Alain Tranoy. Paris, 1974. On this see Thompson, "Roman Spain," 4:19 ff.

Collections of Inscriptions

Otto Fiebiger-Ludwig Schmidt. *Inschriftensammlung zur Geschichte der Ostgermanen*. Denkschriften der Österreichischen Akademie der Wissenschaften in Wien, Phil.-hist. Kl. 60, 3. 1917.

Otto Fiebiger. *Inschriftensammlung zur Geschichte der Ostgermanen: Neue Folge*. Denkschriften der Österreichischen Akademie der Wissenschaften in Wien, Phil.-hist. Kl. 70, 3. 1939.

———. *Inschriftensammlung zur Geschichte der Ostgermanen: Zweite Folge*. Denkschriften der Österreichischen Akademie der Wissenschaften in Wien, Phil.-hist. Kl. 72, 2. 1944.

Vives, José. *Inscripciones cristianas de la España romana visigóda*. Barcelona, 1941/ 1942. 2d ed. Barcelona, 1969.

Ioannes. Lyolus. *On Powers or The Magistracies of the Roman State*. Edited and translated by Anastasius C. Baudy. Philadelphia: American Philosophical Society, 1983.

Ioannis Antiochenus. *Historiae fragmenta*. In FHG 4:538 ff. and 5:27 ff.

Ioannis Malalas. See Malalas.

Isidore of Seville. *Etymologiarum sive originum libri XX*. Edited by Wallace Martin Lindsay. Vols. 1 and 2. 1911.

———. *Historia vel Origo Gothorum*. Edited by Theodor Mommsen. MGH Auctores antiquissimi 11:267 ff. 1894.

———. *Institutionum disciplinae*. Edited by A. E. Anspach. *Rheinisches Museum für Philologie* n.s. 67:557 ff. 1912.

Jerome. *Apologia adversus libros Rufini libri III*. Migne, PL 23:415 ff. 1883. Or: Edited by P. Lardet. CC Ser. Lat. 79. 1982.

———. *Chronicon*. Edited by R. Helm. 2d ed. 1956.

———. *Commentariorum in Ezechielem prophetam libri XIV*. Migne, PL 25:15– 512. 1884.

———. *Epistula* 60. Edited by Isidor Hilberg. CSEL 54:548 ff. 1910.

———. *Epistula* 77. Edited by Isidor Hilberg. CSEL 55: 37 ff. 1912.

———. *Epistulae* 106. Edited by Isidor Hilberg. CSEL 55: 247 ff. 1912.

———. *Liber interpretationis Hebraicorum nominum*. Edited by Paul de Lagarde. CC Ser. Lat. 72, 1. 1969.

John Chrysostom. *Epistolae*. Migne, PG 52:549 ff.

Jordanes. *Romana*. Edited by Theodor Mommsen. MGH Auctores antiquissimi 5, 1:1 ff. 1882.

———. *Getica*. Ibid., 53 ff.

Josephus Flavius. *Antiquitates Iudaicae*. Edited by H. St. J. Thackeray. 6 vols. London, 1966–1977.

M. Junianus Justinus. *Epitoma historiarum Philippicarum Pompei Trogi.* Edited by Otto Seel. Stuttgart, 1972.

Lactantius. *De mortibus persecutorum.* Edited by Samuel Brandt. CSEL 27, 2. 1897.

Laterculus Polemii Silvii. See *Notitia dignitatum,* 254 ff.

Laterculus regum Visigothorum. Edited by Theodor Mommsen. MGH Auctores antiquissimi 13:461 ff. 1898.

Laterculus Veronensis. See *Notitia dignitatum,* 247 ff.

Leges Burgundionum. Edited by Ludwig Rudolf Salis. MGH Leges nationum Germanicarum 2, 1. 1892.

Leges Visigothorum. Edited by Karl Zeumer. MGH Leges nationum Germanicarum 1. 1902.

Lex Romana Visigothorum. Edited by Gustav Haenel. 1849. Reprint, Aalen, 1962.

Liber pontificalis. Edited by Louis Duchesne. Vol. 1. Paris, 1886.

Liberatus. *Breviarium.* Migne, PL 68: 963 ff. 1866.

M. Annaeus Lucanus. *Pharsalia: Belli civilis libri X.* Edited by Alfred Edward Housman. 3d ed. Oxford, 1950.

Malalas, Ioannis. *Chronographia.* Edited by Ludwig Dindorf. Bonn, 1831.

Malchus. *Byzantinae historiae librorum VII fragmenta.* In FHG 4:112 ff.

Marcellinus Comes. *Chronicon.* Edited by Theodor Mommsen. MGH Auctores antiquissimi 11:37 ff. 1894.

Marius of Avenches. *Chronica.* Edited by Theodor Mommsen. MGH Auctores antiquissimi 11:232 ff. 1894.

(Maximinus). *Contra Paganos.* Edited by A. Spagnolo and C. H. Turner. *The Journal of Theological Studies* 17:321 ff. 1916.

Mela Pomponius. *De chorographia libri III.* Edited by Gunnar Ranstrand. Göteborg, 1971.

Menandros Protector. *Historia.* FHG 4:201 ff.

Merobaudes. *Carmina.* Edited by Friedrich Vollmer. MGH Auctores antiquissimi 14:1 ff. 1905.

Namatianus, Claudius Rutilius. *De reditu suo sive iter Gallicum libri II.* Edited by Ernst Doblhofer. Vol. 1. Heidelberg, 1972.

Norwegisches Recht: Das Rechtsbuch des Gulathing. Translated by Rudolf Meissner. *Germanenrechte* 6. 1935.

Notitia dignitatum. Edited by Otto Seeck. Berlin, 1867.

Notitia Galliarum. See *Notitia dignitatum,* pp. 261 ff.

Novellae Valentiniani IX. Edited by Paul M. Meyer. *Leges Novellae ad Theodosianum pertinentes: Codex Theodosianus.* Reprint of 2d ed. Vol. 2. Berlin, 1954.

Olympiodorus of Thebes. *Historiarum librorum XXII fragmenta.* In FHG 4:58 ff.

Origo Gothica. See Jordanes, *Getica.*

Orosius. *Historiarum adversum paganos libri VII.* Edited by Karl Zangemeister. 1889.

XII Panegyrici Latini. Edited by R. A. B. Mynors. Oxford, 1964.

Passio sancti Sabae Gothi. Edited by Hippolyte Delehaye. *Analecta Bollandiana* 31:216 ff. Paris, 1912.

Passio sancti Sigismundi regis. Edited by Bruno Krusch. MGH Scriptores rerum Merovingicarum 2:329 ff. 1888.

Passio sanctorum Innae, Rhimae et Pinae. Edited by Hippolyte Delehaye. *Analecta Bollandiana* 31:215 f. Paris, 1912.

Paulinus of Pella. *Eucharisticos.* Edited by Wilhelm Brandes. CSEL 16:291 ff. 1888.

Paulinus of Périgueux. *De vita Martini libri VI.* Edited by Michael Petschenig. CSEL 16:1 ff. 1888.

Paulinus of Nola. *Carmina.* CSEL 30. 1894

————. *Epistulae.* Edited by Wilhelm Hartel. CSEL 29. 1894.

Paulus Diaconus. *Historia Langobardorum.* Edited by Ludwig Bethmann and Georg Waitz. MGH Scriptores rerum Langobardicarum, 12 ff. 1878.

————. *Historia Romana XI–XVI.* Edited by Hermann Droysen. MGH Auctores antiquissimi 2:183 ff. 1879.

Petrus Patricius. *Historiarum fragmenta.* In FHG 4:184 ff.

Philostorgius. *Historia ecclesiastica.* Edited by Joseph Bidez and Friedhelm Winkelmann. *Die griechischen christlichen Schriftsteller der ersten Jahrhunderte 5.* 2d ed. 1972.

Pliny the Elder. *Historiae naturalis libri XXXVII.* Edited by H. Rackham. Vols. 1–9. Cambridge, Mass., 1949–1952.

Pomponius Mela. See Mela.

Possidius. *Vita s. Augustini.* Edited by Michele Pelegritto. Alba, 1955.

Priscus. *Historiae Byzantinae librorum VIII fragmenta.* In FHG 4:71 ff.

Procopius. *Prokop: Werke.* Vols. 1–5. Edited by Otto Veh.

    De aedificiis. Vol. 5. 1977.

    Anecdota. Vol. 1. 2d ed. 1970.

    De bellis libri VIII. Vols. 2–4. 1966, 1970, 1971.

    De bello Persico I–II.

    De bello Vandalico I–II (III–IV).

    De bello Gothico I–IV (V–VIII).

Prosper Tiro. *Epitoma Chronicon.* Edited by Theodor Mommsen. MGH Auctores antiquissimi 9:341 ff. 1892.

Prosperi continuatio Havniensis. See *Continuatio Prosperi Havniensis.*

Prudentius. *Contra Symmachum libri II.* In Aurelius Prudentius Clemens. *Carmina.* Edited by Maurice P. Cunningham. CC Ser. Lat. 126:182 ff. 1966.

Ptolemy. *Geographica.* Edited by C. F. A. Nobbe. Hildesheim, 1966. Reprint of 1843–1845.

Pytheas Massiliensis. *De Oceano: Pytheas, Fragment.* Edited by Hans Joachim Mette. Berlin, 1952.

Res gestae Divi Saporis. Edited by André Marico. *Syria* 35:295 ff. 1958.

Rufinus. *Eusebii historia ecclesiastica translata et continuata.* Edited by Theodor Mommsen. *Die griechischen christlichen Schriftsteller der ersten Jahrhunderte: Eusebius.* Vol. 2, pt. 1.2. 1903/1908.

Ruricius of Limoges. *Epistulae.* Edited by Bruno Krusch. MGH Auctores antiquissimi 8:299 ff. 1887. Or: Edited by August Engelbrecht. CSEL 21:350 ff. 1891.

Rutilius Namatianus. See Namatianus, Claudius Rutilius.

Salvianus of Marseille. *De gubernatione Dei.* Edited by Karl Halm. MGH Auctores antiquissimi 1. 1877.

Sanctio pragmatica pro petitione Vigilii, chaps. 1–27. Edited by Rudolf Schoell and

Wilhelm Kroll, *Novellae: Appendix constitutionum dispersarum: Corpus iuris civilis* 3:799–802. 1899.

Saxo Grammaticus. *Gesta Danorum.* Edited by J. Olrik and H. Raeder. 2d ed. Vol. 1. Copenhagen, 1931.

Scriptores Historiae Augustae. Edited by Ernst Hohl, Ch. Samberger, and W. Seyfarth. Vols. 1 and 2. Leipzig, 1971.
    20 (Gord.)
    23 (Gall.)
    25 (Claud.)
    26 (Aurel.)
    29 (Firmus)

Servius. *In Vergilii Bucolica et Georgica commentarii.* Edited by Georg Thilo. Leipzig, 1887.

Sidonius Apollinaris. *Carmina.* Edited by Christian Luetjohann. MGH Auctores antiquissimi 8:173 ff. 1887.

———. *Epistulae.* Edited by Christian Luetjohann. MGH Auctores antiquissimi 8:1 ff. 1887.

Sisebut. *De libro rotarum.* Edited by Jacques Fontaine. Paris, 1960.

Snorri Sturluson, *Heimskringla.* Pt. 1: *The Olaf Sagas.* 2 vols. Translated by Samuel Laing. Revised with an introduction and notes by Jacqueline Simpson. London, New York, 1964. Pt. 2: *Sagas of the Norse Kings.* Translated by Samuel Laing. Revised with introduction and notes by Peter Foote. London, New York, 1961.

Socrates. *Historia ecclesiastica.* Migne, PG 67:30 ff. 1859.

Solinus. *Collectanea rerum memorabilium.* Edited by Theodor Mommsen. 2d ed. Berlin, 1895.

Sozomenus. *Historia ecclesiastica.* Edited by Joseph Bidez-Gunther Christian Hansen. *Die griechischen christlichen Schriftsteller der ersten Jahrhunderte* 50. 1960.

Strabo. *Geographica.* Edited by Wolfgang Aly. Vols. 1–4. Bonn, 1957.

Sulpicius Severus. *Chronicon.* Edited by Karl Halm. CSEL 1. 1866.

Synesius of Cyrene. *Epistulae.* Edited by Antonio Garzya. Rome, 1979.

———. *De regno oratio ad Arcadium imperatorem.* Edited and translated by Antonio Garzya. Naples, 1973.

Synkellos, Georgios. See Georgios Synkellos.

Tacitus. *Annalium libri XVI.* Edited by Henry Furneaux. Oxford, 1965.

———. *Germania.* Edited by Michael Winterbottom. Oxford, 1975.

———. *Historiarum libri qui supersunt.* Edited by C. D. Fisher. Oxford, 1911.

Themistius. *Orationes quae supersunt.* Edited by Heinrich Schenkl, Glanville Downey, and Albert Francis Norman. Leipzig, 1965–1974.

Theodoret. *Historia ecclesiastica.* Edited by León Parmentier. Revised by F. Scheidweiler. *Die griechischen christlichen Schriftsteller der ersten Jahrhunderte* 44. 2d ed. Berlin, 1954.

Theophanes Homologetes (Confessor). *Chronographia.* Edited by Carl de Boor. Vols. 1 and 2. Leipzig, 1883/1885.

Flavius Vegetius Renatus. *Epitomae rei militaris libri IV.* Edited by Karl Lang, 2d ed. Leipzig, 1885.

Victor of Vita. *Historia persecutionis Africanae provinciae.* Edited by Karl Halm. MGH Auctores antiquissimi 3:1 ff. 1879.

Vita Orientii. In *Acta Sanctorum,* Mai I: 60 ff. Antwerp, 1680.

Vita sancti Bibiani. Edited by Bruno Krusch. MGH Scriptores rerum Merovingicarum 3:92 ff. 1896.

Vita Vulframni episcopi Senonici. Edited by Bruno Krusch and Wilhelm Levison. MGH Scriptores rerum Merovingicarum 5:657 ff. 1910.

Vita Willibaldi episcopi Eichstettensis. Edited by Oswald Holder-Egger. MGH Scriptores 15, 1:80 ff. 1867.

Vitae Caesarii episcopi Arelatensis libri II. Edited by Bruno Krusch. MGH Scriptores rerum Merovingicarum 3:433 ff. 1896.

Walahfrid Strabo. *Libellus de exordiis et incrementis rerum ecclesiasticarum.* Edited by Alfred Boretius and Viktor Krause. MGH Capitularia regum Francorum 2:471 ff. 1897.

———. *Vita s. Galli.* Edited by Bruno Krusch. MGH Scriptores rerum Merovingicarum 4:280 ff. 1902.

Widsith. See R. W. Chambers (Literature).

Zosimus. *Historia Nova.* Edited by Ludwig Mendelssohn. 1887. Or: *Zosime.* Histoire Nouvelle. Edited and translated by François Paschoud. Vols. 1 and 2. Paris, 1971 and 1979.

Literature

Albert, Gerhard. *Goten in Konstantinopel: Untersuchungen zur oströmischen Geschichte um das Jahr 400 n. Chr.* Studien zur Geschichte und Kultur des Altertums, n.s. I 2. 1984.

Alföldi, Andreas. "Epigraphica." *Archaeologiai Értesitö,* n.s. 52:101–103. 1939.

———. "Nachahmungen römischer Goldmedaillons als germanischer Halsschmuck." *Numizmatikai Közlöny* 28/29:10 ff. 1929/1930.

———. *Studien zur Geschichte der Weltkrise des dritten Jahrhunderts nach Christus.* Darmstadt, 1967.

———. *Der Untergang der Römerherrschaft in Pannonien.* Ungarische Bibliothek 12. 1926.

Altheim, Franz. *Geschichte der Hunnen.* 2d ed. Vol. 1, 1959; vol. 2, 1969; vol. 3, 1961; vol. 4, 1975; vol. 5, Berlin, 1962.

Alzinger, Wilhelm. "Das Municipium Claudium Aguntum." *Aufstieg und Niedergang der römischen Welt: Principat* II 6:380–413. Berlin, 1977.

Ambroz, A. K. "Danubian Elements in the Early Medieval Culture of the Crimea (sixth to eighth centuries)," *Kratkie soobščenija* 113:10–23. 1968. (In Russian).

Bach, Adolf. *Deutsche Namenkunde.* Vol. 1, pt. 1, 1952; vol. 2, pt. 1, 1953; vol. 2, pt. 2, Heidelberg, 1954.

Bachrach, Bernard S[tanley]. *A History of the Alans in the West.* Minneapolis: University of Minnesota Press, 1973.

Bailey, H. W. "A Parthian Reference to the Goths." *English and Germanic Studies* 7:82 f. 1961.

Barral i Altet, Xavier. *La circulation des monnaies suèves et visigotiques. Contribution à l'histoire économique du royaume visigot.* Avec une préface de Jean Lafaurie Beihefte der Francia 4. Munich, 1976.

Barton, Peter F. *Die Frühzeit des Christentums in Österreich und Südostmitteleuropa bis 788.* Studien und Texte zur Kirchengeschichte und Geschichte 1, 1. Vienna, 1975.

Battisti, Carlo. "L'elemento gotico nella toponomastica e nel lessico italiano." *Settimane di studio del Centro italiano di studi sull'alto medioevo* 3:621 ff. Spoleto, 1956.

Beck, Hans-Georg. "Die frühbyzantinische Kirche." *Handbuch der Kirchengeschichte* 2:1 ff. Freiburg, Basle, Vienna, 1975.

Beck, Heinrich, and Nehlsen, Hermann. "belagines." *Reallexikon der germanischen Altertumskunde* 2:205–207. 2d ed. 1976.

Behr, Bruno. *Das alemannische Herzogtum bis 750.* Geist und Werk der Zeiten 41. 1975.

Beninger, Eduard. *Der westgotisch-alanische Zug nach Mitteleuropa.* Mannus-Bibliothek 51. 1931.

Benjamin. "Erelieva." RE 11:412. 1907.

———. "Gundobadus." RE 14:1938–1940. 1912.

Berges, Wilhelm, and Gauert, Adolf. "Die eiserne 'Standarte' und das steinerne 'Szepter' aus dem Grabe eines angelsächsischen Königs bei Sutton Hoo (um 650–60)." In: Percy Ernst Schramm, *Herrschaftszeichen und Staatssymbolik.* Schriften der MGH 13, 1:238 ff. Stuttgart, 1954.

Beumann, Helmut. "Zur Entwicklung transpersonaler Staatsvorstellungen." *Wissenschaft vom Mittelalter. Ausgewählte Aufsätze,* 135 ff. Cologne, Vienna, 1972. Or: *Vorträge und Forschungen* 3:185 ff. 4th reprint. 1973.

Beyerle, Franz. "Die Frühgeschichte der westgotischen Gesetzgebung." *Zeitschrift für Rechtsgeschichte: Germ. Abt.* 67:1 ff. 1950.

Bichir, Gheorghe. *The Archaeology and History of the Carpi.* British Archaeological Reports, suppl. series 16. Oxford, 1976.

Bickerman, Elias J. "Origines gentium." *Classical Philology* 47:65 ff. 1952.

Bierbrauer, Volker. "Alamannische Funde der frühen Ostgotenzeit aus Oberitalien." *Festschrift für Joachim Werner* 2:559 ff. Munich, 1974.

———. "Zur chronologischen, soziologischen und regionalen Gliederung des ostgermanischen Fundstoffs des 5. Jahrhunderts in Südosteuropa." *Denkschriften der Österreichischen Akademie der Wissenschaften in Wien, Phil.-hist. Kl.* 145:131 ff. 1980.

———. "Frühgeschichtliche Akkulturationsprozesse in den germanischen Staaten am Mittelmeer (Westgoten, Ostgoten, Langobarden) aus der Sicht des Archäologen." *Atti del 6° congresso internazionale di studi sull'alto medioevo,* 89 ff. Spoleto, 1980.

———. *Die ostgotischen Grab- und Schatzfunde in Italien.* Biblioteca degli studi medievali 7. Spoleto, 1975.

———. "Zu den Vorkommen ostgotischer Bügelfibeln in Raetia II." *Bayerische Vorgeschichtsblätter* 36:131 ff. 1971.

Birkhan, Helmut. "Altgermanistische Miszellen 'aus funfzehen zettelkästen gezogen.'" *Festgabe für Otto Höfler,* 19 f. Vienna, 1976.

———. "Beizjagd." *Reallexikon der germanischen Altertumskunde* 1:171–173. 2d ed. 1976.

———. *Germanen und Kelten bis zum Ausgang der Römerzeit.* Sitzungsberichte der Österreichischen Akademie der Wissenschaften in Wien, Phil.-hist. Kl. 272. 1970.

———. Review of Piergiuseppe Scardigli, *Die Goten: Sprache und Kultur. Beiträge zur Geschichte der deutschen Sprache und Literatur* 96:339 ff. 1974.

Bodmer, Jean-Pierre. *Der Krieger der Merowingerzeit und seine Welt.* Geist und Werk der Zeiten 2. 1957.

Bodor, Andrei. "Emperor Aurelian and the Abandonment of Dacia." *Dacoromania* 1:29 ff. 1973.

Böhme, Wolfgang H. *Germanische Grabfunde des vierten und fünften Jahrhunderts zwischen unterer Elbe und Loire.* Münchner Beiträge zur Vor- und Frühgeschichte 19. 1974.

Bóna, István. *Der Anbruch des Mittelalters.* Budapest, 1976.

———. "Bemerkungen zur historisch-archäologischen Bearbeitung der Visigotenzeit." *Acta Archaeologica Academiae Scientiarum Hungaricae* 33:363 ff. 1981.

Bonfante, Giuliano. *Latini e Germani in Italia.* Studi grammaticali e linguistici 6. Brescia, 1965.

Bonnassié, Pierre. *La Catalogne du milieu du dixième à la fin du onzième siècle.* Vols. 1 and 2. Toulouse, 1975–1976.

Bornscheuer, Lothar. *Miseriae regum.* Arbeiten zur Frühmittelalterforschung 4. 1968.

Brandis, Carl Georg. "Danuvius." RE 4/2:2103 ff. 1901.

Bremer, Otto. *Ethnographie der germanischen Stämme.* Strasbourg, 1904.

Breschi, Maria Grazia. *La cattedrale ed il battistero degli ariani a Ravenna.* Ravenna, 1965.

Broëns, M. "Le peuplement germanique de la Gaule entre la Méditerranée et l'Océan." *Annales du Midi* 68:17 ff. 1956.

Bruck, Eberhard F. *Caesarius von Arles und die Lex Romana Visigothorum: Über Römisches Recht.* Berlin, 1954.

Brühl, Carlrichard. *Palatium und Civitas.* Vol. 1, Cologne, 1975.

Brunner, Karl. "Der fränkische Fürstentitel im neunten und zehnten Jahrhundert." *Mitteilungen des Instituts für österreichische Geschichtsforschung,* suppl. vol. 24:179 ff. Vienna, 1973.

———. *Oppositionelle Gruppen im Karolingerreich.* Veröffentlichungen des Instituts für österreichische Geschichtsforschung 24. Vienna, 1979.

Brunner, Otto. *Land und Herrschaft.* Reprint of 5th ed. Darmstadt, 1973.

Bruun, Patrick M. *Roman Imperial Coinage.* Vol. 7. London, 1966.

Buchner, Rudolf. *Die Provence in merowingischer Zeit.* Arbeiten zur deutschen Rechts- und Verfassungsgeschichte 9. 1933.

———. *Die Rechtsquellen.* Deutschlands Geschichtsquellen im Mittelalter, Beiheft. 1953.

Büttner, Heinrich. "Studien zum frühmittelalterlichen Städtewesen in Frankreich, vornehmlich im Loire- und Rhonegebiet." *Vorträge und Forschungen* 4:151 ff. 1958.

Bund, Konrad. *Thronsturz und Herrscherabsetzung im Frühmittelalter.* Bonner Historische Forschungen 44. 1979.

Burkitt, Francis Crawford. *Euphemia and the Goth.* London, 1913.

Burns, Thomas S. "The Battle of Adrianople: A Reconsideration." *Historia* 22:336 ff. 1973.

———. *A History of the Ostrogoths*. Bloomington: Indiana University Press, 1984.

———. *The Ostrogoths: Kingship and Society*. Historia Einzelschriften 36. Wiesbaden, 1980.

Cameron, Alan. *Claudian: Poetry and Propaganda at the Court of Honorius*. Oxford, 1970.

Camus, Pierre-Marie. *Ammien Marcellin*. Paris, 1967.

Capelle, Wilhelm. *Das alte Germanien. Die Nachrichten der griechischen und römischen Schriftsteller*. Stuttgart, 1929.

———. *Die Germanen der Völkerwanderung*. Kröners Taschenbuchausgabe 17. Stuttgart, 1940.

Castritius, Helmut. "Die Grenzverteidigung in Rätien und Noricum im 5. Jahrhundert n. Chr. Ein Beitrag zum Ende der Antike." *Denkschriften der Österreichischen Akademie der Wissenschaften in Wien, Phil.-hist. Kl.* 179:17 ff. 1985.

Cesa, Maria. "La politica di Giustiniano verso l'occidente nel giudizio di Procopio." *Athenaeum, studi periodici di letteratura e storia dell'antichità*, n.s. 59:389 ff. Pavia, 1981.

———. "376–382: Romani e barbari sul Danubio." *Studi urbinati*/B 3. 17:63 ff. Urbino, 1984.

Chambers, R. W. *Widsith: A Study in Old English Heroic Legend*. Cambridge, 1912.

Chastagnol, André. *Le sénat romain sous le règne d'Odoacer*. Antiquitas, pt. 3, no. 3. Bonn, 1966.

Chrysos, Evangelos K. "Die Amaler-Herrschaft in Italien und das Imperium Romanum: Der Vertragsentwurf des Jahres 535." *Byzantion* 51:430 ff. 1981.

———. "Die angebliche Abschaffung der städtischen Kurien durch Kaiser Anastasius." *Byzantina* 3:95 ff. 1971.

———. "Ἀντικαῖσαρ" *Byzance: Hommage à A. N. Stratos* 1:73 ff. Athens, 1986.

———. "Οἱ Βησιγότθοι στὴν Πελοπόννησο (396–7 μ.χ.)" *Πράκτικα* 2:181 ff. 1984.

———. Τὸ Βυζάντιον καὶ οἱ Γότθοι. Thessalonica, 1972.

———. "Gothia Romana: Zur Rechtsgrundlage des Föderatenstandes der Westgoten im vierten Jahrhundert." *Dacoromania* 1:52 ff. 1973.

———. "Der Kaiser und die Könige." *Denkschriften der Österreichischen Akademie der Wissenschaften in Wien, Phil.-hist. Kl.* 145:143 ff. 1980.

———. "Zur Reichsideologie und Westpolitik Justinians: Der Friedensplan des Jahres 540." *From Late Antiquity to Early Byzantium*; 41 ff. Proceedings of the Byzantinological Symposion in the Sixteenth International Eirine Conference. Edited by Vladimír Vavřínek, Prague, 1985.

———. Συμβολὴ στὴν Ἰστορία τῆς Ἠπείρου. Ἠπειρωτικὰ Χρονικά 23. Ioannina, 1981.

———. "The Title *Βασιλεύς* in Early Byzantine International Relations." *Dumbarton Oaks Papers* 32:31 ff. 1978.

Classen, Peter. "Der erste Römerzug in der Weltgeschichte." *Historische Forschungen für Walter Schlesinger*, 325 ff. Cologne, Vienna, 1974.

———. "Fortleben und Wandel spätrömischen Urkundenwesens im frühen Mittelalter." *Vorträge und Forschungen* 23:20 ff. 1977.

———. "Kaiserreskript und Königsurkunde II." *Archiv für Diplomatik* 2:1 ff. 1956.

Claude, Dietrich. *Adel, Kirche und Königtum im Westgotenreich*. Vorträge und Forschungen, Sonderband 8. Sigmaringen, 1971.

———. "Zur Ansiedlung barbarischer Föderaten in der ersten Hälfte des fünften Jahrhunderts." *Denkschriften der Österreichischen Akademie der Wissenschaften in Wien, Phil.-hist. Kl.* 193·13 ff. 1987.

———. "Beiträge zur Geschichte der frühmittelalterlichen Königsschätze." *Early Medieval Studies: Antikvariskt Arkiv* 54:8 f. 1973.

———. "comes." *Reallexikon der germanischen Altertumskunde* 5:65 ff. 2d ed. Berlin, New York, 1984.

———. *Geschichte der Westgoten*. Urban Taschenbücher 128. Stuttgart, 1970.

———. *Der Handel im westlichen Mittelmeer während des Frühmittelalters*. Abhandlungen der Akademie der Wissenschaften in Göttingen, Phil.-hist. Kl. III 144, 1985.

———. "Königs- und Untertaneneid im Westgotenreich." *Historische Forschungen für Walter Schlesinger*, 358 ff. Cologne, Vienna, 1974.

———. "Zur Königserhebung Theoderichs des Grossen." *Festschrift für Heinz Löwe*, 1 ff. Cologne, 1978.

———. "Der millenarius." *Denkschriften der Österreichischen Akademie der Wissenschaften in Wien, Phil.-hist. Kl.* 193:17 ff. 1988.

———. "*Millenarius* und *thiuphadus*." *Zeitschrift für Rechtsgeschichte. Germ. Abt.* 88:181 ff. 1971.

———. "Die ostgotischen Königserhebungen." *Denkschriften der Österreichischen Akademie der Wissenschaften in Wien, Phil.-hist. Kl.* 145:149 ff. 1980.

———. "Probleme der vandalischen Herrschaftsnachfolge." *Deutsches Archiv* 30:329 ff. 1974.

———. "Prosopographie des spanischen Suebenreiches." *Francia* 6:648 ff. Munich, 1978.

———. Review of Burns, *The Ostrogoths. Historische Zeitschrift* 234:158 f. 1982.

———. Review of Goffart: *Barbarians and Romans. Francia* 10:753 f. 1980.

———. *Topographie und Verfassung der Städte Bourges und Poitiers bis in das 11. Jahrhundert*. Historische Studien 380. 1960.

———. "Universale und partikulare Züge in der Politik Theoderichs." *Francia* 6:19 ff. 1978.

Clauss, Manfred. *Der magister officiorum in der Spätantike. 4.–6. Jahrhundert*. Vestigia 32. Munich, 1980.

Clavadetscher, Otto P. "Churrätien im Übergang von der Spätantike zum Mittelalter nach den Schriftquellen." *Vorträge und Forschungen* 25:159 ff. 1979.

Clover, Frank H. "Geiseric and Attila." *Historia* 22:104 ff. 1973.

Cohen, Henri. *Description historique des monnaies frappées sous l'empire romain*. Vol. 8. 2d ed. Paris, 1892.

Cortesi, Giuseppe. *La zona e la basilica di S. Severo nel territorio di Classe*. Ravenna, 1964.

Courcelle, Pierre. *Histoire littéraire des grandes invasions germaniques*. 3d ed. Paris, 1964.

Courtois, Christian. "Les politiques navales de l'empire romain." *Revue historique* 186:227 ff. 1939.

————. *Les Vandales et l'Afrique*. Paris, 1955.

Cracco-Ruggini, Lellia. "Vicende rurali dell'Italia antica dall'età tetrarchica ai Longobardi." *Rivista storica italiana* 76:261 ff. 1964. Cf. Ruggini Lellia.

Csendes, Peter. "König Flaccitheus und die Alpenpässe." *Carinthia* I, 155:289 ff. 1965.

Dagron, G. *L'empire romain d'Orient au IVᵉ siècle et les traditions politiques d'Hellénisme*. Travaux et Mémoires 3. Paris, 1968.

Dahlheim, W. "Aëtius." *Reallexikon der germanischen Altertumskunde* 1:91 f. 2d ed. 1973.

Dahn, Felix. *Die Könige der Germanen*. Vols. 3–5. Reprint, Leipzig, 1883. Vol. 6. 2d ed., Leipzig, 1885.

Dalton, O. M. *The Letters of Sidonius*. 2 vols. Oxford, 1915.

Damerau, Paul. *Kaiser Claudius II. Goticus*. Clio, Beiheft 33. Leipzig, 1934.

Danov, Chr. M. "Pautalia." RE suppl. 9:800–824. 1962.

de Baye, J. *Les tombeaux des Goths en Crimée*. Mémoires de la société nationale des antiquaires de France 7. Paris, 1907.

Deér, Josef. "Karl der Grosse und der Untergang des Awarenreiches." *Vorträge und Forschungen* 21:285 ff. 1977.

Deichmann, Friedrich Wilhelm. *Ravenna: Hauptstadt des spätantiken Abendlandes*. Vol. 1. Wiesbaden, 1969.

Deininger, Jürgen. "Neue Forschungen zur antiken Sklaverei (1970–1975)." *Historische Zeitschrift* 222:359 ff. 1976.

Delbrück, Hans, *Geschichte der Kriegskunst im Rahmen der politischen Geschichte*. Vol. 2. 3d ed. Berlin, 1921.

Delehaye, Hippolyte. *Saints de Thrace et de Mésie*. Analecta Bollandiana 31. Paris, 1912.

Demandt, Alexander. "Die Anfänge der Staatenbildung bei den Germanen." *Historische Zeitschrift* 230:265 ff. 1980.

————. "Magister militum." RE, suppl. 12:553–790. 1970.

————. "Der spätrömische Militäradel." *Chiron* 10:609 ff. 1980.

Demougeot, Émilienne. *La formation de l'Europe et les invasions barbares*. Vol. 1, Paris, 1969; vol. 2, pts. 1 and 2, Paris, 1979.

————. "Modalités d'établissement des fédérés barbares de Gratian et de Théodose." *Mélanges d'histoire William Seston*, 143–160. 1974.

————. "À propos des interventions du pape Innocent Ier dans la politique séculière." *Revue historique* 212:23 ff. 1954.

————. *De l'unité à la division de l'empire romain: 395–410*. Paris, 1951.

Diaconu, Gheorghe. *Tîrgşor*. Biblioteca de arheologie 8. Bucharest, 1965.

Diculescu, Constantin. *Die Wandalen und die Goten in Ungarn und Rumänien*. Mannus-Bibliothek 34. 1923.

Diesner, Hans-Joachim. "Die Auswirkungen der Religionspolitik Thrasamunds und Hilderichs auf Ostgoten und Byzantiner." *Sitzungsberichte der Sächsischen Akademie der Wissenschaften zu Leipzig, Phil.-hist. Kl.* 113, 3:4 ff. 1967.

————. "Das Buccellariertum von Stilicho und Sarus bis auf Aëtius (454/455)." *Klio* 54:327 ff. 1972.

————. *Isidor von Sevilla und das westgotische Spanien*. Abhandlungen der Sächsischen Akademie der Wissenschaften zu Leipzig 67, 3:1 ff. 1977.

————. *Kirche und Staat im spätrömischen Reich*. 2d ed. Berlin, 1964.

————. "König Wamba und der westgotische Frühfeudalismus." *Jahrbuch der österreichischen Byzantinistik* 18:22 ff. 1969.

————. "protectores (domestici)." RE, suppl. 11, 1114 ff. 1968.

————. "Vandalen." RE, suppl. 10, 957–992. 1965.

Dilcher, Gerhard. "Gemeinfreie." *Handwörterbuch zur deutschen Rechtsgeschichte* 1:1513–1516. 1971.

Dizionario corografico dell'Italia. Edited by Amato Amati. Vol. 5. Milan, 1868/1878.

Doblhofer, Ernst. *Byzantinische Diplomaten und östliche Barbaren*. Byzantinische Geschichtsschreiber. Vol. 4, Graz, 1955.

d'Ors, Alvaro. *El Código de Eurico: Estudios visigóticos II*. Cuadernos del Instituto Juridico Español 12. Rome, Madrid, 1960.

Dove, Alfred. *Studien zur Vorgeschichte des deutschen Volksnamens*. Sitzungsberichte der Heidelberger Akademie der Wissenschaften, Phil.-hist. Kl., no. 8, 1916.

Dressel, Heinrich. *Die römischen Medaillone des Münzkabinettes der staatlichen Museen zu Berlin*. Edited by Kurt Regling. Vol. 1 (text). Berlin, 1973; vol. 2 (illustrations), Berlin, 1972.

Düwel, Klaus. "Alarich I." *Reallexikon der germanischen Altertumskunde* 1:127 f. 2d ed. 1973.

————. "Alarich II." *Reallexikon der germanischen Altertumskunde* 1:128 f. 2d ed. 1973.

Dunăreanu-Vulpe, Ecaterina. *Der Schatz von Pietroasa*. Bucharest, 1967.

Durliat, Jean. "Du caput antique au manse médiéval." *Pallas* 29:67 ff. 1982.

————. "Le Polyptyque d'Irminon et l'impôt pour l'armée." *Bibliothèque de l'École des Chartes* 141:183 ff. 1983.

————. "Le salaire de la paix sociale dans les royaumes barbares (Ve-VIe siècles)." *Denkschriften der Österreichischen Akademie der Wissenschaften in Wien, Phil.-hist. Kl.* 193:21 ff. 1988.

Dušanić, Slobodan. "Bassianae and Its Territory." *Archaeologia Iugoslavica* 8:67 ff. 1967.

Eckhardt, Karl August. "Die Nachbenennung in den Königshäusern der Goten." *Südostforschungen* 14:41 ff. 1955.

Eckardt, Uwe. *Untersuchungen zu Form und Funktion der Treueidleistungen im merowingischen Frankenreich*. Untersuchungen und Materialien zur Verfassungs- und Landesgeschichte 6. 1976.

Egger, Rudolf. *Der heilige Hermagoras*. Klagenfurt, 1948.

————. "Historisch-epigraphische Studien in Venezien." *Römische Antike und frühes Christentum* 1:45 ff. Klagenfurt, 1962.

————. "Die Zerstörung Pettaus durch die Goten." *Römische Antike und frühes Christentum*: 36 ff. Klagenfurt, 1962.

Eitrem, Samson. "Midas." RE 15.2:1526 ff. 1932.

Ellegård, Alvar. "The Ancient Goths and the Concepts of Tribe and Migration." *Vetenskap och Omvärdering*, 32 ff. Göteborg, 1986.

Engels, Joseph. "La portée de l'étymologie isidorienne." *Studi medievali* III 3:99 ff. 1962.

Ensslin, Wilhelm. "Beweise der Romverbundenheit in Theoderichs des Grossen Aussen- und Innenpolitik." *Settimane di studio del Centro italiano di studi sull'alto medioevo* 3:509 ff. Spoleto, 1956.

——. "Matasuntha." RE 28:2180. 1930.

——. "Mundo." RE 31:559 f. 1933.

——. "Pitzia." RE 40:1889 f. 1950.

——. "Praefectus praetorio." RE 24:2391–2502. 1954.

——. *Theoderich der Grosse.* 2d ed. Munich, 1959.

——. "Theodosius 14." RE II 10:1945. 1934.

——. "Theodimund." RE II 10:1773. 1934.

——. "Thrasamundus." RE II 11:553 f. 1936.

——. "Tribigild." RE 12:2403 ff. 1937.

——. "Tufa." RE I 13:775 f. 1939.

——. "Vallia." RE 15:284 f. 1955.

——. "Victorius." RE II 16:2086 n. 5. 1958.

——. "Vincentius." RE II 16:2189 n. 8. 1958.

——. "Witigis." RE II 17:395 ff. 1961.

Ewig, Eugen. "Zum christlichen Königsgedanken im Frühmittelalter: Spätantikes und fränkisches Gallien." *Beihefte der Francia* 3, 1, 21 ff. Zurich, 1976.

——. "Das Fortleben römischer Institutionen in Gallien und Germanien." *Spätantikes und fränkisches Gallien.* Beihefte der Francia 3, 1:409 ff. 1976.

——. "Die fränkischen Teilungen und Teilreiche (511–613)." *Spätantikes und fränkisches Gallien.* Beihefte der Francia 3, 1:114 ff. 1976.

——. "Die Gebetsklausel für König und Reich in den merowingischen Königsurkunden." *Festschrift für Karl Hauck,* 87 ff. Berlin, New York, 1982.

——. "Probleme der fränkischen Frühgeschichte in den Rheinlanden." *Historische Forschungen für Walter Schlesinger,* 47 ff. Cologne, Vienna, 1974.

——. "Résidence et capitale pendant le haut Moyen Age." *Spätantikes und fränkisches Gallien.* Beihefte der Francia 3, 1:362 ff. 1976. Or: *Revue Historique* 230:25 ff. 1963.

——. "Die Stellung Ribuariens in der Verfassungsgeschichte des Merowingerreichs." Ibid., 1:450 ff. 1976.

——. "Volkstum und Volksbewusstsein im Frankenreich des siebenten Jahrhunderts." Ibid., 1:231 ff. 1976. Or: *Settimane di studio del Centro italiano di studi sull'alto medioevo* 5:587 ff. Spoleto, 1958.

Feist, Sigmund. *Vergleichendes Wörterbuch der gotischen Sprache.* 3d ed. Leiden, 1939.

Fichtenau, Heinrich. *Arenga.* MIÖG suppl. vol. 18., 1957.

——. "Gentiler und europäischer Horizont an der Schwelle des ersten Jahrtausends." *Römische Historische Mitteilungen* 23:277 ff. 1981.

——. "'Politische' Datierungen des frühen Mittelalters." *Intitulatio II.* MIÖG, suppl. vol. 24:453 ff. 1973.

——. *Das Urkundenwesen in Österreich vom 8. bis zum frühen 13, Jahrhundert.* Mitteilungen des Instituts für österreichische Geschichtsforschung, suppl. vol. 23. Vienna, 1971.

Fiebiger, Otto, and Schmidt, Ludwig. *Inschriftensammlung zur Geschichte der Ostgermanen.* Denkschriften der kaiserlichen Akademie der Wissenschaften in

Wien, Phil.-hist. Kl. vol. 60, Abh. 3, Vienna, 1917. Continued by Fiebiger alone in vol. 70, Abh. 3, Vienna, 1939, and vol. 72, Vienna, 1944.

Fluss, Max. "Taifali." RE II 8:2027. 1932.

———. "Tigas." RE II 11:941. 1936.

———. "Tisia." RE II 12:1469–1478. 1937.

Fontaine, Jacques. *Isidore de Seville et la culture classique dans l'Espagne wisigothique.* Vols. 1 and 2. Paris, 1959.

Forstner, Karl. *Das Verbrüderungsbuch von St. Peter in Salzburg.* Graz, 1974.

Fraenkel, Ernst. *Die baltischen Sprachen.* Heidelberg, 1950.

———. *Litauisches etymologisches Wörterbuch.* Vol. 1. Heidelberg, 1962.

Franz, Leonhard. "Hyperboreisches." *Festschrift für Karl Pivec.* Innsbrucker Beiträge zur Kulturwissenschaft 12:65 ff. 1966.

Fridh, Åke. "Die Bekehrung der Westgoten zum Christentum." *Studia Gotica,* 130 ff. Stockholm, 1972.

Friesinger, Herwig. "Die archäologischen Funde der ersten zwei Drittel des fünften Jahrhunderts in Niederösterreich." *Katalog: Germanen, Awaren, Slawen,* 62 ff. Vienna, 1977.

Friesinger, Herwig, and Adler, Horst. *Die Zeit der Völkerwanderung in Niederösterreich.* Wissenschaftliche Schriftenreihe Niederösterreich. 41/42. St. Pölten, 1979.

Fröhlich, Hermann. *Studien zur langobardischen Thronfolge: Von den Anfängen bis zur Eroberung des italienischen Reiches durch Karl den Grossen (774).* Parts 1 and 2. Tübingen, 1980.

Gajdukevič, Viktor Francevič. *Das bosporanische Reich.* 2d ed. East Berlin, 1971.

Gamber, Ortwin. "Dakische und sarmatische Waffen auf den Reliefs der Trajansäule." *Jahrbuch der Kunsthistorischen Sammlungen in Wien* 60:7 ff. 1964.

———. "Grundriss einer Geschichte der Schutzwaffen des Altertums." *Jahrbuch der Kunsthistorischen Sammlungen in Wien* 62:47 ff. 1966.

———. "Kataphrakten, Clibanarier, Normannenreiter." *Jahrbuch der Kunsthistorischen Sammlungen in Wien* 64:27 ff. 1968.

Gamillscheg, Ernst. *Romania Germanica.* Grundriss der germanischen Philologie 11. Vols. 1–3. Berlin, Leipzig, 1934–1936.

Garaud, Marcel. "Le peuplement du Poitou et la conquête franque." *Revue des études anciennes* 52:90 ff. 1950.

García Moreno, L. A. *Prosopografía del reino visigódo de Toledo.* Acta Salmanticensia: Filosofía y letras 77. 1974.

Gaupp, Ernst Theodor. *Die germanischen Ansiedlungen und Landtheilungen in den Provinzen des römischen Westreichs.* Breslau, 1844.

Geiss, Hans. *Geld- und naturalwirtschaftliche Erscheinungsformen im staatlichen Aufbau Italiens während der Gotenzeit.* Stuttgart, 1931.

Geldner, Ferdinand. "Zur Frühgeschichte des Obermain-Regnitz-Landes." *Zeitschrift für bayerische Landesgeschichte* 39:30 ff. 1976.

Giesecke, H.-E. *Die Ostgermanen und der Arianismus.* Leipzig, Berlin, 1939.

Godłowski, Kazimierz. "Das Aufhören der germanischen Kulturen an der mittleren Donau und das Problem des Vordringens der Slawen." *Denkschriften der Österreichischen Akademie der Wissenschaften in Wien, Phil.-hist. Kl.* 145:225 ff. 1980.

———. *The Chronology of the Later Roman and Early Migration Periods in*

Central Europe. 1970.

———. Review of Hachmann. *Goten und Skandinavien. Spranvozdania archeologiczne* 24:533 ff. 1972.

Goffart, Walter, *Barbarians and Romans: Techniques of Accommodation.* Princeton, 1980.

———. *Caput and Colonate: Towards a History of Late Roman Taxation.* Toronto, 1974.

———. "After the Zwettl Conference: Comments on the 'Techniques of Accommodation.'" *Denkschriften der Österreichischen Akademie der Wissenschaften in Wien, Phil.-hist. Kl.* 193:73 ff. 1987.

———. "The Date and Purpose of Vegetius 'De re militari.'" *Traditio* 33:65 ff. 1977.

———. "From Roman Taxation to Medieval Seigneurie: Three Notes." *Speculum* 47:165 ff. and 373 ff. 1972.

———. Review of Thomas S. Burns: *A History of the Ostrogoths. American Historical Review* 90:914 ff. 1985.

———. "Rome, Constantinople, and the Barbarians." *The American Historical Review* 86:275 ff. 1981.

———. "The Supposedly 'Frankish' Table of Nations: An Edition and Study." *Frühmittelalterliche Studien* 17:98 ff. 1983.

———. "Zosimos: The First Historian of Rome's Fall." *American Historical Review* 76:412 ff. 1971.

Gollwitzer, Heinz. "Zum politischen Germanismus des neunzehnten Jahrhunderts." *Festschrift für Hermann Heimpel: Veröffentlichungen des Max-Planck-Instituts für Geschichte* 36,1:282 ff. Göttingen, 1971.

Gostar, Nicolae. "Les titres impériaux Dacicus maximus et Carpicus maximus." *Actes de la conférence internationale d'études classique* "Eirene," 643 ff. Amsterdam, 1975.

Gottlieb, Gunther. Review of Thomas S. Burns: *The Ostrogoths: Kingship and Society. Francia* 10:751 ff. 1982.

Graef. "Amazones." *RE* 1:1755 ff. 1894.

Graf, Heinz-Joachim. *Orientalische Berichte des Mittelalters über die Germanen.* Krefeld, 1971.

Graus, František. *Lebendige Vergangenheit.* Cologne, 1975.

Grierson, Philip. "The Date of Theodoric's Gold Medallion." *Hikuin* 11:19 ff. 1984.

Grönbech, Vilhelm. *Kultur und Religion der Germanen.* Vol. 2. 5th ed. Darmstadt, 1954.

Grosse, Robert. *Römische Militärgeschichte von Gallienus bis zum Beginn der byzantinischen Themenverfassung.* Berlin, 1920.

Gruchmann, Lothar. *Nationalsozialistische Grossraumordnung.* Schriftenreihe der Vierteljahreshefte für Zeitgeschichte 4. 1962.

Grundmann, Herbert. *Geschichtsschreibung im Mittelalter.* Kleine Vandenhoeck-Reihe 209/210. 1965.

Gschwantler, Otto. "Bekehrung und Bekehrungsgeschichte." *Reallexikon der germanischen Altertumskunde* 2:176 f. 2d ed. 1976.

———. "Ermanrich, sein Selbstmord und die Hamdirsage—Zur Darstellung von Ermanrichs Ende in *Getica* 24.129 f." *Denkschriften der Österreichischen Akade-*

mie der Wissenschaften in Wien, Phil.-hist. Kl. 145:187 ff. 1980.

———. *Heldensage in der Historiographie des Mittelalters.* Habilitations-Schrift, University of Vienna, 1971.

———. "Zum Namen der Rosomonen und an. Jónakr." *Die Sprache* 17:164–176. 1971.

Habicht, Christian. "Zur Geschichte Kaiser Konstantins." *Hermes* 86:360 ff. 1958.

Hachmann, Rolf. *Die Goten und Skandinavien.* Quellen und Forschungen zur Sprach- und Kulturgeschichte der germanischen Völker, n.s. 34. Berlin, 1970.

Hagberg, Ulf Erik. "Gotisches Gold in Gotaland." *Denkschriften der Österreichischen Akademie der Wissenschaften in Wien, Phil.-hist. Kl.* 145:205 ff. 1980.

Hahn, Wolfgang. *Moneta Imperii Byzantini I: Von Anastasius I bis Iustinianus I.* Denkschriften der Österreichischen Akademie der Wissenschaften in Wien, Phil.-hist. Kl. 109. 1973.

———. *Moneta Imperii Byzantini II.* Ibid. 119. 1975.

———. *Moneta Imperii Byzantini III.* Ibid. 148. 1981.

Hannestad, Knud. *L'évolution des ressources agricoles de l'Italie du quatrième au sixième siècle de notre ère.* Historisk-filosofiske Meddelelser af det Koneglige Danske Videnskabernes Selskab 40/41. Copenhagen, 1962.

———. "Les forces militaires d'après la guerre gothique de Procope." *Classica et mediaevalia* 21:136 ff. 1960.

Hanslik, Rudolf. "Vibius Trebonianus Gallus Augustus." RE II 16:1984 ff. 1958.

Harhoiu, Radu. "Das norddonauländische Gebiet im 5. Jahrhundert und seine Beziehungen zum spätrömischen Kaiserreich." *Denkschriften der Österreichischen Akademie der Wissenschaften in Wien, Phil.-hist. Kl.* 145:101 ff. 1980.

———. *The Treasure from Pietroasa, Romania.* BAR suppl. series 24. Oxford, 1977.

Harmatta, John. *Studies in the History and Language of the Sarmatians.* Szeged, 1970.

Hartke, Werner. *Römische Kinderkaiser.* Berlin, 1951.

Hartmann, Ludo Moritz. "Amalaricus." RE 2:1715. 1894.

———. *Geschichte Italiens im Mittelalter.* Vol. 1. 2d ed. Gotha, 1923.

Hauck, Karl. "Brustbilder von Königen auf Siegelringen der Völkerwanderungszeit." In Percy Ernst Schramm, *Herrschaftszeichen und Staatssymbolik.* Schriften der MGH 13, 1:239 ff. Munich, 1954.

———. "Halsring und Ahnenstab als herrscherliche Würdezeichen." In: Percy Ernst Schramm, *Herrschaftszeichen und Staatssymbolik.* Schriften der MGH 13, 1:145 ff. Munich, 1954.

———. "Von einer spätantiken Randkultur zum karolingischen Europa." *Frühmittelalterliche Studien* 1:20 ff. 1967.

Hauptfeld, Georg. "Die Gentes im Vorfeld von Ostgoten und Franken im 6. Jahrhundert." *Denkschriften der Österreichischen Akademie der Wissenschaften, Phil.-hist. Kl.* 179:121 ff. 1985.

Hauschild, Richard. *Mistra—die Faustburg Goethes.* Abhandlungen der Sächsischen Akademie der Wissenschaften zu Leipzig, Phil.-hist. Kl. 54, 4. East Berlin, 1963.

Heerklotz, Alexander Theodor. *Die Variae des Cassiodorus Senator als kulturgeschichtliche Quelle.* Heidelberg, 1926.

Heather, Peter. "The Crossing of the Danube and the Gothic Conversion." Greek, Roman, and Byzantine Studies 27:289 ff. Duke University, 1986.

Hefele, Charles Joseph, and Leclercq, Henry. *Histoire des conciles.* Vol. 2. Paris, 1908.

Heidenreich, Robert, and Johannes, Heinz. *Das Grabmal Theoderichs zu Ravenna.* Wiesbaden, 1971.

Heinzel, Richard. "Über die Hervarasaga." *Sitzungsberichte der Österreichischen Akademie der Wissenschaften in Wien, Phil.-hist. Kl.* 114:417 ff. 1887.

———. "Über die ostgotische Heldensage." *Sitzungsberichte der Österreichischen Akademie der Wissenschaften in Wien, Phil.-hist. Kl.* 119:19 ff. 1889.

Heinzelmann, Martin. *Bischofsherrschaft in Gallien: Zur Kontinuität römischer Führungsschichten vom 4. bis zum 7. Jahrhundert.* Beihefte der Francia 5. 1976.

Helbling, Hanno. *Goten und Wandalen.* Zurich, 1954.

Helm, Karl. *Altgermanische Religionsgeschichte.* Vol. 2, pt. 1. Heidelberg, 1937.

———. "Erfundene Götter?" *Festschrift für Friedrich Panzer,* 1 ff. Heidelberg, 1950.

Hermann, Eduard. "Sind der Name der Gudden und die Ortsnamen Danzig, Gdingen and Graudenz gotischen Ursprungs?" *Nachrichten der Akademie der Wissenschaften in Göttingen, Phil.-hist. Kl.,* n.s. 3/8:207 ff. 1941.

Herter, H. "Dirne." *Reallexikon für Antike und Christentum* 3:1204 ff. 1957.

Heuberger, Richard. "Ein angebliches Edikt Theoderichs des Grossen vom Jahr 505 aus dem Castrum Maiense über dem Laureinerberg." *Innsbrucker Beiträge zur Kulturwissenschaft* 12:201 ff. 1966.

———. "Das ostgotische Rätien." *Klio* 30:77 ff. 1937.

———. *Rätien im Altertum und Frühmittelalter.* Innsbruck, 1932.

Heusler, Andreas. "Amelunge." *Reallexikon der germanischen Altertumskunde* 1:77. 1911/1913.

Higounet, Charles. *Bordeaux pendant le Haut Moyen Âge.* Bordeaux, 1963.

Hodgkin, Thomas. *Italy and Her Invaders.* Vol. 1. Oxford, 1880.

Höfler, Otto. "Abstammungstraditionen." *Reallexikon der germanischen Altertumskunde* 1:18 ff. 2d ed. 1973.

———. *Germanisches Sakralkönigtum.* Vol. 1. Tübingen, Münster, 1952.

———. "Der Sakralcharakter des germanischen Königtums." *Vorträge und Forschungen* 3:75 ff. 4th reprint, 1973.

Hörburger, Franz. "Die romanischen und vorromanischen Ortsnamen des Landes Salzburg." *Mitteilungen der Gesellschaft für Salzburger Landeskunde* 107:1 ff. 1967.

Horn, Hans-Jürgen. "Gold." *Reallexikon für Antike und Christentum* 11:895 ff. 1981.

Høst, Gerd. "Spuren der Goten im Osten." *Norwegian Journal of Linguistics* 25:62 ff. 1971.

Hoffmann, Dietrich. *Das spätrömische Bewegungsheer und die Notitia dignitatum.* Epigraphische Studien 7, parts 1 and 2. Düsseldorf, 1969/1970.

Horedt, Kurt. "Apahida II." *Reallexikon der germanischen Altertumskunde* 1:366 f. 2d ed. 1973.

———. "Das archäologische Bild nach der Räumung Dakiens." *Dacoromania* 1:135 ff. 1973.

———. "Beziehungen zwischen Dakern und Germanen." *Festgabe für Kurt Tackenberg,* 167 ff. Bonn, 1974.

———. "Die Datierung des Schatzfundes von Pietroasa." *Acta Musei Napocensis* 6:549 ff. 1969.

———. "Zur Geschichte der frühen Gepiden im Karpatenbecken." *Apulum* 9:705 ff. 1971.

———. "Der Goldfund von Moigrad." *Germania* 55:7 ff. 1977.

———. "Neue Goldschätze des fünften Jahrhunderts aus Rumänien (Ein Beitrag zur Geschichte der Ostgoten und Gepiden)." *Studia Gotica,* 105 ff. Stockholm, 1972.

———. "Quelques problèmes concernant la diffusion de la civilisation de Sîntana-de-Mureş-Tschernéakhov en Roumanie." *Studii şi cercetări de istorie veche şi arheologie* 18:575 ff. 1967.

———. "Wandervölker und Romanen im 5. bis 6. Jahrhundert in Siebenbürgen." *Denkschriften der Österreichischen Akademie der Wissenschaften in Wien, Phil.-hist. Kl.* 145:117 ff. 1980.

——— and Protase, Dimitru. "Ein völkerwanderungszeitlicher Schatzfund aus Cluj-Someşeni (Siebenbürgen)." *Germania* 48:87 ff. 1970.

———. "Das zweite Fürstengrab von Apahida (Siebenbürgen)." *Germania* 50:174 ff. 1972.

Hornstein, Franz. ΙΣΤΡΟΣ ΑΜΑΞΕΥΟΜΕΝΟΣ. Zur Geschichte eines literarischen Topos." *Gymnasium* 64:154 ff. 1957.

Hudeczek, Erich. "Flavia Solva." *Aufstieg und Niedergang der römischen Welt: Principat* II 6:414 ff. 1977.

Hunger, Herbert. *Die hochsprachliche profane Literatur der Byzantiner.* Handbuch der Altertumswissenschaft XII 5, 1 and 2. Munich, 1978.

Iliescu, Vladimir. "Die Räumung Dakiens im Lichte der Schriftquellen." *Dacoromania* 1:5 ff. 1973.

Ioniţă, Ion. "Probleme der Sîntana-de-Mureş-Chernjahov-Kultur auf dem Gebiete Rumäniens." *Studia Gotica,* 95 ff. Stockholm, 1972.

———. *Relations between the Autochthonous Populations and the Migratory Populations on the Territory of Roumania.* Bibliotheca Historica Romaniae, Monographs 16. Bucharest, 1975.

———. "Die Römer-Daker und die Wandervölker im donauländischen Karpatenraum im 4. Jahrhundert." *Denkschriften der Österreichischen Akademie der Wissenschaften in Wien, Phil.-hist. Kl.* 145:123 ff. 1980.

Irsigler, Franz. *Untersuchungen zur Geschichte des frühfränkischen Adels.* Rheinisches Archiv 70. Bonn, 1969.

James, Edward. *Merovingian Archaeology of South-West Gaul.* British Archaeological Reports, suppl. series 25, 1. Oxford, 1977.

———. ed. *Visigothic Spain.* Oxford, 1980.

Jiriczek, Otto Lutpold. *Deutsche Heldensagen.* Strasbourg, 1898.

Johanek, Peter. "Bewaffnung." *Reallexikon der germanischen Altertumskunde* 2:462 ff. 2d ed. 1976.

Jones, A. H. M. *The Later Roman Empire (284–602).* Vols. 1–3. Oxford, 1964.

———. *The Prosopography of the Later Roman Empire: 260–395.* Vol. 1. Cambridge, 1971. Cf. Martindale, *Prosopography.*

Kabell, Aage. "Baugi und der Ringeid." *Arkiv för nordisk filologi* 90:30 ff. 1975.

Kahl, Hans-Dietrich. "Einige Beobachtungen zum Sprachgebrauch von *natio* im mittelalterlichen Latein mit Ausblicken auf das neuhochdeutsche 'Nation.'" *Nationes* 1:63 ff. 1978.

Kampers, Gerd. "Die Genealogie der Könige der Spaniensueben in prosopographischer Sicht." *Frühmittelalterliche Studien* 14:50 ff. 1980.

Karayannopulos, Johannes. *Das Finanzwesen des frühbyzantinischen Staates.* Südosteuropäische Arbeiten 52. 1958.

Karlsson, Gustav. "Goten, die im Osten blieben." *Studia Gotica,* 165 ff. Stockholm, 1972.

Katz, Solomon. *The Jews in the Visigothic and Frankish Kingdoms of Spain and Gaul.* Cambridge, Mass., 1937. Reprint, New York, 1970.

Keller, Hagen. "Fränkische Herrschaft und alemannisches Herzogtum im 6. und 7. Jahrhundert." *Zeitschrift für die Geschichte des Oberrheins* 124:1 ff. 1976.

———. "Spätantike und Frühmittelalter zwischen Genfer See und Hochrhein." *Frühmittelalterliche Studien* 7:10 ff. 1973.

Kienast, Walther. "Magnus = der Ältere." *Historische Zeitschrift* 205:1 ff. 1967.

———. *Studien über die französischen Volksstämme des Frühmittelalters.* Pariser Historische Studien 7. Paris, 1968.

Kiessling, Emil. "Galindai." RE 13:606 f. 1910.

King, P. D. *Law and Society in the Visigothic Kingdom.* Cambridge Studies in Medieval Life and Thought III 5. Cambridge, 1972.

Kiparsky, Valentin. *Die gemeinslavischen Lehnwörter aus dem Germanischen.* Helsinki, 1934.

Kirsten, Ernst. "Cappadocia." *Reallexikon für Antike und Christentum* 2:861 ff. 1954.

———. "Chorbischof." *Reallexikon für Antike und Christentum* 2:1105 ff. 1954.

———. "Dacia." *Reallexikon für Antike und Christentum* 3:558 ff. 1957.

———, and Adolf Lippold. "Donauprovinzen." *Reallexikon für Antike und Christentum* 4:147 ff. 1959.

Klein, Karl Kurt. "Ambrosius von Mailand und der Gotenbischof Wulfila." *Südostforschungen* 22:14 ff. 1963.

———. "Der Auxentiusbrief als Quelle der Wulfilabiographie." *Zeitschrift für deutsches Altertum und deutsche Literatur* 84:116 ff. 1952/1953.

———. "Frithigern, Athanarich und die Spaltung des Westgotenvolks am Vorabend des Hunneneinbruchs (375 n. Chr.)." *Südostforschungen* 19:34 ff. 1960.

———. "Die Goten-Geten-Daken-Sachsengleichung in der Sprachentwicklung der Deutschen Siebenbürgens." *Südostforschungen* 11:84 ff. 1946/1952.

———. "Gotenprimas Wulfila als Bischof und Missionar." *Festschrift für Bischof F. Müller.* Stuttgart, 1967.

———. "Kaiser Valens vor Adrianopel (378 n. Chr.)" *Südostforschungen* 15:58 ff. 1956.

Klinck, Roswitha. *Die Lateinische Etymologie des Mittelalters.* Medium Aevum: Philologische Studien 17. 1970.

Klingenberg, Heinz. *Runenschrift-Schriftdenken-Runeninschriften.* Heidelberg, 1973.

Kneissl, Peter. "Die Siegestitulatur der römischen Kaiser." *Hypomnemata* 23:174 ff. 1969.

Köbler, Gerhard. "Die Freien (*liberi, ingenui*) im alemannischen Recht. Beiträge zum frühalemannischen Recht." *Veröffentlichungen des Alemannischen Instituts Freiburg im Breisgau* 42:38 ff. 1978.

Koenig, Gerd. "Archäologische Zeugnisse westgotischer Präsenz im fünften Jahrhundert." *Madrider Mitteilungen* 21:220 ff. 1980.

Köpke, Rudolph. *Die Anfänge des Königthums bei den Gothen.* Berlin, 1859.

Konecny, Silvia. *Die Frauen des karolingischen Hauses.* Dissertationen der Universität Wien 132. Vienna, 1976.

Kornemann, Ernst. "Dioecesis." RE 9:716–734. 1903.

Kovrig, Ilona. "Nouvelles trouvailles du cinquième siècle découvertes en Hongrie." *Acta archaeologica Academiae scientiarum Hungaricae* 10:209 ff. 1959.

Krahe, Hans. "Einige Gruppen alter Gewässernamen." *Beiträge zur Namenforschung* 6:109 ff. 1955.

Kraus, Andreas. *Bayerische Geschichtswissenschaft in drei Jahrhunderten.* Munich, 1979.

Krause, Wolfgang. *Handbuch des Gotischen.* 3d ed. Munich, 1968.

Kretschmer, Karl. "Scythae." RE II 3:930. 1921.

Kuhn, Hans. "Amaler." *Reallexikon der germanischen Altertumskunde* 1:246. 2d ed. 1973.

———. "Asen." *Reallexikon der germanischen Altertumskunde* 1:457 f. 2nd ed. 1973.

———. Review of Wagner, *Getica,* and Svennung, *Jordanes und Scandia. Anzeiger für deutsches Altertum und deutsche Literatur* 97:152 f. 1968.

———. "Gaut." *Festschrift für Jost Trier.* 417 ff. 1954. Or: *Kleine Schriften* 2:364 ff. Berlin, 1971.

———. "Das römische Kriegswesen im germanischen Wortschatz." *Zeitschrift für deutsches Altertum und deutsche Literatur* 101:36 ff. 1972.

Kunkel, Otto. "Ostsee." RE 36:1700. 1942.

Ladner, Gerhart B. "Aspects of Patristic Anti-Judaism." *Viator* 2:355 ff. 1971.

———. *The Idea of Reform.* Vol. 1. Cambridge, Mass., 1959.

———. "Justinian's Theory of Law and the Renewal Ideology of the Leges Barbarorum." *Proceedings of The American Philosophical Society* 119, 3:195 ff. 1975.

———. "On Roman Attitudes towards Barbarians in Late Antiquity." *Viator* 7:1 ff. 1976.

———. "Der Ursprung und die mittelalterliche Entwicklung der päpstlichen Tiara." *Festschrift für Roland Hampe,* 449 ff. Mainz, 1978.

Lakatos, Pál. *Quellenbuch zur Geschichte der Gepiden.* Opuscula Byzantina 2. Szeged, 1973.

Lechner, Karl. *Die Babenberger.* Veröffentlichungen des Instituts für österreichische Geschichtsforschung 23. Vienna, 1976.

Lechner, Kilian. "Byzanz und die Barbaren." *Saeculum* 6:292 ff. 1955.

Leube, Achim. "Archäologische Formengruppen im nördlichen Elbe-Oder-Gebiet während des ersten bis vierten Jahrhunderts." *Prace archeologiczne* 22:355 ff. Warsaw, Cracow, 1976.

Levison, Wilhelm. "Bischof Germanus von Auxerre und die Quellen zu seiner Geschichte." *Neues Archiv* 29:95 ff. 1904.

———. "Metz und Südfrankreich im frühen Mittelalter." *Aus rheinischer und fränkischer Frühzeit,* 139 ff. Düsseldorf, 1948.

Lhotsky, Alphons. *Thomas Ebendorfer.* Schriften der MGH 15. Munich, 1957.

Lippold, Adolf. "Chlodovechus." RE, suppl. 13:139 ff. 1973.

———. "Goti." *Der kleine Pauly* 2:858 f. 1977.

———. "Narses." RE, suppl. vol. 12:870 ff. 1970.

———. "Review of Wolfram and Daim, *Völker an der Donauo.*" *Zeitschrift für bayerische Landesgeschichte* 44:789 ff. 1981.

———. "Theodosius I." RE, suppl. 13:838 ff. 1973.

———. *Theodosius der Grosse und seine Zeit.* Stuttgart, 1968.

———. "Uldin." RE II 17:510 ff. 1961.

———. "Ulfila." RE II 17:512 ff. 1961.

Löhlein, Georg. *Die Alpen- und Italienpolitik der Merowinger im VI. Jahrhundert.* Erlanger Abhandlungen zur mittleren und neueren Geschichte 17. 1932.

Lönnroth, Erik. "Die Goten in der modernen kritischen Geschichtsauffassung." *Studia Gotica,* 57 ff. Stockholm, 1972.

Löwe, Heinz. "Von Theoderich dem Grossen zu Karl dem Grossen." *Von Cassiodor zu Dante,* 33 ff. Berlin, New York, 1973.

———. "Theoderichs Gepidensieg im Winter 488/489." *Festschrift für Peter Rassow,* 1 ff. Wiesbaden, 1961.

Loewe, Richard. "Gotische Namen in hagiographischen Texten." *Beiträge zur Geschichte der deutschen Sprache und Literatur* 47:407 ff. 1923.

Lot, Ferdinand. "De l'origine et de la signification historique et linguistique des noms de lieux en -ville et en -court." *Romania* 59:199 ff. 1933.

———. "Du régime de l'hospitalité." *Revue belge de philologie et d'histoire* 7:975 ff. 1928.

———. "Que nous apprennent sur le peuplement germanique de la France les récents travaux de toponymie?" *Académie des Inscriptions et Belles-Lettres: Comptes rendus,* 289 ff. Paris, 1945.

Lotter, Friedrich. "Die germanischen Stammesverbände im Umkreis des Ostalpen-Mitteldonau-Raumes nach der literarischen Überlieferung zum Zeitalter Severins." *Denkschriften der Österreichischen Akademie der Wissenschaften in Wien, Phil.-hist. Kl.* 179:29 ff. 1985.

———. "Die historischen Daten zur Endphase römischer Präsenz in Ufernorikum." *Vorträge und Forschungen* 25:27 ff. 1979.

———. "Lauriacum-Lorch zwischen Antike und Mittelalter." *Mitteilungen des Oberösterreichischen Landesarchivs* 11:31 ff. Linz, 1974.

———. "Zur Rolle der Donausueben in der Völkerwanderungszeit." *Mitteilungen des Instituts für österreichische Geschichtsforschung* 76:275 ff. 1968.

———. *Severinus von Noricum: Legende und historische Wirklichkeit.* Monographien zur Geschichte des Mittelalters 12. Stuttgart, 1976.

———. "Die Zwangsbekehrung der Juden von Menorca um 418 im Rahmen der Entwicklung des Judenrechts der Spätantike." *Historische Zeitschrift* 242:291 ff. 1986.

Loyen, André. "Les débuts du royaume wisigoth de Toulouse." *Revue des études latines* 12:406 ff. 1934.

————. *Recherches historiques sur les panégyriques de Sidoine Apollinaire.* Reprint, Rome, 1967.

————. *Sidoine Apollinaire.* Vol. 1, Paris, 1960; vols. 2 and 3, Paris, 1970.

————. *Sidoine Apollinaire et l'esprit précieux en Gaule aux derniers jours de l'empire.* Collection d'études latines, ser. scientifique 20. Paris, 1943.

MacMullen, Ramsay. *Enemies of the Roman Order.* Harvard University Press, 1966.

Maenchen-Helfen, Otto. *The World of the Huns.* University of California Press: Berkeley, Los Angeles, London, 1973.

Manitius, Max. *Geschichte der lateinischen Literatur des Mittelalters.* Vol. 1. 1911.

Martindale, John Robert. *Prosopography of the Later Roman Empire: 395–527.* Vol. 2. Cambridge, 1980. Cf. Jones, *Prosopography.*

Masur, Ingeborg. "Die Verträge der germanischen Stämme." Ph.D. diss., Berlin, 1952.

Matthews, John. *Western Aristocracies and Imperial Court: 364–425.* Oxford, 1975.

McCormick, Michael. "Odoacer, Emperor Zeno and the Rugian Victory Legation." *Byzantion* 47:212 ff. 1977.

————. *Eternal Victory. Triumphal Rulership in Late Antiquity, Byzantium and the Early Medieval West.* (Past and present publications.) Cambridge, Paris: Maison des Sciences de l'Homme and Cambridge University Press, 1986.

Meid, Wolfgang. "Das Suffix -no in Götternamen." *Beiträge zur Namenforschung* 8:72 ff. 1957.

Menéndez Pidal, Ramon. "Los Godos y el origen de la epopeya española." *Settimane di studio del Centro italiano di studi sull'alto medioevo* 3:296 ff. Spoleto, 1956.

————. *Historia de España.* Vol. 3. Madrid, 1940.

Messmer, Hans. *Hispania-Idee und Gotenmythos.* Zurich, 1960.

Meyer, Heinz. *Die Zahlensymbolik im Mittelalter.* Münstersche Mittelalter-Schriften 25. 1975.

Mildenberger, Gerhard. "Probleme der germanischen Frühgeschichte im östlichen Mitteleuropa." *Zeitschrift für Ostforschung* 24:488 ff. 1975.

Miltner, Franz. "Vandalen." RE II 15:298 ff. 1955.

Mirković, Miroslava. "Die Ostgoten in Pannonien nach dem Jahre 445." *Recueil de travaux de la faculté de la philosophie* 10, 1:119 ff. Belgrade, 1968.

Mitrea, Bucur. "Die Goten an der unteren Donau—einige Probleme im III./IV. Jahrhundert." *Studia Gotica,* 81 ff. Stockholm, 1972.

Mócsy, Andreas. "Pannonia." RE, suppl. 9:516 ff. 1962.

————. Review of László Várady, *Das letzte Jahrhundert Pannoniens. Acta archaeologica Academiae scientiarum Hungaricae* 23:347 ff. 1971.

Moisl, Hermann. "Anglo-Saxon Royal Genealogies and Germanic Oral Tradition." *Journal of Medieval History* 7:215 ff. 1981.

Moliner, Maria. *Diccionario de uso del español.* 2 vols. Madrid, 1973/1977.

Momigliano, Arnaldo. "Cassiodorus and Italian Culture of His Time." *Studies in Historiography,* 181 ff. London, 1966.

Mommsen, Theodor. "Ostgothische Studien." *Neues Archiv* 14:451 ff. Hannover, 1889.

―――. "Das römische Militärwesen seit Diocletian." *Gesammelte Schriften* 6:206 ff. Berlin, 1910.

―――. *Römisches Staatsrecht*. Vol. 1. 3d ed. 1952.

Moravcsik, Gyula. *Byzantino-Turcica*. Vol. 2. Berlin, 1958.

Much, Rudolf. *Die Germania des Tacitus*. 3d ed. Heidelberg, 1967.

―――. "Vidivarii." *Reallexikon der germanischen Altertumskunde* 4:418. 1918/1919.

―――. "Völkernamen." *Reallexikon der germanischen Altertumskunde* 4:425 ff. 1918/1919.

Müller, Gunter. "Studien zu den theriophoren Personennamen der Germanen." *Niederdeutsche Studien* 17. 1970.

Müller, Klaus E. *Geschichte der antiken Ethnographie und ethnologischen Theoriebildung*. Studien zur Kulturkunde 52, pt. 1 (1972) and pt. 2 (1980).

Myers, Henry A. *Medieval Kingship*. Chicago, 1982.

Nagl, Assunta. "Odoacer." RE 34:1888 ff. 1937.

―――. "Onoulf." RE 35:526 f. 1939.

―――. "Theia." RE II 10:1602 ff. 1934.

―――. "Theodenanda—Theodenantha." RE II 10:1735. 1934.

―――. "Theoderich der Grosse." RE II 10:1745. 1934.

―――. "Theoderich Strabo." RE II 10:1771 ff. 1934.

―――. "Theudis." RE II 11:246 ff. 1936.

―――. "Totila." RE II 12:1828 ff. 1937.

―――. "Valens." RE II 14:2097 ff. 1948.

Nagy, Tibor. "The Last Century of Pannonia in the Judgment of a New Monograph." *Acta antiqua Academiae scientiarum Hungaricae* 19:299 ff. 1971.

―――. "Reoccupation of Pannonia from the Huns in 427." *Acta antiqua Academiae scientiarum Hungaricae* 15:159 ff. 1967.

Nehlsen, Hermann. "Aktualität und Effektivität germanischer Rechtsaufzeichnungen." *Vorträge und Forschungen* 23:483 ff. 1977.

―――. "belagines." *Reallexikon der germanischen Altertumskunde* 1:206 f. 2d ed. 1976.

―――. "Codex Euricianus." *Reallexikon der germanischen Altertumskunde* 5:42 ff. 2d ed. 1984.

―――. "Lex Visigothorum." *Handwörterbuch zur deutschen Rechtsgeschichte* 2:1966 ff. 1978.

―――. Review of Giulio Vismara, *Edictum Theoderici. Zeitschrift für Rechtsgeschichte: Germ. Abt.* 86:246 ff. 1969.

―――. *Sklavenrecht zwischen Antike und Mittelalter*. Göttingen, 1972.

Noll, Rudolf. *Vom Altertum zum Mittelalter: Katalog der Antikensammlung des Kunsthistorischen Museums, Wien*. Vol. 1. 2d ed. Vienna, 1974.

―――. *Eugippius: Das Leben des heiligen Severin*. 1963. Reprint, Passau, 1981.

Oberhummer, Eugen. "Develtos." RE 9:260. 1903.

―――. "Emathia." RE 10:2480. 1905.

O'Donnell, James J. *Cassiodorus*. Berkeley, Los Angeles, London: University of California Press, 1979.

―――. "The Demise of Paganism." *Traditio* 35:75 ff. 1979.

―――. "Liberius the Patrician." *Traditio* 37:31 ff. 1981.

O'Flynn, John Michael. *Generalissimos of the Western Roman Empire*. Edmonton, Canada: University of Alberta Press, 1983.

Oldenburg, Eugen. "Die Kriegsverfassung der Westgoten." Ph.D. diss., Berlin, 1909.

Oost, Stewart Irvin. *Galla Placidia Augusta: A Biographical Essay*. Chicago, 1968.

Orlandis, José, and Ramos-Lisson, Domingo. *Die Synoden auf der Iberischen Halbinsel bis zum Einbruch des Islam (711)*. Konziliengeschichte. Reihe A: Darstellungen. Edited by Walter Brandmüller. Paderborn, Munich, Vienna, Zurich, 1981.

Oxenstierna, Eric C. G., Graf. *Die Urheimat der Goten*. Leipzig, Stockholm, 1948.

Paschoud, François. *Zosime*. See *Zosimus (Sources)*.

———. "Zosimos." RE II 19:790 ff. 1972.

Patsch, Karl. "Banater Sarmaten. Beiträge zur Völkerkunde von Südosteuropa II." *Anzeiger der Österreichischen Akademie der Wissenschaften in Wien, Phil.-hist. Kl.* 62:181 ff. 1926.

———. "Carpi." RE 6:1608 ff. 1899.

———. "Die Völkerbewegungen an der unteren Donau: Beiträge zur Völkerkunde von Südosteuropa III." *Sitzungsberichte der Österreichischen Akademie der Wissenschaften in Wien, Phil.-hist. Kl.* 208, 2. 1928.

Pavan, Massimiliano. *La politica gotica di Teodosio*. Rome, 1964.

Pepe, Gabriele. *Il medio evo barbarico d'Italia*. 3d ed. Turin, 1971.

Perrin, Odet. *Les Burgondes*. Neuchâtel, 1968.

Pertusi, Agostini. "Ordinamenti militari, guerre in occidente e teorie di guerra dei bizantini (secc. VI–X)." *Settimane di studio del Centro italiano di studi sull'alto medioevo* 15:631 ff. Spoleto, 1968.

Pfeilschifter, Georg. *Der Ostgotenkönig Theoderich der Grosse und die katholische Kirche*. Kirchengeschichtliche Studien III, parts 1 and 2. 1896.

Piel, Joseph M., and Kremer, Dieter. *Hispano-gotisches Namenbuch*. Heidelberg, 1976.

Piltz, Elisabeth. *Kamelaukion et mitra: Insignes byzantines impériaux et écclésiastiques*. Acta Universitatis Upsaliensis: Figura, n.s. 15. Stockholm, 1977.

Pohl, Walter. "Besprechung von Burns, *The Ostrogoths*." MIÖG 89:340 f. 1981.

———. "Die Gepiden und die *gentes* an der mittleren Donau nach dem Zerfall des Attilareiches." *Denkschriften der Österreichischen Akademie der Wissenschaften in Wien, Phil.-hist. Kl.* 145:239 ff. 1980.

Polaschek, Erich. "Ptolemaios als Geograph." RE, suppl. 10:733 ff. 1965.

Popescu, Emilian. "Das Problem der Kontinuität in Rumänien im Lichte der epigraphischen Entdeckungen." *Dacoromania* 1:69 ff. 1973.

Raddatz, Klaus. "Bewaffnung." *Reallexikon der germanischen Altertumskunde* 2:423 ff. 2d ed. 1976.

Ranke, Kurt. "Abstammungstraditionen." *Reallexikon der germanischen Altertumskunde* 1:29. 2d ed. 1973.

———. "Bär." *Reallexikon der germanischen Altertumskunde* 2:46 ff. 2d ed. 1976.

Reindel, Kurt. "Das Zeitalter der Agilolfinger." *Handbuch der bayerischen Geschichte* 1:101 ff. 2d rev. ed. Munich, 1981.

Reinhart, Wilhelm. *Historia general del reino hispanico de los Suevos*. Madrid, 1952.

———. "Die Münzen des tolosanischen Reiches der Westgoten." *Deutsches Jahrbuch für Numismatik* 1:107 ff. 1938.

———. "Sobre el asentamiento de los Visigodos en la Península." *Archivo español de arqueologia* 18:124 ff. 1945.

Riché, Pierre. *Éducation et culture dans l'occident barbare. VIe–VIIIe siècles*. Paris, 1962.

Rogger, Iginio. "La basilica paleocristiana di S. Vigilio VII." *Studi trentini di scienze storiche* 54:3 ff. Trent, 1975.

Roisl, Hans Norbert. "Tadinae." RE, suppl. vol. 14:749 ff. 1974.

———. "Totila." RE, suppl. vol. 14:799 ff. 1974.

———. "Totila und die Schlacht bei den Busta Gallorum, Ende Juni/Anfang Juli 552." *Jahrbuch der österreichischen Byzantinistik* 30:25 ff. 1981.

Roosens, H. "Laeti, Foederati und andere spätrömische Bevölkerungsniederschläge im belgischen Raum." *Archaeologia Belgica* 104:89 ff. 1968.

Rosen, Klaus. *Ammianus Marcellinus*. Erträge der Forschung 183. Darmstadt, 1982.

Rosenfeld, Hellmut. "Dietrichdichtung." *Reallexikon der germanischen Altertumskunde* 5:431 f. 2d ed. 1984.

———. "Ost- und Westgoten." *Die Welt als Geschichte* 17:245 ff. Stuttgart, 1957.

Rostovtzeff, Michail. *Social and Economic History of the Roman Empire*. Vol. 1. 2d ed. Oxford, 1957.

Rothenhöfer, Dieter. "Untersuchungen zur Sklaverei in den ostgermanischen Nachfolgestaaten des römischen Reichs." Ph.D. diss. Tübingen, 1967.

Rouche, Michel. *L'Aquitaine: Des Wisigoths aux Arabes, 418–781: Naissance d'une région*. Paris, 1979.

Rubin, Berthold. "Prokopios von Kaisareia." RE 45:273 ff. 1957.

Ruggini, Lellia. *Economia e società nella Italia annonaria*. Milan, 1960. Cf. Cracco-Ruggini, Lellia.

Russell, Josiah Cox. "That Earlier Plague." *Demography* 5:174 ff. 1968.

Saitta, Biagio. "La rivolta di Ermeneghildo." *Quaderni Catanesi* 1:81 ff. 1979.

Sánchez-Albornoz, Claudio. "La caballería visigoda." *Festschrift für Alphons Dopsch*, 92 ff. Baden, Leipzig, 1938.

———. *En torno a los origines del feudalismo*. Vols. 1 and 3. Mendoza, 1942.

Sandberger, Gertrud. "Bistum Chur in Südtirol." *Zeitschrift für bayerische Landesgeschichte* 40:723 ff. 1977.

Šašel, Jaro(slav). "Antiqui Barbari: Zur Besiedlungsgeschichte Ostnoricums und Pannoniens im fünften und sechsten Jahrhundert nach den Schriftquellen." *Vorträge und Forschungen* 25:125 ff. 1979.

———. "Zur Geschichte der Iulisch-alpischen Militärzone." *Situla* 14/15:255–262. Ljubljana, 1974.

———. "Zur Historischen Ethnographie des mittleren Donauraums." *Denkschriften der österreichischen Akademie der Wissenschaften in Wien, Phil.-hist. Kl.* 145:13 ff. 1980.

———, and Petru, Peter. *Claustra Alpium Iuliarum I*. Fontes. Catalogi et Monographiae 5. Ljubljana, 1971.

Scardigli, Barbara. "Conveniunt itaque Gothi Romanique." *Romanobarbarica* 4:1 ff. 1979.

———. "Die gotisch-römischen Beziehungen im 3. und 4. Jahrhundert n. Chr.: Ein Forschungsbericht 1950–1970." *Aufstieg und Niedergang der römischen Welt* II 5, 1:200 ff. 1976.

Scardigli, Piergiuseppe. *Die Goten: Sprache und Kultur*. Munich, 1973.

———. "Das sogenannte gotische Epigramm." *Beiträge zur Geschichte der deut-*

schen Sprache und Literatur 96:16 ff. 1974.

Schäferdiek, Knut. "Gab es eine gotisch-arianische Mission im süddeutschen Raum?" *Zeitschrift für bayerische Landesgeschichte* 45:239 ff. 1982.

———. "Germanenmission." *Reallexikon für Antike und Christentum* 10:492 ff. Stuttgart, 1977.

———. "Der germanische Arianismus." *Miscellanea historiae ecclesiasticae III: Bibliothèque de la Revue d'histoire écclésiastique* 50:71 ff. Louvain, 1970.

———. *Die Kirchen in den Reichen der Westgoten und Suewen bis zur Errichtung der westgotischen katholischen Staatskirche.* Arbeiten zur Kirchengeschichte 39. Berlin, 1967.

Scheibelreiter, Georg. *Tiernamen und Wappenwesen.* Veröffentlichungen des Instituts für österreichische Geschichtsforschung 24. Vienna, 1976.

Schlesinger, Walter. "Die Entstehung der Nationen: Gedanken zu einem Forschungsprogramm." *Nationes* 1:11 ff. 1978.

———. "Über germanisches Heerkönigtum." *Beiträge zur deutschen Verfassungsgeschichte des Mittelalters* 1:53 ff. Göttingen, 1963. Or: *Vorträge und Forschungen* 3:105 ff. 4th reprint. Sigmaringen, 1973.

Schmid, W. P. "Aisten." *Reallexikon der germanischen Altertumskunde* 1:116 f. 2d ed. 1973.

Schmidt, Ludwig. "Zur Geschichte der Krimgoten." *Schumacher-Festschrift,* 332 ff. Mainz, 1930.

———. "Die letzten Ostgoten." *Wege der Forschung* 249:92 ff. 1972.

———. *Die Ostgermanen.* Rev. reprint 2d ed., Munich, 1941; latest reprint, 1969.

———. "Review of Eduard Beninger, *Der westgotisch-alanische Zug.*" *Historische Zeitschrift* 147:216 f. 1933.

———. *Die Westgermanen.* 2d ed. Vol. 1. Munich, 1938.

Schmidt, P. G. "Barbarus." *Reallexikon der germanischen Altertumskunde* 2:49 f. 2d ed. 1976.

Schmidt-Wiegand, Ruth. "Die volkssprachigen Wörter der Leges barbarorum als Ausdruck sprachlicher Interferenz." *Frühmittelalterliche Studien* 13:56 ff. 1979.

Schneider, Reinhard. *Königswahl und Königserhebung im Frühmittelalter.* Monographien zur Geschichte des Mittelalters 3. Stuttgart, 1972.

Schönfeld, Moriz. "Goti." RE, suppl. vol. 3:797 ff. 1918.

———. *Wörterbuch der altgermanischen Personen- und Völkernamen.* Heidelberg, 1911.

Schramm, Gottfried. "Eine hunnisch-germanische Namenbeziehung?" *Jahrbuch für fränkische Landesforschung* 20:129 ff. 1960.

———. *Nordpontische Ströme.* Göttingen, 1973.

———. "Die nordöstlichen Eroberungen der Russland-Goten (Merens-Mordens und die anderen Völkernamen bei Jordanes, *Getica* XXIII 116)." *Frühmittelalterliche Studien* 8:3 ff. 1974.

Schramm, Percy Ernst. *Herrschaftszeichen und Staatsymbolik.* Schriftenreihe der MGH 13, 1–3. 1954.

Schulze, Hans Kurt. "Mediävistik und Begriffsgeschichte." *Festschrift für Helmut Beumann,* 388 ff. Sigmaringen, 1977.

Schwab, Ute. "Bilaif im Gotischen Kalender (29. Oktober)." *Helikon* 7:357 ff. Rome, 1967.

Schwarcz, Andreas. "Nachrichten über den lateinischen Westen bei Prokopios von

Kaisareia." Diss. Institut für österreichische Geschichtsforschung. Vienna, 1983.

———. "Reichsangehörige Personen gotischer Herkunft: Prosopographische Studien." Ph.D. diss. Vienna, 1984.

Schwarz, Ernst. *Germanische Stammeskunde.* Heidelberg, 1956.

———. *Goten, Nordgermanen, Angelsachsen: Studien zur Ausgliederung der germanischen Sprachen.* Bibliotheca Germanica 2. 1951.

———. "Die Herkunftsfrage der Goten." *Wege der Forschung* 249:287 ff. 1972.

———. "Die Krimgoten." *Wege der Forschung* 249:202 ff. 1972. Or: *Saeculum* 4:156 ff. 1953.

———. "Die Urheimat der Goten und ihre Wanderungen ins Weichselland und nach Südrussland." *Saeculum* 4:13 ff. 1953.

Schwöbel, Heide. *Synode und König im Westgotenreich.* Dissertationen zur mittelalterlichen Geschichte 1. 1982.

Ščukin, M. B. "About the Initial Date of the Černjachov Culture." *Prace archeologiczne* 22:303 ff. 1976.

———. "Das Problem der Černjachov-Kultur in der sowjetischen Forschung." *Zeitschrift für Archäologie* 9:25 ff. 1975.

Scythians, From the Land of the. The Metropolitan Museum of Art Bulletin XXXII 5. New York, 1975.

Seeck, Otto. "Ablabius." RE 1:103 f. 1893.

———. "Aiulfus." RE 1:1129 f. 1893.

———. "Alatheus." RE 1:1295. 1893.

———. "Athaulf." RE 4:1939 ff. 1896.

———. "Comites." RE 17:648 ff. 1900.

———. "Dux." RE 10:1869 ff. 1905.

———. *Geschichte des Untergangs der antiken Welt.* Vol. 5. 2d ed. Stuttgart, 1920.

———. "Gundiocus." RE 14:1937 f. 1912.

———. "Iovinus." RE 18:2012 f. 1916.

———. "Ragnahilda." RE II 1:127. 1914.

———. *Die Regesten der Kaiser und Päpste für die Jahre 311–476 n. Chr.* Stuttgart, 1919.

———. "Sarus." RE II 3:54. 1921.

Seibt, Werner. "Bleisiegel des Kaisers Markianos (450–457) aus österreichischem Boden." *Römisches Österreich* 2:61 ff. 1974.

Sevin, Heinrich. *Die Gebiden.* 1955.

Seyfarth, Wolfgang. *Ammianus Marcellinus: Römische Geschichte.* Vol. 1. 3d ed. Darmstadt, 1975.

Siems, Harald. "Codex Theodosianus." *Reallexikon der germanischen Altertumskunde* 5:47 ff. 2d ed. 1984.

———. "Lex Romana Visigothorum." *Handwörterbuch zur deutschen Rechtsgeschichte* 2:1940 ff. 1978.

Simon, Günther. "Die Reform der Reiterei unter Kaiser Gallien." *Kölner Historische Abhandlungen* 28:435 ff. 1980.

Soliva, Claudio. "Die Lex Romana Curiensis und die Stammesrechte." *Beiträge zum frühalemannischen Recht* 42:73 ff. Freiburg, 1978.

Spitzer, Leo. "Das Suffix -one im Romanischen." *Biblioteca dell'Archivum Romanicum* II 2:183 ff. 1921.

Staab, Franz. "Ostrogothic Geographers at the Court of Theodoric the Great: A Study of Some Sources of the Anonymous Cosmographer of Ravenna." *Viator* 7:27 ff. 1976.

Stallknecht, Bernt. *Untersuchungen zur römischen Aussenpolitik in der Spätantike.* Habelts Dissertationsdrucke. Reihe Alte Geschichte 7. Bonn, 1969.

Stearns, MacDonald. *Crimean Gothic. Studia linguistica et philologica* 6. 1980.

Stein, Ernst. *Histoire du Bas-Empire.* Vol. 1, 2d ed., Paris, 1959; vol. 2, Paris, 1949.

———. "Untersuchungen zur spätrömischen Verwaltungsgeschichte." *Rheinisches Museum für Philologie* n.s. 74:347 ff. 1925.

———. "Der Verzicht der Galla Placidia auf die Präfektur Illyricum." *Wiener Studien* 36:344 ff. 1914.

Stein, Friedrich. "Carpicus." RE 6:1610. 1899.

———. "Gothicus." RE 14:683 ff. 1912.

Steinbach, Franz. *Studien zur westdeutschen Stammes- und Volksgeschichte.* 1962. Neudruck von Schriften des Instituts für Grenz- und Auslandsdeutschtum an der Universität Marburg 5. 1926.

Steinhauser, Walter. "Kultische Stammesnamen in Ostgermanien." *Die Sprache* 2:13 ff. 1950/1952.

———. "Der Name der Leitha und die Hunnenschlacht am Nedao." *Jahrbuch für Landeskunde von Niederösterreich* 36:844 ff. 1964.

Stengel, Edmund Ernst. "Der Heerkaiser (Den Kaiser macht das Heer)." *Abhandlungen und Untersuchungen zur Geschichte des Kaisergedankens im Mittelalter.* Cologne, Graz, 1965.

Stevens. "Tolosa." RE II 12:1689. 1937.

Stock, Klaus. "Review of Bachrach: *The Alans.*" *Francia* 5:852 ff. 1977.

Straub, Johannes. *Heidnische Geschichtsapologetik in der christlichen Spätantike.* Bonn, 1963.

———. *Regeneratio Imperii: Aufsätze über Roms Kaisertum und Reich im Spiegel der heidnischen und christlichen Publizistik.* Darmstadt, 1972.

———. *Studien zur Historia Augusta.* Bern, 1952.

Streitberg, Wilhelm. *Die gotische Bibel.* Vols. 1 and 2. 6th ed. Darmstadt, 1971.

Stroheker, Karl Friedrich. *Eurich.* Stuttgart, 1937.

———. *Germanentum und Spätantike.* Zurich, Stuttgart, 1965.

———. *Der senatorische Adel im spätantiken Gallien.* 2d ed. Darmstadt, 1970.

Strzelczyk, Jerzy. *Goci: Rzeczwisto i legenda.* Warsaw, 1984.

Stutz, Elfriede. "Codices Gotici." *Reallexikon der germanischen Altertumskunde* 5:52 ff. 2d ed. 1982.

———. "Fragmentum Spirense—Recto." *Zeitschrift für Vergleichende Sprachforschung* 85:85 ff. 1971.

———. "Fragmentum Spirense—Verso." *Zeitschrift für Vergleichende Sprachforschung* 87:1 ff. 1973.

———. "Die germanistische These vom 'Donauweg' gotisch-arianischer Missionare im 5. und 6. Jahrhundert." *Denkschriften der Österreichischen Akademie der Wissenschaften in Wien, Phil.-hist. Kl.* 145:207 ff. 1980.

———. *Gotische Literaturdenkmäler.* Stuttgart, 1966.

Suerbaum, Werner. *Vom antiken zum frühmittelalterlichen Staatsbegriff.* 2d ed. Münster, 1970.

Sundwall, Johannes. *Abhandlungen zur Geschichte des ausgehenden Römertums.* Helsingfors, 1919. Reprint, New York, 1975.

Svennung. Josef. *Zur Geschichte des Goticismus.* Uppsala, 1967.

———. "Jordanes und die gotische Stammsage." *Studia Gotica,* 20 ff. Stockholm, 1972.

———. *Jordanes und Scandia.* Stockholm, 1967.

———. *Skandinavien bei Plinius und Ptolemaios.* Uppsala, 1974.

Sybel, Heinrich. *Entstehung des Deutschen Königthums.* Frankfurt, 1881.

Szádeczky-Kardoss, Samuel. "Bagaudae." RE, suppl. vol. 11:346 ff. 1968.

Szydłowski, Jerzy. "Zur Anwesenheit der Westslawen an der mittleren Donau im ausgehenden 5. und 6. Jahrhundert." *Denkschriften der Österreichischen Akademie der Wissenschaften, Phil.-hist. Kl. in Wien* 145:233 ff. 1980.

Teillet, Suzanne. *Des Goths à la nation gothique: Les origines de l'idée de nation en Occident du Vᵉ au VIIᵉ siècle.* Paris: Belles-Lettres, 1984. Cf. Wolfram, "Review," 724 ff.

Thompson, Edward Arthur. "Barbarian Kingdoms in Gaul and Spain." *Nottingham Medieval Studies* 7:3 ff. 1963.

———. *The Early Germans.* Oxford, 1965.

———. "The End of Roman Spain I–IV." *Nottingham Medieval Studies* 20:3 ff. 1976; 21:3 ff. 1977; 22:3 ff. 1978; 24:1 ff. 1979.

———. *The Goths in Spain.* Oxford, 1969.

———. *The Historical Work of Ammianus Marcellinus.* Cambridge, 1947.

———. *A History of Attila and the Huns.* Oxford, 1948.

———. *Romans and Barbarians: the Decline of the Western Empire.* University of Wisconsin Press, 1982.

———. "The Settlement of the Barbarians in Southern Gaul." *The Journal of Roman Studies* 46:65 ff. 1956.

———. "The Visigoths from Fritigern to Euric." *Historia* 12:105 ff. 1963.

———. *The Visigoths in the Time of Wulfila.* Oxford, 1966.

Thürlemann, Felix. "Die Bedeutung der Aachener Theoderich-Statue für Karl den Grossen (801) und bei Walahfrid Strabo (829)." *Archiv für Kulturgeschichte* 59:25 ff. 1977.

Thurnwald, Richard. *Die menschliche Gesellschaft in ihren ethnosoziologischen Grundlagen.* 5 vols. Berlin, 1931–1934.

Tiefenbach, Heinrich. *Studien zu Wörtern volkssprachlicher Herkunft in karolingischen Königsurkunden.* Munich, 1973.

Timpe, Dieter. "comes." *Reallexikon der germanischen Altertumskunde* 5:63 ff. 2d ed. 1982.

Tischler, Johann. *Neu- und wiederentdeckte Zeugnisse des Krimgotischen.* Innsbruck, 1978.

Tjäder, Jan-Olof. "Der Codex Argenteus und der Buchmeister Viliaric." *Studia Gotica,* 144 ff. Stockholm, 1972.

———. *Die nichtliterarischen Papyri Italiens aus der Zeit 475–700.* Vol. 2. Stockholm, 1982.

Tomasini, Wallace. *The Barbaric Tremisses in Spain and Southern France: Anastasius to Leovigild.* Numismatic Notes and Monographs 152. New York, 1964.

Tóth, Endre. "Geschichte der Oberen Wart im ersten Jahrtausend." *Die Obere Wart,* 77 ff. Oberwart, 1977.

———. "Zur Geschichte des nordpannonischen Raums im fünften bis sechsten Jahrhundert." *Denkschriften der Österreichischen Akademie der Wissenschaften in Wien, Phil.-hist. Kl.* 145:91 ff. 1980.

The Transformation of the Roman World. Edited by Lynn T. White. UCLA, Center for Medieval and Renaissance Studies: *Contributions.* 3. Berkeley, Los Angeles, 1966.

Toynbee, Arnold. *A Study of History.* Vol. 1. Abridgment of vols. 1–6 by D. C. Somerell. New York, London: Oxford University Press, 1947.

Tudor, Dumitru. "Preuves archéologiques attestant la continuité de la domination romaine au nord du Danube après l'abandon de la Dacie sous Aurélian." *Dacoromania* 1:149 ff. 1973.

Uiblein, Paul. *Studien zur Passauer Geschichtsschreibung des Mittelalters.* Archiv für österreichische Geschichte 121. Vienna, 1955.

Ulrich-Bansa, Otto. *Moneta Mediolanensis.* Venice, 1949.

Várady, László. *Epochenwechsel um 476.* Budapest, Bonn, 1984.

———. "Jordanes-Studien." *Chiron* 6:1 ff. 1976.

———. *Das letzte Jahrhundert Pannoniens: 376–476.* Amsterdam, 1969.

Vasil'ev, Alexander Alexandrovich. *The Goths in the Crimea.* Cambridge, Mass., 1936.

Vasmer, Max. "Review of Ernst Fraenkel: *Die baltischen Sprachen.*" *Zeitschrift für Litauische Philologie* 22:216 ff. 1953.

———. *Russisches etymologisches Wörterbuch.* Vol. 1. Heidelberg, 1953; vol. 3. Heidelberg, 1958.

Vercauteren, Fernand. *Études sur les civitates de la Belgique seconde.* Brussels, 1934.

Vetters, Hermann. *Dacia ripensis.* Österreichische Akademie der Wissenschaften in Wien: Schriften der Balkankommission 11. 1950.

———. "Virunum." *Aufstieg und Niedergang der römischen Welt: Principat* II 6:302 ff. 1977.

———. "Der Vogel auf der Stange." *Jahreshefte des Österreichischen Archäologischen Instituts* 37:131 ff. Vienna, 1948.

Vinski, Zdenko. "Archäologische Spuren ostgotischer Anwesenheit im heutigen Bereich Jugoslawiens." *Problemi seobe naroda u Karpatskoj kotlini,* 33 ff. Novisad, 1978.

Vismara, Giulio. *Edictum Theoderici.* Ius Romanum Medii Aevi I, 2b, aa. Milan, 1967.

———. "El 'edictum Theoderici.'" *Estudios visigóticos* I. Cuadernos del Instituto juridico Español 5:49 ff. Rome, Madrid, 1956.

———. "Romani e Goti di fronte al diritto nel regno ostrogoto." *Settimane di studio del Centro italiano di studi sull'alto medioevo* 3:409 ff. Spoleto, 1956.

———. *Scritti di storia giuridica. Fonti del diritto nei regni germanici* 1. Milan, 1987.

Vives, José. "Die Inschrift an der Brücke von Merida unter Bischof Zenon." *Römische Quartalschrift für christliche Altertumskunde und für Kirchengeschichte* 46:57 ff. 1941.

Vogt, Joseph. "Christenverfolgung." *Reallexikon für Antike und Christentum* 2:1184–1188. 1954.

———. "Der Lebensbericht des Paulinus von Pella." *Kölner Historische Abhandlungen* 28:527 ff. 1980.

von Gebhardt, Oscar. *Die Akten der edessischen Bekenner Gurjas, Samonas und*

Abibos. Texte und Untersuchungen zur Geschichte der altchristlichen Literatur III 7, 2. 1911.

von Heland, Madeleine. "The Golden Bowl from Pietroasa." *Stockholm Studies in History of Art* 24:58 ff. 1973.

von Matt, Leonhard. *Ravenna.* 1971.

von Ungern-Sternberg, J. "Bagaudes." *Lexikon des Mittelalters* 1:1344 f. 1980.

von Uslar, Rafael. *Germanische Sachkultur in den ersten Jahrhunderten nach Christus.* Cologne, 1975.

Vulpe, Radu, "Considerations historiques autour de l'évacuation de la Dacie." *Dacoromania* 1:41 ff. 1973.

————. *Le vallum de la Moldavie inférieure et le "mur" d'Athanaric.* The Hague, 1957.

Wagner, Norbert. "Bemerkungen zur Amalergenealogie." *Beiträge zur Namenforschung,* n.s. 14:26 ff. 1979.

————. "Gausus und Harodus." *Beiträge zur Namenforschung,* n.s. 13:241 ff. 1978.

————. "Germanische Namengebung und kirchliches Recht in der Amalerstammtafel." *Zeitschrift für deutsches Altertum und deutsche Literatur* 99:1 ff. 1970.

————. *Getica.* Berlin, 1967.

————. "Ich armer Dietrîch: Die Wandlung von Theoderichs Eroberung zu Dietrichs Flucht." *Zeitschrift für deutsches Altertum* 109:209 ff. 1980.

————. "Zu einigen Personennamen aus Quellen zur gotischen Geschichte." *Würzburger Prosastudien* 2:27 ff. 1975.

————. "Review of Piel and Kremer, *Hispano-gotisches Namenbuch.*" *Göttingische Gelehrte Anzeigen* 230:242 ff. 1978.

Wartburg, Walther von. *Die Entstehung der romanischen Völker.* 2d ed. Halle, 1951.

Wattenbach, Wilhelm; Levison, Wilhelm; and Löwe, Heinz. *Deutschlands Geschichtsquellen im Mittelalter.* Vol. 1: *Vorzeit und Karolinger.* 1952.

Weber, Max. *Wirtschaft und Gesellschaft.* Vol. 2. 5th ed. Tübingen, 1976.

Weiler, Ingomar. "Zum Schicksal der Witwen und Waisen bei den Völkern der Alten Welt." *Saeculum* 31:157 ff. 1980.

Weissensteiner, Johann. "Quellenkundliche Abhandlungen zu Jordanes." Diss., Institut für österreichische Geschichtsforschung, Vienna, 1980.

Wellhausen, Julius. *Reste arabischen Heidentums.* 2d ed. Berlin, 1927.

Wenskus, Reinhard. "Adel." *Reallexikon der germanischen Altertumskunde,* 1:60 ff. 2d ed. 1973.

————. "Alanen." *Reallexikon der germanischen Altertumskunde* 1:122 ff. 2d ed. 1973.

————. "Alarich (Erulerkönig)." *Reallexikon der germanischen Altertumskunde* 1:129. 2d ed. 1973.

————. "Amaler." *Reallexikon der germanischen Altertumskunde* 1:246 ff. 2d ed. 1973.

————. "Athaulf." *Reallexikon der germanischen Altertumskunde* 1:464 f. 2d ed. 1973.

————. "Balthen." *Reallexikon der germanischen Altertumskunde* 2:13 f. 2d ed. 1976.

———. "Bastarnen." *Reallexikon der germanischen Altertumskunde* 2:88 ff. 2d ed. 1976.

———. "Bevölkerung." *Reallexikon der germanischen Altertumskunde* 2:359 ff. 2d ed. 1976.

———. "Bewaffnung." *Reallexikon der germanischen Altertumskunde* 2:458 ff. 2d ed. 1976.

———. "Germanische Herrschaftsbildungen des fünften Jahrhunderts." *Handbuch der europäischen Geschichte* 1:213 ff. Stuttgart, 1976.

———. "Zum Problem der Ansippung." *Festschrift für Otto Höfler*. Vienna, Stuttgart, 1976.

———. "Probleme der germanisch-deutschen Verfassungs- und Sozialgeschichte im Lichte der Ethnosoziologie." *Festschrift für Walter Schlesinger,* 19 ff. Cologne, 1974.

———. "Sachsen-Angelsachsen-Thüringer." *Wege der Forschung* 50:483 ff. Darmstadt, 1967.

———. *Stammesbildung und Verfassung*. 2d ed. Cologne, 1977.

Werner, Joachim. "Die archäologischen Zeugnisse der Goten in Südrussland, Ungarn, Italien und Spanien." *Settimane di studio del Centro italiano di studi sull'alto medioevo* 3:127 ff. Spoleto, 1956.

———. *Beiträge zur Archäologie des Attila-Reiches*. Bayerische Akademie der Wissenschaften, Abhandlungen der Phil.-hist. Kl., n.s. 38 A. Munich, 1956.

———. "Herkuleskeule und Donar-Amulett." *Jahrbuch des Römisch-Germanischen Zentralmuseums Mainz* 11:176 ff. 1964.

———. "Zur Herkunft und Ausbreitung der Anten und Sklavenen." *Actes du VIIIe Congrès International des Sciences Préhistoriques et Protohistoriques* 1:243 ff. Belgrade, 1971.

———. *Die Langobarden in Pannonien*. Bayerische Akademie der Wissenschaften, Abhandlungen der phil.-hist. Kl., n.s. 55 A, 1962.

———. "Studien zu Grabfunden des fünften Jahrhunderts aus der Slowakei und der Karpatenukraine." *Slovenska archeologia* 7:422 f. 1959.

———. "Zwei prismatische Knochenanhänger ('Donar-Amulette') von Zlechov." *Časopis Moravského Musea: Acta Musei Moraviae* 57:33 ff. 1972.

Werner, Robert. "Zur Herkunft der Anten: Ein ethnisches und soziales Problem der Spätantike." *Kölner Historische Abhandlungen* 28:573 ff. 1980.

Wes, M. A. *Das Ende des Kaisertums im Westen des römischen Reichs*. The Hague, 1967.

Wieacker, Franz. *Allgemeine Zustände und Rechtszustände gegen Ende des weströmischen Reichs*. Ius Romanum Medii Aevi I 2a. Milan, 1963.

———. "Lateinische Kommentare zum Codex Theodosianus." *Symbolae Friburgenses in honorem Ottonis Lenel,* 259 ff. Leipzig, 1931.

———. *Recht und Gesellschaft in der Spätantike*. Stuttgart, 1964.

———. *Vulgarismus und Klassizimus im Recht der Spätantike*. Sitzungsberichte der Heidelberger Akademie der Wissenschaften, Phil.-hist. Kl. 3. Abhandlung. 1955.

Wiesner, Joseph. *Die Thraker*. Stuttgart, 1963.

Wilkes, J. J. *Dalmatia*. London, 1969.

Wimmer, Jan. *Der Entsatz von Wien 1683*. Warsaw, 1983.

Wirth, Gerhard. "Anmerkungen zur Vita des Severin von Noricum." *Quaderni*

Catanesi 1:217 ff. 1979.

———. "Attila und Byzanz." *Byzantinische Zeitschrift* 60:41 ff. 1967.

———. "Buc(c)ellarii." *Lexikon des Mittelalters* 2:802. Munich, Zurich, 1983.

———. "Review of Wolfram, *Goten.*" *Bonner Jahrbücher des Rheinischen Landesmuseums,* 695 ff. 1981.

White, Lynn, jr. *Medieval Technology and Social Change.* Oxford, 1965.

Wohlhaupter, Eugen. "Das germanische Element im altspanischen Recht und die Rezeption des römischen Rechts in Spanien." *Zeitschrift für Rechtsgeschichte: Roman. Abt.* 66:135–264. 1948.

Wolfram, Herwig. "Zur Ansiedlung reichsangehöriger Föderaten." *MIÖG* 91:5 ff. 1983.

———. "Athanaric the Visigoth: Monarchy or Judgeship? A Study in Comparative History." *Journal of Medieval History* 1:1 ff. 1975.

———. "Die Aufnahme germanischer Völker ins Römerreich: Aspekte und Konsequenzen." *Settimane di studio del Centro italiano di studi sull'alto medioevo* 29:87 ff. Spoleto, 1983.

———. "Constantin als Vorbild für den Herrscher des hochmittelalterlichen Reiches." *MIÖG* 68:226 ff. Vienna, 1959.

———. *Conversio Bagoariorum et Carantanorum: Das Weissbuch der Salzburger Kirche über die erfolgreiche Mission in Karantanien und Pannonien.* Vienna, 1979.

———. "Ethnogenesen im Donau- und Ostalpenraum (6.–10. Jahrhundert)." *Frühmittelalterliche Ethnogenese im Alpenraum. Nationes* 5:97 ff. Sigmaringen, 1985.

———. "Fortuna in mittelalterlichen Stammesgeschichten." *MIÖG* 72:1 ff. 1964.

———. *Die Geburt Mitteleuropas. Geschichte Österreichs vor seiner Entstehung.* Vienna, Berlin, 1987.

———. "Gegenstände des politischen Briefwechsels zwischen Ferdinand I. und seinen Geschwistern Karl V. und Maria von Ungarn." *Veröffentlichungen des Instituts für österreichische Geschichtsforschung* 20:84 ff. Vienna, 1974.

———. "Gothic History and Historical Ethnography." *Journal of Medieval History* 7:309 ff. 1981.

———. "Gotische Studien I–III." *MIÖG* 83:1–32. 1975; 83:289–324. 1975; 84:239–261. 1976.

———. "Gotisches Königtum und römisches Kaisertum von Theodosius dem Großen bis Justinian I." *Frühmittelalterliche Studien* 13:1 ff. Berlin, New York, 1979.

———. *Intitulatio I and II.* MIÖG, suppl. vols. 21 and 24. Vienna, 1967 and 1973.

———. "Libellus Virgilii: Ein quellenkritisches Problem der ältesten Salzburger Güterverzeichnisse." *Vorträge und Forschungen* 20:177 ff. 1974.

———. "Methodische Fragen zur Kritik am 'sakralen' Königtum germanischer Stämme." *Festschrift für Otto Höfler* 2:473 ff. Vienna, 1968.

———. "Mittelalterliche Politik und adelige Staatssprache." *MIÖG* 76:1 ff. 1968.

———. "Review of Jaroslav Šašel. *Antiqui barbari.*" *MIÖG* 89:107 ff. 1981.

———. "Review of Suzanne Teillet. *Des Goths à la nation gothique.*" *Francia* 13:724 ff. 1985.

———. "The Shaping of the Early Medieval Kingdom." *Viator* 1:1 ff. Berkeley, Los Angeles, London, 1970.

————. *Splendor Imperii*. MIÖG, suppl. vol. 20, 3. Vienna, 1963.

————. "Theogonie, Ethnogenese und ein kompromittierter Grossvater im Stammbaum Theoderichs des Grossen." *Festschrift für Helmut Beumann,* 80 ff. Sigmaringen, 1977.

————. "Die Zeit der Agilolfinger: Rupert und Virgil." *Geschichte Salzburgs* 1:121 ff. Salzburg, 1981.

Wolfram, Herwig, and Schwarcz, Andreas, ed. *Anerkennung und Integration. Zu den wirtschaftlichen Grundlagen der Völkerwanderungszeit (400–600).* Denkschriften der Österreichischen Akademie der Wissenschaften in Wien, Phil.-hist. Kl. 193. 1988.

Woloch, Michael G. "A Survey of Scholarship on Ostrogothic Italy. (A.D. 489–552)." *Classical Folia: Studies in the Christian Perpetuation of the Classics* 25:320 ff. 1971.

Wozniak, Frank E. "East Rome, Ravenna and Western Illyricum: 454–536 A.D." *Historia* 30:351 ff. 1981.

Wrede, Ferdinand. *Über die Sprache der Ostgoten in Italien.* Quellen und Forschungen zur Sprach- und Culturgeschichte der germanischen Völker 68. 1891.

Wüst, Walter. "Goten in Indien?" In: Franz Altheim, *Geschichte der Hunnen* 3:141 ff. 2d ed. 1961.

Zeiller, Jacques. *Les origines chrétiennes dans les provinces danubiennes de l'empire romain.* Paris, 1918.

Zeiss, Hans. "Review of Eduard Beninger, *Der westgotisch-alanische Zug.*" *Germania* 16:249 ff. 1932.

————. "Die Nordgrenze des Ostgotenreichs." *Germania* 12:25 ff. 1928.

Zeumer, Carl. "Geschichte der westgothischen Gesetzgebung." Parts 1–4. *Neues Archiv* 23:419 ff. 1898; 24:39 ff. and 571 ff. 1899; 26:91 ff. 1901.

————. "Über zwei neuentdeckte westgothische Gesetze." *Neues Archiv* 23:75 ff. 1898.

Zeuss, Johann Kaspar. *Die Deutschen und die Nachbarstämme.* Munich, 1837. Reprint, Heidelberg, 1925.

Zibermayr, Ignaz. *Noricum, Baiern und Österreich.* 2d ed. Horn, 1956.

Zimmermann, Franz Xaver. "Der Grabstein der ostgotischen Königstochter Amalafrida Theodenanda in Genazzano bei Rom." *Festschrift für Rudolf Egger* 1:330 ff. Klagenfurt, 1953.

Zöllner, Erich. *Geschichte der Franken bis zur Mitte des sechsten Jahrhunderts.* Munich, 1970.

————. *Die politische Stellung der Völker im Frankenreich.* Veröffentlichungen des Instituts für österreichische Geschichtsforschung 13. Vienna, 1950.

————. "Review of Rolf Weiss, *Chlodwigs Taufe.*" MIÖG 83:175 ff. 1975.

————. "Zusammenfassung: Noricum und Raetien I." *Vorträge und Forschungen* 25:255 ff. 1979.

Index Abbreviations

b.	bishop	p.	pope
br.	brother	pat.	patricius
c.	comes	pat. praes.	patricius praesentalis
ch.	chief(tain)	PPO	praefectus praetorio
cos.	consul	q.	queen
e.	emperor	s.	son
f.	father	si.	sister
k.	king	St.	Saint
ME	magister equitum	tr.	tribe
MM	magister militum	v.i.	vir inluster
MP	magister peditum	v.s.	vir spectabilis
MVM	magister utriusque militiae		

Index

Maps

Map 1

Gothiscandza, Gotland and Götaland

Map 2

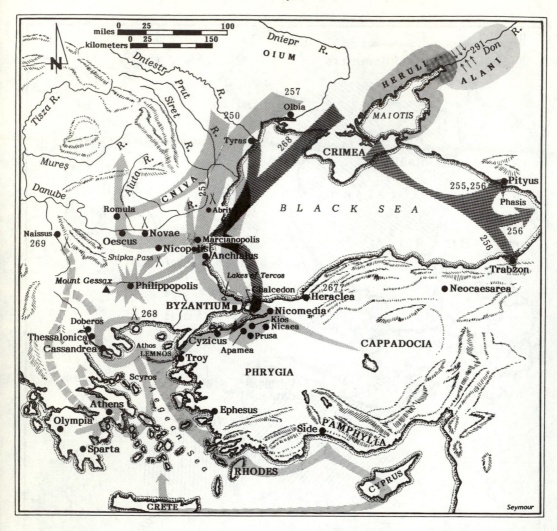

The Goths in the Third Century

Map 3

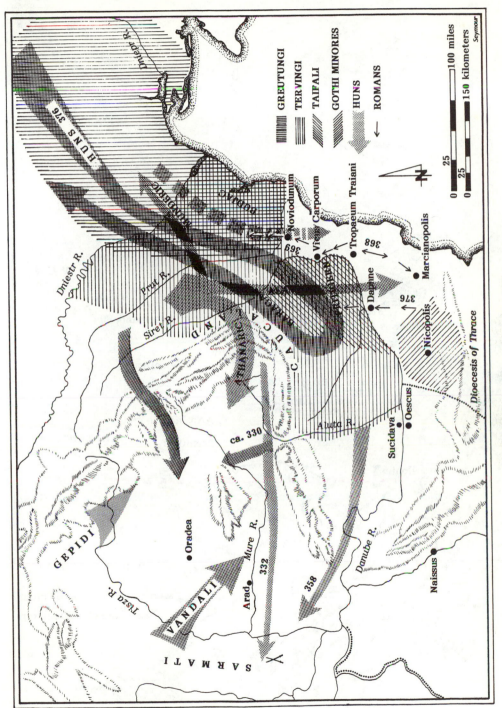

Gothic Realms outside the Roman Empire

Map 4

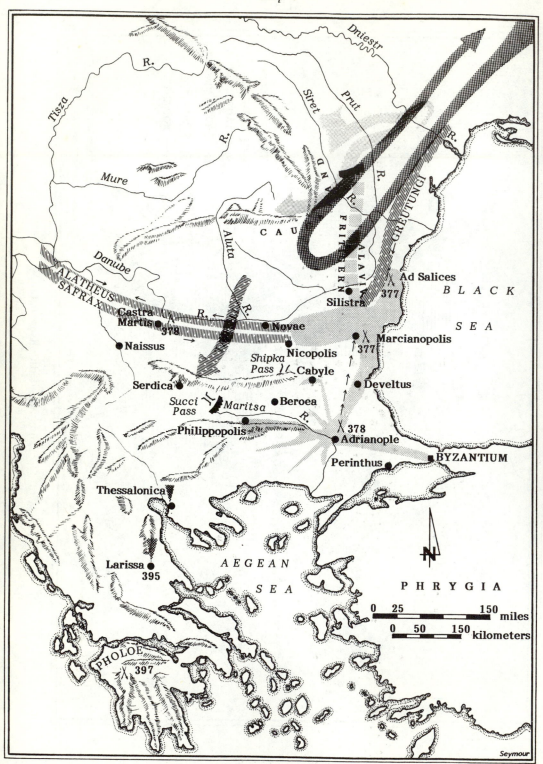

The Goths after 376

Map 5

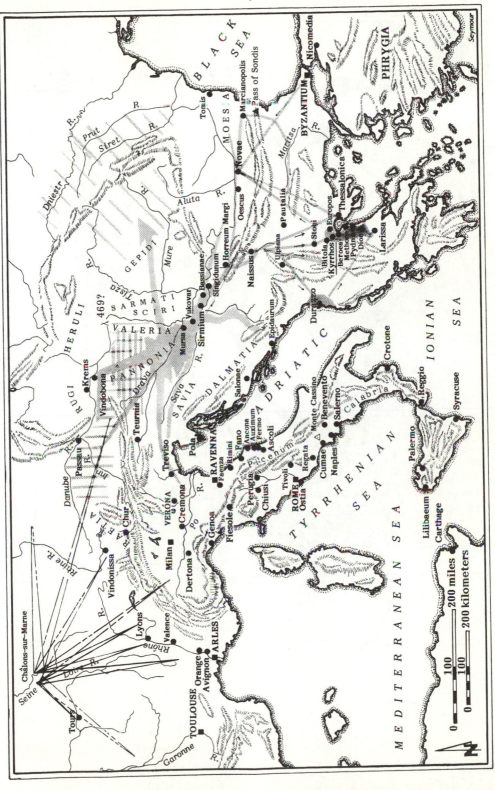

The Ostrogoths

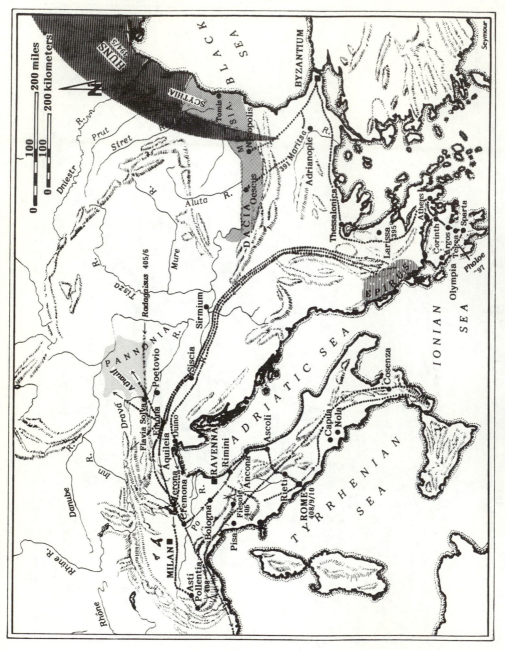

The Visigoths in the Balkans and in Italy

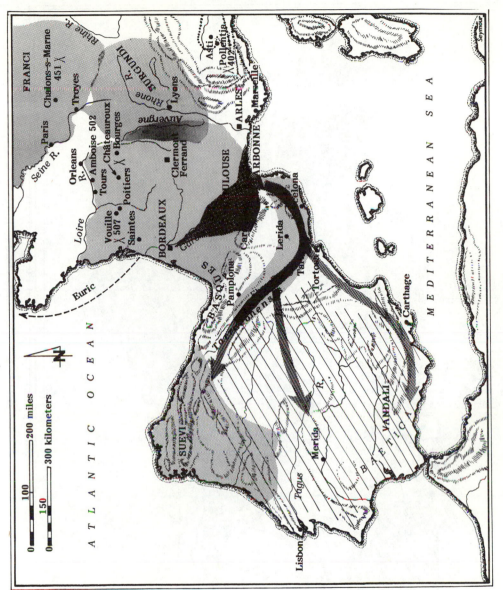

The Visigoths in France and Spain

Map 7

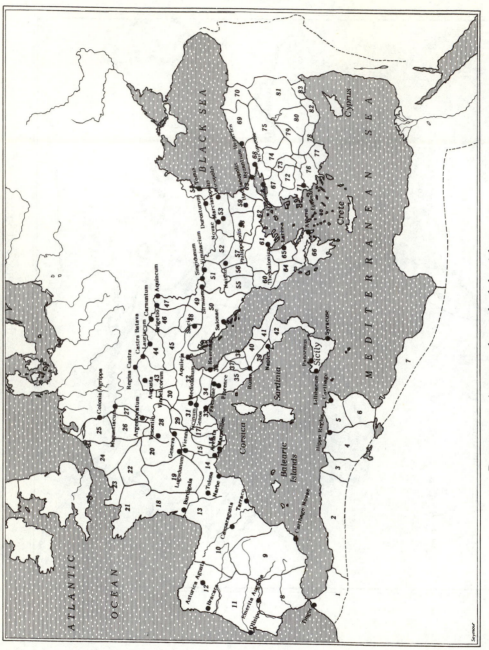

Roman provinces at the end of the 4th century
(after L. Schmidt, Ostgermanen)

1. Tingitana
2. Mauretania Caesariensis
3. Mauretania Siti-fenis
4. Numidia
5. Africa proconsularis
6. Byzacena
7. Tripolis
8. Baetica
9. Carthaginiensis
10. Tarraconensis
11. Lusitania
12. Gallaecia
13. Novempopulana
14. Narbonensis I
15. Viennensis
16. Narbonensis II
17. Alpes maritimae
18. Aquitania II
19. Aquitania I
20. Lugdunensis I
21. Lugdunensis III
22. Lugdunensis Senonia
23. Lugdunensis II
24. Belgica II
25. Germania II
26. Belgica I
27. Germania I
28. Maxima Sequanorum
29. Alpes Graiae et Poe-ninae
30. Raetia I
31. Liguria
32. Venetia et Histria
33. Alpes Cottiae
34. Aemilia
35. Tuscia et Umbria
36. Flaminia et Picenum annonarium
37. Valeria
38. Picenum subur-bicarium
39. Campania
40. Samnium
41. Apulia et Calabria
42. Lucania et Bruttii
43. Raetia II
44. Noricum ripense
45. Noricum mediter-raneum
46. Pannonia I
47. Valeria
48. Savia
49. Pannonia II
50. Dalmatia
51. Moesia I
52. Dacia ripensis
53. Moesia II
54. Scythia
55. Praevalitana
56. Dardania
57. Dacia medit.
58. Thracia
59. Haemimontus
60. Epirus nova
61. Macedonia
62. Rhodope
63. Europa
64. Epirus vetus
65. Thessalia
66. Achaia
67. Hellespontus
68. Bithynia
69. Paphlagonia
70. Pontus
71. Asia
72. Lydia
73/74. Phrygia
75. Galatia
76. Caria
77. Lycia
78. Pamphylia
79. Pisidia
80. Lycaonia
81. Cappadocia
82. Isauria
83. Cilicia

Designer: Joanna Hill
Compositor: Prestige Typography
Text: 10/13 Sabon
Display: Sabon

GOTHIC
SETTLEMENTS
AND KINGDOMS

NORTH SEA

SC

ATLANTIC

OCEAN

Seine R.

Paris   • Châlons-sur-Marne

Loire   Orléans
         Tours   • Troyes
         • Amboise
         Châteauroux   Rhine R.
         Bourges   Danube   R.
Poitiers   Castra Bat
                                          Passau
                Clermont   R.   Irn
                Ferrand   Vindonissa   R.
         BORDEAUX   Chur
                            Lyons   Teurnia
                                          Aquileia Emo
                    Po R.   Milan Verona Treviso
                            Asti Pavia   Cremona Dui
                    Valence Pollentia Dertona
Pamplona TOULOUSE Viviers
                    Orange Riez Genoa Bologna Pola
Duero R.   Avignon   Fiesole RAVENNA
                    ARLES   Pisa   Faenza Rimini
                                          Fano
Lisbon   Tagus   Larida   Perugia Ancona
         Merida R.   Barcelona   Chiusi Auxim
                    Tort   Spoleto Fermo
                                          Rieti   Ascoli
         Guadalquivir R.   ROME • Tivoli
                                          Regata
                    Cartagena   Cumae
                                          Capua
                                          Naples
         Septem   MEDITERRANEAN   SEA

                    Lilybaeum   Palermo
                    Carthage   Catania

Seymour